WOMEN AND SOCIETY

To Robin, the watch bird, watching me. . . .

MBR-D

To Rebecca, who liberated me. . . .
and to the women and men who are working
to eliminate social arrangements and
states of mind that prevent human
fulfillment. . . .

LVB

Marie Barovic Rosenberg majored in law at Stanford University where she received her B.A. in 1944. After marriage and three children, and twenty years in business and industry, she returned to the University of Washington, completing her doctorate in political science in 1973. During her graduate school years she taught fulltime for six years at Seattle Central Community College. In 1972 she received a joint appointment as assistant professor in the Institute of Governmental Affairs, University of Wisconsin–Extension (Madison), and in the School of Business, University of Wisconsin–Eau Claire. Dr. Rosenberg is active in national and regional political science associations and has served in various positions, including the presidency of Women's Caucus for Political Science. She has critiqued manuscripts for a number of major publishers, and her own publications are listed in the Index.

Len Bergstrom was appointed to the Department of History at the University of Wisconsin–Eau Claire in 1971, where he teaches courses in Chinese and Japanese History. He has contributed a number of reviews to professional journals. Dr. Bergstrom was educated at Stanford University, the University of Oregon, and the University of Leeds, England, and was a research fellow at St. Antony's College, Oxford University. He is a member of numerous professional organizations, and in addition to having traveled and studied in the Far East and Europe, he speaks five languages fluently, including Chinese and Japanese. Dr. Bergstrom has been involved in women's studies for several years.

WOMEN AND SOCIETY

A Critical Review
of the Literature with a Selected
Annotated Bibliography

Compiled and Edited by

MARIE BAROVIC ROSENBERG
LEN V. BERGSTROM

University of Wisconsin

SAGE PUBLICATIONS / Beverly Hills / London

For information address:

SAGE PUBLICATIONS, INC.
275 South Beverly Drive
Beverly Hills, California 90212

SAGE PUBLICATIONS LTD
St George's House / 44 Hatton Garden
London EC1N 8ER

Printed in the United States of America

International Standard Book Number 0-8039-0248-4

Library of Congress Catalog Card No. 73-77874

FIRST PRINTING

CONTENTS

Page Numbers

PREFACE   1

INTRODUCTION: A SELECTIVE REVIEW OF THE LITERATURE
Women in History   6
Women at Work   13
Women in Politics   19

Citation Numbers

I.   SOCIOLOGY
A. Sex Roles, Characteristics and Differences   1- 132
B. Family   133- 215
C. Marriage and Divorce   216- 271
D. Life Styles   272- 392
E. Sexuality   393- 472
F. Class and Status   473- 567
G. Education and Socialization   568- 704
H. Women in Education   705- 766
I. Birth Control, Abortion and Demographic Studies   767- 877

II.   POLITICAL SCIENCE
A. Women as Socializers   878- 886
B. Victorian Attitudes   887- 890
C. Social Reformers
    1. General   891- 927
    2. Social Reformers—Abolitionists   928- 933
    3. Social Reformers—Peace   934- 939
    4. Social Reformers—Prohibition   940- 953
    5. Social Reformers—Prostitution   954- 960
D. Feminism, Equal Rights
    1. General   961-1075
    2. Feminism: Equal Rights—Committees on the Status of Women   1076-1116
    3. Feminism: Equal Rights—Marriage and Divorce   1117-1144
    4. Feminism: Equal Rights—Property   1145-1148
    5. Feminism: Equal Rights—Legal Status   1149-1209
    6. Feminism: Equal Rights—Employment   1210-1240
    7. Feminism: Equal Rights—Education   1241-1260
    8. Feminism—Innovative   1251-1260
    9. Feminism—Radical   1261-1287
E. Women as Voters
    1. General   1288-1313
    2. Women as Voters—Extent of Participation   1314-1327
    3. Women as Voters—Stand on Issues   1328-1331
F. Woman Suffrage
    1. General   1332-1370
    2. Woman Suffrage—Leaders   1371-1401
    3. Woman Suffrage—Opponents   1402-1418
    4. Woman Suffrage—Allies   1419-1424
    5. Woman Suffrage—Effects of the Movement   1425-1430

G. Politicians
   1. General   1431-1465
   2. Politicians—Elective Office   1466-1506
   3. Politicians—Appointive Office   1507-1518
   4. Politicians—Party Activists   1519-1533
   5. Politicians—Interest Groups and Voluntary Associations   1534-1542

III.   **HISTORY**
A. Women in Society   1543-1618
B. The Position of Women   1619-1679
C. Women—From Ancient Times Through Victorian   1680-1714
D. Women—Manners and Customs   1715-1737
E. Women in Folklore and Witchcraft   1738-1774
F. Woman and Fashion   1775-1824
G. Modern Women—Social and Moral Questions   1825-1949
H. Women in Revolutionary and Changing Societies   1950-1987
I. Women as Colonists and Pioneers   1988-2043
J. Women as Soldiers and Spies   2044-2081
K. Women in Ethnic Minorities   2082-2129
L. Women as Rulers   2130-2174

IV.   **WOMEN IN PHILOSOPHY AND RELIGION**   2175-2296

V.   **WOMEN IN MEDICINE AND HEALTH**   2297-2382

VI.   **WOMEN IN BIOGRAPHY, AUTOBIOGRAPHY AND MEMOIRS**   2383-2691

VII.   **WOMEN IN LITERATURE AND THE ARTS**   2692-2827

VIII.   **WOMEN IN PSYCHOLOGY**   2828-2938

IX.   **WOMEN IN ANTHROPOLOGY**   2939-3051

X.   **WOMEN IN ECONOMICS**
A. The Economic Position of Women—General   3052-3193
B. Women and Job Discrimination   3194-3237
C. Economic Effects of the Employment of Married Women   3238-3267
D. Women's Labor Unions and Organizations   3268-3298
E. Women in Domestic Labor   3299-3306
F. Women in Business, Industry and Production   3307-3365
G. Women in the Professions   3366-3399
H. Women in the Semiprofessions   3400-3432

XI.   **GENERAL REFERENCE WORKS ON WOMEN**
A. Bibliographies   3433-3503
B. Biographical Dictionaries   3504-3513
C. Directories of Women's Organizations and Institutes   3514-3550
D. Women's Periodicals and Newspapers   3551-3578
E. Women's Collections and Libraries   3579-3600

   Page Numbers
XII.   **ADDENDUM**   292

AUTHOR - ORGANIZATION INDEX   307

INDEX OF JOURNAL ISSUES ENTIRELY DEVOTED TO WOMEN   338

INDEX OF PERSONS NOT CITED AS AUTHORS   339

INDEX OF PLACES, SUBJECTS AND TOPICS   344

PREFACE

Leibnitz, it has been said, was the last man to know everything.
Though this is certainly a gross exaggeration, it is a statement with
considerable pertinence, for, while the old philosopher may have been
able to encompass the whole science of his day, and to absorb a broad
culture as well, our century has seen the proliferation of specialized
fields of interest, and the researches of an ever-increasing number of
scholars have diverged. From time to time since the growth of speciali-
zation, broad movements have arisen in reaction to this trend, seeking
unity and attempting integration. There are signs of such a movement
today in the area of women's studies. An awareness of a certain inter-
relatedness of a group of studies is growing, originally diverse and dis-
connected, but all related. Indeed, the present state of scholarship on
the changing social, economic, and political roles of women almost
dictates such an integrative, comprehensive approach, for the evolving
field is characterized more by basic "factual" research than by sweeping interpretive writing.

This present state is largely the result of the "assault" on women's
history by the international scholarly community in the past several
decades. Confronted with such a vast field of investigation, many researchers have naturally been inclined to concentrate on particularities
rather than generalities, in the hope of creating a sound factual foundation that might subsequently support interpretive superstructures. This
is a proper attitude and approach. It is, perhaps, because "life is a
swallow, and theory a snail," that scholars want the basic documents
and data of women's history to be presented objectively, as untainted
by interpretation as possible. In the future all the possible facts of
women's experience, influence, and achievement in the current of

history will have been neatly established, classified, and defined, only
to await incorporation into some grand interpretive edifice of as yet
unforeseeable outlines.

Something of this "omnibus" spirit persists in every bibliographer
who sets out to summarize the general literary scene he has surveyed,
but it is an extraordinarily ambitious and unrealizable goal. The bibliographic genre is becoming increasingly popular, so great is this desire
for unification and movement toward larger explanatory patterns.
This great abstracting and indexing service carries with it a certain
danger; bibliographic chaos, unnecessary duplication, and concentra-
tion on search rather than research. But the demand for convenient
bibliographic systems has been insistent. With a similar purposeful
approach, and while we have strived for a degree of unity in this survey
of the literature on women, we have had to be continually selective. Because we can never have the total perspective to evaluate definitively
the vast range of materials pertaining to women in this volume, we
have had to restrain our survey within narrow margins.

The focus adopted here centers on providing for scholars and the
general public alike a selected annotated bibliography of the scholarly
and applied research efforts from the major disciplines in the form of
generally authoritative and available books, journals, pamphlets, and
reference articles on women in a cross-national and cross-cultural
perspective. Our main purpose is to guide the interested readers to the
best works in which they can pursue in detail any subject pertaining
to women which attracts them in principle. We have selected those
works that contribute to a general understanding of the economic,
political, legal, military, social, moral, religious, educational, scientific,
medical, philosophic, literary, and artistic aspects of women's roles
in society. Trends in interpretation were given secondary attention,
because we hesitated to presume to be able to judge knowledgeably or
thoroughly the methods, questions, and results of analysis and description emerging from the selections.

Having forewarned the readers of the limitations inherent in the
nature of all bibliographies, we consider it more constructive to suggest that they assume the unavoidable task of being their own historian,
and to integrate the facts of women's history by analyzing the bibliographic sources illustrating the different aspects or themes of that
tradition. We believe that the content and format of this volume are
logical and orderly, and that our choice of themes enables the reader
to follow a particular concern or interest with an economy of effort.
This bibliography depends for its effectiveness on the total pattern
built up by its parts.

The variety of documents that the reader will face is enormous. Entries are arranged topically, so that the reader, by consulting the comprehensive table of contents, can readily retrieve those books and articles pertaining to any particular subject of individual interest. Within each section, entries are further divided among subsections that have been suggested by the subject matter. The sequence of subsections reflects a combination of chronological and topical groupings. The reader may best begin surveying the references by taking note of the whole of each subsection, not its first listing only. Although an effort to make each subsection a complete unit in itself has resulted in some duplication of entries, there nevertheless remains a need for some cross-referencing from category to category and from subsection to subsection as many of the works have multidisciplinary applications.

Every document may be studied from various perspectives. Each author and subject have certain social and cultural contexts, purposes, structures, and methods, and a relationship with and affiliation to other sources. In each broad category we have supplied explanatory headnotes to aid the reader of a given document to consider it as an effect of earlier developments or a cause of subsequent research. Some references are combined with other sources of the same period to form a trend. They have been grouped in countless ways, but we have, in most cases, cited works whose authors share both similar and opposite values and biases, works reflecting certain social and cultural milieu, and more broadly, those involving ideas and values held during whole historical eras. By moving back and forth between categories and documents the reader can interpret and generalize from the original readings.

Because we cannot hope that the choices we have made will content every reader, we should explain the method of our choice, particularly because the method of this bibliography is intimately related to the method of choice. We did not intend this book to be exhaustive or completely authoritative. One defect of a select bibliography is that the reader who independently discovers a book that is relevant but unlisted does not know whether it has been rejected as bad or simply overlooked. Absence of a work does not imply that it was of little or no value, and any exclusions of entries were the results of difficult judgments guided by our conscious desire to achieve a representative balance within assigned limits.

We have felt free to add a number of popularized works from our respective fields of political science and history along with special items of interest and humor in the literatures of numerous specialties. Not all of our citations aim simply to tell the truth. Many of them, through the use of rhetorical devices or disciplinary predilections, are designed to win a case, whether in court, in formal debate, or in a wider forum of opinion. Many are pitched to special audiences to get some point across, some are justifications of actions already taken, others are exhortations for the future. Clearly, all research is intelligible only in terms of the purpose or function it intends to serve and of the audience it attempts to reach.

Nevertheless, we hope that what we have assembled will be a contribution, no matter how limited its scope, for as Francis Bacon wisely observed, "Truth will sooner come out from error than from confusion." But if this bibliography gives some notion of the diverse studies of women, together with some idea of the unification which exists (even more important, the differences of opinion, controversies, lack of unification, and the gaps that remain to be explored), then this bibliography will have achieved its objective.

A number of people have helped in many ways in the preparation of this book, and we have profited from many of our colleagues in various disciplines. We thank Professor Robert B. Dishman for his warm and helpful response to our original conception of this volume and for the many hours he contributed in verifying citations for articles involving women and their legal rights. Our thanks go out also to Dan Peterson of Seattle Central Community College and Dean James Wenner of the University of Wisconsin—Eau Claire for their personal and administrative support; Eugene Engeldinger and Richard Bell, librarians at the University of Wisconsin, for their technical advice. The most perceptive aid has come from Rebecca Bergstrom and Bob Dishman, whose response to what we have done has been sympathetic, critical, and richly sustaining. Sage Publications, and particularly Connie Greaser, have been consistently patient and courteous to us in our relations, while at the same time granting us the widest latitude in matters of content, composition, and organization. At the close of a long task it is good to remember the cooperation of many publishing houses and scholars in the field of women's studies, whose suggestions and contributions lightened the inevitable drudgeries of research. Their advice in fields of which they are masters was gratuitous and stimulating.

We wish also to thank Tim Burns, David Thoms, Rozanna Hanson, Fran Podmolik, Roseann Wilde, Cheryl Huenink, Jean Luedtke, Gail Kramer, Carol and Ron Rubenzer, JoAnn Een and Peter Jauquet for the many hours of assistance they contributed in the often tedious and sometimes droll tasks of citation verification.

Finally, the authors wish to acknowledge each other. Only the intriguing subject matter, the refreshing review of scholarly publications in all fields, a ready humor, and the inspiration that comes from long and regular association and understanding could sustain us in such a prolonged and trying venture. We are conscious of how incomplete this effort is, yet how rewarding to us. We hope it deserves to be read, then revised and up-dated, and to that end we welcome criticisms and further suggestions from anyone working in this field. We want, finally, to repeat that the methodological judgments represented in the choice of categories, entries, and annotation are our sole responsibility for which neither the publishers nor our colleagues can justly be blamed.

M.B.R.
L.V.B.

INTRODUCTION: A SELECTIVE REVIEW
OF THE LITERATURE

WOMEN IN HISTORY

Our prefatory remarks will have already suggested that no detailed authoritative history of women has yet appeared in a Western language. This is a field of study where science rivals philosophy in uncertainty of knowledge and fertility of hypothesis. Much research remains to be done to trace the positive achievements of women, their social roles, and their contributions to community life. Despite these qualifications, the special problem of surveying the available literature on women remains. Restrictions of space preclude our analyzing but a few of the works cited in this volume. We shall synthesize our general approach by examining some of the works dealing with women's historical, political, and economic roles. It is in these three areas that we feel most competent to deal consistently with the wide range of observations and insights, as well as with the general long-term goals of women's historic quest for equal rights.

Modern as woman may be in her economic and social situation, she has not as yet broken with all traditions of an authoritarian and patriarchal past. Remnants of age-old historical and biological traditions regarding women as the intellectually weaker sex, less able to shoulder responsibilities in politics or the labor market, still stand in the way of that true equality. Generally speaking, women throughout the world today are confronted with social and psychological problems that largely arise out of the disharmony between a demanding present and an unmastered past—in short, the conflict between pre-industrial roles and the demands of modern life.

Of general histories, Johann Bachofen's *Das Mutterecht* (The Mother Right, 1861) [1546], though outdated and superseded by more recent and thorough anthropological and historical evidence, has led to a theory of patriarchal and matriarchal societies that is still held by many social scientists. Stated briefly, Bachofen's thesis was that the mother in prehistoric times fulfilled most of the parental functions. Primitive families were at first organized on the assumption that the position of the man in the family was superficial and incidental, while that of the woman was fundamental and supreme. In early forms of "matrilocal marriage," the husband left his clan and went to live with the clan and family of his wife. Descent was traced through the female line and inheritance was through the mother. This "mother-right" was not matriarchal in the sense that women ruled over men. Women in primitive societies exercised a certain authority, arising from their importance in the home.

Attempts to schematize the history of human institutions in universal developmental frameworks resulted in more empirical theories of social change and social evolution. One of the best pieces of evidence against Bachofen's matriarchal-patriarchal theories can be found in Edward Westermarck's *History of Human Marriage* [268], published in 1891. His investigation of primitive social institutions, carefully and systematically tested, drove the "armchair" evolutionists and theory-makers out of business. No matriarchal societies have ever been discovered, he said, although some matrilocal and matrilineal communities existed. Therefore, Westermarck concluded, because no matriarchies have existed, all theories based on the idea of their existence had to be dropped. Nor was there a consistent pattern in earlier societies of relating private property with hunting or agricultural systems, he added. Uncontrolled sexual communism had never been discovered, nor is there evidence it ever existed. About the only broad generalization Westermarck makes is that all societies have rules of sexual behavior, have families consisting of some variation of the nuclear family, practice exogamy, and usually proscribed homosexual practices.

Robert Briffault was the last anthropologist to take Bachofen's theories seriously with his book *The Mothers* [142], written in 1927. His interpretation of the historical evidence concluded that when woman with her industry and inventiveness finally enabled man to live in security in a woman-dominated civilization, man then established the custom of taking over her ideas and commercializing them. Woman thus became subservient to man. Scientific anthropology, sociology, and critical history have reduced almost every aspect of his theories to rubble.

The scientific methods of Westermarck and the later intensive field studies and theoretical analysis of Bronislaw Malinowski, Franz Boaz, Margaret Mead, and other investigators, were sometimes carried to extremes. Many researchers were content to rely on data gathered by all varieties of collectors whose interpretations had since been disproven by more reliable scientific methods. Several speculative and partisan studies of women in primitive society have been published. Helen Diner, in *Mothers and Amazons* (1965) [1564], pays enthusiastic support to Bachofen's findings and makes many of the same invalid uses of mythological interpretation in order to understand prehistorical social processes, contradicting the "certainties" of sociologists with her insights, views, and often pseudo-scientific perspective of other disciplines. Eva Figes, in her *Patriarchal Attitudes* (1970) [1567], criticizes the masculine attitudes that have subjugated women. Her survey of the purely patriarchal character of our civilization develops in a one-sided conception that women's inferior social and sexual position resulted from the interaction of psychic and social factors. Her solution to the patriarchal problem is to abolish the institution of marriage. Elizabeth Gould Davis's *The First Sex* (1971) [1561] seeks to restore to women their "ancient dignity and pride" as the superior and dominant sex. In trying to prove women's superiority, she relegates man to a position of inferiority. This would be a flight from reality and could have revolutionary psychosociological repercussions. Unfortunately today, many of the past and present "theoretical cloud cathedrals" of nineteenth-century anthropology are still accepted by educated laymen and even social scientists outside anthropology.

Simone de Beauvoir's *The Second Sex* (1949) [26] explores a comparable historic theme. Rejecting some of Bachofen's theory, keeping some of Engels and Bebel, and adding some "pseudo-anthropology" of her own, she concludes that "society has always been in the hands of men." Reviewing the data of prehistoric research and ethnography in the light of existentialist philosophy, de Beauvoir asserts that woman "submitted passively to her biologic fate," for it is not in giving life but in risking life that man was raised above woman. Men presumed to create a "feminine domain . . . only in order to lock up women therein." By her use of the "existentialist perspective," women can understand more clearly how the biological and economic condition of primitive society led to male supremacy. Woman traditionally has been defined only in relation to man, not as she in herself. Man, de Beauvoir says, is the "Subject, the Absolute— she is the Other." Woman found herself "living in a world where men

compel her to assume the status of the Other. They propose to sta-
bilize her as object . . . " Prevented by her weakness and inferior productive capacity in primitive society, woman could not become a
fellow workman with the man. Since "he did not accept her" because
she seemed in his eyes to have the aspect of the *other,* "man could
not be otherwise than her oppressor. The male will to power and expansion made of woman's incapacity a curse."

Marred occasionally by its dogmatic tendencies, *The Second Sex*
clarifies many ideas of woman's relation to man and how she has been
pushed into a secondary, inferior position, resulting in severe alienation in herself and in society. It has played an important role in the
new feminist movement's initiative for organized agitation for a life
as full human beings. The literature of the women's movement demands that women be liberated not only from the legal, occupational,
and educational barriers in their lives, but also from the false self-
concepts they have acquired in one way or another. Women today
seek liberation from sexually, rather than humanly, oriented socialization processes; from laws, customs, and traditions locked into and
handed down by male-dominated societies; from parents, from the
men in their lives, from advisers reflecting uncritically a patriarchal
order of things. The new feminist movement is obviously a means to
the end of self-discovery and identity.

Women of today undertake careers in a mentally harassing situation while still under the personal burdens implied historically by
their femininity. Paradoxically, their modern independent status has
given rise to an inferiority complex. Their femininity makes them
doubtful of their professional future. As a result of this defeatist
attitude, women have become reconciled to moderate successes; they
do not dare aim too high. As de Beauvoir says, "What women essentially lacks today for doing great things is forgetfulness of herself and
her past. Newly come into the world of men, poorly seconded by
them, woman is still too busily occupied to search for herself." We
shall refer to this problem again in the review of the literature on
women's economic activities in our century.

While Simone de Beauvoir's study is the source, as much as any
other single work, of the rationale for this century's sexual and
social revolution, that movement may very well have been born with
Mary Wollstonecraft, the daughter of a brutal authoritarian father
and a martyr of a mother, in eighteenth-century England. In statements that have a familiar modern ring to them, she asserted that
women must be free to compete with men on their own grounds.
Let society recognize new roles for women, she says.

It is time to effect a revolution in female manners—time to restore to them
their lost dignity—and make them, as part of the human species, labour by
reforming themselves, to reform the world. . . . They might also study
politics . . . Business of various kinds, they might likewise pursue. . . . The
few employments open to women, so far from being liberal, are menial . . .

We can see in her *Vindication of the Rights of Women* (1792)
[1065], the bible of feminism, and her demand for equality for
women is repeated by present-day feminists. From her pen spring not
only the works of Simone de Beauvoir, but also the feminist scholarship of Vivian Gornick and Barbara J. Moran, editors of *Woman in
Sexist Society* (1971) [501], an anthology of essays showing how
acceptance of the female role continues to dictate women's lives today. It is a recommended reader of some of the best contemporary
materials. Note particularly such writers as Naomi Weisstein, "Kinder,
Küche, Kirche as Scientific Law," "Psychology Constructs the Fe-
male," and "Woman as Nigger," and Gornick, "Woman as Outsider."
Several other anthologies may be mentioned here as being relevant.
The sociologists Cynthia F. Epstein and William J. Goode, in their
The Other Half: Roads to Women's Equality (1971) [33], have put
together a varied selection of readings with intelligent introductions.
Some variety of primary and secondary sources may be found also in
Anne Koedt and Shulamith Firestone's *Notes from the Third Year:
Women's Liberation* (1971) [1002], an interesting selection of essays
on women in literature, black feminism, lesbianism, women's legal
inequities, and the women's rights movement, to name only a few.
See also Nancy Reeves's *Womankind: Beyond the Stereotypes* (1971)
[104], a collection of sources with an excellent introductory text
highlighted by a short.photographic essay. In addition, *Feminism:
The Essential Historical Writings,* edited by Miriam Schneir in 1972
[1043], contains excerpts of documents which appeared between the
Revolutionary War period and 1929, and is a recommended text for
introductory courses in women's studies programs, Roberta Salper's
Female Liberation: History and Current Politics (1972) [1924], views
the first and second women's movements in America, with a scholarly
introduction describing the limitations as well as the achievements of
past and present feminists.

A frequent accusation of contemporary scholars of the feminist
movement is that its "radicals" envy and hate male superiority. In
Modern Woman, The Lost Sex (1947) [439], Ferdinand Lundberg
and Marynia Farnham give a prejudiced and often inaccurate rebuttal
to the extreme feminist position. Their analysis of the feminist mood

is that it is hostile to heterosexual love, hostile to sex, hostile to motherhood, and most of all, hostile to women.

> What the feminists were actually aiming for was definitely not justice. It was, as Mary Wollstonecraft flatly said . . . *masculinity*. And a female who attempts to achieve masculinity is psychically ill in the same way as a male who attempts to achieve feminity.

For a more reasoned discussion of women's liberation viewpoints, consult Betty Friedan's *The Feminine Mystique* (1963) [41].

In the eighteenth and nineteenth centuries feminism was often inseparable from other radical and utopian movements, and had influences in matters of sex, marriage, and sex roles. Not only in our time, but in the early nineteenth century, there was still almost universal mockery of feminism. Many American and European reformers devoted themselves to the abolition of the "feminine problem," and as a result, feminism gained in strength and militance, with the political rather than the sexual-freedom faction controlling the movement in most countries.

Historical scholarship dealing with the feminist movement both here and abroad has been made accessible to students by the works of a number of researchers. Eleanor Flexner's *Century of Struggle* (1959) [1445] traces the story of the women's rights movement in America, and its activists, "not as presidents, inventors, generals, or business leaders, but as mothers and homemakers, producers, reformers, and eventually as citizens." While the author admits that her book is only a limited step toward filling the gap in the historical research of the feminist movement, it presents a well-balanced and scholarly effort to chart its slow development, beginning in the nineteenth century, down to the passage of the suffrage amendment to the United States Constitution in 1920. Women's involvement in the many reform movements of the nineteenth century is well documented in Robert Riegel's *American Feminists* (1968) [1423], and in such studies as Gerda Lerner's *The Grimké Sisters from South Carolina: Rebels Against Slavery* (1967) [2554]. Eileen Kraditor's *The Ideas of the Woman Suffrage Movement* (1969) [943] and the *History of Woman Suffrage* [1366], a six-volume essential study edited by the women who fought for the movement, Elizabeth Cady Stanton, Susan B. Anthony, Ida Husted Harper, and Matilda Joslin Gage, and published between 1881 and 1922, are definitive works. William L. O'Neill's *Everyone Was Brave: The Rise and Fall of Feminism in America* (1969) [884] is a well-researched, interpretive study, but William H. Chafe's *The American Woman: Her Changing Social, Economic, and Political Role, 1920-1970* (1972) [878] is so far the only recent study that focuses on the history of the American woman since 1920.

Also usable as general histories of women's progress in gaining the vote are Ray Strachey's book *The Cause* (1928) [1049], Emmeline Pankhurst's *My Own Story* (1915) [2595], and her sister Sylvia's study, *The Suffragette Movement* (1931) [1915], which describe the British suffrage struggle.

The changes in the position of women are dealt with in such works as Suzanne La Follette's *Concerning Women* (1926) [1578], Mary Beard's *Woman as Force in History* (1946) [1547] and her earlier book *On Understanding Women* (1931) [1624]. *A Brief History of the Condition of Women* (1854) [1628] by Lydia Child deals with the position of women in 53 countries. Eugene Hecker's *Short History of Women's Rights* (1914) [1640], which has just been reprinted, begins with women during the Roman period and concludes with the history of women's rights to the end of World War I. Many studies of the changing roles and position of women in earlier Western societies have been published. Several dated but worthwhile monographs are Mitchell Carroll's *Greek Women* (1908) [1688], Pierce Butler's study of *Women in Medieval France* (1908) [1685], John Effiger's portraits of *Women in the Romance Counties* (1908) [1721], Edward Pollard's *Oriental Women* (1908) [1593], and Jermann Schoenfeld's *Women of the Teutonic Nations* (1908) [1599], to mention a few. Modern times are covered adequately in *Women of India* (1958) [1623] by Iara Baig, *Facts about Women in Norway* (1960) [1663] by Ellen B. Seip, *Political Status of Women in the Other American Republics* (1957) [1674], a U.S. Government publication, *Italian Women* (1939) [1957] by Maria Castellani, *Women in the New Asia* (1963) [1944] by Barbara Ward, *Women in the USSR* (n.d.) [1983] by Nadezhda Tatarinova, and *Women of Algeria* (1968) [1963] by David Gordon. These are only a few of the studies focusing on women's changing social, political, and economic roles in foreign countries.

In our assessment of the works on women's contributions, we noted the absence of any comprehensive cross-cultural references, but Anna Garlin Spencer's *Woman's Share in Social Culture* (1925) [1602], William Alexander's encyclopedic compendium of women from earliest antiquity to the year of its publication in 1799 [1544], along with Harriet Bradbury's *Civilization and Womanhood* (1916) [1551], are excellent for their discussions of women's contributions toward the progress of civilization. The studies of Anna de Koven (1941) [1562], Sarah Josepha Hale (1855) [1572], William King (1903) [1646], and the classic study of woman's share in primitive culture by Otis T. Mason (1895) [1699] provide insights into a variety of cultures.

A similar hiatus exists in the study of women's scientific contributions to civilization, but Edna Yost's *American Women of Science* (1955) [2690] and *Women of Modern Science* (1959) [2691] give credit where it has long been overdue.

Women have a history worth knowing. Individually and collectively, the investigations so far of the literature describing women's contributions, their position in society, and the way society has looked upon them confirm the importance of all women in our social heritage. The ways in which women have struggled to solve their problems, the various institutions they have established, and the ideas they have developed about the world and their place in it are part of the background of our own period. The rich historical literature on women enables us to indicate the major landmarks in the development and progress of women through the ages, and in understanding this background better, we learn to understand ourselves and our society better.

L.B.

WOMEN AT WORK

The most conspicuous central theme in the literature concerned with the economic position of women is one of growing discontent. This is not the image projected by the mass media in most of the developed nations of the world. There, women are usually depicted as contented if slightly bored housewives. The reality, of course, is to be found elsewhere—in the reports of the various Commissions on the Status of Women, in hearings before legislative committees on discrimination in employment, and in lawsuits in the courts. It is even reflected in the statistical compilations of Departments of Labor and in the most objective of scholarly articles. Together, they make clear a fact already known to most women—that as housewives their work is undervalued, and as workers and professionals they are underpaid relative to men doing the same work. Revealed also are the depth and extent of societal limitations on the productive capacities of females because they are females—to say nothing of limitations on the monetary and psychological rewards they receive.

The growing unrest among women and an increasing awareness of their unrest on the part of scholars, politicians, and business managers has led to a burgeoning literature on the subject in the past twenty years. Some of the more recent literature is scholarly and objective, but much of it is frankly and understandably polemic and partisan. Increasingly, women themselves are challenging not only the pattern of discrimination but also the social attitudes, public policies, and economic institutions that reinforce it. Pultizer prize-winning Stanford historian Carl Degler perceptively assessed the cumulative impact of this ferment as a social "Revolution Without Ideology" (1964) [297]. The implications of this revolution may be even greater in the economic and social spheres than in the political because they portend fundamental changes in the basic relations between the sexes and in the economic structure itself.

Throughout the centuries preceding the full impact of the Industrial Revolution, women's roles were largely confined to domestic chores and agricultural production. Technology propelled most women, who along with their menfolk were replaced by machines on the farm, into tending machines in the factories. Some of their number, of course, remain on the farms today. A miniscule few "made it" in an uphill battle into the ranks of the professions. Others, too, were "promoted" by the Ladies Home Journalists of their day into an idealized housewifery that John Kenneth Galbraith describes as a "cryptoservant class" ("The Equitable Household and Beyond," *Economics and the Public Purpose,* Boston: Houghton Mifflin, 1973). While one need not agree with the parameters of Galbraith's own vision of the life of the housewife, nor even with his tentative proposals for corrective measures (which include professionally prepared food, public transportation, and professional entertainment), he has accurately assessed the assigned value of her present occupational status. It was Alva Myrdal and Viola Klein (1956, 1966) [95] who earlier focused attention on the demands and frequent conflict between the two predominant societal roles of the woman: her role in the home and her role in the economy. Nor is this conflict in women's roles to be found only in Western, capitalistic societies. In a recent study ("Women in the Soviet Economy," *Review of Radical Political Economics,* vol. 4, no. 3, July 1972), Marilyn Power Goldberg found much the same kind of conflict in the Soviet Union. Soviet women have found that their economic role as workers or professionals does not relieve them from their roles as housewives and mothers. She denotes their condition as one of double exploitation: they are expected by their men to accept almost complete responsibility for home and family, and they are channeled by state planners and managers, mostly males, into the lowest paid and least prestigious jobs and professions.

Whatever their country or marital status, women still encounter two kinds of discrimination on the job. First, certain occupations or careers may be closed to them either partly, as under a quota system based arbitrarily on sex, or completely, as when the qualifications for a job are drawn so as effectively to bar women. Where overt exclusion is forbidden by law, as it now is in the United States, it may

still be accomplished indirectly through an informal "old boy" network, and perhaps less obviously by societal perceptions of "appropriate" women's work. Second, even when they gain entry into a field,
women are not treated equally with men in the conditions of their
employment. Their pay scales and salaries, rates and levels of advancement, fringe benefits, and job security tend to be lower than men's
even in those jobs into which women have been purposively channeled.

In the past 150 years three basic strategies have been tested by advocates of humanitarian and equalitarian persuasion. The earliest
efforts were directed at self-help through trade union organization and
negotiation, but they were not, for the most part, effective. Whatever
gains the labor movement may have achieved for men, it did little to
protect women against discrimination by either their employer or
their male co-workers. Many unions, indeed, barred women from
membership, and those that did not were usually ineffective. Even in
those trades and professions which have employed predominantly
females, unions have been slow to organize and to bargain effectively
with management. The International Ladies Garment Worker's Union,
indeed, is a notable exception. Though research on the subject has
been relatively sparse, there are several general accounts of the early
attempts to organize and politicize workers in industrial mills. As an
example of women's activities on behalf of unionization, see A.J.G.
Perkins and Theresa Wolfson, *Frances Wright: Free Inquirer* (1939)
[1397]. A later and more general treatise, *The Trade Union Women*
(1915) [3280] by Alice Henry, though somewhat dated, is a useful
reference, as is *The Woman Worker and the Trade Unions* (1926)
[3298] by Theresa Wolfson. Alice H. Cook, *Women and American
Trade Unions* (1968) [3276], and Lucretia M. Dewey, "Women in
Labor Unions" (*Monthly Labor Review*, vol. 94, no. 2, February,
1971), provide more recent statistics on membership and service as
officers.

Disappointed in their efforts at self-help through trade unions,
working women and their middle-class allies, men and women, next
turned to their government for protection. In the United States this
meant largely state governments because only they in strict constitutional theory, were armed with the police power, that is, the power to
regulate private persons and their property in order to foster, protect,
and promote the general welfare, health, safety, morals, and convenience. During the Progressive Era many states responded to the call by
giving working women protection which for many years was denied to
men. Though these laws were invariably challenged as "mere meddle-
some interferences" with property rights, many were upheld by the

courts. Thus, in 1908 the U.S. Supreme Court upheld a maximum hours law (*Muller* v. *Oregon,* 208 U.S. 412, 1908), and in 1937 a minmum wage law (*West Coast Hotel Co.* v. *Parrish,* 300 U.S. 379, 1939), which applied to women in certain classifications of jobs, but neither of which applied to men.

Other decisions of the Supreme Court upheld laws which had the effect, if not the intent, of forcing women to compete at a disadvantage with men. In *Radice* v. *New York* (264 U.S. 292, 1924), it was a state law forbidding women to work at night in large cities; in *Goeseart* v. *Cleary* (335 U.S. 464, 1948) [1216] a state law forbidding women to tend bar unless their father or husband owned the establishment. While these, and cases in a similar vein, did not go to the heart of the issues of entry into and inequality within a variety of occupations, they were lauded for a time in the belief they improved the lot (to say nothing of protecting the morals) of women who had to work for a living. The irony was, as Kathleen Lucas Barber[1] states, "While women labor leaders and (largely) male legislators have continued to advocate these laws to protect women, their effect has been to channel women into the lowest status jobs in the economy, to deny them advancement and the privileges earned through seniority, and in the case of minimum wage laws, to bring them to the exalted status . . . in which full-time employed women earn about sixty percent of what similarly employed men receive."

In effect stalemated in this strategy, women turned from protective legislation to legislation with an emphasis on equality. Once again they had to go through the exercise of documenting existing discriminatory practices and conditions, and pressuring legislative bodies and their constituencies alike for remedial legislation.

Probably the most comprehensive single work cataloging in detail the extent, and to a degree, the consequences of discriminatory policies and practices against women are the public hearings conducted in 1970 (supplemental hearings 1972) by Congresswoman Edith Green, chairperson of the Special Subcommittee on Education of the U.S. House of Representatives [3235]. The committee's primary focus was on discrimination against women in the field of education. In fact, because education in one place or another is the de facto source of formal learning, is at least an influence on informal learning throughout our culture, and is relied upon as our single greatest instrument for implementing social change, the hearings mirrored the greater societal scope of women's concerns and women's plight.

Somewhat similar in nature and importance are the 1973 hearings before the Joint Economic Committee, Congress of the United States on *Economic Problems of Women* (93rd Cong. 1st sess. pts. i, ii, iii,

1973). These hearings catalog the handicaps women face in their efforts to function as individual or group economic units as either consumers, employees, or entrepreneurs. For a recent study emphasizing the elements contributing to the success of women entrepreneurs in West Germany, see Heinz Hartmann, *Die Unternehmerin* (Cologne, 1968), a section of which is available in English translation, "The Enterprising Woman: A German Model" (*Columbia Journal of World Business,* vol. 5, no. 2, March-April 1970). Extremely useful, too, are the many publications of the U.S. Department of Labor, Women's Bureau (established in 1922). While these reports at times reflect the somewhat less urgent perspective of a more complacent period in women's history, the statistics kept by the bureau are our best source for base-line data and measurement of change. The most recent compendium, now out of print but, one would hope, to be updated soon, is the *Handbook on Women Workers* (1969) [3165]. For a useful comparison but slightly different perspective, see the National Manpower Council's publication, *Womanpower* (1957) [3112]. For syntheses that provide an overview and some historical perspective, see Robert W. Smuts, *Women and Work in America* (1959) [3135], Marjorie B. Turner and Irvine Bernstein, eds., *Women and Work* (1964) [3144], and Esther Petersen, "Working Women" (1964) [297].

Though there had been prior advocates of general concern and specific measures to ameliorate women's lot, the federal government's official awakening on the subject was symbolized by President John F. Kennedy's 1961 Statement Establishing a Commission on the Status of Women. The commission report [693, 1105-1113; see also Mead and Kaplan (1965), 1085] produced shock in some and serious concern in many. It, together with Commission on the Status of Women reports from a number of other jurisdictions (for example, see Washington [1114-1116], New Hampshire [1087], the United Nations [1098-1102]) and a growing number of countries (see Maj-Britt Sandlin, Sweden [1096]), began to stir the public sector into action as these and other works mobilized an increasing number of individuals and groups in the private sector into overt prodding including lobbying. The swelling volume of literature noted such contributions as Caroline Bird's *Born Female: The High Cost of Keeping Women Down* (1968) [1834]; National Labour Market Board of Sweden, "Women and the Labour Market" (1968) [3361]; Valerie Kincade Oppenheimer, *The Female Labor Force in the United States: Demographic and Economic Factors Governing Its Growth and Changing Composition* (1970) [3353]; and Jessie Bernard's *Women and the Public Interest: An Essay on Policy and Protest* (1971) [3058].

These, and the efforts of many others, had their effects in fostering legislative response. Passage of "landmark legislation" does not guarantee change, but it does help by providing both the climate and the mechanics for affecting behavior and further policy provisions. Thus it was that in 1963, after many years of delay, the U.S. Congress passed the Equal Pay Act, limited to be sure, but requiring all establishments subject to the Fair Labor Standards Act of 1938 to provide equal pay for equal work. Though the classification sex originally was added to the Civil Rights Act of 1964 in a maneuver to defeat its passage, the climate—and the publicity—facilitated its passage instead. The addition of the 1972 Amendment to the Equal Pay Act extended its provisions to persons in the professions. These laws, together with Presidential Executive Order 11246 as amended by Executive Order 11375, Executive Order 11478, and amendment provisions known as Revised Order 4 (*Federal Register,* vol. 36, no. 234, December 4, 1971), prohibit discrimination against women and minorities. Together they provide for agencies to administer the provisions of the laws and the regulations devised to implement them. The agencies with major responsibilities for these tasks are the Division of Higher Education of the Office for Civil Rights in the Department of Health, Education and Welfare; the Office of Federal Contract Compliance; the Equal Employment Opportunity Commission; and the U.S. Civil Service Commission. They require reports, issue guidelines, investigate complaints, and pursue legal remedies when violations are substantiated. The laws and regulations preempt any conflicting state or local laws and are applicable to contractors and agencies receiving federal funds.

The same patterns of discrimination and attempts to remedy them can also be seen in other countries. By 1955 the British had decided to introduce equal pay for nonmanual civil servants, gradually extending the coverage to include their counterparts in local government, nationalized industries, the health services, and the teaching professions. Equal pay for manual workers is restricted mainly to public transport and some of the textile trades. As of 1971 about 12 percent of employed women in the United Kingdom were receiving equal pay, while time rates of pay for the rest of the working women averaged about 80 percent of men's pay. Legislation was effected as of May 1970 aimed at implementation of equal pay by the end of 1975 leaving employers free to decide their own programs of implementation. The law extends coverage to government employees with special provisions for the extension to armed forces and police. It does not cover pension rights nor does it preempt existing "protective" legislation.

See C. A. Larsen, "Equal Pay for Women in the United Kingdom," *International Labor Review,* vol. 103, no. 1, January 1971.

Norton Dodge, in *Women in the Soviet Economy* (1966) [3075], provides some cogent observations on the discrepancies among Soviet pronouncements, policies, and practices relative to equality for women. He chronicles discriminatory practices in matters of pay, equal access to privileged ranks of employment, and relief from the burdens of double exploitation—on the job and in the home. One recourse denied to Soviet women, resort to litigation in the ordinary courts, is available to British and American women. Once, "the rules of law" and supporting regulations have been established, interpretation, as we have seen, is ultimately left to the courts. While there have been several recent cases which have denied the right to discriminate against women under specific conditions and circumstances (see *Reed* v. *Reed,* 404 U.S. 71, 1971, upholding designation of a woman as administratrix of an estate where the Idaho law gave preference to a man, and *Phillip* v. *Martin Marietta,* 400 U.S. 542, 1971, where the court held the burden of proof was on the company to show preschool children would affect a woman's job performance any more than it would a man's), these cases do not demonstrate any great shift toward egalitarian positions by the court. To date there has been no equivalent for women of *Korematsu* v. *U.S.* (323 U.S. 214, 1944) in which the court observed that classification by race is inherently suspect.

M.B.R.

WOMEN IN POLITICS

A thoughtful examination and evaluation of the substantial number of citations which have been classified herein as pertaining to women in politics reveals that many of these works are descriptive of women's individual or group actions perceived to be directly or indirectly political in nature. Few are analytical. Fewer still are the result of rigorous or even systematic scholarly research into the political behavioral patterns of women; practically none investigate the causes of such behavior. Even among the "classics" of political behavior there is still much to be desired in scope and breadth of research, adequacy of methodology, and impartiality in approach, to say nothing ofconcernfor women as a majority of the body politic.

With rare exceptions, the major works to be reviewed here, significant because they are so frequently cited as authoritative, take one proposition as proven: that politically women behave differently from men. Gabriel Almond and Sidney Verba have both described and, "on the whole, confirmed," this finding in their *Civic Culture* (1965) [1290]. "Somewhat more frequently" than men, they say, women are "apathetic, parochial, conservative, and sensitive to the personality, emotional and esthetic aspects of political life and electoral campaigns." For some years the evidence cited to support this type of finding came largely from two pioneering studies. The older is Herbert Tingsten's *Political Behavior* (1937) [1326], which was first published as volume 7 of the Stockholm Economic Studies. Today, after nearly forty years, the work is still notable for the breadth and rigor of its analysis. It covers parliamentary elections and a few referenda and local elections in eleven countries where it was possible to distinguish the votes cast by women from those cast by men. He concludes that "the women nowhere make use of their vote to the same extent as the men," that woman suffrage seems to have "favored the bourgeois parties, particularly those having a religious tint," and that "in general woman suffrage has acted as a conservative factor in politics, though its importance in this respect may have varied a good deal in different countries." He made no attempt to offer "general explanations" of these tendencies, though he did point out "certain obvious connections" between them. One such connection, that between women's "religious tendencies" and their voting behavior, he left entirely to social psychologists to explain.

The second study is Maurice Duverger's *The Political Role of Women* (1955) [1443]. Though the organization and conclusions, not to mention the writing style, are unmistakably his, the study is essentially a report of a survey conducted by the International Political Science Association for UNESCO's Department of the Social Sciences in 1952 and 1953. The Duverger report is both like and unlike the Tingsten study. Both are based largely on aggregate election data in countries where a separate count was kept of men and women voters; but whereas the earlier study covered eleven countries, the Duverger was limited to four—France, the German Federal Republic, Norway, and Yugoslavia—all chosen by UNESCO. Only in Norway was an accurate breakdown of the vote available for both parliamentary and municipal elections. In Yugoslavia the women's vote was available for only one election, in France for only two districts, and Germany for only those relatively few districts which continued the practice started under the Weimar Republic of distinguishing between men and women voters. In Duverger's own words, the documentary material was generally "scanty" and "not adequate to provide a basis for any definite conclusion. The variety of our sources makes the comparisons we have tried to draw between different countries even less reliable." The report itself, moreover, was "drafted with extreme speed, which is hardly conducive to scientific methods." Though the "pioneer work" done for the survey was "important," in his judgment, "its results cannot be more than fragmentary and hypothetical. Scientific integrity compels most of the matter in this general report to assume the form of questions. The report raises, in fact, more questions than it answers."

Notwithstanding Duverger's modest—and prudent—disclaimers, his work is still cited often as *the* authoritative source for an understanding of women's political roles. He himself reached conclusions which went far beyond his "scanty" documentation. But not even the most ardent feminist can fault his empathy for the plight of women who attempt to play a political role.

> If the majority of women are little attracted to political careers, it is because everything tends to turn them away from them; if they allow politics to remain essentially a man's business, it is because everything conduces to this belief—tradition, family life, education, religion, and literature. . . . The small part played by women in politics merely reflects and results from the secondary place to which they are still assigned by the customs and attitudes of our society and which their education and training tend to make them accept as the natural order of things.

Yet on occasion the Frenchman in him triumphs over the political sociologist. One example has been widely quoted:

> While women have, legally ceased to be minors, they still have the mentality of minors in many fields and, particularly in politics, they usually accept paternalism on the part of men. The man—husband, fiance, lover, or myth— is the mediator between them and the political world.

It may be, as Fred Greenstein (*Children and Politics*, New Haven: Yale University Press, 1965) suggests, that Duverger was simply being "charmingly Gallic" or that, as Almond and Verba maintain, he was expressing an attitude which was "essentially continental European." In either event, the comment is neither as charming nor as valid as it no doubt seemed twenty years ago.

More recent investigations have attempted, with varying success, to avoid the methodological limitations of the Tingsten and Duverger studies. In the past two decades the sample survey has largely replaced the reliance on aggregate election data which characterized almost all of the earlier voting studies. Surveys make it possible to study the attitudes of nonvoters as well as voters and to do so at any time, not only at elections at which votes are tabulated or otherwise distinguished on the basis of the voter's sex.

The most comprehensive study of voting based on survey data is Angus Campbell et al., *The American Voter* [1295], published in 1960.

Not the least of its many virtues are its scope and replicability, sum-marizing, as it does, the findings of the University of Michigan's Sur-vey Research Center over three presidential elections. In general, *The American Voter* confirms the findings of earlier studies that women turn out at the polls about 10 percent less frequently than men, but it qualifies its findings as some of the others do not. Outside the South there was very little "average difference" in turnout among college graduates or young people without children. To the extent that women are not as politically involved as men, the study shows it is not owing to any lack of a sense of duty on their part; indeed, women are about as likely as men to be loyal to their political party and con-scious of their civic duty to vote. Only in their sense of political efficacy were women found to be markedly different from men.

> Men are more likely than women to feel that they can cope with the com-plexities of politics and to believe that their participation carries some weight in the political process.

In the Campbell study, women's relatively weak sense of politi-cal competence is said to reflect the different sex roles which men and women have acquired by the time they come of political age. As they describe these "role beliefs," Campbell and his associates are as Gallic as Duverger but not nearly as charming:

> The man is expected to be dominant in action directed toward the world outside the family; the woman is to accept his leadership passively. She is not expected, therefore, to see herself as an effective agent in politics.

The evidence cited in support of this differentiation of sex roles is not impressive. Indeed, on closer examination, it is not "the woman" in general who accepts "the man's leadership passively" but merely the "dependent wife . . . tends to leave not only the sifting of information up to her husband but abides by his ultimate decision about the direction of the vote as well." In the end, Campbell and his associates conclude: "Of course some wives, as well as some women without husbands, do strike out on their own politically." These "liberated women," in the authors' phrase, may well be as sophisticated as men in their political evaluations. The inference to be drawn should be clear: as more and more women "strike out on their own," they can be expected to show the same level of sophistication as men, however high or low that level may be. Nevertheless, Campbell and associates come down on the side of "male dominance" in determination of the voting behavior of women.

Jean Grossholtz and Susan C. Bourque recently presented a carefully prepared critique[2] of *The American Voter* and other relatively recent major studies detailing the notable shortcomings and gaps in the works on women's participation, pointing out that "Women are caught in a damned if you do and damned if you don't situation." They conclude that:

> those who study elites assume that those elites will be men and seem little concerned to investigate the few women who do appear. By ignoring these women in the elite structure, political scientists lend support to the thesis that males dominate in politics and maintain the notion that women are not politically active.

The reader is heartily recommended to their selective review.

Grossholtz and Bourque found a larger proportion of studies of women's political participation, and furthermore studies by political scientists, than did Louise M. Young twelve years earlier in her 1961 bibliographical essay, "The American Woman at Mid-Century" [1073]. Young, herself trained in political psychology, political sociology, and political theory, and author of several books and articles on politics, could find little beyond Lazarsfeld and Campbell, as political scientists concerned with women in politics, to mention in her review. She notes, "No thorough investigation of the nature and scope of American Women's direct and indirect participation in political life has yet been made by historians, or political scientists though several studies are in progress." Nonetheless, her essay continues to be valuable for its assessments of the many first-person historical accounts, biographies, and autobiographies of women actively involved in social and political reform movements. These "will always remain an immense grab bag of valuable source material." Her judgment can as well be applied to the more recent volumes in the same genre. In addition she reviews the works of historians, sociologists, educators, social psychologists, psychologists, cultural anthropologists, and economists whose research on women is significant to political scientists, or should be in the absence of their own.

Carrying on in this tradition, Wilma Rule Krauss has prepared an extensive bibliographical overview, exploring the cumulative literature on what might be described as the cultural aspect of behavioral causation. Her paper, "Politics and Gender Roles: Some Perspectives in Contemporary Literature"[3] provides a most useful survey of the research on sex roles and some of the studies in which it has been applied. Krauss, like Grossholtz and Bourque, points out the gaps to which specific research needs to be applied.

It would be a mistake to conclude that no substantive work is being produced on women. All of the fields and most of the authors mentioned by Young plus a number new to the subject are evident in the quickened flow of research to the public. Not the least in presenting these efforts are the professional journals. Foremost among them for continued interest, attention, and a focus on politics over the years are the *Annals* of the American Academy of Political and Social Sciences [279, 392, 1074, 1349, 3296] with periodical issues devoted entirely to the subject. Other professional journals are opening their covers to studies both about women and by women. Among them are *Politics and Society*. Lynn Iglitzin (1972) [1448] pinpoints serious shortcomings in the political education of women that result in their responding politically less than men. She is not the first in her concern over the socialization processes. In 1962, in the *Journal of Politics,* Fred Greenstein [882] explored "Sex-Related Political Differences in Childhood." He is to be credited for a serious approach to the subject, though some of his conclusions, tempered by a stricture that "further research is needed to learn in detail just what these underpinnings are," remain questionable. He departs from his own documented research to opine "politics, although not of deep interest to children of either sex, is more resonant with the 'natural' enthusiasm of boys." Unfortunately, most of the works on political socialization between 1961 and 1972 either ignore the sex of the socializers or of the socialized as a significant variable, if they treat it at all. An exception is M. Kent Jennings and Richard G. Niemi, "The Divisions of Political Labor between Mothers and Fathers," *American Political Science Review* (1971) [883].

Jennings's interest in sex-based political comparisons was evidenced as well in an earlier work, "Men and Women in Party Elites: Social Roles and Political Resources," *Midwest Journal of Political Science* (1968) [66]. He was predated by Emmy Werner "Women in Congress: 1917-1964," *Western Political Quarterly* (1966) [1504]. Werner's work broke a long political science journal drought on women in public office. It has been journals of other disciplines which have aired important aspects of women's political profile and still do. The *Journal of Social Issues* (1972) brought out Edmond Constantini and Kenneth H. Craik's study, "Women as Politicians: The Social Background, Personality, and Political Issues" [1475].

However, it is still true that the three richest sources for the current researcher are as yet unpublished dissertations, unpublished theses, and unpublished papers (presented in increasing numbers) at professional association regional, and national meetings. For the latter, some associations, such as the American Political Science Association, have initiated the practice of copyrighting and submitting complete sets of the papers (regularly available through their distribution centers at annual meetings) to University Microfilms. For the rest, and for papers presented at earlier meetings, it is still necessary to comb the programs and contact the authors. Unpublished theses are listed in university library card files which are seldom published. Thus a valuable research resource is largely lost. The unpublished dissertations are, happily, more accessible. Xerox printouts of dissertations on file with University Microfilms, Ann Arbor, Michigan, are available on order for a fee. Even better is the announcement of March 1974 that a thirty-seven volume "Comprehensive Dissertation Index" (key title word and author index) listing more than 417,000 doctoral dissertations accepted by United States colleges and universities and a number of foreign institutions is now available. The index should be most valuable in ascertaining what has and what has not been done in all disciplines. For the dissertations under way, one may be grateful for the periodic listings printed (as submitted by graduate students or graduate departments) in professional association journals.

Particular note should be made of the legal aspects of women's political, economic, and social status. While a number of university law reviews have presented important contributions to the literature, especially on the Equal Rights Amendment [Harvard 1862, Yale 1153, Denver 1187, Cornell 1193, Michigan 1206, *George Washington Law Review* 1185, New York University 1170], *Valparaiso University Law Review* has devoted an entire symposium issue to the subject of Women and the Law [1204]. The most comprehensive single work on women and the law thus far is *Sex-Roles in Law and Society: Cases and Materials* (1973) [1172] by Leo Kanowitz, who has long been interested in the subject.

Space limitations preclude us from mentioning but several of the published significant broader works relating to women in politics. Among the recent volumes is Hope Chamberlin, *A Minority of Members: Women in the U.S. Congress* (1973) [1471], notable for efforts to include a brief assessment of the congressional performance and effectiveness, as well as a biographical sketch, of every woman who has served for any period through the elections of November 1972. Irene Murphy's *Public Policy on the Status of Women* (1973) [1184] deals with decision-making on the national level related to sex discrimination. Finally, we note Martin Gruberg [1481] whose *Women in American Politics* (1968) stands as the first and still the most comprehensive source book on the subject of women in public political life since the adoption of the Women's Suffrage Amendment to the Constitution in 1920.

Many worthy items have been left unmentioned here, including a substantial literature on women of other countries. They offer the researcher-reader tantalizing browsing through significant contributions, as well as provide indications of the many aspects yet to be adequately explored.

M.B.R.

NOTES

1. Kathleen Lucas Barber, "Equal Rights and the Double-Edged Sword of Protection," paper delivered at Midwest Political Science Association, Annual Meeting, Chicago, Illinois, May 3-5, 1974.

2. Jean Grossholtz and Susan C. Bourque, "Politics as an Unnatural Practice: Political Science Looks at Female Participation," paper presented at the American Political Science Association Annual Meeting, New Orleans, September 6, 1973.

3. Wilma Rule Krauss, "Politics and Gender Roles: Some Perspectives in Contemporary Literature," Political Science Department, Northern Illinois University, DeKalb, Ill., November 1973.

BIBLIOGRAPHY

I. SOCIOLOGY

The titles discussed under this heading fall into several groups, and in a sense are a microcosm of the entire bibliography. They range from doctrinaire survey texts that ask whether we understand sufficiently what is implied by the term "womanhood" to some rather strident studies of women today, their conflicts, frustrations, and fulfillments. It would be impossible to suggest that the sources cited here fully describe woman's "experience" in any period, but we may assume that the diversity of literature in this category and its subdivisions reflects a broad range of views on the part of both sexes which speak of anatomical, historical, and psychological facts.

A. Sex Roles, Characteristics and Differences

There are few Noras in contemporary American society because women have deluded themselves that the doll's house is large enough to find complete personal fulfillment within it.

—Alice Rossi

1. Adams, Elsie, and Mary Louise Briscoe, (eds.) UP AGAINST THE WALL, MOTHER. . . . Beverly Hills: Glencoe Press, 1971. A women's liberation reader.
2. Aldous, Joan. "Children's Perceptions of Adult Role Assignment: Father-Absence, Class, Race, and Sex Influences," JOURNAL OF MARRIAGE AND THE FAMILY, Vol. 34 (Feb. 1972), pp. 55+. Interviews concerning conventional adult roles.
3. Almquist, Elizabeth M., and Shirley S. Angrist. "Role Model Influences on College Women's Career Aspirations," MERRILL-PALMER QUARTERLY, vol. 17 (July 1971), pp. 263-279. Interviews with 110 female students concerning broad views of adult female roles.
4. Arnott, Catherine. COMMITMENT AND CONGRUENCY IN THE ROLE PREFERENCE OF MARRIED WOMEN: AN INTERPERSONAL APPROACH. Los Angeles: Univ. of Southern California Press, 1971. Reconciling work and marriage goals.

5. Atherton, Gertrude. CAN WOMEN BE GENTLEMEN? Boston: Houghton Mifflin, 1938. 208 pp. A defense of women's roles in the world outside the home.

6. Backman, Margaret E. "Patterns of Mental Abilities: Ethnic, Socioeconomic, and Sex Differences," AMERICAN EDUCATIONAL RESEARCH JOURNAL, vol. 9 (Winter 1972), pp. 1-12. Achievement and role patterns, by sex.

7. Barry, Herbert, Margaret K. Bacon, and Irvin L. Child. "A Cross-Cultural Survey of Some Sex Differences in Socialization," JOURNAL OF ABNORMAL AND SOCIAL PSYCHOLOGY, vol. 55 (1957) pp. 327-332.

8. Baumrind, Diana. "From Each According to Her Ability," SCHOOL REVIEW, vol. 80 (Feb. 1972), pp. 161-197. A review of sex-role research.

9. Bennett, John W., Herbert Passin, and Robert K. McKnight, IN SEARCH OF IDENTITY. Minneapolis: Univ. of Minnesota Press, 1958. Changing social roles of Japanese women.

10. Bernard, Jessie. THE SEX GAME. New York: Atheneum, 1972. Reissue of an earlier study of aspects of role performance linked to sex.

11. Bieliauskas, Vytautas J. "Masculinity-Feminity and Self-Concept," PERCEPTUAL AND MOTOR SKILLS, vol. 34 (Feb. 1972), pp. 163-167.

12. Biller, Henry. "Fathering and Female Sexual Development," MEDICAL ASPECTS OF HUMAN SEXUALITY, vol. 5 (Nov. 1971), pp. 126-138. Attitudes toward marriage, sex, and career in the father-daughter relationship.

13. Buck, Ross W. "Differences in Social Learning Underlying Overt-Behavioral, Self-Report, and Physiological Responses to Emotion." ERIC. Pittsburgh: Carnegie-Mellon Univ., 1971. 11 pp. Review of sex differences in emotional respondings.

14. Calderone, Mary S. "New Roles for Women," SCHOOL REVIEW, vol. 80 (Feb. 1972), pp. 275-280.

15. Cassara, Beverly, (ed.) AMERICAN WOMEN: THE CHANGING IMAGE. Boston: Beacon Press, 1962. Collection of articles on women's changing roles.

16. Chafetz, Janet S. MASCULINE/FEMININE OR HUMAN: AN OVERVIEW OF THE SOCIOLOGY OF SEX ROLES. Itasca, Ill.: Peacock, 1974. Deals with lesbianism.

17. "Change and Choice for the College Woman," AMERICAN ASSOCIATION OF UNIVERSITY WOMEN JOURNAL (Eightieth Anniversary Issue), vol. 55, no. 4 (May 1962), Washington, D.C. Issue devoted to training for women's roles.

18. Chesler, Phyllis. WOMEN AND MADNESS. New York: Doubleday. 1972. 359 pp. Interviews with 60 women on the effects of sex-role stereotypes.

19. Chesney, Kellow. THE ANTI-SOCIETY: AN ACCOUNT OF THE VICTORIAN UNDERWORLD. Boston: Gambit, 1972. 398 pp. Describes how women were subordinated, insulted, and silenced in the Victorian man's world.

20. Cleaver, Eldridge. "White Woman, Black Man." Pp. 155-210 in E. Cleaver SOUL ON ICE. New York: McGraw-Hill, 1968.

21. Conant, Margaret M. "Learning to Be a Boy, a Girl, or a Person," PTA MAGAZINE, vol. 6 (Mar. 1972), pp. 18-21. The effects of parents' concepts of sex-roles in child-rearing.

22. Coolidge, Mary R. WHY WOMEN ARE SO. New York: Henry Holt, 1912. 371 pp. Reflections on feminine roles.
23. Cooper, Jean. "Women's Liberation and the Black Woman," JOURNAL OF HOME ECONOMICS, vol. 63 (Oct. 1971), pp. 521-523. Various viewpoints between the races on male-female relationships.
24. Dahlstrom, Edmund, ed. THE CHANGING ROLES OF MEN AND WOMEN. London: Duckworth, 1967; Boston: Beacon Press, 1971. 302 pp. Collected articles on sex roles and socialization.
25. Davis, Angela. "Reflections on the Black Woman's Role in the Community of Slaves," THE BLACK SCHOLAR, vol. 3 (Dec. 1971), pp. 2-16. Dispels the myth of the passive and submissive black woman.
26. deBeauvoir, Simone. THE SECOND SEX. New York: Knopf, 1957. 732 pp. Comprehensive examination of the physiological, sexual, and social roles of women past and present.
27. Decter, Midge. THE NEW CHASTITY AND OTHER ARGUMENTS AGAINST WOMEN'S LIBERATION. New York: Coward, McCann and Geoghegan, 1972. 188 pp. An indictment of the counterproductive attitudes of the women's movement in its repudiation of feminine roles.
28. Drake, St. Clair. BLACK METROPOLIS: A STUDY OF NEGRO LIFE IN A NORTHERN CITY. New York: Harcourt, Brace, 1945. 809 pp. Studies of the roles of Negro women in the structure and organization of the Negro community.
29. Elder, Glen H. "Role Orientations, Marital Age, and Life Patterns in Adulthood," MERRILL-PALMER QUARTERLY, vol. 18 (Jan. 1972), pp. 3-24.
30. Ellmann, Mary. THINKING ABOUT WOMEN. New York: Harcourt, Brace and Jovanovich, 1968. 240 pp. Criticism of the various ways we stereotype women.
31. Empey, Lamar T. "Role Expectations of Young Women Regarding Marriage and a Career," MARRIAGE AND FAMILY LIVING, vol. 20 (1958), pp. 152-155.
32. Epstein, Cynthia F. WOMAN'S PLACE: OPTIONS AND LIMITS IN PROFESSIONAL CAREERS. Los Angeles: Univ. of California Press, 1971. 221 pp. Data drawn from law, medicine, science, engineering, and academia.
33. Epstein, Cynthia F., and William J. Goode, eds. THE OTHER HALF: ROADS TO WOMEN'S EQUALITY. Englewood Cliffs, N.J.: Prentice-Hall, 1971. 207 pp. Anthology of 17 previously published articles emphasizing women's position today.
34. Erskine, Hazel G. "The Polls: Women's Role," PUBLIC OPINION QUARTERLY, vol. 35 (Summer 1971), pp. 275-290. Women's role in society, focusing on data from 1937-1970.
35. Farber, Seymour M., and Roger H. L. Wilson, eds. THE CHALLENGE TO WOMEN, New York: Basic Books, 1966. 176 pp. Anthology relevant to role concepts.
36. ———, eds. THE POTENTIAL OF WOMEN, New York: McGraw-Hill, 1963. 328 pp. Anthology by 34 specialists defining women's new roles.
37. Feminists on Children's Media. "Sexism in Children's Literature," EDCENTRIC, vol. 3 (Dec. 1971), pp. 9-15.

38. Firestone, Shulamith. DIALECTIC OF SEX. New York: Morrow, 1970. Asserts that the eradication of sex roles in our society is a political problem and that feminism may be the ideological means of uniting society.

39. Folsom, Joseph K. THE FAMILY AND DEMOCRATIC SOCIETY. New York: Wiley, 1934. Advocates reforms in the family system and in the relations between men and women.

40. Fredriksson, Ingrid. "Sex Roles and Education in Sweden," NEW YORK UNIVERSITY EDUCATION QUARTERLY, vol. 3 (Winter 1972), pp. 17-25. Sweden's move toward career, family, and political roles undifferentiated by sex.

41. Friedan, Betty. THE FEMININE MYSTIQUE. New York: Norton, 1963. 410 pp. Analysis of the media, Freud, and anthropological studies of women.

42. Gerber, Ellen W. "The Changing Female Image: A Brief Commentary in Sport Competition for Women," JOURNAL OF HEALTH, PHYSICAL EDUCATION, AND RECREATION (Oct. 1971), pp. 59-61. Survey of women's increased participation in sports activities.

43. Gilman, Charlotte Perkins. THE MAN-MADE WORLD: OR OUR ANDROCENTRIC CULTURE. New York: Source Book Press, 1970. Reprint of the 1911 edition. 260 pp. How one sex has monopolized human activities.

44. Gove, Walter, and Jeannette Tudor. "Adult Sex Roles and Mental Illness," AMERICAN JOURNAL OF SOCIOLOGY, vol. 78, no. 4 (Jan. 1973), pp. 812-835. Study of patterned variations in rates of mental illness in men and women due to sex roles.

45. Greer, Germaine. THE FEMALE EUNUCH. New York: McGraw-Hill, 1971. 349 pp. All-inclusive study of women's cultural history, psychological development, and relationships to men.

46. Groves, Ernest R. THE AMERICAN WOMAN: THE FEMININE SIDE OF A MASCULINE CIVILIZATION. New York: Emerson Books, 1944. 465 pp. Focuses on the anonymous women invisible in traditional histories of America.

47. Harbeson, Gladys E. CHOICE AND CHALLENGE FOR THE AMERICAN WOMAN. Cambridge, Mass.: Schenkman, 1967. 185 pp. Survey of career patterns today and traditional roles in the past.

48. Harding, M. Esther. THE WAY OF ALL WOMEN. New York: G. P. Putnam's Sons, 1970. 314 pp. Revision of the 1933 edition stressing Jungian theories of women's roles.

49. Harris, J. S. "The Position of Women in a Nigerian Society," TRANSACTIONS OF THE NEW YORK ACADEMY OF SCIENCES, vol. 2, no. 5 (1940), pp. 141-148. Ibo women's roles.

50. Hartley, C. Gasquoine. MOTHERHOOD AND THE RELATIONSHIP OF THE SEXES. New York: Dodd, Mead, 1917. 402 pp.

51. Hartley, Ruth. "A Development View of Female Sex-Role Definition and Identification," MERRILL-PALMER QUARTERLY, vol. 10 (1964), pp. 3-16.

52. Hartley, Ruth, and Frances Hardesty. "Children's Perceptions of Sex Role in Childhood," JOURNAL OF GENETIC PSYCHOLOGY, vol. 105, no. 1 (1964), pp. 43-51.

53. Hays, H. R. THE DANGEROUS SEX: THE MYTH OF FEMININE EVIL. New York: G. P. Putnam's Sons, 1964; Pocket Books, 1965. Literate account of man's fear of women and women's institutionalization of that fear.
54. Herschberger, Ruth. ADAM'S RIB. New York: Pellegrini and Cudahy, 1948. 221 pp. Reprinted by Harper and Row, 1970, 238 pp. Posits that passive and submissive stereotypes have resulted in frigid and frustrated women.
55. Hochschild, Arlie. "A Review of Sex Role Research," AMERICAN JOURNAL OF SOCIOLOGY, vol. 78, no. 4 (Jan. 1973), pp. 1011-1029. Discusses sex differences, sex roles, women as minority group, and the sociological implications thereof. [see 339]
56. Hoffman, Lois W. "Effects of the Employment of Mothers on Parental Power Relations and the Division of Household Tasks," MARRIAGE AND FAMILY LIVING, vol. 22 (1960), pp. 27-35.
57. Holter, H. SEX ROLES AND SOCIAL STRUCTURE. London: Pall Mall Press, 1970. A British view.
58. Horner, Matina S., et al. THE FEMININE PERSONALITY IN CONFLICT. Belmont, Calif.: Brooks/Cole, 1971. Studies of sex roles.
59. Hottel, Althea, ed. "Women Around the World," THE ANNALS OF THE AMERICAN ACADEMY OF POLITICAL AND SOCIAL SCIENCE, vol. 375 (Jan. 1968), 263 pp. Comprehensive anthology with articles on women's roles. See entry 337.
60. Howe, Florence. "Sexual Stereotypes Start Early," SATURDAY REVIEW, vol. 54 (Oct. 16, 1971), pp. 76-77+. How schools reinforce sexual stereotypes.
61. Hunt, Morton M. HER INFINITE VARIETY: THE AMERICAN WOMAN AS LOVER, MATE, AND RIVAL. New York: Harper and Row, 1962. Sex Roles.
62. Jacobson, Alver H. "Conflict of Attitude Toward the Roles of the Husband and Wife in Marriage," AMERICAN SOCIOLOGICAL REVIEW, (1952), pp. 146-150.
63. Jahoda, Marie, and Joan Havel. "Psychological Problems of Women in Different Social Roles—A Case History of Problem Formulation in Research," EDUCATIONAL RECORD, vol. 36 (1955), pp. 325-335.
64. Janeway, Elizabeth. MAN'S WORLD, WOMAN'S PLACE. New York: Morrow, 1971. Sex roles.
65. Jenkin, Noel, and Karen Vroegh. "Contemporary Concepts of Masculinity and Femininity," PSYCHOLOGICAL REPORTS, vol. 25 (1969), pp. 679-697.
66. Jennings, M. Kent, and Norman Thomas. "Men and Women in Party Elites: Social Roles and Political Resources," MIDWEST JOURNAL OF POLITICAL SCIENCE, vol. 7, no. 4 (Nov. 1968), pp. 469-492. Empirical study of sex differences in political behavior.
67. Kalish, R. A., M. Maloney, and A. Arkoff. "Cross-Cultural Comparisons of College Student Marital-Role Preferences," JOURNAL OF SOCIAL PSYCHOLOGY, vol. 68, pp. 41-47.
68. Kally, Maureen M. "Attitudes Toward the Dual Role of The Married Professional Woman," AMERICAN PSYCHOLOGIST, Mar. 26, 1971, pp. 301-306. Investigation of negative attitudes toward professional women.

69. Key, Ellen. THE CENTURY OF THE CHILD. New York: Arno Press, 1972. Reprint of the 1909 edition. 339 pp. Swedish feminist attacks traditional mother role.

70. Key, Mary R. "The Role of Male and Female in Children's Books—Dispelling All Doubt," WILSON LIBRARY BULLETIN, vol. 46 (Oct. 1971), pp. 167-176. Reprinted in AMERICAN TEACHER.

71. Kirschner, Betty Frankle. "Introducing Students to Women's Place in Society," AMERICAN JOURNAL OF SOCIOLOGY, vol. 78, no. 4 (Jan. 1973), pp. 1051-1054. Critique of ten books presenting traditional views of women.

72. Klein, Viola. THE FEMININE CHARACTER: HISTORY OF AN IDE-OLOGY. New York: International Universities, 1946, 1948. Scholarly history of the idea of femininity as revealed in early studies in psychology and sociology.

73. Kolle, Oswalt. TU MUJER ESA DESCONOCIDA [Mother, the Stranger]. Barcelona, Spain: Bruguera, 1971. 334 pp. Sex roles of the Spanish mother.

74. Komarovsky, Mirra. "Cultural Contradictions and Sex Roles," AMERICAN JOURNAL OF SOCIOLOGY, vol. 52 (1946), pp. 184-189.

75. ———. "Cultural Contradictions and Sex Roles: The Masculine Case," AMERICAN JOURNAL OF SOCIOLOGY, vol. 78 (Jan. 1973), pp. 873-884. Updated, with emphasis on male attitudes toward working wives.

76. Kurtz, R. M. "Body Image—Male and Female," TRANS-ACTION, (Dec. 1968), pp. 25-27

77. Ladner, Joyce A. TOMORROW'S TOMORROW: THE BLACK WOMAN. New York: Doubleday, 1971. Sex roles among 30 adolescent girls in a St. Louis ghetto.

78. Lazarsfield, Sofie. WOMAN'S EXPERIENCE OF THE MALE. London: Encyclopaedic Press, 1967. 446 pp. Sex roles among British women.

79. Leijon, Anna-Greta. SWEDISH WOMEN—SWEDISH MEN. Stockholm: Swedish Institute for Cultural Relations with Foreign Countries, 1968. Results of efforts to alter Swedish sex-role stereotypes.

80. LeMoyne, Jean. "Women and French Canadian Civilization." In CONVERGENCES: ESSAYS FROM QUEBEC. Translated by Philip Strafford. Toronto: Ryerson, 1966. Examination of the Quebec matriarch's role.

81. Levine, Lena, and David Loth. THE EMOTIONAL SEX: WHY WOMEN ARE THE WAY THEY ARE TODAY. New York: Morrow, 1964. 186 pp.

82. Lipman-Blumen, Jean. "How Ideology Shapes Women's Lives," SCIENTIFIC AMERICAN, vol. 226 (Jan. 1972), pp. 34-52. Data on 1,012 wives on appropriate roles with respect to men.

83. Lynn, David B. "Determinants of Intellectual Growth in Women," SCHOOL REVIEW, vol. 80 (Feb. 1972), pp. 241-260. Hypothesis for the causes of "female" intellectual development.

84. Maccoby, Eleanor. THE DEVELOPMENT OF SEX DIFFERENCES. Stanford: Stanford Univ. Press, 1966. Standard reference with bibliography.

85. Mathur, Mary E.F. "Who Cares that a Woman's Work is Never Done?" INDIAN HISTORY, vol. 4 (Summer 1971), pp. 11-15. Marital roles of Indian women.

86. McDonald, Donald. "The Liberation of Women," CENTER MAGAZINE, Center for the Study of Democratic Institutions, vol. 5, no. 3 (May-June 1972), pp. 25-42. Concludes that the changes currently in motion in the sex roles of women are a healthy social development.

87. McKee, J. P., and A. C. Sherriffs. "Men and Women's Beliefs, Ideals, and Self-Concepts," AMERICAN JOURNAL OF SOCIOLOGY, vol. 64 (1959), pp. 356-363.

88. Mead, Margaret. MALE AND FEMALE. New York: Morrow, 1949, 1967. Stresses biologically based cultural complements of sex roles in a cross-cultural study of seven Pacific islands.

89. Mehta, Nandini. "Women's Liberation Movement: Chapati-Maker to Chappal-Phenkar," ILLUSTRATED WEEKLY OF INDIA, vol. 92 (Oct. 24, 1971), pp. 8-13. Changing roles of Indian women.

90. Michaelson, Evelyn J., and Walter Goldschmidt. "Female Roles and Male Dominance Among Peasants," SOUTHWESTERN JOURNAL OF ANTHROPOLOGY, vol. 27 (Winter 1972), pp. 330-352.

91. Millman, Marcia. "Observations on Sex Role Research," JOURNAL OF MARRIAGE AND THE FAMILY, vol. 33 (Nov. 1971), pp. 772-776. Critical review on recent research with alternative approaches.

92. Milner, Esther. "Effects of Sex Roles and Social Status on the Early Adolescent Personality," GENETIC PSYCHOLOGY MONOGRAPHS, vol. 40 (1949), pp. 235-325.

93. Montagu, Ashley. THE NATURAL SUPERIORITY OF WOMEN. New York: Macmillan, 1962. 205 pp. The facts, according to Montagu, seem to prove that women are superior to men.

94. Morgan, Elaine. THE DESCENT OF WOMAN. New York: Stein and Day, 1972. Evolutionary approach toward the development of the female sex.

95. Myrdal, Alva, and Viola Klein. WOMEN'S TWO ROLES: HOME AND WORK. London: Routledge and Kegan Paul, 1956. An influential study, but with no radical proposals for change.

96. Neisser, Edith. MOTHERS AND DAUGHTERS. New York: Harper and Row, 1967. Roles.

97. Oakley, Ann. SEX, GENDER, AND SOCIETY. London: Temple-Smith, 1971. 220 pp. Statistical differences in men and women, rooted in gender or sex, inherent or societal.

98. Parkhurst, Jessie W. "The Role of the Black Mammy in the Plantation Household," THE JOURNAL OF NEGRO HISTORY, vol. 23 (Jan. 1938), pp. 349-369.

99. Parsons, Elsie Clews. THE OLD-FASHIONED WOMAN: PRIMITIVE FANCIES ABOUT THE SEX. New York: Arno Press, 1972. Reprint of the 1913 edition. Primitive ideas about femininity, discrimination, girl babies, honeymoons, and superiority and inferiority.

100. Parsons, Talcott. "Age and Sex in the Social Structure of the United States," AMERICAN SOCIOLOGICAL REVIEW, vol. 7 (Oct. 1942), pp. 604-616. Sociological study of sex roles and the consequences if women choose "masculine" patterns of competitive careers.

101. Peck, Robert F. "A Cross-national Comparison of Sex and Socioeconomic Differences in Aptitude and Achievement." ERIC. Washington, D.C.: U.S. Office of Education, 1971. 13 pp. Originally published by the University of Texas in Austin, Texas. Comparisons among eight countries.

102. Poole, Howard E. "A Study of Sex Role and Learning in a Changing Society ," WEST AFRICAN JOURNAL OF EDUCATION, vol. 15 (Oct. 1971), pp. 167-169.

103. Pratt, Lois. "Conjugal Organization and Health," JOURNAL OF MARRIAGE AND THE FAMILY, vol. 34 (Feb. 1972), pp. 85-95. States that happy families, i.e., ones in which roles are undifferentiated, are healthy families.

104. Reeves, Nancy. WOMANKIND: BEYOND THE STEREOTYPES. Chicago: Aldine, 1971. 434 pp. Stereotypes seen not to be decreed by history, anatomy, or feminine psychology.

105. Riegel, Robert E. AMERICAN WOMEN: A STORY OF SOCIAL CHANGE. Teaneck, N.J.: Fairleigh Dickinson Univ. Press, 1970. 376 pp. Origins and decline of female inequality in male-oriented society.

106. Robinson, Marie N. THE POWER OF SEXUAL SURRENDER. New York: New American Library, 1969. Implications of subordinate role casting.

107. Rose, Arnold. "The Adequacy of Women's Expectations for Adult Roles," SOCIAL FORCES, vol. 30 (Oct. 1951), pp. 69-77. Sociological study of the causes of women's confusion of preadult expectations.

108. Rosenberg, Carroll S. "Beauty, the Beast and the Militant Woman: A Case Study in Sex Roles and Social Stress in Jacksonian America," AMERICAN QUARTERLY, vol. 23 (Oct. 1971), pp. 562-584. Discussion of the double standard and male dominance.

109. Roszak, Theodore, and Betty Roszak, eds. MASCULINE/FEMININE. New York: Harper Torchbooks, 1969. Anthology of readings in sexual mythology and the liberation of women.

110. Sagarin, Edward, ed. "Sex and the Contemporary American Scene," THE ANNALS, vol. 376 (Mar. 1968), pp. 1-232. Entire issue devoted to sex and sex roles.

111. Scully, Diane, and Pauline Bart. "A Funny Thing Happened on the Way to the Orifice: Women in Gynecology Textbooks," AMERICAN JOURNAL OF SOCIOLOGY, vol. 78, no. 4 (Jan. 1973), pp. 1045-1050. Analysis of 27 gynecological texts reveals a persistent bias toward maintaining traditional sex-role stereotypes.

112. Seward, Georgene A., and Robert C. Williamson, eds. SEX ROLES IN CHANGING SOCIETY. New York: Random House, 1970. 419 pp. Anthology.

113. Spacks, Patricia M. "Free Women," THE HUDSON REVIEW, vol. 24 (Winter 1971-1972), pp. 559-573. Distinguished emancipated women who write about themselves often reveal the persistent hindrances to their equality.

114. Spinner, Stephanie, ed. FEMININE PLURAL: STORIES BY WOMEN ABOUT GROWING UP. New York: Macmillan, 1972. Anthology.

115. Stephens, Kate. WORKFELLOWS IN SOCIAL PROGRESSION. New York: Sturgis and Walton, 1916. 328 pp. Articles devoted to advocates of women's collegiate education and to the uses and abuses of the words female and woman.

116. Stoller, R. J. SEX AND GENDER: THE DEVELOPMENT OF MASCU-
LINITY AND FEMININITY. New York: Science House, 1968.
117. Stuart, Dorothy M. THE GIRL THROUGH THE AGES. London: George
G. Harrap, 1933. 263 pp. From ancient Babylonia to Victorian England,
illustrated.
118. Sullerot, Evelyne. WOMEN, SOCIETY, AND CHANGE. New York:
McGraw-Hill, 1971. Description of the changes with a selected bibliography.
119. Talmon, Yonina. "Sex-Role Differentiation in an Equalitarian Society."
In Thomas E. Laswell, et al., LIFE IN SOCIETY. Chicago: Scott, Foresman, 1965. Asks whether it is possible for society to do away with sex-
role and status differences, even if it wants to.
120. Thompson, Mary Lou, ed. VOICES OF THE NEW FEMINISM. Boston:
Beacon Press, 1971. 246 pp. Anthology of current problems, ideology,
and sex roles.
121. Trumpeter, Margo, and Linda D. Crowe. "Sexism in Picture Books,"
ILLINOIS LIBRARY, vol. 53 (Sept. 1971), pp. 499-503.
122. UNESCO. "Images of Women in Society," New York: INSTITUTE OF
SOCIAL SCIENCES JOURNAL, vol. 14, no. 1 (1962), pt. 1, pp. 7-70.
123. Vaerting, Mathilde, and Mathias Vaerting. THE DOMINANT SEX: A
STUDY IN THE SOCIOLOGY OF SEX DIFFERENTIATION. London:
Allen and Unwin, 1923.
124. Walker, Kenneth, and Peter Fletcher. SEX AND SOCIETY. London: Allen
and Unwin, 1955; Penguin edition, 1969. 250 pp. Sex roles and the
psychology of sex.
125. Wallin, Paul. "Cultural Contradictions and Sex Roles: A Repeat Study,"
AMERICAN SOCIOLOGICAL REVIEW, vol. 15 (April 1950), pp. 288-
293. Revision of Mirra Komarovsky's 1943 study of the incompatibility
of sex roles in the social life of the college woman.
126. Walsh, William. DIALOGUE CONCERNING WOMEN, BEING A DE-
FENSE OF THE SEX. London: n.p., 1691. One of the earliest accounts.
134pp. Preface by John Dryden.
127. Welter, Barbara. "The Cult of True Womanhood," AMERICAN QUARTER-
LY, (Summer 1966), pp. 151-174.
128. Werner, Peter. "The Role of Physical Education in Gender Identification,"
THE PHYSICAL EDUCATOR, vol. 20 (Mar. 1972), pp. 27-28. Sex
roles involved in games and other activities.
129. West, Anne Grant. "Women's Liberation or Exploding the Fairy Princess
Myth," SCHOLASTIC TEACHER, (Nov. 1971), pp. 6-11. Students and
how they adapt to sex roles prescribed in our culture, with a chauvinist
index for educators.
130. Winick, Charles. "The Beige Epoch: Depolarization of Sex Roles in America," THE ANNALS, vol. 376 (Mar. 1968), pp. 18-24.
131. Wortis, Helen, and Clara Rabinowitz, eds. THE WOMEN'S MOVEMENT:
SOCIAL AND PSYCHOLOGICAL PERSPECTIVES. New York: AMS
Press, 1972. 151 pp. Collection of new essays examining the entire
social structure and goals pertaining to changing roles of women.
132. Ziv, Avner. "Sex Differences in Performance as a Function of Praise and
Blame," THE JOURNAL OF GENETIC PSYCHOLOGY, vol. 120
(Mar. 1972), pp. 111-119.

B. Family

People having this common saying—"The kingdom, the State, the family." The root of the kingdom is in the State. The root of the State is in the family. The root of the family is in the person of its Head.

—Mencius (372-289 B.C.)

133. Abbott, John S.C. THE MOTHER AT HOME: OR, THE PRINCIPLES OF MATERNAL DUTY. New York: Arno Press, 1972. Reprint of the London, 1834 edition. Advice to mothers and the history of the American family.

134. Abrams, Ray H., ed. THE AMERICAN FAMILY IN WORLD WAR II. New York: Arno Press, 1972. Reprinted from THE ANNALS, vol. 229 (Sept. 1943). Measures the impact of the war on American society, and particularly upon women.

135. Ackworth, E. THE NEW MATRIARCHY. London: Peter Gollancz, 1965. Mothers and the family.

136. American Sociological Society. THE FAMILY. Reprinted from PUBLI-CATIONS OF THE AMERICAN SOCIOLOGICAL SOCIETY, vol. 3 (1909). New York: Arno Press, 1972. Changes in the American family at the beginning of the twentieth century.

137. Bell, Norman W., and Ezra F. Vogel, eds. A MODERN INTRODUCTION TO THE FAMILY. New York: Free Press, 1968. An anthology with an excellent bibliography.

138. Bernstein, Rose. HELPING UNMARRIED MOTHERS. New York: Assoc-iation Press, 1971. 186 pp. Socialization and the family.

139. Billingsley, Andrew. BLACK FAMILIES IN WHITE AMERICA. Engle-wood Cliffs, N.J.: Prentice-Hall, 1968.

140. Bogue, Mary F. ADMINISTRATION OF MOTHER'S AID IN TEN LOCALITIES: WITH SPECIAL REFERENCE TO HEALTH, HOUS-ING, EDUCATION, AND RECREATION, in THE FAMILY AND SOCIAL SERVICE IN THE 1920's. New York: Arno Press, 1972. Re-print of the Washington, D.C., 1928 edition. The earliest version of a modern Aid to Dependent Children program.

141. Breckinridge, Sophonisba P. THE FAMILY AND THE STATE: SELECT DOCUMENTS. New York: Arno Press, 1972. Reprint of the 1934 edition. Traces the changing legal and social relationships between the family and the broader society by the associate of Jane Addams.

142. Briffault, Robert. THE MOTHERS: A STUDY OF THE ORIGINS OF SENTIMENTS AND INSTITUTIONS. 3 vols. New York: Macmillan, 1927. One of the definitive works.

143. Calhoun, Arthur. A SOCIAL HISTORY OF THE AMERICAN FAMILY. 3 vols. in 1. New York: Barnes and Noble, 1945. Well-documented historical study from colonial times to the early twentieth century.

144. Canada, Department of Labour. MATERNITY-LEAVE POLICIES: A SURVEY. Ottawa, 1969. Comprehensive study of Canadian practices.

145. ———. WORKING MOTHERS AND THEIR CHILD-CARE ARRANGE-MENTS. Ottawa, 1970. Fact book.

146. Central Statistical Board of the USSR, Council of Ministers. WOMEN AND CHILDREN IN THE USSR: BRIEF STATISTICAL RETURNS. Moscow: Foreign Languages Publishing House, 1963. 195 pp.

147. Chombart de Lauwe, P.-H., et al. FAMILLES D'AUJOURD'HUI: COLLOQUE CONSACREA LA SOCIOLOGIE DE LA FAMILLE. Brussels: Institut de Sociologie de l'universite Libre de Bruxelles, 1968. 196 pp. European focus.
148. Chombart de Lauwe, P.-H. "La Fin de la Famille?" LA NEF, no. 46/47 (Feb.-May 1972), pp. 21-44. The family and divorce.
149. Dirks, Sabine. LA FAMILLE MUSULMANE TURQUE [The Moslem Turk Family]. Paris: Mouton, 1969. 168 pp. Changes in the Moslem family today.
150. Dodziuk-Kitynska, Ann, and Danuta Markowska. THE POLISH URBAN FAMILY. Warsaw: Institute of Philosophy and Sociology of the Polish Academy of Sciences, 1971. 322 pp. Informative, with a good bibliography.
151. Doo-hun Kim. "Family Life in Korea," KOREANA, vol. 13 (Spring-Summer 1971), pp. 64-68.
152. Engels, Friedrich. THE ORIGINS OF THE FAMILY, PRIVATE PROPERTY, AND THE STATE. Translated by E. Untermann. Chicago: Charles Kerr, 1902. Matrilineal theory for the origins of the state and society.
153. Fletcher, R. THE FAMILY AND MARRIAGE IN BRITAIN. London: Penguin, 1969. Comprehensive and contemporary.
154. Fogarty, Michael P., Rhona Rapoport, and Robert N. Rapoport. SEX, CAREER AND FAMILY. Beverly Hills: Sage Publications, 1971. An international review of men and women in the family.
155. Folsom, Joseph K. THE FAMILY AND DEMOCRATIC SOCIETY. New York: Wiley, 1943.
156. Fox, Ann. "The Child Care Deduction: Issues Raised by Michael and Elizabeth Nammack and the Pending Amendment to Section 214," BOSTON COLLEGE INDUSTRIAL AND COMMERCIAL LAW REVIEW, vol. 13 (Dec. 1971), pp. 270-288.
157. Frazier, E. Franklin. THE NEGRO FAMILY IN THE UNITED STATES. Chicago: Univ. of Chicago Press, 1939. Classic study of the sequence of social conditions that shaped the Negro family.
158. Geertz, Hildred. THE JAVANESE FAMILY. Glencoe, Ill. Free Press, 1961.
159. Geiger, H. Kent. THE FAMILY IN SOVIET RUSSIA. Cambridge: Harvard Univ. Press, 1968. 381 pp. Historical and well documented.
160. Gibson, Colin. "A Note on Family Breakdown in England and Wales," BRITISH JOURNAL OF SOCIOLOGY, vol. 22 (Sept. 1971), pp. 322-325.
161. Gilman, Charlotte Perkins. THE HOME: ITS WORK AND INFLUENCE. New York: Source Book Press, 1970. Reprint of the 1903 edition. Brilliant exposition of the home as a human institution.
162. Goode, William J. THE FAMILY. Englewood Cliffs, N.J.: Prentice-Hall, 1964. Comprehensive sociological study of the family system.
163. ———. WORLD REVOLUTION AND FAMILY PATTERNS. New York: Collier-Macmillan, 1963.
164. Gossmann, Elisabeth. MANN UND FRAU IN FAMILIE UND OFFENTLICHKEIT [Man and Woman in the Family and State]. Munich: n.p., 1964. Changes in the German family.
165. Gough, Kathleen. "The Origin of the Family," JOURNAL OF MARRIAGE AND THE FAMILY, vol. 33 (Nov. 1971), pp. 760-770.

166. Haldane, Charlotte. MOTHERHOOD AND ITS ENEMIES. New York: Doubleday, 1928. 253 pp. A history of contemporary motherhood.

167. Hani, Setsuko. THE JAPANESE FAMILY, AS SEEN FROM THE STANDPOINT OF JAPANESE WOMEN. Tokyo: Japan Institute of Pacific Studies, International Publishing Company, 1948. Changes in the family before and after the war.

168. Hathway, Marion. THE MIGRATORY WORKER AND FAMILY LIFE: THE MODE OF LIVING AND PUBLIC PROVISION FOR THE NEEDS OF THE FAMILY OF THE MIGRATORY WORKER IN SELECTED INDUSTRIES OF THE STATE OF WASHINGTON. New York: Arno Press, 1972. Reprint of the 1934 edition. Analysis of their difficulties and their inability to avoid them.

169. Heiss, Jerold. "On the Transmission of Marital Instability in Black Families," AMERICAN SOCIOLOGICAL REVIEW, vol. 37 (Feb. 1972), pp. 82-92

170. Hessel, Vitia. "La Mere et son Fils," LA NEF, vol. 29 (Feb.-May 1972), pp. 147-154.

171. Hewitt, M. WIVES AND MOTHERS IN VICTORIAN SOCIETY. London: Barrie, 1958. Traditional roles and expectations.

172. Hjorth, Roland L. "A Tax Subsidy for Child Care: Section 210 of the Revenue Act of 1971," TAXES: THE TAX MAGAZINE, vol. 50 (Mar. 1972), pp. 133-145.

173. Jackson, Jacquelyne J. "But Where are the Men?" BLACK SCHOLAR, vol. 3 (Dec. 1971), pp. 30-41. Counters the myth of black matriarchy.

174. Key, Ellen. THE RENAISSANCE OF MOTHERHOOD. New York: Source Book Press, 1970. Reprint of the 1914 edition. 171 pp. Women's contributions to the moral standards of society, the glory of motherhood, and education for motherhood.

175. Kingsbury, Susan H., and Mildred F. Fairchild. FACTORY, FAMILY AND WOMEN IN THE SOVIET UNION. New York: G. P. Putnam's Sons, 1935. 334 pp.

176. Kirkpatrick, C. NAZI GERMANY: ITS WOMEN AND FAMILY LIFE. Indianapolis: Bobbs-Merrill, 1938. The rise of female employment and its effects on family life.

177. Kollontai, Alexandra. COMMUNISM AND THE FAMILY. New York: Herder and Herder, n.d. Important work but unavailable. See Iring Fetscher, ed., MARX AND MARXISM, New York: Herder and Herder, 1971.

178. Lacey, W. K. THE FAMILY IN CLASSICAL GREECE. New York: Cornell Univ. Press, 1968. 342 pp.

179. Laing, Ronald D. THE POLITICS OF THE FAMILY AND OTHER ESSAYS. New York: Pantheon, 1969. 133 pp.

180. Lang, Olga. CHINESE FAMILY AND SOCIETY. New Haven: Yale Univ. Press, 1946. One of the early studies of pre-World War II family structures and functions.

181. Levy, Marion J., Jr. THE FAMILY REVOLUTION IN MODERN CHINA. Cambridge: Harvard Univ. Press, 1949. Sociological analysis of traditional family structure and the changes in its character during a time of increasing industrialization and urbanization.

182. Lin, Yüeh-hua. THE GOLDEN WING: A SOCIOLOGICAL STUDY OF CHINESE FAMILISM. London: Kegan Paul, Trench, and Trubner, 1948. Excellent sociological study with bibliography.
183. Mace, David, and Vera Mace. THE SOVIET FAMILY. Garden City: Doubleday, 1963. 367 pp.
184. Makarenko, A. S. THE COLLECTIVE FAMILY. Translated by R. Daglish. Garden City: Doubleday, 1967. The Soviet family.
185. Mitscherlich, Alexander. SOCIETY WITHOUT THE FATHER. Translated by E. Mosbacher. New York: Harcourt, Brace and World, 1969.
186. Monroe, Ernest R. FAMILY DISORGANIZATION: AN INTRODUCTION TO A SOCIOLOGICAL ANALYSIS. New York: Arno Press, 1972. Reprint of 1927 edition. Research in the position of women in America for understanding the dynamics of family and society.
187. Morris, Clyde P. "Yavapai-Apache Family Organization in a Reservation Context," PLATEAU, vol. 44 (Winter 1972), pp. 105-110. Study of 41 households.
188. Moynihan, Daniel P. "The Negro Family: The Case for National Action." Office of Policy Planning and Research, U.S. Dept. of Labor. Washington, D.C.: SUDOC, GPO, 1965.
189. Orga, Irfan. PORTRAIT OF A TURKISH FAMILY. New York: Macmillan, 1950. 306 pp.
190. Parsons, Talcott, and Robert F. Bales. FAMILY, SOCIALIZATION AND INTERACTION PROCESS. New York: Free Press, 1955. 422 pp. Sociology of the family and its place in American society.
191. Rainwater, Lee. BEHIND GHETTO WALLS: FAMILY LIFE IN A FEDERAL SLUM. Chicago: Aldine, 1970. 488 pp. Excellent statement of the causes, conditions, and solutions of an overriding social issue in our country.
192. Ramu, G.N. "Geographic Mobility, Kinship and the Family in South India," JOURNAL OF MARRIAGE AND THE FAMILY, vol. 34 (Feb. 1972), pp. 147-152.
193. Reed, Ruth. THE ILLEGITIMATE FAMILY IN NEW YORK CITY: ITS TREATMENT BY SOCIAL AND HEALTH AGENCIES. New York: Arno Press, 1972. Reprint of 1934 edition. Historical information on illegitimacy, the fate of children, and effective responses to their needs.
194. Richardson, Stephen, and Alan Guttnacher, eds. CHILDBEARING: ITS SOCIAL AND PSYCHOLOGICAL ASPECTS. Baltimore: Williams and Wilkins, 1967. 334 pp. Anthology of articles.
195. Roberts, Robert W. THE UNWED MOTHER. New York: Harper and Row, 1966. 270 pp.
196. Sanger, Margaret. MOTHERHOOD IN BONDAGE. London: Brentano, 1928. 446 pp. A plea by the advocate of birth control.
197. Scanzoni, John H. THE BLACK FAMILY IN MODERN SOCIETY. Rockleigh, N.J.: Allyn and Bacon, 1971. 353 pp.
198. Schur, Edwin M., ed. THE FAMILY AND THE SEXUAL REVOLUTION. Bloomington: Indiana Univ. Press, 1964. 427 pp. Collection of articles in the area of social changes affecting the family.
199. Shorter, Edward. "Illegitimacy, Sexual Revolution, and Social Change in Modern Europe," JOURNAL OF INTERDISCIPLINARY HISTORY, vol. 2 (Aug. 1972), pp. 237-272. A review of changes in the European family.

200. Skolnick, Arlene S., and Jerome H. Skolnick, eds. FAMILY IN TRANSI-
     TION. Boston: Little, Brown, 1971. 542 pp. Anthology of articles.
201. Spiro, Melford E. KIBBUTZ: VENTURE IN UTOPIA. New York:
     Schocken Books, 1963. 266 pp. The kibbutz as a communal society.
202. Staples, Robert. "The Matricentric Family System: A Cross-Cultural
     Examination," JOURNAL OF MARRIAGE AND THE FAMILY,
     vol. 34 (Feb. 1972), pp. 156-165.
203. Trotsky, Leon. WOMEN AND THE FAMILY. New York: Pathfinder
     Press, 1972. A pamphlet. Reprint.
204. U.S. Congress, Senate. Committee on Finance. "Child Care," hearings on
     S. 2003, 92d Cong., 1st sess. September 22, 23, and 24, 1971. Washing-
     ton, D.C.: SUDOC, GPO. Hearings on what can be done to improve
     child care.
205. U.S. Department of Labor. "Day Care Services: Industry Involvement."
     Washington, D.C.: SUDOC, GPO, 1971. 33 pp. Discusses the need for
     services for children of working mothers and reports on past and present
     contributions of industry.
206. U.S. Office of the President. "Day Care: Resources for Decision." Wash-
     ington, D.C.: SUDOC, GPO, 1971. 484 pp. Data on day care experience
     in other countries and in America.
207. van der Valk, M. H. CONSERVATISM IN MODERN CHINESE FAMILY
     LAW. Leiden: Brill, 1956.
208. Vincent, Clark E. UNMARRIED MOTHERS. New York: Free Press, 1961.
     308 pp.
209. Wadsworth, Benjamin. THE WELL-ORDERED FAMILY: OR RELATIVE
     DUTIES. Boston, 1712. In THE COLONIAL AMERICAN FAMILY. New
     York: Arno Press, 1972. Family life and domestic relations.
210. Winch, Robert F., Robert McGinnis, and Herbert R. Barringer, eds.
     SELECTED STUDIES IN MARRIAGE AND THE FAMILY. New York:
     Holt, Rinehart and Winston, 1962.
211. Wiseman, Jacqueline P., ed. PEOPLE AS PARTNERS: INDIVIDUAL AND
     FAMILY RELATIONSHIPS IN TODAY'S WORLD. San Francisco: Can-
     field, 1971. 497 pp. Articles on the contemporary family in society.
212. Wolf, Margery. WOMEN AND THE FAMILY IN RURAL TAIWAN. Stan-
     ford: Stanford Univ. Press, 1972. 235 pp.
213. Yang, C. K. THE CHINESE FAMILY IN THE COMMUNIST REVOLUTION.
     Cambridge: M.I.T. Press, 1959. Standard sociological account.
214. Young, Donald, ed. THE MODERN AMERICAN FAMILY. New York:
     Arno Press, 1972. Reprint of the entire issue from THE ANNALS, vol.
     160 (Mar. 1932). pp. 1-222. Entire issue devoted to the family, court-
     ship, marriage and the law, the bereaved family, and education of children.
215. Young, Leontine. OUT OF WEDLOCK. New York: McGraw-Hill, 1954.
     261 pp. Classic study of the unmarried mother.

C. Marriage and Divorce

Men's vows are women's traitors.
—Shakespeare

If it were not for the presents, an elopement would be preferable.
—George Ade

216. Alcott, William A. THE YOUNG HUSBAND: OR, DUTIES OF MAN IN THE MARRIAGE RELATION. New York: Arno Press, 1972. Reprint of the 1839 edition. An early guidebook for the newly married man.
217. ———. THE YOUNG WIFE: OR, DUTIES OF WOMEN IN THE MARRIAGE RELATION. New York: Arno Press, 1972. Reprint of the 1837 edition. Companion to the young husband's guidebook; epitomizes the viewpoint for which nineteenth- and twentieth-century feminists battled.
218. Astell, Mary. SOME REFLECTIONS UPON MARRIAGE. New York: Source Book Press, 1970. 176 pp. Reprint of the 1694 and 1730 editions. Contradicts the traditional view that women ought to marry.
219. Bernard, Jessie. THE FUTURE OF MARRIAGE. New York: World, 1972. 367 pp. Study of the nature and probable future of marriage; bibliography.
220. ———. MARRIAGE AND FAMILY AMONG NEGROES. Englewood Cliffs, N.J.: Prentice-Hall, 1966.
221. Bird, Caroline. "Women Who Make Great Success Have Husbands Who Make Coffee," NEW WOMAN, vol. 1 (Nov. 1971), pp. 64-67+.
222. Blake, Nelson M. THE ROAD TO RENO: A HISTORY OF DIVORCE IN THE UNITED STATES. New York: Macmillan, 1962. 269 pp. Scholarly and progressive in its views.
223. Bohannan, Paul, ed. DIVORCE AND AFTER. Garden City: Doubleday, 1970. 301 pp. Eleven studies covering the sociological aspects of divorce, including articles on divorce among Swedish men and women, and among Eskimos.
224. Briffault, Robert, and B. Malinowski. MARRIAGE: PAST AND PRESENT. Boston: Porter Sargent, 1956. 99 pp. The first chapter, "What is A Family?" makes the book worth publishing.
225. Burr, Andrew. "Engagement is not Marriage: Perspectives on Cultural Conflict in East Africa," MOSAIC, vol. 5 (Winter 1972), pp. 65-79.
226. Calverton, V. F. THE BANKRUPTCY OF MARRIAGE. New York: Arno Press, 1972. Reprint of the 1928 edition. 341 pp. Traces the new morality which challenged men's superior position in the marriage.
227. Chesser, Eustace. MARRIAGE AND FREEDOM. London: Rich and Cowan, 1952. 175 pp.
228. Coleman, Emily R. "Medieval Marriage Characteristics: A Neglected Factor in the History of Medieval Serfdom," JOURNAL OF INTERDISCIPLINARY HISTORY, vol. 2 (Aug. 1971), pp. 205-219. Rich in demographic information and references on 2,000 family marriage patterns of the servile population.
229. Couch, Elsbeth H. JOINT AND FAMILY INTERVIEWS IN THE TREATMENT OF MARITAL PROBLEMS. New York: Family Service Association of America, 1969. 330 pp. Well-documented study.
230. Das, Sonya Ruth. THE AMERICAN WOMAN IN MODERN MARRIAGE. New York: Philosophical Library, 1948. 185 pp. Sees the family as

having been transformed from a patriarchal to a democratic institution, with a new individuality among American women.

231. Davids, Leo. "North American Marriage: 1990," CURRENT, vol. 136 (Jan. 1972), pp. 33-42. Projections of changes in marriage or nonmarriage in child-raising patterns.

232. DeLora, Joann, and Jack DeLora. INTIMATE LIFE STYLES: MARRIAGE AND ITS ALTERNATIVES. Pacific Palisades, Calif.: Goodyear, 1972. A contemporary view.

233. Dixon, Ruth B. "Explaining Cross-Cultural Variations in Age at Marriage and Proportions Never Marrying," POPULATION STUDIES, vol. 25 (July 1971), pp. 215-230. Develops a framework for studying variations in timing and quantity of marriages.

234. Edmonds, Vernon H., Glenn Withers, and Beverly Dibatista. "Adjustment, Conservatism, and Marital Conventionalization," JOURNAL OF MARRIAGE AND THE FAMILY, vol. 34 (Feb. 1972), pp. 96-103.

235. Glasse, R. M., and M. J. Meggitt, eds. PIGS, PEARLSHELLS, AND WOMEN: MARRIAGES IN THE NEW GUINEA HIGHLANDS. Englewood Cliffs, N.J.: Prentice-Hall, 1970. 246 pp. Collection of articles.

236. Glen, Norval D., and Margaret S. Keir. "Divorce Among Sociologists Married to Sociologists," SOCIAL PROBLEMS, vol. 19 (Summer 1971), pp. 57-67.

237. Goode, William J. AFTER DIVORCE. Glencoe, Ill.: Free Press, 1956. Personal histories of divorcees and studies of the post-divorce experience.

238. Havens, Elizabeth M. "Women, Work, and Wedlock: A Note on Female Marital Patterns in the United States," AMERICAN JOURNAL OF SOCIOLOGY, vol. 78, no. 4 (Jan. 1973), pp. 975-981. Census data indicating diverse marital patterns for women by occupation and income categories.

239. Henshel, Anne-Marie. "Swinging: A Study of Decision Making in Marriage." AMERICAN JOURNAL OF SOCIOLOGY, vol. 78, no. 4 (Jan. 1973), pp. 885-891. Sample of 25 Toronto housewives as to who makes the final decision to "swing."

240. Herskovits, M. J. "A Note on 'Woman Marriage' in Dahomey," AFRICA, vol. 10 (1973), pp. 335-341. Marriages between women also exist in Nigeria, Sudan, and in the Transvaal.

241. Hollis, Florence. WOMEN IN MARITAL CONFLICT: A CASEWORK STUDY. New York: Family Service Association of America, 1949. 236 pp.

242. Howard, G. E. A HISTORY OF MATRIMONIAL INSTITUTIONS. 3 vols. Chicago: Univ. of Chicago Press, 1904. An early sociological study.

243. Kandel, Denise B., and Gerald S. Lesser. "Marital Decision-Making in American and Danish Urban Families," JOURNAL OF MARRIAGE AND THE FAMILY, vol. 34 (Feb. 1972), pp. 134-138.

244. Kapur, Promilla. MARRIAGE AND THE WORKING WOMEN IN INDIA. Delhi: Vikas, 1970. Survey research.

245. Key, Ellen. LOVE AND MARRIAGE. New York: Source Book Press, 1970. 418 pp. Reprint of the 1911 edition. By the well-known Swedish critic, appealing for both conservatives and radicals, by virtue of her worship of motherhood, and her defense of motherhood for single women.

246. Kohler, M. MARRIAGE CUSTOMS IN SOUTHERN NATAL. Pretoria, S. Africa: Department of Native Affairs, Ethnological Publications 4, 1933.

247. Komarovsky, Mirra. BLUE-COLLAR MARRIAGE. New York: Random House, 1964.

248. Kuper, H. "The Marriage of a Swazi Princess," AFRICA, vol. 15, no. 3 (1945), pp. 145-156. Description of the wedding ceremony and the bride's position after marriage.

249. Lefcowitz, Myron J. "Differences Between Negro and White Women in Marital Stability and Family Structures: A Multiple Regression Analysis," AMERICAN STATISTICAL ASSOCIATION (1967), pp. 245-253.

250. Lindsey, Ben B., and Wainwright Evans. THE COMPANIONATE MARRIAGE. New York: Arno Press, 1972. Reprint of 1927 edition. Proposed trial marriage in an attempt to link new ideas on women's rights and romantic love to the family.

251. Lopata, Helena Z. "The Secondary Features of a Primary Relationship," HUMAN ORGANIZATION (1965), pp. 116-125.

252. MacGregor, O. DIVORCE IN ENGLAND. London: Heinemann, 1970.

253. MacLennan, John F. PRIMITIVE MARRIAGE. Chicago: Univ. of Chicago Press, 1970. Reprint of a sociological and anthropological study.

254. "Marriage Can Be Many Things," SCANDINAVIAN TIMES, vol. 5 (Nov. 1971), pp. 27-28. Discusses the moral and ethical concepts of divorce in Denmark and Sweden.

255. McKain, Walter C. "A New Look at Older Marriages," THE FAMILY COORDINATOR, vol. 21 (Jan. 1972), pp. 61-69. Surveys the ingredients that lead to marital success or failure.

256. Mead, Margaret. MARRIAGE FOR MODERNS. New York: Henry A. Bowman, 1942.

257. Mpongo, Laurent. POUR UNE ANTHROPOLOGIE CHRETIENNE DU MARIAGE AU CONGO [Christian Anthropology of Marriage in the Congo]. Kinshasa: Editions du C.E.P., 1968. 201 pp.

258. O'Brien, John E. "Violence in Divorce Prone Families," JOURNAL OF MARRIAGE AND THE FAMILY, vol. 33 (Nov. 1971), pp. 692-698. A sample of 150 individuals.

259. O'Neill, William. DIVORCE IN THE PROGRESSIVE ERA. New Haven: Yale Univ. Press, 1967. 295 pp. Challenges the conventional interpretation by claiming that divorce became a safety valve for preserving the conjugal family system.

260. "A Rot That Persists (Dowry)," LINK, vol. 14 (Oct. 1971), p. 41. Describes the archaic practice of dowry in India and its effect on discrimination in education and on inheritance.

261. Ruiz, Alonso Celia. EMANCIPACION Y MATRIMONIO. Madrid: Editorial Alameda, 1971. 60 pp. Spanish marriage and divorce.

262. Russell, Bertrand. MARRIAGE AND MORALS. New York: Bantam Press, 1970. New edition of the 1929 book. A radical view by the British philosopher.

263. Sheresky, Norman, and Marya Mannes. UNCOUPLING: THE ART OF COMING APART. New York: Viking Press, 1972. Falling out of love and marriage.

264. Speer, David C. "Marital Dysfunctionality and Two-Person, Non-Zero-Sum Game Behavior," JOURNAL OF PERSONALITY AND SOCIAL PSY-

CHOLOGY, vol. 21 (1972), pp. 18-24. Study of the relationship between marital communication and choices in the Prisoner's Dilemma game.

265. Tegg, William. THE KNOT TIED: MARRIAGE CEREMONIES OF ALL NATIONS. London: William Tegg, 1877. 410 pp. Descriptions of hundreds of little-known rituals, laws, and customs relating to marriage in every era.

266. Tjan, Tjoe-som. PO HU-T'ING: THE COMPREHENSIVE DISCUSSIONS IN THE WHITE TIGER HALL. 2 vols. Leiden: Brill (Sinica Leidensia), 1949. "Han Marriage Regulations", vol. 1, pp. 244-263, is very interesting.

267. Urlin, Ethel L. A SHORT HISTORY OF MARRIAGE: MARRIAGE, CUSTOM, AND FOLKLORE IN MANY COUNTRIES AND ALL AGES. London: D. Rider, 1913. 276 pp. Borneo, Abyssinia, Arabia, and ancient Chaldea are among the countries from which are gathered the interesting traditions reported here.

268. Westermarck, E. THE HISTORY OF HUMAN MARRIAGE. 3 vols. 5th ed. London: Macmillan, 1922. Scholarly study of historical changes in marriage by a Finnish antropologist. Extensive bibliography.

269. ———. THE FUTURE OF MARRIAGE IN WESTERN CIVILIZATION. London: Macmillan, 1936. A sequel to and revision of the earlier work.

270. Winch, Robert F, Robert McGinnis, and Herbert R. Barringer, eds. SELECTED STUDIES IN MARRIAGE AND THE FAMILY. New York: Holt, Rinehart and Winston, 1962.

271. Young, Ann Eliza. WIFE NO. 19, OR THE STORY OF A LIFE IN BONDAGE, BEING A COMPLETE EXPOSE OF MORMONISM, AND REVEALING SORROWS, SACRIFICES AND SUFFERINGS OF WOMEN IN POLYGAMY. New York: Arno Press, 1972. Reprint of the 1875 edition. She escaped and told all—the nature of male rule, the social life of Young's wives, and the raising of children.

D. Life Styles

He who has nothing to assert has no style and can have none.
—Shaw

272. Acton, William. PROSTITUTION. Edited by Peter Fryer. New York: Praeger, 1971. 251 pp. Originally published London: Frank Cass, 1857. 302 pp. Pioneer study of Victorian prostitution by a social reformer.

273. "A Girl's Life in India: A Hundred Years Ago," CALCUTTA REVIEW, vol. 95 (July 1892), pp. 51-56. By a British observer.

274. ASIAN WOMEN. Berkeley, Calif.: Univ. of California Press, 1971. 144 pp. (No author cited.) Collection of essays, stories, poems, and photographs of women examining their identities as Asians and as women.

275. Astin, Helen S. PERSONAL AND ENVIRONMENTAL FACTORS IN CAREER DECISIONS OF YOUNG WOMEN: FINAL REPORT. Washington, D.C.: Bureau of Social Research, 1970.

276. Beatty, Jerome. THE GIRLS WE LEAVE BEHIND: A TERRIBLY SCIENTIFIC STUDY OF AMERICAN WOMEN AT HOME. New York: Doubleday, 1963. 183 pp. The world of the American commuter's wife.

277. Bell, Ernest A. FIGHTING THE TRAFFIC IN YOUNG GIRLS OR WAR ON THE WHITE SLAVE TRADE. No publisher cited, 1910. 481 pp.

278. Bernard, Jessie. "Changing Family Lifestyles: One Role, Two Roles, Shared Roles," ISSUES IN INDUSTRIAL SOCIETY, vol. 2, no. 1 (1971), pp. 21-28. The conclusions of a 1957 survey on employment status of women, especially equal rights.

279. Booth, Viva B., ed. "Woman in the Modern World," THE ANNALS, vol. 143 (May 1929). Entire issue devoted to changing life-styles of women, in marriage, employment, and education.

280. Bowne, Eliza S. GIRL'S LIFE EIGHTY YEARS AGO. New York: Charles Scribner's Sons, 1888. 239 pp. Selections from the author's letters.

281. Bragdon, Elizabeth, ed. WOMEN TODAY: THEIR CONFLICTS, THEIR FRUSTRATIONS, AND THEIR FULFILLMENTS. Indianapolis: Bobbs-Merrill, 1953. 335 pp. Collection of articles.

282. Brown, Alberta. "Message to the Black Woman," AFRICAN TEACHERS FORUM, Nov. 1968. 4 pp. Proposals for changes in life-styles.

283. Bullough, Vern L. THE HISTORY OF PROSTITUTION. New Hyde Park, N.Y.: State Univ. of New York, 1964. 304 pp. Chronological study with an excellent bibliographical essay and notes.

284. Burton, Gabrielle. I'M RUNNING AWAY FROM HOME BUT I'M NOT ALLOWED TO CROSS THE STREET: A PRIMER ON WOMEN'S LIBERATION. Pittsburgh: KNOW, 1972. 206 pp.

285. Business and Professional Women's Association. THE DUAL PROFES—SION FAMILY: RESEARCH SUMMARY. Washington, D.C.: Business and Professional Women's Association, 1971.

286. Butler, Josephine E.G. PERSONAL MEMORIES OF A GREAT CRUSADE. London: H. Marshall, 1896. 409 pp. Social and moral questions and prostitution in Great Britain are discussed.

287. Callahan, Sidney Cornelia. THE ILLUSION OF EVE: MODERN WOMAN'S QUEST FOR IDENTITY. New York: Sheed and Ward, 1965. 214 pp. A proposal that women do what they want, either following traditional roles as housewife, or working, or both.

288. Carson, Josephine. SILENT VOICES: THE SOUTHERN NEGRO WOMAN TODAY. New York: Delacorte, 1969. 273 pp. The Negro woman and her concern for employment and status.

289. Chew, Peter T. "Faithful Old Jane Faces Middle Age and Her Mirror," THE NATIONAL OBSERVER, Nov. 27, 1971, pp. 1, 16. Identity crisis of middle-aged women outgrown by their husbands and children.

290. Clawson, Augusta. SHIPYARD DIARY OF A WOMAN WELDER. New York: Penguin Books 1944. 181 pp. World War II working woman.

291. Cooper, Elizabeth. THE HARIM AND THE PURDAH: STUDIES OF ORIENTAL WOMEN. New York: Century, 1915. 309 pp. Informative and well written.

292. Cooperman, Irene G. "Second Careers: War Wives and Widows," THE VOCATIONAL GUIDANCE QUARTERLY, vol. 20 (Dec. 1971), pp. 103-111.

293. Crow, Duncan. THE VICTORIAN WOMAN. New York: Stein and Day, 1972. 351 pp.

294. Cudden, J. A. "In the Seraglio," CONTEMPORARY REVIEW, vol. 194 (Oct. 1958), pp. 196-199.

295. Cummings, Gwenna. "Black Women—Often Discussed but Never Understood." In THE BLACK POWER REVOLT, edited by Floyd Barbour. Boston: Porter Sargent, 1968, pp. 235-239. A study of the inner complexities of being black.

296. Cunnington, C. W. FEMININE ATTITUDES IN THE 19TH CENTURY. London: Heinemann, 1935. Life-styles in Britain.

297. DAEDALUS. "The Woman in America," DAEDALUS: JOURNAL OF THE AMERICAN ACADEMY OF ARTS AND SCIENCES, vol. 93, no. 2 (Spring 1964), pp. 579-801. Entire issue devoted to women in America. Contributors: Lotte Bailyn, Jill Conway, Carl N. Degler, Erik H. Erikson, Joan M. Erikson, Esther Peterson, David Riesman, Alice C. Rossi, and Edna G. Rostow.

298. Dalla Costa, Mariarosa. "Women and the Subversion of the Community," RADICAL AMERICA, vol. 6 (Jan.-Feb. 1972), pp. 67-102. Offers alternatives to relieve women of their isolation in the community.

299. Davey, R.P.B. "Present Condition of Muhammedan Women in Turkey," FORTNIGHTLY REVIEW (London), vol. 64 (July 1895), pp. 53-66.

300. ———. "Sultan and His Harem," FORTNIGHTLY REVIEW, vol. 64 (Nov. 1895), pp. 790-799.

301. Davis, Kingsley. "Sexual Behavior." In CONTEMPORARY SOCIAL PROBLEMS, edited by Robert K. Merton and Robert A. Nisbet. New York: Harcourt, Brace and Jovanovich, 1971, pp. 322-372. Prostitution.

302. Decter, Midge. THE LIBERATED WOMAN AND OTHER AMERICANS. New York: Coward, McCann and Geohegan, 1971. Anthology of essays and reviews.

303. deRham, Edith. HOW COULD SHE DO THAT? New York: Clarkson N. Potter, 1969. A study of female criminality.

304. Dorys, Georges. LA FEMME TURQUE. Paris: Plon-Nouritt et Cie, 1902. 299 pp. Changing life-styles of Turkish women.

305. Dowty, Nancy. "To Be a Woman in Israel," SCHOOL REVIEW, vol. 80 (Feb. 1972), pp. 319-332.

306. Dunbar, J. THE EARLY VICTORIAN WOMAN. London: Harrap, 1953. Sociological study of life-styles in Victorian England.

307. Eckenstein, Lina. WOMAN UNDER MONASTICISM. Cambridge: Cambridge Univ. Press, 1896. Chapters on convent life between A.D. 500 and A.D. 1500.

308. Eley, G. THE RUINED MAID: MODES AND MANNERS OF VICTORIAN WOMEN. Chicago: Priory Press, 1970.

309. Ellington, George. THE WOMEN OF NEW YORK: OR THE UNDERWORLD OF THE GREAT CITY. New York: Arno Press, 1972. Reprint of 1869 edition. Lives of women of fashion, women of pleasure, pickpockets, female models, etc. Illustrated.

310. Ellis, Evelyn. "Social Psychological Correlates of Upward Social Mobility among Unmarried Career Women," AMERICAN SOCIOLOGICAL REVIEW, vol. 17 (1952), pp. 558-563.

311. Fairchild, J. E. WOMEN, SOCIETY, AND SEX. London: Wentworth-Rohr, Linton and Starr, 1962. A history of prostitution.

312. Franken, Van Driel P. EUROPEES VROUWENLEVEN [Lives of European Women]. Amsterdam: n.p., 1955.

313. Gallup, George, and Evan Hill. "The American Woman," SATURDAY EVENING POST, (Dec. 22, 1962), pp. 15-32. Changes in women's life-styles.

314. Gavron, Hannah. THE CAPTIVE WIFE: CONFLICTS OF HOUSEBOUND MOTHERS. London: Routledge and Kegan Paul, 1966. A plea for the reintegration of the young mother into society.

315. Gawthorpe, A. UP HILL TO HOLLOWAY. U.K.: Traversity Press, 1962. Women in prison.

316. Gerson, Menachem. "Women in the Kibbutz," AMERICAN JOURNAL OF ORTHOPSYCHIATRY, vol. 41 (July 1971), pp. 566-573. Asserts that most of the goals of the women's liberation in America have been realized by Israeli kibbutz woman.

317. Ginzberg, Eli. LIFE STYLES OF EDUCATED WOMEN. New York: Columbia Univ. Press, 1966. 224 pp. Attitudes, involvement, and problems of contemporary educated women within American society.

318. Ginzberg, Eli, and Alice M. Yohalem. EDUCATED AMERICAN WOMEN: SELF-PORTRAITS. New York: Columbia Univ. Press, 1966. 198 pp. Anthology of articles on American women intellectuals, internal values and goals.

319. Goldberg, Dorothy. THE CREATIVE WOMAN. Washington, D.C.: Robert B. Luce, 1963. 204 pp.

320. Goldman, Nancy. "The Changing Role of Women in the Armed Forces," AMERICAN JOURNAL OF SOCIOLOGY, vol. 78, no. 4 (Jan. 1973), pp. 892-911. Examines the organizational resistance and role strains associated with the increase of women in the armed forces.

321. Gordon, David C. WOMEN OF ALGERIA: AN ESSAY ON CHANGE. Harvard Middle Eastern Monographs, no. 19. Cambridge: Harvard Univ. Press, 1968. 98 pp.

322. Greenwald, Harold. THE ELEGANT PROSTITUTE: A SOCIAL AND PSYCHOANALYTICAL STUDY. New York: Walker, 1970.

323. Gross, Irma H., ed. POTENTIALITIES OF WOMEN IN THE MIDDLE YEARS. E. Lansing: Michigan State Univ. Press, 1956.

324. Guelaud-Leridon, Francoise. RECHERCHES SUR LA CONDITION FEMININE DANS LA SOCIETE D'AUJOURD'HUI [Researches into the Condition of Women in Society Today] . Paris: Travaus et Documents, cahier No. 48, Presses Universitaires de France, 1967.

325. Haavis, Mannila E. "Some Consequences of Women's Emancipation," JOURNAL OF MARRIAGE AND THE FAMILY, vol. 31 (Feb. 1969), pp. 125-134.

326. Hagood, Margaret J. MOTHERS OF THE SOUTH: PORTRAITURE OF THE WHITE TENANT FARM WOMAN. Chapel Hill: Univ. of North Carolina Press, 1939. 252 pp. Answers many questions in regard to their quality of life.

327. Hall, Granville S. SENESCENCE: THE LAST HALF OF LIFE. New York: Arno Press, 1972. Reprint of the 1912 edition. Traces the treatment of the aged in other societies, past and present.

328. Hamid, M. A. "Purdah," MOSLEM WORLD, vol. 25 (July 1935), pp. 276-282. Changes in the traditional custom.

329. Harper's Magazine. "The American Female," HARPER'S MAGAZINE (Special Supplement), Oct. 1962, pp. 117-180. Contributors: Esther Raushenbush, Bruno Bettelheim, Patricia Cayo Sexton, Midge Decter, Florence B. Robin, and Marion K. Sanders.

330. Harris, Sara. HOUSE OF 10,000 PLEASURES: A MODERN STUDY OF THE GEISHA AND OF THE STREETWALKER OF JAPAN. London: Allen and Unwin, 1962. 222 pp.

331. Harry, M. "Visit to a Harem: Wives of the Sultan of Yemen," LIVING AGE (Boston), vol. 354 (May 1938), pp. 249-253.

332. Hauferlin, C. "La Vie d'une Femme Dans un Village de Dahomey," LE COURIER DE L'UNESCO (Paris), Mar. 1957, pp. 4-10; also in May 1957, pp. 14-15, 32-33. Traditional daily life.

333. Haug, Marie R., and Marvin R. Sussman. "The Second Career—Variant of a Sociological Concept," JOURNAL OF GERONTOLOGY, Oct. 1967, pp. 439-444.

334. Henriques, Fernando. PROSTITUTION AND SOCIETY, New York: Citadel, 1962.

335. ———. STEWS AND STRUMPETS: A SURVEY OF PROSTITUTION. London: MacGibbon and Kee, 1961; New York: Grove Press, 1962, 1968. Primitive, classical, and oriental prostitution.

336. Himmelheber, U. SCHWARZE SCHWESTER [Black Sister]. Bremen: Schunemann, 1956. The life-styles of the Dan women of Liberia.

337. Hottel, Althea K., special editor. "Women Around the World," THE ANNALS, vol. 375 (Jan. 1968). Special issue devoted to women. Contributors: Althea K. Hottel, Jessie Bernard, Jeanne C. Ridley, Julia J. Henderson, Lakshmi N. Menon, Inger M. Pederson, Rosamonde R. Boyd, Nelly Festini, Marcelle S. Derand, Kamila Chylinska, Beraet Z. Ungor, Angie E. Brooks, Amari Rakasataya, Taki Fujita, Ada Norris, Elizabeth Johnstone, Alison R. Lanier, Alice H. Cook, Nicole M. Friderich, Jeanne H. Chaton, Ina M. Beasley, and Margaret K. Bruce.

338. Hubback, J. WIVES WHO WENT TO COLLEGE. London: Heinemann, 1957. Life-styles of British women graduates.

339. Huber, Joan, ed. "Changing Women in a Changing Society: A Special Issue," AMERICAN JOURNAL OF SOCIOLOGY, vol. 78, no. 4 (Jan. 1973). Entire issue consisting of articles by Bernard, Freeman, Komarovsky, Lopata, et al. on such subjects as women in work, the origins of the liberation movement, and women in the book industry.

340. Ilejiani, O. "My Father's Harem in Nigeria," CORONET, vol. 37 (Dec. 1954), pp. 35-40.

341. Jafri, S.N.S. "Purdah in India," ASIATIC REVIEW (London), vol. 33 (July 1937), pp. 533-538.

342. Jolson, Marvin A., and Martin J. Gannon. "Wives—A Critical Element in Career Decisions," BUSINESS HORIZONS, vol. 15 (Feb. 1972), pp. 83-88.

343. Jones, Claudia. AN END TO THE NEGLECT OF THE PROBLEMS OF THE NEGRO WOMAN. New York: National Women's Commission, 1949. 19 pp. Proposals for change in Negro women's life-styles.

344. Jones, Violet R. S., and L. Bevan Jones. WOMAN IN ISLAM: A MANUAL WITH SPECIAL REFERENCE TO CONDITIONS IN INDIA. Lucknow: Lucknow Publishing House, 1941. 455 pp. Excellent sociological study with documentation.

345. Joslyn, Kersten, and Arlene K. Daniels. "The Place of Voluntarism in the Lives of Women," n.d. Available from Scientific Analysis Corporation, 4339 California Street, San Francisco, Calif., 94118.

346. Jutting, Van Bethem. "Prostitution of Minors and Means to Combat It," REEDUCATION, 1970, n.p. Pamphlet proposing preventive measures.
347. Kalish, Richard A. "Value Similarities and Differences in Three Generations of Women," JOURNAL OF MARRIAGE AND THE FAMILY, vol. 34 (Feb. 1972), pp. 49-54
348. Key, Ellen. THE MORALITY OF WOMAN AND OTHER ESSAYS. Translated by M. B. Borthwick. Chicago: Ralph F. Seymour, 1911. 78 pp. Life-styles and liberation from traditional roles.
349. Kirchwey, Freda, ed. OUR CHANGING MORALITY: A SYMPOSIUM. New York: Arno Press, 1972. Reprint of the 1930 edition. Explores the links between changing life-styles and the growing freedom of women.
350. Kollontai, Alexandra. RED LOVE. New York: Seven Arts, 1927. By the early advocate of free love and the liberation of Soviet women.
351. ———. FREE LOVE. New York: Herder, 1932.
352. Krueger, Lillian. MOTHERHOOD ON THE WISCONSIN FRONTIER. Madison: State Historical Society of Wisconsin, 1946, 1951. 48 pp. Pioneering women and their life-styles.
353. Lemaire, C. AFRICAINES: CONTRIBUTION A L'HISTOIRE DE LA FEMME EN AFRIQUE. Brussels: C. Bulens, 1897. 256 pp. Description of African women and their way of life.
354. Lewis, Edwin. DEVELOPING WOMEN'S POTENTIAL. Ames: Iowa State Univ. Press, 1969. Originally TOWARD A NEW FEMININITY. Changes in women's life-styles.
355. Lopata, Helena Z. "Social Relations of Black and White Widowed Women in a Northern Metropolis," AMERICAN JOURNAL OF SOCIOLOGY, vol. 78, no. 4 (Jan. 1973), pp. 1003-1010. Contrasts the social situation and life-styles of black and white women.
356. ———. OCCUPATION HOUSEWIFE. New York: Oxford Univ. Press, 1971. 387 pp. Sociological study of the life-style of mothers, at home and in the community.
357. Martin, Del, and Phyllis Lyon. LESBIAN/WOMAN. New York: Bantam Press, 1972. States that lesbianism is a natural and viable life-style; interesting data for discussion of female life-styles.
358. Mayhew, Henry. LONDON LABOUR AND THE LONDON POOR. 4 vol. New York: Dover Press, 1972. 504 pp. Victorian prostitution and its economic causes.
359. Mishima, Sumie Seo. THE BROADER WAY: A WOMAN'S LIFE IN THE NEW JAPAN. New York: n.p., 1953. Reprinted by Greenwood Press, Westport, Conn. 247 pp. By an emancipated Japanese woman on the new Japanese woman, her ideas and goals.
360. Myrdal, Jan. REPORT FROM A CHINESE VILLAGE. New York: New American Library, 1966; London: Heinemann, 1965. 397 pp. Interviews with Chinese women on their lives before and since the coming of the Communists.
361. Neuss, Margret. "Die Seitosha: Der Ausgangspunkt der Japanischen Frauenbewegung in Seinen Zeitgeschichtlichen und Sozialen Bedingungen" [The Seitosha: The Origins of the Japanese Feminist Movement in Its Contemporary and Social Circumstances], ORIENS EXTREMUS, vol. 18 (July 1971), pp. 1-66.

362. O'Neill, Barbara P. CAREERS FOR WOMEN AFTER MARRIAGE AND CHILDREN. New York: Macmillan, 1965. 401 pp.
363. Orth, Penelope. AN ENVIABLE POSITION: THE AMERICAN MISTRESS FROM SLIGHTLY KEPT TO PRACTICALLY MARRIED. New York: McKay, 1972. A serious attempt at surveying the mistress in contemporary American society.
364. Pollack, Otto. THE CRIMINALITY OF WOMEN. Philadelphia: Univ. of Pennsylvania Press, 1950. A bit out of date but good for background information and references to prostitution.
365. Pruette, Lorine. WOMEN AND LEISURE: A STUDY OF SOCIAL WASTE. Introduction by Harry Elmer Barnes. New York: Arno Press, 1972. Reprint of the 1924 edition. Veblenesque sociological study of women released from household drudgery by mechanical advances to face useless leisure.
366. Rainwater, Lee, et al. WORKINGMAN'S WIFE: HER PERSONALITY, WORLD, AND LIFE STYLE. Chicago: Social Research, 1958. 238 pp.
367. Rover, C. LOVE, MORALS AND THE FEMINISTS. London: Routledge and Kegan Paul, 1970.
368. Russ, Lavinia. A HIGH OLD TIME OR HOW TO ENJOY BEING A WOMAN OVER SIXTY. New York: Saturday Review Press, 1972. 160 pp.
369. Sagarin, Edward, special editor. "Sex and the Contemporary Scene," THE ANNALS, vol. 376 (Mar. 1968). Entire issue devoted to women, with articles by Edward Sagarin, Erwin D. Smigel and Rita Seiden, Charles Winick, J. Richard Udry, Robert Boyers, Mary S. Calderone, Bernard Rosenberg and Joseph Bensman, Theodore Ferdinand, Isadore Rubin, Albert Ellis, John H. Gagnon and William Simon, T. C. Esselstyn, Edwin M. Schur, and Donald E. J. MacNamara.
370. Saghaphi, M.M.K. "Imperial Harem," ASIA, vol. 28 (April 1928), pp. 306-312.
371. Salazar, Fernando. LA MUJER SOLTERA [The Unmarried Woman]. Madrid: Editorial Alameda, 1971. 60 pp.
372. Scott, A. C. THE FLOWER AND THE WILLOW WORLD: THE STORY OF THE GEISHA. New York: Orion, 1960. 208 pp.
373. Seeley, John R., R. Alexander Sim, and Elizabeth W. Loosley. CRESTWOOD HEIGHTS. Toronto: Univ. of Toronto Press, 1963. Landmark sociological study of the affluent, pre-Friedan housewife of the fifties in Canada.
374. Silverman, Phyllis R. "Widowhood and Preventive Intervention," THE FAMILY COORDINATOR, vol. 21 (Jan. 1972), pp. 95-102. The transition from the role of wife to that of widowhood.
375. Sister Mary Ethel. FORGOTTEN WOMEN. Middleton, Idaho: Boise Valley Herald, 1938. 124 pp. Pleas for the emancipation of the convent nun.
376. Slaughter, Diana T. "Becoming an Afro-American Woman," SCHOOL REVIEW, vol. 80 (Feb. 1972), pp. 299-318. New life-styles for black women.
377. "The Spinster," LINK, vol. 14 (Sept. 19, 1971), p. 14. Compares the attitudes of the West on unmarried women to those in India.

378. Starke, Barbara. BORN IN CAPTIVITY: THE STORY OF A GIRL'S ESCAPE. Indianapolis: Bobbs-Merrill, 1931. 301 pp. The first nonfictionalized commentary on the morality of the "open road" as experienced by a woman.

379. "Study on Traffic in Persons and Prostitution," Dept. of Economic and Social Affairs, Secretariat. New York: United Nations Publications, 1959. 57 pp.

380. Sweet, James A. "The Living Arrangements of Separated, Widowed, and Divorced Mothers," DEMOGRAPHY, vol. 9 (Feb. 1972), pp. 143-157.

381. Tallman, I. "Working Class Wives in Suburbia: Fulfillment or Crises?" JOURNAL OF MARRIAGE AND THE FAMILY, vol. 31 (Feb. 1969), pp. 65-72.

382. Tarbell, Ida M. THE BUSINESS OF BEING A WOMAN. New York: Macmillan, 1912. 242 pp. Essays in defense of new life-styles for women.

383. ———. THE WAYS OF WOMAN. New York: Macmillan, 1915. Supplementary essays on the author's earlier book, THE BUSINESS OF BEING A WOMAN.

384. Tchernavin, Tatiana. WE SOVIET WOMEN. Translated by N. Alexander. New York: Dutton, 1936. 304 pp. Sketches of various types of women and their life-styles in the USSR.

385. Van Rensselaer, Mrs. John King. THE GOEDE VROUW OF MANA-HA-TA: AT HOME AND IN SOCIETY, 1609-1760. New York: Arno Press, 1972. Reprint of 1898 edition. Records of the daily life and household activities of women in early New York.

386. Vidal, Mirta. WOMEN: NEW VOICE OF LA RAZA: CHICANAS SPEAK OUT. New York: Pathfinder Press, 1972. Radical solutions to problems of life-style. 16 pp.

387. Weingarten, Violet. THE MOTHER WHO WORKS OUTSIDE THE HOME. New York: Child Study Association of America, 1961.

388. Wharton, Edith. "Harems and Ceremonies," YALE REVIEW, vol. 9 (Oct. 1919), pp. 47-71.

389. "Women in Transition," AMERICAN ASSOCIATION OF UNIVERSITY WOMEN JOURNAL, vol. 64, no. 2 (Nov. 1970). Entire issue devoted to women. 48 pp. Collected articles dealing with women in all walks of life.

390. Woodsmall, Ruth Frances. MOSLEM WOMEN ENTER A NEW WORLD. New York: Round Table Press, 1936. 432 pp. Publication of the American University of Beirut, Social Science Series, no. 14.

391. ———. WOMEN AND THE NEW EAST. Foreword by Bayer Dodge. Washington, D.C.: Middle East Institute, 1960. 436 pp. Changes in life-styles of women in Turkey, Iran, Pakistan, Afghanistan, Indonesia, and India.

392. Young, Louise M., ed. "Women's Opportunities and Responsibilities," THE ANNALS, vol. 251 (May 1947), pp. 1-224. Entire issue devoted to women in society, their changing economic, political, and educational roles, and the search for new values.

E. Sexuality

Feminine passion is to masculine as an epic to an epigram.
                                                    —Karl Kraus

393. Barker-Benfield, Ben. THE HORRORS OF THE HALF-KNOWN LIFE. New York: Harper Torchbooks, 1973. Homosexuality and lesbianism.

394. ———. "The Spermatic Economy: A Nineteenth Century View of Sexuality," FEMINIST STUDIES (New York), vol. 1, no. 1 (Summer 1972), pp. 45-74. Believes that men project their sexual anxieties onto women.

395. Bartell, Gilbert D. GROUP SEX. New York: Peter H. Wyden, 1971. 298 pp.

396. Beach, F. A., ed. SEX AND BEHAVIOR. New York: Wiley, 1965.

397. Bell, Robert R. PREMARITAL SEX IN A CHANGING SOCIETY. Englewood Cliffs, N.J.: Prentice-Hall, 1966. 182 pp. Sociological framework for examining premarital sexual values and behavior.

398. Bengis, Ingrid. COMBAT IN THE ERONGENOUS ZONE. New York: Knopf, 1972. 260 pp. The war between and among the sexes; the battleground, the bedroom and the psyche.

399. Calverton, V. F., and S. D. Schmalhausen. SEX IN CIVILIZATION. New York: MacCauley, 1929.

400. Carpenter, Edward. LOVE'S COMING OF AGE. London: Allen and Unwin, 1923. 221 pp. A somewhat philosophical study of sex and love.

401. Caspari, E. W. "The Evolutionary Importance of Sexual Processes and of Sexual Behavior." Pp. 34-52 in SEX AND BEHAVIOR, edited by F. A. Beach. 1966. New York: John Wiley.

402. Chesser, Eustace. SEX AND THE MARRIED WOMAN. London: W. H. Allen, 1968. 231 pp. A physician's view of fulfillment in sex.

403. ———. UNMARRIED LOVE. New York: D. McKay, 1965, 177 pp.

404. ———. WOMAN AND LOVE. London: Jarrolds, 1962. 175 pp.

405. Chesser, Eustace, Joan Maizels, et al. THE SEXUAL, MARITAL, AND FAMILY RELATIONSHIP OF THE MARRIED WOMAN. London: Hutchinsons, 1956. 642 pp.

406. Chideckel, Maurice. FEMALE SEX PERVERSION: THE SEXUALLY ABERRATED WOMAN AS SHE IS. New York: Brown, 1935, 1966. 331 pp.

407. Chou, Eric. THE DRAGON AND THE PHOENIX: LOVE, SEX, AND THE CHINESE. New York: Arbor House, 1971. 222 pp. Sexuality in the Chinese culture revealed in erotica, pornography, and sexual pharmacology.

408. Clephane, E. TOWARD SEX FREEDOM. London: Bodley Head, 1938. A liberal approach to freedom in sexual relations.

409. Cuber, John, and Peggy Harroff. SEX AND THE SIGNIFICANT AMERICANS: A STUDY OF SEXUAL BEHAVIOR AMONG THE AFFLUENT. Baltimore: Penguin, 1966. 204 pp. Descriptive anthropology of twentieth century man and woman.

410. Dank, Barry M. "Six Homosexual Siblings," ARCHIVES OF SEXUAL BEHAVIOR, vol. 1, no. 3 (1971), pp. 193-204.

411. Davis, Katharine Bement. FACTORS IN THE SEX LIFE OF TWENTY-TWO HUNDRED WOMEN. New York: Arno Press, 1972. Reprint of 1929 edition. The first careful and formal study in this field.

412. Deutsch, Ronald M. THE KEY TO FEMININE RESPONSE IN MARRIAGE. New York: Random House, 1968. Replaces modern myths and confusion about women's sexuality.

413. Ditzion, Sidney. MARRIAGE, MORALS AND SEX IN AMERICA. New York: Octagon Books, 1953. A history of ideas.

414. Ellis, Albert. THE AMERICAN SEXUAL TRAGEDY. New York: Grove Press, 1962.

415. ———. THE FOLKLORE OF SEX. New York: Grove Press, 1955.
416. Ellis, Havelock. THE PSYCHOLOGY OF SEX. New York: New American Library edition, 1933, 1938. 272 pp. Good one-volume study.
417. Ferdinand, Theodore N. "Sex Behavior and the American Class Structure: A Mosaic," THE ANNALS, vol. 376 (Mar. 1968), pp. 76-85. Changes in sexual mores and behavior are a result of changes in the social class structure.
418. Ferm, Deane William. RESPONSIBLE SEXUALITY NOW. New York: Seabury Press, 1971. 179 pp. Studies the Swedish sexual revolution as a model for ours.
419. Filler, W., and N. Drezner. "The Results of Surgical Castration in Women under Forty," AMERICAN JOURNAL OF OBSTETRICS AND GYNECOLOGY, vol. 47 (1944), pp. 122-124.
420. Fisher, S., and Howard J. Osofsky. "Sexual Responsiveness in Women: Physiological Correlates," PSYCHOLOGICAL REPORTS, vol. 22 (1968), pp. 215-226.
421. Ford, Clellan S., and Frank A. Beach. PATTERNS OF SEXUAL BEHAVIOR. New York: Harper, 1951. 307 pp. A study of 190 different societies of humans.
422. Francoeur, Robert. EVE'S NEW RIB: 20 FACES OF SEX, MARRIAGE AND FAMILY. New York: Harcourt, Brace and Jovanovich, 1972.
423. Freud, Sigmund. "Female Sexuality," INTERNATIONAL JOURNAL OF PSYCHOANALYSIS, vol. 13 (1932), pp. 281-297.
424. ———. "The Psychogenesis of a Case of Homosexuality in a Woman." Pp. 202-231 in COLLECTED PAPERS, vol. 2. London: Hogarth Press, 1948.
425. Gagnon, John H., and William Simon, eds. THE SEXUAL SCENE. Chicago: Aldine, 1970. 150 pp. Scientific, nonscientific, and provocative discussions on sexual behavior.
426. Gittelson, Natalie. THE EROTIC LIFE OF THE AMERICAN WIFE: A SURVEY OF HER SEXUAL MORES. New York: Delacorte, 1972. 400 pp. Two years of cross-country study of the emerging, ambivalent frame of mind of married American women.
427. Gordon, Michael, and Penelope J. Shankweiler. "Different Equals Less: Female Sexuality in Recent Marriage Manuals," JOURNAL OF MARRIAGE AND THE FAMILY, vol. 33 (Aug. 1971), pp. 459-466. Eighteen of the best-selling marriage manuals over the last 20 years consider women to have less interest and experience in sex than men.
428. Gulik, Robert H. Van. LA VIE SEXUELLE DANS LA CHINE ANCIENNE [Sexual Life in Ancient China]. Paris: Gallimard, 1961. 466 pp.
429. Hennessey, Caroline. THE STRATEGY OF SEXUAL STRUGGLE. New York: Lancer Books, 1971.
430. Henriques, Fernando. LOVE IN ACTION: THE SOCIOLOGY OF SEX. New York: Dutton, 1960.
431. Hunt, Morton. THE AFFAIR: A PORTRAIT OF EXTRA-MARITAL LOVE IN CONTEMPORARY AMERICA. New York: World, 1969. 317 pp. Based upon interviews of 91 men and women.
432. ———. HER INFINITE VARIETY: THE AMERICAN WOMAN AS LOVER, RIVAL, AND MATE. New York: Harper and Row, 1962.
433. Johnson, Arthur. "Roundtable: The Significance of Extramarital Relations," MEDICAL ASPECTS OF HUMAN SEXUALITY, vol. 3, no. 10

(1969), p. 33+. Concerning reasons for extramarital relations, their effects on the marriage relationship, and their relationship to our changing social scene.

434. Karlen, Arno. SEXUALITY AND HOMOSEXUALITY: A NEW VIEW. New York: Norton, 1971, 666 pp. Interesting insight into the historical and biological, as well as familial, influences on sex behavior.

435. Kinsey, Alfred C., et al. SEXUAL BEHAVIOR IN THE HUMAN FEMALE. Philadelphia: W. B. Saunders, 1953. A classic.

436. Kirkendall, Lester A., and Robert N. Whitehurst, eds. THE NEW SEXUAL REVOLUTION. New York: W. Brown, 1971. 236 pp. Contributions by 19 specialists ranging from a new sexual bill of rights to evolving sexual ethics within a democratic society.

437. Koupernik, Cyrille. "Le Couple Homophile," LA NEF, vol. 29 (Feb.-May 1972), pp. 127-145. An account of lesbianism in France.

438. Kronhausen, Phyllis, and Eberhard Kronhausen. THE SEXUALLY RESPONSIVE WOMAN. New York: Ballantine Books, 1964. 288 pp. Female sexuality from the point of view of happiness, mental health, and social progress, with an excellent bibliography.

439. Lundberg, Ferdinand, and Marynia Farnham. MODERN WOMAN: THE LOST SEX. New York: Grosset and Dunlap, 1947. 497 pp. Psychosocial history of women and sexuality; excellent bibliography.

440. Malfetti, James L., and Elizabeth M. Eidlitz. PERSPECTIVES ON SEXUALITY: A LITERARY COLLECTION. New York: Holt, Rinehart and Winston, 1972. 611 pp. Portrays many facets of sexuality.

441. Malinowski, Bronislaw. SEX AND REPRESSION IN SAVAGE SOCIETY. New York: Humanities Press, 1927. Classic functional approach of primitive sexualism.

442. ———. SEX, CULTURE AND MYTH. New York: Harcourt, Brace and World. 1962.

443. Marchand, Henry L. THE SEXUAL HISTORY OF FRANCE. New York: Tower Books, 1968. 250 pp. French sexuality and eroticism from medieval to modern times, for the serious student.

444. Marcuse, Herbert. EROS AND CIVILIZATION. Boston: Beacon Press, 1955. Marxian critique of Freud's theories of repression, calling for a nonrepressive reality principle.

445. Marmor, Judd. "Normal and Deviant Sexual Behavior," AMERICAN MEDICAL ASSOCIATION JOURNAL, vol. 217 (July 12, 1971), pp. 165-170. An effort to divorce the terms from the value systems of contemporary society.

446. Masters, William H., and Virginia E. Johnson. HUMAN SEXUAL INADEQUACY. Boston: Little, Brown, 1970. Sound clinical study of human sexuality.

447. ———. HUMAN SEXUAL RESPONSE. Boston: Little, Brown, 1966. Key empirical study.

448. Meyer, Jon K., Norman J. Knorr, and Dietrich Blumer. "Characterization of a Self-Designated Transsexual Population," ARCHIVES OF SEXUAL BEHAVIOR, vol. 1, no. 3 (1971), pp. 219-230.

449. Mohr, R. "Ricerche Sull' Etica Sessuale di Alcune Popolazioni dell' Africa Centrale e Orientale," ARCHIVIO PER L'ANTHROPOLOGIA E LA ETNOLOGIA, vol. 69, nos. 3-4 (Florence, 1939), pp. 157-315. Premarital and marital sexual ethics among the people of the Upper Nile.

450. Money, John, ed. SEX RESEARCH: NEW DEVELOPMENTS. New York: Rinehart and Winston, 1965. Collection of articles.
451. Pearsall, Ronald. THE WORM IN THE BUD: THE WORLD OF VICTORIAN SEXUALITY. New York: Macmillan, 1972. 560 pp. Everything from aristocratic perversions to menstrual cycles, but no social diagnosis. Good bibliography.
452. Reich, Wilhelm. THE SEXUAL REVOLUTION. New York: Farrar, Straus and Giroux, 1965. 269 pp. Important work by an important researcher.
453. ———. THE FUNCTION OF THE ORGASM. New York: Noonday Press, 1961.
454. Schwendinger, Julia, and Herman Schwendinger. "Sociology's Founding Fathers: Sexists to a Man," JOURNAL OF MARRIAGE AND THE FAMILY, vol. 33 (Nov. 1971), pp. 78-99. Critique of Lester Ward's and W. I. Thomas's sexist paradigms for analyzing sexual relationships.
455. Scott, Clifford H. "A Naturalistic Rationale for Women's Reform: Lester Frank Ward on the Evolution of Sexual Relations," HISTORIAN, vol. 33 (1970), pp. 54-67. A sociobiological defense of the women's movement and how to bring women into full equality.
456. Seaman, Barbara R. FREE AND FEMALE: THE SEX LIFE OF THE CONTEMPORARY WOMAN. New York: Coward, McCann and Geoghegan, 1972. Case studies of women.
457. Sherfey, Mary Jane. THE NATURE OF EVOLUTION AND FEMALE SEXUALITY. New York: Random House, 1971.
458. Sorensen, Robert C. ADOLESCENT SEXUALITY IN CONTEMPORARY AMERICA: PERSONAL VALUE AND SEXUAL BEHAVIOR AGES 13-19. New York: World, 1973. The first comprehensive, nationwide study of this subject.
459. Sorokin, Pitirim A. THE AMERICNA SEX REVOLUTION. Boston: Porter Sargent, 1956. 186 pp. Critical review of sexualization in American society, its far-reaching individual and sociocultural consequences, and programs for progress from sex anarchy to sex order.
460. Taylor, G. Rattray. SEX IN HISTORY. London: Thames and Hudson, 1953; New York: Vanguard, 1954. Scholarly and with an excellent bibliography.
461. Thompson, Norman L., Boyd R. McCandless, and Bonnie R. Strickland. "Personality Adjustment of Male and Female Homosexuals," JOURNAL OF ABNORMAL PSYCHOLOGY, vol. 78 (Oct. 1971), pp. 237-240. Much information about the female homosexual and matched heterosexuals.
462. Tobin, Kay, and Rany Wicker. THE GAY CRUSADERS. New York: Paperback Press, 1972. Men and women seeking the repeal of discriminatory laws and the rethinking of traditional sexuality.
463. Todd, John. CONJUGAL SINS. New York: J. S. Redfield, 1870. Women and sexual intercourse and antimasturbatory arguments.
464. ———. THE STUDENT'S MANUAL. Northampton, Mass.: Hopkins and Bridgman, 1835. Preaches avoidance of contact with women which is addictive and debilitating.
465. von Krafft-Ebing, Richard. PSYCHOPATHIA SEXUALIS. New York: G. P. Putnam's Sons, 1969. A reprint of an 1886 classic study of sexuality.
466. Walker, Kenneth and Peter Fletcher. SEX AND SOCIETY. London: Allen and Unwin, 1955; Penguin edition, 1969. 250 pp. The psychology of sexuality.

467. Watts, Alan. NATURE, MAN, AND WOMAN. New York: Pantheon, 1958. The nature of sexuality and its manifestations from an eastern philosophical viewpoint.

468. Weininger, O. SEX AND CHARACTER. London: Heinemann, 1966. Psychosexual study with bibliography.

469. Wright, Helena. SEX AND SOCIETY. Seattle: Univ. of Washington Press, 1968. 140 pp. Problems of unhappiness in sexual relations examined and solutions offered.

470. Wughtman, John. "Film Modalities of Sex," ENCOUNTER (London), vol. 38 (Mar. 1972), pp. 32-35.

471. Wulffen, E. WOMAN AS A SEXUAL CRIMINAL. New York: Falstaff Press, 1935.

472. Young, Wayland. EROS DENIED: SEX IN WESTERN SOCIETY. New York: Grove Press, 1964. Historical and sociological study, with a defense of pornography.

F. Class and Status

There may be said to be two classes of people in the world: those who constantly divide the people of the world into two classes, and those who do not.
—Robert Benchley

473. Andreas, Carol. SEX AND CASTE IN AMERICA. Englewood Cliffs, N.J.: Prentice-Hall, 1971. 146 pp. A study of sex roles and the education process and how it prevents the full development of modern society.

474. Anonymous. AN ESSAY IN DEFENCE OF THE FEMALE SEX. New York: Source Book Press, 1970. 136 pp. Reprint of the 1696 edition. A critique of their isolation from male-dominated activities.

475. Anthony, Katherine S. FEMINISM IN GERMANY AND SCANDINAVIA. New York: Holt, 1915. Devoted to status and legal issues.

476. Bart, Pauline B. "Sexism and Social Science: From the Gilded Cage to the Iron Cage, or, The Perils of Pauline," JOURNAL OF MARRIAGE AND THE FAMILY, vol. 33 (Nov. 1971), pp. 734-745.

477. Benson, Mary S. WOMEN IN EIGHTEENTH-CENTURY AMERICA: A STUDY OF OPINION AND SOCIAL USAGE. New York: Columbia Univ. Press, 1935. 345 pp. Study of the status of early American women through legislation, politics, and the church.

478. Blanc, Madame Marie Therese de Solms. THE CONDITION OF WOMAN IN THE UNITED STATES: A TRAVELLER'S NOTES. Translated by Abby Langdon Alger. New York: Arno Press, 1972. Reprint of the 1895 edition. Interviews with organized women's groups, accounts of visits to women's colleges, clubs, and homes, with perceptive observations on class and status.

479. Borgese, Elizabeth Mann. THE ASCENT OF WOMEN. New York: George Braziller, 1962. Essays on changes in women's status.

480. Breckenridge, Sophonisba P. WOMEN IN THE TWENTIETH CENTURY: A STUDY OF THEIR POLITICAL, SOCIAL AND ECONOMIC ACTIVITIES. New York: McGraw-Hill, 1933. Changes in women's status.

481. Brown, Donald R., ed. THE ROLE AND STATUS OF WOMEN IN THE SOVIET UNION. New York: Teachers College, Columbia Univ., 1968.

139 pp. Collection of essays concerned with the legal, social, economic, and political status of Soviet women.

482. Cassara, Beverly B., ed. AMERICAN WOMEN: THE CHANGING IMAGE. Boston: Beacon Press, 1962. Includes essays on changing women's status.

483. Cavan, S. "The Status of Women in the Professions Relative to the Status of Men," QUARTERLY OF THE AMERICAN INTERPROFESSIONAL INSTITUTE, Winter 1956-1957.

484. Chandrasekhar, Sripati. "Women in New China." Pp. 74-87 in RED CHINA: AN ASIAN VIEW (same author). New York: Praeger, 1961. Summary of women's changing status, legal and economic.

485. Citizen's Advisory Council on the Status of Women. "The Proposed Equal Rights Amendment to the United States Constitution: A Memorandum," Washington, D.C.: SUDOC, GPO, 1970. 18 pp. History of the equal rights amendment.

486. Clignet, Remi. MANY WIVES, MANY POWERS: AUTHORITY AND POWER IN POLYGAMOUS FAMILIES. Evanston, Ill.: Northwestern Univ. Press, 1970. Concubinage and status in other societies.

487. Cooper, Anna J.H. A VOICE FROM THE SOUTH. Westport, Conn.: Greenwood Press, 1970. Reprint of Xenia, Ohio, 1892 edition. 304 pp. The status and position of women at the close of the nineteenth century, particularly the status of black women.

488. Cooper, Elizabeth. THE WOMEN OF EGYPT. New York: Stokes, 1914. 380 pp. Scholarly study of the changes experienced by Egyptian women.

489. Coughlin, Richard J. POSITION OF WOMEN IN VIETNAM. New Haven: Yale Univ. Press, 1950. Traditional and new roles of women.

490. Cutler, John H. WHAT ABOUT WOMEN?: AN EXAMINATION OF THE PRESENT CHARACTERISTICS, NATURE, STATUS, AND POSITION OF WOMEN AS THEY HAVE EVOLVED DURING THIS CENTURY. New York: Washburn, 1961. 241 pp. A good overview.

491. Datta, Kali Kinkar. "Position of Women in Bengal in the Mid-Eighteenth Century," CALCUTTA REVIEW, vol. 37 (Oct. 1930), pp. 17-32. From contemporary Indian literature and British observations.

492. David, O. THE EDUCATION OF WOMEN: SIGNS FOR THE FUTURE. Washington, D.C.: American Council on Education, 1957. Changes in women's status through education.

493. DeRham, Edith. THE LOVE FRAUD: A DIRECT ATTACK ON THE STAGGERING WASTE OF EDUCATION AND TALENT AMONG AMERICAN WOMEN. New York: Pegasus, 1965. 219 pp. Excellent chapter on the question of social class in the women's movement.

494. Dollard, John. CASTE AND CLASS IN A SOUTHERN TOWN. New Haven: Yale Univ. Press, 1937. Chapter entitled "The Sexual Gain" deals with moral and social questions concerning sexual relations between blacks and whites.

495. Fanon, Frantz. STUDIES IN A DYING COLONIALISM. New York: Grove Press, 1967. Revolutionary Algerian women and their change in status dealt with thoughout.

496. Fenberg, M. "Blame Coke and Blackstone," WOMEN LAWYERS JOURNAL, vol. 34, no. 2 (1948), p. 7. Examines the historical roots of women's legal inequality.

497. Frost, D., and A. Jay. "Women." In THE ENGLISH. New York: Avon Books, 1969. A look at the changing status of British women.

498. Fussell, G. E., and K. R. Fussell. THE ENGLISH COUNTRYWOMAN: A FARMHOUSE SOCIAL HISTORY, A.D. 1500-1900. New York: Benjamin Blom, 1953. 221 pp. A history of relatively few changes in 400 years, from Cromwell to Victoria.

499. Goldberg, Philip. "Are Women Prejudiced Against Women?" TRANSACTION, April 1968.

500. Goncourt, Edmond de and Jules de Goncourt. THE WOMAN OF THE EIGHTEENTH CENTURY: HER LIFE, FROM BIRTH TO DEATH, HER LOVE AND HER PHILOSOPHY IN THE WORLDS OF SALON, SHOP AND STREET. Translated by Jacques Le Clercq and Ralph Roeder. London: Allen and Unwin, 1928. 347 pp.

501. Gornick, Vivian, and Barbara K. Moran. WOMAN IN SEXIST SOCIETY. New York: Basic Books, 1971. 515 pp. Collection of 29 essays showing that woman's condition is the result of years of entrenched and pervasive cultural-political decisions that women are merely child-bearing and sex objects.

502. Hacker, Helen M. "Women as a Minority Group," SOCIAL FORCES, vol. 30 (Oct. 1951), pp. 60-69. An early assessment. Also available in Bobbs-Merrill reprints.

503. Halle, Fannina W. WOMEN IN THE SOVIET EAST. New York: Dutton, 1938. 363 pp. An expanded version of her earlier WOMEN IN SOVIET RUSSIA, dealing with the emancipation of women. Excellent bibliography.

504. Houghton, Ross C. WOMEN OF THE ORIENT: AN ACCOUNT OF THE RELIGIOUS, INTELLECTUAL, AND SOCIAL CONDITION OF WOMEN IN JAPAN, EGYPT, SYRIA AND TURKEY. Cincinnati: Walden and Stowe, 1877. 496 pp. Dated but historically relevant.

505. Jaulin, R. "Elements et Aspects Divers de l'Organisation Civile et Penale des Groupes du Moyen-Chari: Groupe Sara Madjingaye et Groupe Mbaye," BULLETIN DE L'IFAN, vol. 20, nos. 1-2 (Dakar, 1958), pp. 170-184. The position of Sara women and their search for emancipation.

506. Jones, Beverly, and Judith Brown. TOWARD A FEMALE LIBERATION MOVEMENT. Cambridge, Mass.: New England Free Press, 1968. Puts forth sensible and realizable programs for changes in women's status.

507. Joseph, G. "Condition de la Femme en Cote D'Ivoire," BULLETINS ET MEMOIRES DE LA SOCIETE D'ANTHROPOLOGIE DE PARIS, vol. 14, no. 5 (Paris, 1913), pp. 585-589. Customs regulating women's status in marriage and homelife.

508. Karim, Abdul K. N. CHANGING SOCIETY IN INDIA AND PAKISTAN: A STUDY IN SOCIAL CHANGE AND SOCIAL STRATIFICATION. Dacca: Oxford Univ. Press, 1956. 173 pp.

509. Kellersberger, J. S. CONGO CROSSES: A STUDY OF CONGO WOMANHOOD. Boston: Central Committee of United States and Foreign Missions, 1936. 222 pp. Discusses the life of Congolese women, their role in society, their occupations, and the influence of the missionary movement in changing their status.

510. Knudsen, Dean D. "The Declining Status of Women: Popular Myths and the Failure of Functionalist Thought," SOCIAL FORCES, (Dec. 1969), pp. 183-192.

511. Koeume, E. THE AFRICAN HOUSEWIFE AND HER HOME. Nairobi: Eagle Press, 1952. 186 pp. Changes in the traditional status of Kenyan women.

512. Koyama, Takashi. THE CHANGING SOCIAL POSITION OF WOMEN IN JAPAN. Geneva, Switzerland: UNESCO, 1961.

513. Labarge, Margaret W. THE CULTURAL TRADITION OF CANADIAN WOMEN. Ottawa: Royal Commission on the Status of Women in Canada, 1971. Historical summary of prevailing attitudes toward class and status.

514. Labouret, H. "Situation Materielle, Morale, et Coutumiere de la Femme dans l'Ouest Africain," AFRICA, vol. 13 (1940), pp. 97-124. Women's position in the household, her legal status in customary marriage, female solidarity, and the effects of education on changing their traditional status.

515. Lambton, Ann K.S. ISLAMIC SOCIETY IN PERSIA. London: School of Oriental and African Studies, 1954. 32 pp. Women's place in Persian society.

516. Landes, R. "Negro Slavery and Female Status," AFRICAN AFFAIRS, vol. 53, no. 206 (1953), pp. 54-57. Posits a continuity between African women's status and social position and of American negro slaves.

517. Lantz, Joanne B. "On the Position of Women in Society," AMERICAN PERSONNEL AND GUIDANCE ASSOCIATION, 1971. 8 pp. An intelligent, brief, and well-documented examination of discrimination against women.

518. Larrabee, Eric, and Rolf Meyersohn, eds. MASS LEISURE. Glencoe, Ill.: Free Press, 1958. 429 pp. A sequel to their MASS CULTURE, emphasizing the changes in social status afforded by mass leisure.

519. Letourneau, C. LA CONDITION DE LA FEMME. Paris: V. Giard et E. Briere, 1903. 508 pp. Chapters on women in Africa, their position and legal status.

520. Lewis, Edwin C. DEVELOPING WOMAN'S POTENTIAL. Ames: Iowa State Univ., 1971. If changes in the role and status of women in our society are to take place, they must be initiated by the women concerned. Excellent bibliography.

521. Little, K. L. "The Poro Society as an Arbiter of Culture (Sierra Leone)," AFRICAN STUDIES, vol. 7, no. 1 (1948), pp. 1-15.

522. Louis Harris and Associates, Inc. THE 1970 VIRGINIA SLIMS AMERICAN WOMEN'S OPINION POLL: A SURVEY OF THE ATTITUDES OF WOMEN ON THEIR ROLE IN AMERICAN SOCIETY. New York: Louis Harris Associates, 1970, 82 pp. Efforts to assess women's status.

523. ———. THE 1972 VIRGINIA SLIMS AMERICAN WOMEN'S OPINION POLL: A SURVEY OF THE ATTITUDES OF WOMEN ON THEIR ROLE IN POLITICS AND THE ECONOMY. New York: Louis Harris Associates, 1972, 117 pp. Women as citizens, in the economy and their stand on equal rights.

524. Makonga, B. "La Position Sociale de la Mere," PROBLEMES SOCIAUX CONGOLAIS, vol. 17 (Elisabethville, 1951), pp. 243-259. Among the Luba-Katanga, women, especially in their role as mothers, are the basic element in society.

525. Mandle, Joan D. "Women's Liberation: Humanizing Rather Than Polarizing," THE ANNALS, vol. 397 (Sept. 1971), pp. 118-128. Exploration of the social causes of the inferior position of women in society.

526. Mannin, Ethel E. WOMEN AND THE REVOLUTION. New York: Dutton, New York, 1939. 314 pp. Study of the social changes in women's status.

527. Marcuse, Herbert and Peter Furth, "Herbert Marcuse und Peter Furth, Emanzipation der Frau," DAS ARGUMENT, vol. 4, no. 23 (Oct.-Nov. 1962), n.p.

528. Marie-Andre Du Sacre-Coeur, Sister. "La Femme Mossi, La Situation Juridique," L'ETHNOGRAPHIE, Paris, vol. 23-24 (1938) pp. 15-33. Respect for native custom has prevented reforms in the status of women in Nigeria.

529. ———. LA FEMME NOIRE EN AFRIQUE OCCIDENTALE [The Black Woman in Western Africa]. Paris: Payot, 1939. 278 pp. Women in West African society: legal status and economic life of women under Western influences.

530. Mauny, R. "Masques Mende de la Societe Bundu (Sierra Leone)," NOTES AFRICAINES, vol. 51 (Dakar, 1959), pp. 8-13. Bundu society is a women's society which exerts considerable political influence. Illustrated.

531. Maxeke, C. M. "Social Conditions Among Bantu Women and Girls," CHRISTIAN STUDIES AND MODERN SOUTH AFRICA (Fort Hare, 1930), pp. 111-117.

532. Mercier, P. "La Femme et Les Societes Africaines," TROPIQUES, no. 379 (Paris 1955), pp. 21-28. The economic functions and the status of African women in different societies. Illustrated.

533. Milton, Nancy. "Women in China," BERKELEY JOURNAL OF SOCIOLOGY, vol. 16 (1971-1972), pp. 106-121.

534. Myrdal, Gunnar. AN AMERICAN DILEMMA. 2 vols. New York: Harper and Row, 1962. Revised edition with an appendix devoted to changing roles of black women.

535. Nadarajah, Devapoopathy. WOMEN IN TAMIL SOCIETY: THE CLASSICAL PERIOD. Kuala Lumpur: Univ. of Malaya, 1966. 189 pp. Historical study of the changes of status among women in the Madras region.

536. Nearing, Scott. WOMEN AND SOCIAL PROGRESS. New York: Macmillan, 1912. By the American socialist on the opportunities for women in the future.

537. NEW RESEARCH ON WOMEN. Proceedings of a Conference on Women, Univ. of Michigan, Ann Arbor, Mar. 15, 1973. Papers on the history, status, and psychology of women.

538. Nicod, A. LA FEMME AU CAMEROUN. Paris: Societe des Missions Evangeliques, 1927. 82 pp. Notes on the status of women in Cameroon and changes taking place since 1917.

539. O'Hara, Albert R. THE POSITION OF WOMEN IN EARLY CHINA, INCLUDING TRANSLATION OF THE LIEH NU CHUAN. Hong Kong, 1955. Annotated translation of a Han dynasty guide for girls along with idealized biographies of virtuous women.

540. Parsons, Talcott. "Age and Sex in the Social Structure of the United States," AMERICAN SOCIOLOGICAL REVIEW, vol. 7, no. 5 (Oct. 1942), pp. 604-616. The importance of male and female youth culture in the United States and the isolation of the old aged from participation in the most important social structures and interests.

541. Patai, Raphael. WOMEN IN THE MODERN WORLD. New York: Free Press, 1967. 519 pp. Women's status in various countries.
542. Pescatello, Ann, ed. FEMALE AND MALE IN LATIN AMERICA. Pittsburgh: Univ. of Pittsburgh Press, 1973. Changing roles and status of women and men.
543. Pollera, Alberto. LA DONNA IN ETIOPIA. Rome: Grafia, 1922. 85 pp. New opportunities for women.
544. Popova, Nina. WOMEN IN THE LAND OF SOCIALISM. Moscow: Foreign Languages Publishing House, 1949. 264 pp.
545. "A Report on the Way Women View Their Portrayal in Today's Television and Magazine Advertising." Unpublished advertising study. New York: Foote, Cone and Belding Marketing Information Service, Nov. 1972. 23 pp. The extent to which women feel that television and magazine advertising depicts them accurately and how they react to this portrayal.
546. Rossi, Alice, ed. ESSAYS ON SEX EQUALITY. Chicago: Univ. of Chicago Press, 1970. Anthology of articles on women's changing status.
547. Sarasvati, Pundita Ramabai. THE HIGH CASTE HINDU WOMAN. Philadelphia: n.p., 1887. 119 pp.
548. Seagoe, May V., ed. "Professional Women in Modern Society," JOURNAL OF SOCIAL ISSUES, vol. 6, no. 3 (1950). Whole issue devoted to women's status.
549. Smith, Anna Greene. THE NEGRO PROFESSIONAL WOMAN: A STUDY IN CONTINUITY AND CHANGE, 1945-1970. Study, available from Department of Sociology, Agnes Scott College, Decatur, Georgia. 1971.
550. Smith, Jessica. WOMAN IN SOVIET RUSSIA. New York: Vanguard, 1928. 216 pp. This study and the one by Alexandra Kollontai are the first general studies of the subject.
551. Snow, Helen. WOMEN IN MODERN CHINA. New York: Humanities Press, 1968. Changes in the status of Chinese women.
552. Sontag, Susan. "The Double Standard of Aging," SATURDAY REVIEW OF THE SOCIETY, vol. 55, no. 39 (Oct. 1972), pp. 29-38. To liberate themselves, women must disobey this convention.
553. Timms, Duncan W.B., and Elizabeth A. Timms. "Anomie and Social Participation Among Suburban Women," PACIFIC SOCIOLOGICAL REVIEW, vol. 15 (Jan. 1972), pp. 123-142. The position of women in a local social network and their anomie.
554. U.S. Citizen's Advisory Council on the Status of Women. REPORT TO THE CITIZEN'S ADVISORY COUNCIL ON THE STATUS OF WOMEN. Washington, D.C.: SUDOC, GPO, 1968. 139 pp.
555. ———. WOMEN AND THEIR FAMILIES IN OUR RAPIDLY CHANGING SOCIETY: REPORT TO THE CITIZEN'S ADVISORY COUNCIL ON THE STATUS OF WOMEN. Washington, D.C.: SUDOC, GPO, 1968. 59 pp.
556. Veblen, Thorstein. "The Barbarian Status of Women," AMERICAN JOURNAL OF SOCIOLOGY, vol. 4, no. 4 (Jan. 1899), pp. 503-514.
557. Vickland, Ellen Elizabeth. WOMEN OF ASSAM. Philadelphia: Judson Press, 1928. 179 pp. Changes in the status of Indian women during the British Raj.

558. Wägner, Elin. VACKARKLOCKA [The Alarm Clock] . Stockholm: Albert Bonnier, 1942. 339 pp. A study of the position of women in Sweden by the early Swedish feminist (d. 1949).
559. Ware, Caroline Farrar. WOMEN TODAY: TRENDS AND ISSUES IN THE U.S. New York: Bureau of Communication, YMCA. 1963.
560. Weiss-Rosmarin, Trude. "Women in the Jewish Community," THE JEWISH SPECTATOR, vol. 37 (Feb. 1972), pp. 6-8+.
561. Whyte, William H. "Wives of Management." In AMERICA AS A MASS SOCIETY, edited by P. Olson. Glencoe, Ill.: Free Press, 1963. Study of the social position of corporation wives.
562. Witke, Roxanne. FEMINISM IN MODERN CHINA. Forthcoming.
563. WOMEN IN NEW CHINA. Peking: Foreign Languages Press, 1950. 55 pp. Changes in the status of women after the rise of Mao.
564. "Women's Lib and the American Housewife: A Qualitative Study." Unpublished advertising study. New York: Dancer-Fitzgerald-Sample, June 1972. 53 pp. Examines the effects of the movement on the American housewife.
565. WOMEN OF PAKISTAN. Karachi: Pakistan Publications, 1949. 98 pp. Changes in status since partition.
566. Woodsmall, Ruth Frances. WOMEN AND THE NEW EAST. Beirut, Lebanon: Middle East Institute, 1933. Study of women at all social and educational levels in Iran, Turkey, Afghanistan, Pakistan, India, and Indonesia, with excellent bibliography.
567. Yamada, Waka. THE SOCIAL STATUS OF JAPANESE WOMEN. Tokyo: Kokusai Bunka Shinkokai, 1937.

G. Education and Socialization

You teach your daughters the diameters of planets, and wonder when you have done that they do not delight in your company.
—Samuel Johnson

568. Addams, Jane. THE LONG ROAD OF WOMEN'S MEMORY. New York: Macmillan, 1916. 168 pp. Details the role women have played in shaping society's norms.
569. American Association of University Women. "Change and Choice for the College Woman," AAUW JOURNAL, vol. 55 (May 1962). Issue devoted to education of women.
570. Astell, Mary. A SERIOUS PROPOSAL TO THE LADIES, FOR THE ADVANCEMENT OF THEIR TRUE AND GREATEST INTEREST. New York: Source Book Press, 1971. 176 pp. Reprint of the 1694 edition. The first considered proposal for higher education for English women.
571. Bakke, E. Wight. "Graduate Education for Women at Yale: Excerpts from a Report by E. Wight Bakke," reprinted from VENTURES MAGAZINE, Yale Graduate School, vol. 9, no. 2 (Fall 1969).
572. Barth, Ilene. "College Careers: The Explosion in Women's Studies," SEVENTEEN, vol. 31 (Feb. 1972), pp. 40+.
573. Beecher, Catherine E. THE DUTY OF AMERICAN WOMEN TO THEIR COUNTRY. New York: Harper, 1845. Concerning the education of women, by a major reformer of American education.

574. ———. AN ESSAY ON THE EDUCATION OF FEMALE TEACHERS. New York: Van Nostrand and Dwight, 1835. N.p.
575. ———. "Female Education," THE AMERICAN JOURNAL OF EDUCATION FOR 1827, vol. 2, p. 9. A plea.
576. ———. THE TRUE REMEDY FOR THE WRONGS OF WOMEN. Boston: Phillips, Sampson, 1851. 263 pp. Concerning the education or lack of education of women.
577. Bem, Sandra L., and Daryl J. Bem. "Case Study of a Non-Conscious Ideology: Training the Woman to Know Her Place." In D. J. Bem, BELIEFS, ATTITUDES, AND HUMAN AFFAIRS. Belmont, Calif.: Brooks/Cole, 1970. 11 pp.
578. Bennett, John. STRICTURES ON FEMALE EDUCATION, CHIEFLY AS IT RELATES TO THE CULTURE OF THE HEART. New York: Source Book Press, 1970. 128 pp. Reprint of the 1795 edition. One of the few strong pleas for advanced education for women toward the close of the colonial period.
579. Berry, Jane, and Sandra Epstein. CONTINUING EDUCATION OF WOMEN: NEEDS, ASPIRATIONS, AND PLANS. Kansas City: Univ. of Missouri at Kansas City, 1963. 41 pp.
580. Blandin, I.M.E. HISTORY OF HIGHER EDUCATION OF WOMEN IN THE SOUTH PRIOR TO 1860. New York: Neal, 1909.
581. Brackett, Anna Callender, ed. THE EDUCATION OF AMERICAN GIRLS. CONSIDERED IN A SERIES OF ESSAYS. New York, 1874. Reprinted by Greenwood Press, Westport, Conn., 1971.
582. Breasted, Mary. OH! SEX EDUCATION! New York;Praeger,1970. 343 pp.
583. Brittain, Vera. THE WOMEN AT OXFORD: A FRAGMENT OF HISTORY. New York: Macmillan, 1960. 272 pp. Women's struggle for equal educational rights and intellectual achievement at Oxford.
584. Brownlee, Jean. "Where is the Professional Woman?" WOMEN LAWYERS JOURNAL, vol. 53, no. 1 (Winter 1967), p. 14.
585. Burton, John. LECTURES ON FEMALE EDUCATION AND MANNERS. New York: Source Book Press, 1970. 502 pp. Reprint of the 1793 edition.
586. Business and Professional Women's Association. INFO-DIGEST: EDUCATION OF WOMEN AROUND THE WORLD. Washington, D.C., 1971.
587. Cannon, Mary Agnes. THE EDUCATION OF WOMEN DURING THE RENAISSANCE. Washington, D.C.: National Capitol Press, 1916. Emergence of a humanistic approach toward the education of women.
588. Center for Continuing Education of Women. NEW CAREERS IN COMMUNITY SERVICE: PROCEEDINGS OF THE CONFERENCE WORKSHOP, Mar. 27, 1968. Ann Arbor: Univ. of Michigan, 1968. 144 pp. Papers devoted to education and socialization.
589. Chabaud, Jacqueline. THE EDUCATION AND ADVANCEMENT OF WOMEN. Paris: UNESCO, 1970. 155 pp. Discusses the deficiencies evident in the education of women in all countries.
590. Chester, Eliza [Harriet E. Paine]. CHATS WITH GIRLS ON SELF-CULTURE. New York: Dodd, Mead, 1891. 213 pp.
591. Child, Lydia. THE MOTHER'S BOOK. New York: Arno Press, 1972. Reprint of the Boston 1831 edition. By the female Spock of Jacksonian America.

592. Clarke, Amy K. A HISTORY OF CHELTENHAM LADIES COLLEGE. London: Faber and Faber, 1953. 193 pp. Education of British girls from 1853 to 1953.

593. Cobbe, Frances P. THE DUTIES OF WOMEN: A COURSE OF LECTURES. Boston: Ellis, 1882. 193 pp. By the ardent supporter of higher education for women in nineteenth century England.

594. Cole, Arthur C. A HUNDRED YEARS OF MOUNT HOLYOKE COLLEGE: THE EVOLUTION OF AN EDUCATIONAL IDEAL. New Haven: Yale Univ. Press, 1940. 426 pp. Education for women at one of America's first women's colleges.

595. Converse, Florence. THE STORY OF WELLESLEY. Boston: Little, Brown, 1919. 284 pp.

596. Council for Exceptional Children. EXCEPTIONAL CHILDREN CONFERENCE PAPERS: GIFTED AND DEVELOPMENTAL POTENTIAL IN WOMEN AND THE DISADVANTAGED. ERIC. Arlington, Va.: Council for Exceptional Children, 1971. 39 pp. Papers dealing with the current trends and opportunities for education of women based on a review of related studies.

597. Crawford, Mary Caroline. THE COLLEGE GIRL OF AMERICA AND THE INSTITUTONS WHICH MAKE HER WHAT SHE IS. Boston: L. C. Page, 1905. 319 pp. Advocates public and higher education of women in the United States.

598. Crockford, Richard E. "The Forgotten Sex in Education," JUNIOR COLLEGE JOURNAL, vol. 42 (Oct. 1971), pp. 17-19. Looks at the importance of coeducation with both sexes on equal terms.

599. Dall, Caroline W. THE COLLEGE, THE MARKET, AND THE COURT: OR WOMAN'S RELATION TO EDUCATION, LABOR, AND LAW. Concord, N.H.: Rumford Press, 1914. 511 pp.

600. Davies, Emily. THE HIGHER EDUCATION OF WOMEN. London: Alexander Stahan, 1866. 191 pp. Instrumental work in helping women to achieve higher education in nineteenth century England.

601. Dickinson, Louisa. FORESHADOWINGS OF SMITH COLLEGE. Privately printed, 1928. 44 pp. Selections from letters of 1856-1857 discussing higher education for American girls.

602. Dolan, Eleanor F. "Educated Women," EDUCATIONAL FORUM, vol. 20 (Jan. 1956), pp. 219-228.

603. Dubrovina, L. WOMEN'S RIGHT TO EDUCATION IN THE SOVIET UNION: REPORT. Moscow: Foreign Languages Publishing House, 1956. 28 pp.

604. "Education Emphasized for Delinquent Girls," PENNSYLVANIA EDUCATION, vol. 3 (Nov.-Dec. 1971), pp. 10-12.

605. "Education for Womanhood in East Africa," IMPROVING COLLEGE AND UNIVERSITY TEACHING, vol. 22 (Winter 1972), pp. 68-70. Traditional attitudes toward women influence girls' attitudes toward schooling, possibilities of employment, and participation in community life in East Africa.

606. Evans, J. D. "Education of the Sudanese Girl," OVERSEAS EDUCATION, vol. 2 (1930), pp. 25-32. Socialization and education.

607. Farello, Elene Wilson. A HISTORY OF EDUCATION OF WOMEN IN THE UNITED STATES. New York: Vantage Press, 1970. 586 pp.

Rich in factual data and biographies of women who pioneered in the field of education for women.

608. Farence, Patricia S. "Vocational Interests of High Ability College Women," JOURNAL OF COLLEGE STUDENT PERSONNEL, vol. 12 (Nov. 1971), pp. 430-437. Studies at different levels of vocational interests conducted at the University of Minnesota.

609. Farley, Jennie. "Graduate Women: Career Aspirations and Desired Family Size," AMERICAN PSYCHOLOGIST, vol. 25 (Dec. 1970), pp. 1099-1100. Education as a social influence on family size.

610. FEMINIST STUDIES, vol. 1, no. 1 (Summer 1972). 119 pp. Entire issue devoted to women. Articles by Betty Levy, Carol Brown, Ben Barker-Benfield, Mary Eastwood, Judith R. Walkowitz, and Erica Harth.

611. Feminists on Children's Media, compiler. LITTLE MISS MUFFET FIGHTS BACK: RECOMMENDED NON-SEXIST BOOKS ABOUT GIRLS FOR YOUNG READERS. New York: Author, 1971. 48 pp.

612. Fidell, Linda S., and John DeLamater, eds. "Women in the Professions: What's all the Fuss About?" AMERICAN BEHAVIORAL SCIENTIST, vol. 15, no. 2 (Nov.-Dec. 1971). Special issue devoted to the subject. Contributors: John DeLamater, Linda S. Fidell, Jane Prather, Joyce M. Mitchell, Rachel R. Starr, Irene Tinker, Victoria Wilson, Bernard M. Bass, Judith Kresell, Ralph A. Alexander, Teresa Levitin, Robert P. Quinn, Graham L. Staines, William M. Mandel, and Ruth M. Oltman.

613. Freeman, Jo. "Women's Liberation and Its Impact on the Campus," LIBERAL EDUCATION, vol. 57 (Dec. 1971), pp. 468-478. Higher education has been a direct cause of the movement.

614. Friedan, Betty, and Anne Grant West. "Sex Bias Maims the Public Schools," AMERICAN SCHOOL BOARD JOURNAL, vol. 159 (Oct. 1971), pp. 16-20. Discussion of bias in the public schools in keeping women out of various classes and activities.

615. Galkin, K. THE TRAINING OF SCIENTISTS IN THE SOVIET UNION. Moscow: Foreign Languages Publishing House, 1959. 204 pp. Education of women for scientific professions.

616. Gerstein, Hannelore. STUDIERENDE MADCHEN [Women Students]. Munich, Germany, 1965. Education and socialization of German women students.

617. Grady, Elaine, John J. Dempsey, and Alice Wilson. "Pregnant Adolescents: Educational Oportunities," NASSP BULLETIN, vol. 56 (April 1972), pp. 55-63. Describes the growth and development of the San Francisco school program.

618. Greenfield, Lois B. "Women in Engineering Education," CONTEMPORARY EDUCATION, vol. 43 (Feb. 1972), pp. 224-226. An explanation for the lack of women in engineering education.

619. Grey, Mrs. William. PAPER ON THE STUDY OF EDUCATION AS A SCIENCE. London: William Ridgway, 1874. 26 pp. A plea for education for women.

620. Hale, Beatrice Forbes-Robertson. WHAT'S WRONG WITH OUR GIRLS? THE ENVIRONMENT, TRAINING AND FUTURE OF AMERICAN GIRLS. New York: Stokes, 1923. 158 pp. Practical suggestions to improve girls' training and education.

621. Haney, Jack N., et al. "Sex Related Variables Associated with Choice and Evaluation of Options in An Introductory Psychology Course," JOURNAL OF EDUCATIONAL RESEARCH, vol. 65 (Dec. 1971), pp. 168-172. Choice and opportunities for women in psychological careers.

622. Higginson, Thomas Wentworth. WOMEN AND THE ALPHABET: A SERIES OF ESSAYS. New York: Arno Press, 1972. Reprint of the 1900 edition. A plea for full education for women by the famous New England minister and antislavery advocate.

623. Hoernle, A. W. "An Outline of the Native Conception of Education in Africa,"AFRICA,vol. 4 (1931), pp. 145-163. The education of young girls is under strict social control and is carried out within the framework of the age classes.

624. Holding, E. M. "Women's Institutions and the African Church," INTERNATIONAL REVIEW OF MISSIONS, vol. 31, no. 123 (Edinburgh, 1942), pp. 290-300. The importance of education and socialization in solving certain social problems.

625. Hopwood, Katherine. "Expectations of University College Women," PERSONNEL AND GUIDANCE JOURNAL, vol. 52 (1954), pp. 464-469.

626. Hosford, Frances Juliette. FATHER SHEPHERD'S MAGNA CHARTA: A CENTURY OF COEDUCATION IN OBERLIN COLLEGE. Boston: Marshall, 1937. 180 pp.

627. Hoshino, Ai. "The Education of Women." In WESTERN INFLUENCES IN MODERN JAPAN, edited by Nitoba Inazo. Chicago: Univ. of Chicago Press, 1931. Education and socialization of Japanese women.

628. Howe, Florence. "The Education of Women," LIBERATION, Aug.-Sept. 1969, n.p.

629. Howe, Julia Ward, ed. SEX AND EDUCATION: A REPLY TO DR. E. H. CLARKE'S "SEX IN EDUCATION." New York: Arno Press, 1972. Reprint of 1874 edition. Clarke concluded that intellectual aspirations could wreck a woman; Mrs. Howe was determined to open more college doors for women in higher education.

630. Husbands, Sandra A. "Women's Place in Higher Education," SCHOOL REVIEW, vol. 80 (Feb. 1972), pp. 261-274.

631. Hutchinson, Emilie J. WOMEN AND THE PH.D.: FACTS FROM THE EXPERIENCES OF 1,025 WOMEN WHO HAVE TAKEN THE DEGREE OF DOCTOR OF PHILOSOPHY SINCE 1877. Institute of Women's Professional Relations Bulletin, no. 2. Greensboro: North Carolina College for Women, 1930. 212 pp.

632. International Federation of University Women. THE POSITION OF THE WOMAN GRADUATE TODAY (1956-1965). Washington, D.C.: International Federation of University Women, 1966. A survey of the gains and goals yet to be achieved.

633. Itasca Conference on the Continuing Education of Women. EDUCATION AND A WOMAN'S LIFE. Washington, D.C.: American Council on Education, 1963. 153 pp. Papers presented at the Itasca, Minnesota, Conference in 1962, pleading for more equal educational opportunites for women.

634. Komarovsky, Mirra. WOMEN IN THE MODERN WORLD: THEIR EDUCATION AND THEIR DILEMMAS. Boston: Little, Brown, 1953. 319 pp.

635. Koontz, Elizabeth D. "A New Look at Education for Girls," CONTEM-PORARY EDUCATION, vol. 43 (Feb. 1972), pp. 195-197. Suggestions for changes.
636. "Lagos Women's Play," NIGERIA, vol. 58 (1958), pp. 225-237. The Lagos Child Welfare Mother's Union makes use of the theatre as a means of educating and socializing women against the lax morals of town life, and to glorify feminine qualities.
637. Leonard, Eugenie A. PROBLEMS OF FRESHMAN COLLEGE GIRLS: A STUDY OF MOTHER-DAUGHTER RELATIONSHIPS AND SOCIAL ADJUSTMENTS OF GIRLS ENTERING COLLEGE. New York: Teachers College, Columbia Univ., 1932. 140 pp. Education and social-ization.
638. Leslie, Eliza. MISS LESLIE'S BEHAVIOUR BOOK: A GUIDE AND MANUAL FOR LADIES. New York: Arno Press, 1972. Reprint of the 1859 edition. The Julia Child of her day; generations of women cooked and behaved as she told them to behave.
639. Lever, Janet, and Pepper Schwartz. WOMEN AT YALE: LIBERATING A COLLEGE CAMPUS. Indianapolis: Bobbs-Merrill, 1971. 274 pp. Analysis of the impact of the influence of women on the institution and the effects on the women themselves.
640. Manis, Laura G., and June Mochizuki. "Search for Fulfillment: A Program for Adult Women," THE PERSONNEL AND GUIDANCE JOURNAL, vol. 50 (Mar. 1972), pp. 594-599. Education for fulfillment.
641. Mather, Cotton. "Elizabeth in Her Holy Retirement: An Essay to Pre-pare a Pious Woman for Her Lying-in." In THE COLONIAL AMERI-CAN FAMILY. New York: Arno Press, 1972. Reprint of the 1710 edition.
642. Mayer, P. "Gusii Initiation Ceremonies: Initiation of Girls," JOURNAL OF THE ROYAL ANTHROPOLOGICAL INSTITUTE, vol. 83 (1953), pp. 26-36. Initiation rites and educational training for womanhood in Kenya.
643. McBreaty, James C. "Kitchen Revolution: New Careers for American Women," ARIZONA REVIEW, vol. 21 (Jan. 1972), pp. 10-14. States that women should be qualified for more jobs than technical schools will allow them to train for.
644. McClure, Robert F. "Birth Order, Income, Sex and School-Related Attitudes," JOURNAL OF EXPERIMENTAL EDUCATION, vol. 39 (Summer 1971), pp. 73-74. Education and socialization.
645. Meigs, Cornelia. WHAT MAKES A COLLEGE: A HISTORY OF BRYN MAWR. New York: Macmillan, 1956. 277 pp. History of women's education and programs at Bryn Mawr.
646. Miller, Nora. THE GIRL IN THE RURAL FAMILY. Chapel Hill: Univ. of North Carolina Press, 1935. 108 pp. Eight types of rural families in-vestigated to see how their way of living affects the girl who is no longer going to school.
647. Millett, Kate. TOKEN LEARNING: A STUDY OF WOMEN'S HIGHER EDUCATION IN AMERICA. New York: National Organization for Women (NOW), 1968.
648. Mills, Herbert E., et al. COLLEGE WOMEN AND THE SOCIAL SCIENCES. New York: John Day, 1934. 324 pp. Study of education of women, compiled by Mills's former students.

649. Minuchin, Patricia. "The Schooling of Tomorrow's Women," SCHOOL REVIEW, vol. 80 (Feb. 1972), pp. 199-208. Defines goals that are relevant to the development of a liberated young female in the elementary schools.

650. More, Hannah. STRICTURES ON THE MODERN SYSTEM OF FEMALE EDUCATION WITH A VIEW OF THE PRINCIPLES AND CONDUCT PREVALENT AMONG WOMEN OF RANK AND FORTUNE. 2 vols. in 1. Boston: Joseph Bumstead, 1802. 312 pp.

651. Morris, Roger R. "New Horizons for Women," PARENTS, vol. 47 (Jan. 1972), pp. 46-47+. Study of new courses in U.S. colleges that prepare women for meaningful jobs outside the home.

652. Mueller, Kate. EDUCATING WOMEN FOR A CHANGING WORLD. Minneapolis: Univ. of Minnesota Press, 1964. Study of higher education in America for women.

653. Mullins, Carolyn. "The Plight of the Boardwoman," AMERICAN SCHOOL BOARD JOURNAL, vol. 159 (Feb. 1972), pp. 27-28+. Efforts to educate young women for careers.

654. National Merit Scholarship Corporation. REVIEW OF RESEARCH, vol. 6, no. 1 (Evanston, Ill., 1970). Studies from 1957 through 1969 of six differences in levels of aspiration and achievement.

655. National Organization for Women. "Academic Discrimination Kit." Mimeographed. Chicago: NOW, 1971. Available from NOW, 1952 E. 73rd St., Chicago, Ill., 60649. Materials relevant to increasing educational opportunity for women.

656. ———. "A Preliminary Report on the Status of Women at Princeton University," New York: NOW, 1971. 24 pp. History and Philosophy of coeducation at Princeton, with important data.

657. Newcomer, Mabel. A CENTURY OF HIGHER EDUCATION FOR WOMEN. New York: Harpers, 1959. Details the lack of progress in education.

658. Noble, Jeanne L. THE NEGRO WOMAN'S COLLEGE EDUCATION. New York: Teachers College, Columbia University, 1956. 163 pp. A good summary with bibliography and some comments on the literature of education for black women.

659. Nuita, Yoko. "Continuing Education of Women in Japan," IMPROVING COLLEGE AND UNIVERSITY TEACHING, vol. 22 (Winter 1972), pp. 66-68. Discusses ways in which the adult population in Japan improved opportunities for education.

660. Olin, Helen R. THE WOMEN OF A STATE UNIVERSITY: AN ILLUSTRATION OF THE WORKING OF COEDUCATION IN THE MIDDLE WEST. New York: Putnam, 1909. 308 pp. An illustration of how coeducation has flourished at Wisconsin University.

661. Oltman, Ruth M. CAMPUS 1970: WHERE DO WOMEN STAND? Washington, D.C.: American Association of University Women, 1970. Evaluates the activities of women administrators, faculty, trustees, and students and the general attitudes of administration regarding women on American campuses.

662. ———. "The Evolving Role of the Women's Liberation Movement in Higher Education," Washington, D.C. American Association of University Women, 1971. Results of a questionnaire concerning aspects of the role of women in higher education.

663. Packer, Barbara, and Karen Waggoner. "Yale and the New Sisterhood," YALE ALUMNI MAGAZINE, April 1970, pp. 26-31. What Yale University can do about the women's liberation movement.

664. Parker, Franklin. "New Wisdom on Women's Education: U.S.A. and World View," NATIONAL ASSOCIATION OF SECONDARY SCHOOL PRINCIPALS BULLETIN, vol. 55 (Nov. 1971), pp. 32-39 Calls for more progress in women's education.

665. ———. "Women's Education: Historical and International View," CONTEMPORARY EDUCATION, vol. 43 (Feb. 1972), pp. 198-201. The changing social attitudes about women's roles and the vast potential to be derived by educating women.

666. Patterson, Samuel White. HUNTER COLLEGE: EIGHTY-FIVE YEARS OF SERVICE. New York: Lantern Press, 1955. 263 pp. History of educational reforms instituted for women.

667. Pekin, L. B. COEDUCATION IN ITS HISTORICAL AND THEORETICAL SETTING. London: Hogarth, 1939. 208 pp. Historical discussion of British coeducational opportunities.

668. Pietrofesa, John J., and Nancy K. Schlossberg. COUNSELOR BIAS AND THE FEMALE OCCUPATIONAL ROLE. Detroit: College of Education, Wayne State Univ., 1970.

669. Roby, Pamela. "Women and American Higher Education," THE ANNALS, vol. 404 (Nov. 1972), pp. 118-139. Traces the history of the development of higher educational opportunities for women in the United States.

670. Royce, Marion, "Higher Education of Women in Britain," IMPROVING COLLEGE AND UNIVERSITY TEACHING, vol. 22 (Winter 1972), pp. 61-62.

671. Royden, Agnes M. WOMEN AT THE WORLD'S CROSSROADS. New York: Woman's Press, 1922. Talks to young women on their part in the world and methods, such as education, to achieve their future roles.

672. Salper, Roberta. "The Theory and Practice of Women's Studies," EDCENTRIC, vol. 3 (Dec. 1971), pp. 4-8. Case study of the first program at San Diego State College, how it was set up, the opposition it met, and the research that must be done by women.

673. Sandlund, Maj-Britt. "Adult Education of Women in Sweden," IMPROVING COLLEGE AND UNIVERSITY TEACHING, vol. 22 (Winter 1972), pp. 64-65.

674. Schmidt, Earl R., and Dolores B. Schmidt. "The Invisible Women: The Historian as Professional Magician; An Analysis, Quantitative and Qualitative of 27 Textbooks Designed for College Survey Courses in American History." Mimeographed. Fall, 1971. 14 pp. Available from the authors, California State College, California, Pa., and Slippery Rock State College, Slippery Rock, Pa.

675. Scott, Ann F. "The Half-Eaten Apple," THE REPORTER, 1970, 16 pp. A sophisticated study of academic bias, with proposals for ending it.

676. Seelye, L. Clark. THE EARLY HISTORY OF SMITH COLLEGE, 1871-1910. Boston: Houghton, 1923. 242 pp.

677. Shridevi, S. "Women's Higher Education in India Since Independence," IMPROVING COLLEGE AND UNIVERSITY TEACHING, vol. 22 (Winter 1972), pp. 71-72.

678. Simon, Rita, Shirley Clark, and Katherine Galway. "The Woman Ph.D.: A Recent Profile," SOCIAL PROBLEMS, vol. 15 (Fall 1966), pp. 221-256.

679. Somerville, Rose M. "Women's Studies," TODAY'S EDUCATION, National Education Association Journal, vol. 60, no. 8 (Nov. 1971), pp. 35-37. Discusses the future of women's studies courses and programs.

680. Stavsova, Helen. "How Russian Women Won the Right to Higher Education," SOVIET WOMAN, vol. 4 (July-Aug. 1946), pp. 49-50.

681. Stuart, Janet Erskine. THE EDUCATION OF CATHOLIC GIRLS. New York: Longmans, 1927. 257 pp.

682. Sumner, William G. FOLKWAYS. Boston: Atheneum, 1906. 692 pp. A revolutionary book analyzing the importance of custom or channeled behavior in society, dealing with women throughout.

683. Taylor, James M., and Elizabeth H. Haight. VASSAR. New York: Oxford Univ. Press, 1915. 232 pp. A history of the famous Eastern women's college.

684. Taylor, Jean Anne M. SPECIAL REPORT ON WOMEN AND GRADUATE STUDY. Resources for Medical Research Report, no. 13. 1968. 99 pp. ERIC. Sample of 41,000 college seniors polled in 135 colleges and universities in 1961.

685. Trecker, Janice Law. "Women's Place is in the Curriculum," SATURDAY REVIEW, vol. 54 (Oct. 16, 1972), pp. 81-86+. Women's studies and their relation to the overall university program are discussed.

686. Trow, JoAnne J. "Higher Education for Women," IMPROVING COLLEGE AND UNIVERSITY TEACHING, vol. 22 (Winter 1972), pp. 19-22.

687. Tryon, Ruth W. INVESTMENT IN CREATIVE SCHOLARSHIP, 1890-1956. Washington, D.C.: American Association of University Women, 1957. A history of the AAUW fellowship program, with an excellent account of the professional achievements of many women who have been recipients.

688. United Nations. ACCESS OF WOMEN TO HIGHER EDUCATION. New York: United Nations Economic and Social Commission, 1958. 67 pp. Summary of measures to improve the education of women in many countries.

689. ———. "Study on UNESCO Activities of Special Interest to Women," New York: United Nations Economic and Social Commission on the Status of Women, 1972. Covers three years of the UNESCO long-term program to ensure equality of access of girls and women to education.

690. U.S., Department of Health, Education and Welfare. SPECIAL REPORT ON WOMEN AND GRADUATE STUDY. HEW Report no. 13. Washington, D.C.: SUDOC, GPO, June 1968.

691. U.S. Department of Labor. CONTINUING EDUCATION PROGRAMS AND SERVICES FOR WOMEN. Washington, D.C.: Women's Bureau (SUDOC, GPO), 1971. 172 pp. Lists nearly 450 continuing education programs for women, in operation in early 1971.

692. ———. TRENDS IN EDUCATIONAL ATTAINMENT OF WOMEN, 1965-1969. Washington, D.C.: SUDOC, GPO, 1969. 19 pp. Charts the high school, bachelor's, and professional degrees of women, 1900-1968.

693. U.S. President's Commission on the Status of Women. REPORT OF THE COMMITTEE ON EDUCATION TO THE PRESIDENT'S COMMISSION ON THE STATUS OF WOMEN, COMMITTEE ON EDUCATION. Washington, D.C.: SUDOC, GPO, 1964. 71 pp.

694. Useem, Ruth Hill. "Where are the Women?" THE MICHIGAN STATE UNIVERSITY MAGAZINE (East Lansing), vol. 7 (Mar. 1962), pp. 16-18+.

695. Vassar College. "Coeducation: Alan Simpson on Vassar," COLLEGE BOARD REVIEW, vol. 82 (Winter 1971-1972), pp. 17-23.

696. ———. THE FIFTIETH ANNIVERSARY OF THE OPENING OF VASSAR COLLEGE, OCTOBER 10-13, 1915: A RECORD. Poughkeepsie, N.Y.: Vassar College, 1916. 337 pp.

697. Warren, Constance. A NEW DESIGN FOR WOMEN'S EDUCATION. New York: Stokes, 1940. 277 pp. The president of Sarah Lawrence College tells of the experiment in women's education at Sarah Lawrence and other "progressive" women's schools.

698. Wells, Jean A. CONTINUING EDUCATION PROGRAMS AND SERVICES FOR WOMEN. Pamphlet no. 10. Washington, D.C.: U.S. Department of Labor, Women's Bureau, 1968. 104 pp.

699. White, Lynn J. EDUCATING OUR DAUGHTERS. New York: Harper, 1950. Illuminates masculine bias of the present educational system.

700. "A Whole New Vision for the Educated Woman," AMERICAN ASSOCIATION OF UNIVERSITY WOMEN JOURNAL, vol. 63, no. 2 (Jan. 1970). Entire issue devoted to women in education and advancement in the professions.

701. WOMEN IN COLLEGE AND UNIVERSITY TEACHING. Madison, Wis., 1965. 54 pp. Papers from a symposium on staff needs and opportunities in higher education, held under the auspices of the School of Education, University of Wisconsin.

702. "Women on Campus, 1970: A Symposium." Papers presented at a symposium held at Ann Arbor, Mich., Oct. 14, 1970. Among other topics the papers concerned women graduate students, and the university and women.

703. Woody, Thomas. A HISTORY OF WOMEN'S EDUCATION IN THE UNITED STATES. 2 vols. New York: Science Press, 1929. Comprehensive work, devoting much attention to colonial and early Jacksonian education; bibliography.

704. Zapoleon, Marguerite Wykoff. OCCUPATIONAL PLANNING FOR WOMEN. New York: Harper, 1966. Education for women outside the home.

H. Women in Education

Thus, then, whilst they [the Americans] have allowed the social inferiority of woman to subsist, they have done all they could to raise her morally and intellectually to the level of man; and in this respect they appear to me to have excellently understood the true principle of democratic improvement.

—Alexis de Tocqueville

705. American Anthropological Association. NEWSLETTER OF THE AMERICAN ANTHROPOLOGICAL ASSOCIATION, vol. 2, no. 9 (Nov.) 1970. Survey of positions of women in anthropology in 14 major institutions, conducted by the AAA's Committee on the Status of Women in Anthropology.

706. American Association of University Professors. ANNUAL REPORT, April 1971. Washington, D.C.: American Association of University Professors,

Committee on the Status of Women in the Professions. An assessment of gains and losses in the struggle for equality. See also AAUP Bulletin (Summer 1973), 1972-73 Report.

707. American Association of University Women. "College Presidents React to AAUW Guidelines on Equality," AAUW JOURNAL, Jan. 1972. 5 pp. Includes studies on the employment of women on American campuses and the institutional policies relating to health services, more women trustees and faculty members, and child-care centers.

708. ———. "Standards for Women in Higher Education: Affirmative Policy in Achieving Sex Equality in the Academic Community," Washington, D.C.: AAUW, 1971. 9 pp. Standards stated in terms of general objectives for women students, faculty, and administration to provide means of assessing the achievement of those objectives.

709. ———. THE WOMAN TRUSTEE: A REPORT ON A CONFERENCE FOR WOMEN MEMBERS OF COLLEGE AND UNIVERSITY GOVERNING BOARDS. Washington, D.C.: AAUW Educational Foundation, 1965. Symposium on the future of women's education, women in higher education, and women as university faculty.

710. American Historical Association. FINAL REPORT, May 25, 1971. American Historical Association, Committee on the Status of Women. Washington, D.C. Report of current status of American women historians in the profession.

711. ———. "Report by the Ad Hoc Committee on the Status of Women Historians," AHA NEWSLETTER, Sept. 1971. Summary of findings and its recommendations for improvements.

712. American Political Science Association. "APSA 1971 Survey of Political Science Departments." Mimeographed. Washington, D.C.: APSA, May 24, 1972. Survey dealing with statistics on the percentage of faculty members who are female, by rank, with the alarming fact that women are virtually missing in the professorial and associate ranks.

713. Association for Women Psychologists. PSYCHOLOGY AND THE NEW WOMAN: STATEMENT OF THE ASSOCIATION FOR WOMEN PSYCHOLOGISTS TO THE AMERICAN PSYCHOLOGICAL ASSOCIATION. Washington, D.C.: American Psychological Association, Sept. 1970. 6 pp. Summary of figures on women in the profession.

714. Astin, Helen. THE WOMAN DOCTORATE IN AMERICA: ORIGINS, CAREERS AND FAMILY. New York: Russell Sage Foundation, 1969. Well-documented survey.

715. Batho, Edith C. A LAMP OF FRIENDSHIP, 1918-1968: A SHORT HISTORY OF THE INTERNATIONAL FEDERATION OF UNIVERSITY WOMEN. Eastbourne, England: Sumfield and Day, 1969. The history of the IFUW, with lists of officers, programs, and conferences.

716. Bazell, Robert J. "Sex Discrimination: Campuses Face Contract Loss Over HEW Demands," SCIENCE, vol. 170 (Nov. 20, 1970), pp. 834-835.

717. Bernard, Jessie. ACADEMIC WOMEN. University Park: Pennsylvania State Univ. Press, 1964. 331 pp. Highlights various career patterns of academic women, with their effects on professional and family life.

718. Berry, J. "Life Plans of College Women," JOURNAL OF THE NATIONAL ASSOCIATION OF DEANS OF WOMEN, vol. 18 (1955), pp. 76-80.

719. Bettelheim, Bruno. WOMAN AND THE SCIENTIFIC PROFESSIONS. Cambridge: M.I.T. Press, 1965. A symposium on American women in science and engineering.

720. Borchers, G. L. "Some Investigations Concerning the State of Faculty Women in America." In V. Totaro, WOMEN IN COLLEGE AND UNIVERSITY TEACHING. Madison: Univ. of Wisconsin, 1965. 54 pp.

721. Brackett, Anna Callender, ed. WOMAN AND THE HIGHER EDUCATION. New York, 1893. Reprinted by Greenwood Press, Westport, Conn., 1971. 214 pp. Discrimination against women in higher education.

722. Brown, David G. THE MOBILE PROFESSORS. Washington, D.C.: American Council on Education, 1967. 113 pp. Women and men in the academic world of tenure and greener pastures.

723. Bryan, A. I., and E. G. Boring. "Women in American Psychology: Factors Affecting their Professional Careers," THE AMERICAN PSYCHOLOGIST, vol. 2 (1947), pp. 3-20.

724. Business and Professional Women's Association. SEX DISCRIMINATION IN THE ACADEMIC WORLD: RESEARCH SUMMARY. Washington, D.C.: BPWA, 1970.

725. Caplow, T., and Reece McGee. THE ACADEMIC MARKET PLACE. New York: Basic Books, 1958. Women in the professions.

726. Cockburn, P. WOMEN UNIVERSITY GRADUATES IN CONTINUING EDUCATION AND EMPLOYMENT: AN EXPLORATORY STUDY INITIATED BY THE CANADIAN FEDERATION OF UNIVERSITY WOMEN. Toronto, 1966.

727. Collins, M. WOMEN GRADUATES AND THE TEACHING PROFESSION. Manchester, England: Manchester Univ. Press, 1964.

728. Davis, Ann E. "Women as a Minority Group in Higher Academics," THE AMERICAN SOCIOLOGIST, May 1969, pp. 95-99.

729. Eckert, Ruth E. "Academic Woman Revisited," LIBERAL EDUCATION, Vol. 57 (Dec. 1971), pp. 479-487. Study of faculty members in Minnesota throws light on when and why women chose academic careers.

730. Fava, S. "The Status of Women in Professional Sociology," AMERICAN SOCIOLOGICAL REVIEW, vol. 25 (1960), pp. 271-276.

731. Fischer, Ann, and Peggy Golde. "The Position of Women in Anthropology," AMERICAN ANTHROPOLOGIST, vol. 70 (April 1968), pp. 338-343. The proportion of full-time women faculty members in graduate anthropology was low.

732. Fraser, Leila. "Guidelines on Filing Complaints of Sex Discrimination in Education Employment." Mimeographed. American Political Science Association, Women's Caucus for Political Science, Oct. 1972. Copy available from the APSA, Washington, D.C.

733. Fuller, Ann L. "The Status of Women at Oberlin College," OBERLIN ALUMNI MAGAZINE, Sept.-Oct. 1972, pp. 8-11. Indicates the forms of discrimination against women at Oberlin and efforts being made to recruit women faculty members and administrators.

734. Gardner, Jo-Ann Evans, and Elsa McKeithan. "Patterns of Feminist Action in Professional Associations." Paper presented at an Eastern Psychological Association symposium entitled "Sex and Professional Employment: Present and Future," held on April 15, 1971, and organized by Jane W. Torrey.

735. Gruchow, Nancy. "Discrimination: Women Charge Universities, Colleges with Bias," SCIENCE, vol. 169 (Sept. 25, 1970), pp. 1284-1290.

736. Harris, Ann Sutherland. "The Second Sex in Academe," EDCENTRIC, vol. 3 (Dec. 1971), pp. 21-31. See Lewis and Perkins.

737. ———. "Response to Edwin Lewis's Article, 'The Second Sex in Academe,' " AAUP BULLETIN, vol. 57, no. 1 (Mar. 1971).

738. Hornig, Lilli S. "Women in Higher Education: Affirmative Action Through Affirmative Attitudes." Paper from a conference sponsored by the New York State Education Department, Albany, N.Y., 1973. 18 pp. Discrimination against women in higher education.

739. League of Academic Women. SEX BASED DISCRIMINATION IN ACADEMIA AND WHAT YOU CAN DO ABOUT IT, Berkeley, Calif.: League of Academic Women, 1971.

740. Lewis, Edwin C. "The Second Sex in Academe," AAUP BULLETIN, vol. 57, no. 1 (Mar. 1971). See Harris and Perkins.

741. Loeb, Jane, and Marianne Ferber. "Sex as Predictive of Salary and Status on a University Faculty," JOURNAL OF EDUCATIONAL MANAGE-MENT, vol. 8 (Winter 1971), pp. 235-244.

742. Michigan State University. "A Compilation of Data on Faculty Women and Women Enrolled at Michigan State University." E. Lansing: Michigan State Univ., 1970. 56 pp. Data covering total instructional staff, salaries, new faculty, the rate of promotion of faculty women, length of service, etc.

743. Mitchell, Mildred B. "Status of Women in the American Psychological Association," AMERICAN PSYCHOLOGIST, vol. 6 (June 1951), pp. 193-201.

744. National Science Foundation. WOMEN IN SCIENTIFIC CAREERS. Washington, D.C.: SUDOC, GPO, 1961.

745. Neugarten, Bernice. WOMEN IN THE UNIVERSITY OF CHICAGO: RE-PORT OF THE COMMITTEE ON UNIVERSITY WOMEN. Chicago: Univ. of Chicago, May 1970.

746. Park, Dabney. "Down With Tenure," CHANGE, vol. 4 (Mar. 1972), pp. 32-37. Male tenure practices exclude women and are clearly discriminatory.

747. Parrish, John B. "Women in Top Level Teaching and Research," JOUR-NAL OF THE AMERICAN ASSOCIATION OF UNIVERSITY WO-MEN, vol. 55, no. 2. (Jan. 1962), pp. 99-106.

748. Perkins, Lisa H. "Response to Edwin Lewis's Article, 'The Second Sex in Academe,' " AAUP BULLETIN, vol. 57, no. 1 (Mar. 1971). See Lewis and Harris.

749. Robinson, Lora H. "The Status of Academic Women." Washington, D.C.: ERIC. Clearinghouse on Higher Education, April 1971. Review-5. 30 pp. Comprehensive description of academic women and their struggle for equal opportunities in higher education.

750. Romer, Karen T. and Cynthia Secor, "The Time is Here for Women's Liberation," THE ANNALS, vol. 397 (Sept. 1971), pp. 129-139. Discusses sex role limitations on women and the importance of male assistance in overcoming inequalities in higher education.

751. Rossi, Alice. "Discrimination and Demography Restrict Opportunities for Academic Women," COLLEGE AND UNIVERSITY BUSINESS, Feb. 1970, p. 78.

752. ———. "Status of Women in Graduate Departments of Sociology, 1968-69," THE AMERICAN SOCIOLOGIST, vol. 5 (Feb. 1970), pp. 1-12. A concerted commitment to the hiring and promotion of women sociologists to correct the present imbalance.

753. Rossi, Alice, and Ann Calderwood, eds. ACADEMIC WOMEN ON THE MOVE. New York: Russell Sage Foundation, 1973. Very useful reference volume on higher education and career development for women.
754. Schuck, Victoria. "Women in Political Science: Some Preliminary Observations," POLITICAL SCIENCE, vol. 2 (Fall 1969), pp. 642-653.
755. Shaffer, Harry G., and Juliet P. Shaffer. "Job Discrimination Against Faculty Wives," JOURNAL OF HIGHER EDUCATION, vol. 37 (Jan. 1966), pp. 10-15.
756. Simon, Rita, Shirley Clark, and Katherine Galway. "Of Nepotism and the Pursuit of an Academic Career," SOCIOLOGY OF EDUCATION, vol. 39, no. 4 (Fall 1966), pp. 334-358.
757. "Study of the Status of Women Faculty at Indiana University, Bloomington Campus." ERIC, 1971. 55 pp. Study of women faculty hiring, promotion, salary, and power position.
758. Truax, Ann, et al. RESEARCH ON THE STATUS OF FACULTY WOMEN, UNIVERSITY OF MINNESOTA. Minneapolis, Minn. Office of Student Affairs, May 1970.
759. University of California, Berkeley. "Report of the Subcommittee on the Status of Academic Women on the Berkeley Campus," May 19, 1970, pp. 38-41. Univ. of California, Berkeley, Committee on Senate Policy.
760. University of Washington. A REPORT ON THE STATUS OF WOMEN AT THE UNIVERSITY OF WASHINGTON, PART I: FACULTY AND STAFF; PART II: UNDERGRADUATE AND GRADUATE STUDENTS, 1971. Available from the ASUW Women's Commission, Univ. of Washington, Seattle.
761. University of Wisconsin. FINAL REPORT ON THE STATUS OF ACADEMIC WOMEN. Madison: Univ. of Wisconsin, 1971. 490 pp. Study of all 16 campuses of the University of Wisconsin to determine if women are distributed across the academic levels in a similar pattern to their male colleagues.
762. Van Fleet, David D. "Salaries of Males and Females: A Sample of Conditions at the University of Akron." ERIC. Univ. of Akron, 1970. 17 pp. Data regarding rank, sex, and salaries.
763. Weitzman, Lenore, et al. "Women on the Yale Faculty." ERIC. 1971. 33 pp. Reviews eleven departments and concludes that there are significantly fewer women on the faculty than in other prestigious institutions.
764. "Women Faculty in the University of Pennsylvania." ERIC. Philadelphia: Univ. of Pennsylvania, 1971. 36 pp.
765. "Women in Michigan: Academic Sexism Under Siege," SCIENCE, 24 Nov. 1972. President's evaluation of the extent of sex discrimination against women faculty members.
766. Yale University, Committee on the Status of Professional Women. "Report to the President from the Committee on the Status of Professional Women at Yale." New Haven, Yale Univ., 1971. 44 pp.

I. **Birth Control, Abortion and Demographic Studies**

It is to the laws of nature, therefore, and not to the conduct and institutions of man, that we are to attribute the necessity of a strong check on the natural increase of population.

—Thomas Malthus

"Gott macht Kinder, der wird sie auch ernähren"—God makes children, and He will also nourish them.

—Martin Luther

767. "Abortion: I. Nurses Talk About Abortion; II. Administrative Guidelines for an Abortion Service; III. Personal Experience at a Legal Abortion Center," AMERICAN JOURNAL OF NURSING, vol. 72 (Jan. 1972), pp. 106-112.

768. "Abortion—Health Care: A Discussion," YALE REVIEW OF LAW AND SOCIAL ACTION, vol. 2 (Fall 1971), pp. 69-76.

769. Abramowicz, Marc. "L'Avortement en Milieu Etudiant [Studies in Abortion Today], REVUE DE L'INSTITUTE DE SOCIOLOGIE, no. 3 (1971), pp. 357-362.

770. American Friends Service Committee. WHO SHALL LIVE? MAN'S CONTROL OVER BIRTH AND DEATH. New York: Hill and Wang, 1970. 144 pp.

771. Aptekar, H. ANJEA: INFANTICIDE ABORTION AND CONTRACEPTION IN SAVAGE SOCIETY. New York: Goodwin, 1931. An early study with bibliography.

772. "Avortement: Aspects—Medico—Psychologiques et Aspects Socio-Juridiques, Debats, et Synthese" [Abortion—Psychological, Medical, and Socio-Legal Aspects—Debates and Synthesis], REVUE DE L'INSTITUT DE SOCIOLOGIE, no. 3 (1971), pp. 365-459. Issue devoted to abortion, birth control methods, and government programs of population control education.

773. Banks, Joseph, and Olive Banks. FEMINISM AND FAMILY PLANNING IN VICTORIAN ENGLAND. New York: Schocken Books, 1964.

774. Beebe, Gilbert Wheeler. CONTRACEPTION AND FERTILITY IN THE SOUTHERN APPALACHIANS. New York: Arno Press, 1972. Reprint of the 1942 edition. Describes the results of birth control education among West Virginia families in 1939.

775. Breslin, John B. "Birthright—Alternative to Abortion," AMERICA, vol. 125 (Sept. 4, 1971), pp. 116-119. Takes a look at the Birthright Centers in New York City established by Cardinal Cooke.

776. Bromley, Dorothy Dunbar. BIRTH CONTROL: ITS USE AND MISUSE. New York: Harper, 1934. 304 pp. A sympathetic, intelligent view.

777. Brown, Norman K., et al. "How Do Nurses Feel About Euthanasia and Abortion," AMERICAN JOURNAL OF NURSING, vol. 71 (July 1971), pp. 1413-1416.

778. Calderone, Mary S., ed. ABORTION IN THE UNITED STATES. New York: Harper and Row, 1958. Methods and medical-legal problems.

779. Campbell, Arthur A. "Fertility and Family Planning Among Nonwhite Married Couples in the United States," EUGENICS QUARTERLY, vol. 12 (1965), pp. 124-131. Data on the birthrates and birth control education among members of a Negro population.

780. Carleton, R. O. "Fertility Trends, and Differentials in Latin America," MILBANK MEMORIAL FUND QUARTERLY, vol. 43, no. 4 (pt. 2), 1965.

781. Carroll, Charles. "Liberalized Abortion: A Critique," CHILD AND FAMILY, vol. 7, no. 2 (Spring 1968), pp. 157-169.

782. Chandrasekhar, Sripati. POPULATION AND PLANNED PARENTHOOD IN INDIA. 2d ed. London: Allen and Unwin, 1961.

783. Char, Walter F., and John F. McDermott, Jr. "Abortions and Acute Identity Crises in Nurses," AMERICAN JOURNAL OF PSYCHIATRY, vol. 128 (Feb. 1972), pp. 952-957.

784. Chasteen, Edgar R. THE CASE FOR COMPULSORY BIRTH CONTROL. Englewood Cliffs, N.J.: Prentice-Hall, 1971. 230 pp.

785. Collyer, A. O. BIRTH RATES IN LATIN AMERICA. Research Series no. 7. Berkeley, Calif.: Institute of International Studies, Univ. of California, 1965. Data on birth control measures as well.

786. Commander, Lydia Kingsmill, THE AMERICAN IDEA. New York: Arno Press, 1972. Reprint of the 1907 edition. Helps the reader to understand Margaret Sanger and the birth control movement.

787. Committee on Psychiatry and Law, Group for the Advancement of Psychiatry. THE RIGHT TO ABORTION: A PSYCHIATRIC VIEW. New York: Charles Scribner's Sons, 1970. 75 pp.

788. David, Henry P. "Abortion in Psychological Perspective," AMERICAN JOURNAL OF ORTHOPSYCHIATRY, vol. 42 (Jan. 1972), pp. 61-68. Well-balanced view.

789. Delgado Garcia, Ramiro. "Perspectives of Family Planning Programs in Latin America." Pp. 214-227 in POPULATION DILEMMA IN LATIN AMERICA, edited by J. Mayone Stycos and Jorge Arias. Washington, D.C.: American Assembly, Potomac Books, 1966.

790. Dienes, C. Thomas. "The Progeny of Comstockery—Birth Control Laws Return to the Court," THE AMERICAN UNIVERSITY LAW REVIEW, vol. 21 (Sept. 1971), pp. 1-129. Issue devoted to the abortion-legal controversy.

791. Dixon, Ruth. "Hallelujah the Pill?" TRANS-ACTION, vol. 8, nos. 1-2 (1970), pp. 44-49. Preaches a stage of demographic diversity of a new sort—choice of family and size of family.

792. Dourlen-Rollier, Anne-Marie. "L'Avortement" [Abortion], REVUE DE L'INSTITUT DE SOCIOLOGIE, no. 3 (1971), pp. 321-326. A French view.

793. El-Badry, M. A. "Trends in the Components of Population Growth in the Arab Countries of the Middle East: A Survey of Present Information," DEMOGRAPHY, vol. 2 (1965), pp. 140-186.

794. Etzioni, Amitai, "Sex Control, Science and Society," SCIENCE, vol. 148 (1968), pp. 1107-1112. The consequences and progress realized from effective birth control.

795. Felton, Gerald, and Roy Smith. "Administrative Guidelines for an Abortion Service," AMERICAN JOURNAL OF NURSING, vol. 72 (Jan. 1972), pp. 108-109.

796. Ferris, P. THE NAMELESS: ABORTION IN BRITAIN TODAY. London: Hutchinson, 1967.

797. Ficarra, Bernard J. NEWER ETHICAL PROBLEMS IN MEDICINE AND SURGERY. Westminster, Md.: Newman Press, 1951. 168 pp. Roman Catholic view on abortion, sterilization.

798. Florence, Lella Secor. PROGRESS REPORT ON BIRTH CONTROL. London: Heinemann, 1956. 260 pp. British study of programs and progress.

799. Ford, Charles V., Pietro Castelnuovo-Tedesco, and Kahlila D. Long. "Abortion: Is It a Therapeutic Procedure in Psychiatry?" JOURNAL OF THE AMERICAN MEDICAL ASSOCIATION, vol. 218 (Nov. 22, 1971), pp. 1173-1178. Discusses 40 women of lower socioeconomic status who had requested therapeutic abortion.

800. Fryer, Peter. THE BIRTH CONTROLLERS. New York: Stein and Day, 1966. 384 pp.; London: Corgi Press, 1957. A history of leading women advocates of birth control and abortion; bibliography.

801. Furstenberg, Frank F. "Birth Control Experience Among Pregnant Adolescents: The Process of Unplanned Parenthood," SOCIAL PROBLEMS, vol. 19 (Fall 1971), pp. 192-203. Interviews with 337 unmarried black teenagers confirming that premarital pregnancy is often unwanted.

802. Fyfe, Henry H. REVOLT OF WOMEN. New York: Rich and Cowan, 1933. 275 pp. Birth control and population planning.

803. Geairain, Jeanine. "Le Controle des Naissance" [Birth Control], REVUE DE L'INSTITUT DE SOCIOLOGIE, no. 3 (1971), pp. 353-356.

804. Gebhard, P. H., W. B. Pomeroy, C. Martin, and C. Christenson. PREGNANCY, BIRTH AND ABORTION, New York: Harper and Row, 1958.

805. Gendell, Murray. "The Influence of Family-Building Activity on Women's Rate of Economic Activity." Pp. 283-287 in PROCEEDINGS of the United Nations World Population Conference, Belgrade, vol. 4. New York, 1967.

806. Glass, D. V. POPULATION POLICIES AND MOVEMENTS IN EUROPE. Oxford: Clarendon Press, 1940. Good history and bibliography of birth control movements in Europe.

807. Hardin, Garrett. "Abortion—Or Compulsory Pregnancy?" JOURNAL OF MARRIAGE AND THE FAMILY, vol. 30, no. 2 (May 1968), pp. 246-251. Argues that the experience of the Scandinavian laws may be an alternative to ours.

808. ———. POPULATION, EVOLUTION AND BIRTH CONTROL: A COLLAGE OF CONTROVERSIAL IDEAS. San Francisco, Calif.: W. H. Freeman, 1969. 386 pp.

809. Hawkins, Everett. "Indonesia's Population Problems." Pp. 119-145 in S. Chandrasekhar, POPULATION AND PLANNED PARENTHOOD IN INDIA. London: Allen and Unwin, 1961.

810. Heer, David M. "Abortion, Contraception, and Population Policy in the Soviet Union," DEMOGRAPHY, vol. 2 (1965), pp. 531-539. Recent trends in the Soviet Union.

811. Jaiswal, R. H. "Family Planning—A Fresh Approach," THE MODERN REVIEW, Sept. 1971, pp. 222-224. Suggests several approaches in improving the success of the Indian family planning program.

812. Jakobovits, Immanuel, Chief Rabbi of England. "A Jewish View of Abortion," CHILD AND FAMILY, vol. 7 (1968), pp. 142-156.

813. *Jane Roe et al., Appellants v. Henry Wade,* (Jan. 22, 1973) 410 U.S. 113. Landmark case declared the unconstitutionality of the Texas criminal abortion laws which have been in effect for over a century.

814. Jenness, Linda, and Caroline Lund. ABORTION: A WOMAN'S RIGHT. New York: Pathfinder Press, 1972. 16 pp.

815. Knowlton, Charles. FRUITS OF PHILOSOPHY. 3d ed. by Charles Bradlaugh and Mrs. Annie Besant, 1878. In BIRTH CONTROL AND MORALITY IN NINETEENTH CENTURY AMERICA. New York: Arno Press, 1972. The morality of birth control discussed by a Boston physician before the Civil War.

816. Kopp, Marie E. BIRTH CONTROL IN PRACTICE. New York: Arno Press, 1972. Reprint of the 1934 edition. Evaluates the Margaret Sanger birth clinics; historically important account of the appeal and success of the early years of the birth control movement.

817. Koya, Yoshio. "A Family Planning Program in a Large Population Group," MILBANK MEMORIAL FUND QUARTERLY, vol. 40 (1962), pp. 319-327. Japanese birth control efforts.

818. Lader, Lawrence. ABORTION II: MAKING THE REVOLUTION. Boston: Beacon Press, 1973. An updating of Lader's earlier book, a powerful diatribe for reform of our abortion laws.

819. Langmyhr, George, and Walter C. Rogers. LEGAL ABORTION: A GUIDE FOR WOMEN IN THE UNITED STATES. New York: Planned Parenthood, 1970.

820. Lee, N. H. THE SEARCH FOR AN ABORTIONIST. Chicago: Univ. of Chicago Press, 1969.

821. Lochner, Jim W., and J. M. Gotta. "Premarital Pregnancies and the Choice Process," SCHOOL HEALTH REVIEW, vol. 3 (Jan.-Feb. 1972), pp. 18-22.

822. Lucas, Roy. "Federal Constitutional Limitations on the Enforcement and Administration of State Abortion Statutes," NORTH CAROLINA LAW REVIEW, vol. 46, no. 4 (June 1968).

823. Mead, Margaret, et al. THE PEACEFUL REVOLUTION: BIRTH CONTROL AND THE CHANGING STATUS OF WOMEN. New York: Planned Parenthood-World Population, 1967. Series of articles on planned parenthood in various countries.

824. Meyer, Adolf, ed. BIRTH CONTROL: FACTS AND RESPONSIBILITIES: A SYMPOSIUM DEALING WITH THIS IMPORTANT SUBJECT FROM A NUMBER OF ANGLES. Baltimore: Williams and Wilkins, 1925. 157 pp. Includes an essay by Margaret Sanger.

825. Mitchell, Robert E. "Husband-Wife Relations and Family-Planning Practices in Urban Hong Kong," JOURNAL OF MARRIAGE AND THE FAMILY, vol. 34 (Feb. 1972), pp. 139-146.

826. Moody, Howard. "Abortion: Woman's Right and Legal Problem," THEOLOGY TODAY, vol. 28 (Oct. 1971), pp. 337-346. A Christian point of view.

827. More, Adelyne. UNCONTROLLED BREEDING OR FECUNDITY VERSUS CIVILIZATION: A CONTRIBUTION TO THE STUDY OF OVERPOPULATION AS THE CAUSE OF WAR AND THE CHIEF OBSTACLE TO THE EMANCIPATION OF WOMEN. New York: Critic and Guide, 1917. 108 pp.

828. Myrdal, Alva. NATION AND FAMILY: THE SWEDISH EXPERIMENT IN DEMOCRATIC FAMILY AND POPULATION POLICY. Cambridge: M.I.T. Press, 1968.

829. O'Malley, Austin. THE ETHICS OF MEDICAL HOMICIDE AND MUTI-
        LATION. New York: Devin-Adair, 1919. 273 pp. An antiabortion book
        written by a Catholic physician.

830. Orleans, Leo A. "Birth Control: Reversal or Postponement?" CHINA
        QUARTERLY (London), no. 3 (1960), pp. 59-73. Trends and figures
        for China Mainland.

831. ———. "Evidence from Chinese Medical Journals on Current Population
        Policy," CHINA QUARTERLY, no. 40 (1969), pp. 137-146. Concludes
        that the population explosion is being brought under control in main-
        land China as a by-product of successful modernization.

832. Osofsky, Joy D., and Howard J. Osofsky. "The Psychological Reaction of
        Patients to Legalized Abortion," AMERICAN JOURNAL OF ORTHO-
        PSYCHIATRY, vol. 42 (Jan. 1972), pp. 61-68.

833. Peck, Ellen. "Advertisers, Unite! Strike a Blow Against Motherhood,"
        ADVERTISING AGE, vol. 43 (Jan. 24, 1972), pp. 33-34. Discusses the
        use of television commercials as a means to promote zero population
        growth.

834. Pelrine, Eleanor Wright. ABORTION IN CANADA. Toronto: New Press,
        1971. Comprehensive medical data; reviews Canadian law, includes re-
        ports of surveys in hospitals, and of women who have had abortions.

835. Planned Parenthood-World Population. A SELECTED BIBLIOGRAPHY
        FOR PROFESSIONALS ON FAMILY PLANNING AND RELATED
        SUBJECTS. New York: Planned Parenthood, 1967.

836. Rainwater, Lee, and Karole K. Rainwater. AND THE POOR GET
        CHILDREN—SEX, CONTRACEPTION, AND FAMILY PLANNING IN
        THE WORKING CLASS, Chicago: Quadrangle Books, 1960.

837. Resnik, H. L., and Byron J. Resnik. "Abortion and Suicidal Behaviors:
        Observations on the Concept of 'Endangering the Mental Health of the
        Mother,' " MENTAL HYGIENE, vol. 55, no. 1 (Jan. 1971), pp. 10-20.
        Broadly interpretive.

838. Roberts, Thomas D., ed. CONTRACEPTION AND HOLINESS: THE
        CATHOLIC PREDICAMENT. New York: Herder and Herder, 1964.

839. Robinson, Caroline Hadley. SEVENTY BIRTH CONTROL CLINICS: A
        SURVEY AND ANALYSIS INCLUDING THE GENERAL EFFECTS OF
        CONTROL ON THE SIZE AND QUALITY OF POPULATION. Balti-
        more: Williams and Wilkins, 1930. 351 pp. Excellent data on some early
        birth control clinics.

840. Robinson, Victor. PIONEERS OF BIRTH CONTROL IN ENGLAND
        AND AMERICA. New York: Voluntary Parenthood League, 1919. 107
        pp. Biographies and programs of some early advocates.

841. Rongy, A. J. ABORTION: LEGAL OR ILLEGAL? New York: Vanguard,
        1933. 212 pp. Calls for the repeal of abortion laws; estimated that there
        were two million abortions at that time, annually.

842. Rosen, Harold, ed. ABORTION IN AMERICA. Boston: Beacon Press,
        1972. Historical account of birth control efforts and the present legal
        controversies surrounding it.

843. "Rosen v. Louisiana State Board of Medical Examiners" (U.S. District
        Court), THE U.S. LAW WEEK, vol. 39, (Sept. 8, 1970), pp. 2126-2127.
        Decision upholding the Louisiana Medical Practice Act which prohibits
        a physician from performing an abortion unless done for the relief of a

woman whose life appears in peril. Dr. Rosen argued that the phrase was unconstitutionally vague and indefinite; the Court ruled that it was not.

844. Rossi, Alice. "Abortion and Social Change," DISSENT, July-Aug. 1969, pp. 338-346.

845. ———. "Abortion Laws and Their Victims," TRANSACTION, Sept.-Oct. 1966.

846. Rutko, Victor. "Radio in Family Planning Education in Africa," EDUCA-TIONAL BROADCASTING INTERNATIONAL, vol. 5 (Dec. 1971), pp. 243-245.

847. Sanger, Margaret. THE PIVOT OF CIVILIZATION. New York: Brentano's, 1922. 284 pp. By the pioneer proponent of abortion and family planning in America.

848. ———. WHAT EVERY GIRL SHOULD KNOW. London: Jonathan Cape, 1922. 109 pp. A guide for young girls.

849. ———. WOMAN AND THE NEW RACE. Preface by Havelock Ellis. New York: Brentano, 1920. 234 pp.

850. Sarker, Subhash C. "Population Planning in China," POPULATION RE-VIEW, vol. 2 (1958), pp. 49-58.

851. Schur, Edwin M. "Abortion and the Social System," SOCIAL PROB-LEMS, Oct. 1955, pp. 94-99.

852. Sikora, Mitchell. "Abortion: An Environmental Convenience or a Constitu-tional Right?" ENVIRONMENTAL AFFAIRS, vol. 1 (Nov. 1971), pp. 469-527.

853. Simms, Madeleine. "The Abortion Act After Three Years," POLITICAL QUARTERLY, vol. 42 (July-Sept. 1971), pp. 269-286. Discusses the results of the British Abortion Act, with many facts and figures.

854. Smith, D. L. ABORTION AND THE LAW. Cleveland: Case Western Reserve Press, 1967. Factual and offers programs.

855. "State v. Barquet" (Florida Supreme Court), THE U.S. LAW WEEK, vol. 40 (Mar. 14, 1972), pp. 2585-2586. A discussion of the Florida statute prohibiting abortions as "not necessary to preserve the mother's life," which violates the 14th Amendment.

856. Stockham, Alice B. KAREZZA: ETHICS OF MARRIAGE. Chicago: Author, 1896. 136 pp. Advocates this method as the way to achieve maximum happiness in marriage. Karezza was practiced by the Oneida Colony in nineteenth century New York State.

857. Stopes, Marie Carmichael. CONTRACEPTION (BIRTH CONTROL): ITS THEORY, HISTORY AND PRACTICE; A MANUAL FOR THE MEDI-CAL AND LEGAL PROFESSIONS. London: Putnam, 1931, 487 pp.

858. ———. "THE FIRST FIVE THOUSAND": BEING THE FIRST REPORT OF THE FIRST BIRTH CONTROL CLINIC IN THE BRITISH EMPIRE, THE MOTHER'S CLINIC' FOR CONSTRUCTIVE BIRTH CONTROL. London: Bale, 1925. 67 pp. By the British popularizer of birth control.

859. Storrer, Anne-Marie. "Les Femmes Juristes Devant Le Probleme" [Women Jurists Confront the Problem], REVUE DE L'INSTITUT DE SOCIOLOGIE, no. 3 (1971), pp. 337-341. French legal questions on the matter of abortion.

860. Stuart, Martha, and William T. Liu, eds. THE EMERGING WOMAN: THE IMPACT OF FAMILY PLANNING. Boston: Little, Brown, 1970. 360 pp. The effects of birth control and contraception on women and society.

861. Swedish Institute for Cultural Relations with Foreign Countries. THERA-PEUTIC ABORTION AND THE LAW IN SWEDEN, 1964. Available from author, Box 3306, Stockholm 3, Sweden.

862. Thomson, Judith J. "A Defense of Abortion," PHILOSOPHY AND PUB-LIC AFFAIRS, vol. 1 (Fall 1971), pp. 47-66. The author rejects the premise that the fetus is a person from the moment of conception, and concludes that the impermissibility of abortion based upon that premise is invalid.

863. Tien, H. Yuan. "Birth Control in Mainland China: Ideology and Politics," MILBANK MEMORIAL FUND QUARTERLY, vol. 41 (1963), pp. 269-290.

864. Tietze, C. SELECTED BIBLIOGRAPHY OF CONTRACEPTION: 1940-1960. New York: National Committee on Maternal Health, 1960.

865. ———. BIBLIOGRAPHY OF FERTILITY CONTROL: 1950-1965. New York: National Committee on Maternal Health, 1965.

866. ———. "History of Contraceptive Methods," JOURNAL OF SEX RE-SEARCH, vol. 1 (1965), pp. 69-85.

867. Tietze, C., and H. Lehfeldt. "Legal Abortion in Eastern Europe," JOURNAL OF THE AMERICAN MEDICAL ASSOCIATION, vol. 175 (1961), pp. 1149-1154.

868. Toussiant, Philippe. "Pour une Legalisation de L'Avortement," REVUE DE L'INSTITUT DE SOCIOLOGIE, no. 3 (1971), pp. 343-351. Legalization of abortion in France.

869. Trussell, James, and Dr. Robert A. Hatcher. FIVE WOMEN IN NEED. New York: Macmillan, 1972. 192 pp. Discusses the societal-legal aspects of contraception, abortion, sterilization, and family planning.

870. Tuan Chi-hsien. "Reproductive Histories of Chinese Women in Rural Taiwan," POPULATION STUDIES, vol. 12 (1958), pp. 40-50.

871. U.S., Bureau of the Census. ESTIMATES AND PROJECTIONS OF THE POPULATION OF THE USSR AND OF THE COMMUNIST COUNTRIES OF EASTERN EUROPE BY AGE AND SEX. Washington, D.C.: SUDOC, GPO, April 1964. 143 pp.

872. U.S., Department of Health, Education and Welfare. THE FEDERAL PROGRAM IN POPULATION RESEARCH: INVENTORY OF POPU-LATION RESEARCH SUPPORTED BY FEDERAL AGENCIES DUR-ING FISCAL YEAR 1970. Washington, D.C.: SUDOC, GPO, December 31, 1970.

873. Westoff, Charles F., and Raymond H. Potvin. COLLEGE WOMEN AND FERTILITY VALUES. Princeton: Princeton Univ. Press, 1967. Includes valuable data and bibliographical materials.

874. Woodhull, Victoria Claflin. A PAGE OF AMERICAN HISTORY, 1870: THE ALCHEMY OF MATERNITY: STIRPICULTURE OR, THE SCIENTIFIC PROPAGATION OF THE HUMAN RACE; SOME THOUGHTS ABOUT AMERICA. Tewkesbury, England: Manor House Club, 1889. 39 pp. Some early ideas about birth control by a pioneer feminist.

875. Wright, Eleanor. ABORTION IN CANADA. Toronto: New Press, 1971. 133 pp.

876. Yaukey, David. FERTILITY DIFFERENCES IN A MODERNIZING COUNTRY: A SURVEY OF LEBANESE COUPLES. Princeton: Princeton Univ., 1961.

877. "YWCA v. Kugler" (U.S. District Court—N.J.), THE U.S. LAW WEEK, vol. 40 (Mar. 21, 1972), pp. 2617-2620. Discussion of abortion in terms of a woman's constitutional right to privacy as provided for in the 9th and 14th Amendments, with various legal precedents cited. Court ruled that the New Jersey statute which prohibits abortion unless legally justified constituted unreasonable state intervention and, therefore, rendered the statute invalid.

II. POLITICAL SCIENCE

The titles included in the nine categories of this section have a common char-
acteristic with the Sociology section, in that they, too, chronologically span the
period from the early nineteenth century to the present. The setting up of sections, and allocation of entries to them, is at best an arbitrary and procrustean
procedure. A number of important topics for which the volumes we analyzed
were too few to constitute a separate section have been included in the general
categories of each subsection. For example, we have nearly 40 entries under section
C.1 (Social Reformers—General) on the leadership and ideas of women reformers,
and only 7 entries under section C.5 on prostitution reforms. This anomaly has
been allowed to stand as evidence of the multiplicity of references under the former topic and the scarcity under the latter. Some relevant sources may go un-
noted, but on further investigation by specialists, a rich body of materials may
be added from the fragments of sources we have dredged up from the sea of books
assembled here.

A. Women as Socializers

Marriage is to politics what the lever is to engineering. The State is not founded upon
single individuals but upon couples and groups.
　　　　　　　　　　　　　　　　　　　　　—Baron Novalis

878. Chafe, William J. THE AMERICAN WOMAN: HER CHANGING SOCIAL,
ECONOMIC, AND POLITICAL ROLES, 1920-1970. New York: Oxford
Univ. Press, 1972. 351 pp. Predicts that the classic differences between
men and women will disappear as both sexes take on the same roles in
the economic and political spheres.
879. Communist Party of Canada. CANADA'S WOMEN: THE HOME, AT
WORK, CHILDREN, EQUALITY, PEACE. Toronto: Progress Books,
1963. 24 pp. Published by the National Women's Committee of the
Communist party and calls for changes in all aspects of women's lives.
880. Dell, Floyd. WOMEN AS WORLD BUILDERS: STUDIES IN MODERN
FEMINISM. Chicago: Forbes, 1913. 104 pp. Attempts to interpret the
feminist movement through the personalities of Jane Addams, Beatrice
Webb, and others.
881. Froman, Lewis A. "Personality and Political Socialization," JOURNAL
OF POLITICS, vol. 23 (1961), pp. 341-352. Develops a conceptual
scheme of political socialization by considering environment, personality,
and behavior, and their interrelationships.
882. Greenstein, Fred. "Sex-Related Political Differences in Childhood,"
JOURNAL OF POLITICS, vol. 23 (May 1961), pp. 353-371. Concludes
that political sex differences among children tend to follow the roles of
adult parents, and that girls find political behavior unfeminine.
883. Jennings, M. Kent, and Richard G. Niemi. "The Division of Political
Labor between Mothers and Fathers," AMERICAN POLITICAL
SCIENCE REVIEW, vol. 65, no. 1 (Mar. 1971).
884. O'Neill, William L. EVERYONE WAS BRAVE: THE RISE AND FALL
OF FEMINISM IN AMERICA. Chicago: Quadrangle Books, 1969. 369

pp. Posits the concept of "social feminism" to combat the obstacles to women's emancipation.

885. Ossoli, Mrs. Sarah Margaret Fuller. WOMAN IN THE NINETEENTH CENTURY, AND KINDRED PAPERS RELATING TO THE SPHERE, CONDITION, AND DUTIES OF WOMAN. Boston, 1874. Reprinted by Greenwood Press, Westport, Conn. One of the principal works of Fuller, and a valuable reference to her career as a social reformer and a pioneer feminist.

886. Schmalhausen, Samuel D., and Victor F. Calverton, eds. WOMAN'S COMING OF AGE: A SYMPOSIUM. New York: Horace Liveright, 1931. 569 pp. Collection of essays which conclude that social environment and tradition must be changed before deciding what women can do to change their social and political rights.

B. Victorian Attitudes

The Victorians were lame giants: the strongest of them walked on one leg a little shorter than the other. . . . There is a moment when Carlyle turns suddenly from a high creative mystic to a common Calvinist. There are moments when George Eliot turns from a prophetess into a governess. There are also moments when Ruskin turns into a governess, without even the excuse of sex.
—G. K. Chesterton

887. Bryant, Willa C. "Discrimination Against Women in General: Black Southern Women in Particular," CIVIL RIGHTS DIGEST, vol. 4 (Summer 1971), pp. 10-11. The concept of woman as biologically and socially inferior to men was conceived to justify the oppression and indignities to which women were subjected.

888. Dodge, Mary [Gail Hamilton]. WOMAN'S WRONGS: A COUNTER-IRRITANT. New York: Arno Press, 1972. Reprint of the 1868 edition. Early study of women's rights and how they have been disregarded.

889. Grimes, Alan Pendleton. THE PURITAN ETHIC AND WOMAN SUFFRAGE. New York: Oxford Univ. Press, 1967. 159 pp. Well-documented thesis that the franchise of women coincided with a fundamental change in earlier social values concerning the role of women in American life, i.e., puritan values which could contribute to the purification of politics and help end corruption in government.

890. Scott, Anne Firor. THE SOUTHERN LADY: FROM PEDESTAL TO POLITICS, 1830-1930. Chicago: Univ. of Chicago Press, 1970. 247 pp. A study of the history and conditions of women in the Southern states, with an excellent bibliography.

C. Social Reformers

1. General

Reform, n. A thing that mostly satisfies reformers opposed to reformation.
—Ambrose Bierce

891. Addams, Jane. DEMOCRACY AND SOCIAL ETHICS. New York: Macmillan, 1916. Concerned with questions of ethical progress and the

growth of democratic thought, sentiment, and institutions, and with the expansion of women's roles in society.

892. Athey, Louis. "Florence Kelley and the Quest for Negro Equality," JOURNAL OF NEGRO HISTORY, vol. 56 (Oct. 1971), pp. 249-261. Friend of Jane Addams; investigated Chicago slums and made herself a foe of child and woman labor and the problems of racial prejudice.

893. Birney, Catherine H. THE GRIMKE SISTERS. SARAH AND ANGELINE GRIMKE, THE FIRST AMERICAN WOMEN ADVOCATES OF ABOLITION AND WOMAN'S RIGHTS. Westport, Conn.: Greenwood Press, 1970. Reprint of 1885 edition. 319 pp. The first women to challenge the status of women with demands for reform.

894. Brinkley, Mrs. Hugh L. WOMEN IN CIVIL SERVICE REFORM. New York: American News Co., 1882. 45 pp. For its time, a revolutionary pamphlet.

895. Chester, Giraud. EMBATTLED MAIDEN: THE LIFE OF ANNA DICK-INSON. New York: G. P. Putnam's Sons, 1951. 307 pp. Leading woman lecturer of mid-nineteenth century who advocated prohibition, abolition, and politics and suffrage for women.

896. "Congrés Constitutif de l'Union des Femmes de l'Ouest Africain (U.F.O.A.)," Bamako, Mali, July 20-23,1959. In LA VIE AFRICAINE vol. 4, (Paris, 1959), no. 7, n.p. Congress held to form groups to unite the women of Africa in the fight for freedom; defense of the rights of women, child welfare, cultural and social activities, and unity of Negro Africa.

897. D'Arusmont, Frances Wright. LIFE, LETTERS AND LECTURES: 1834, 1844. New York: Arno Press, 1972. Reprint of two volumes of 1834 and 1844. Disturbing talks, exploring birth control, the redistribution of wealth, free education, and equal rights for women.

898. Duffus, R. L. LILLIAN WALD NEIGHBOR AND CRUSADER. New York: Macmillan, 1939. 371 pp. Public health nurse, founder of National Children's Bureau, Henry Street Settlement House, supporter of woman suffrage, the peace movement, and other humanitarian causes.

899. Gattey, Charles Neilson. THE BLOOMER GIRLS. New York: Coward-McCann, 1968. Early American reformer, most notable today for intro-ducing, in 1849, bloomers.

900. Gilman, Charlotte Perkins. THE LIVING OF CHARLOTTE PERKINS GILMAN: AN AUTOBIOGRAPHY. Foreword by Zona Gale. New York: Arno Press, 1972. Reprint of 1935 edition. By the prolific writer on emancipation of women, though always on the periphery of the suffrage movement.

901. Goldman, Emma. ANARCHISM AND OTHER ESSAYS. Port Washington, N.Y.: Kennikat Press, 1969. Collection of essays dealing with prostitu-tion, women's emancipation, suffrage, and marriage and love.

902. ———. LIVING MY LIFE. New York: AMS Press, 1970. Reprint of the 1934 edition. Memoirs of the Russian-born anarchist who challenged many of America's social, intellectual, and political convictions.

903. Goldmark, Josephine. IMPATIENT CRUSADER: FLORENCE KELLEY'S LIFE STORY. Urbana: Univ. of Illinois Press, 1953. 217 pp. Interpreta-tion of the life and achievements of the reformer.

904. James, Bessie Rowland. ANNE ROYALL'S U.S.A. New Brunswick, N.J.: Rutger's Univ. Press, 1972. Early nineteenth-century traveler and jour-

nalist who campaigned against graft and for freedom of the press. She
was once bailed out of jail by Andrew Jackson.

905. Johnston, Johann. MRS. SATAN: THE INCREDIBLE SAGA OF
VICTORIA WOODHULL. New York: Macmillan, 1967. One of America's most unconventional reformers who first published Marx's *Communist Manifesto* in America.

906. Jones, Mary Harris. THE AUTOBIOGRAPHY OF MOTHER JONES.
Edited by Mary Field Parton, Chicago: Charles H. Kerr, 1925. 242 pp.
Irish-born daughter of a railroad worker whose political efforts and
sympathies were with miners, their wives, and children.

907. Levine, Daniel. JANE ADDAMS AND THE LIBERAL TRADITION.
Madison: State Historical Society of Wisconsin, 1971. 277 pp. Emphasizes her role as a publicist, persuader, and reformer within the liberal
tradition.

908. Linn, James Weber. JANE ADDAMS: A BIOGRAPHY. New York, 1935.
Reprint by Greenwood Press, Westport, Conn. 1970. 457 pp. The
authorized biography by her nephew.

909. Miller, Jean Baker. "New Political Directions for Women," SOCIAL
POLICY, vol. 2 (July-Aug. 1971), p. 32. Criticizes women's movement
for its shallow involvement in making changes in the social order.

910. Nathan, Maud. ONCE UPON A TIME AND TODAY. New York: Putnam's,
1933. 327 pp. Cites Mrs. Nathan's work for the Consumer's League, the
working woman, the suffrage movement in New York State, and the
International Suffrage Alliance for women.

911. Oakley, Violet. CATHEDRAL OF COMPASSION: DRAMATIC OUTLINE
OF THE LIFE OF JANE ADDAMS, 1860-1935. Philadelphia: Women's
International League for Peace and Freedom, 1955. 104 pp.

912. Pannell, Anne Gary, and Dorothea E. Wyatt. JULIA S. TUTWILER AND
SOCIAL PROGRESS IN ALABAMA. Auburn: Univ. of Alabama Press,
1961. 158 pp. Southern campaigner against alcoholism; advocate for
improving prisons, expanding state teacher training, and establishing a
state college for women.

913. Prior, Margaret. WALKS OF USEFULNESS, OR REMINISCENCES OF
MRS. MARGARET PRIOR. New York: American Female Moral Reform Society, 1847. 324 pp. One of the leaders of the American Female Moral Reform Society.

914. Rathbone, Eleanor R. THE DISINHERITED FAMILY: A PLEA FOR
THE ENDOWMENT OF THE FAMILY. London: Edward Arnold, 1924.
332 pp. The author became the first Independent woman member of
England's Parliament in 1929.

915. Robertson, Constance Noyes, ed. ONEIDA COMMUNITY: AN AUTO-
BIOGRAPHY, 1851-1876. Syracuse: Syracuse Univ. Press, 1970.
Oneida's—and John Humphrey Noyes's—views of the role of women
were so far in advance of what had been achieved up to that time.
Volume 2, ONEIDA COMMUNITY: THE BREAKUP, 1876-1881,
offers excellent views of the Oneida Commune's advanced theories on
women and marriage.

916. Schulman, Alix Kates. RED EMMA SPEAKS. New York: Random
House, 1972. Collected writings and speeches of Emma Goldman on
woman suffrage and other topics.

917. Sessions, Ruth H. SIXTY-ODD: A PERSONAL HISTORY. Brattleboro, Vt.: Stephen Daye Press, 1936. 429 pp. Mother of the composer Roger Sessions, and advocate of woman suffrage.

918. Spencer, Anna Garlin. WOMAN'S SHARE IN CULTURE. New York: Arno Press, 1972. Reprint of 1913 edition. The first female ordained minister in Rhode Island, concerned with factory laws, child labor and prostitution, and with women as ladies, geniuses, spinsters, workers, and postgraduate mothers.

919. Stewart, William Rhinelander, compiler. THE PHILANTHROPIC WORK OF JOSEPHINE SHAW LOWELL, CONTAINING A BIOGRAPHICAL SKETCH OF HER LIFE TOGETHER WITH A SELECTION OF HER PUBLIC PAPERS AND PRIVATE LETTERS. New York: Macmillan, 1911. 584 pp. Much of her work was devoted to improving the condition of women in reformatories and institutions for the feeble-minded.

920. Strachey, Rachel Conn (Costelloe). A QUAKER GRANDMOTHER. New York: Fleming H. Revell, 1914. About the activist Mrs. Pearsall Smith, the author's grandmother (1832-1911).

921. Suhl, Yuri. ERNESTINE L. ROSE AND THE BATTLE FOR HUMAN RIGHTS. New York: Reynal, 1959. 310 pp. Polish-born daughter of a Rabbi who was a pioneer in the great reform movements of the nineteenth century; abolition, woman's rights, free education, and Utopian socialism.

922. Swisshelm, Jane Grey. CRUSADER AND FEMINIST: LETTERS OF JANE GREY SWISSHELM, 1858-1865. St. Paul: Minnesota Historical Society, 1934. 327 pp. By the ardent supporter of woman's rights and antislavery.

923. ———. HALF A CENTURY. New York: Source Book Press, 1970. Reprint of 1880 edition. 363 pp.

924. Terry, Ellen. THE THIRD DOOR: THE AUTOBIOGRAPHY OF AN AMERICAN NEGRO WOMAN. Westport, Conn.: Greenwood Press, 1969. Reprint of the 1955 edition. Details her efforts to improve race relations through her work in Harlem with Catherine de Huech, founder of the International Friendship House.

925. Tims, Margaret. JANE ADDAMS OF HULL HOUSE, 1860-1935: A CENTENARY STUDY. New York: Macmillan, 1961. 166 pp. Much bibliographical information.

926. Waterman, William Randall. FRANCES WRIGHT. New York: Columbia Univ. Press, 1924. 267 pp.

927. Woodhull, Victoria (Claflin), and Tennessee C. Claflin. THE HUMAN BODY THE TEMPLE OF GOD. London: n.p. 1890. The philosophy of sociology and other essays dealing with the rights of women and other social and moral questions.

2. Social Reformers—Abolitionists

But for equality their [the Americans'] passion is ardent, insatiable, incessant, invincible; they call for equality in freedom; and if they cannot obtain that, they will call for equality in slavery.

—de Tocqueville

928. Beecher, Catherine Esther. AN ESSAY ON SLAVERY AND ABOLITIONISM, WITH REFERENCE TO THE DUTY OF AMERICAN FEMALES.

Boston: Perkins and Marvin, 1837. Includes comments on controversial literature circulated in 1837.

929. Bernard, Jacqueline. JOURNEY TOWARD FREEDOM. New York: Dell, 1967. 271 pp. Biography of Sojourner Truth, champion of the abolitionist and women's rights movements.

930. Bradford, Sarah H. SCENES IN THE LIFE OF HARRIET TUBMAN, OR HARRIET TUBMAN: THE MOSES OF HER PEOPLE. New York: Corinth Books, 1961. 149 pp. Story of the famous Negro abolitionist, and conductor of the "Underground Railroad."

931. Lutz, Alma. CRUSADE FOR FREEDOM: WOMEN OF THE ANTI-SLAVERY MOVEMENT. Boston: Beacon Press, 1968. 338 pp. A scholarly account of the women who helped organize antislavery societies, such as Lucretia Mott, the Grimké sisters, and Maria Weston Chapman.

932. Pauli, Hertha. HER NAME WAS SOJOURNER TRUTH. New York: Avon Books, 1972. Negro woman born into slavery who won her freedom and struggled for the liberty and dignity of her people.

933. Stowe, Harriet Beecher. UNCLE TOM'S CABIN. New York: Washington Square Press, 1963. Originally published in 1851, this novel became the most telling document in the abolitionist propaganda attack.

3. Social Reformers—Peace

934. Addams, Jane, Emily G. Balch, and Alice Hamilton. WOMEN AT THE HAGUE: THE INTERNATIONAL CONGRESS OF WOMEN AND ITS RESULTS. New York: Garland, 1972. Reprint of the 1915 edition. What European and American women tried to do to bring about peace during World War I.

935. Degen, Marie Louise. THE HISTORY OF THE WOMAN'S PEACE PARTY. Baltimore: Johns Hopkins Press, 1939. 266 pp. The oldest continually active peace organization in the United States, founded by Jane Addams, Carrie Chapman Catt, and Fanny Fern Andrews.

936. Ladd, William. ON THE DUTY OF FEMALES TO PROMOTE THE CAUSE OF PEACE. New York: Garland, 1971. 48 pp. Reprint of the Civil War pamphlet. Interesting because Ladd was anti-women's liberation, but he asks the ladies to educate children at home in the principles of peace, procure and distribute peace tracts, and to found Female Peace Societies.

937. Norris, Kathleen. WHAT PRICE PEACE? A HANDBOOK OF PEACE FOR AMERICAN WOMEN. New York: Doubleday, 1928. 71 pp. The power to end war rests with women, she concludes.

938. Sewall, May Wright. WOMEN, WORLD WAR, AND PERMANENT PEACE. San Francisco: Newbegin, 1915. 206 pp. Proceedings of the International Conference of Women workers to Promote Permanent Peace, held in San Francisco in 1915.

939. Spaull, Hebe. WOMEN PEACE-MAKERS. London: Harrap, 1924. 124 pp. Biographies of European women and their contributions to the furthering of world peace.

4. Social Reformers—Prohibition

A prohibitionist is the sort of man one wouldn't care to drink with—even if he drank.
—Mencken

940. Asbury, Herbert. CARRY NATION. New York: Knopf, 1929. 314 pp. Witty, in-depth biography detailing her role in the temperance movement at the turn of the century.

941. Dillon, Mary Earhart. FRANCES WILLARD: FROM PRAYERS TO POLITICS. Chicago: Univ. of Chicago Press, 1944. 417 pp. Founder of the Women's Christian Temperance Union.

942. Hartley, Ralph Waldo. THE AGE OF UNREASON: PROHIBITION AND WOMEN AND WHAT THEY'RE DOING. Boston: Meador, 1936. 228 pp. Fanatical, amusing book which sees the emancipation of women as the root of society's ills.

943. Kraditor, Aileen S. THE IDEAS OF THE WOMAN SUFFRAGE MOVEMENT, 1890-1920. New York: Columbia Univ. Press, 1965. 313 pp. Deals with two major suffragist arguments, the link between temperance and suffrage, with excellent bibliographical section.

944. Paulson, Ross E. WOMEN'S SUFFRAGE AND PROHIBITION: A COMPARATIVE STUDY OF EQUALITY AND SOCIAL CONTROL. Glenview, Ill.: Scott, Foresman, 1973.

945. Root, Grace C. WOMEN AND REPEAL: THE STORY OF THE WOMEN'S ORGANIZATION FOR NATIONAL PROHIBITION REFORM. New York: Harper, 1934. 217 pp.

946. Stewart, Mrs. Eliza Daniel. MEMORIES OF THE CRUSADE: A THRILLING ACCOUNT OF THE GREAT UPRISING OF THE WOMEN OF OHIO IN 1873 AGAINST THE LIQUOR CRIME, BY MOTHER STEWART. New York: Arno Press, 1972. Reprint of the 1889 edition. Case studies of the deterioration of family life, the sexual violence and abuse of wives and children, the degradation of the worker by drink, and the nation's failure to act.

947. Strachey, Rachel Conn (Costelloe). FRANCES WILLARD. London: T. F. Unwin, 1912. The life and work of the opponent of intemperance, Frances E. Willard (1830-1898).

948. Trowbridge, Lydia Jones. FRANCES WILLARD OF EVANSTON. Chicago: Willett, Clark, 1938. 207 pp. Life of the temperance advocate and later supporter of women's suffrage.

949. Willard, Frances E. WOMAN AND TEMPERANCE: OR, THE WORK AND WORKERS OF THE WOMAN'S CHRISTIAN TEMPERANCE UNION. Hartford, Conn.: Park, 1883. 648 pp.

950. ———. GLIMPSES OF FIFTY YEARS: THE AUTOBIOGRAPHY OF AN AMERICAN WOMAN. New York: Source Book Press, 1970. Reprint of the 1889 edition. 724 pp.

951. ———. MY HAPPY HALF-CENTURY: THE AUTOBIOGRAPHY OF AN AMERICAN WOMAN. Edited by Frances E. Cook. London: Ward, Lock and Bowden, 1894. 392 pp.

952. Willard, Frances E., and Mary A. Livermore, eds. A WOMAN OF THE CENTURY: FOURTEEN HUNDRED-SEVENTY BIOGRAPHICAL SKETCHES . . . OF LEADING AMERICAN WOMEN IN ALL WALKS

OF LIFE. Buffalo, N.Y.: Moulton, 1893. Excellent short sketches of women in suffrage, reform, and temperance activities.
953. Wittenmyer, Annie. HISTORY OF THE WOMAN'S TEMPERANCE CRUSADE. A COMPLETE OFFICIAL HISTORY OF THE WONDERFUL UPRISING OF THE CHRISTIAN WOMEN OF THE UNITED STATES AGAINST THE LIQUOR TRAFFIC, WHICH CULMINATED IN THE GOSPEL TEMPERANCE MOVEMENT. Introduction by Frances E. Willard. Philadelphia: Christian Women, 1878. 794 pp.

5. Social Reformers—Prostitution

Prisons are built with stones of law, brothels with bricks of religion.
—Blake

954. Addams, Jane. A NEW CONSCIENCE AND AN ANCIENT EVIL. New York: Arno Press, 1972. Reprint of the 1912 edition. Helped to start the Progressive attack on prostitution.
955. Butler, A.S.G. PORTRAIT OF JOSEPHINE BUTLER. London: Faber and Faber, 1954. 222 pp. Biography of the social reformer in England whose principal cause was the plight of the prostitute.
956. Clarke, Charles Walter. TABOO: THE STORY OF THE PIONEERS OF SOCIAL HYGIENE. Washington, D.C.: Public Affairs Press, 1961. 109 pp. Includes a chapter on Josephine Butler, the British champion of antiprostitution legislation and the fight against venereal diseases.
957. Roby, Pamela A. "Politics and Criminal Law: Revision of the New York State Penal Law on Prostitution," SOCIAL PROBLEMS, (Summer 1969), pp. 83-109.
958. ———. "Politics and Prostitution: A Case Study of the Revision, Enforcement, and Administration of the New York State Penal Laws on Prostitution," CRIMINOLOGY, vol. 9 (Feb. 1972), pp. 425-447.
959. United Nations. SUMMARIES OF ANNUAL REPORTS OF GOVERNMENTS ON TRAFFIC IN WOMEN AND CHILDREN. New York: United Nations Publications, 1946, 1947, 1948, 1949, 1950.
960. ———. "International Convention for the Suppression of Traffic in Women of Full Age," New York: United Nations Publications, 1945-1966.

D. Feminism, Equal Rights

1. General

All animals are equal, but some animals are more equal than others.
—George Orwell

961. Adams, Abigail. FAMILIAR LETTERS OF JOHN ADAMS AND HIS WIFE ABIGAIL. 2 vols. Boston: Somerset, 1840. Abigail wrote to her husband who was attending the first Continental Congress, to enact new laws which would give some consideration to the rights of women along with the rights of mankind.
962. Altbach, Edith Yoshino, ed. FROM FEMINISM TO LIBERATION. Cambridge, Mass.: Schenkman, 1971. Anthology of previously published

articles from the issue devoted to women in RADICAL AMERICA (Feb. 1970).

963. Anthony, Susan B. "Woman's Half-Century of Evolution," NORTH AMERICAN REVIEW, vol. 175 (July-Dec., 1902), pp. 800-810. Resume of the progress made by the women's rights movement in the fifty-year period following the first woman's rights movement in 1848.

964. Atkins, Martha. THE HIDDEN HISTORY OF THE FEMALE: THE EARLY FEMINIST MOVEMENT IN THE UNITED STATES. Toronto: Hogtown Press, 1971. 36 pp. A brief history of the advances made by the early feminists.

965. Awobajo, Theophilus D. "African Version of Women's Liberation," AFRICAN PROGRESS MAGAZINE, vol. 1 (Sept.-Oct. 1971), pp. 21-22. A look at African women and how they are winning battles for equality in becoming secretaries, nurses, journalists, and businesswomen.

966. Banerji, J. "Four Goals of Women's Lib," ILLUSTRATED WEEKLY OF INDIA, vol. 92 (Oct. 24, 1971), pp. 14-17.

967. Blackwell, Alice. LUCY STONE: PIONEER OF WOMEN'S RIGHTS. Boston: Gale, 1972. Reprint of 1930 edition. Pioneer of women's rights for female laborers and mill workers.

968. Blease, Walter Lyon. THE EMANCIPATION OF ENGLISH WOMEN. New York: Benjamin Blom, 1910. 294 pp. Study of how the English have, through their religious practices, literature, legal system, and their educational institutions, denied women equality from the Restoration through the 1880s and 1890s.

969. Bloor, Ella Reeve. WOMEN IN THE SOVIET UNION. New York: Workers Library, 1938.

970. Bosmajian, Hamida, ed. THIS GREAT ARGUMENT: THE RIGHTS OF WOMEN. New York: Canfield Press, 1972. Essays, court decisions, speeches, drama, poetry, journal articles, and commission recommendations on the rights of women.

971. Branagan, Thomas. THE EXCELLENCY OF THE FEMALE CHARACTER VINDICATED: BEING AN INVESTIGATION RELATIVE TO THE CAUSE AND EFFECTS OF THE ENCROACHMENTS OF MEN UPON THE CIVIL RIGHTS OF WOMEN, AND THE TOO FREQUENT DEGRADATION AND CONSEQUENT MISFORTUNES OF THE FAIR SEX. New York: Arno Press, 1972. Reprint of the 1808 edition. A moving tract in advance of its time.

972. Bryant, Willa C. "Discrimination Against Women in General: Black Southern Women in Particular," CIVIL RIGHTS DIGEST, vol. 4 (Summer 1971), pp. 10-11. The concept of women as biologically and socially inferior to men was conceived to justify the oppression and indignities to which black women were subjected.

973. Claflin, Tennessee E. CONSTITUTIONAL EQUALITY, A RIGHT OF WOMEN: OR A CONSIDERATION OF THE VARIOUS RELATIONS WHICH SHE SUSTAINS AS A NECESSARY PART OF THE BODY OF SOCIETY AND HUMANITY. New York: Woodhull, Claflin, 1871. 148 pp. By the sister of Victoria Woodhull, herself a radical women's rights leader.

974. Conrader, Constance. "Women—Attaining Their Birthright," WORLD ORDER, vol. 6, no. 4 (Summer 1972), pp. 43-59. The problem of increasing equality of women by a Baha'i writer. Baha'is have long advocated women's rights.

975. Corbin, John. THE RETURN OF THE MIDDLE CLASS. New York: Scribner's, 1922. 353 pp. Much of the book deals with equal rights for women.

976. Cudlipp, Edythe. UNDERSTANDING WOMEN'S LIBERATION. New York: Paperback Library, 1971. 220 pp. Series of chapters dealing with women's legal rights, women's liberation groups, and how to liberate yourself to become equal, or at least to be treated like a human.

977. Davis, Angela Y. IF THEY COME IN THE MORNING: VOICES OF RESISTANCE. New York: Third Press, 1971. 281 pp. Collection of writings about black American women who have become the symbol of resistance to political oppression all over the world.

978. Davis, Paulina Wright. A HISTORY OF THE NATIONAL WOMAN'S RIGHTS MOVEMENT. New York: Source Book Press, 1970. Reprint of the 1871 edition. 152 pp. Includes the proceedings of the 1870 meeting of the national women's rights movement, as well as reports and addresses of the movement's leaders.

979. De Carturla Bru, Victoria. LA MUJER EN LA INDEPENDENCIA DE AMERICA. Havana: Jesus Montero, 1945. Discusses the need to liberate women in Latin America if the revolution is to succeed.

980. Decter, Midge. THE NEW CHASTITY AND OTHER ARGUMENTS AGAINST WOMEN'S LIBERATION. New York: Coward, McCann and Geoghegan, 1972. Provocative broadside of the women's liberation movement, contending that the movement is retreating from the amount of freedom that they have recently won. Liberation for men and women cannot come in movements, but only through the constant use of intelligence and choice.

981. Dixon, Marlene. "Why Women's Liberation." In THE UNDERSIDE OF AMERICAN HISTORY: OTHER READINGS, Vol. II: SINCE 1865, edited by Thomas R. Frazier. New York: Harcourt, Brace and Jovanovich, 1971. An analytical summary of the roots of women's liberation.

982. Dornberg, John. THE NEW TSARS: RUSSIA UNDER STALIN'S HEIRS. New York: Doubleday, 1972. Changes Russian women have encountered since the Revolution of 1917.

983. Flexner, Eleanor. MARY WOLLSTONECRAFT: A BIOGRAPHY. New York: Coward, McCann and Geoghegan, 1972. 307 pp. Excellent biography of the English woman who first challenged the image of women as the weaker and subservient sex, and who was instrumental in starting the movement for women's equal rights.

984. Gardiner, Lady. "Some More Equal than Others," CONTEMPORARY REVIEW, vol. 220 (Jan. 1972), pp. 32-36. Seeks to establish equality between the sexes on economic, legal, social, moral, occupational, and political levels, as proposed by the Six-Point Group in England.

985. Gaudio, Attilio. LA REVOLUTION DES FEMMES EN ISLAM. Paris: Julliard, 1957. 250 pp. Excellent summary of changes in women's rights in Arab countries, with bibliography.

[94] WOMEN AND SOCIETY

986. Gordon, David C. WOMEN OF ALGERIA: AN ESSAY ON CHANGE. Cambridge: Harvard Univ. Press, 1968.

987. Greene, Gael. "The Insatiable Critic: Was McSorley's Worth Liberating?" NEW YORK MAGAZINE, vol. 4 (Dec. 20, 1971), pp. 124-125. The famous men's bar that spurred the Court's orders that male bars admit women.

988. Greeting, Corinne. "Tyranny of Women's Liberation," ETC., vol. 28 (Sept. 1971), pp. 357-361. Criticizes the label "Women's Liberation" for its negative connotations, and suggests that women truly dedicated to the movement should separate themselves from the term.

989. Grimke, Sarah M. LETTERS ON THE EQUALITY OF THE SEXES, AND THE CONDITION OF WOMEN. New York: Source Book Press, 1970. 128 pp. Reprint of the 1838 edition. The first serious discussion of women's rights by an American woman activist.

990. Gwyn, Sandra. "Woman." In Robert Fulford, David Godfrey, and Abraham Rotstein, READ CANADIAN: A BOOK ABOUT CANADIAN BOOKS. Toronto: James Lewis and Samuel, 1972, pp. 144-153. Discusses women in Canadian literature, nonfiction, the economy, education, and politics, with an excellent bibliography.

991. Hackett, Amy. "The German Women's Movement and Suffrage, 1890-1914: A Study of National Feminism." Pp. 354-386 in MODERN EUROPEAN SOCIAL HISTORY, edited by Robert J. Bezucha. Lexington, Mass.: D. C. Heath, 1972. Comparative study of the German feminist movement with the U.S. and British movements, concluding that the Germans placed minor emphasis on women's political rights.

992. Her Majesty's Stationery Office. CONVENTION OF THE POLITICAL RIGHTS OF WOMEN. London: H.M.S.O., 1967. Report of the convention.

993. Hopper, Janice H. "Paper on Latin American Women and Public Policy," cited in AMERICAN SOCIOLOGIST. McLean, Va.: Human Sciences Research, June 1971. 48 pp.

994. Horrell, Muriel, compiler. THE RIGHTS OF AFRICAN WOMEN: SOME SUGGESTED REFORMS. Johannesburg, S.A.: Institute of Race Relations, 1968. 18 pp.

995. "How Women Fare in Foreign Lands," AMERICAN ASSOCIATION OF UNIVERSITY WOMEN JOURNAL, (Oct. 1971), pp. 3 passim. Women from France, Lebanon, Nigeria, Argentina, Japan, the USSR, and India make statements on the status of women in their countries.

996. Howe, Florence, and Paul Lauter. THE CONSPIRACY OF THE YOUNG. New York: World, 1970. 399 pp. An examination of the inequalities in the social and political structure of the United States.

997. Hudson, K. MEN AND WOMEN, FEMINISM AND ANTI-FEMINISM TODAY. Devon, England: David and Charles, 1968. A survey of English attitudes.

998. Hynes, Maureen. A HISTORY OF THE RISE OF WOMEN'S CONSCIOUSNESS IN CANADA AND IN QUEBEC . . . WITH SOME CONCLUSIONS DRAWN CONCERNING THE STRUGGLE OF CANADIAN WOMEN TODAY. Toronto: Hogtown Press, 1971.

999. International Institute of Differing Civilizations. WOMEN'S ROLE IN THE DEVELOPMENT OF TROPICAL AND SUBTROPICAL COUNTRIES. Brussels: I.I.D.C., 1958. Report of the 31st meeting held in Brussels, September 1958.

1000. Katayama, Tetsu. WOMEN'S MOVEMENT IN JAPAN. Tokyo: Foreign Affairs Association of Japan, 1938.

1001. Kiba, Simon. "Les Femmes D'Afrique au Centre International du Mont Carmel en Israel," AFRIQUE NOUVELLE, no. 1260,(Sept.29, 1971). A conference in Haifa in which women from Africa, Asia, and Mediterranean lands discussed the role of women in the developing countries.

1002. Koedt, Anne, and Shulamith Firestone, eds. NOTES FROM THE THIRD YEAR: WOMEN'S LIBERATION. New York: Notes, 1971. 152 pp. Anthology of radical feminist topics ranging from the nineteenth century women's rights movement, women in literature, black feminism, children's books, prostitution, lesbianism, and legal inequities, to problems of the middle-aged, women in the labor force, the media, religion, etc.

1003. Komisar, Lucy. THE NEW FEMINISM. New York: Warner Paperback Library, 1971. 206 pp. A primer on the women's movement for teenagers, exploring the thoughts, ideas, and aspirations of young women searching for femininity and freedom.

1004. Korshunova, Y., and M. Rumyantseva. THE RIGHTS OF SOVIET WOMEN. Moscow: Trade Union Publishing House, 1962. 53 pp.

1005. Krasnopolskii, A., and G. Sverdlov. THE RIGHTS OF MOTHER AND CHILD IN THE USSR. Moscow: Foreign Languages Publishing House, 1953. 80 pp.

1006. Levy, Richard G. WHY WOMEN SHOULD RULE THE WORLD. New York: Vantage Press, 1952. 152 pp. Sees the destruction of the world if women are not permitted to rule.

1007. Lewis, Helen M. THE WOMAN MOVEMENT AND THE NEGRO MOVEMENT: PARALLEL STRUGGLES FOR RIGHTS. Charlottesville: Univ. of Virginia Press, 1949. 89 pp.

1008. Long, Priscilla, ed. THE NEW LEFT: A COLLECTION OF ESSAYS. Boston: Porter Sargent, 1969. Anthology of radical writing on the women's movement.

1009. Mandel, William. "Soviet Women and Their Self-Image," SCIENCE AND SOCIETY, vol. 35 (Fall 1971), pp. 286-310. Attempts to determine whether there is anything in the USSR today like the women's liberation movement.

1010. Mandle, Joan. "Women's Liberation: Humanizing Rather Than Polarizing," THE ANNALS, vol. 397 (Sept. 1971), pp. 118-128.

1011. Mayreader, Rosa. A SURVEY OF THE WOMEN PROBLEM. Translated from German by Herman Scheffauer. New York: Doran, 1913. 275 pp. Well-developed philosophy of feminism, advocating the freedom of feminine individuality to express and realize itself in a world of fact rather than in a fancified world of outworn ideals.

1012. Mestre, Carmen. "La Emancipacion de La Mujer: Conquista o Alienacion?" [The Emancipation of Women: Conquest or Alienation?] , CUADERNOS PARA EL DIALOGO (Madrid), no. 95 (Aug. 1971), pp. 11-13. Discovers that the fight for women's emancipation may not be a revolutionary one, although there is a need for radical change.

1013. Michelet, Jules. THE WOMEN OF THE FRENCH REVOLUTION. Phila-
      delphia: H. G. Baird, 1855. 371 pp. Classic study of the role of the
      women in the French Revolution.
1014. Mill, John Stuart. ON LIBERTY, REPRESENTATIVE GOVERNMENT,
      AND THE SUBJECTION OF WOMEN. London: Oxford Univ. Press,
      1869, 1912. Three seminal essays exploring the social and moral ques-
      tions concerning women's rights and representation.
1015. Mill, John Stuart, and Harriet Taylor Mill. ESSAY ON SEX EQUALITY.
      Introduction by Alice Rossi. Chicago: Univ. of Chicago Press, 1970.
      242 pp. Mill and his wife denied the traditional belief that women's
      character was the opposite of men's. Both pleaded for less submission,
      less control of each other.
1016. Millard, Betty. WOMAN AGAINST MYTH. New York: International
      Publishers, 1948. A communist view of women's efforts to achieve
      equality in the United States.
1017. Miller, Casey, and Kate Swift. "De-Sexing the Language," CURRENT,
      vol. 138 (Mar. 1972), pp. 43-47.
1018. Mitchell, Juliet. WOMEN'S ESTATE. Baltimore: Penguin Books, 1973.
      An historical summary of women's inequality.
1019. Miyake, Yujiro. "The Woman Movement in Japan," THE JAPAN MAGA-
      ZINE, vol. 12 (Oct. 1921), pp. 238-240.
1020. Morgan, Robin, ed. SISTERHOOD IS POWERFUL. New York: Random
      House, 1971. 602 pp. Excellent anthology of the women's liberation
      movement. Fifty-seven of the 75 articles are published for the first time.
1021. Ogg, Elizabeth. WHY SOME WOMEN STAY SINGLE. New York: Public
      Affairs Committee, 1951. 31 pp. Explains why there are many women
      who have never married and stresses the need for contributions by
      women to the nation, outside marriage and children.
1022. Pan-American Union. DERECHOS CIVILES Y POLITICOS DE LA
      MUJER DE AMERICA, PRIMERA PARTE: DERECHOS POLITICOS
      [Civil and Political Rights of the American Woman, First Part: Political
      Rights]. Report presented to the 10th Inter-American Conference.
      Washington, D.C.: Pan-American Union, 1954. Emphasizes the dicho-
      tomy between the Roman legal system and English canon law and its
      influence on granting political rights to women.
1023. ———. INFORME PRESENTADO POR LA COMISION INTERAMERI-
      CANA DE MUJERES AL SEMINARIO DE LAS NACIONES UNIDAS
      SOBRE PARTICIPACION DE LA MUJER EN LA VIDA PUBLICA.
      Bogota, Colombia, 1959. Washington, D.C.: Pan-American Union, 1959.
1024. ———, Tenth Inter-American Conference. "Participation of Women in the
      Organs of the Inter-American System," FINAL ACT. Caracas, Venezuela,
      1954. Washington, D.C.: Pan-American Union, 1954. 66 pp.
1025. Petrova, L., and S. Gilevskaya, eds. EQUALITY OF WOMEN IN THE
      USSR: MATERIALS OF INTERNATIONAL SEMINAR. Moscow:
      Foreign Languages Publishing House, 1957. 362 pp. Results of a
      symposium held between September 15 and October 1, 1956.
1026. Pollard, Penelope. "The Inequality of Cuban Women in the Nineteenth
      and Early Twentieth Century." Unpublished paper prepared for the
      Pacific Coast Conference of Latin American Studies session, The
      Female in Latin America: Her Role Past and Present, Monterrey,

California, October 27, 1972. A study of the isolation and segregation of Cuban women from men.

1027. Racz, Elizabeth. "The Women's Rights Movement in the French Revolution," SCIENCE AND SOCIETY, vol. 16, no. 2 (Spring 1952), pp. 28-32, 64.

1028. Ramelson, Marian. THE PETTICOAT REBELLION: A CENTURY OF STRUGGLE FOR WOMEN'S RIGHTS. London: Lawrence and Wishart, 1967. 208 pp.

1029. Ravenel, Florence Leftwich. WOMEN AND THE FRENCH TRADITION. New York: Macmillan, 1918. 234 pp. Antifeminist viewpoint.

1030. Rhondda, Viscountess. NOTES ON THE WAR. London: Macmillan, 1937. 221 pp. Essays by Lady Rhondda, editor of the progressive weekly, TIME AND TIDE, concerning women and their rights.

1031. Richmond, Mary E., and Fred S. Hall. MARRIAGE AND THE STATE: BASED UPON FIELD STUDIES OF THE PRESENT DAY ADMINISTRATION OF MARRIAGE LAWS IN THE UNITED STATES. New York: Russell Sage Foundation, 1929. 395 pp.

1032. Robins, Elizabeth. WAY STATIONS. New York: Dodd, 1913. 371 pp. Speeches and essays by a prominent English member of the woman's movement.

1033. Roper, Elmo. "Women in America, The *Fortune* Survey," part 1, FORTUNE MAGAZINE, vol. 34, no. 2 (Aug. 1946), pp. 5-14; part 2, vol. 34, no. 3, (Sept. 1946) pp. 5-6. Presents a detailed picture of attitudes toward women in the United States showing that men and women agree more than not in their appraisal of their own and the opposite sex.

1034. Rosenberg, Marie Barovic. "Affirmative Action—Equal Employment Opportunity: Evolving Public Policy." Madison, Wis.: Institute of Governmental Affairs, Univ. of Wisconsin—Extension, 1975. Bibliography traces development of concepts, legislation, and practices.

1035. Ross, Susan Deller. THE RIGHTS OF WOMEN. New York: Avon Books, 1973. One of a series of American Civil Liberties Union Handbooks.

1036. Rotzoll, Christa, et al. EMANZIPATION UND EHE [Emancipation and Marriage]. Munich: Delp, 1968. The rights of women in society, employment, marriage, with bibliography.

1037. Rover, C. THE PUNCH BOOK OF WOMEN'S RIGHTS. London: Hutchinson, 1967. Overview of British brand of humor centering around women's rights.

1038. Rowbotham, Sheila. WOMEN: THE WHOLE PEOPLE QUESTION. London: May Day Manifesto, 1969.

1039. Royden, Agnes M., and Victor Gollancz, eds. THE MAKING OF WOMEN: OXFORD ESSAYS IN FEMINISM. London: G. Allen and Unwin, 1917.

1040. Rugg, Winnifred King. UNAFRAID: A LIFE OF ANNE HUTCHINSON. Boston: Houghton, 1930. 263 pp. The story of the woman who first raised the question of equal status for women in New England.

1041. Russell, Dora, Harriet Unwin, and Emma Goldman. IN A MAN'S WORLD. London: Freedom Press, 1965, reprint. 31 pp. Four articles on the woman question.

1042. Sartin, Pierrette. LA FEMME LIBEREE? Paris: Stock, 1968. 288 pp. Women's rights, with a bibliography.

1043. Schneir, Miriam, ed. FEMINISM: THE ESSENTIAL HISTORICAL WRITINGS. New York: Random House, 1972. 360 pp. Collection of essays, fiction, and memoirs of feminist writers, including Wollstonecraft, Stanton, Anthony, and Sanger. Must for the reader or specialist in feminism.

1044. Scott, Ann Firor, ed. THE AMERICAN WOMAN: WHO WAS SHE? Englewood Cliffs, N.J.: Prentice-Hall, 1971. Provocative excerpts from the writings of many women and men on the history of the women's movement. Informative, but no bibliography.

1045. Serebrennikov, G. N. THE POSITION OF WOMEN IN THE USSR. London: Gollancz, 1937. 288 pp. Changes in the status of Soviet women.

1046. Sinclair, Andrew. THE BETTER HALF: THE EMANCIPATION OF THE AMERICAN WOMAN. New York: Harper and Row, 1965. 401 pp. A history of the struggle for equality, privilege, suffrage, and dignity for the American woman.

1047. Soong, Ching-ling. "Women's Liberation in China," PEKING REVIEW, vol. 15 (Feb. 11, 1972), pp. 6-7. By the widow of Dr. Sun Yat-sen.

1048. Stanton, Theodore, ed. THE WOMAN QUESTION IN EUROPE. New York: Source Book Press, 1970. Reprint of the 1884 edition. 496 pp. Essays summarizing the social and legal status of women in every European country.

1049. Strachey, Rachel Conn (Costelloe). THE CAUSE. London: G. Bell Sons, 1928. 429 pp. American title: STRUGGLE: THE STIRRING STORY OF A WOMAN'S ADVANCE IN ENGLAND. Brief history of the woman's rights movement in England.

1050. ———. OUR FREEDOM AND ITS RESULTS. London: Leonard and Virginia Woolf (Hogarth Press), 1936. The story of changes in law, employment, sex morality, and social and public life in England with respect to women.

1051. Swaminathan, V. S. "Women's Movement in India," CONTEMPORARY REVIEW, vol. 174 (July 1948), pp. 26-30. Changes in women's rights during the first year of Partition.

1052. Thompson, Mary Lou, ed. VOICES OF THE NEW FEMINISM. Boston: Beacon Press, 1970. 246 pp. Articles covering the history of the feminist movement, its ideology, problems, and goals, with programs for the future. Partially annotated bibliography section.

1053. Todd, Rev. John. WOMAN'S RIGHTS. Boston: Lee and Shepard, 1867. Rather antifeminist in its viewpoint.

1054. United Nations, CHARTER OF THE UNITED NATIONS AND STATUTES OF THE INTERNATIONAL COURT OF JUSTICE. New York: Department of Public Information, United Nations, 1945. The United Nations' position on the recognition of women's political rights is confirmed by two basic documents: the Charter itself and also the Universal Declaration of Human Rights.

1055. ———. CIVIC AND POLITICAL EDUCATION OF WOMEN. New York: United Nations Publications, 1971. 87 pp. An account of the work of the UN in advancing civil and political rights for women around the world.

1056. ———. THE CONVENTION ON THE POLITICAL RIGHTS OF WOMEN, HISTORY AND COMMENTARY. New York: United Nations, Department of Economic and Social Affairs, 1955.

1057. ———. RESOURCES AVAILABLE TO MEMBER STATES FOR THE ADVANCEMENT OF WOMEN. New York: United Nations, 1971. 82 pp.

1058. U.S. Department of Labor. THE REPORT OF PRESIDENT NIXON'S TASK FORCE ON WOMEN'S RIGHTS AND RESPONSIBILITIES. Washington, D.C.: SUDOC, GPO, 1970.

1059. Vavich, Dee Ann. "The Japanese Woman's Movement: Ichikawa Fusae," MONUMENTA NIPPONICA, vol. 22 (1967), pp. 403-436.

1060. "Vietnamese Women," VIETNAMESE STUDIES, no. 10. Hanoi: Democratic People's Republic of Vietnam, 1966. Available from China Books and Periodicals, San Francisco, California.

1061. Williams, Fannie Barrier. "Present Status and Intellectual Progress of Colored Women." Address delivered before the Congress of Representative Women, World's Congress Auxiliary of the World's Columbian Exposition. Chicago, n.p., 1898. 15 pp.

1062. Williams, Maxine, and Pamela Newman. BLACK WOMEN'S LIBERATION. New York: Pathfinder Press, 1972. 16 pp. Outlines the rise of the black woman's liberation movement and explains its relationship to the other struggles for social change.

1063. Wilson, B. M. "The Position of Women in South Africa," THE EAST AND THE WEST, vol. 14 (1916), pp. 61-68. Contemporary account of the changes in African women's rights.

1064. Wipper, Audrey. "Equal Rights for Women in Kenya?" MODERN AFRICAN STUDIES, vol. 9, no. 3 (1971), pp. 429-442.

1065. Wollstonecraft, Mary. A VINDICATION OF THE RIGHTS OF WOMEN. New York: Source Book Press, 1970. Reprint of the 1792 edition. 471 pp. Feminist classic.

1066. WOMEN IN CHINA TODAY. Peking: All-China Democratic Women's Federation, 1952. Series of ten pamphlets describing the Chinese woman's change in status, new roles, and responsibilities.

1067. WOMEN IN OUR WORLD. Sydney, Australia: Current Book Distributors, 1947. 32 pp. Pamphlet sponsored by the Australian Communist party.

1068. "Women in Politics: Catholic Collegiate Attitudes," SOCIAL ORDER, vol. 3 (Oct. 1953), pp. 361-366.

1069. Women's International Democratic Federation. FOR THEIR RIGHTS AS MOTHERS, WORKERS, CITIZENS. Berlin: Author, 1952. 62 pp. An international look at the rights of women.

1070. Woodward, Helen Beal. THE BOLD WOMEN. Freeport, N.Y.: Books for Libraries Press, 1971. Reprint of 1953 edition. 373 pp. Anthology of brief biographical episodes in the lives of nineteenth century feminists, such as Frances Wright, Delia Bacon, Kate Field, Eliza W. Farnham, etc., with excellent documentation of the historical roots of modern feminist protests.

1071. Yamakawa, Kikue. "Are Japanese Women Advancing?" THE JAPAN MAGAZINE, vol. 12 (Dec. 1921), pp. 358-360.

1072. Ying-chao Teng. WOMEN OF CHINA BUILD FOR PEACE. Peking: All-China Democratic Women's Federation, 1952. 26 pp.

1073. Young, Louise M. "The American Woman at Mid-Century," AMERICAN REVIEW, vol. 2 (Dec. 1961), pp. 121-138. Review essay on the research and the literature in politics up to 1961.

1074. ———, ed. "Women's Opportunities and Responsibilities," THE ANNALS, vol. 251 (May 1947), pp. 1-185. Entire issue devoted to women's rights, edited by author.
1075. Yu-lan Lu. "Liberation of Women," PEKING REVIEW, no. 10 (March 10, 1972), pp. 10-12.

2. *Feminism: Equal Rights—Committees on the Status of Women*

Living movements do not come of committees.
—Cardinal Newman

1076. Bilshai, Vera. THE STATUS OF WOMEN IN THE SOVIET UNION. Moscow: Foreign Languages Publishing House, 1957. 106 pp.
1077. Boatwright, Eleanor. "The Political and Civil Status of Women in Georgia, 1783-1860," GEORGIA HISTORICAL QUARTERLY, vol. 25 (Dec. 1941).
1078. Canada. REPORT OF THE ROYAL COMMISSION ON THE STATUS OF WOMEN IN CANADA. Ottawa, Information Canada, 1970. 346 pp.
1079. Citizen's Advisory Council on the Status of Women. "Women in 1970." ERIC. Washington, D.C.: SUDOC, GPO, March 1971. 52 pp. Highlights the advances made by women in 1970; originally a memo presented on the proposed equal rights amendment to the U.S. Constitution.
1080. D.-Johnson, Micheline. HISTORY OF THE STATUS OF WOMEN IN THE PROVINCE OF QUEBEC. Royal Commission on the Status of Women in Canada. Ottawa, 1971. Good on the powerful role of the single woman in Quebec society.
1081. Gallaher, Ruth A. LEGAL AND POLITICAL STATUS OF WOMEN IN IOWA: AN HISTORICAL ACCOUNT OF THE RIGHTS OF WOMEN IN IOWA FROM 1838 to 1919. Iowa City: State Historical Society, 1918. 300 pp.
1082. Kok, G.H.S. "Rapport sur la Situation Politique, Sociale, Civique de la Femme en Europe." Strasbourg, France: Conseil de l'Europe, 1967.
1083. MacClellan, Margaret E. HISTORY OF WOMAN'S RIGHTS IN CANADA. Royal Commission on the Status of Women in Canada. Ottawa, 1971. A selection of bills enacted to improve the status of women.
1084. Marton, Elizabeth Homer. "Raising the Status of Canadian Women," QUEEN'S QUARTERLY, vol. 78 (Summer 1971), pp. 30-38.
1085. Mead, Margaret, and Frances B. Kaplan, eds. AMERICAN WOMEN: THE REPORT OF THE PRESIDENT'S COMMISSION ON THE STATUS OF WOMEN AND OTHER PUBLICATIONS OF THE COMMISSION. New York: Scribners, 1965. 274 pp. Reports of seven committees investigating women's civil and political rights, employment, education, protective labor legislation, and other related aspects.
1086. National Conference of Governors' Commissions on the Status of Women. 1968: A TIME FOR ACTION. 4th Conference. Washington, D.C.: U.S. Women's Bureau, 1969. 97 pp. Reports of three conferences, 1966, 1967, and 1968, available from SUDOC, GPO. Washington, D.C.
1087. New Hampshire State Commission on the Status of Women. REPORT OF THE HEARINGS HELD BY THE NEW HAMPSHIRE COMMISSION ON THE STATUS OF WOMEN, Spring 1971. Resumé of hearings

consisting of detailed outlines of recognized areas of discrimination and rank ordering of priorities for action.

1088. New York City Commission on Human Rights. WOMEN'S ROLE IN CONTEMPORARY SOCIETY. New York: Avon Books, 1972. Testimony by Margaret Mead, Shirley Chisholm, Bella Abzug, Betty Friedan, Gloria Steinem, Kate Millett, Sally Kempton, etc., with recommendations and findings.

1089. Organization of American States, Inter-American Commission of Women. HISTORICAL REVIEW ON THE RECOGNITION OF THE POLITICAL RIGHTS OF AMERICAN WOMEN. Washington, D.C.: General Secretariat of the Organization of American States, 1965. 29 pp.

1090. Pan-American Union, Ninth International Conference of American States, Bogota, Columbia, 1948. FINAL ACT. Approval of the resolution to establish the OAS Secretariat General for an Inter-American Commission of Women to study the economic position of working women in Latin America and the United States. Available from the Pan-American Union, Washington, D.C.

1091. ———. INFORME DE LA COMISION INTERAMERICANA DE MUJERES A LA NOVENA CONFERENCIA INTERNACIONAL AMERICANA SOBRA DERECHOS CIVILES Y POLITICOS DE LA MUJER. Washington, D.C.: Pan-American Union, 1948.

1092. ———. INFORME SOBRE DERECHOS POLITICOS Y CIVILES DE LA MUJER PARA LA ACCION DE LA SEPTIMA CONFERENCIA INTERNACIONAL AMERICANA DE ACUERDO CON LA RESOLUCION DE LA SEXTA CONFERENCIA. Washington, D.C.: Pan-American Union, 1933.

1093. ———. REPORT OF THE CIVIL AND POLITICAL RIGHTS OF WOMEN IN THE AMERICAN REPUBLICS (SUMMARY). Prepared for the 11th Inter-American Conference. Washington, D.C.: Pan-American Union, 1959.

1094. ———. Inter-American Commission of Women. REPORT PRESENTED TO THE THIRTEENTH SESSION OF THE UNITED NATIONS COMMISSION OF THE STATUS OF WOMEN, New York: Mar. 1959. Washington, D.C.: Pan-American Union, 1959.

1095. Rothman, Betsy. "Women in Canada," SOCIAL EDUCATION, vol. 35 (Oct. 1971), pp. 617-619. Clear and vivid picture of the situation in an interview with Anne Francis.

1096. Sandlund, Maj-Britt. THE STATUS OF WOMEN IN SWEDEN. Stockholm: Swedish Institute, 1968. Report to the United Nations, 1968. 22 pp. Changes in women's status brought about by Swedish legislation.

1097. Schlesinger, Benjamin. "Status of Women in Canada: Summary of Commission Recommendation," FAMILY COORDINATOR, vol. 20 (July 1971), pp. 253-258. Presents 167 recommendations dealing with sex education, poverty, job discrimination, equal status, and representation for women in politics.

1098. United Nations, Commission on the Status of Women. CONSTITUTIONS, ELECTORAL LAWS AND OTHER LEGAL INSTRUMENTS RELATING TO THE POLITICAL RIGHTS OF WOMEN. New York: United Nations, 1968. 147 pp.

1099. ———. "The Status of the Unmarried Mother: Law and Practice." New York: United Nations, 1971. Study showing that discrimination against unmarried mothers still exists in law and fact in many countries.

1100. ———. "Implementation of the Declaration on the Elimination of Discrimination Against Women." New York: United Nations, 1971. Measures that have been taken to implement the Declaration and the problems faced by the unmarried mother and her child.

1101. ———. "International Instruments and National Standards Relating to the Status of Women." New York: United Nations, 1972. Study showing to what extent existing international conventions contain provisions relating to women's rights.

1102. ———. WHAT THE UNITED NATIONS IS DOING FOR THE STATUS OF WOMEN. New York: United Nations, 1949.

1103. U.S. Citizen's Advisory Council. Task Force on Family Law and Policy. REPORT TO THE CITIZEN'S ADVISORY COUNCIL ON THE STATUS OF WOMEN. Washington, D.C.: SUDOC, GPO, 1968, 69 pp.

1104. U.S. Interdepartmental Committee on the Status of Women. REPORT ON PROGRESS ON THE STATUS OF WOMEN. Annual volumes, beginning 1963. Available from Washington, D.C.: SUDOC, GPO.

1105. U.S. President's Commission on the Status of Women. THE AMERICAN WOMEN. Washington, D.C.: SUDOC, GPO, 1963. 86 pp. See also: Mead, Margaret, and Frances B. Kaplan.

1106. U.S. President's Commission on the Status of Women, Committee on Federal Employment Policies and Practices. REPORT OF THE COMMITTEE ON FEDERAL EMPLOYMENT TO THE PRESIDENT'S COMMISSION ON THE STATUS OF WOMEN. Washington, D.C.: SUDOC, GPO, 1963. A report on women in the U.S. Civil Service.

1107. U.S. President's Commission on the Status of Women, Committee on Home and Community. REPORT. Washington, D.C.: SUDOC, GPO, 1963. Women in the home and community, with bibliographic footnotes.

1108. U.S. President's Commission on the Status of Women, Committee on Private Employment. REPORT OF THE COMMITTEE ON PRIVATE EMPLOYMENT TO THE PRESIDENT'S COMMISSION ON THE STATUS OF WOMEN. Washington, D.C.: SUDOC, GPO, 1964.

1109. U.S. President's Commission on the Status of Women, Committee on Protective Labor Legislation. REPORT TO THE PRESIDENT'S COMMISSION ON THE STATUS OF WOMEN. Washington, D.C.: SUDOC, GPO, 1963. 38 pp.

1110. U.S. President's Commission on the Status of Women, Committee on Social Insurance and Taxes. REPORT Washington, D.C.: SUDOC, GPO, 1963. 81 pp.

1111. U.S. President's Commission on the Status of Women, Committe on Civil and Political Rights. REPORT OF THE COMMITTEE ON CIVIL AND POLITICAL RIGHTS TO THE PRESIDENT'S COMMISSION ON THE STATUS OF WOMEN. Washington, D.C.: SUDOC, GPO, 1964. 83 pp.

1112. U.S. President's Commission on the Status of Women. A REPORT. Washington, D.C.: SUDOC, GPO, 1963. 51 pp.

1113. U.S., President's Commission on the Status of Women, Task Force on Women's Rights and Responsibilities. A MATTER OF SIMPLE JUSTICE: THE REPORT. Washington, D.C.: SUDOC, GPO, 1970.

1114. Washington State, Governor's Commission on the Status of Women. REPORT. Olympia, Wash.: Office of the Governor, Dec. 1963. 40 pp. One of the first typical Governor's commissions set up to evaluate the status of women.

1115. Washington State, Governor's Commission on the Status of Women, Interagency Committee on the Status of Women. INTERIM REPORT. Olympia, Wash.: Office of the Governor, Oct. 1970. 18 pp.

1116. Washington State, Governor's Commission on the Status of Women. THE STATUS OF WOMEN IN THE STATE OF WASHINGTON. Olympia, Wash.: Office of the Governor, 1963. 40 pp. Report relating to areas of concern to women. Typical of many state reviews conducted to determine the status of women.

3. Feminism: Equal Rights—Marriage and Divorce

Nature has given women so much power that the law has very wisely given them little.
—Samuel Johnson

1117. Anonymous. AN ESSAY ON MARRIAGE: OR THE LAWFULNESS OF DIVORCE. Philadelphia, 1788. In THE COLONIAL AMERICAN FAMILY. New York: Arno Press, 1972. The first American effort to confront the problem of divorce in a republican society.

1118. Anonymous. SHOULD WOMEN OBEY?: A PROTEST AGAINST IMPROPER MATRIMONIAL AND PRENATAL CONDITIONS, SHOWING CAUSES, PREVENTION AND REMEDY OF NEEDLESS INHARMONIES, UNHAPPINESS, ETC. Chicago: Ernest Lommis, 1900. 144 pp. The author supports equal rights for women in all spheres and protests against the double standard.

1119. Carlier, Auguste. MARRIAGE IN THE UNITED STATES. New York: Arno Press, 1972. Reprint of the Boston, 1867 edition. Courtship, styles of domestic life, divorce, general morality, and democratic institutions and their effects on American life.

1120. Center for a Woman's Own Name, compiler. BOOKLET FOR WOMEN WHO WISH TO DETERMINE THEIR OWN NAMES AFTER MARRIAGE. Barrington, Ill.: Center for a Woman's Own Name, 1974. 56 pp. A historical review of the name issue, referrals to the common law, statutes, court decisions, and court procedures.

1121. Curry, Douglas L. "Personal Jurisdiction in Divorce Proceedings: Stucky v. Stucky, 186 Nebraska, 636 (1971)" NEBRASKA LAW REVIEW, vol. 51 (Fall 1971), pp. 159-171.

1122. Deech, Ruth L. "Comparative Approaches to Divorce: Canada and England," THE MODERN LAW REVIEW, vol. 35 (Mar. 1972), pp. 113-128.

1123. Djamour, J. MALAY KINSHIP AND MARRIAGE IN SINGAPORE. London: n.p., 1959.

1124. Edmiston, Susan. "How to Write Your Own Marriage Contract," MS. MAGAZINE (Spring 1972), pp. 66-72. Also in NEW YORK MAGAZINE, vol. 4 (Dec. 20, 1971), pp. 66-72.

1125. Freeman, M.D.A. "Adultery and Intolerability: Goodrich v. Goodrich," THE MODERN LAW REVIEW, vol. 35 (Jan. 1972), pp. 98-103.

1126. Gorecki, Jan. DIVORCE IN POLAND: A CONTRIBUTION TO THE SOCIOLOGY OF LAW. The Hague: Mouton, 1970. 156 pp.

1127. Greene, Felix. "A Divorce Trial in China." Boston: New England Free Press, n.d., n.p.

1128. Her Majesty's Stationery Office, Royal Commission on Marriage and Divorce. REPORT, 1951-1955. London: H.M.S.O., 1956. 405 pp.

1129. Lichtenberger, J. P. DIVORCE: A SOCIAL INTERPRETATION. New York: Arno Press, 1972. Reprint of 1931 edition. Wide-ranging study of divorce in American and other societies.

1130. "Marriage—Grounds for Firing a Woman?" SOVIET WOMAN, no. 5 (May 1960), p. 12.

1131. McAleavy, Henry. "Some Aspects of Marriage and Divorce in Communist China." Pp. 34-38 in FAMILY LAW IN ASIA AND AFRICA, edited by J.N.D. Anderson. London: Allen and Unwin, 1968.

1132. Meijer, M. J. MARRIAGE LAW AND POLICY IN THE CHINESE PEOPLE'S REPUBLIC. Hong Kong: Univ. of Hong Kong Press, 1971. How the PRC's Marriage Law has been used to destroy the old "feudal" marriage institutions and to build a new political and social morality.

1133. Pederson, Inger Margrete. "Status of Women in Private Law," THE ANNALS, vol. 375 (Jan. 1968), pp. 44-57. Deals with the problems of protecting women's rights, especially in the areas of marriage and divorce law.

1134. Phillips, Arthur, and Henry F. Morris. MARRIAGE LAWS IN AFRICA. London: Oxford Univ. Press, 1971. 229 pp.

1135. Pilpel, Harriet, and Theodora Zavin. YOUR MARRIAGE AND THE LAW. New York: Collier, 1952; revised 1965.

1136. Rac, Frank. "The Modern Theory and Practice of Antenuptial Agreements," THE JOHN MARSHALL JOURNAL OF PRACTICE AND PROCEDURE, vol. 5 (Winter 1971), pp. 179-204.

1137. Seidelson, David E. "Interest Analysis and Divorce Actions," BUFFALO LAW REVIEW, vol. 21 (Winter 1972), pp. 315-337. Perceptive analysis of the basis of court jurisdiction in cases where husbands and wives may be domiciled in different states; important work on conflict of laws.

1138. Smith, Raymond. "Recognition of Foreign Divorce Decrees—the Problem of Retroactivity," INTERNATIONAL AND COMPARATIVE LAW QUARTERLY, vol. 20 (July 1971), pp. 557-563.

1139. Spargo, John. SOCIALISM AND MOTHERHOOD. New York: Huebsch, 1914. 128 pp. Allays the fear that socialism is a threat to monogamic marriage and private family life, despite the theories of love and marriage by sociologists such as Bebel and Bax.

1140. Sverdlov, G. M. LEGAL RIGHTS OF THE SOVIET FAMILY: MARRIAGE, MOTHERHOOD AND FAMILY IN SOVIET LAW. London, 1945.

1141. Trumball, Benjamin. AN APPEAL TO THE PUBLIC: ESPECIALLY TO THE LEARNED, WITH RESPECT TO THE UNLAWFULNESS OF DIVORCE. New Haven, 1788, in THE COLONIAL AMERICAN FAMILY. New York: Arno Press, 1972. Edited by David J. Rothman and Sheila H. Rothman.

1142. United Nations. NATIONALITY OF MARRIED WOMEN. Revised. New York: United Nations Publications, 1971. 121 pp. Figures and breakdowns of marriage and divorce in the world (conflicting laws).

1143. ———. CONVENTIONS ON THE NATIONALITY OF MARRIED WOMEN. New York: United Nations Publications, 1971. 75 pp.

1144. Wilner, Charles. ALIMONY: THE AMERICAN TRAGEDY. New York: Vantage Press, 1952. 329 pp. Sees present-day feminism as being at the heart of today's alimony laws, and recommends that men reestablish themselves as the head of the family.

4. Feminism: Equal Rights—Property

List, you shall hear the gifts of price that lie
Gathered and bound within the marriage tie.
                    —Cardinal Newman

1145. Doukhan-Landau, Leah. "Husbands and Wives as Co-Owners of Immovable Property," ISRAEL LAW REVIEW, vol. 6 (Oct. 1971), pp. 487-516.

1146. Ebbott, John F. "Allocatory Trusts May Cause the Marital Deduction to Be Elusive," JOURNAL OF TAXATION, vol. 36 (Jan. 1972), pp. 11-15. Deals with property rights of women regarding inheritance.

1147. Moore, Malcolm A. "Taking Advantage of a Community Property Estates Marital Deduction Possibilities," JOURNAL OF TAXATION, vol. 36 (Jan. 1972), pp. 8-10.

1148. Richards, Britten D. "Discrimination Against Married Couples Under Present Income Tax Law," TAXES: THE TAX MAGAZINE, vol. 49 (Sept. 1971), pp. 526-531. Discusses the way in which rates work to the disadvantage of married couples.

5. Feminism: Equal Rights—Legal Status

It is a crime for a woman to engage in prostitution but not for her customer to use her services. She is breaking the law, it seems, while he is only doing what comes naturally.
                    —Faith A. Seidenberg

1149. Abbott, Edith, and Sophonisba P. Breckinridge. THE ADMINISTRATION OF THE AID-TO-MOTHERS LAW IN ILLINOIS. Children's Bureau Publication, no. 82 (Washington, D.C., 1921). In THE FAMILY AND SOCIAL SERVICE IN THE 1920'S. New York: Arno Press, 1972. The fate of this program and a look at public relief practices for women and children in the 1920s.

1150. Bayles, George James. WOMAN AND THE LAW. New York, 1901. Reprinted by Greenwood Press, Westport, Conn., 1971. 274 pp. An early twentieth-century treatise on women's legal rights.

1151. Breckinridge, Sophonisba P. MARRIAGE AND THE CIVIC RIGHTS OF WOMEN: SEPARATE DOMICILE AND INDEPENDENT CITIZENSHIP. Chicago: Univ. of Chicago Press, 1931. 158 pp.

1152. ———. "Neglected Widowhood in the Juvenile Court," THE AMERICAN JOURNAL OF SOCIOLOGY, July 1910.

1153. Brown, Barbara A., Thomas I. Emerson, Gail Falk, and Ann E. Freedman. "The Equal Rights Amendment: A Constitutional Basis for Equal Rights for Women," THE YALE LAW JOURNAL, vol. 80, no. 5 (April 1971), pp. 871-985. Thorough review of the need for constitutional legislation on equal rights.

1154. Cassell, Kay Ann. "The Legal Status of Women," LIBRARY JOURNAL, vol. 96 (Sept. 1971), pp. 2600-2603. Looks at protective laws and how they actually allow discrimination against some women.

1155. Chisholm, Shirley. "Racism and Anti-Feminism," THE BLACK SCHOLAR, vol. 1, no. 3-4 (Jan.-Feb. 1970), pp. 40-45. Laws can be used to provide protection and to begin the process of evolutionary change by forcing the insensitive majority to reexamine its unconscious attitudes.

1156. David, Pauline G. "Divorce—Constitutionality of a Residency Require- ment in a State Divorce Law (Wymelenberg v. Syman)," DICKINSON LAW REVIEW, vol. 76 (Fall 1971), pp. 183-196.

1157. Davidson, Kenneth M., Ruth B. Ginsburg, and Herma H. Kay. SEX-BASED DISCRIMINATION: TEXT, CASES, AND MATERIALS. St. Paul, Minn.: West, 1974. 1031 pp. The most current major legal American text on the subject.

1158. Dilts, Thomas H. "Sex-Plus: The Failure of the Attempt to Subvert the Sex Provision of the Civil Rights Act of 1964," GONZAGA LAW RE- VIEW, vol. 7 (Fall 1971), pp. 83-105.

1159. Fishman, Nathaniel. MARRIED WOMAN'S BILL OF RIGHTS. New York: Liveright, 1943. 282 pp. Explains many points of American law which may affect the married woman.

1160. Francis, Philip. LEGAL STATUS OF WOMEN. Legal Almanac Series, no. 53. New York: Oceana Publications, 1963. 92 pp. Survey of U.S. political and civil rights, contracts, debts, property rights, inheritance, and marriage and divorce rights.

1161. Green, Edith. "Omnibus Post-Secondary Education Act of 1970," CON- GRESSIONAL RECORD, HR 16098, 1970. Would amend Title VI, Sec. 601, and Title VII, Sec. 702, of the Civil Rights Act of 1964; Sec. 104 of the Civil Rights Act of 1957, and Sec. 13(a) of the Fair Labor Stan- dards Act of 1938, to strengthen the provisions against discrimination on grounds of sex. Oregon Congresswoman.

1162. Grossman, Joel B., and Richard S. Wells. CONSTITUTIONAL LAW AND JUDICIAL POLICY MAKING. New York: Wiley, 1972. Especially pp. 810-822, dealing with the constitutional rights of women; articles by Kanowitz, P. Murray, Eastwood, and others.

1163. Hardie, Keir. THE CITIZENSHIP OF WOMEN. London: Independent Labor Party Press, 1906. Leading Labor parliamentarian and one of the founders of the London School of Economics.

1164. Heide, Wilma Scott. "Feminism: The Sine Qua Non for a Just Society," VITAL SPEECHES, vol. 38 (1972), pp. 403-409. The Equal Rights Amendment and why there is opposition to it.

1165. Hoyt v. Florida, 386 U.S. 57 (1961). Case in which the Supreme Court up- held the constitutionality of a Florida statute exempting women from jury duty unless they volunteer for it.

1166. Hufstedler, Shirley M. "Crinolines, Courts, and Cleavers," WOMEN LAWYERS JOURNAL, Fall 1969.

1167. Javits, Jacob K. "Women's Lib in Congress," ESQUIRE, vol. 76 (Oct. 1971), pp. 76+. States reasons for the defeat of the Equal Rights Amendment earlier in Congress.
1168. Jessup, Henry Wynans. LAW FOR WIVES AND DAUGHTERS: THEIR RIGHTS AND THEIR OBLIGATIONS. New York: Macmillan, 1927, 208 pp.
1169. Johnson, Julia T., compiler. SOCIAL LEGISLATION FOR WOMEN. New York: H. W. Wilson, 1926. 142 pp.
1170. Johnston, John D., and Charles Knapp. "Sex Discrimination by Law: A Study in Judicial Perspective," NEW YORK UNIVERSITY LAW REVIEW, vol. 46 (Oct. 1971), pp. 675-747. The authors analyze many cases in which the courts have dealt with sex discrimination by law, and conclude that the judicial record in this area has ranged from "poor to abominable."
1171. Kanowitz, Leo. "Sex-Based Discrimination in American Law: I. The Law and the Single Girl," ST. LOUIS UNIVERSITY LAW JOURNAL, vol. 11 (Spring 1967); II. "The Law and the Married Woman," vol. 12, no. 1 (Fall 1967), p. 3.
1172. ———. SEX ROLES IN LAW AND SOCIETY: CASES AND MATERIALS. Albuquerque: Univ. of New Mexico Press, 1973.
1173. ———. "Title VII of the 1964 Civil Rights Act and the Equal Pay Act of 1963," HASTINGS LAW REVIEW, vol. 20 (Nov. 1968), pp. 305-360.
1174. ———. WOMEN AND THE LAW: THE UNFINISHED REVOLUTION. Albuquerque: Univ. of New Mexico Press, 1969. 312 pp. First major synthesis of legal status of women, with excellent bibliographical references.
1175. Krause, Harry D. ILLEGITIMACY: LAW AND SOCIAL POLICY. Indianapolis: Bobbs-Merrill, 1971. 379 pp.
1176. Lamb, Anthony B. "Family Law—Blood—Grouping Tests and the Presumption of Legitimacy," THE NORTH CAROLINA LAW REVIEW, vol. 50 (Dec. 1971), pp. 163-172.
1177. "Le Role de la Femme Africaine dans la Vie Publique" [The Role of the African Woman in Public Life], JEUNE AFRIQUE, no. 554 (Aug. 1971), pp. 3+. Talks about women and the factors that prevent them from exercising their rights in Africa.
1178. Lewis, John Wilson, ed. MAJOR DOCTRINES OF COMMUNIST CHINA. New York: Norton, 1964. Women's rights and the law in China are discussed.
1179. Lund, Caroline, and Betsey Stone. WOMEN AND THE EQUAL RIGHTS AMENDMENT. New York: Pathfinder Press, 1972.
1180. MacDonald, John Marshall. RAPE OFFENDERS AND THEIR VICTIMS. Springfield, Ill.: Thomas, 1971.
1181. McVeety, Jean. "Law and the Single Woman," WOMAN LAWYERS JOURNAL, vol. 53 (Winter 1967), pp. 10+.
1182. Miller, Robert Stevens. "Sex Discrimination and Title VII of the Civil Rights Act of 1964," MINNESOTA LAW REVIEW, vol. 51 (1967), pp. 877-897. Section II especially good for Rep. Edith Green's stand on the women's rights amendment to the Civil Rights Act of 1964.
1183. Morris, Richard B. STUDIES IN THE HISTORY OF AMERICAN LAW, WITH SPECIAL REFERENCE TO THE 17TH AND 18TH CENTURIES.

New York: Columbia Univ. Press, 1930. Bibliographic essay and sections on "Women—Legal Status, Laws," etc.

1184. Murphy, Irene Lyons. PUBLIC POLICY ON THE STATUS OF WOMEN. Lexington, Mass.: Lexington, 1973. Analysis of contemporary issue of sex discrimination and the major factors involved in decision-making on the national level.

1185. Murray, Pauli, and Mary O. Eastwood, "Jane Crow and the Law: Sex Discrimination and Title VII," THE GEORGE WASHINGTON LAW REVIEW, vol. 34 (Dec. 1965), pp. 232-253.

1186. Nagel, Stuart, and Lenore J. Weitzman. "Double Standard of American Justice," SOCIETY, vol. 19, no. 5 (1972), pp. 18-25, 62-63. Analyzes 363 cases in which women were discriminated against in the law courts.

1187. Oldham, James C. "Sex Discrimination and State Protective Laws," DENVER LAW REVIEW, vol. 44 (Summer 1967), pp. 344.

1188. Ostrogorskii, Moiseii Akovievich. THE RIGHTS OF WOMEN: A COMPARATIVE STUDY IN HISTORY AND LEGISLATION. London, 1893. Reprinted by Greenwood Press, Westport, Conn. 1971. 232 pp.

1189. Pan-American Union, Seventh International Conference of American States, Montevideo, Uruguay, 1933. "Nationality of Women," FINAL ACT. Washington, D.C.: Pan-American Union, 1933. First International Treaty by the Inter-American Commission of Women for women's rights which eliminated the distinction based on sex and which recognized the general principle of equal rights with men.

1190. "The Proposed Equal Rights Amendment to the United States Constitution: A Memorandum," Washington, D.C.: Citizen's Advisory Council on the Status of Women, Mar. 1970. SUDOC, GPO.

1191. Ransel, D. L. "Catherine II's Instruction to the Commission on Laws," THE SLAVONIC AND EAST EUROPEAN REVIEW, vol. 50 (Jan. 1972), pp. 10-28.

1192. Reeve, Tapping. THE LAW OF BARON AND FEMME, 3d ed. New York: Source Book Press, 1970. Reprint of the 1862 edition. 678 pp. Thorough summary of laws concerning husbands, wives, children, masters, and servants.

1193. Seidenberg, Faith A. "The Submissive Majority: Modern Trends in the Law Concerning Women's Rights," CORNELL LAW REVIEW, vol. 55, (1970), pp. 262-271. Interesting discussion of the discrimination against women in criminal law.

1194. "Sex Discrimination and Equal Protection: Do We Need a Constitutional Amendment?" HARVARD LAW REVIEW, vol. 84, (1971), pp. 1499-1524.

1195. Shah, Diane K. "Women Attack Rape Justice," THE NATIONAL OBSERVER, (Oct. 9, 1971).

1196. Sharwin, Robert. "The Law and Sexual Relationships," JOURNAL OF SOCIAL ISSUES, (April 1968), p. 115. How laws on prostitution discriminate against the female.

1197. Simons, H. J. AFRICAN WOMEN: THEIR LEGAL STATUS IN SOUTH AFRICA. Evanston, Ill.: Northwestern Univ. Press, 1968. 299 pp.

1198. Smith, Ethel M. TOWARD EQUAL RIGHTS FOR MEN AND WOMEN. Washington, D.C.: National League of Women Voters, Committee on the Legal Status of Women. 1929. 139 pp.

1199. Smith, Julia E. ABBEY SMITH AND HER COWS. WITH A REPORT OF THE LAW CASE DECIDED CONTRARY TO THE LAW. New York: Arno Press, 1972. Reprint of the 1877 edition. The story of two spinsters who rebelled when they were levied taxes for being unmarried. They became ardent women's rightists.

1200. Snyder, Eloise C. "Sex Role Differential and Juror Decisions," MENTAL HEALTH DIGEST, vol. 3 (Dec. 1971), pp. 51-52.

1201. Sprague, Henry H. WOMEN UNDER THE LAW OF MASSACHUSETTS: THEIR RIGHTS, PRIVILEGES, AND DISABILITIES. Boston: Little, Brown, 1903. 100 pp.

1202. United Nations. CONSTITUTIONS, ELECTORAL LAWS AND OTHER LEGAL INSTRUMENTS RELATING TO THE POLITICAL RIGHTS OF WOMEN. New York: United Nations Publications, 1971. 147 pp. An international digest.

1203. U.S. Congress, House, Committee on Rules. CIVIL RIGHTS, hearing on H.R. 7152, 88 Cong., 2d sess. 2 vols. Washington, D.C.: SUDOC, GPO, 1964.

1204. VALPARAISO UNIVERSITY LAW REVIEW, vol. 5, no. 2 (Symposium Issue), 1971. An issue devoted to Women and the Law, with articles by Jo Freeman, Pauli Murray, Mary Eastwood, Faith A. Seidenberg, Caruthers Gholson Berger, Sonia Pressman Fuentes, Patsy T. Mink, Aleta Wallach, Ruth Bader Ginsburg, and student notes. 285 pp.

1205. Velimesis, Margery L. "Criminal Justice for the Female Offender," AAUW JOURNAL, vol. 63, no. 1 (Oct. 1969), pp. 13-16. Story of the AAUW's investigation of criminal justice for women offenders in Pennsylvania.

1206. White, James J. "Women in the Law," MICHIGAN LAW REVIEW, vol. 65 (1966), pp. 1051-1122.

1207. Wilson, Jennie L. THE LEGAL AND POLITICAL STATUS OF WOMEN IN THE UNITED STATES. Cedar Rapids, Iowa: Torch Press, 1912. 336 pp.

1208. Women's Equity Action League. SUMMARY OF EXECUTIVE ORDER 11246 AS AMENDED BY EXECUTIVE ORDER 11375: HOW THESE ORDERS RELATE TO SEX DISCRIMINATION IN UNIVERSITIES AND COLLEGES THAT HAVE FEDERAL CONTRACTS. Washington, D.C.: Women's Equity Action League, n.d. Available from above offices, 1504 44th Street, N.W.

1209. Zuker, Marvin A., and June Callwood. CANADIAN WOMEN AND THE LAW. Toronto: Copp Clark, 1971. Chapter 1, "How to Get A Legal Abortion," and other topics, such as divorce, labor legislation, welfare regulations; handbook rather than reference.

6. Feminism: Equal Rights–Employment

> *For nothing lovelier can be found*
> *In woman, than to study household good,*
> *And good works in her husband to promote.*
> *—Milton*

1210. Allen, Virginia. "A Matter of Simple Justice," ADVANCED MANAGE-MENT JOURNAL, vol. 36 (Oct. 1971), pp. 49-52. Government Task Force outlines what the woman's role in business should be in an 11-

point business action program with a target date of 1976 to achieve elimination of discrimination against women.

1211. Amundsen, Kirsten Steinmo. THE SILENCED MAJORITY: WOMEN AND AMERICAN DEMOCRACY. Englewood Cliffs, N.J.: Prentice-Hall, 1971. An indictment of the American democratic system which ignores women in the political process while capitalizing on their economic and social contributions.

1212. Archibald, Kathleen. SEX AND THE PUBLIC SERVICE. Ottawa: Public Service Commission, 1970. How Canada's largest single employer treats women, and how, in Canada, men are rated more equal than women.

1213. Chase, Judy. "Inside HEW: Women Protest Sex Discrimination," SCIENCE, vol. 174 (Oct. 15, 1971), pp. 270-274. A look at how HEW systematically relegates women to second-class status.

1214. Dall, Caroline. THE COLLEGE, THE MARKET, AND THE COURT: OR, WOMAN'S RELATION TO EDUCATION, LABOR, AND LAW. New York: Arno Press, 1972. Reprint of 1867 edition. Traces the Anglo-American traditions, cultural influences, and religious attitudes against which women had to contend in seeking entry into male professions and fields of work.

1215. Falk, Ruth, Frances Maraventano, and Diane Ralph. A WOMAN'S PLACE, AN UPDATING OF WOMEN'S LIBERATION. Washington, D.C.: National Institute of Mental Health, Office of Youth and Study Affairs, 1970. 18 pp. Summary of major trends in the women's lib movement, especially the work of professional women's caucuses and federal women's programs.

1216. "Goesaert, et al. v. Cleary, et al." Members of the Michigan Liquor Control Commission, 335 U.S. 464 (1948). The Supreme Court upheld a Michigan law which forbids any female to act as a bartender unless she is the wife or daughter of the male owner of a licensed liquor establishment.

1217. Goldstein, Mark L. "Blue-Collar Women and American Labor Unions," INDUSTRIAL AND LABOR RELATIONS FORUM, vol. 7 (Oct. 1971), pp. 1-35. Part I discusses the history and Part II presents the arguments pro and con legislation.

1218. Grunfeld, Judith. "Women's Work in Russia's Planned Economy," SOCIAL RESEARCH, vol. 9, no. 1 (Feb. 1942), pp. 22-45.

1219. Hays, Elinor Rice. MORNING STAR: A BIOGRAPHY OF LUCY STONE, 1818-1893. New York: Harcourt, Brace and World, 1961. 339 pp. About the opponent of harsh mill conditions for working girls and women.

1220. Kennedy, John F. "Memorandum on Equal Opportunity for Women in the Federal Service," PUBLIC PAPERS OF THE PRESIDENTS, Item 304, July 24, 1962. Washington, D.C.: SUDOC, GPO.

1221. Lapin, Eva. MOTHERS IN OVERALLS. New York: Workers Library, 1943. 30 pp. A call for women to get into overalls and production lines to aid the war effort.

1222. May, Charles Paul. WOMEN IN AERONAUTICS. New York: Thomas Nelson, 1962. Stories of pioneer women aviators.

1223. Meikle, Wilma. TOWARDS A SANE FEMINISM. London: McBride, 1916. Argues that women should enter into commerce and business on a large scale because a dependent class must become economically influential before it can have political power.

1224. Pressman, Sonia. "Sex Discrimination in Employment and What You Can Do About It," WOMEN LAWYERS JOURNAL, vol. 54, no. 4 (Fall 1968), p. 6.

1225. "Revolution II. Thinking Female," COLLEGE AND UNIVERSITY BUSINESS, vol. 48 (Feb. 1970), pp. 51-86.

1226. Roe, Dorothy. THE TROUBLE WITH WOMEN IS MEN. Englewood Cliffs, N.J.: Prentice-Hall, 1961. 207 pp. Advocates careers for women and attacks male critics of women, indicating that women's troubles are created by men themselves.

1227. Sartin, Pierrette. LA PROMOTION DE FEMMES. Paris: Hachette, 1964. 303 pp. Women in employment in France; bibliographic section.

1228. Seaman, Barbara. "Ideas for Living No. 5: An Interview With Congresswoman Martha Griffiths," FAMILY CIRCLE, Feb. 1972. Discusses Mrs. Griffiths's two-career family and her successful challenge of airline discrimination against married stewardesses.

1229. Shapley, Deborah. "Women's Rights: Whose Feet Are Dragging?" SCIENCE, vol. 175 (Jan. 14, 1972), pp. 151-154. Talks about the need for universities to end discrimination in employing women on faculties, suggesting strong enforcement action on universities who continue to discriminate.

1230. Sigworth, Heather. "The Legal Status of Anti-Nepotism Regulations," AAUP BULLETIN, vol. 58 (Spring 1972), pp. 31-34. How anti-nepotism unfairly limits the opportunities of faculty relatives (almost always wives) to pursue their professions and deprives communities of qualified faculty on the basis of inappropriate criteria.

1231. STATEWIDE CONFERENCES ON THE CHANGING STATUS OF WOMEN, OHIO UNIVERSITY. Columbus: Ohio State Univ. 1965. 61 pp. Focus on employment of women.

1232. U.S. Bureau of Labor. LAWS RELATING TO THE EMPLOYMENT OF WOMEN AND CHILDREN IN THE UNITED STATES. Washington, D.C.: SUDOC, GPO, 1907. 150 pp.

1233. U.S. Civil Service Commission. INVESTIGATING COMPLAINTS OF DISCRIMINATION IN FEDERAL EMPLOYMENT, ON GROUNDS OF RACE, COLOR, RELIGION, SEX, AND NATIONAL ORIGIN. Washington, D.C.: SUDOC, GPO, 1967. 28 pp.

1234. ———. STUDY OF EMPLOYMENT OF WOMEN IN THE FEDERAL SERVICE. Washington, D.C.: SUDOC, GPO, 1969. Of 2,610,128 civil service employees, 717,549 were women.

1235. U.S. Congress, Senate, Judiciary Committee. HEARINGS ON THE EQUAL RIGHTS AMENDMENT. Washington, D.C.: SUDOC, GPO, Sept. 1970. 433 pp. Covers nearly all aspects of women's rights— politics, education, family services, working conditions, etc.

1236. U.S. Department of Labor, Women's Bureau. ACTION FOR EQUAL PAY. Washington, D.C.: Department of Labor, 1965. On equal pay for women working in jobs equivalent to male jobs.

1237. ———. LAWS ON SEX DISCRIMINATION IN EMPLOYMENT. Washington, D.C.: SUDOC, GPO, 1970.
1238. ———. "State Action Since Title VII," FEDERAL EMPLOYMENT REPORT, Oct. 11, 1971. 192 pp. Washington, D.C.: SUDOC, GPO, 1971.
1239. ———. "What You Want in a State Equal Pay Bill." Washington, D.C.: Women's Bureau, Mar. 1969.
1240. U.S. Equal Employment Opportunity Commission. HELP WANTED . . . OR IS IT? A LOOK AT WHITE COLLAR JOB INEQUALITIES FOR MINORITIES AND WOMEN. Washington, D.C.: SUDOC, GPO, 1968. 15 pp.

7. Feminism: Equal Rights—Education

When a woman is intellectually inclined there is usually something wrong with her sex.
—Nietzsche

1241. Burton, Hester. BARBARA BODICHON, 1827-1891. London: Murray, 1949. 220 pp. Biography of a woman who worked for higher education for women in Britain.
1242. Clough, Blanche Athena. A MEMOIR OF ANNE JEMINA CLOUGH. London: Edward Arnold, 1897. 344 pp. About one of the leaders in the fight for higher education for women in England.
1243. Conrad, Earl. HARRIET TUBMAN: NEGRO SOLDIER AND ABOLITIONIST. New York: International Press, 1968. The definitive biography of the Negro abolitionist, military leader, and suffragist.
1244. "Guidelines for Improving the Image of Women in Textbooks," New York: Scott, Foresman, 1972. Pamphlet edited by the publishers defining sexism in textbooks.
1245. Her Majesty's Stationary Office. CIVIC AND POLITICAL EDUCATION OF WOMEN. London: H.M.S.O., 1965.
1246. Irwin, Inez Hayes. ANGELS AND AMAZONS: A HUNDRED YEARS OF AMERICAN WOMEN. Garden City: Doubleday, Doran, 1933. The development of American women between 1833 and 1933 in education and women's rights.
1247. Lutz, Alma. EMMA WILLARD: DAUGHTER OF DEMOCRACY. Boston: Houghton, 1929. 291 pp. The authoritative biography of the woman who played an important role in gaining higher education for women through legislation.
1248. Mottahedeh, Mildred R. "Educating Women for their Rights," WORLD ORDER, vol. 6, no. 3 (Spring 1972), pp. 45-50. By a Baha'i writer in the Baha'i magazine, which has long advocated women's rights.
1249. New York. Governor's Committee on the Education and Employment of Women. NEW YORK WOMEN AND THEIR CHANGING WORLD. Albany: State of New York, 1964. 96 pp. A new way to encourage the education of women and the education of the community to make full use of its trained and talented women.
1250. U.S. President's Commission on the Status of Women. REPORT OF THE COMMITTEE ON EDUCATION TO THE PRESIDENT'S COMMISSION ON THE STATUS OF WOMEN. Washington, D.C.: SUDOC, GPO, 1964. Education of women with bibliographic references on women's careers and education.

8. Feminism: Innovative

Nothing in progression can rest on its original plan. We may as well think of rocking a grown man in the cradle of an infant.
                                                                —Burke

1251. Benston, Margaret. "The Political Economy of Women's Liberation," MONTHLY REVIEW (Sept. 1969), pp. 13-27. Clear, short analysis of the economic roots of the oppression of women from a Marxian perspective.

1252. Castro, Fidel, and Linda Jenness. WOMEN AND THE CUBAN REVOLUTION. New York: Pathfinder Press, 1972.

1253. Lilienthal, Meta. WOMEN OF THE FUTURE. New York: Socialist Literature Co., 191 31 pp. Women under Socialism.

1254. Mitchell, Juliet. "The Longest Revolution," NEW LEFT REVIEW, vol. 40 (Nov.-Dec. 1966). Studies the role of women in socialist countries and argues that women fare poorly.

1255. Purcell, Susan Kaufman. "Modernizing Women for A Modern Society: The Cuban Case." In FEMALE AND MALE IN LATIN AMERICA, edited by Ann Pescatello. Pittsburgh: Univ. of Pittsburgh Press, 1973.

1256. Rue, Vincent M. "A U.S. Department of Marriage and the Family," JOURNAL OF MARRIAGE AND THE FAMILY, vol. 35, (Nov. 1973) pp. 689-699.

1257. Salaff, Janet Wietzer, and Judith Merkle. "Woman and Revolution: The Lessons of the Soviet Union and China," SOCIALIST REVOLUTION, vol. 1, no. 4 (July-Aug. 1970), pp. 39-72. From a Marxist, but also a feminist perspective.

1258. Schuster, Alice. "Women's Role in the Soviet Union: Ideology and Reality," THE RUSSIAN REVIEW, vol. 30 (July 1971), pp. 260-267. Discusses the possibility of women becoming equal with men in reality and well as ideologically.

1259. "Women in Latin America," JOURNAL OF MARRIAGE AND THE FAMILY, vol. 35, no. 2 (May 1973), special section, pp. 299-354. Articles by Nora Scott Kinzer, Evelyn P. Stevens, Lucy M. Cohen, Elsa M. Chaney, and Jane E. Jaquette.

1260. Zetkin, Clara. LENIN ON THE WOMAN QUESTION. New York: International Publishers, 1936. 31 pp. By one of the founders of the German Communist party. Lenin unequivocally supported the complete equality of women as an improvement over their previous status under the Czarist government, but today, women hold few if any positions in top government positions.

9. Feminism: Radical

How much longer is one form of society and life to content itself with the morality made for another? We have had the morality of submission, and the morality of chivalry and generosity; the time is now come for the morality of justice.
                                                                —John Stuart Mill

1261. Briscoe, Mary L., and Elsie Adams. UP AGAINST THE WALL, MOTHER. Beverly Hills, Calif.: Glencoe Press, 1971. 521 pp. An anthology of essays, articles, and poems illustrating that the role of women has been traditionally defined by custom and culture as one of inferiority.

1262. Bryant, Louise. MIRRORS OF MOSCOW. New York: n.p., 1923. Chapter entitled "Madame Alexandra Kollontai and the Women's Movement."

1263. Clark, Ida Clyde, ed. WOMEN OF 1923: INTERNATIONAL. Chicago: John C. Winston, 1923. 224 pp.

1264. Day, Dorothy. FROM UNION SQUARE TO ROME. Silver Spring, Md.: Preservation of the Faith Press, 1942. 173 pp. Recounts the author's early radical life and comments on her association with many of the leading radicals of the 1920s and 1930s.

1265. DeCrow, Karen. THE YOUNG WOMAN'S GUIDE TO LIBERATION: ALTERNATIVES TO A HALF-LIFE WHILE THE CHOICE IS STILL YOURS. Indianapolis: Bobbs-Merrill, 1971. 200 pp. Witty, well-written anthology dealing with female roles, economic enslavement, "Barbie Dolls," sexism on TV, and women's magazines, among other things.

1266. Dixon, Marlene. "Public Ideology and the Class Composition of Women's Liberation (1966-1969)," BERKELEY JOURNAL OF SOCIOLOGY, vol. 16 (1971-1972), pp. 149-167.

1267. Drinnon, Richard. REBEL IN PARADISE. Chicago: Univ. of Chicago Press, 1961. 349 pp. Biography of Emma Goldman, the Russian-born anarchist and advocate of women's rights.

1268. Firestone, Shulamith. THE DIALECTIC OF SEX: THE CASE FOR FEMINIST REVOLUTION. New York: Morrow, 1970. On Marxian definitions of women, sex, but mostly on American feminism, Freud's errors, children, and the male culture.

1269. Flynn, Elizabeth Gurley. DAUGHTERS OF AMERICA: ELLA REEVE BLOOR AND ANITA WHITNEY. New York: Workers Library, 1942. 14 pp. Pamphlet.

1270. Frölich, Paul. ROSA LUXEMBOURG: HER LIFE AND WORK. New York: Howard Fertig, 1969. 339 pp. Excellent biography of the Polish communist who struggled against the male-centered society of her time and became a leading political figure and leader until her tragic assassination.

1271. Goldman, Emma. MY DISILLUSIONMENT IN RUSSIA. Garden City: Doubleday, Page, 1923. 242 pp. An indictment of the Communist Revolution in Russia.

1272. Hole, Judith, and Ellen Levine. REBIRTH OF FEMINISM. New York: Quadrangle Books, 1971. 488 pp. Comes close to being a one-volume Woman Studies Program, starting with the rebirth of feminism in the 1960s and reviewing legislation, historical backgrounds, ideas, issues, and areas of action.

1273. Jenness, Linda. FEMINISM AND SOCIALISM. New York: Pathfinder Press, 1972. Essays dealing with the feminist movement by socialist writers.

1274. Landy, Laurie. WOMEN IN THE CHINESE REVOLUTION. New York: International Socialist Book Service, 1970.

1275. Lee, George. "Rosa Luxembourg and the Impact of Imperalism," THE ECONOMIC JOURNAL, vol. 81 (Dec. 1971), pp. 847-862.

1276. Morgan, Robin, ed. WOMEN IN REVOLT. New York: Random House, 1969. Extensive compendium of writings on psychology, education, birth control, sexuality, etc.

1277. Nies, Judith. MESSAGE TO THE FUTURE: THE TRADITION OF RAD-
ICAL WOMEN IN AMERICA. New York: Holt, Rinehart and Winston,
1974. Studies of women in radical social movements in America from
the abolitionists to the Catholic Workers Movement.

1278. O'Neill, William L. "Feminism as a Radical Ideology." In THE UNDER-
SIDE OF AMERICAN HISTORY: OTHER READINGS, edited by
Thomas R. Frazier, vol. 2. New York: Harcourt, Brace and Jovanovich,
1971.

1279. Rappaport, Philip. LOOKING FORWARD: A TREATISE ON THE
STATUS OF WOMAN AND THE ORIGIN AND GROWTH OF THE
FAMILY AND STATE. Chicago: Kerr, 1906. 234 pp. Marxian approach
to the woman question.

1280. Reed, Evelyn. PROBLEMS OF WOMEN'S LIBERATION: A MARXIST
APPROACH. New York: Merit Publishers, 1969. Traces the subjugation
of women to the rise of private property and the development of the
family.

1281. Sheehy, Gail. "The Fighting Women of Ireland," NEW YORK MAGA-
ZINE, vol. 4 (Mar. 13, 1972), pp. 45-55.

1282. Stambler, Sookie, ed. WOMEN'S LIBERATION-BLUEPRINT FOR THE
FUTURE. New York: Ace Books, 1970.

1283. Stone, Lucy, compiler. WOMAN'S RIGHTS TRACTS. Rochester, N.Y.:
n.p., n.d. (1850s?) Five tracts on Freedom for Women, Public Function
of Women, Enfranchisement of Women, Women and Her Wishes, and
Responsibilities of Women.

1284. TANIA: THE UNFORGETTABLE GUERILLA. New York: Random House,
1971. 212 pp. Scrapbook of a Cuban revolutionary who died with Che
Guevara in Bolivia, edited by Marta Rojas and Mirta Rodriguez Calderon.

1285. Taylor, G. R. Stirling. MARY WOLLSTONECRAFT: A STUDY IN
ECONOMICS AND ROMANCE. London: Secker and Warburg, 1911.
210 pp. Wollstonecraft is the date from which historians date the
woman question as a political force.

1286. Thomas, Edith. THE WOMEN INCENDIARIES. New York: G. Braziller,
1966. About the condition and history of women in Paris during the
Paris Commune period.

1287. Zetkin, Clara. LES BATAILLES REVOLUTIONAIRES, DE L'ALLE-
MAGNE EN 1919 [The Revolutionary Battles in Germany in 1919].
Issue no. 9. Paris: L'Internationale, Feb. 1920. Describes the role of
women in the struggles.

E. Women as Voters

1. General

> Politics we bar,
> They are not our bent:
> On the whole we are
> Not intelligent,
>
> —Gilbert and Sullivan (Princess Ida)

1288. Abrahams, Sir Adolphe. WOMEN: MAN'S EQUAL? London: Christopher Johnson, 1954. Women and their role in politics and society.
1289. Allen, William H. WOMAN'S PART IN GOVERNMENT: WHETHER SHE VOTES OR NOT. New York: Dodd, 1911. 377 pp. Woman must use the vote once she has achieved it, and she must participate in government to rid herself of inequality.
1290. Almond, Gabriel A., and Sidney Verba. THE CIVIC CULTURE: POLITICAL ATTITUDES AND DEMOCRACY IN FIVE NATIONS. Boston and Toronto: Little, Brown, 1965. 379 pp. A study in political socialization and civic competence in the United States, Great Britain, Italy, Germany, and Mexico.
1291. Berelson, Bernard R., Paul F. Lazarsfeld, and William N. McPhee. VOTING: A STUDY OF OPINION FORMATION IN A PRESIDENTIAL CAMPAIGN. Chicago: Univ. of Chicago Press, 1964. The extent to which women's voting influenced the election outcome.
1292. Blair, Emily Newell. "Woman at the Conventions," CURRENT HISTORY MAGAZINE, (Oct. 1920).
1293. Brown, Nona B. "Women's Vote: The Bigger Half?" NEW YORK TIMES MAGAZINE, (Oct. 21, 1956).
1294. Brumbaugh, Sara Barbara. DEMOCRATIC EXPERIENCE AND EDUCATION IN THE NATIONAL LEAGUE OF WOMEN VOTERS. New York: Teachers College Bureau of Publications, 1946.
1295. Campbell, Angus, et al. THE AMERICAN VOTER. New York: Wiley, 1960. Includes some information on women.
1296. Cassara, Beverly, ed. AMERICAN WOMEN: THE CHANGING IMAGE. Boston: Beacon Press, 1962. Discussion of women and voting, among other topics.
1297. Chomel, Marie Cecile. "Does the Wife Vote Like Her Husband?" LADIES' HOME JOURNAL, (May 1919).
1298. Colton, Olive A. "Adventures of a Woman Voter," SURVEY, (Sept. 1, 1928).
1299. Fisher, Marguerite J. "If Women Only Voted," CHRISTIAN SCIENCE MONITOR MAGAZINE, (Oct. 30, 1948).
1300. Gerould, Katherine Fullerton. "Some American Women and the Vote," SCRIBNER'S MAGAZINE, (May 1925).
1301. Good, Josephine L. THE HISTORY OF WOMEN IN REPUBLICAN NATIONAL CONVENTIONS AND WOMEN IN THE REPUBLICAN NATIONAL COMMITTEE. Washington, D.C.: Women's Division of the Republican National Committee, 1963.
1302. Hastings, Philip K. "Hows and Howevers of the Woman Voter," NEW YORK TIMES MAGAZINE, (June 12, 1960).

1303. Kruschke, Earl R. THE WOMAN VOTER: AN ANALYSIS BASED UPON PERSONAL INTERVIEWS, Washington, D.C.: Public Affairs Press, 1955.
1304. League of Women Voters. FACTS ABOUT THE LEAGUE OF WOMEN VOTERS. Publication no. 221. Washington, D.C.: LWV, 1964.
1305. ———. HANDBOOK FOR CITIZENS. Raleigh, N.C.: LWV, 1963.
1306. ———. THE MEMBER AND THE LEAGUE. Publication no. 264. Washington, D.C.: LWV, 1960.
1307. Lindsay, Malvina. "Mrs. Grundy's Vote," NORTH AMERICAN REVIEW, (June 1932).
1308. Low, A. Maurice. "Women in the Election," YALE REVIEW, (Jan. 1921).
1309. Martin, Anne. "Woman's Vote and Woman's Chains," SUNSET MAGAZINE, (April 1922).
1310. Merriam,Charles E., and Harold F. Gosnell. NON-VOTING: CAUSES AND METHODS OF CONTROL. Chicago: Univ. of Chicago Press, 1924.
1311. Moyer-Wing, Alice C. "The Vote: Our First Comeback," SCRIBNER'S MAGAZINE, (Sept. 1928).
1312. Sanders, Marion K. THE LADY AND THE VOTE. Boston: Houghton Mifflin, 1956.
1313. Tart, Marjorie. THE EDUCATION OF WOMEN FOR CITIZENSHIP: SOME PRACTICAL SUGGESTIONS. Basel, Switzerland: UNESCO, 1954.

2. *Women as Voters: Extent of Participation*

> *Ring out a slowly dying cause,*
> *And ancient forms of party strife;*
> *Ring in the nobler modes of life,*
> *With sweeter manners, purer laws.*
> *—Tennyson*

1314. Boyd, Mary Sumner. THE WOMAN CITIZEN. New York: Stokes, 1918. 260 pp. Handbook of how women should go about acquiring the right to vote and how to apply their right to vote.
1315. Brown, Mrs. Raymond. YOUR VOTE AND HOW TO USE IT. New York: Harper, 1918. 263 pp. By a woman who helped win the vote in New York.
1316. Catt, Carrie Chapman. HOW TO WORK FOR SUFFRAGE IN AN ELECTION DISTRICT OR VOTING PRECINCT. New York: National Woman Suffrage Publishing Co., 1917. 12 pp.
1317. Communist Party, U.S.A., National Election Campaign Committee. WORKING WOMEN AND THE ELECTIONS. New York: Workers Library, 1932. 16 pp. How women can use their votes and participate in elections more fruitfully.
1318. Cutler, Amelia MacDonald. HOW TO REACH THE RURAL VOTER. New York: National Woman Suffrage Publishing Co. 1917. 11 pp.
1319. "L'Evolution de la Femme Africaine," L'AFRIQUE EN MARCHE, vols. 22-23 (1958), pp. 38-40. Historical outline of votes for women, their political role, and percentage of women's votes.

1320. Livermore, Henrietta W. THE "BLUE BOOK" SUFFRAGE SCHOOL COURSE FOUNDED ON 'WOMAN SUFFRAGE—HISTORY, ARGU-MENTS AND RESULTS'. New York: National Woman Suffrage Publishing Co., 1917. 12 pp.
1321. ———. HOW TO RAISE MONEY FOR SUFFRAGE. New York: National Woman Suffrage Publishing Co., 1917. 15 pp.
1322. ———. A SUFFRAGE TRAINING SCHOOL. New York: National Woman Suffrage Publishing Co., 1916, 12 pp.
1323. Means, Ingunn Norderval. "Norwegian Women Wield Ballots," THE CHRISTIAN SCIENCE MONITOR, Nov. 2, 1971, p. 10. Describes the impressive increase in the number of Norwegian women voting.
1324. Rokkan, Stein, and Henry Valen. "The Mobilization of the Periphery: Data on Turnout, Party Membership and Candidate Recruitment in Norway," ACTA SOCIOLOGICA, vol. 6 (nos. 1-2, 1962), pp. 136+. Maintains that for women voting is an act of compliance, whereas running for office is competitive, thus, contrary to established cultural norms for women.
1325. Stern, Meta Lilienthal. VOTES FOR WORKING WOMEN. Socialist Literature Company, 191–? 31 pp.
1326. Tingsten, Herbert. POLITICAL BEHAVIOR. Totowa, N.J.: Bedminister Press, 1963. A pioneering study, first published in 1937, of voting behavior in a number of countries, especially Scandinavia, Germany and Austria, and the United States. Chapter 1 deals with "Electoral Participation and Political Attitude [sic] of Women," pp. 10-78.
1327. Wilson, Justina Leavitt. SUFFRAGE ARGUMENT: OUTLINE FOR SPEECH OR DEBATE. New York: National Woman Suffrage Publishing Co., 1917. 19 pp.

3. Women as Voters: Stand on Issues

1328. Cole, Margaret. "The Women's Vote: What Has It Achieved?" POLITICAL QUARTERLY, vol. 33 (Jan.-Mar. 1962), pp. 74-83. By an Alderman of the London County Council.
1329. Evans, Wainwright. "When Lovely Woman Votes 'Thumbs Down!' " WORLD'S WORK, (Feb. 1929).
1330. Kirk, Russell. THE INTELLIGENT WOMAN'S GUIDE TO CONSERVA-TISM. New York: Devin-Adair, 1957. 122 pp. Rather specious argument that women are conservative by nature. Liberals or radicals offer America no solutions, but women will restore the Republic to its original goals, which have been taken over by the socialists and communists.
1331. Royden, Agnes M. VOTES AND WAGES. London: National Union of Women's Suffrage Societies, 1912. 14 pp. How woman suffrage will improve the economic position of women.

F. Woman Suffrage

1. General

To get the word "male" in effect out of the Constitution cost the women of the country fifty-two years of pauseless campaign ... During that time they were forced to conduct fifty-six campaigns of referenda to male voters; 480 campaigns to get Legislatures to submit suffrage amendments to voters; 47 campaigns to get State constitutional conventions to write woman suffrage into state constitutions; 277 campaigns to get State party conventions to include woman suffrage planks; 30 campaigns to get presidential party conventions to adopt woman suffrage planks in party platforms, and 19 campaigns with 19 successive Congresses.

—Carrie Chapman Catt

1332. Adams, Mildred. THE RIGHT TO BE PEOPLE. Philadelphia: Lippincott, 1967. 248 pp. A history of woman suffrage in the United States, and the concern with the status of women after passage of the 19th Amendment.

1333. Blackburn, Helen. WOMEN'S SUFFRAGE: A RECORD OF THE WOMEN'S SUFFRAGE MOVEMENT IN THE BRITISH ISLES. New York: Source Book Press, 1970. Reprint of the 1902 edition. 314 pp. A retrospective of the social development which brought about the woman's suffrage movement.

1334. Catt, Carrie Chapman. WOMAN SUFFRAGE BY FEDERAL CONSTITUTIONAL AMENDMENT. New York: National Woman Suffrage Publishing Co., 1917. 100 pp.

1335. Catt, Carrie Chapman, and Nettie R. Shuler. WOMAN SUFFRAGE AND POLITICS: THE INNER STORY OF THE WOMAN SUFFRAGE MOVEMENT. Seattle: Univ. of Washington Press, 1969. Reprint of the 1929 edition. 504 pp.

1336. Cleverdon, Catherine L. THE WOMAN SUFFRAGE MOVEMENT IN CANADA. Toronto: Univ. of Toronto Press, 1950. 324 pp. By an American, very factual, but not very useful on the personalities of the women involved, or of the ambience in which they lived.

1337. Coolidge, Olivia E. WOMEN'S RIGHTS: THE SUFFRAGE MOVEMENT IN IN AMERICA, 1848-1920. New York: Dutton, 1966. 189 pp. By an early suffragist.

1338. Dangerfield, George. THE STRANGE DEATH OF LIBERAL ENGLAND. New York: Capricorn Books, 1961. 449 pp. Part II, Chapter 3, "The Women's Rebellion," pp. 139-213; Part III, Chapter 3, "The Pankhursts Provide a Clew," pp. 364-388. Leading suffragists of the World War I period.

1339. Davies, H. O. "Emancipation of Women in West Africa," WEST AFRICAN REVIEW (Liverpool), (Feb. 1938), pp. 13-15.

1340. Faber, Doris. PETTICOAT POLITICS: HOW AMERICAN WOMEN WON THE RIGHT TO VOTE. New York: Lothrop, Lee and Shepard, 1967. 192 pp.

1341. Fawcett, Millicient G. WOMAN'S SUFFRAGE. New York: Source Book Press, 1970. Reprint of the 1912 edition. 94 pp. A short, popular history by the President of the National Union of Women's Suffrage Societies in Great Britain.

1342. ———. THE WOMAN'S VICTORY AND AFTER. London: Sidgwick and Jackson, 1920.

1343. Fulford, R. VOTES FOR WOMEN: THE STORY OF A STRUGGLE. London: Faber and Faber, 1957. 343 pp. Captures the militancy of women's quest for suffrage in England.

1344. Guazon-Mendoza, Maria Paz. THE DEVELOPMENT AND PROGRESS OF THE FILIPINO WOMAN. Manila: n.p., 1951.

1345. Harper, Ida Husted. STORY OF THE NATIONAL AMENDMENT FOR WOMAN SUFFRAGE. New York: National Woman Suffrage Publishing Co., 1919. 38 pp.

1346. Hobman, D. GO SPIN, YOU JADE! London: Watts, 1957. 152 pp. Studies in the emancipation of British women.

1347. Kraditor, Aileen. IDEAS OF THE WOMAN SUFFRAGE MOVEMENT, 1890-1920. New York: Columbia Univ. Press, 1965. A seminal work on the history of the movement, with studies of the older and younger suffragists.

1348. Leonard, Eugenie. THE DEAR-BOUGHT HERITAGE. Philadelphia: Univ. of Pennsylvania Press, 1965. 658 pp.

1349. Lichtenberger, James P., ed. "Women in Public Life," THE ANNALS, vol. 56, no. 145 (Nov. 1914), p. 194. Special issue devoted to women in public life before the suffrage amendment was passed.

1350. Lloyd, Trevor. SUFFRAGETTES INTERNATIONAL: THE WORLD-WIDE CAMPAIGN FOR WOMEN'S RIGHTS. New York: American Heritage Press, 1971. 127 pp. Study of women's liberation movements in Britain and America from the eighteenth century to post-World War I.

1351. Maule, Frances, and Annie G. Porritt, eds. WOMAN SUFFRAGE: HISTORY, ARGUMENTS, AND RESULTS. New York: National Woman Suffrage Publishing Co., 1917.

1352. Mill, John Stuart. ENFRANCHISEMENT OF WOMEN. Numerous editions. In a famous address to Parliament, Mill argued not only for the right of women to vote, but on the larger question of full social equality.

1353. Miller, Alice D. ARE WOMEN PEOPLE? A BOOK OF RHYMES FOR SUFFRAGE TIMES. New York: Doran, 1915.

1354. *Minor* v. *Happersett,* 21 Wallace 162, 88 U.S. 627 (1875). Supreme Court decision which upheld the Constitution and laws of Missouri to resrtict voting to male citizens, thus denying that such laws abridged women's privileges and immunities as American citizens.

1355. Mitchell, Hannah. THE HARD WAY UP: THE AUTOBIOGRAPHY OF HANNAH MITCHELL, SUFFRAGETTE AND REBEL. London: Faber and Faber, 1967. 260 pp. Personal account of a British woman dedicated to equal rights in labor and suffrage.

1356. Morton, Ward M. WOMAN SUFFRAGE IN MEXICO. Gainesville: Univ. of Florida Press, 1962. 160 pp. A history with portraits of leading Mexican women leaders in the movement.

1357. National American Woman Suffrage Association. VICTORY: HOW WOMEN WON IT: A CENTENNIAL SYMPOSIUM, 1840-1940. New York: H. W. Wilson, 1940. 174 pp. Biographies and bibliographical references.

1358. Noun, Louise R. STRONG-MINDED WOMEN. Ames: Iowa State Univ. Press, 1969. 322 pp. Specific study of the political actions and attitudes of various suffrage leaders.

1359. O'Neill, William L. THE WOMAN MOVEMENT: FEMINISM IN THE UNITED STATES AND ENGLAND. London: Allen and Unwin; New

York: Barnes and Noble, 1969. 208 pp. History with documents of American and British suffragettes.

1360. Pankhurst, Christabel. PRESSING PROBLEMS OF THE CLOSING AGE. London: Morgan and Scott, 1924. 194 pp. The difficulties encountered in obtaining women's enfranchisement.

1361. Pankhurst, E. Sylvia. THE SUFFRAGETTE: THE HISTORY OF THE WOMEN'S MILITANT SUFFRAGE MOVEMENT. New York: Source Book Press, 1970. Reprint of the 1911 edition. 534 pp. A narrative of a young suffragette written at the height of the suffrage battle in England.

1362. Patrick M. M. "Emancipation of Mohammedan Women," NATIONAL GEOGRAPHIC MAGAZINE, vol. 20 (Jan. 1909), pp. 42-66.

1363. Porter, Kirk Harold. A HISTORY OF SUFFRAGE IN THE UNITED STATES. Chicago, 1918. Reprinted by Greenwood Press, New York, 1969. 260 pp. Chronicles the history of suffrage, ending with the movement to grant the right to vote to women.

1364. Robinson, Harriet H. MASSACHUSETTS IN THE WOMAN SUFFRAGE MOVEMENT: A GENERAL, POLITICAL, LEGAL AND LEGISLATIVE HISTORY FROM 1774 to 1881. Boston: Roberts, 1881. 265 pp.

1365. Slosson, Preston W. THE GREAT CRUSADE AND AFTER, 1914-1928. New York: Macmillan, 1930. 486 pp. Chapter on the fight for women's suffrage.

1366. Stanton, Elizabeth Cady, Susan B. Anthony, Matilda J. Gage, and Ida H. Harper. HISTORY OF WOMAN SUFFRAGE. 6 vol. New York: Source Book Press, 1970. Originally published,,1882-1922. 4530 pp. A historical record of the woman suffrage movement, beginning with the World Anti-Slavery Convention in London in 1840, including the Woman's Rights Convention in Seneca Falls in 1848, with reminiscences and brief biographical sketches of the women involved in the long struggle for the vote, and ending with passage of the amendment granting suffrage to women.

1367. Terrell, May Church. "The Progress of Colored Women." Washington, D.C.: Smith Brothers, 1898. 15 pp. An address delivered before the National American Women's Suffrage Association, Feb. 18, 1898.

1368. Vreede de Stuers, C. L'EMANCIPATION DE LA FEMME INDONES-IENNE. Paris: n.p., 1949.

1369. Williams, Jesse Lynch. A COMMON-SENSE VIEW OF WOMAN SUFFRAGE. New York: National American Woman Suffrage Association, n.d. 19 pp. Reprinted from THE LADIES WORLD.

*1370. THE WOMEN'S CONQUEST OF NEW YORK: BEING AN ACCOUNT OF THE RISE AND PROGRESS OF THE WOMEN'S RIGHTS MOVE-MENT OF THE GRANT OF FEMALE SUFFRAGE . . . by a Member of the Committee of Safety of 1908. New York: Harper, 1894, 1953. 84 pp.

2. Woman Suffrage: Leaders

> *A name like Curtius' shall be his,*
> *On fames' loud trumpet blown,*
> *Who with a wedding kiss shuts up*
> *The mouth of Lucy Stone.*
>   *—Alice Stone Blackwell*

1371. Algeo, Sara M. THE STORY OF A SUB-PIONEER. Providence, R.I.: Snow and Harnham, 1925. 318 pp. About the author's fight for woman suffrage in Rhode Island.

1372. Beard, Mary R. AMERICA THROUGH WOMEN'S EYES. Westport, Conn.: Greenwood Press, 1969. 558 pp. The story of the educational, political, and social roles of women from such writers as Edith Abbott, Jane Addams, Alice Baldwin, Julia Ward Howe, and Edith Wharton.

1373. Blatch, Harriet Stanton, and Alma Lutz. CHALLENGING YEARS: THE MEMOIRS OF HARRIET STANTON BLATCH. New York: G. P. Putnam's Sons, 1940. 347 pp. Insider's story of the woman suffrage movement.

1374. Breckinridge, Sophonisba P. MADELINE McDOWELL BRECKINRIDGE: A LEADER IN THE NEW SOUTH. Chicago: Univ. of Chicago Press, 1921. 275 pp. Biography of the Kentucky leader in the struggle to achieve suffrage.

1375. Brown, Leando. MRS. RAFORD, HUMANIST: A SUFFRAGE DRAMA. New York: L. E. Landone, 1912. 137 pp. A plea for women to work as the equals of men in conquering social evil.

1376. Brown, Olympia, ed. DEMOCRATIC IDEALS. Washington, D.C.: Federal Suffrage Association, 1917. 116 pp. Biographical sketch of Clara B. Colby, a leading suffragette in the late nineteenth century, detailing her philosophy, religion, and talents to work to achieve equality under the law for all women.

1377. Burlingame-Cheney, Emeline. AN APPEAL TO WOMAN'S MISSIONARY SOCIETIES: TEN THOUGHTS FOR YOU. Washington, D.C.: National Woman's Christian Temperance Union, n.d. Pamphlet with a militant plea for the vote.

1378. Burnett, Constance B. FIVE FOR FREEDOM: ELIZABETH CADY STAN- TON, LUCY STONE, SUSAN B. ANTHONY, CARRIE CHAPMAN CATT, AND LUCRETIA MOTT. New York: Abelard Press, 1953. 317 pp.

1379. Cromwell, Otelia. LUCRETIA MOTT. Cambridge: Harvard Univ. Press, 1958. 241 pp. Biography of the Quaker woman (1793-1880) who be- came the orator of the woman's movement.

1380. Dorr, Rheta L. SUSAN B. ANTHONY: THE WOMAN WHO CHANGED THE MIND OF A NATION. New York: AMS Press, 1970. 367 pp. Reprint of 1928 edition.

1381. Doyle, Helen MacKnight. MARY AUSTIN: WOMAN OF GENIUS. New York: Gotham House, 1939. 302 pp. Popular novelist who also struggled for women's right to career and ballot.

1382. Duniway, Abigail Scott. PATH BREAKING: AN AUTOBIOGRAPHICAL HISTORY OF THE EQUAL SUFFRAGE MOVEMENT IN PACIFIC COAST STATES. New York: Source Book Press, 1970. Reprint of the 1915 edition. 291 pp. Famed Oregon suffragist.

1383. Graham, Abbie. LADIES IN REVOLT. New York: Woman's Press, 1934. 222 pp. Sketches and speeches of celebrated leaders of the women's rights movement.

1384. Hare, Lloyd C.M. THE GREATEST AMERICAN WOMAN, LUCRETIA MOTT. Westport, Conn.: Greenwood Press, 1970. Reprint of the 1937 edition. 307 pp. Describes Lucretia Mott as the real founder and the soul of the woman's rights movement in America and England.

1385. Haskell, Oreola Williams. BANNER BEARERS: TALES OF THE SUFFRAGE CAMPAIGNS. Geneva, N.Y.: W. F. Humphrey, 1920. 350 pp. Stories of the experiences and struggles of the women in the suffrage movement.

1386. Hays, Elinor R. MORNING STAR: A BIOGRAPHY OF LUCY STONE, 1818-1893. New York: Harcourt, Brace and World, 1961. 339 pp. Early American feminist, abolitionist, and suffragist.

1387. Howe, Julia Ward. REMINISCENCES, 1819-1899. Boston, 1899. Reprint by Greenwood Press, Westport, Conn., 1969. 465 pp. Valuable for any student of the suffrage struggle.

1388. Howe, M.A. DeWolfe. CAUSES AND THEIR CHAMPIONS. Boston: Little, 1926. 331 pp. Chapters on Frances Willard and Susan B. Anthony.

1389. Kenney, Annie. MEMORIES OF A MILITANT. New York: Longmans, 1924. 308 pp. Member of the militant movement for woman suffrage in England, emphasizing her moral and emotional reasons for involvement.

1390. Livermore, Mary A. MY STORY OF THE WAR: A WOMAN'S NARRATIVE OF FOUR YEARS PERSONAL EXPERIENCE AS NURSE IN THE UNION ARMY, AND IN RELIEF WORK AT HOME, IN HOSPITALS, CAMPS, AND AT THE FRONT, DURING THE WAR OF THE REBELLION. New York: Arno Press, 1972. Reprint of the 1889 edition. After the war, she gave her talents to the battle for woman suffrage, which she saw as the key to finding solutions for such problems as war, liquor, and other social ills.

1391. Lutz, Alma. CREATED EQUAL: A BIOGRAPHY OF ELIZABETH CADY STANTON, 1815-1902. New York: John Day, 1940. 345 pp. Extensive and scholarly account of Mrs. Stanton's role.

1392. ———. SUSAN B. ANTHONY: REBEL, CRUSADER, HUMANITARIAN. Boston: Beacon Press, 1959. 340 pp. The definitive biography of the prominent leader in achieving passage of the suffrage amendment.

1393. Lytton, Constance, and Jane Warton. PRISONS AND PRISONERS: SOME PERSONAL EXPERIENCE. London: Heinemann, 1914. 337 pp. Lady Lytton was a militant English suffragist associated with the Pankhursts; imprisoned three times.

1394. Maison, Margaret. "Insignificant Objects of Desire," THE LISTENER, vol. 36 (July 22, 1971), pp. 105-107. Traces the history of the leaders of the suffrage movement in England.

1395. McClung, Nellie L. IN TIMES LIKE THESE. Toronto: McLeod and Allen, 1915. 218 pp. A leader of the woman suffrage movement in Manitoba.

1396. Mott, James, and Lucretia Mott. LIFE AND LETTERS. Boston: Houghton, 1884. 566 pp. A look at the lives of the Motts; Mr. Mott was a staunch abolitonist, Mrs. Mott was an outspoken advocate of women's rights.

1397. Perkins, A.J.G., and Theresa Wolfson. FRANCES WRIGHT: FREE ENQUIRER. THE STUDY OF A TEMPERAMENT. New York: Harper, 1939. 393 pp. Sketches of the famous British-American reformer and free thinker.

1398. Stanton, Elizbeth Cady. EIGHTY YEARS AND MORE (1815-1897). New York: Source Book Press, 1970. Reprint of the 1898 edition. 486 pp. Reminiscences of one of the most important suffragettes.

1399. Stanton, Theodore, and Harriet Stanton Blatch, eds. ELIZABETH AS REVEALED IN HER LETTERS, DIARY AND REMINISCENCES. 2 vols. New York: Harper, 1922. 362 and 369 pp.

1400. Strachey, Rachel Conn (Costelloe). MILLICENT GARRETT FAWCETT. London: J. Murray, 1931. Mrs. Fawcett (1847-1929) was in the woman suffrage movement in Great Britain.

1401. Walker, Lola C. THE SPEECHES AND SPEAKING OF CARRIE CHAPMAN CATT. Cambridge: Harvard College Library, 1959.

3. Woman Suffrage: Opponents

Women in this country by their elevated social position, can exercise more influence upon public affairs than they could coerce by the use of the ballot ... The woman who undertakes to put her sex in an adversary position to man, who undertakes by the use of some independent political power to contend and fight against man, displays a spirit which would, if able, convert all the now harmonious elements of society into a state of war, and make every home a hell on earth.
—Senator Williams (Oregon), 1866

1402. Anonymous. VOTES FOR MEN. New York: Duffield, 1913. 80 pp. Antisuffrage pamphlet which closes: "The yellow banner 'Votes for Women' is the last insult which the New Woman has offered to the intelligence of civilized man."

1403. Archer, Stevenson. WOMAN SUFFRAGE—NOT TO BE TOLERATED ALTHOUGH ADVOCATED BY THE REPUBLICAN CANDIDATE FOR THE VICE-PRESIDENCY. Speech of Hon. S. Archer of Maryland in the House of Representatives, May 30, 1872. Washington, D.C.: F. and J. Rives and Geo. A. Bailey, 1872. 20 pp.

1404. Beecher, Catherine Esther. WOMAN'S PROFESSION AS MOTHER AND EDUCATOR WITH VIEWS IN OPPOSITION TO WOMAN SUFFRAGE. Philadelphia and Boston: G. MacLean, 1872.

1405. Bernbaum, Ernest, ed. ANTI-SUFFRAGE ESSAYS BY MASSACHUSETTS WOMEN. Boston: Haien, 1916. 152 pp.

1406. Bernheim, Nicole. "Les Algeriennes," JEUNE AFRIQUE, no. 551 (July 27, 1971), p. 61. Describes why feminine emancipation remains a forbidden topic in Algeria.

1407. Brockett, L. P. WOMAN: HER RIGHTS, WRONGS, PRIVILEGES, AND RESPONSIBILITIES. Hartford: Stebbins, 1869. 447 pp. Reprinted 1970 by Books for Libraries Press, Freeport, N.Y. Woman's relation to man in England, France, and the United States; her position in education, employment, and professional life, and with a long section on woman suffrage, which the author considered folly.

1408. Bushnell, Horace. WOMEN'S SUFFRAGE: THE REFORM AGAINST NATURE. New York: Scribner's, 1869. 184 pp. One of the earliest studies of the suffrage cause.

1409. Crannell, Mrs. W. Winslow. WYOMING. Albany, N.Y.: Albany Anti-Suffrage Association, 1895. Women voted for the first time in Wyoming in 1870.

1410. Goodwin, Grace Duffield. ANTI-SUFFRAGE: TEN GOOD REASONS. New York: Duffield, 1912. 142 pp. Women, she feels, should be able to get their wishes if they are willing to work, without the ballot.

1411. Hamilton, Gail [Mary Abigail Dodge, 1833-1896]. WOMAN'S WRONGS: A COUNTER-IRRITANT. Boston: Ticknor and Fields, 1868. 212 pp. Rather backward on the woman question, believing women's influence on politics should be indirect.

1412. Kenneally, J. "Catholics and Woman Suffrage in Massachusetts," CATHOLIC HISTORICAL REVIEW, vol. 53 (1967), pp. 43-57. The Catholic clergy tried to prevent suffrage on the grounds that it would lead to moral deterioration and upset the political and social climate.

1413. Lombroso, Gina. THE SOUL OF WOMAN (L'ANIMA DELLA DONNA): REFLECTIONS OF LIFE. New York: Dutton, 1923. 269 pp. Rather old-worldish, antifeminist, and antisuffrage.

1414. Ludovici, Anthony M. LYSISTRATA OR WOMAN'S FUTURE AND FUTURE WOMAN. New York: Dutton, 1925. 110 pp. Sees a decline in masculinity and an eventual take-over of the world by women unless a new breed of men will reassert their old mastery.

1415. ———. WOMAN: A VINDICATION. New York: Knopf, 1923. 331 pp. Antifeminist account extolling women's negative qualities such as love of petty power, vanity, and sensuality.

1416. Smith, Munroe. THE CONSENT OF THE GOVERNED. New York: Academy of Political Science, 1914. Reprinted from Publications of the Academy of Political Science, vol. 5, no. 1. A rejection of woman suffrage on the grounds that the operation of government and acquiescence to majority voting decisions depends upon implicit threat of force. Since women are not fit to fight, they have no right to vote.

1417. Trevelyan, Janet Penrose. THE LIFE OF MRS. HUMPHREY WARD, BY HER DAUGHTER. New York: Dodd, Mead, 1923. 317 pp. Mrs. Ward, a novelist of note, was an ardent opponent of suffrage for women.

1418. Wright, Sir Almroth E. THE UNEXPURGATED CASE AGAINST WOMAN SUFFRAGE. New York: Paul B. Hoeber, 1913. 188 pp.

4. Woman Suffrage: Allies

Men, their rights and nothing more; women, their rights and nothing less!
—Motto of THE REVOLUTION, a weekly
edited by Anthony and Stanton

1419. Feeler, Felix [Rev. L. E. Keith]. FEMALE FILOSOFY: FISHED OUT AND FRIED. Cleona, Penn.: G. Holzapfel, 1894, 1897. 336 pp. A forceful, folksy affirmation of woman suffrage.

1420. Higginson, Thomas Wentworth. COMMON SENSE ABOUT WOMEN. Westport, Conn.: Greenwood Press, 1971. Reprint of the Boston, 1882 edition. 403 pp. Higginson was very favorably influenced by the women's rights movement.

1421. Johnson, Helen. WOMAN AND THE REPUBLIC: A SURVEY OF THE WOMAN SUFFRAGE MOVEMENT IN THE UNITED STATES AND A DISCUSSION OF THE CLAIMS AND ARGUMENTS OF ITS FOREMOST ADVOCATES. New York: Appleton, 1897. 327 pp.

1422. Larson, T. A. "Dolls, Vassals, and Drudges—Pioneer Women in the West," WESTERN HISTORICAL QUARTERLY, vol. 3 (Jan. 1972), pp. 5-16. Discusses the West's priority in woman suffrage starting in the pioneer days.

1423. Riegel, Robert E. AMERICAN FEMINISTS. Lawrence: Univ. of Kansas Press, 1968.

1424. Sinclair, Andrew. THE BETTER HALF: THE EMANCIPATION OF THE AMERICAN WOMAN. New York: Harper and Row, 1965.

5. *Woman Suffrage: Effects of the Movement*

Even in the seventeen states where equal pay laws are on the statute books, unequal pay continues to be the rule for women.

—Eleanor Flexner

1425. Catt, Carrie Chapman, and Nettie Rogers Shuler. WOMEN SUFFRAGE AND POLITICS. Seattle: Univ. of Washington Press, 1969. 504 pp. One of the most adequate views of what the woman suffrage movement was about, and what it accomplished.

1426. Gigliotti, Cairoli. WOMAN SUFFRAGE: ITS CAUSES AND POSSIBLE CONSEQUENCES. Chicago: Barnard and Miller Press, 1914.

1427. Grimes, Alan P. THE PURITAN ETHIC AND WOMAN SUFFRAGE. New York: Oxford Univ. Press, 1967. Stresses the woman suffrage movement as a weapon in the hands of nativists organizing against the large groups of foreign immigrants.

1428. Porritt, Mrs. Annie G. LAWS AFFECTING WOMEN AND CHILDREN IN THE SUFFRAGE AND NON-SUFFRAGE STATES. New York: National Woman Suffrage Publishing Co., 1916.

1429. Woodbury, Helen L. S. EQUAL SUFFRAGE: THE RESULTS OF AN INVESTIGATION IN COLORADO MADE FOR THE COLLEGIATE EQUAL SUFFRAGE LEAGUE OF NEW YORK STATE. New York: Arno Press, 1972. Reprint of 1909 edition. Twelve years of woman suffrage in Colorado; how women dealt with political machines, attitudes and prejudices, and how practical politics and women's ideals contended with each other.

1430. Zacharis, John C. "Emmeline Pankhurst: An English Suffragette Influences America," SPEECH MONOGRAPHS, vol. 38 (Aug. 1971), pp. 198-206. Describes the influence of Mrs. Pankhurst when she came to the United States in 1909.

G. Politicians

1. General

I suppose you'd say I don't care too much about which one gets in. I always say they're all gentlemen when they go in as President but rascals when they come out. . . . I don't vote myself. I leave that to the menfolks.

—A Georgia Housewife

We mustn't be too hard on the men. After all, they're the only opposite sex we've got.
—Jean Mann, M.P.

1431. Addams, Jane. NEWER IDEALS OF PEACE. London: Macmillan, 1907. 243 pp. Utilization of women in city government.

1432. Armstrong, Ann. BERLINERS. New Brunswick, N.J.: Rutger's Univ. Press, 1973. Includes research about Berlin women who play a valuable and prominent role in politics, business, and society.

1433. Bach, Patricia Gorence. "Women in Public Life in Wisconsin: A Preliminary Report." ERIC. Alverno Research Center on Women, 1971. 30 pp. A data analysis from a 12-page questionnaire answered by 294 of the 592 women holding public office at the state and local level.

1434. Boals, Kay. "On Getting Feminine Qualities into the Power Structure," UNIVERSITY: A PRINCETON QUARTERLY, no. 54 (Fall 1972), pp. 6-12. Discusses the need for the large-scale entry of women into public and political life to achieve "infusion of feminine qualities into the power structure of America."

1435. THE BOOK OF WOMAN'S POWER. Introduction by Ida M. Tarbell. New York: Macmillan, 1911. 285 pp. Women in government, men and women in society, industry, and the political value of the family.

1436. Braun, Lily. DIE FRAUEN UND DIE POLITIK [Women and Politics]. Berlin: Expedition der Buchhandlung Vorwarts, 1903. An early German account of the role of women in politics.

1437. "The Chieftainship in Basutoland," AFRICAN STUDIES (Johannesburg, S.A.), vol. 4, no. 4 (1945), pp. 157-159. Judgment in a case brought against the chief wife of a deceased Sotho chief upon her having assumed the regency; the fact that the judgment was in her favor is proof of the changes taking place among the tribes in their defense of the rights of women.

1438. Clarkson, Adrienne. "The Female Style in Politics." In A GUIDE TO THE PEACEABLE KINGDOM, edited by William Kilbourn. Toronto: Macmillan, 1970. A perceptive review of women's liberation in Canada.

1439. Davis, Kenneth. "Miss Eleanor Roosevelt," AMERICAN HERITAGE, vol. 22 (Oct. 1971), pp. 48-59. Biographical article.

1440. Depatie, Francine. PARTICIPATION OF WOMEN IN POLITICS IN QUEBEC. Studies of the Royal Commission on the Status of Women in Quebec. Ottawa, 1972. Study of the forces that have shaped the Canadian women's political and legal consciousness.

1441. deTocqueville, Alexis. DEMOCRACY IN AMERICA. New York: Harper and Row, 1965. Observations on the more restrictive nature of marital status of American women compared with their European counterparts. Contrasts the greater freedom allowed American single women, but their lack of access to political roles.

1442. Dunn, Erica, and Judy Klein. "Women in the Russian Revolution," reprinted from WOMEN: A JOURNAL OF REVOLUTION, vol. 1, no. 4 (Summer 1970), pp. 22-23. Traces the growth of the women's movement in Russia during the Bolshevik Revolution.

1443. Duverger, Maurice. THE POLITICAL ROLE OF WOMEN. Paris: M. Blondin (UNESCO), 1955. 221 pp. Analyzes the prevailing powerlessness of women in politics and considers the main obstacles to female influence in government: female inertia and male chauvinism. Use with caution, noting Duverger's reservations.

1444. Festini, Nelly. "Women in Public Life in Peru," THE ANNALS, vol. 375 (Jan. 1968), pp. 58-60. Political participation of Peruvian women (granted some years ago), falls short of that of men because women are confronted with the dilemma of their roles as mother and housewife.

1445. Flexner, Eleanor. A CENTURY OF STRUGGLE. Cambridge: Harvard Univ. Press, 1959; New York: Atheneum, 1968. 384 pp. Scholarly history of the women's rights movement in America from its beginnings to 1920.

1446. Hareven, Tamara. ELEANOR ROOSEVELT: AN AMERICAN CONSCIENCE. New York: Quadrangle Books, 1968. One of the first searching appraisals of her role in the New Deal and her impact on American life.

1447. International Institute of Differing Civilizations (INCIDI). WOMEN'S ROLE IN THE DEVELOPMENT OF TROPICAL AND SUBTROPICAL COUNTRIES. Brussels: INCIDI, 1959.

1448. Jaquette, Jane S., ed. WOMEN IN POLITICS. New York: Wiley, 1974. Anthology of essays and studies of women around the world. Contributors include: Cornelia B. Flora, Naomi B. Lynn, Mary M. Lepper, Susan Kaufman Purcell, Jo Freeman, Barbara Jancar, Lynne B. Iglitzen, Emmy B. Werner, Louise Bachtold, Mary C. Porter, Ann B. Matasar, Marjorie Lansing, Warren Farrell, Nancy McWilliams, Temma Kaplan, Eleanor C. Smeal, Judith van Allen, Audrey S. Wells, JoAnn F. Aviel, Kay Boals, and Elsa Chaney.

1449. "Les Femmes Togolaises: Une Participation Active Autant Qu'Originale a La Vie Economique at Politique," FRANCE OUTREMER, no. 502 (Nov. 1971), pp. 26-27.

1450. Marie-André du Sacre-Coeur, Sister. "L'Activité Politique de la Femme en Afrique Noire," REVUE JURIDIQUE ET POLITIQUE DE L'UNION FRANCAISE (Paris), Oct.-Dec. 1954, pp. 476-497.

1451. Marvick, Dwaine. "The Political Socialization of the American Negro," THE ANNALS, vol. 361 (Sept. 1965), pp. 112-127. Noteworthy in that no mention is made of female contributions or the state of female political socialization, much less of black females as political beings.

1452. McCulloch, Albert. SUFFRAGE AND ITS PROBLEMS. Baltimore: Warwick and York, 1929. 185 pp. A 1929 look at the influence of the Negro women, and foreign immigrants in American life, with a good exploration of the suffrage struggle from the early 1600s to 1929.

1453. Means, Ingunn Norderval. "Political Recruitment of Women in Norway," THE WESTERN POLITICAL SCIENCE QUARTERLY, vol. 25, no. 3 (Sept. 1972), pp. 491-521. The results of 1971 municipal elections indicates that a larger proportion of women are being recruited into national service.

1454. ———. "Women in Local Politics: The Norwegian Experience," CANADIAN JOURNAL OF POLITICAL SCIENCE, vol. 5, no. 3 (Sept. 1972).

1455. Muggeridge, Kitty. BEATRICE WEBB: A LIFE, 1858-1943. London: Secker and Warburg, 1967. 271 pp. Biography of one of the founders of the London School of Economics and THE NEW STATESMAN; crusader for social reform in Britain over a period of 50 years.

1456. Pickles, Dorothy. "The Political Role of Women," INTERNATIONAL SOCIAL SCIENCE BULLETIN, (Mar. 1953), pp. 75-103. Study of the political roles of women in Norway, France, Yugoslavia, and West Germany, particularly their voting records, roles in parliaments and local government, and their influence in the public, judicial, and educational systems. This article led to the UNESCO inquiry on women's political roles, written by Maurice Duverger.

1457. Roosevelt, Eleanor. THIS IS MY STORY. New York: Harper, 1937. 365 pp. The story of the personal growth and official duties of the wife of F.D.R., up to 1924.
1458. ———. THIS I REMEMBER. New York: Harper, 1949. 387 pp. Continuation of her THIS IS MY STORY, the years in the White House, family problems, and the defense of her husband against his innumerable critics.
1459. ———. TOMORROW IS NOW. New York: Harper, 1963. 139 pp. The last writings of one of the busiest women in the world, or as Adlai Stevenson said, "one of God's noblest, strongest creations."
1460. Rosenberg, Marie Barovic. "Women in Politics: Participation in Chippewa and Eau Claire Counties." Madison, Wis.: Institute of Governmental Affairs, 1975. 20 pp.
1461. Rover, C. WOMEN'S SUFFRAGE AND PARTY POLITICS IN BRITAIN, 1866-1914. London: Routledge and Kegan Paul, 1967.
1462. Rowbotham, Sheila. WOMEN'S LIBERATION AND THE NEW POLITICS. London: May Day Manifesto, 1970. 32 pp.
1463. Tart, Marjorie. THE EDUCATION OF WOMEN FOR CITIZENSHIP: SOME PRACTICAL SUGGESTIONS. Paris: UNESCO, 1954. 106 pp.
1464. Weis, Jessica M. "Organizing the Women." In POLITICS U.S.A., edited by James Cannon. New York: Doubleday, 1960. 348 pp.
1465. WHO'S WHO IN AMERICAN POLITICS, 1971-1972. New York: R. R. Bowker, 1971. 1171 pp. Very important resource book on men and women in politics.

2. Politicians: Elective Office

Democracy substitutes election by the incompetent many for appointment by the corrupt few.
—G. B. Shaw

1466. Abzug, Bella. BELLA—MS. ABZUG GOES TO WASHINGTON. Edited by Mel Ziegler. New York: Saturday Review Press, 1972. Record of Bella Abzug's campaign for the House of Representatives, in diary form.
1467. Alpha Kappa Alpha Sorority, Incorporated. WOMEN IN POLITICS. Booklet no. 2. Chicago: Alpa Kappa Alpha Sorority, July, 1969. Series of short biographical sketches of 14 Negro women who served in state or national elective office.
1468. Betts, Annabel (Paxton). WOMEN IN CONGRESS. Richmond, Va.: Dietz, 1945. 140 pp. Biographies of congresswomen.
1469. Brookes, Pamela. WOMEN AT WESTMINSTER: 1918-1966. London: Peter Davies, 1967. Women who have served in the British Parliament.
1470. Bullock, Charles S., and Patricia Findley Heys. "Recruitment of Women for Congress: A Research Note," WESTERN POLITICAL SCIENCE QUARTERLY, vol. 25, no. 3 (Sept. 1972), pp. 416-423. Congresswomen who win regular elections have backgrounds different from those of widows elected to fill their husbands' vacancies. The first, like their male counterparts, come from similar educational, professional, and political backgrounds, while the widows usually come from a housewife class.
1471. Chamberlin, Hope. A MINORITY OF MEMBERS: WOMEN IN THE U.S. CONGRESS. New York: Praeger, 1973. A biographical sketch of each woman who has served in the U.S. Congress.

1472. Chisholm, Shirley. UNBOUGHT AND UNBOSSED. Boston: Houghton Mifflin, 1970. Autobiographical account of her family background, education, political apprenticeship, and election to Congress.

1473. ———. THE GOOD FIGHT. New York: Harper and Row, 1973. On her presidential campaign and on her continuing battle for the reform of American politics.

1474. Cole, Margaret. SERVANT OF THE COUNTRY. London: Dennis Dobson, 1956. 200 pp. Describes her work as alderman of the London County Council.

1475. Constantine, Edmond, and Kenneth H. Craik. "Women as Politicians: The Social Background, Personality, and Political Careers of Female Party Leaders," JOURNAL OF SOCIAL ISSUES, vol. 28, no. 2 (1972), pp. 217-236.

1476. Dreifus, Claudia. "Women in Politics: An Interview with Edith Green," SOCIAL POLICY (Jan.-Feb. 1972), pp. 16-22. Describes her discriminatory treatment by her male colleagues in Congress, especially since her espousal of the Equal Rights Amendment.

1477. Gehlen, Frieda L. Foote. "Roll Stress and Cultural Resources: A Study of the Role of the Woman Member of Congress." Ph.D dissertation, Mighican State Univ., 1967. Univ. Microfilms, Ann Arbor, Mich. An exhaustive and definitive study of the women members of the 88th Congress replete with comparative analyses of a representative sampling of their male colleagues.

1478. ———. "Women in Congress: Their Power and Influence in a Man's World," TRANSACTION, Oct. 1969, pp. 36-40. Indicates that the few female members of Congress are represented on the higher-status committees and in small formal groups, but their participation in powerful "informal relationships" has been blocked.

1479. Gilfond, Duff. "Gentlewomen of the House," THE AMERICAN MERCURY, vol. 18, no. 70 (Oct. 1929), pp. 151-160. Short, waspish, and condescending biographies of a number of Congresswomen newly elected to the House.

1480. Graham, Frank. MARGARET CHASE SMITH: WOMAN OF COURAGE. New York: John Day, 1964. 188 pp. Informal biography of the Maine senator.

1481. Gruberg, Martin. WOMEN IN AMERICAN POLITICS: AN ASSESSMENT AND SOURCEBOOK. Oshkosh, Wis.: Academia Press, 1968. 336 pp. Statistical compilations with brief sketches on outstanding American women political activists.

1482. Kirkpatrick, Jeane. POLITICAL WOMAN. New York: Basic Books, 1974. New Brunswick, N.J.: Rutger's Univ., Center for the American Woman in Politics, Eagleton Institute. Study stemming from a 1972 conference of women legislators.

1483. "Lady Paramount Chief: Mme. Ella Koblo Gulama, from the Mende of Sierra Leone," WEST AFRICA, no. 2141 (1958), p. 391. A biographical note on the first district head and woman deputy in Sierra Leone.

1484. Lampson, Peggy. FEW ARE CHOSEN: AMERICAN WOMEN IN POLITICAL LIFE TODAY. Boston: Houghton Mifflin, 1968. 240 pp. Concentrates on ten women who have entered the political arena, and how they got there. Discusses Senator Margaret Chase Smith, Congresswomen Patsy Mink, Frances Bolton, Martha Griffiths, and Ambassador Eugenie Anderson.

1485. Loth, David. A LONG WAY FORWARD: THE BIOGRAPHY OF CON-
GRESSWOMAN FRANCES P. BOLTON. New York: Longmans, Green
1957.
1486. Mann, Jean. WOMEN IN PARLIAMENT. London: Oldhams Press, 1962.
Autobiographical account of her role in Westminster and British politics.
1487. Mann, Peggy. GOLDA: THE LIFE OF ISRAEL'S PRIME MINISTER.
New York: Coward, McCann and Geoghegan, 1971. 287 pp. The
woman whose life is dramatically interwoven with the creation of Israel.
1488. Miller, Judy Ann. "The Representative is a Lady," THE BLACK POLITI-
CIAN, vol. 1, no. 2 (Fall 1969), pp. 17-18. About Iowa's Representative A. June Franklin, Minority House Whip, first black lawmaker in the
history of American politics to be elected to a leadership position.
1489. Mitchell, A. "America's First Woman Mayor," OHIO STATE ARCHEO-
LOGICAL AND HISTORICAL QUARTERLY, vol. 53 (Columbus,
Ohio), 1944, pp. 52-54.
1490. Nader, Ralph. RALPH NADER CONGRESS PROJECT: CITIZENS LOOK
AT CONGRESS. 9 vols. Washington, D.C.: Grossman Publishers, 1972.
Series of portraits of women members of the House of Representatives:
Marcia Abramson, "Martha Griffiths (D.-Mich.)"; Nancy Gates, "Patsy
T. Mink (D.-Hawaii)"; Ken Jarin and James Burkhardt, "Ella Grasso (D.-
Conn.)"; Joan Kuriansky, "Louise Day Hicks (D.-Mass.)"; Joan Kurian-
sky and Catherine Smith, "Shirley St. Hill Chisholm (D.-N.Y.)"; Jack
Lyness, "Margaret M. Heckler (R.-Mass.)"; Dale Pullen, "Margaret Chase
Smith (R.-Maine)"; Robert Sussman, "Leonor K. Sullivan (D.-Missouri)";
and Nancy Weinberg and Pauline Jennings, "Bella S. Abzug (D.-N.Y.)";
Ruth Darmstadter, "Julia Butler Hansen (D.-Washington)"; Louise
Wides, "Edith Green (D.-Oregon)."
1491. Nies, Judith. "The Abzug Race: A Lesson in Politics," MS. MAGAZINE,
Feb. 1973. A criticism of the many efforts of liberals to prevent her from
returning to Congress.
1492. Norris, Marianna. DONA FELISA: A BIOGRAPHY OF THE MAYOR OF
SAN JUAN. New York: Dodd, Mead, 1969. 95 pp.
1493. Rosenberg, Marie Barovic. "Women in Politics: A Comparative Study of
Congresswomen Edith Green and Julia Butler Hansen." Ph.D dissertation,
Univ. of Washington, 1973. University Microfilms, Ann Arbor, Michigan.
1494. Ross, J.F.S. "Women and Parliamentary Elections," BRITISH JOURNAL
OF SOCIOLOGY, vol. 4, no. 1 (1953), pp. 14-24. Study of female
candidates for Parliament, showing a tendency to select a woman over a
man if there appears to be any chance of victory.
1495. Smith, Margaret Chase. DECLARATION OF CONSCIENCE. New York:
Doubleday, 1972. 512 pp. Statement by Senator from Maine.
1496. Stocks, Mary D. ELEANOR RATHBONE: A BIOGRAPHY. London:
Gollancz, 1950. 376 pp. The story of the early British suffragist and
member of Parliament.
1497. Summerskill, Edith. A WOMAN'S WORLD. London: Heinemann, 1967.
258 pp. Autobiography of a feminist and socialist physician, a member
of Parliament, and an advocate of abortion reform in Britain.
1498. Sweetman, Maude. WHAT PRICE POLITICS: THE INSIDE STORY OF
WASHINGTON STATE POLITICS. Seattle: White and Hitchcock, 1927.
150 pp. Author served three terms in the Washington State House of
Representatives from 1923-1927.

1499. Syrkin, Marie. GOLDA MEIR: ISRAEL'S LEADER. New York: G. P. Putnam's Sons, 1963. Biography of the prime minister and world leader.
1500. U.S. Department of Labor. WOMEN OF THE 80TH-90TH CONGRESS, 1946-67. Washington, D.C.: Women's Bureau, SUDOC, GPO, 1967. 12 pp.
1501. Valen, Henry. "The Recruitment of Parliamentary Nominees in Norway," SCANDINAVIAN POLITICAL STUDIES, vol. 1 (1966), pp. 131 ff. Argues that Norwegian parties will place women in marginal positions on the lists in the hopes that women candidates will attract the female vote.
1502. ———, and Daniel Katz. POLITICAL PARTIES IN NORWAY. Oslo: Universitetsforlaget,1964. Indicates that women's chances for election are better than in American society.
1503. Werner, Emmy. "Personality Characteristics of Women in State Legislatures and Congress." In WOMEN IN POLITICS edited by Jane Jaquette. New York: Wiley, 1974. Compilation and analysis of statistics available on women who have served as legislators.
1504. ———. "Women in Congress: 1917-1964," WESTERN POLITICAL QUARTERLY, vol. 19, no. 1 (Mar. 1966), pp. 16-30. Examination of biographical information available on U.S. Congresswomen to identify trends and prospects for increased representation.
1505. Willcoxen, Harriet. FIRST LADY OF INDIA: THE STORY OF INDIRA GANDHI. Garden City, N.Y.: Doubleday, 1969.
1506. "Women in Public Office," COMMONWEAL, vol. 24 (Jan. 13, 1939), p. 311.

3. Politicians: Appointive Office

Whenever a man has cast a longing eye on offices, a rottenness begins in his conduct.
—Thomas Jefferson

1507. Ade, Ginny. "One-Year Job: White House Fellow," PROGRESSIVE WOMAN, vol. 2 (Feb. 1972), pp. 14-17+.
1508. Alpha Kappa Alpha Sorority, Inc. NEGRO WOMEN IN THE JUDICIARY. Booklet no. 1. Chicago: Alpha Kappa Alpha Sorority, 1969. Series of short biographies of the careers of ten Negro women in the judiciary.
1509. Anderson, Mary. WOMAN AT WORK: THE AUTOBIOGRAPHY OF MARY ANDERSON AS TOLD TO MARY N. WINSLOW. Minneapolis: Univ. of Minnesota Press, 1951. 266 pp. The story of the director of the Women's Bureau, U.S. Department of Labor, for 25 years, until 1944.
1510. Harriman, Florence. FROM PINAFORE TO POLITICS. New York: Holt, 1923. 359 pp. Reminiscences of her life in New York society in the 1890s and her political involvement as the only woman member of President Wilson's Industrial Relations Commission.
1511. Jeffreys, Margot. "Married Women in the Higher Grades of the Civil Service and Government-Sponsored Research Organizations," BRITISH JOURNAL OF SOCIOLOGY, vol. 3 (Dec. 1952), pp. 361-364. Study of appointment procedures and policies.
1512. Judek, Stanislauw. WOMEN IN THE PUBLIC SERVICE: THEIR UTILIZATION AND EMPLOYMENT. Ottawa: Department of Labour, 1968. How the Canadian Public Service discriminates against women in employment.

1513. Kollontai, Alexandra. AUTOBIOGRAPHY OF A SEXUALLY EMANCI-
PATED WOMAN AND AN ESSAY ON THE NEW WOMAN. New York:
Herder, 1971. 135 pp. Story of the first Russian woman appointed
ambassador and of her fight for women's rights in the Soviet Union.

1514. McFadden, Judith Nies. "Women's Lib on Capitol Hill," THE PRO-
GRESSIVE, Dec. 1970, pp. 22-25. Discriminatory attitudes toward
women on Congressional staffs and committees.

1515. Mead, Margaret. "Women in National Service," TEACHERS COLLEGE
RECORD, vol. 73 (Sept. 1971), pp. 59-63. Discusses national services
for women.

1516. "Meet Ten Women Ministers," SOVIET WOMAN, no. 1 (Jan. 1957),
pp. 6-7.

1517. Perkins, Frances. THE INTERNATIONAL LABOR ORGANIZATION AS
AN AGENCY OF DEMOCRACY. Philadelphia: n.p., 1939. Presented
March 27, 1939 before the Democratic Women's Luncheon Club. Description of the appointive roles of women in international labor
organizations.

1518. "Women in Public Life," STATE GOVERNMENT, vol. 10 (Oct. 1937).
Entire issue devoted to the subject. Articles by Frances Perkins, Secretary of Labor; Hattie Caraway, U.S. Senator; Katherine F. Lenroot, Chief
of the Children's Bureau; Bernice T. Van Der Vries, Illinois State Representative; Jean Charters, Personnel Secretary, Public Administration
Clearing House; and Marion E. Martin, Maine State Representative.

4. Politicians: Party Activists

I always voted at my party's call,
And I never thought of thinking for myself at all.
—Gilbert and Sullivan
(H.M.S. Pinafore)

1519. Beard, Charles A. "The Woman's Party," THE NEW REPUBLIC, vol. 7,
no. 91 (July 29, 1916), pp. 329-331. The story of the formation of the
Woman's Party at Chicago in 1916 and the statement of the woman's
cause which won from the Republicans the strong endorsement of the
principle of woman suffrage on the ground of justice.

1520. Belden, Jack. CHINA SHAKES THE WORLD. New York: Monthly Review Press, 1970. 524 pp. Reprint of the 1949 edition. Chapters discussing the role of Chinese women in the Chinese Revolution and in the
Communist party.

1521. Erskine, Hazel. "The Polls: Women's Role," PUBLIC OPINION QUARTER-
LY, vol. 35 (Summer 1971), pp. 275-290. Womens role in Society 1937-1970.

1522. Flynn, Elizabeth Gurley. ALDERSON STORY: MY LIFE AS A POLITI-
CAL PRISONER. New York: International Publishing Co., 1972. Biography of a political activist and rebel.

1523. Frumkin, S. A WOMAN'S PARTY. London: Goldston, 1938. 159 pp. A
plea for the formation of a woman's political party.

1524. Irwin, Inez Hayes. UPHILL WITH BANNERS FLYING: THE STORY OF
THE WOMAN'S PARTY. Penobscot, Maine: Traversity Press, 1964.
Official history of the party that kept the Equal Rights Amendment
battle going, alone, for 40 years.

1525. Jennings, M. Kent, and Norman Thomas. "Men and Women in Party Elites: Social Roles and Political Resources," MIDWEST JOURNAL OF POLITICAL SCIENCE, vol. 7, no. 4 (Nov. 1968).

1526. Molle, Jessie. "The National Convention and the Woman's Movement," INTERNATIONAL SOCIALIST REVIEW, vol. 8, no. 11 (May 1908), pp. 688-690. A plea for a socialist party to work as a whole toward women's rights, rather than as a separate association of women's clubs, conventions, etc.

1527. Phillips, Marion, ed. WOMEN AND THE LABOUR PARTY. New York: Huebsch, 1918. 110 pp.

1528. Pritchard, Ada. "Speech," LEGISLATURE OF ONTARIO DEBATES, official report, daily edition, 1st sess., 28th Legislature, July 18, 1968, p. 5976. Alleges that parties in Canada tend to nominate women only in areas they consider to be certain losses.

1529. Proxmire, Ellen. ONE FOOT IN WASHINGTON: THE PERILOUS LIFE OF A SENATOR'S WIFE. Washington, D.C.: Robert B. Luce, 1963. Autobiography of her participation in Democratic party politics as precinct committeewoman, to the state executive committee.

1530. Republican Party, National Committee. THE HISTORY OF WOMEN IN REPUBLICAN NATIONAL CONVENTIONS. Washington, D.C.: Republican National Committee, Women's Division, 1963.

1531. Richmond, Al. NATIVE DAUGHTER: THE STORY OF ANITA WHITNEY. San Francisco: Anita Whitney 75th Anniversary Committee, 1942. 199 pp. Biography of a prominent communist leader.

1532. Spargo, John. "Women and the Socialist Movement," INTERNATIONAL SOCIALIST REVIEW, Feb. 1908, pp. 449-455.

1533. THE STRUGGLE BETWEEN TWO LINES AT THE MOSCOW WORLD CONGRESS OF WOMEN. Peking: Foreign Languages Press, 1963. 61 pp.

5. Politicians: Interest Groups and Voluntary Associations

"It is possible—that it may not come, during our lives. . . . We shall not see the triumph."
[Defarge] "We shall have helped it," returned madame."
—Dickens (A Tale of Two Cities)

1534. Beard, Mary R. WOMAN'S WORK IN MUNICIPALITIES. New York: Arno Press, 1972. Reprint of the 1915 edition. Evaluates the female force for good in civic works, and contributions being made by women in social movements for community improvement, education, public health, integration, social services, and the fight against social evils.

1535. Breckinridge, Sophonisba P. WOMEN IN THE TWENTIETH CENTURY: A STUDY OF THEIR POLITICAL, SOCIAL AND ECONOMIC ACTIVITIES. New York: Arno Press, 1972. Reprint of the 1933 edition. 364 pp. Surveys the changing roles of women's clubs, national organizations, occupational and professional groups, by the leading associate of Jane Addams.

1536. Golding, Elizabeth B., and Dallas Johnson. DON'T UNDERESTIMATE WOMAN POWER: A BLUE-PRINT FOR INTER-GROUP ACTION. New York: Public Affairs Committee, 1951. 32 pp. Pamphlet describing what women's groups can accomplish politically, both nationally and locally, by working together.

1537. McFarland, C. K. "Crusade for Child Laborers: 'Mother' Jones and the March of the Mill Children," PENNSYLVANIA HISTORY, vol. 38 (July 1971), pp. 283-296. Biographical article on Mother Jones.

1538. Nestor, Agnes. WOMEN'S LABOR LEADER: AN AUTOBIOGRAPHY. Rockford, Ill.: Bellevue Books, 1954. 307 pp. Agnes Nestor was president of the Woman's Trade Union League of Chicago from 1913 until her death in 1948.

1539. Phillips, Ruth, ed. FORTY YEARS OF A GREAT IDEA. Washington, D.C.: League of Women Voters of the United States, 1960. 51 pp. Story of the LWV since 1920; the creative forces, purpose, and history of a national organization.

1540. Rothschild, Joan A. "On Building a Female Constituency: The Case of Massachusetts." Mimeographed. Boston: Women's Research Center of Boston, part 1, (Sept. 1972), 13 pp.; part 2, (Nov. 1973), 13 pp. Description of the many service-oriented groups that are specifically feminist in terms of the projects and services they offer, i.e., women's centers, birth control counseling centers, free and co-op stores, day care, etc.

1541. ———, et al. WHO RULES MASSACHUSETTS WOMEN: AN ANALYSIS OF POLICIES AND POLICY-MAKERS IN STATE GOVERNMENT. Boston: Women's Research Center of Boston, Aug. 1972.

1542. WOMEN'S RIGHTS CONVENTIONS: SENECA FALLS AND ROCHESTER, 1848. New York: Arno Press, 1969. Proceedings of both conventions, with the texts and signatories of members present at the first Women's Rights Conventions.

III. HISTORY

The following sections indicate some of the potentialities and certain inadequacies of the literature surveyed in this volume. Faced with the difficult task of selecting and editing the materials, we have attempted to construe the history of women in its widest sense by maintaining a chronological and topical balance between useful general works and scholarly monographs of interest to the specialist. Since it is neither possible nor desirable to impose absolute uniformity on the various sections, we have been guided by the state of the literature. History, as one of the social sciences, is indebted to economics, political science, psychology, cultural anthropology, sociology, philosophy, biography, and the humanities for special insights into selected aspects of women's role in society. The history of women, as revealed in the following chapter, is the study of a unique sequence of unique individuals, events, situations, ideas, and institutions—the record of the progress of women, socially as individuals, politically as citizens—from ancient times, when woman was little more than a household drudge, to the present day, when woman is at last given the right to stand beside men and have a voice in regulating and deciding affairs. We can now grasp the main landmarks in the development and progress of women through the ages from a variety of sources and disciplines. What follows is a bare outline, with many inevitable omissions.

One final technical remark: the references are as specific as possible, but with occasional exceptions, complete citations were not available for some editions of earlier works.

A. Women in Society

... history can legitimately play a role in providing for women—and for men— heroines and models, it can be a source of forgotten alternatives, and also a chart of shallow water and treacherous rocks. History, after all, should be a liberating force.

—Alan Graebner

1543. Agrippa, Marcus Vipsanius. DE NOBILITATE ET PRAECELLENTIA FOEMINEI SEXUS [The Nobility and Pre-Eminence of the Feminine Sex]. Translated by David Clapham, 1542. By the Roman statesman and general, victor over Antony and Cleopatra at Actium. An early pro-feminist view.

1544. Alexander, William. THE HISTORY OF WOMEN FROM THE EARLIEST ANTIQUITY; GIVING SOME ACCOUNT OF ALMOST EVERY INTERESTING PARTICULAR CONCERNING THAT SEX, AMONG ALL NATIONS ANCIENT AND MODERN. 2 volumes. London: n.p., 1779. An encyclopedic compendium.

1545. ARAMCO WORLD MAGAZINE, vol. 22, no. 2 (Mar.-April 1971). Special issue devoted to women in the Arab world. 40 pp. Twelve articles by such authors as Leslie Farmer, Anne Bruno, Katsy Thomas, and Penny Williams on "The Arab Woman at War," "The Arab Woman in History," and "The Arab Woman—A Traditional View."

1546. Bachofen, J. J. DAS MUTTERECHT [The Mother Right]. Stuttgart, 1861. An influential historical and sociological study that uncovered evidences of a frequent matriarchal stage of family organization prior to the historical patriarchal family.

1547. Beard, Mary Ritter. WOMEN AS FORCE IN HISTORY: A STUDY OF TRADITIONS AND REALITIES. New York: Macmillan, 1946. 369 pp. Comprehensive study of women's influence through the ages, with informative chapters on women's and men's attitudes, the force of women in medieval economic and social life, with an excellent bibliography.

1548. Bebel, Auguste. WOMAN: PAST, PRESENT AND FUTURE. New York: Boni and Liveright, 1918. 512 pp. Marxist classic that contains radical nineteenth-century views on women.

1549. Bond, R. Warwick, ed. WILLIAM BERCHER'S NOBILITY OF WOMEN. London: Roxburghe Club, 1904. Originally written in 1529 in Latin, translated in 1542. A classic quoted by English writers on behalf of women.

1550. Booth, Meyrich. WOMAN AND SOCIETY. New York: Longmans Green, 1929. 256 pp. Because women are physically and psychologically inferior to men, Booth contends that they should be educated for house-keeping and childbirth, and not for business or the professions.

1551. Bradbury, Harriet B. CIVILIZATION AND WOMANHOOD. Richard Badger, 1916. 229 pp. A discussion of the position of women in the past and the contributions they have made to the progress of civilization.

1552. Braithwaite, Richard. THE ENGLISH GENTLEWOMAN. London: n.p., 1631. Modesty, piety, and skill were needed to keep her husband's love, and caring for her family in health and sickness were the chief obliga-tions of the perfect gentlewoman.

1553. Breckinridge, Sophonisba P. WOMEN IN THE TWENTIETH CENTURY: A STUDY OF THEIR POLITICAL, SOCIAL AND ECONOMIC ACTIVITIES. New York: Arno Press, 1972. Reprint of the 1933 edition. A survey of the changing and expanding roles of women in the first two decades of the twentieth century, by an associate of Jane Addams.

1554. Brittain, Alfred, and Mitchell Carroll. WOMEN OF EARLY CHRISTIAN-ITY. Philadelphia: Rittenhouse Press, 1908. 390 pp. Historical view of women, their customs, and their contributions to early Christian institutions.

1555. Brophy, Brigid. DON'T NEVER FORGET. New York: Holt, Rinehart and Winston, 1961. 319 pp. Anthology of essays on women in general, marriage, and monogamy, with biographical sketches of such women as Jane Austen, Louisa M. Alcott, and Simone de Beauvoir.

1556. Campo de Alange, Maria de los Reyes Laffitte de Salamanca, Condesa del. LA MUJER EN ESPAGNA: CIEN ANOS DE SU HISTORIA, 1860-1960. Madrid: Aguilar, 1963. 389 pp. History of women in Spain, with contributions of Spanish women to society.

1557. Chombart de Lauwe, Paul-Henry. IMAGES DE LA FEMME DANS LA SOCIETE: RECHERCHE INTERNATIONALE SOUS LA DIRECTION DE PAUL-HENRY CHOMBART DE LAUWE. Paris: Editions Ouvrieres, 1964. 280 pp. An international portrait of women's roles in society.

1558. Coolidge, Mary Roberts. WHY WOMEN ARE SO. New York: Arno Press, 1972. Reprint of the 1912 edition. An analysis by a social historian of the development of feminine behavior and the social forces that molded them to meet masculine expectations.

1559. Cudderford, G. WOMEN AND SOCIETY: FROM VICTORIAN TIMES TO THE PRESENT DAY. London: Hamish Hamilton, 1967. 120 pp. The condition and progress of women in Great Britain.

1560. Darcie, Abraham. THE HONOUR OF LADIES: OR, A TRUE DESCRIP-TION OF THEIR NOBLE PERFECTIONS. London: n.p., 1622. An early pro-feminist tract of the Elizabethan period.

1561. Davis, Elizabeth Gould. THE FIRST SEX. New York: G. P. Putnam's Sons, 1971. 382 pp. Develops the thesis that women are not only the equal of men, but that their contribution to civilization has been superior. In developing this theory, the author draws from mythology, archeology, and history.

1562. de Koven, Anna. WOMEN IN THE CYCLES OF CULTURE: A STUDY OF "WOMEN'S POWER" THROUGH THE CENTURIES. New York: G. P. Putnam's Sons, 1941. An attack upon the male-dominated society, with evidences of women's contributions to culture and civilization.

1563. Dexter, Elizabeth A. CAREER WOMAN OF AMERICA, 1776-1840. Francetown, N.H.: Marshall Jones, 1950. History of women and their careers, emphasizing their struggle for professional and employ-ment equality.

1564. Diner, Helen. MOTHERS AND AMAZONS: THE FIRST FEMININE HISTORY OF CULTURE. New York: Julian Press, 1965. 254 pp. Published more than 40 years ago in Germany, a brilliant study of primitive social organization, based on biology, mythology, psychology, and sociology, and ranging from the Sumerians and Babylonians to Greece and Rome, Asia and the Americas.

1565. Dingwall, Eric John. THE AMERICAN WOMAN: A HISTORICAL STUDY. London: G. Duckworth, 1956. 286 pp. His thesis is that woman's basic conflict is sexual, and that she is oppressed by the roles imposed upon her by society.

1566. Donovan, Frank R. THE WOMEN IN THEIR LIVES: THE DISTAFF SIDE OF THE FOUNDING FATHERS. New York: Dodd, Mead, 1966. 339 pp. Personalities and influences of the women in the lives of Franklin, Washington, Adams, Jefferson, Hamilton, and Madison.

1567. Figes, Eva. PATRIARCHAL ATTITUDES. Greenwich, Conn.: Fawcett, 1970. Historical attitudes toward women by Freud and Rousseau, among others, are examined by an English novelist.

1568. Fuller, Margaret. WOMAN IN THE NINETEENTH CENTURY, AND KINDRED PAPERS RELATING TO THE SPHERE, CONDITION AND DUTIES OF WOMAN. New York: Source Book Press, 1970. Re-print of the 1855 edition. Influential work which maintained that women must independently fulfill themselves as individuals, by the first woman staff member of the NEW YORK TRIBUNE.

1569. Furuya, Tsunetake. "Meiji Women: Landmarks They Have Left," JAPAN QUARTERLY, vol. 14 (1967), pp. 318-325. Description of significant contributions by women in social, political, and economic development of Japan during the period 1868-1912.

1570. Gage, Matilda Joslyn. WOMAN, CHURCH AND STATE: A HISTORICAL ACCOUNT OF THE STATUS OF WOMEN THROUGH THE CHRIS-TIAN AGES; WITH REMINISCENCES OF THE MATRIARCHATE. New York: Arno Press. 1972. Reprint of the 1900 edition. A scholarly critique of theological complicity in women's subjugation through the ages.

1571. Gordon, Ann D., Mari Jo Buhle, and Nancy E. Schrom. "Women in American Society: An Historical Contribution," RADICAL AMERICA, vol. 5 (July-Aug. 1971), pp. 3-66. Historians, who largely limited themselves to writing about the powerful, study a history without women.
1572. Hale, Sarah Josepha. WOMEN'S RECORD; OR, SKETCHES OF ALL DISTINGUISHED WOMEN, FROM THE CREATION TO A.D. 1854. 2 vols. New York: Source Book Press, 1970. 945 pp. Reprint of the 1855 edition. Brief biographies and selected writings of 2,000 women in history, by the editor of GODEY'S LADY'S BOOK.
1573. Heywood, Thomas. NINE BOOKS OF VARIOUS HISTORY CONCERNINGE WOMEN. London: n.p., 1624. Reissued in 1657 as THE GENERAL HISTORY OF WOMEN. "Here thou mayest reade of all degrees, from the Scepter in the Court to the Sheepehooke in the Cottage: of all times from the first Rainbow to the last blazing Starre."
1574. Hill, Georgiana. WOMEN IN ENGLISH LIFE. 2 vols. London: R. Bentley, 1896. The record of women in British culture and traditions.
1575. Humphrey, Grace. WOMEN IN AMERICAN HISTORY. Indianapolis: Bobbs-Merrill, 1919. The role of American women in the struggle for liberation.
1576. James, Bartlett Burleigh. WOMEN OF ENGLAND. Philadelphia: Rittenhouse Press, 1908. 425 pp.
1577. Kirkpatrick, Clifford. NAZI GERMANY: ITS WOMEN AND FAMILY LIFE. Indianapolis: Bobbs-Merrill, 1938. 353 pp. The Nazi theories of family life and the role of women under National Socialism.
1578. La Follette, Suzanne. CONCERNING WOMEN. New York: Arno Press, 1972. Reprint of the 1926 edition. Places the struggle for women's liberation within the framework of the struggle for economic justice, and criticizes home, marriage, work, and legislation to prevent women's fulfillment.
1579. Langdon-Davies, John. A SHORT HISTORY OF WOMEN. New York: Literary Guild of America, 1927. 382 pp. Women in primitive society, ancient civilization, the early Christian Church, and in the modern period.
1580. Larus, John Rouse. WOMEN OF AMERICA. Philadelphia: Rittenhouse Press, 1908. 389 pp. Sketches of women and their lives in the nineteenth and early twentieth centuries.
1581. Lederer, Wolfgang. THE FEAR OF WOMEN. New York: Grune and Stratton, 1968. 360 pp. A historical, philosophical, and psychological view of how women are seen by men, and of the oscillation between love and fear that reinforces man's supposed superiority to women.
1582. Logan, Mary S. THE PART TAKEN BY WOMEN IN AMERICAN HISTORY. New York: Arno Press, 1972. Reprint of the 1912 edition. Especially valuable sections on outstanding Catholic and Jewish women, along with hundreds of other entries of famous and little-known women.
1583. Luetkens, Charlotte. WOMAN AND A NEW SOCIETY. New York: Duell, 1946. 128 pp. Illustrates the progress of women during the past generation and its excessive costs.
1584. Mackenzie, Norman I. WOMEN IN AUSTRALIA: A REPORT TO THE SOCIAL SCIENCE RESEARCH COUNCIL OF AUSTRALIA. London: Angus, 1963. Progress in the liberation of Australian women from several centuries of economic, political, and social subjugation.

1585. Martineau, Harriet. SOCIETY IN AMERICA. 3 vols. London, 1837; Gloucester, Mass.: Peter Smith, 1968. The English observer of American life
looked at women, American marriage, and social life, and predicted that
women's condition would long remain unchanged.

1586. McCracken, Elizabeth. THE WOMEN OF AMERICA. New York:
Macmillan, 1904. 397 pp. Interesting accounts of pioneer women,
women in small towns, the Southern woman, women of letters, women
on the farm, and the social ideals of women.

1587. M'Rabet, Fadela. LA FEMME ALGERIENNE. Paris: F. Maspero, 1964.
140 pp. Women in Algeria.

1588. O'Faolain, Julia, and Lauro Martines, eds. NOT IN GOD'S IMAGE:
WOMEN IN HISTORY FROM THE GREEKS TO THE VICTORIANS.
New York: Harper and Row, 1973. 362 pp. Scholarly study of women,
their status, social roles, degrees of freedom and subordination. Basically
a book of readings, including sections on women in Greece and Byzantium,
early Hebrew women, medieval women, biological and medical views on
women, German philosophers on women, and feminism in history.

1589. Oriege, Guy d'. HISTOIRE ET GEOGRAPHIE DE LA FEMME. Paris:
Editions du Scorpion, 1958. 285 pp. General history of women.

1590. Parsons, Alice B. WOMAN'S DILEMMA. New York: Crowell, 1926.
Opposes the idea that woman is inferior to man, in mind or body.

1591. Parsons, Elsie Clews. THE OLD-FASHIONED WOMAN: PRIMITIVE
FANCIES ABOUT THE SEX. New York: Arno Press, 1972. Reprint of
the 1913 edition. Study of the primitive ideas behind femininity and
discrimination in such topics as girl babies, debutantes, harems, honeymoons, spinsters, and women's fashions.

1592. Plato. THE REPUBLIC. Any edition. Book V discusses certain objections
to the equality of women with men in education and occupations, and
to the proposed community of women and children, which would mean
for the ruling class the abolition of the family.

1593. Pollard, Edward B. ORIENTAL WOMEN. Philadelphia: Rittenhouse
Press, 1908. 372 pp. A history of women in the East.

1594. Putnam, Emily James. THE LADY: STUDIES OF CERTAIN SIGNIFI-
CANT PHASES OF HER HISTORY. Chicago: Univ. of Chicago Press,
1970. Reprint of the 1910 edition. 323 pp. How various societies have
treated women and what women have done to combat social attitudes;
deals with Greek women, the women of the Renaissance, the lady of
the salon, and the lady of the slave states.

1595. Reich, Emil. WOMAN THROUGH THE AGES. 2 vols. London: n.p.,
1908. History of women in various countries with short biographical
sketches.

1596. Reische, Diana L., ed. WOMEN AND SOCIETY. New York: H. W. Wilson,
1972. 234 pp.

1597. Rosenberg, Carroll Smith. "Beauty, the Beast and the Militant Woman: A
Case Study in Sex Roles and Social Stress in Jacksonian America."
In Ari Hoogenboom and Olive Hoogenboom, AN INTERDISCIPLINARY
APPROACH TO AMERICAN HISTORY, vol. 1. Englewood Cliffs, N.J.:
Prentice-Hall, 1973. Article on the early beginnings of the feminist
movement.

1598. Scheinfeld, Amram. WOMEN AND MEN. New York: Harcourt, Brace, 1943; London: Chatto and Windus, 1943. Cross-cultural account of many assumptions about men and women, including their sexuality.

1599. Schoenfeld, Jermann. WOMEN OF THE TEUTONIC NATIONS. Philadelphia: Rittenhouse Press, 1908. 412 pp.

1600. Scobie, Alistair. WOMEN OF AFRICA. London: Cassell, 1960. 184 pp. Social and economic progress of African women.

1601. Simkins, Francis, and James W. Patton. THE WOMEN OF THE CONFEDERACY. Richmond and New York: Garrett and Massey, 1936. Economic and social conditions of women during the Civil War period.

1602. Spencer, Anna Garlin. WOMAN'S SHARE IN SOCIAL CULTURE. Philadelphia: Lippincott, 1925. A historical review.

1603. Stammler, Wolfgang. FRAU WELT. Univeritaetsverlag Freiburg in der Schweiz, 1959.

1604. Stenton, Doris Mary. THE ENGLISH WOMAN IN HISTORY. London: Allen and Unwin, 1957. 363 pp. Begins with women in the Germanic tribes and ends with the publication of Mills' SUBJECTION OF WOMEN in 1869. Chapters on the country woman, women in the English Revolution, and the rise of modern feminist movements. Excellent source book.

1605. ———. "The Place of Women in Anglo-Saxon Society," TRANSACTIONS OF THE ROYAL HISTORICAL SOCIETY, 4th series, vol. 25 (1943), pp. 1-13. Study of the place-names in England reveals a number of examples which show women in possession of land, and something of their position in society.

1606. Theobald, Robert, ed. DIALOGUE ON WOMEN. Indianapolis: Bobbs-Merrill, 1967. Anthology.

1607. Thieme, Hugo P. WOMEN OF MODERN FRANCE. Philadelphia: Rittenhouse Press, 1908. 414 pp.

1608. Tickner, F. W. WOMEN IN ENGLISH ECONOMIC HISTORY. London: J. M. Dent, 1923. The part women have played in the economy of England.

1609. Turkey. Ministry of the Interior. THE TURKISH WOMAN IN HISTORY. Ankara: Guzel Sanatlar Matbaasi, 1937. 33 pp. A review of women's changing roles.

1610. Varigny, Charles V. THE WOMEN OF THE UNITED STATES. Translated by Arabella Ward. New York: n.p., 1895. Reprinted by Greenwood Press, Westport, Conn., 1971. 277 pp.

1611. Vigman, Fred K. BEAUTY'S TRIUMPH: OR, THE SUPERIORITY OF THE FAIR SEX INVINCIBLY PROVED. . . . Boston: Christopher Publishing House, 1966. 202 pp. A social history of the rise of sex equalitarianism, feminism, and modern women from the Renaissance to modern times.

1612. Waagenaar, Sam. WOMEN OF ISRAEL. Tel Aviv: L. Kahn, 1961. 46 pp. Review of the status changes of Israeli women.

1613. Wakamori, Taro, and Yamoto Fujie. NIHON NO JOSEI SHI [A History of Women in Japan]. Tokyo: Shuei Sha, 1966.

1614. Wieth-Knudsen, K. A. UNDERSTANDING WOMEN: A POPULAR STUDY OF THE QUESTION FROM ANCIENT TIMES TO THE PRESENT DAY. Translated from the Danish by Arthur G. Chater. New York: Elliot Holt, 192? (stet). 324 pp. Antifeminist point of view.

1615. Winter, Alice Ames. THE HERITAGE OF WOMEN. New York: Minton, Balch, 1927. 303 pp. Good survey of women from ancient times to 1927.

1616. "Women," JAPAN TODAY AND TOMORROW, vol. 2 (Dec. 1928), pp. 60-63. Brief review of women's status during the Showa period (1926 to present).

1617. "Women in History: A Re-Creation of our Past," WOMEN: A JOURNAL OF LIBERATION, vol. 1, no. 3 (Spring 1970). Issue devoted to women in history, such as the "Women of Heian Japan," Sarah and Angelina Grimké, Harriet Tubman, Emma Goldman, Margaret Sanger, and Elizabeth Gurley Flynn.

1618. Wormser-Migot, Olga. LES FEMMES DANS L'HISTOIRE. Paris: Corrêa, 1952.

B. The Position of Women

I'd like to see the day when a mediocre woman can go as far as a mediocre man.
—Another woman

1619. Altekar, A. S. THE POSITION OF WOMEN IN HINDU CIVILIZATION. Delhi: Motilal Banarsidass, 1962. 468 pp. History and condition of Hindu women from pre-history to the present.

1620. Anonymous. THE LAWES RESOLUTIONS OF WOMENS RIGHTS OR THE LAWES PROVISION FOR WOMEN. London: n.p., 1632. Written during the last years of Elizabeth I, probably one of the first books to deal with women's legal inequalities.

1621. Aptheker, Herbert. "The Negro Woman," MASSES AND MAINSTREAM, (Feb. 1949), pp. 10-17. Descriptions of black women in the working class, as females, and as blacks, illustrating the tasks that must be performed to eliminate the oppression of black women.

1622. Austin, William. HAEC HOMO WHEREIN THE EXCELLENCY OF THE CREATION OF WOMEN IS DESCRIBED BY WAY OF AN ESSAIE. London, 1638. Argues that "homo" stands equally for man and woman, that each have souls, which are equal before God; but he wants to keep women where feudal law had placed them, in submission.

1623. Baig, Tara Ali, ed. WOMEN OF INDIA. Delhi: Ministry of Information and Broadcasting, Publications Division, 1958. Chapters on women in the home, the professions, the threatre, education, and in the struggle for emancipation.

1624. Beard, Mary R. ON UNDERSTANDING WOMEN. Westport, Conn.: Greenwood Press, 1970. Reprint of 1931 edition. 541 pp. Traces the history and condition of women throughout civilization, highlighting women's achievements which have been previously minimized.

1625. Benson, Mary Sumner. WOMEN IN EIGHTEENTH-CENTURY AMERICA: A STUDY OF OPINION AND SOCIAL USAGE. Port Washington, N.Y.: Kenikat Press, 1966. 343 pp. Aspects of the position and condition of women in America, with an excellent bibliographical essay.

1626. Bott, Alan, ed. OUR MOTHERS: A CAVALCADE IN PICTURES, QUOTATION AND DESCRIPTION OF LATE VICTORIAN WOMEN, 1870-1900. London: Gollancz, 1932. History and condition of women in pictures.

1627. Branch, E. Douglas. THE SENTIMENTAL YEARS, 1836-1860. New York: Hill and Wang, 1934, 1962. 432 pp. See especially Chapter 7, "Garlands and Chains," dealing with the position of women in industry, medicine, and woman suffrage and including literary tributes to women in American society.
1628. Child, Lydia Maria. A BRIEF HISTORY OF THE CONDITION OF WOMEN. New York and Boston: C. S. Francis, 1854. Historical facts on the position of women in 53 countries.
1629. Chumacero, Rosalia d'. PERFIL Y PENSAMIENTO DE LA MUJER MEXICANA. Mexico City, 1961. Translated as PROFILES AND THOUGHTS ON MEXICAN WOMEN.
1630. Cobbledick, M. Robert. THE STATUS OF WOMEN IN PURITAN NEW ENGLAND, 1630-1660. New Haven: Yale Univ. Press, 1936.
1631. Cutler, John Henry. WHAT ABOUT WOMEN? AN EXAMINATION OF THE PRESENT CHARACTERISTICS, NATURE, STATUS, AND POSITION OF WOMEN AS THEY HAVE EVOLVED DURING THIS CENTURY. New York: I. Washburn, 1961. 241 pp.
1632. Du Bois, W.E.B. DARK WATER: VOICES FROM WITHING THE VEIL. New York: Schocken Books, 1969. First published in 1920, this anthology speaks to the oppression and resilience of black women in American society.
1633. Ellington, George. THE WOMEN OF NEW YORK: OR THE UNDER-WORLD OF THE GREAT CITY. New York: Arno Press, 1972. Reprint of the 1869 edition. "Rips the veil from shame and explores the evils that drag innocent women into sin and honorable men into disease and moral destruction."
1634. Elliott, Grace L. WOMEN AFTER FORTY; THE MEANING OF THE LAST HALF OF LIFE. New York: Holt, 1936. 213 pp. Deals with topics such as crises in middle age, achievement in later life, deprivation of women's basic needs, and the condition of women in the last half of life.
1635. Ferrers, Richard. THE WORTH OF WOMEN. London, 1622. Typical Elizabethan attitudes toward women as obedient and submissive.
1636. Goncourt, Edmond, and Jules de Goncourt. THE WOMAN OF THE EIGHTEENTH CENTURY. New York: Minton, Balch, 1927. 347 pp. Discusses women in the upper, middle, and lower classes with respect to religion, and cultural and social life.
1637. Hansen, Henny Harald. DAUGHTERS OF ALLAH: AMONG MOSLEM WOMEN IN KURDISTAN. London: Allen and Unwin, 1960. 191 pp. The position of women and changing status in modern times.
1638. ———. THE KURDISH WOMAN'S LIFE: FIELD RESEARCH IN A MUSLIM SOCIETY, IRAQ. Kobenhavn, Denmark: Nationalmuseet, 1961. 213 pp.
1639. Hare, Nathan, and Julia Hare. "Black Woman 1970," TRANS-ACTION, vol. 8, no. 1/2 (Nov./Dec. 1970), pp. 65-68, 90. Special issue on American women, with emphasis in this article on the triple exploitation resulting from being black, female, and poor.
1640. Hecker, Eugene Arthur. A SHORT HISTORY OF WOMEN'S RIGHTS FROM THE DAYS OF AUGUSTUS TO THE PRESENT TIME, WITH SPECIAL REFERENCE TO ENGLAND AND THE UNITED STATES.

2d ed., rev. New York, 1914. Reprinted by Greenwood Press, Westport, Conn. 313 pp. Begins with women under Roman law, and traces the history of women's rights down to World War I. Excellent footnotes of original sources make this an important reference work.

1641. Hect, J. THE DOMESTIC SERVANT CLASS IN 18TH CENTURY ENGLAND. London: Routledge and Kegan Paul, 1956. The position of women in the household drudge occupations.

1642. Holtby, Winifred. WOMEN AND A CHANGING CIVILIZATION. New York: Longmans, Green, 1935. 213 pp. Detailed account of the development of the English woman's sense of awareness concerning her condition and rights as a social entity, and the progress made as a result of this consciousness.

1643. Issaev, B. LA MASCULINIZACION DE LA MUJER. Buenos Aires: Editorial Nova, 1961. 171 pp. History and condition of Argentine women.

1644. Kaplan, Justin, ed. WITH MALICE TOWARD WOMEN: A HANDBOOK FOR WOMEN-HATERS DRAWN FROM THE BEST MINDS OF ALL TIME. London: W. H. Allen, 1953. Many of the attitudes that have kept women in a state of inequality are herein described.

1645. Kellen, Konrad. THE COMING AGE OF WOMAN POWER. New York: Peter H. Wyden, 1972. Maintains that the 1980s will be the "golden age of woman power."

1646. King, William C. WOMAN: HER POSITION, INFLUENCE, AND ACHIEVEMENT THROUGHOUT THE CIVILIZED WORLD. . . . Springfield, Mass.: King-Richardson, 1903. 667 pp. History of women before the Christian era, during the Dark Ages, condition and position of women at the dawn of woman's power, and the contribution of women to modern civilization.

1647. Lerner, Gerda. "The Lady and the Mill Girl: Changes in the Status of Women in the Age of Jackson," MIDCONTINENT AMERICAN STUDIES JOURNAL, vol. 10, no. 1 (Spring 1969), pp. 5-15.

1648. Lerner, Max. AMERICA AS A CIVILIZATION. 2 vols. New York: Simon and Schuster, 1957. Especially chapter 6, vol. 2, "The Ordeal of the American Woman," which discusses women being caught between a man's world and a world of their own in which they find it difficult to achieve fulfillment.

1649. Lester, Julia. TO BE A SLAVE. New York: Dial Press, 1968. 160 pp. Compilations of the writings of former slaves.

1650. Marshall, D. THE ENGLISH DOMESTIC SERVANT IN HISTORY. London: Historical Association, 1968. Short pamphlet on the conditions of the domestic classes.

1651. Mayer, August. EMANZIPATION, FRAUENTUM, MUTTERTUM FAMILIE UND GESELLSCHAFT [Emancipation, Womanhood, Motherhood, Family and Society]. Stuttgart: F. Enke, 1962. 63 pp. History and condition of women in Germany.

1652. Norton, Caroline. ENGLISH LAWS FOR WOMEN IN THE NINETEENTH CENTURY. London: n.p., 1854. By the daughter of Richard Brinsley Sheridan; a treatise against the inequalities of the law which governed the relations between husband and wife, and of the celebrated law case in which she was involved.

1653. O'Hara, A. R. POSITION OF WOMAN IN EARLY CHINA, INCLUD-
ING A TRANSLATION OF LIEH NU CHUAN. Hong Kong, 1955. Contains many idealized biographies of virtuous women in early China,
with descriptions of their status.

1654. Parsons, Alice. WOMAN'S DILEMMA. New York: Crowell, 1926. 309 pp.
Attacks the idea that women are inferior to men; many examples of
male attitudes toward the position of women in society.

1655. Plant, Marjorie. THE DOMESTIC LIFE OF SCOTLAND IN THE 18TH
CENTURY. Chicago: Aldine, 1952. Interesting chapters on the
position of women.

1656. Potter, David M. "American Women and the American Character." In
AMERICAN CHARACTER AND CULTURE, edited by John A. Hague.
Deland, Fla.: Stetson Univ. Press, 1964. An important summary of the
history of women in America, pp. 65-84.

1657. Pullai, Arpad. "The Party and the Equality of Women," WORLD
MARXIST REVIEW, vol. 14 (Nov. 1971), pp. 45-53. Argues that
capitalist exploitation was and remains the cause of woman's oppressed
status.

1658. Rafiq, Bashir Ahmed. THE STATUS OF WOMEN IN ISLAM. London:
London Mosque, 1965. 16 pp.

1659. Rainwater, Lee, and William L. Yancey. THE MOYNIHAN REPORT
AND THE POLITICS OF CONTROVERSY. Cambridge: M.I.T. Press,
1967. Includes the Moynihan Report, as well as reactions of civil rights
leaders, the press, intellectuals, etc., to the status of Negro men and
women in American society.

1660. Ramos, Maria. MULHERES DA AMERICA. Rio de Janeiro: J. Alvaro,
1964. 180 pp. History and condition of women in Latin America.

1661. Salmon, Lucy Maynard. DOMESTIC SERVICE. New York: Arno
Press, 1972. Reprint of the 1897 edition. Analyzes the lives of
thousands "trapped in subservience to master and mistress."

1662. Schuller, Mary Craig, and Elizabeth H. Wheeler, ed. THE ROLE OF
WOMEN IN AFRICA. New York: African-American Institute, 1959.
36 pp.

1663. Seip, Ellen Bonnevie. FACTS ABOUT WOMEN IN NORWAY. Oslo:
Norwegian Joint Commission on International Social Policy, 1960. 42
pp. Review of changes in the status of women.

1664. Seler, Cecilia. DIE FRAU IM MEXICO. Berlin: n.p., 1893. A pioneer
study.

1665. Sewall, Samuel E. THE LEGAL CONDITION OF WOMEN IN
MASSACHUSETTS. Boston: C. K. Whipple, 1869.

1666. Smith, Lillian. KILLERS OF THE DREAM. New York: Norton, 1949.
See especially her chapter, "The Women," pp. 134-152.

1667. Smith, T. R., compiler and ed. THE WOMAN QUESTION. New York:
Boni, 1918. 229 pp. Anthology of essays by Ellen Key, Anna E.
Dickinson, and others on women's position.

1668. Stern, Bernhard J., and Margaret Mead. "Women, Position in Society,"
ENCYCLOPEDIA OF THE SOCIAL SCIENCES, vol. 15 (1934), pp.
442 ff. A valuable historical sketch tracing the evolution of women's
rights, with an extensive bibliography.

1669. Thomas, Paul. INDIAN WOMEN THROUGH THE AGES: A HISTORICAL SURVEY OF THE POSITION OF WOMEN AND THE INSTITUTIONS OF MARRIAGE AND FAMILY IN INDIA FROM REMOTE ANTIQUITY TO THE PRESENT DAY. Delhi: Asia Publishing House, 1964.

1670. Thompson, William. APPEAL OF ONE HALF OF THE HUMAN RACE, WOMEN, AGAINST THE PRETENSIONS OF THE OTHER HALF, MEN, TO RETAIN THEM IN POLITICAL, AND THENCE IN CIVIL AND DOMESTIC SLAVERY. New York: Source Book Press, 1970. Reprint of the 1825 edition. 241 pp. Important early pro-feminist tract.

1671. Trevelyan, George M. ENGLISH SOCIAL HISTORY. London: Longmans, 1945. Social history, with references to the status of British women from the late eighteenth century to the twentieth.

1672. U.S. Department of Commerce. Bureau of the Census. WE THE AMERICAN WOMEN. Washington, D.C.: SUDOC, GPO, 1973. 16 pp. The female population of America, as of 1970, is equal to the population of Japan! Women comprise 51.3 percent of the population.

1673. U.S. Department of Labor. HISTORICAL REVIEW ON THE RECOGNITION OF THE POLITICAL RIGHTS OF AMERICAN WOMEN. Washington, D.C.: SUDOC, GPO, 1957.

1674. –––. POLITICAL STATUS OF WOMEN IN THE OTHER AMERICAN REPUBLICS. Washington, D.C.: SUDOC, GPO, 1957.

1675. Veblen, Thorstein. THE THEORY OF THE LEISURE CLASS. New York: Macmillan, 1899. Many sections of this classic are devoted to women's consumption and leisure, standards of feminine beauty, women's fashions, and the underlying motives of the nineteenth-century woman's movement.

1676. Vicinus, Martha, ed. SUFFER AND BE STILL: WOMEN IN THE VICTORIAN AGE. Bloomington: Indiana Univ. Press, 1972. 256 pp.

1677. Wetch, Galbraith. AFRICA BEFORE THEY CAME: THE CONTINENT, NORTH, SOUTH, EAST, AND WEST, PRECEDING THE COLONIAL POWERS. New York: Morrow, 1965. 396 pp. Chapters on the history and position of women in many African nations.

1678. Whitton, Mary O. THESE WERE THE WOMEN: U.S.A., 1776-1860. New York: Hastings House, 1954. 288 pp. Biographical and historical sketches of significant women in America, with summaries of women's position during the colonial and succeeding periods.

1679. Willard, Emma, and Catherine Beecher. THE WOMAN'S BOOK, DEALING PRACTICALLY WITH THE MODERN CONDITIONS OF HOME-LIFE, SELF-SUPPORT, EDUCATION, OPPORTUNITIES, AND EVERYDAY PROBLEMS. 2 vols. New York: Charles Scribner's Sons, 1894.

C. Women—From Ancient Times Through the Renaissance

Dux femina facti.
    —AENEID, i, 364.

1680. Abram, A. "Women Traders in Medieval London," ECONOMIC JOURNAL, (June 1916), pp. 276 ff.

1681. Bader, Clarisse. WOMEN IN ANCIENT INDIA: MORAL AND LITER-ARY STUDIES. Varanasi, India: Chowkhamba Sanskrit Series, 1964. 338 pp.
1682. Bainton, Roland. WOMEN OF THE REFORMATION: IN GERMANY AND ITALY. Minneapolis: Augsburg Press, 1971. 279 pp. Biographical information concerning women considered most influential in the Protestant and Catholic reformation movement in the sixteenth century. Bibliography included.
1683. Balsdon, John P. V. D. ROMAN WOMEN: THEIR HISTORY AND HABITS. New York: John Day, 1963. 351 pp. Historical study of women from Rome's founding in 753 B.C. to A.D. 337. Discusses the importance of women in public and social life, with a good account of the history of emancipation of Roman women from a burdening and restrictive marriage system.
1684. Bradford, Gamaliel. ELIZABETHAN WOMEN. Cambridge, 1936. Reprinted by Books for Libraries, 1969, under the editorship of Harold O. White. Excellent bibliographical sources for the collection of biographies cited.
1685. Butler, Pierce. WOMEN OF MEDIEVAL FRANCE. Philadelphia: Rittenhouse Press, 1908. 472 pp.
1686. Camden, Carroll. THE ELIZABETHAN WOMAN. New York: Elsevier Press, 1952. 333 pp. The nature of Elizabethan women, their place in society, in marriage, and in the household, the Elizabethan version of the eternal female and other controversies over women; with an excellent bibliography.
1687. Cannon, Mary A. EDUCATION OF WOMEN DURING THE RENAISSANCE. Washington, D.C.: Capitol Press, 1916.
1688. Carroll, Mitchell. GREEK WOMEN. Philadelphia: Rittenhouse Press, 1908. 391 pp. Another in a series about women in all ages and in all countries.
1689. Clark, Alice. THE WORKING LIFE OF WOMEN. New York: Harcourt, Brace, 1920. The life of women in transition from medieval to modern times.
1690. Clavière, R. de Maulde la. THE WOMEN OF THE RENAISSANCE: A STUDY OF FEMINISM. Translated by George H. Ely. New York: Putnam, 1901. 510 pp. A scholarly work on the position of women and the feminist movement in the sixteenth century in Italy and France.
1691. Dale, Marian K. "The London Silkwomen of the Fifteenth Century," ECONOMIC HISTORICAL REVIEW (London), vol. 4, (n.d.), pp. 324-335.
1692. Donaldson, James. WOMAN: HER POSITION AND INFLUENCE IN ANCIENT GREECE AND ROME, AND AMONG THE EARLY CHRISTIANS. London: Longmans, Green, 1907. 278 pp. A readable account of the various ideals of women prevailing throughout Greek, Roman, and Christian times, with many of the typical historical misconceptions.
1693. Gagé, Jean. MATRONALIA: ESSAI SUR LES DEVOTIONS ET LES ORGANIZATIONS CULTUELLES DES FEMMES DANS L'ANCIENNE ROME. Bruxelles: Latomus, Révue d'Etudes Latines, 1963. 289 pp.
1694. Hill, Georgiana. WOMEN IN ENGLISH LIFE FROM MEDIEVAL TO MODERN TIMES. 2 vols. London: R. Bentley, 1896. Aspects of economy touched upon, with chapters on women in guilds, as petitioners before Parliament, women's political influence, and women in trade.

1695. Kaberry, Phyllis M. ABORIGINAL WOMAN SACRED AND PROFANE. Philadelphia: Blakiston, 1939. The roles of women in primitive societies, especially Africa.
1696. Lagno, Isadoro Del. WOMEN OF FLORENCE. Translated by Mary Steegman. London: Chatto and Windus, 1907.
1697. Latour, Therese Louis. PRINCESSES, LADIES AND ADVENTURESSES OF THE REIGN OF LOUIS XIV. New York: Knopf, 1924. 358 pp. Brief lives of prominant women during the period.
1698. Marygrove College. INTO HER OWN: THE STATUS OF WOMAN FROM ANCIENT TIMES TO THE END OF THE MIDDLE AGES. Detroit: Marygrove College, 1946. 66 pp.
1699. Mason, Otis T. WOMAN'S SHARE IN PRIMITIVE CULTURE. New York: Appleton, 1895. 296 pp. Classic work on women in primitive cultures.
1700. McRobbie, Kenneth. "Women and Love: Some Aspects of Competition in Late Medieval Society," MOSAIC, vol. 5 (Winter 1972), pp. 139-168.
1701. Ormsbee, T. H. "The Women Silversmiths of England," AMERICAN COLLECTION,(May 1938), pp. 8-9.The importance of women in the early English silversmith's guilds.
1702. Power, Eileen. MEDIEVAL NUNNERIES. Cambridge: Cambridge Univ. Press, 1922. Women in early Christian convent life.
1703. ———. "The Position of Women." In THE LEGACY OF THE MIDDLE AGES, edited by C. G. Crump and E. F. Jacob. Oxford: Oxford Univ. Press, 1926.
1704. Reynolds, Myra. THE LEARNED LADY IN ENGLAND, 1650-1760. Boston: Houghton Mifflin, 1920. Women in medieval and renaissance intellectual life.
1705. Rodocanachi, E. LA FEMME ITALIENNE A L'EPOQUE DE LA RENAISSANCE. Paris, 1907.
1706. Rhumer, W. THEORIEN UBER FRAUENBILDUNG IM ZEITALTER DER RENAISSANCE [Theories on Women's Education in the Age of the Renaissance]. Bonn: n.p., 1915.
1707. Schreiber, S. E. GERMAN WOMAN IN THE AGE OF THE ENGLIGHTEN-MENT. New York: King's Crown Press, 1948. 257 pp.
1708. Seltman, Charles. WOMEN IN ANTIQUITY. New York: St. Martin's Press, 1955. 224 pp. Women in ancient Mediterranean civilizations, along with discussions of primitive and Near Eastern women, ending with an assessment of how women have been treated in the Western world.
1709. Spencer, Anna Garlin. "Primitive Working Woman," FORUM, vol. 46 (1911), pp. 546-558.
1710. Walker, Arda Susan. THE LIFE AND STATUS OF A GENERATION OF FRENCH WOMEN, 1150-1200. Ann Arbor, Mich.: University Microfilms, 1959. Microfilm AC-1, No. 58-5974.
1711. Williams, Mary W. SOCIAL LIFE IN SCANDINAVIA IN THE VIKING AGE. New York: Macmillan, 1920. The family, marriage, and the place of women in Viking society.
1712. Williamson, G. C. LADY ANN CLIFFORD. London: Kendal, 1922. Position of women in the feudal world, with a biography of Ann, Countess of Pembroke (1590-1676).

1713. Wright, Thomas. WOMANKIND IN WESTERN EUROPE. London: Grombridge, 1869. 340 pp. History and condition of women in Europe from the ancient period to the seventeenth century.

1714. Zahm, John Augustine. GREAT INSPIRERS. New York: Appleton, 1917. 271 pp. Focuses upon the ancient Latin accounts of Paula and her daughter Eustochium, who collaborated with St. Jerome in translating the Bible, and Dante and his relation with Beatrice.

D. Women: Manners and Customs

A healthy appetite for righteousness, kept in due control by good manners, is an excellent thing; but to "hunger and thirst" after it is often merely a symptom of spiritual diabetes.

—C. D. Broad

The longing to be primitive is a disease of culture; it is archaism in morals. To be so preoccupied with vitality is a symptom of anemia.

—Santayana

1715. Aretz, Gertrude. THE ELEGANT WOMAN: FROM THE ROCOCO PERIOD TO MODERN TIMES. New York: Harcourt, Brace, 1932. 315 pp. History of fashionable women, manners and customs of high society from the mid-eighteenth century to the modern period.

1716. Bateson, Mary. "Manners and Customs." In SOCIAL ENGLAND, edited by Henry D. Traill and James S. Mann. 6 vols. Westport, Conn.: Greenwood Press, 1964. Reprint of the 1902-04 edition. See vol. 3, sec. 2.

1717. Beecher, Catherine, and Harriet Beecher Stowe. THE AMERICAN WOMAN'S HOME. New York: J. B. Ford, 1869. Written with her sister, Harriet Beecher Stowe, it includes chapters on the wide-ranging duties of women, home decoration, care of infants, and the blessedness of aiding to sustain a truly Christian home.

1718. Catlin, George. MANNERS, CUSTOMS AND CONDITIONS OF THE NORTH AMERICAN INDIANS. London: n.p., 1844. Many sections dealing with women's customs and manners.

1719. Dubois, J. A. HINDU MANNERS, CUSTOMS, AND CEREMONIES. Translated by Henry R. Beauchamp. Oxford: Oxford Univ. Press, 1906.

1720. Dyer, T. F. Thistleton. POPULAR BRITISH CUSTOMS. London: n.p., 1876. Women are dealt with throughout the book.

1721. Effiger, John R. WOMEN OF THE ROMANCE COUNTRIES. Philadelphia: Rittenhouse Press, 1908. 405 pp. Manners and customs of women in Southern Europe.

1722. Finck, Henry T. ROMANTIC LOVE AND PERSONAL BEAUTY: THEIR DEVELOPMENT, CAUSAL RELATIONS, HISTORIC AND NATIONAL PECULIARITIES. New York: Macmillan, 1912. 560 pp. Excellent summary of the development of manners and customs around the world.

1723. Furness, Clifton J., ed. THE GENTEEL FEMALE: AN ANTHOLOGY. Ann Arbor, Mich.: Finch Press Reprints, 1931. 306 pp. Study of the American woman in the nineteenth century, her fashions, manners, and literary tastes.

1724. Grinnell, George N. "Cheyenne Women Customs," THE AMERICAN ANTHROPOLOGIST, vol. 4 (1902).

1725. Hale, Sarah J. MANNERS: OR, HAPPY HOMES AND GOOD SOCIETY ALL THE YEAR ROUND. New York: Arno Press, 1972. 377 pp. Reprint of 1868 edition. Sets down the rules of good conduct, correct conversation, and obligations of ladies, by the exercise of which the world might be improved.

1726. Halifax, Lord. ADVICE TO A DAUGHTER. London: n.p., 1688. Discourse on religion, husband, house, family and children, behavior, friendships, vanity, pride, and diversions. Timeless and indicative of early English conceptions of woman's role in society.

1727. Hamilton, Cicely M. MARRIAGE AS A TRADE. New York: Moffat, Yard, 1909. Reprinted by Singing Tree Press, Gale Research Company (Detroit), 1971. 257 pp. The trade aspect of wifehood and motherhood in marriage customs.

1728. Holliday, Carl. WOMAN'S LIFE IN COLONIAL DAYS. Detroit: Gale Research Co., 1970. 319 pp. Reprint of the 1922 edition. Interesting chapters on colonial women and the home, dress, and social life.

1729. Hosie, Dorothea. TWO GENTLEMEN OF CHINA. London: Seeleg, Service, 1929. 5th ed. Late Imperial Chinese upper-class home life from a feminine point of view.

1730. Leslie, Eliza. MISS LESLIE'S BEHAVIOUR BOOK: A GUIDE AND MANUAL FOR LADIES. New York: Arno Press, 1972. Reprint of the 1859 edition. Generations of American women behaved as this early Emily Post told them to behave.

1731. Levy, Howard S. CHINESE FOOTBINDING: HISTORY OF A CURIOUS CUSTOM. New York: Walton Rawls, 1966. 352 pp.

1732. ———. HAREM FAVORITES OF AN ILLUSTRIOUS CELESTIAL. Taipei, Taiwan: Chung-t'ai Printing Co., 1958. Interesting vignettes of Emperor Hsuan Tsung's palace women, and a short history of the custom of concubinage in China.

1733. Penzer, Norman M. THE HAREM: AN ACCOUNT OF THE INSTITUTION AS IT EXISTED IN THE PALACE OF THE TURKISH SULTANS WITH A HISTORY OF THE GRAND SERAGLIO FROM ITS FOUNDATION TO MODERN TIMES. London: Spring Books, 1966. 277 pp.

1734. Quisumbing, Lourdes R. MARRIAGE CUSTOMS IN RURAL CEBU. Cebu City, Philippines: Univ. of San Carlos, n.d. 77 pp. Marriage customs, beliefs, and practices among the Filipinos.

1735. Rice, Clara C. PERSIAN WOMEN AND THEIR WAYS, London: n.p., 1923. Unique marriage and social customs among Iranian women.

1736. Thomas, Antoine Leonard. AN ACCOUNT OF THE CHARACTER, THE MANNERS, AND THE UNDERSTANDING OF WOMEN, IN DIFFERENT AGES, AND DIFFERENT PARTS OF THE WORLD. Translated from French by Mrs. Kindersley. London: n.p., 1800.

1737. Wright, Frances. VIEWS OF SOCIETY AND MANNERS IN AMERICA. Cambridge: Harvard Univ. Press, 1963. A famous traveler from England records her memories of American society and morals.

E. Women in Folkore and Witchcraft

"But, my loving master, if any wind will not serve, then I wish I were in Lapland, to buy a good wind of one of the honest witches, that sell so many winds there and so cheap."
—*MACBETH, Act I, Scene 3.*

All witchcraft comes from carnal lust, which in women is insatiable.
—*St. John Chrysostom*

1738. Baroja, Julio Caro. THE WORLD OF THE WITCHES. Chicago: Univ. of Chicago Press, 1961, 1964. A history of witches and witchcraft.

1739. Batchelor, J. THE AINU AND THEIR FOLKLORE. London: n.p., 1901. Sections on Ainu women and superstitious practices.

1740. Best, E. "The Lore of the Whare-Kohanga," JOURNAL OF POLYNESIAN SOCIETY (New Plymouth, New Zealand), vol. 14 (1905), pp. 211 ff. The Maori believe that the moon is the permanent husband of all women.

1741. Burr, George Lincoln, ed. NARRATIVES OF THE WITCHCRAFT CASES, 1648-1706. New York: Barnes and Noble, 1914, 1952. 467 pp. Good history of American witch episodes, citing hundreds of women witches.

1742. Campbell, J. G. WITCHCRAFT AND SECOND SIGHT IN THE HIGH-LANDS AND ISLANDS OF SCOTLAND. Glasgow, Scotland, 1902. Celebrated witches and incidents cited.

1743. Child, Frank S. A COLONIAL WITCH: A STUDY OF THE BLACK ART IN CONNECTICUT. New York: Baker and Taylor, 1897.

1744. Crooke, W. POPULAR RELIGION AND FOLKLORE OF NORTHERN INDIA. London: Westminster, 1896. Women are dealt with in many sections.

1745. DeForest, John W. WITCHING TIMES. New Haven: College and Univ. Press, 1967. 336 pp. A novel—historically accurate—of the Salem witchcraft delusions.

1746. Drake, Samuel G. ANNALS OF WITCHCRAFT IN NEW ENGLAND. Boston: Elliott Woodward, 1869.

1757. Ewen, Cecil Henry L'Estrange. WITCHCRAFT AND DEMONIANISM . . . OF ENGLAND AND WALES. London: Heath Cranston, 1933, 1970. 495 pp. Accounts of famous witches.

1748. Folsom, Joseph F. "Witches in New Jersey," NEW JERSEY HISTORICAL SOCIETY PROCEEDINGS, New Series, vol. 7 (1922), pp. 293-305.

1749. Frazer, Sir James George. FOLKLORE IN THE OLD TESTAMENT. London: Macmillan, 1919. 476 pp. On the subject in general, with many references to women, especially Isa. 24: 5; Jer. 3: 1, 2, 9; and Psalms 106: 38.

1750. ———. THE NEW GOLDEN BOUGH. Edited by Theodor H. Gaster. New York: Criterion Books, 1959. 738 pp. An abridged version of the classic study of folklore through the ages, with many references to women.

1751. Fritscher, John. POPULAR WITCHCRAFT, STRAIGHT FROM THE WITCH'S MOUTH. Bowling Green, Ohio: Bowling Green Univ. Popular Press, 1972. 123 pp. Includes bibliographic references.

1752. Garnett, Lucy. THE WOMEN OF TURKEY AND THEIR FOLKLORE. 2 vols. London: D. Nutt, 1890. Women as rainmakers, etc.

1753. Georgeakis, G., and Léon Pineau. FOLK-LORE DE LESBOS. Paris: J. Maissonneuve, 1894. 372 pp. Lesbos and Lesbians lauded.

1754. Harding, M. Esther. WOMAN'S MYSTERIES: ANCIENT AND MOD-ERN. New York: G. P. Putnam's Sons, 1971. 256 pp. A psychological interpretation of femininity as portrayed in myth, story, and dreams.

1755. Harrison, G. B., ed. THE TRIAL OF THE LANCASTER WITCHES, A.D. MDCXII. London: Peter Davies, 1929. 188 pp. English witches Elizabeth Sowtherns, Elizabeth Device, Ann Redferne, Janes Wilkinson, Margaret Lyon, and others.

1756. Hoadly, Charles J. "A Case of Witchcraft in Hartford," CONNECTICUT MAGAZINE, vol. 5 (1899), pp. 557-561.

1757. Hole, Christina. WITCHCRAFT IN ENGLAND. New York: Charles Scribner's Sons, 1947.

1758. James, E. O. THE CULT OF THE MOTHER GODDESS: AN ARCHEO-LOGICAL AND DOCUMENTARY STUDY. London: Thames and Hudson, 1959; New York: Barnes and Noble, 1961. A look at her prehistoric image and at her superimposed, condensed image throughout the ages and up to the present time. Includes an extensive bibliographic section.

1759. Krige, E. J., and J. D. Krige. THE REALM OF THE RAIN-QUEEN. London: n.p., 1947. Folklore in Lovedu society.

1760. Linton, E. Lynn. WITCH STORIES. London: Chapman and Hall, 1861. Reprinted by Frederick Muller, 1972. 428 pp. Tales of witches in Scotland and England, taken from actual court transcripts and trials.

1761. Miquell, Violeta. WOMAN IN MYTH AND HISTORY. New York: Vantage Press, 1962. 153 pp.

1762. Moret, A. DU CARACTERE RELIGIEUX DE LA ROYAUTE PHARAONIQUE. Paris, 1902. Folk and magic cults in ancient Egypt; see especially his chapter on the sacred marriage, pp. 48-73.

1763. Murray, Margaret Alice. THE GOD OF THE WITCHES. London: Oxford Univ. Press, 1970, 1931. 212 pp.

1764. ———. THE WITCH CULT IN WESTERN EUROPE. Oxford: Clarendon Press, 1921. Very good bibliography is included in this scholarly study.

1765. Napier, J. FOLK-LORE, OR SUPERSTITIOUS BELIEFS IN THE WEST OF SCOTLAND. Paisley, Scotland, 1879. Many examples of women cited.

1766. Nevins, Winfield S. WITCHCRAFT IN SALEM VILLAGE IN 1692. Salem, Mass.: Salem Press, 1916.

1767. Panofsky, Dora, and Erwin Panofsky. PANDORA'S BOX. New York: Pantheon Press, 1956. Traces the fate of Pandora and the legend through art.

1768. Parrinder, Edward Geoffrey. WITCHCRAFT: EUROPEAN AND AFRICAN. London: Faber and Faber, 1963. 215 pp.

1769. Reik, Theodor. THE CREATION OF WOMAN. New York: George Braziller, 1960. 159 pp. A psychoanalytical approach to the eternal question of Eve as manifested in initiation rites, religion, folklore, etc.

1770. Swan, Helena. GIRLS' CHRISTIAN NAMES: THEIR HISTORY, MEANIN MEANING AND ASSOCIATION. London: Swan Sonnenschein, 1900. 516 pp. Reprinted by Gale Research Co., Detroit, 1968. Curious details on more than 1,000 girls' names in legend and history.

1771. Upham, Charles W. SALEM WITCHCRAFT. 2 vols. Williamstown, Mass.: Corner House, 1971. Reprint of the 1867 edition. Accounts of many Salem witches of the seventeenth and early eighteenth centuries.

1772. Van Buren, E. Douglas. "The Sacred Marriage in Ancient Mesopotamia," ORIENTALIA, vol. 13 (1944), pp. 1 ff.

1773. Worthen, Samuel C. "Witches in New Jersey and Elsewhere," NEW JERSEY HISTORICAL SOCIETY PROCEEDINGS, New Series, vol. 8 (1923), pp. 139-143.

1774. Zimmer, Heinrich. THE KING AND THE CORPSE. New York: Meridian Books, 1948, 1960. Interesting legends about men and women throughout history and in many cultures.

F. Women and Fashion

Hearts may fail, and Strength outwear, and Purpose
   turn to Loathing,
But the everyday affair of business, meals, and clothing,
Builds a bulkhead 'twixt Despair and the Edge of Nothing.
                    —Kipling

1775. Angelino, H., L. A. Barnes, and C. L. Shedd, "Attitudes of Mothers and Adolescent Daughters Concerning Clothing and Grooming," JOURNAL OF HOME ECONOMICS, vol. 48 (Dec. 1956), pp. 779-782. What, if any, differences exist between mothers' and daughters' opinions concerning clothing and grooming.
1776. "Art and the Well-Dressed Woman," PRACTICAL HOME ECONOMICS, vol. 27 (May 1949), pp. 263-265. The relationship of art to the portraiture of well-dressed women.
1777. Ballin, A. S. THE SCIENCE OF DRESS. London: Sampson Low, Marston, Searle, and Rivington, 1885. A book on dress written for women by a woman.
1778. Barber, B., and L. S. Lobel. " 'Fashion' in Women's Clothes and the American Social System," SOCIAL FORCES, vol. 31 (Dec. 1952), pp. 124-131. Discussion of the meaning of fashion as a function in the American social system, in the economic system, in sex-role structures, and in the class system.
1779. Bartley, L., and J. Warden. "Clothing Preferences of Women 65 and Older," JOURNAL OF HOME ECONOMICS, vol. 54 (Oct. 1962), pp. 716-717.
1780. Bell, Quentin. ON HUMAN FINERY. London: Hogarth Press, 1947. Theoretical treatment using Veblen's leisure-class concepts; with material on moral standards, fashion, fashion changes, and sexual differentiation in dress.
1781. Bergler, E. FASHION AND THE UNCONSCIOUS. New York: Brunner, 1953. Argues that clothes are a masculine invention forced upon women, and that they are man's reassurance against his own repressed fears of woman's body.
1782. Binder, P. MUFFS AND MORALS. New York: Morrow, 1954. Emphasizes moral attitudes toward clothing, especially women's dress, age and sex-roles, hairdressing, cosmetics, and fashion trends.
1783. Blanc, C. ART IN ORNAMENT AND DRESS. London: Chapman and Hall, 1877. Analysis of design principles for clothing of men and women.
1784. Boehn, M. von. MODES AND MANNERS. Translated by J. Joshua. 4 vols. Philadelphia: Lippincott, 1932. Description of men's and women's fashions from the middle ages to the eighteenth century.
1785. Brew, M. AMERICAN CLOTHING CONSUMPTION, 1879-1909. Chicago: Univ. of Chicago Press, 1948. Contrasts the clothing habits of women in 1879 and 1909, maintaining that clothing customs are culturally determined.

1786. Carlyle, Thomas. SARTOR RESARTUS. New York: Charles Scribner's Sons, 1921. Classic work on the symbolism of clothing and fashions of society.
1787. "Church Decrees in Women's Dress," LITERARY DIGEST, vol. 87 (Nov. 21, 1925), p. 32. A decree by Pope Pius XI on modesty in women's dress.
1788. Cunnington, C. W. FEMININE ATTITUDES IN THE 19th CENTURY. New York: Macmillan, 1936. Extensive comments on women and fashion.
1789. ———. WHY WOMEN WEAR CLOTHES. London: Faber and Faber, 1941. Psychological explanations for women's wearing clothes with emphasis on the purpose of sexual attraction.
1790. de Megri, E. "Yoruba Women's Costume," NIGERIA MAGAZINE, no. 72 (Mar. 1962), pp. 4-12. Claims that Yoruba fashions are an indication of the social and economic attitudes of the people.
1791. Dooley, W. H. CLOTHING AND STYLE. New York: Heath, 1930. Pages 81-88, 220, and 251-273 deal with women's clothing, emotional influences on changes in fashions, and other factors influencing dress, modesty, custom, religion, and commercial interests.
1792. Ellis, Albert. THE AMERICAN SEXUAL TRAGEDY. New York: Grove Press, 1962. Pages 15-65 devoted to the argument that women must dress "romantically, fashionably, distinctively, extensively, sex-enticingly, and properly."
1793. Flower, B. O. "The Next Step Forward for Women: Or Thoughts on the Movement for Rational Dress," ARENA, vol. 6 (Oct. 1892), pp. 635-644. Relates the movement for rational dress to the general movement for women's rights.
1794. Flugel, J. C. "Clothes Symbolism and Clothes Ambivalence," INTERNATIONAL JOURNAL OF PSYCHO-ANALYSIS, vol. 10 (April-July 1929), pp. 205-217. Phallic symbolism of various objects of clothing, and vaginal and uterine symbolism are discussed; concludes that this symbolism relates to modesty and protection in dress.
1795. Garma, A. "The Origin of Clothes," PSYCHOANALYTIC QUARTERLY, vol. 18 (April 1949), pp. 173-190. The symbolism of clothes in dreams of pregnancy. Clothes are unconsciously perceived as maternal protection.
1796. Goodhart, C. B. "A Biological View of Toplessness," NEW SCIENTIST, vol. 23 (Sept. 1964), pp. 558-560. Attributes hesitancy of women to bare their breasts to biological reasons; concludes that breasts serve as "releasers" of erotic behavior because of coloration.
1797. Gregory, P. M. "An Economic Interpretation of Women's Fashions," SOUTHERN ECONOMIC JOURNAL, vol. 14 (Oct. 1947), pp. 148-162. Relates fashion trends to economic fluctuations.
1798. Hall, C. FROM HOOPSKIRTS TO NUDITY. Caldwell, Idaho: Caxton Printers, 1938. Review of fashions of the past 70 years.
1799. Harnick, E. J. "Pleasure in Disguise, the Need for Decoration and the Sense of Beauty," THE PSYCHOANALYTIC QUARTERLY, vol. 1 (April 1932), pp. 216-264. Psychoanalytic orientation of clothing as sexual symbolism.
1800. Hawes, E. IT'S STILL SPINACH. Boston: Little, Brown, 1954. Interesting statements on women's dress, nightgowns, hats, shoes, makeup, bras,

and why people dress. Sequel to her 1938 book, FASHION IS
SPINACH.

1801. Hiler, H., and M. Hiler. BIBLIOGRAPHY OF COSTUME. New York: H.
W. Wilson, 1939. Extensive index of costume references, and various
approaches to the study of clothing among men and women.

1802. Hirning, L. C. "Clothing and Nudism." Pp. 268-283 in THE ENCYCLO-
PEDIA OF SEXUAL BEHAVIOR, edited by Albert Ellis and A.
Abarbanel, 2nd edition. New York: Hawthorn Books. Argues that
primary function of clothing is decorative and sexually symbolic.

1803. Hoper, L. H. "Fig Leaves and French Dresses," GALAXY, vol. 18 (Oct.
1874), pp. 504-510. Blames Elias Howe and the sewing machine for the
fact that women must now be conspicuous to be considered well-
dressed.

1804. Hurlock, Elisabeth. THE PSYCHOLOGY OF DRESS: AN ANALYSIS OF
FASHION AND ITS MOTIVE. New York: Ronald Press, 1929. 224 pp.

1805. Jackson, M. "The Function of Clothes," THE SPECTATOR, vol. 155
(Nov. 8, 1935), p. 772. Women derived the use of dress as ornament
from men.

1806. Katz, Elihu and Paul F. Lazarsfeld. PERSONAL INFLUENCE. Glencoe, Ill.:
Free Press, 1964. 400 pp. Fashion leadership in the community is examined
in relation to life-cycle position, fashion interest, and social status. See
pp. 247-270.

1807. Kroeber, Alfred L. "On the Principle of Order in Civilization as Exemplified by Changes in Fashion," AMERICAN ANTHROPOLOGIST, vol.
21 (1919), pp. 235-263. Classic interpretation of women and fashions.

1808. Langdon-Davies, J. LADY GODIVA: THE FUTURE OF NAKEDNESS.
London: Harper, 1928. Satirical projection to a time when nudity
will be the vogue.

1809. Lebeuf, Jean-Paul. VETEMENTS ET PARURES DU CAMEROUN
FRANCAIS. Paris: Aux Editions Arc-en-Ciel, 1946. An album of
colored illustrations of clothes and ornaments of the French Cameroun
natives.

1810. Monro, I. S., and D. E. Cook. COSTUME INDEX. New York: H. W.
Wilson, 1937. Bibliography of references to women's and men's clothing.

1811. National Council of Women of the United States. "Symposium on
Women's Dress," pts. 1 and 2, ARENA, vol. 6 (Sept.-Oct. 1892), pp.
488-507, 621-634. Nineteenth-century discussion of suitable dress for
women in different walks of life.

1812. Packard, Vance. THE STATUS SEEKERS. New York: David McKay,
1959. Pages 128-138 talk about the class structure of American society,
especially the symbols of status-rank, and refer to men's and women's
clothing fashions.

1813. Reik, Theodor. "Men, Women, and Dresses," PSYCHOANALYSIS, vol.
1 (Winter 1953), pp. 3-16. An attempt to relate a woman's statement,"
"I have nothing to wear," to a little girl's complaint about her lack of
male sex organs.

1814. Richardson, Jane, and Alfred L. Kroeber. THREE CENTURIES OF
WOMEN'S DRESS FASHIONS: A QUANTITATIVE ANALYSIS. Berkeley: Univ. of California, Anthropological Records, vol. 5, no. 2, 1940.

1815. Rickert, E. CHAUCER'S WORLD. New York: Columbia Univ. Press, 1948. Interesting passages on male and female fashions and shopping in fourteenth-century London.

1816. Riegel, Robert E. "Women's Clothes and Women's Rights," AMERICAN QUARTERLY, vol. 15 (Fall 1963), pp. 390-401. History of dress reform in the middle and late nineteenth century. Concludes that as women gained more freedom and rights, changes in dress codes followed rapidly.

1817. Roach, Mary Ellen, and Joanne Bubolz Eicher, eds. DRESS, ADORN-MENT, AND THE SOCIAL ORDER. New York: Wiley, 1965. 429 pp. Collection of readings regarding the relationship between the social order and dress. Some classic statements with an annotated bibliography of 529 items, emphasizing women and fashion.

1818. Rothfeld, O. WOMEN OF INDIA. Bombay: D. B. Taraporeuata, n.d. Pages 177-196 comment on functions of dress and the quasi-religious sanction of dress in India.

1819. Russell, F. "A Brief Survey of the American Dress Reform Movements of the Past with Views of Representative Women," ARENA, vol. 6 (Aug. 1892), pp. 325-339. Views of Amelia Bloomer, Elizabeth Cady Stanton, and Frances E. Willard.

1820. Ryan, M. S. PSYCHOLOGICAL EFFECTS OF CLOTHING. PART I: A SURVEY OF THE OPINION OF COLLEGE GIRLS. Cornell Univ. Agricultural Experiment Station Bulletin, no. 882. Ithaca, N.Y.: Cornell Univ., 1952. Survey of college girls to determine how and in what way they think clothing affects them, degree of interest in clothing, and their attitudes toward the importance of being well-dressed.

1821. Trahey, Jane. HARPER'S BAZAAR: 100 YEARS OF THE AMERICAN FEMALE. New York: Random House, 1967. 307 pp. An excellent illustrated view of women's changing fashions in America.

1822. Veblen, Thorstein. "The Economic Theory of Women's Dress," POPULAR SCIENCE MONTHLY, vol. 46 (Dec. 1894), pp. 198-205. Veblen considered women to be chattel who displayed their wealth through dress, a conspicuously unproductive expenditure.

1823. Wykes-Joyce, M. COSMETICS AND ADORNMENT: ANCIENT AND CONTEMPORARY. New York: Philosophical Library, 1961. Historical study, with comments on hair fashions, beards, tattooing, perfumes, and cosmetic surgery.

1824. Young, K. HANDBOOK OF SOCIAL PSYCHOLOGY. New York: Appleton-Century-Crofts, 1960. Pages 310-329 are a thorough discussion of fashion and its relation to culture, with attention to women's fashions.

G. Modern Women—Social and Moral Questions

Liberty is the mother of virtue, and if women be, by their very constitution, slaves, and not allowed to breathe the sharp invigorating air of freedom, they must ever languish like exotics, and be reckoned beautiful flaws in nature.
—Mary Wollstonecraft

1825. Addams, Jane. A CENTENNIAL READER. New York: Macmillan, 1960. 330 pp. Selections from the writings of Jane Addams on the position of women, child welfare, and social work.

1826. ———. PEACE AND BREAD IN TIME OF WAR. New York: Garland, 1972. 267 pp. Reprint. Concerns the Women's Peace Party, Women's International League for Peace and Freedom.

1827. ———. SECOND TWENTY YEARS AT HULL HOUSE. New York: Macmillan, 1930. Her concepts of education and current events, with analyses of the Negro problem and social progress.

1828. "American Woman: What Price Liberation?" NEW GENERATION, vol. 51 (Fall 1969). Entire issue devoted to women and women's liberation.

1829. Anthony, Susan B. "The Status of Women Past, Present, and Future," THE ARENA, May 1897, n.p.

1830. Banks, J. A. and Olive Banks. FEMINISM AND FAMILY SOCIAL PLANNING IN VICTORIAN ENGLAND. New York: Schocken Books, 1964.

1831. Barnes, Earl. WOMAN IN MODERN SOCIETY. New York: Huebsch, 1912. 257 pp. Asserts that both sexes will achieve happiness and freedom if they recognize their sex differences and use them.

1832. Bell, Ralcy Husted. WOMAN FROM BONDAGE TO FREEDOM. New York: Critic and Guide, 1921. 230 pp. The emancipation and progress of women, economically and socially.

1833. Billington, George, and Theresa Billington. THE MILITANT SUFFRAGE MOVEMENT. London: Frank Palmer, 1911. The history of British suffrage struggles.

1834. Bird, Caroline. BORN FEMALE: THE HIGH COST OF KEEPING WOMEN DOWN. New York: David McKay, 1968. Feminist overview, with emphasis on women's status in employment and the economy.

1835. Blatch, Harriet Stanton and Alma Lutz. CHALLENGING YEARS. New York: G. P. Putnam's Sons, 1940. 347 pp. Biography by the daughter of Elizabeth Cady Stanton, a leader of the early suffragist movment in England and America. Much history of the movement in the late nineteenth century and early twentieth.

1836. Bloor, Ella Reeve. WE ARE MANY: AN AUTOBIOGRAPHY. New York: International Publishers, 1940. 319 pp. The memoirs of a 78-year-old Communist and organizer of the American labor movement.

1837. Blumberg, Dorothy R. FLORENCE KELLEY: THE MAKING OF A SOCIAL PIONEER. New York: A. M. Kelley, 1966. 194 pp. Biography of one of the founders of the NAACP, a vice-president of the National Woman Suffrage Association, and the women who initiated the struggle against child labor in America.

1838. Boulting, William. WOMEN IN ITALY: FROM THE INTRODUCTION OF THE CHIVALROUS SERVICE OF LOVE TO THE APPEARANCE OF THE PROFESSIONAL ACTRESS. New York: Brentano's, 1910. 356 pp. Intensive study of the Italian woman's life-style from birth to death, based upon Italian documents.

1839. Bradbrook, Muriel C. THAT INFIDEL PLACE: A SHORT HISTORY OF GIRTON COLLEGE. London: Chatto and Windus, 1969. 265 pp. A history of one of Britain's first women's colleges, with accounts of women's struggle for equal educational opportunities.

1840. Brittain, Vera. LADY INTO WOMAN: A HISTORY OF WOMEN FROM VICTORIA TO ELIZABETH II. New York: Macmillan, 1953. 256 pp. The changing roles of women in Britain and throughout the world during a period of vigorous struggle for woman suffrage and greater equality of the sexes.

1841. Brown, Charles Brockden. ALCUIN: A DIALOGUE. New York: T. and J. Swords, 1798. 77 pp. Conversation between Brown and Mrs. Carter, representing the ideas of one of the earliest champions of the rights of women in America.

1842. Buckley, J. M. THE WRONG AND PERIO OF WOMEN SUFFRAGE. New York: Fleming H. Revell, 1909. An anti-suffrage point of view.

1843. Bullough, Vern L. THE HISTORY OF PROSTITUTION. New Hyde Park, N.Y.: University Books, 1964. 304 pp. Includes some very important bibliographical references on prostitution, along with a survey of the problem.

1844. Bunch-Weeks, Charlotte. A BROOM OF ONE'S OWN. Washington, D.C.: Women's Liberation, 1970. 19 pp. A housewife's manifesto, and a take-off of Virginia Woolf's A ROOM OF ONE'S OWN.

1845. Buytendijk, F.J.J. WOMEN: A CONTEMPORARY VIEW. Translated by Denis J. Barrett. Glen Rock, N.J.: Newman Press, 1968. By a noted Dutch psychologist and philosopher on how women talk, move, and react to men. Chapters on "The Intuitive Notion of the Essence of Femininity" and "How Woman Manifests Herself."

1846. Chopin, Kate. THE AWAKENING. Chicago and New York: H. S. Stone, 1899. Autobiographical account of the Southern writer of Creole stories and her awakening to the feminist movement.

1847. Clark, F. I. THE POSITION OF WOMEN IN CONTEMPORARY FRANCE. London: P. S. King, 1937.

1848. Conway, Jill. "Women Reformers and American Culture, 1870-1930." In Ari Hoogenboom and Olive Hoogenboom, AN INTERDISCIPLINARY APPROACH TO AMERICAN HISTORY, vol. 2. Englewood Cliffs, N.J.: Prentice-Hall, 1973. The early reformers failed to question sexual stereotypes, the author concludes.

1849. Cooke, Joanne, Charlotte Bunch-Weeks, and Robin Morgan, eds. THE NEW WOMEN: A MOTIVE ANTHOLOGY ON WOMEN'S LIBERA-TION. Greenwich, Conn.: Fawcett, 1971. 217 pp. Prose, poems, and polemics by 15 writers. Good bibliography.

1850. Coolidge, Olivia. WOMEN'S RIGHTS: THE SUFFRAGE MOVEMENT IN AMERICA, 1848-1920. New York: Dutton, 1966. 189 pp.

1851. Cooper, James, and Sheila McIsaac Cooper. THE ROOTS OF AMERICAN FEMINISM. Boston: Allyn and Bacon, 1973. 300 pp. An anthology of writings by such feminists as Wollstonecraft, Grimké, Fuller, John Stuart Mill, Gilman, Sanger, and Suzanne LaFollette.

1852. Cott, Nancy F., ed. ROOT OF BITTERNESS: DOCUMENTS OF THE SOCIAL HISTORY OF AMERICAN WOMEN. New York: Dutton, 1972. 373 pp. Excellent anthology of women from colonial times to the turn of the century, containing documents of some feminist arguments from journals, fiction, and autobiography.

1853. Cusack, Dymphna. CHINESE WOMEN SPEAK. Australia: Angus and Robertson, 1958. Changes in the status of Chinese women since 1949.

1854. Davis, Paulina Wright. A HISTORY OF THE NATIONAL WOMEN'S RIGHTS MOVEMENT. New York: Source Book Press, 1970. Reprint of the 1871 edition. 152 pp.

1855. Degler, Carl N. "Charlotte Perkins Gilman on the Theory and Practice of Feminism," AMERICAN QUARTERLY, vol. 8, no. 1 (Spring, 1956).

Charlotte Gilman was called "the most original and challenging mind which the women movement produced."

1856. Dell, Floyd. WOMEN AS WORLD BUILDERS. Chicago: Forbes, 1913. Studies in early twentieth-century feminism, with short biographical studies of such women as Gilman, Pankhurst, Addams, Webb, Goldman, and others.

1857. Dixon, Marlene. "Why Women's Liberation," RAMPARTS (Dec. 1969), pp. 58-63. Summary of the purposes of women's lib. [see 1900]

1858. Dorr, Rheta C. WHAT EIGHT MILLION WOMEN WANT. Boston: Small, Maynard, 1910. 339 pp. Women wanted suffrage.

1859. ———. A WOMAN OF FIFTY. New York: Funk and Wagnalls, 1924. 451 pp. The story of her struggle for freedom and her years as a militant suffragist, and as a war correspondent in Revolutionary Russia.

1860. Drier, Mary. MARGARET DREIER ROBINS: HER LIFE, LETTERS, AND WORK. New York: Island Press Cooperative, 1950. 278 pp. Biography of the president of the National Women's Trade Union League, who brought to national attention the problems women were encountering in getting employment.

1861. Epstein, Cynthia Fuchs, and William J. Goode, eds. THE OTHER HALF: ROADS TO WOMEN'S EQUALITY. Englewood Cliffs, N.J.: Prentice-Hall, 1971. 207 pp. Essays exploring the social, psychological, biological, and political issues involved in the fight for women's rights.

1862. "Equal Rights for Women: A Symposium on the Proposed Constitutional Amendment," HARVARD CIVIL RIGHTS—CIVIL LIBERTIES LAW REVIEW, (Mar. 1971). pp. 215-287. Six articles on the ERA by Pauli Murray, Norman Dorsen, Thomas Emerson, Paul Freund, and others.

1863. Farmer, Lydia, ed. THE NATIONAL EXPOSITION SOUVENIR: WHAT AMERICA OWES TO WOMEN. Buffalo and Chicago: Moulton, 1893. 505 pp. A discussion of women's rights and suffrage.

1864. Farnam, Anne. "Isabella Beecher Hooker as a Woman Suffragist: A Centennial Frame of Reference," CONNECTICUT REVIEW, vol. 5 (Oct. 1971), pp. 70-82.

1865. Firestone, Shulamith, and Anne Koedt, eds. NOTES FROM THE SECOND YEAR: WOMEN'S LIBERATION. New York: Radical Feminists, 1970. Major writings of the Radical Feminists on women's theories of feminism and how to found a movement.

1866. Flexnor, Eleanor. A CENTURY OF STRUGGLE: THE WOMAN'S RIGHTS MOVEMENT IN THE UNITED STATES. Cambridge: Harvard Univ. Press, 1959. 384 pp. Most complete history of the women's rights movement up to 1920.

1867. Frazier, Thomas R. ed. THE UNDERSIDE OF AMERICAN HISTORY: OTHER READINGS. Vol. 2. New York: Harcourt, Brace and Jovanovich, 1971. Several articles on "Feminism as a Radical Ideology,"and "Why Women's Liberation."

1868. Freeman, Jo. "The Origins of the Women's Liberation Movement," AMERICAN JOURNAL OF SOCIOLOGY, vol. 78, no. 4 (Jan. 1973), pp. 792-811. Description of the essential elements contributing to the emergence of women's liberation in the mid-sixties.

1869. Fukichi Shigetaka. KINDAI NIHON JOSEI SHI [The History of Women in Modern Japan]. Tokyo: Sekkasha, 1963. Excellent Japanese-language source of the role of women in modern Japanese society.

1870. Gamble, Eliza Burt. THE EVOLUTION OF WOMAN. New York: G. P. Putnam's Sons, 1894. Feminist biology and anthropology, fantastic and ludicrous in parts, but a central work of feminist theory.

1871. Giele, Janet. "Centuries of Childhood and Centuries of Womanhood: An Evolutionary Perspective on the Feminist Role." Paper published by the Radcliffe Institute, Cambridge, Mass., 1971. A historical summary.

1872. Gilchrist, B. B. THE LIFE OF MARY LYON. Boston: Houghton Mifflin, 1910. 462 pp. Valuable biography of a pioneer in the field of women's education and the founder of Mount Holyoke College.

1873. Grimke, Sarah. LETTERS ON THE EQUALITY OF THE SEXES AND THE CONDITION OF WOMAN. Boston: Isaac Knapp, 1838. Pamphlet whose central theme is woman's moral responsibility to act for the good of mankind.

1874. Hale, Beatrice Forbes-Robertson. WHAT WOMEN WANT: AN INTER-PRETATION OF THE FEMINIST MOVEMENT. New York: Stokes, 1914. 307 pp. The historical origins of the movement, its effects in altering women's status, the present condition of women, and prospects for the future.

1875. Hale, Sarah J. MANNERS: OR, HAPPY HOMES AND GOOD SOCIETY ALL THE YEAR ROUND. New York: Arno Press, 1972. Reprint of the 1868 edition. By the literary editor of GODEY'S LADY'S BOOK. By means of education and good manners women can be a moral force through which the world may be improved.

1876. Hansberry, Lorraine. THE MOVEMENT: A DOCUMENTARY OF THE STRUGGLE FOR EQUALITY. New York: Simon and Schuster, 1964. 127 pp. Black and white women's liberation, by the short-lived author of A RAISIN' IN THE SUN.

1877. Hernton, Calvin. SEX AND RACISM IN AMERICA. New York: Grove Press, 1965. 180 pp. Chapters on social and moral questions, and also good for studies of the sexual aspects of race relations.

1878. Houghton, Walter. VICTORIAN FRAME OF MIND. New Haven: Yale Univ. Press, 1957. 467 pp. Chapter describing women's function and impact in the familial, sexual, and social aspects of Victorian life; bibliography.

1879. Humphrey, Grace. WOMEN IN AMERICAN HISTORY. Indianapolis: Bobbs-Merrill, 1919. 223 pp. Short biographies of 15 American women who displayed unusual degrees of achievement, courage, and dedication to their causes.

1880. Inman, Mary. IN WOMEN'S DEFENSE. Los Angeles, Calif.: Committee to Organize the Advancement of Women, 1940. 174 pp. Study of social questions—equality, equal opportunity—relating to women.

1881. ———. WOMAN POWER. Los Angeles, Calif.: Committee to Organize the Advancement of Women, 1942. 88 pp.

1882. Irwin, Inez. ANGELS AND AMAZONS. Garden City, N.Y.: Doubleday, Doran, 1933. 531 pp. The progress of American women from 1833 to 1933 in biographies of some of the more influential women and the problems to which they addressed themselves.

1883. ———. THE STORY OF THE WOMAN'S PARTY. New York: Harcourt, Brace, 1921. 486 pp. The story of the struggle for woman suffrage in the United States.

1884. Japanese Woman's Commission. JAPANESE WOMEN. Chicago: A. C. McClure, 1893. Descriptive account of the Japanese woman in Japanese traditional and modern society, written for the Chicago World's Columbian Exposition.

1885. Jensen, Oliver. THE REVOLT OF AMERICAN WOMEN. New York: Harcourt Brace, 1952.

1886. Jones, Beverly, and Judith Brown. TOWARD A FEMALE LIBERATION MOVEMENT. Boston: New England Free Press, 1968. 32 pp.

1887. Kamm, Josephine. RAPIERS AND BATTLE AXES: THE WOMEN'S MOVEMENT AND ITS AFTERMATH. London: Allen and Unwin, 1966. 240 pp. The history of the women's rights movement in England.

1888. Katz, Maude W. "The Negro Woman and the Law," FREEDOMWAYS, vol. 2 (Summer 1962), pp. 278-286. The status of women before the law and efforts being made to improve it.

1889. Kaur, Manmohan. THE ROLE OF WOMEN IN THE FREEDOM MOVE-MENT. Delhi: Sterling, 1968. A history of the work done by Indian women from 1857 to 1947, the year of India's independence.

1890. Kenyatta, Mary. "On Liberation and Black Women," CHURCH AND SOCIETY, (Jan.-Feb. 1972), pp. 21-24. The role of black women in the feminist movement.

1891. Kerstin, Aner. SWEDISH WOMEN TODAY: A PERSONAL APPRAISAL. Stockholm: Swedish Institute for Cultural Relations with Foreign Countries, 1966. The changing roles of women in Sweden.

1892. Key, Ellen. THE WOMAN MOVEMENT. New York: G. P. Putnam's Sons, 1912. A discussion of women's contributions to the fight for suffrage and equality.

1893. King, Clyde L., ed. "Women in the Modern World," THE ANNALS, vol. 143 (May 1929), pp. 1-396. An entire issue devoted to women—the women's movement, women in the modern home, women's work outside the home, in industry, the professions—and their achievements in integrating career and family life.

1894. Koyama, Takashi. THE CHANGING SOCIAL POSITION OF WOMEN IN JAPAN. Geneva: La Tribune de Geneve, UNESCO, 1961. Status and institutional changes from 1950-1960, with summary of the increased participation by Japanese women in civic activities.

1895. Kraditor, Aileen S. UP FROM THE PEDESTAL: SELECTED DOCU-MENTS FROM THE HISTORY OF AMERICAN FEMINISM. Chicago: Quadrangle Books, 1968. An anthology on such topics as women's spheres, religion and status, marriage, divorce, women in government, and equal rights.

1896. Lansing, Marjorie. "Women: The New Political Class." In WOMEN IN POLITICS, edited by Jane Jaquette. New York: Wiley, 1974.

1897. Lasch, Christopher. THE NEW RADICALISM IN AMERICA, 1889-1963. New York: Knopf, 1965. 349 pp. Summary of the feminist movements.

1898. ———, ed. THE SOCIAL THOUGHT OF JANE ADDAMS. Indianapolis: Bobbs-Merrill, 1965. 266 pp. Collection of writings of the Nobel Peace

Prize winner on politics, the city, the revolt of youth, immigrants, social work, civil rights, pacifism and family life.

1899. Lawrenson, Helen. "The Feminine Mistake," ESQUIRE, vol. 75, no. 1 (Jan. 1971), pp. 82 ff. Criticizes the women's liberation movement for misdirecting its attention against men rather than more important social concerns.

1900. Leffler, Ann, and Dair L. Gillespie. "A Feminist Reply: We Deny the Allegations and Defy the Allegator (Reply to M. Dixon)," BERKELEY JOURNAL OF SOCIOLOGY, vol. 16 (1971-1972), pp. 68-79. An answer to Marlene Dixon's question, "Why Women's Liberation," previously cited [1857].

1901. Livermore, Mary. THE STORY OF MY LIFE. Hartford, Conn.: n.p., 1897. Civil War nurse, temperance and suffrage leader, and lecturer, 1820-1905.

1902. Marine, Gene. A MALE GUIDE TO WOMEN'S LIBERATION. New York: Holt, Rinehart and Winston, 1973. 312 pp. An attempt to explain the feminist indictment of society to the uncomprehending and often hostile male audience.

1903. Martin, Edward S. THE UNREST OF WOMEN. New York: Appleton, 1913. 146 pp. Such topics as self-supporting wives, Jane Addams, feminine equality, etc.

1904. McCrimmon, Abraham L. THE WOMAN MOVEMENT. Philadelphia and Boston: Griffith and Rowland, 1915. 254 pp. Includes an excellent bibliography.

1905. Menzies, Sutherland. POLITICAL WOMEN. 2 vols. London: Henry S. King, 1873. The debate about women's participation and enfranchisement in politics.

1906. Mitchell, David J. MONSTROUS REGIMENT: THE STORY OF THE WOMEN OF THE FIRST WORLD WAR. New York: Macmillan, 1965. 400 pp. The story of the woman peace movement in Great Britain.

1907. Montefiore, Dora. FROM A VICTORIAN TO A MODERN. London: E. Archer, 1927.

1908. Munaker, Sue, Evelyn Goldfield, and Naomi Weisstein. "A Woman is a Sometime Thing." Pp. 263-271 in THE NEW LEFT: A COLLECTION OF ESSAYS, edited by Priscilla Long. Boston: Porter Sargent, 1969. An attack on the media and all other degrading institutions, beauty contests, playboy clubs, hair sprays, TRUE ROMANCE magazines, false breasts, Norman Mailer, feminine mystiques, brides' magazines, etc.

1909. Nathan, Maud. THE STORY OF AN EPOCH MAKING MOVEMENT. New York: Doubleday, 1926. 245 pp. How the Consumer's League, founded in 1890, grew into more than 20 affiliates in the various states, and how the league facilitated the improvement of working conditions for women and girls.

1910. National American Woman Suffrage Association. VICTORY: HOW WOMEN WON IT: A CENTENNIAL SYMPOSIUM; 1840-1940. New York: H. W. Wilson, 1940. 174 pp.

1911. Novack, George. REVOLUTIONARY DYNAMICS OF WOMEN'S LIBERATION. New York: Pathfinder Press, 1972. A Marxian approach.

1912. O'Malley, I. B. WOMEN IN SUBJECTION. London: Duckworth, 1933. Feminist history presented with a feminist bias.

1913. O'Neill, William L. EVERYONE WAS BRAVE: THE RISE AND FALL OF FEMINISM IN AMERICA. Chicago: Quadrangle Books, 1969. 369 pp. A criticism of marriage, family, and sexual permissiveness as hindering further emancipation after suffrage.

1914. Ostrogorskii, Moiseii A. THE RIGHTS OF WOMEN. London: Swann Sonnenschein, 1893.

1915. Pankhurst, E. Sylvia. THE SUFFRAGETTE MOVEMENT: AN INTIMATE ACCOUNT OF PERSONS AND IDEALS. New York: Longmans, Green, 1931.

1916. Panther Women. "Panther Sisters on Women's Liberation," THE MOVEMENT, (Sept. 1969), n.p. Several Black Panther women discuss women in revolutionary struggles.

1917. Parker, Gail, ed. THE OVEN BIRDS: AMERICAN WOMEN ON WOMANHOOD, 1820-1920. Writings of early American feminists on the rise and fall of the women's movement in America.

1918. Porter, Kirk H. HISTORY OF SUFFRAGE IN THE UNITED STATES. Chicago: Univ. of Chicago Press, 1918.

1919. Racz, Elizabeth. "The Women's Rights Movement in the French Revolution." Available from KNOW, Inc., P.O. Box 10197, Pittsburg, Pa., 1971.

1920. Renard, Marie Thérese. LA PARTICIPATION DES FEMMES A LA VIE CIVIQUE. Paris: Editions Ouvriéres, 1965. 175 pp. History of the political participation of French women.

1921. Rischbieth, Bessie Mabel. MARCH OF AUSTRALIAN WOMEN: A RECORD OF FIFTY YEARS' STRUGGLE FOR EQUAL CITIZENSHIP. Perth, Australia: Paterson Brokensha Party, 1964. 177 pp.

1922. Roesch, Roberta F. WOMEN IN ACTION: THEIR QUESTIONS AND THEIR ANSWERS. New York: John Day, 1967. 249 pp. Questions and answers to the problems of women's lib.

1923. Rossi, Alice, ed. ESSAYS ON SEX EQUALITY. Chicago: Univ. of Chicago Press, 1970. One volume edition of all the writings of Harriet Taylor Mill and John Stuart Mill on problems and solutions to the women problem.

1924. Salper, Roberta, ed. FEMALE LIBERATION: HISTORY AND CURRENT POLITICS. New York: Knopf, 1972. 246 pp. An anthology designed to given an introductory view of the nineteenth-century women's rights movement along with the contemporary women's liberation movement.

1925. Sanger, William W. THE HISTORY OF PROSTITUTION: ITS EXTENT, CAUSES AND EFFECTS THROUGHOUT THE WORLD. New York: Arno Press, 1972. Reprint of the 1859 edition. A massive survey, based on interviews with 2,000 women.

1926. Schneir, Miriam, ed. FEMINISM: THE ESSENTIAL HISTORICAL WRITINGS. New York: Vintage Press, 1972. 320 pp. An anthology of books, essays, speeches, letters, and documents on feminism by such individuals as George Sand, Susan B. Anthony, Engels, Virginia Woolf, and others.

1927. Schurman, Ann Maria à. THE LEARNED MAID OR WHETHER A MAID MAY BE A SCHOLAR? London: n.p., 1641, 1659. Translated by Clement Barksdale. An early feminist plea for the education of girls.

1928. Scott, Anne Firor. "The 'New Woman' in the New South," SOUTH ATLANTIC QUARTERLY, vol. 61 (Autumn 1962), pp. 473-483. The effects of reform on the lives of contemporary Southern women.
1929. ———. "After Suffrage: Southern Women in the Twenties," JOURNAL OF SOUTHERN HISTORY, vol. 30, no. 3 (Aug. 1964), pp. 298-318. Discusses the 19th Amendment and concludes that Southern women achieved only a partial change in the social structure and still are confronted with difficulties in obtaining full participation in public life.
1930. Sillen, Samuel. WOMEN AGAINST SLAVERY. New York: Masses and Mainstream, 1955. 102 pp. Contains sketches of 16 women abolitionists.
1931. Smith, Page. DAUGHTERS OF THE PROMISED LAND. Bosgon: Little, Brown, 1971. 392 pp. Anecdotal for the most part, but informative. For example, "In the late 19th century a mother prepared her daughter for sexual intercourse by telling the young lady she must lie quietly on her wedding bed and think of the British Empire."
1932. Sochen, June. THE NEW FEMINISM IN TWENTIETH CENTURY AMERICA. Lexington, Mass.: Heath, 1971. 214 pp. Places the contemporary issue of women's liberation in historical perspective.
1933. Stearns, Bertha Monica. "Reform Periodicals and Female Reformers," AMERICAN HISTORICAL REVIEW, vol. 37 (July 1932), pp. 678-699.
1934. Stern, Madeline B. WE THE WOMEN: CAREER FIRSTS OF NINE-TEENTH CENTURY AMERICA. New York: Schulte, 1962. 403 pp. Accounts of notable women who broke the employment and discrimination barriers to pursue careers outside the home.
1935. Swords, Betty. "Your Stake in Women's Liberation," PROGRESSIVE WOMAN, vol. 2 (Jan. 1972), pp. 18-24.
1936. Symons, H. J. AFRICAN WOMEN: THEIR LEGAL STATUS IN SOUTH AFRICA. London: C. Hurst, 1968. The author looks at such issues as separate development, polygamy, unmarried mothers, inheritance laws, and the increase of women in politics.
1937. ———. "The Status of African Women." In Peter J.M. McEwan and Robert B. Sutchliffe, MODERN AFRICA. New York: Crowell, 1965. Pp. 326-331. With particular emphasis on South Africa, author discusses the status changes of African women which followed from a weakening in their economic functions.
1938. Tanner, Leslie B., ed. VOICES FROM WOMEN'S LIBERATION. New York: Signet Books, 1970. 445 pp. Anthology of essays by women on feminists of the past, politics, jobs, childrearing, lesbianism, racism, sexism, and other issues of women's liberation.
1939. Taylor, James M. BEFORE VASSAR OPENED: A CONTRIBUTION TO THE HISTORY OF THE HIGHER EDUCATION OF WOMEN IN AMERICA. Boston: Houghton Mifflin, 1914. 287 pp.
1940. U.S. Congress. House Committee on Rules. CREATING COMMITTEE ON WOMAN SUFFRAGE IN THE HOUSE OF REPRESENTATIVES. Hearings on House Resolution 12, May 18, 1917. Washington, D.C.: SUDOC, GPO, 1917. 24 pp. The debate initiating the committee on woman suffrage.
1941. Vicinus, Martha, ed. SUFFER AND BE STILL: WOMEN IN THE VICTORIAN AGE. Bloomington: Indiana Univ. Press, 1972. 256 pp. Essays on the psychological, biological, sociological, and literary attitudes toward women in the Victorian period.

1942. Vreed de Stuers, Cora. THE INDONESIAN WOMAN. The Hague: Mouton, 1960. Indonesian women today and the problems of the women's movement—education, marriage laws, and how to use the talents of Indonesian women in solving national problems.

1943. Wadia, A. R. THE ETHICS OF FEMINISM. New York: Doran, 1923.

1944. Ward, Barbara E. WOMEN IN THE NEW ASIA. Paris: UNESCO, 1963. Study of the impact of the new status of women in Burma, Ceylon, India, Laos, Malaya, Pakistan, the Philippines, Singapore, Thailand, and Vietnam.

1945. White, Jean Bickmore. "Gentle Persuaders: Utah's First Women Legislators," UTAH HISTORICAL QUARTERLY, vol. 38, no. 1 (Winter 1970), pp. 31-49. The elections and subsequent legislative records of three women elected to the Utah State Legislature in 1896. Dr. Martha Hughes Cannon, the first state senator of the female sex is featured.

1946. Woodroofe, Debby. SISTERS IN STRUGGLE, 1848-1920. New York: Pathfinder Press, 1972. 32 pp. A socialist viewpoint.

1947. Woodward, Helen, B. THE LADY PERSUADERS. New York: Harcourt, Brace, 1929. 189 pp. A history of women's magazines stressing their influence on women and society.

1948. Woody, Thomas. A HISTORY OF WOMEN'S EDUCATION IN THE UNITED STATES. 2 vols. New York: Octagon Press, 1971. Reprint of the 1929 edition. A short history, with documents, of changes in women's education, with emphasis on women's colleges. Excellent bibliography.

1949. Ziebarth, Marilyn. "Woman's Rights Movement," MINNESOTA HISTORY, vol. 33 (Summer 1971), pp. 225-30. An illustrated book from the Minnesota Historical Society showing women as they fought for the vote, worked, and wore new types of clothes during the ninteenth century. Commentaries on the photographs.

H. Women in Revolutionary and Changing Societies

We take as our source the hitherto unrecognized culture of women, a culture which from long experience of oppression developed an intense appreciation for life, a sensitivity to unspoken thoughts and the complexity of simple things, a powerful knowledge of human needs and feelings. . . . We regard our feelings as our most important source of political understanding. We see the key to our liberation in our collective wisdom and our collective strength.

—New York Radical Women

1950. Baraka, Imamu Amiri. "Black Women," THE BLACK WORLD (formerly NEGRO DIGEST), 1970. No volume or pagination given. Argues the need for black women to develop a level of consciousness which will help unify black women in their revolutionary struggle for liberation.

1951. Beard, Mary R. THE FORCE OF WOMEN IN JAPANESE HISTORY. Washington, D.C.: Public Affairs Press, 1953. 196 pp. How Japanese women have helped to change their society.

1952. Bebel, Auguste. WOMAN UNDER SOCIALISM. New York: Labor News Press, 1904. Women's civic and political status under socialism.

1953. Belden, Jack. "Gold Flower's Story." Pp. 275-307 in Jack Belden, CHINA SHAKES THE WORLD. New York: Monthly Review Press,

1970. Argues that the Communists' drive for power was "touched at almost every point by women, their feelings, by their relationship to men, by their social status, by their symbol as an object of property, religion and sex."

1954. Bouvier, Jeanne. LES FEMMES PENDANT LA REVOLUTION [Women During the Revolution]. Paris: n.p., 1931. Women in the French Revolution.

1955. Browning, Hilda. WOMEN UNDER FASCISM AND COMMUNISM. London: n.p., 1934.

1956. Buhle, Mari Jo. "Women and the Socialist Party, 1901-1914," RADICAL AMERICA, Feb. 1970, n.p.

1957. Castellani, Maria. ITALIAN WOMEN. Rome: n.p., 1939. A defense of Italian fascism and women's roles in Italy.

1958. Chisholm, Shirley. "Race, Revolution and Women," BLACK SCHOLAR, vol. 3, no. 4 (Dec. 1971), pp. 17-21. Women in America must become revolutionaries, but the goal must be more than political freedom or economic freedom, but rather total freedom to build a worldwide society based on the positive values of all human life.

1959. Coughlin, Richard J. THE POSITION OF WOMEN IN VIETNAM. New Haven: Yale Univ. Southeast Asia Studies, 1965. 45 pp. Data culled from French language studies of the legal, economic, and social position of Vietnamese women since World War II.

1960. Davis, Angela. IF THEY COME IN THE MORNING: VOICES OF RESISTANCE. New York: Third Press, 1971. Comprehensive collection of writings by black priosners and their lawyers on the revolutionary struggle of black prisoners against the courts and prisons. Essays by Angela Davis and Ericka Huggins, and Angela Davis's lawyer, Margaret Burnham, are particularly interesting.

1961. Ellet, Elizabeth F. L. THE WOMEN OF THE AMERICAN REVOLUTION. New York: Haskell House, 1969, reprint, 1850 edition.

1962. Figner, Vera. MEMOIRS OF A REVOLUTIONIST. New York: International Publishers, 1927. Autobiography of a Russian woman, b. 1852.

1963. Gordon, David C. WOMEN OF ALGERIA: AN ESSAY ON CHANGE. Harvard Middle Eastern Monographs, no. 19. Cambridge: Harvard Univ. Press, 1968, 98 pp. Good historical study of traditional Algerian society under French rule, with discussions of the changes in the position of women as a result of their participation in the Algerian revolution.

1964. Hinton, William. FANSHEN: A DOCUMENTARY OF REVOLUTION IN A CHINESE VILLAGE. New York: Monthly Review Press, 1966. 637 pp. In the process of describing the revolutionary changes, Hinton gives some interesting materials on the position of women in parts of rural China.

1965. Hulton, Ann. LETTERS OF A LOYALIST LADY. New York: Arno Press, 1970. Reprint of the 1927 edition. Observations of society during the American Revolution, by a pro-British woman.

1966. INTERNATIONAL LABOUR REVIEW, eds. "African Conferences on the Role of Women in National Development," INTERNATIONAL LABOUR REVIEW, vol. 104 (Dec. 1971), pp. 555-557.

1967. Johnson, Olive M. WOMAN AND THE SOCIALIST MOVEMENT. New York: Socialist Labor Party, 1918. Marxian argument that women's place in society depends upon its economic arrangements; therefore, after private property and the family relations it has produced are abolished, full equality for women will result.

1968. Kaneko, Josephine C. "The Activity of Socialist Women," THE SOCIAL-IST WOMAN, Jan. 1908.

1969. Klimpel Alvarado, Félicitas. LA MUJER CHILENA: EL APORTE FEMININO AL PROGRESO DE CHILE, 1910-1960 [Chilean Women: The Feminine Contribution to the Progress of Chile, 1910-1960]. Santiago: Editorial Andrés Bello, 1962.

1970. Ladner, Joyce, "Tanzanian Women and Nation-Building," BLACK SCHOLAR, vol. 3, no. 4 (Dec. 1971), pp. 22-28. Pleas for the opportunity for women to participate in the home, community, and nation to eliminate the destructive forces of racism, human exploitation, and the last vestiges of neocolonialism.

1971. Le Duan. ON THE SOCIALIST REVOLUTION IN VIETNAM. Vol. 3. Hanoi: Foreign Languages Publishing House, 1967. By the Premier of North Vietnam, on Vietnamese women and the revolution.

1972. Leith-Ross, L. "The Rise of a New Elite Amongst the Women of Nigeria." In AFRICA: SOCIAL PROBLEMS OF CHANGE AND CONFLICT, edited by Pierre L. Van Den Berghe. San Francisco: Chandler, 1965. Contrasts the changes between "primitive" Ibo women and today's modern, sophisticated women, the product of revolutionary changes.

1973. Leith-Ross, Sylvia. AFRICAN WOMEN: A STUDY OF THE IBO OF NIGERIA. New York: Praeger, 1965. 367 pp.

1974. Lucas, Christopher. WOMEN OF CHINA. Hong Kong: Dragonfly Press, 1965. Anticommunist look at equality and emancipation of the Chinese woman as a life of constant turmoil, drabness, and loss of femininity.

1975. Ma, Hsin-teh. CHINESE WOMEN IN THE GREAT LEAP FORWARD. Peking: Foreign Languages Press, 1960. Portraits of women in Communist China—telephone operators, housewives, farmers—and discussion of the part women have played in the Chinese Revolution.

1976. Marx, Karl, Friedrich Engels, Vladimir Lenin, and Joseph Stalin. THE WOMAN QUESTION. New York: International Publishers, 1951. 96 pp. Collection of excerpts on the position of women in society under both capitalism and socialism.

1977. Michael, Franz. THE TAIPING REBELLION. Vol. 1. Seattle: Univ. of Washington Press, 1965. 256 pp. Interesting proposals put forward by the Taiping Rebels in China regarding equality for women predate the Communist period by 100 years.

1978. Morris, Margaret. PRIVATE JOURNAL KEPT DURING A PORTION OF THE REVOLUTIONARY WAR. New York: Arno Press, 1970. Reprint of the 1836 edition. View of social changes that occurred after the Revolution, with a forecast of changes for women in the new society.

1979. Paulme, Denise, ed. WOMEN OF TROPICAL AFRICA. London: Routledge and Kegan Paul, 1963, 308 pp. Collection of essays, all by women anthropologists, dealing with African women in their everyday lives in traditional settings, and what the future offers African women. Excellent bibliography. [see 3031].

1980. Reed, Evelyn. PROBLEMS OF WOMAN'S LIBERATION: A MARXIST APPROACH. New York: Pathfinder Press, 1970. Discussion of matriarchal periods in history, how women have been subjected in the past, and prospects for the future.

1981. Reimar, Robert Fernandez, ed. CASA DE LAS AMERICAS [Home of the Americas], Havana (Mar.-June 1971). Issue devoted to women includes articles on black women in Cuba since Castro's rise to power, women in Brazil, and Vietnamese women.

1982. Stephens, Winifred. WOMEN OF THE FRENCH REVOLUTION. London: n.p., 1922.

1983. Tatarinova, Nadezhda. WOMEN IN THE USSR. Moscow: Novosti Press, n.d. 110 pp. Summary of women in the Soviet economy, highlighting changes since the Russian Revolution in women's participation in political and public life.

1984. Weinstein, James. THE DECLINE OF SOCIALISM IN AMERICA, 1912-1925. New York: Monthly Review Press, 1967. See his chapter on "Women and Socialism."

1985. "Women in Revolution," WOMAN: A JOURNAL OF LIBERATION, vol. 1, no. 4 (1969), pp. 2-32, 64. Issue devoted to women in Asia, Cuba, France, and Vietnam.

1986. WOMEN OF VIETNAM. Nos. 1, 2, 3, and 4. Hanoi: Vietnam Women's Union, 1967. Series of pamphlets on women in the revolution, Ho Chi Minh on the emancipation of women, and illustrations of changes in the lives of women in North Vietnam.

1987. Yetman, Norman. LIFE UNDER THE PECULIAR INSTITUTION: SELECTIONS FROM THE SLAVE NARRATIVE COLLECTION. New York: Holt, Rinehart and Winston, 1970. Many selections by women slaves before and after abolition.

I. Women as Colonists and Pioneers

It is particularly intriguing that social and economic historians of the past century have overlooked women, for during that time one of the most impressive social and economic facts has been the rapid change in the part women have played in the society and the economy.

—Ann Firor Scott

The power of a woman is in her dependence, flowing from the consciousness of that weakness which God has given her for her protection.

—The Congregational Clergy of Massachusetts

1988. Acrelius, Israel. A HISTORY OF NEW SWEDEN OR THE SETTLEMENTS ON THE RIVER DELAWARE. Stockholm: Harberg and Hassellberg, 1759. The part women played in the settlements is discussed throughout the book.

1989. Adams, James T. THE FOUNDING OF NEW ENGLAND. Boston: Atlantic Monthly Press, 1921. Women in the founding of the early colonies.

1990. Augur, Helen. AN AMERICAN JEZEBEL: LIFE OF ANNE HUTCHINSON. New York: Brentano, 1930. A biography of the early colonist in the Massachusetts Bay Colony who was exiled to Rhode Island, and who later migrated to the shores of Long Island where she and her family were killed by Indians.

1991. Baird, Charles W. HISTORY OF HUGUENOT EMIGRATION TO AMERICA. 2 Volumes. New York: Dodd, Mead, 1893. Women who played a part in the emigration movement are mentioned.

1992. Barnard, Ella Kent. DOROTHY PAYNE, QUAKERESS. Philadelphia: Ferris and Leach, 1909. A pioneer in the settlement of Pennsylvania.

1993. Bayer, Henry G. THE BELGIANS: FIRST SETTLERS IN NEW YORK AND IN THE MIDDLE STATES. New York: Devin-Adair, 1925. The narrative of women who helped settle the region are discussed.

1994. Beedy, Helen C. MOTHERS OF MAINE. Portland, Maine: Thurston, 1895. Pioneer women of Maine.

1995. Bibbins, Ruth M. THE BEGINNINGS OF MARYLAND IN ENGLAND AND AMERICA. Baltimore: Remington, 1934. Women in the colonies are dealt with briefly.

1996. Blumenthal, Walter H. BRIDES FROM BRIDEWELL: FEMALE FELONS SENT TO COLONIAL AMERICA. Rutland, Vt.: C. E. Tuttle, 1962. 139 pp.

1997. Bolton, Herbert E. ANZA'S CALIFORNIA EXPEDITION. 2 vols. Berkeley: Univ. of California Press, 1930. Anza's first expedition to California in 1774 included a few women, but his second in 1776 included 29 wives of soldiers, who became the first permanent Spanish settlement in the region.

1998. Brailsford, Mabel R. QUAKER WOMEN, 1650-1690. London: Duckworth, 1915. History of the influence and achievements of a number of Quaker women in the American colonies, mainly as religious zealots and homesteaders.

1999. Bridenbaugh, Carl. CITIES IN THE WILDERNESS: THE FIRST CENTURY OF URBAN LIFE IN AMERICA, 1625-1742. New York: Ronald Press, 1938. Some mention is given to the role of women in the colonization and development of urban society and culture.

2000. Brooks, Geraldine. DAMES AND DAUGHTERS OF COLONIAL DAYS. New York: Crowell, 1914. 290 pp.

2001. Bruce, H. Addington. WOMEN IN THE MAKING OF AMERICA. Boston: Little, Brown, 1928. 347 pp.

2002. Chapman, Charles E. FOUNDING OF SPANISH CALIFORNIA. New York: Macmillan, 1916. Stories of pioneer men and women in California.

2003. Clapp, Thomas. "Womanhood in Early America," CONNECTICUT MAGAZINE, vol. 12 (1908), pp. 233-239. The contributions of women to the colonization efforts in America.

2004. Clement, Jesse, ed. NOBLE DEEDS OF AMERICAN WOMEN. Buffalo, N.Y.: Derby, 1851.

2005. Dexter, Elizabeth A. COLONIAL WOMEN OF AFFAIRS. Boston: Houghton Mifflin, 1924. 203 pp. Stories of colonial women in various walks of life, with several sections on early pioneers, such as Elizabeth Poole, founder of the town of Taunton, Massachusetts; Lady Deborah Dunche Moody, leader of a colony on Long Island in 1643; and Elizabeth Haddon Estaugh, pioneer woman in New Jersey (1680-1762).

2006. Drinker, Sophie H. HANNAH PENN AND THE PROPRIETORSHIP OF PENNSYLVANIA. Philadelphia: National Society of Colonial Dames of

America in Pennsylvania, 1958. 207 pp. The story of Hannah Callowhill Penn, wife of William Penn, the founder of Pennsylvania, who for the last 6 years of Penn's life, managed his affairs in the colony.

2007. ———. "The Two Elizabeth Carterets," NEW JERSEY HISTORICAL PROCEEDINGS, vol. 79, no. 2 (1961), pp. 95-110. The Carteret family established a colony in eastern New Jersey.

2008. Earle, Alice. COLONIAL DAMES AND GOOD WIVES. Boston: Houghton Mifflin, 1895. Reprinted by Frederick Ungar Publishing Co., 1962. 315 pp.

2009. Ellet, Elizabeth F. L. PIONEER WOMEN OF THE WEST. New York: Scribner's, 1854. 434 pp. Story of the settlements from Tennessee to Michigan in American history, with accounts of women who went along to colonize the territory.

2010. Farnham, Eliza Woodson. LIFE IN PRAIRIE LAND. New York: Arno Press, 1972. Reprint of the 1846 edition. Women as homemakers and civilizers on the American frontier.

2011. Fiske, John. DUTCH AND QUAKER COLONIES IN AMERICA. 2 vols. Boston: Houghton Mifflin, 1899. Women of note are cited throughout the book.

2012. Fowler, William W. WOMAN ON THE AMERICAN FRONTIER. New York: Source Book Press, 1970. 527 pp. A history of American women as pioneers, patriots, adventuresses, heroines, missionaries, soldiers, teachers, and wives.

2013. Gersch, Harry. WOMEN WHO MADE AMERICA GREAT. Philadelphia: Lippincott, 1962. 224 pp. Biographical sketches.

2014. Green, Harry Clinton, and Mary Wolcott Green. PIONEER MOTHERS. 3 vols. New York: G. P. Putnam's Sons, 1912. Excellent survey of the women who helped to make America.

2015. Hammond, George P. DON JUAN DE ONATE AND THE FOUNDING OF NEW MEXICO. Santa Fe: Historical Society of New Mexico, 1927. Contains stories of the first settlements in New Mexico, with an account of the sixteenth-century woman pioneer and colonist Doña Ana de Zaldivar y Mendoza.

2016. Hanaford, Phoebe A. C. DAUGHTERS OF AMERICA. Augusta, Maine: True, 1882.

2017. Holliday, Carl. WOMAN'S LIFE IN COLONIAL DAYS. Boston: Cornhill, 1922.

2018. Hotten, John C. THE ORIGINAL LIST OF PERSONS OF QUALITY WHO WENT FROM GREAT BRITAIN TO THE AMERICAN PLANTA-TIONS, 1600-1700. London: Chatto and Windus, 1874. Includes women who went to the New World.

2019. Leonard, Eugenie A., Sophie H. Drinker, and Miriam Y. Holden. THE AMERICAN WOMAN IN COLONIAL AND REVOLUTIONARY TIMES, 1565-1800: A SYLLABUS WITH A BIBLIOGRAPHY. Philadelphia: Univ. of Pennsylvania Press, 1962. 169 pp. Excellent source materials with a bibliography.

2020. Magoffin, Susan. DOWN THE SANTA FE TRAIL AND INTO MEXICO: THE DIARY OF SUSAN SHELBY MAGOFFIN, 1846-47. Edited by Stella M. Drumm. New Haven: Yale Univ. Press, 1962. 294 pp. Biography of an early American woman pioneer.

2021. Majors, Monroe A. NOTED NEGRO WOMEN, THEIR TRIUMPHS AND ACTIVITIES. Chicago: Donohue and Henneberry, 1971; Freeport, N.Y.: Books for Libraries Press, 1971. 365 pp. Written by a black physician in 1893; an important compilation of brief information on 312 black women; illustrated.

2022. Marble, Ann R. THE WOMEN WHO CAME IN THE MAYFLOWER. Boston: Pilgrim Press, 1920.

2023. Marcus, Jacob R. EARLY AMERICAN JEWRY, 1649-1794. 2 vols. Philadelphia: Jewish Publishing Society, 1951-1955. Many outstanding Jewish women are featured.

2024. Moller, Herbert. "Sex Composition and Correlated Culture Patterns of Colonial America," WILLIAM AND MARY QUARTERLY, vol. 2, ser. 3 (1945), pp. 113-153.

2025. Morgan, Edmund S. THE PURITAN FAMILY: ESSAYS ON RELIGION AND DOMESTIC RELATIONS IN 17TH CENTURY NEW ENGLAND. Boston: Boston Public Library, 1944.

2026. Noyes, Ethel J.R.C. THE WOMEN OF THE MAYFLOWER AND WOMEN OF PLYMOUTH COLONY. Detroit: Gale Research Co., 1971. 197 pp. Reprint of the 1921 edition. History of the women who fed, clothed, and encouraged their people in the hazardous days of Plymouth Colony, with the story of the twentieth-century descendants of the Pilgrim women.

2027. O'Sullivan-Beare, Nancy. LAS MUJERES DE LOS CONQUISTADORES: LA MUJER ESPANOLA EN LOS COMIENZOS DE LA COLONIZA-CION AMERICANA [The Women of the Conquistadores: Spanish Women in the Beginning of American Colonization]. Madrid: Compañia Bibliografica Española, 1956.

2028. Pryor, Sara C. THE MOTHER OF WASHINGTON AND HER TIMES. New York: Macmillan, 1903. Biography of the mother of the first president, and the accounts of her hardships in the new colony of Virginia.

2029. Robertson, James A. TRUE RELATION OF THE HARDSHIPS SUFFER-ED BY GOVERNOR FERNANDO DE SOTO AND CERTAIN PORTU-GUESE GENTLEMEN DURING THE DISCOVERY OF THE PROVINCE OF FLORIDA BY A GENTLEMAN OF ELVAS. 2 vols. Tallahassee: Florida State Historical Society, publication no. 11, 1933. Includes an account of Francisca Hinestrosa who came on DeSoto's expedition to Florida with her husband. She was killed by Chickasaw Indians.

2030. Ross, Nancy Wilson. WESTWARD THE WOMEN. New York: Random House, 1944. 196 pp. Narcissa Whitman, Sacajawea, Mary Walker, Eliza Spalding, Abigail Scott Duniway, Bethenia Owens, and others are featured.

2031. Sale, Edith T. OLD TIME BELLES AND CAVALIERS. Philadelphia: Lippincott, 1912. Men and women in the colonial period.

2032. Sioussat, Anna M. COLONIAL WOMEN OF MARYLAND. Baltimore: Lord Baltimore Press, 1911.

2033. Sprague, William Forrest. WOMEN AND THE WEST: A SHORT SOCIAL HISTORY. New York: Arno Press, 1972. Reprint of the 1940 edition. A scholarly social history of the hardships and achievements of women pioneers.

2034. Spruill, Julia C. WOMEN'S LIFE AND WORK IN THE SOUTHERN COLONIES. Chapel Hill: Univ. of North Carolina Press, 1938. 426 pp. Discusses their function in the colonies, their social life, recreation, occupations, and the manner in which they were regarded by the law and society in general.

2035. ———. "Women in the Founding of the Southern Colonies," NORTH CAROLINA HISTORICAL REVIEW, vol. 13 (1936), pp. 202-218.

2036. Stewart, Elinore. LETTERS OF A WOMAN HOMESTEADER. Lincoln: Univ. of Nebraska Press, 1961. 281 pp.

2037. Thomas, Anna L. B. NANCY LLOYD: JOURNAL OF A QUAKER PIONEER. New York: Frank Maurice, 1927. Story of the pioneering Lloyd family in Pennsylvania.

2038. Torbert, Alice C. ELEANOR CALVERT AND HER CIRCLE. New York: William Frederick Press, 1950. The life and times of one of the founding families of Maryland.

2039. Van Laer, Arnold J. E. CORRESPONDENCE OF MARIA VAN RENSSELAER, 1669-1689. Albany: Univ. of the State of New York Press, 1935. The descriptive letters of life and society in early Dutch colonial New York.

2040. Wharton, Ann H. COLONIAL DAYS AND DAMES. Philadelphia: Lippincott, 1908.

2041. ———. SALONS: COLONIAL AND REPUBLICAN PHILADELPHIA. Philadelphia: Lippincott, 1900.

2042. White, Elizabeth N. MARY BROWNE: THE TRUE LIFE AND TIMES OF THE DAUGHTER OF MR. JOHN BROWNE, GENT.,—WIFE OF THE FIRST ENGLISH MAYOR OF NEW YORK. Providence, R.I.: Roger Williams Press, 1935.

2043. Wright, Richardson. FORGOTTEN LADIES. Philadelphia: Lippincott, 1928. Interesting accounts of early women colonists and heroines.

J. Women as Soldiers and Spies

And out of the light a Voice spoke, the voice of an angel as she firmly believed, and the wondering girl heard the words: "Jeanne, you must go to the help of the King of France, and it is you who shall give him back his kingdom."
—Joan of Arc

2044. AAF Historical Office. "Women Pilots with the AAF," 1941-1944. In ARMY AIR FORCES HISTORICAL STUDIES, no. 55. Washington, D.C., n.d.

2045. Andrews, Matthew P. VIRGINIA, OLD DOMINION. Garden City, N.Y.: Doubleday, Doran, 1937. Includes accounts of many colonial women who fought Indians, followed their husbands in the struggle for independence, and died for freedom.

2046. Braddon, Russell. WOMEN IN ARMS: THE STORY OF NANCY WAKE. London: Collins, 1963. 192 pp.

2047. Brice, Raoul. LA FEMMES ET LES ARMEES DE LA REVOLUTION ET DE L'EMPIRE, 1792-1815. Paris: n.p., 1913. Women who fought during the French Revolution and with Napoleon's armies.

2048. Bunce, Oliver B. THE ROMANCE OF THE REVOLUTION. New York: Bunce, 1854. Accounts of women who fought in the American Revolution. See esp. pp. 110-117, 147-150, 162-165, 236-252, 273-275, 323-326.

2049. Campbell, Amelia D. "Women of New York State in the Revolution," NEW YORK STATE HISTORICAL ASSOCIATION QUARTERLY, vol. 3 (1922), pp. 155-168.

2050. Chun, Victor K. "The Origin of the WASPS," JOURNAL OF THE AMERICAN AVIATION HISTORICAL SOCIETY, vol. 14, no. 4 (Winter 1969), pp. 259-262. The story of how women got into aviation during World War II.

2051. Cometti, Elizabeth. "Women in the American Revolution," NEW ENGLAND QUARTERLY, vol. 20 (1947), pp. 329-346.

2052. Corcos, Fernand. LES FEMMES EN GUERRE. Montaigne, France: n.p., 1926.

2053. Coulter, Ellis M. "Nancy Hart, Georgia Heroine of the Revolution," GEORGIA HISTORICAL QUARTERLY, vol. 39 (1955), pp. 118-151. She fought beside her husband, Capt. Benjamin Hart, in the American Revolution.

2054. Darrach, H. "Lydia Darrah," PENNSYLVANIA MAGAZINE OF HISTORY AND BIOGRAPHY, vol. 23 (1899), pp. 86-91. Story of a pioneer woman and fighter in the American Revolution.

2055. de Beaumont, E. WOMEN AND CRUELTY. London: n.p., 1905. The sword and womankind, descriptions of lady duellists and soldiers.

2056. Duparcq, de la Barre. HISTOIRE MILITAIRE DES FEMMES. Paris: n.p., 1869.

2057. Egle, William H. SOME PENNSYLVANIA WOMEN DURING THE WAR OF THE REVOLUTION. Harrisburg, Pa.: Harrisburg Publishing Co., 1898. 208 pp.

2058. Ellet, Elizabeth F. THE WOMEN OF THE AMERICAN REVOLUTION. 3 vols. New York: Baker and Scribner, 1848-50. Includes accounts of Margaret C. Corbin, Lydia Darragh, Deborah Sampson Gannett, Nancy Hart, Rebecca Motte, Catherine Schuyler, and other women who fought in the Revolution. [see 1961]

2059. Engle, Bernice Schultz. "The Amazons in Ancient Greece," PSYCHO-ANALYTIC QUARTERLY, vol. 11 (1942), pp. 512-554. The legendary race of Greek women warriors analyzed from a sociopsychological point of view.

2060. Gribble, Francis G. WOMEN IN WAR. New York: Dutton, 1917. Accounts of brave women and their daring exploits from the time of Boadicea to Florence Nightingale.

2061. Hansbrough, Henry Clay. WAR AND WOMEN. New York: Duffield, 1915. 121 pp. Maintains that women, in partnership with men, will eventually put an end to war.

2062. Holden, James A. "The Influence of the Death of Jane McCrea on the Burgoyne Campaign," NEW YORK STATE HISTORICAL ASSOCIATION PROCEEDINGS, vol. 12 (1913), pp. 249-294. Jane McCrea, a New York heroine in the Revolution, was able to foil Gen. Burgoyne's two-pronged attack along both the Mohawk and upper Hudson approaches to Albany. Burgoyne was defeated at the Battle of Saratoga, a decisive battle.

2063. Hutton, J. Bernard. WOMEN IN ESPIONAGE. New York: Macmillan, 1972. 192 pp. A completely documented account of the female spy in Eastern and Western secret services.

2064. Jones, Katherine. WHEN SHERMAN CAME: SOUTHERN WOMEN AND THE 'GREAT MARCH.' Indianapolis: Bobbs-Merrill, 1964. 353 pp. How Southern women impeded Sherman's March to the Sea during the Civil War.

2065. Laffin, John. WOMEN IN BATTLE. London and New York: Abelard-Schuman, 1967. 192 pp. Joan of Arc, Nancy Wake, Kit Welsh, Hannah Snell, and Molly Pitcher.

2066. Las Cases, Comte Emile. LA FEMME SOLDAT [The Woman Soldier]. Rouen, France: n.p., 1900.

2067. Levine, Isaac Don. YASHKA. New York: Stokes, 1919. A transcription of the autobiography of Maria Botchkareva, commander of the Russian women's Battalion of Death.

2068. Lyman, Susan E. "Three New York Women of the Revolution," NEW YORK HISTORICAL SOCIETY QUARTERLY, vol. 29 (1945), pp. 77-82.

2069. Mann, Herman. THE FEMALE REVIEW: LIFE OF DEBORAH SAMPSON, THE FEMALE SOLDIER IN THE WAR OF THE REVOLU-TION. New York: Arno Press, 1972. Reprint of the 1797 edition. Story of the young girl who joined the Revolutionary Army in 1782, served as an orderly and Indian fighter, was shot in the leg, and finally granted a $4 monthly pension through Congressional action.

2070. McArthur, J. L. "Women of the Revolution," NEW YORK STATE HISTORICAL ASSOCIATION PROCEEDINGS, vol. 5 (1905), pp. 153-161.

2071. Mills, Emma L. "How Molly Saved the Fort," GRANITE MONTHLY, vol. 14 (1892), pp. 276-281. Molly Pitcher besieged Fort Clinton (N.Y.) with her husband and fired the last gun at the British after her husband was shot. She saved the fort from falling to the British, was made a sergeant by Washington, and after the war was pensioned.

2072. Moore, Frank. WOMEN OF THE WAR: THEIR HEROISM AND SELF-SACRIFICE. Hartford, Conn.: n.p., 1866. 596 pp. Civil War women.

2073. Myers, Albert Cook, ed. SALLY WISTER'S JOURNAL: A TRUE NARRATIVE, BEING A QUAKER MAIDEN'S ACCOUNT OF HER EXPERIENCES WITH OFFICERS OF THE CONTINENTAL ARMY, 1777-1778. New York: Arno Press, 1972. Reprint of the 1902 edition.

2074. Parker, Amelia C. "Baroness Riedesel and Other Women in Burgoyne's Army," NEW YORK STATE HISTORICAL ASSOCIATION PRO-CEEDINGS, vol. 26 (1928), pp. 109-119.

2075. Power, James R. BRAVE WOMEN AND THEIR WARTIME DECORA-TIONS: A STUDY. New York: Vantage Press, 1959. 97 pp.

2076. Reinach, Adolphe. L'ORIGINE DES AMAZONES. Paris: n.p., 1913.

2077. Romain, Col. Charles Armand. LES GUERRIERES. Paris: n.p., 1931. Sketches of women warriors in legend, antiquity, in the middle ages, and in modern times, with emphasis on French women. Bibliography.

2078. Taylor, Susie King. REMINISCENCES OF MY LIFE IN CAMP WITH THE 33RD UNITED STATES COLORED TROOPS, LATE 1ST SOUTH CAROLINA VOLUNTEERS. New York: Arno Press, 1972. Reprint of the 1902 edition.

2079. Tweedie, Ethel B. WOMEN AND SOLDIERS. London: John Lane, 1918. 184 pp. British women during World War I.

2080. U.S. Women's Bureau. CAREERS FOR WOMEN IN THE ARMED FORCES. Compiled by Helen J. Robinson, Special Services and Publications Division. Washington, D.C.: Department of Defense, 1955. 46 pp.

2081. Velazquez, Loreta Janeta. THE WOMAN IN BATTLE: A NARRATIVE OF THE EXPLOITS, ADVENTURES, AND TRAVELS OF MADAME LORETA JANETA VELAZQUEZ, OTHERWISE KNOWN AS LIEUTENANT HARRY T. BUFORD, CONFEDERATE STATES ARMY. Edited by C. J. Worthington. New York: Arno Press, 1972. Reprint of the 1876 edition. Amazing story of the battles she participated in as a confederate officer, her career as a spy and blockade-runner, her adventures as a miner, stockbroker, resident among the Mormons, and her numerous love affairs.

K. Women in Ethnic Minorities

Here is a great mass of people, yet it takes an effort of the intellect and will even to see them.

—Michael Harrington

2082. Aptheker, Herbert, ed. A DOCUMENTARY HISTORY OF THE NEGRO PEOPLE IN THE UNITED STATES. 2 vols. New York: Citadel Press, 1951. Both volumes are indexed.

2083. Bardolph, Richard. THE NEGRO VANGUARD. New York: Rhinehart, 1959. Biographical data and generalizations about Afro-Americans from 1790-1959. Many black women included.

2084. Beauchamp, W. M. "Iroquois Women," JOURNAL OF AMERICAN FOLKLORE (Boston), vol. 13 (1901).

2085. Bennett, Lerone, ed. "The Negro Woman," EBONY, 1963. This special issue is devoted to black women in American society.

2086. ———. PICTORIAL HISTORY OF BLACK AMERICA. 3 vols. Chicago: Johnson Publishing Co., 1971. Many references and illustrations of black womens' lives.

2087. Bogardus, Emory S. IMMIGRATION AND RACE ATTITUDES. New York: Heath, 1928. An analysis of the varied forms of anti-Mexican racism in America.

2088. Botkin, Benjamin A. LAY MY BURDEN DOWN: A FOLK HISTORY OF SLAVERY. Chicago: Univ. of Chicago Press, 1945. 285 pp. Collection of narratives written by black men and women.

2089. ———. THE MEXICAN IN THE UNITED STATES. New York: Arno Press, 1970. Reprint of the 1934 edition.

2090. Buckmaster, Henrietta. LET MY PEOPLE GO. New York: Harper, 1941. 398 pp. The story of the abolition movement and the underground railroad.

2091. Cade, Toni, ed. THE BLACK WOMAN. New York: Signet Books, 1970. 256 pp. Wide-ranging anthology by 26 black women on racism, sexism, and the politics of liberation.

2092. Carr, Lucien. "On the Social and Political Position of Women Among the Huron-Iroquois Tribes," REPORT OF THE PEABODY MUSEUM OF AMERICAN ARCHEOLOGY AND ETHNOLOGY, vol. 3. Cambridge, Mass.: Harvard Univ. Press, 1880-1887. See esp. pp. 207-232.

2093. Chisholm, Shirley. "Racism and Anti-Feminism," THE BLACK SCHOL-AR (Jan.-Feb.1970), pp. 40-45. Explores the relationship between racism and discrimination and antifeminism a black woman encounters in the political arena.

2094. Chung, Wen-hui. CHANGING SOCIAL-CULTURAL PATTERNS OF THE CHINESE COMMUNITY IN LOS ANGELES. Los Angeles: Univ. of Southern California Press, 1952. Description of how Chinese families have been acculturated in this West Coast area.

2095. Cleaver, Eldridge. SOUL ON ICE. New York: Dell, 1968. 210 pp. Chapter entitled "To All Black Women, From All Black Men" examines the status of black women in American society.

2096. Crummell, Alexander. THE BLACK WOMAN OF THE SOUTH—HER NEGLECTS AND HER NEEDS. Washington, D.C.: B. S. Adams, 1883.

2097. Fanon, Frantz. BLACK SKINS, WHITE MASKS. New York: Grove Press, 1967. Classic study of alienation and identity caused by colonialism and racism. See esp. chapters 2 and 3 which deal with black women in Algeria.

2098. Fuchs, Lawrence H., ed. AMERICAN ETHNIC POLITICS. New York: Harper Torchbooks, 1968. A good background to the politics of ethnic discrimination.

2099. Gamio, Manuel. MEXICAN IMMIGRATION TO THE UNITED STATES. Chicago: Univ. of Chicago Press, 1930. Describes the migration of millions of refugees from poverty and frustration in southern Mexico to the American Southwest, and how the men and women suffered as fully in this country.

2100. Hewitt, John N. "Status of Women in Iroquois Polity Before 1784," SMITHSONIAN ANNUAL REPORT, 1932. pp. 475-488. The Iroquois are a matriarchal society, and the role of women is influential.

2101. Higham, John. STRANGERS IN THE LAND: PATTERNS OF AMERICAN NATIVISM, 1860-1925. New York: Atheneum, 1963. 431 pp. A scholarly study of the ideological roots of anti-Catholic, anti-radical, and Anglo-Saxon traditions against the immigrants coming into America. Excellent bibliography of sources for many foreign groups in America.

2102. Hoggan, Frances. AMERICAN NEGRO WOMEN DURING THEIR FIRST FIFTY YEARS OF FREEDOM. London: n.p. 1913.

2103. Ichihashi, Yamoto. JAPANESE IN THE UNITED STATES: A CRITICAL STUDY OF THE PROBLEMS OF THE JAPANESE IMMIGRANTS AND THEIR CHILDREN. Stanford: Stanford Univ. Press, 1932. A social history of the Japanese in Hawaii and the United States to 1930. Japanese women are singled out in many cases throughout the book.

2104. Iga, Mamoru. "Japanese Social Structure and the Source of Mental Strain of Japanese Immigrants in the United States," SOCIAL FORCES, vol. 35 (1957), pp. 271-278. Analysis of personality conflicts derived from certain elements of tension in Japanese and American social organization.

2105. Jacobs, Milton. A STUDY OF CULTURE STABILITY AND CHANGE: THE MOROCCAN JEWESS. Washington, D.C.: Catholic Univ. of America, 1956. The status of Jewish women within the Mohammedan community.

2106. Ladner, Joyce. TOMORROW'S TOMORROW. Garden City: Doubleday, 1971. Topics covered include Black Womenhood in Historical Perspective, Growing Up Black, and Racial Oppression and the Black Girl; with an extensive bibliography.

2107. Landes, Ruth. THE OJIBWA WOMAN. New York: AMS Press, 1969. 247 pp. The life and social status of the Ojibwa woman from birth to death.

2108. La Violette, Forest E. AMERICANS OF JAPANESE ANCESTRY: A STUDY OF ASSIMILATION IN THE AMERICAN COMMUNITY. Toronto: Canadian Institute of International Affairs, 1945. Survey of Japanese in American communities and the problems of assimilation.

2109. Lebeson, Anita Libman. JEWISH PIONEERS IN AMERICA, 1492-1848. New York: Brentano, 1931. The stories of Jewish men and women struggling against anti-Semitism to build lives in America.

2110. Linderman, Frank B. PRETTY SHIELD: MEDICINE WOMAN OF THE CROWS. New York: John Day, 1972. 256 pp. Autobiography as told by Pretty Shield, about life for women among the Crow Indians.

2111. Lurie, Nancy O., ed. MOUNTAIN WOLFWOMAN, SISTER OF CRASHING THUNDER. Ann Arbor: Univ. of Michigan Press, 1961. 142 pp. An account of the life of a Winnebago Indian woman.

2112. Madsen, William. THE MEXICAN-AMERICANS OF SOUTH TEXAS. New York: Holt, Rinehart and Winston, 1964. 112 pp. Women and their position in the social setting are discussed throughout the book.

2113. McKenzie, Marjorie. 50 YEARS OF PROGRESS FOR NEGRO WOMEN. Pittsburg, Pa.: Pittsburgh Courier, 1950. 11 pp. The changes, if any, in the status of black women in America.

2114. Michelson, Truman. THE NARRATIVE OF A SOUTHERN CHEYENNE WOMAN. Washington, D.C.: Smithsonian Institute, 1932. Small study of one of the last survivors of the traditional Cheyenne way of life by a prominent ethnologist.

2115. Noble, Jeanne L. "The American Negro Woman," pp. 522-547 in THE AMERICAN NEGRO REFERENCE BOOK, edited by John P. Davis. Englewood Cliffs, N.J.: Prentice-Hall, 1966. Compilation of useful factual material on sex and age distribution, labor, income, marriage, and family life.

2116. Reid, Inez Smith. TOGETHER BLACK WOMEN. New York: Emerson Hall, 1971. In-depth interviews with some 200 black women in seven different states.

2117. Rendon, Armando B. CHICANO MANIFESTO: THE HISTORY AND ASPIRATIONS OF THE SECOND LARGEST MINORITY IN AMERICA. New York: Macmillan, 1971. A study of the burgeoning self-awareness and militancy of the Mexican-Americans in our society.

2118. Samora, Julian. LA RAZA: FORGOTTEN AMERICANS. South Bend, Ind.: Univ. of Notre Dame, 1966. One of the few books on urban life and its problems for Mexican-Americans.

2119. Sibler, Iriven, ed. VOICES OF NATIONAL LIBERATION. Brooklyn, N.Y.: Central Book Co., 1970, 326 pp. Cultural Congress of Havana, January, 1968. Revolutionary writings of artis and intellectuals, with many references to black women, such as "The New Woman in Revolutionary Cuba," by Elena Diaz and Natasha Klein.

2120. Sone, Monica. NISEI DAUGHTER. Boston: Little, Brown, 1953. Autobiography of a second-generation Japanese-American.

2121. Stampp, Kenneth. THE PECULIAR INSTITUTION: SLAVERY IN THE
ANTE-BELLUM SOUTH. New York: Random House, 1956. 435 pp.
A classic study of the impact of slavery on nineteenth-century American
society, with detailed accounts of the conditions of slaves.

2122. Steiner, Stan. LA RAZA: THE MEXICAN AMERICANS. New York:
Harper and Row, 1969. 418 pp.

2123. Stern, Elizabeth G. I AM A WOMAN—AND A JEW. New York: Arno
Press, 1972. Reprint of the 1926 edition.

2124. Thomas, Dorothy S., and Richard S. Nishimoto. THE SPOILAGE. Vol. 1
of JAPANESE-AMERICAN EVACUATION AND RESETTLEMENT.
Berkeley: Univ. of California Press, 1946. An excellent history of the
West Coast evacuation of the Japanese, and the social and psychological
effects of the internment.

2125. Vasquez, Enriqueta Lonquae. "The Mexican American Woman." Pp.
379-384 in SISTERHOOD IS POWERFUL: AN ANTHOLOGY OF
WRITINGS FROM THE WOMEN'S LIBERATION MOVEMENT, edited
by Robin Morgan. New York: Vintage, 1970. The role of the women of
La Raza.

2126. Wallace, Anthony F. C. "The Heyday of the Iroquois." In Ari Hoogenboom and Olive Hoogenboom, AN INTERDISCIPLINARY APPROACH
TO AMERICAN HISTORY, vol. 1, Englewood Cliffs, N.J.: Prentice-
Hall, 1973. An article dealing with sexual roles, child behavior, and the
importance of dreams in Iroquois culture.

2127. Williams, Maxine. "Why Women's Liberation is Important to Black
Women," THE MILITANT, July 1970. Describes the reasons women's
liberation is not attractive to black women and how certain aspects of
women's lib are relevant to her sisters.

2128. Winks, Robin W. THE BLACKS IN CANADA: A HISTORY. New Haven:
Yale Univ. Press, 1971. 546 pp. Detailed historical investigation of
Negroes in Canadian history and in the total pattern of the Canadian
community.

2129. Wong, Jade Snow. FIFTH CHINESE DAUGHTER. New York: Harper
and Row, 1950. Autobiographical account of a Chinese family in San
Francisco.

L. Women as Rulers

*Cleopatra's nose: if it had been shorter the whole face of the earth would have been
different.*

—Pascal (Pensées)

*Sir, there is one thing in all our fancy, and that now shall ye know: We desire of men,
above all manner of things, to have the sovereignty.*

—Dame Ragnell to King Arthur

2130. Adelman, Joseph. FAMOUS WOMEN: AN OUTLINE OF FEMININE
ACHIEVEMENT THROUGH THE AGES WITH LIFE STORIES OF
FIVE HUNDRED NOTED WOMEN. New York: Pictorial Review Pub-
lishers, 1926. 238 pp. Contains a section on "Rulers, Empresses, Queens,"

with short biographies of such rulers as Cleopatra, Semiramis of Assyria, Wilhelmina of Holland, Elizabeth of Austria, Esther, Queen of Israel, and many others.

2131. Almedingen, E. M. CATHERINE THE GREAT. London: Hutchinson, 1963. Biography of the Russian Empress (1729-1796).

2132. Anthony, Katherine Susan. CATHERINE THE GREAT. New York: Knopf, 1925. 331 pp.

2133. Atherton, Gertrude F. H. DIDO, QUEEN OF HEARTS. New York: Horace Liveright, 1929. 384 pp. Dido, a Phoenician princess, sister of Pygmalion, King of Tyre. In 850 B.C., she founded the city of Carthage.

2134. Buttles, Janet R. QUEENS OF EGYPT. London: n.p., 1908. Cleopatra, Nefertiti, and others.

2135. Cartwright, Julia. CHRISTINA OF DENMARK. London, 1913. Reprinted by AMS Press, 1970. Christina, Duchess of Milan and Lorraine (1522-1590).

2136. Castelot, Andre. JOSEPHINE: QUEEN OF FRANCE. New York: Harper and Row, 1967. 506 pp. The life of the Empress Josephine, Napoleon's consort.

2137. –––. QUEEN OF FRANCE: A BIOGRAPHY OF MARIE ANTOINETTE. New York: Harper and Row, 1957. 434 pp.

2138. Cole, Hubert. JOSEPHINE. London: Heinemann, 1962. 324 pp. Biography of Napoleon's wife.

2139. Collis, Maurice. THE MOTHERLY AND AUSPICIOUS. New York: Putnam, 1944. Biography of Tz'u Hsi, last (Dowager) Empress of China.

2140. Crankshaw, Edward. MARIE THERESA. New York: Viking Press, 1969. 366 pp. Biography of the Empress of Austria (1740-1780), whose struggle with Frederick the Great of Prussia over the seizure of Silesia brought Austria into the Seven Years' War.

2141. Crawford, Marion. ELIZABETH THE QUEEN: THE STORY OF BRITAIN'S NEW SOVEREIGN. Englewood Cliffs, N.J.: Prentice-Hall, 1952. 236 pp.

2142. Delayen, Baston. CLEOPATRA. New York: Dutton, 1934. Biography of one of the most fascinating queens in history (69-30 B.C.)

2143. de Serviez, T. R. Nicholas. THE ROMAN EMPRESSES: THE HISTORY OF THE LIVES AND SECRET INTRIGUES OF THE WIVES OF THE TWELVE CAESARS. 2 vols. New York: Nichols, 1913.

2144. Diener, Bertha. IMPERIAL BYZANTIUM. Translated by Eden and Cedar Paul. Boston: Little, Brown, 1938. Biographies of the queens and kings of Byzantium.

2145. Ewart, Andrew. THE WORLD'S WICKEDEST WOMEN. New York: Taplinger, 1965. See especially, pp. 76-96, for a biography of Theodora, "The Harlot Queen" who became Empress of Byzantium. Also, see pp. 228-242, "Jezebel of the Balkans," for the biography of Queen Draga of Serbia, wife of King Alexander. Both were assassinated by the rival Karageorgovic faction.

2146. Ferrara, Guglielmo. THE WOMEN OF THE CAESARS. New York: Loring and Mussey, 1911.

2147. Fitzgerald, C. P. THE EMPRESS WU. London: Cresset, 1968. The best English-language biography of China's early Empress in the T'ang Dynasty (ca. 690-705 A.D.)

2148. Fraser, Lady Antonia. MARY, QUEEN OF SCOTS. New York: Delacorte, 1969. 613 pp. A scholarly account of the Catholic Queen who ruled from 1553 to 1558.

2149. Gregorovius, Ferdinand. LUCRETIA BORGIA. New York: Benjamin Blom, 1903. 401 pp. Scholarly use of contemporary letters and documents to fathom the woman behind the legend.

2150. Guedalla, Philip. THE QUEEN AND MR. GLADSTONE. Garden City, N.Y.: Doubleday, Doran, 1934. 793 pp. Queen Victoria.

2151. Henderson, Thomas F. MARY, QUEEN OF SCOTS: HER ENVIRONMENT AND TRAGEDY, A BIOGRAPHY. 2 vols. New York: Haskell House, 1969.

2152. Hume, Martin A. S. QUEENS OF OLD SPAIN. London: n.p., 1906.

2153. Jenkins, Elizabeth. ELIZABETH THE GREAT. New York: Coward-McCann, 1958. 336 pp. Biography of Queen Elizabeth I.

2154. Lamb, Harold. THEODORA AND THE EMPEROR: THE DRAMA OF JUSTINIAN. Garden City, N.Y.: Doubleday, 1952.

2155. Lee, Sir Sidney. QUEEN VICTORIA: A BIOGRAPHY. New York: Macmillan, 1903. 611 pp.

2156. Levine, Joseph M. ELIZABETH I. Englewood Cliffs, N.J.: Prentice-Hall, 1969. 177 pp.

2157. Lindsay, Jack. CLEOPATRA. New York: Coward-McCann, 1970. 560 pp. An up-to-date and scholarly study.

2158. Longford, Elizabeth. QUEEN VICTORIA: BORN TO SUCCEED. New York: Harper and Row, 1965. 635 pp.

2159. Ludwig, Emil. CLEOPATRA: THE STORY OF A QUEEN. New York: Viking Press, 1937. 342 pp.

2160. Macurdy, Grace H. HELLENISTIC QUEENS: A STUDY OF WOMAN-POWER IN MACEDONIA, SELEUCID SYRIA, AND PTOLEMAIC EGYPT. Baltimore: Johns Hopkins Press, 1932.

2161. ———. "Queen Eurydice and the Evidence for Woman-Power in Early Macedonia," AMERICAN JOURNAL OF PHILOLOGY, vol. 48 (1927), pp. 201 ff.

2162. Masson, Frederic. JOSEPHINE: EMPRESS AND QUEEN. Paris: Goupil, 1899. 278 pp. Biography of Napoleon's queen.

2163. Mattingly, Garrett. CATHERINE OF ARAGON. New York: Vintage Books, 1941. 415 pp. Story of the first wife of Henry VIII.

2164. Miron, E. L. THE QUEENS OF ARAGON: THEIR LIVES AND TIMES. New York: Brentano, 1913.

2165. Mundt, Klara Muller. LOUISA OF PRUSSIA AND HER TIMES. New York: McClure, 1868. Life of the queen of Prussia (1776-1810), mother of William I, Emperor of Germany.

2166. Oliva, Lawrence J., ed. CATHERINE THE GREAT. Englewood Cliffs, N.J.: Prentice-Hall, 1971. 184 pp. Scholarly studies and critical essays about the great Russian Empress.

2167. Paul, John E. CATHERINE OF ARAGON AND HER FRIENDS. New York: Fordham Univ. Press, 1966. 263 pp.

2168. Phillips, James E. "The Woman Ruler in Spencer's Fairie Queene," HUNTINGTON LIBRARY QUARTERLY, vol. 5 (1942), pp. 211-234.

2169. Staley, Edgcumbe. THE DOGARESSAS OF VENICE. New York: Scribner's, 1910. History of the women rulers of Venice.

2170. Strachey, Lytton. QUEEN VICTORIA. New York: Harcourt, Brace, 1921. 434 pp.

2171. Taylor, Ida Ashworth. CHRISTINA OF SWEDEN. London: Hutchinson, n.d. 336 pp. Biography of the famous Swedish queen who abdicated her throne.

2172. Walsh, William. ISABELLA OF SPAIN: THE LAST CRUSADER. New York: R. M. McBride, 1930. 515 pp.

2173. Weibull, Curt Hugo J. CHRISTINA OF SWEDEN. Stockholm: Bonniers, 1966. 186 pp.

2174. Woodham-Smith, Cecil. QUEEN VICTORIA. New York: Knopf, 1972. The most recent biography of the British monarch.

IV. WOMEN IN PHILOSOPHY AND RELIGION

A great portion of the history of mankind finds its counterpart in Holy Scripture. Ten centuries of evolution in the conception of women have resulted in an attitude of the Church toward women which seems to be based solely on the writings in the Bible and of St. Paul. The following books and articles record both the scriptural development of this conception of women and its contemporary re-examination as regards her entrance into the Christian ministry and her place in the other major religions of the world.

Because the cosmos needs a hostess, we recommend: Father, Son, and Holy Ghostess.

—Rev. Robbins Ralph

2175. Achtemeier, Elizabeth. THE FEMININE CRISIS IN CHRISTIAN FAITH. New York: Abingdon Press, 1965. 160 pp. A look at the history of women's Christian activities, concluding, without a strong basis of supportable fact, that women are theologically well grounded.

2176. Addams, Jane. SOCIAL APPLICATION OF RELIGION. Cincinnati: Jennings and Graham, 1908. Women, through religious inculcation, could adapt themselves to changing women's condition, and world conditions, thus winning moral superiority over men.

2177. Alberione, James. WOMAN: HER INFLUENCE AND ZEAL AS AN AID TO THE PRIESTHOOD. Boston: St. Paul Editions, 1964. 316 pp.

2178. Ali, Ameer. "The Influence of Women in Islam," NINETEENTH CENTURY MAGAZINE, May 1899, pp. 755-774.

2179. Bacon, Francis D. WOMEN IN THE CHURCH. London: Butterworth, 1945. 146 pp. The argument for and against women's entrance into the ministry.

2180. Bailey D. S. THE MAN-WOMAN RELATIONSHIP IN CHRISTIAN THOUGHT. London: Longmans, 1959. 314 pp. Takes as its starting point a couple made in the image of God, jointly charged with overcoming and controlling the forces of nature.

2181. Barot, Madelaine. COOPERATION OF MEN AND WOMEN IN CHURCH, FAMILY, AND SOCIETY. Geneva: World Council of Churches, 1964. 48 pp. Motherhood has within itself a vitality which forces it to transcend itself in a messianic and spiritual maternity.

2182. Battis, Emery. SAINTS AND SECRETARIES: ANNE HUTCHINSON AND THE ANTI-NOMIAN CONTROVERSY IN THE MASSACHUSETTS BAY COLONY. Williamsburg: Univ. of Virginia Press, 1962. 379 pp. The history of the conflict between Puritan orthodoxy and Anne Hutchinson's crusade for the doctrine of free grace.

2183. Beaver, Robert Pierce. ALL LOVES EXCELLING: AMERICAN PROTESTANT WOMEN IN WORLD MISSIONS. Grand Rapids, Mich.: Eerdman's, 1968. Short history of the missionary efforts of Protestant women.

2184. Bjerregaard, C.H.A. THE GREAT MOTHER: A GOSPEL OF THE ETERNALLY-FEMININE: OCCULT AND SCIENTIFIC STUDIES AND EXPERIENCES IN THE SACRED AND SECRET LIFE. New York: Inner-Life, 1913. 330 pp. Religious-occult view which claims the superiority of women and advocates a return to matriarchy.

2185. Blavatsky, Helena P. SECRET DOCTRINE. 2 vols. Chicago: Theosophical Publishing House, 1970. Studies in occultism and religion by one of the founders of the science of theosophy.

2186. Bliss, Kathleen. THE SERVICE AND STATUS OF WOMEN IN THE CHURCHES, London: SCM Press, 1952. 208 pp.

2187. Bode, Edward Lynn. THE FIRST EASTER MORNING: THE GOSPEL ACCOUNTS OF THE WOMEN'S VISIT TO THE TOMB OF JESUS. ANALECTA BIBLICA 45. Rome: Biblical Institute Press, 1970. 217 pp.

2188. Bode, Mabel. WOMEN LEADERS OF THE BUDDHIST REFORMATION. London: Royal Asiatic Association, 1893.

2189. Bragdon, Claude. "Delphic Women." In Claude Bragdon, THE NEW IMAGE AND OLD LAMPS FOR NEW. New York: Knopf, 1936. Anthology of 12 essays.

2190. Brown, Norman O. LIFE AGAINST DEATH. New York: Random House, 1959. An effort to go beyond Freud's theory of patricidal-castration-guilt complex to a "maternal reality principle," but one which contributes a view of women as separate from the world of natural phenomena.

2191. Burkill, T. A. "Two into One: The Notion of Carnal Union in Mark 10:8, Cor. 6:16, Eph. 5:31," ZEITSCHRIFT FUR DIE NEUTESTAMETLICHE WISSENSCHAFT [Journal of New Testament Studies] , vol. 62, no. 1-2 (1971), pp. 115-120.

2192. Buytendijk, F.J.J. WOMAN: A CONTEMPORARY VIEW. Glen Rock, N.J.: Newman Press, 1968. 362 pp. A scholarly religious phenomenology.

2193. Calkins, Grace Gilkey. FOLLOW THOSE WOMEN. New York: United Church Women, 1961. 108 pp. History of the cooperation and work among women in the Protestant Church in America.

2194. Callahan, Sidney C. BEYOND BIRTH CONTROL: THE CHRISTIAN EXPERIENCE OF SEX. New York: Sheed and Ward, 1968. 248 pp. Deals with such topics as sexuality, celibacy, family planning and child-rearing in a Christian framework.

2195. Cavert, Inez. WOMEN IN AMERICAN CHURCH LIFE. New York: Friendship Publishers, 1951. 93 pp. Short survey of the role women play in American Christian churches.

2196. Ceballa Lopez, Fermin. LA MUJER COMO SUB-IGLESIA [Women within the Church] . Madrid: Editorial Alameda, 1971. 59 pp.

2197. Central Advisory Council for the Ministry of the Church Assembly. GENDER AND THE MINISTRY. Oxford, England: Church Army Press, 1962. Argument for the advancement of women into the liturgical ministry.

2198. Church of England, Commission Appointed by the Archbishop of Canterbury and York. WOMEN AND HOLY ORDERS. London: Central Board of Finance, Church of England, 1966. 134 pp. Objections to women in the Anglican ministry.

2199. CONCERNING THE ORDINATION OF WOMEN. Geneva: World Council of Churches, 1964. Considers the question of women's role in the church ministry.

2200. Cox, Harvey. "Eight Theses on Female Liberation," CHRISTIANITY AND CRISIS, vol. 31 (Oct. 4, 1971), pp. 199-202. Describes the influence that a liberated society can have upon changing the presently structured society. Predicts a trend toward Christian socialism.

2201. Crook, Margaret. WOMEN AND RELIGION. Boston: Beacon Press, 1964. 272 pp. Theological view of women and Christianity; compares the love of God with that of the husband and the submission to the Church with that of the wife.

2202. Culver, Elsie Thomas. WOMEN IN THE WORLD OF RELIGION: FROM PAGAN PRIESTESSES TO ECUMENICAL DELEGATES. Garden City, N.Y.: Doubleday, 1967. 340 pp. Detailed study of women in all aspects of religion and the feminine qualities they lend to church organization.

2203. Cunneen, Sally. SEX: FEMALE; RELIGION: CATHOLIC. New York: Holt, Rinehart and Winston, 1968. 171 pp. Study of how American Catholic women are responding to the challenge to relate their faith to their world of experience; based on information derived from 4,627 questionnaires.

2204. Daly, Mary. THE CHURCH AND THE SECOND SEX. New York: Harper and Row, 1968. 187 pp. History of antifeminism in the Church from ancient times, emphasizing the insensitivity of various Popes to the problems of women and the Christian acceptance of a "masculine" God.

2205. ———. BEYOND GOD THE FATHER: TOWARD A PHILOSOPHY OF WOMEN'S LIBERATION. Boston: Beacon Press, 1973, 225 pp.

2206. ———. "The Church and Women: An Interview with Mary Daly," THEOLOGY TODAY, vol. 28 (Oct. 1971), pp. 349-354. The author of THE CHURCH AND THE SECOND SEX and associate professor of theology at Boston College answers such questions as: Will the Second Coming be feminine? Will new symbols—a new Mary—lead to the development of a new Woman?

2207. Daniel, E., and B. Olivier. WOMAN IS THE GLORY OF MAN. Westminster, Md.: Newman Press, 1966. Refutes the ideas in Genesis that woman was created from man; instead they are seen as partners, created at the same time in order to share in the same enterprise: the emancipation of mankind.

2208. Danielou, Jean. MINISTRY OF WOMEN IN THE EARLY CHURCH. London: Faith Press, 1961. 31 pp. Small pamphlet stating that women's exclusion from the Church can be refuted by evidence in the Bible.

2209. Deen, Edith. ALL OF THE WOMEN OF THE BIBLE. New York: Harper and Row, 1955. 410 pp. Short biographies and studies of women in the Bible—Mary, Ruth, Miriam, Esther, etc.

2210. Devaux, Andre A. TEILHARD AND WOMANHOOD. Glen Rock, N.Y.: Paulist Press, 1968. A critical study of Teilhard de Chardin's attitudes toward women in his theological studies THE PHENOMENON OF MAN, MAN'S PLACE IN NATURE, and other writings.

2211. D'Héricourt, Madame. A WOMAN'S PHILOSOPHY OF WOMAN: OR WOMAN AFFRANCHISED: AN ANSWER TO MICHELET, PROUDHON, GIRARDIN, LEGOUVE, COMTE, AND OTHER MODERN INNOVATORS. Translated from the last Paris edition. New York: Carleton, 1864. 317 pp. A very militant view of the woman question, with highly supportable arguments against the antifeminine prejudices of her contemporary French colleagues.

2212. Doely, Sarah Bentley, ed. WOMEN'S LIBERATION AND THE CHURCH. New York: Association Press, 1970. 158 pp. A look at the demands of women to be allowed to participate in the church ministry, and an attempt to gauge that participation and impact on the future of the church. Good anthology with sources.
2213. Douglas, William. MINISTER'S WIVES. New York: Harper and Row, 1965. 265 pp.
2214. Dumas, Francine. MAN AND WOMAN: SIMILARITY AND DIFFER-ENCE. Geneva: World Council of Churches, 1966. 88 pp. Concerning the various roles of women, women in the Old Testament, the myth of Eve, the meaning of sexual differentiation in Christian terms.
2215. Eberhard, Wolfram. GUILT AND SIN IN TRADITIONAL CHINA. Berke-ley: Univ. of California Press, 1967. 141 pp. Based largely on Ming Dynasty morality books; a good study of sin in Chinese folk religion.
2216. Eckenstein, Lina. THE WOMEN OF EARLY CHRISTIANITY. London: n.p., 1935. 159 pp. The role women played in the spread of Christianity.
2217. ———. WOMAN UNDER MONASTICISM. Cambridge: Cambridge Univ. Press, 1896. 496 pp. Convent life from A.D. 500 to A.D. 1500.
2218. Eddy, Mary Baker. MISCELLANEOUS WRITINGS, 1883-1896. Boston: Christian Science Publishing House, 1898. Many revisions. The social gospel of the founder of Christian Science.
2219. Ermath, Margaret S. ADAM'S FRACTURED RIB: OBSERVATIONS OF WOMEN IN THE CHURCH. Philadelphia: Fortress Press, 1970. 159 pp. Study of the role of women in the life of the church and the possible ordination of women; concludes that the church is not sure, has not been responding to women as it should, and that the Holy Spirit is trying to tell the church something!
2220. Evans, Frederick. ANN LEE, THE FOUNDER OF THE SHAKERS. Mt. Lebanon, N.Y.: Author, 1858. 190 pp. Biography of the woman who founded the Shakers, an American religious-communistic celibate sect.
2221. Farley, Luke A. SAINTS FOR THE MODERN WOMAN: A UNITED NATIONS OF HOLINESS FOR THE WOMAN OF TODAY. Boston: St. Paul Editions, 1961. 276 pp. Moral and ethical examples for today's women to emulate.
2222. Faulhaber, Michael Cardinal. THE WOMEN OF THE BIBLE. Edited by Rev. Brendan Keogh. Westminster, Md.: Newman Press, 1955. 248 pp.
2223. Fell, Margaret. WOMEN'S SPEAKING JUSTIFIED, PROVED, AND ALLOWED OF BY THE SCRIPTURES. London: n.p., 1666. Short pamphlet advocating a voice for women, rather than subordination as called for in scriptural canon.
2224. Fifield, Emily. HISTORY OF THE ALLIANCE. Boston: The Alliance of Unitarian and other Liberal Christian Women, 1915. 150 pp.
2225. Fitzsimmons, John. WOMAN TODAY. New York: Sheed and Ward, 1952. 192 pp. Thesis that women have lost their position, but can gain it back by following Christian precepts of equality.
2226. Foster, Warren Dunham, ed. HEROINES OF MODERN RELIGION. Free-port, N.Y.: Books for Libraries Press, 1970. Reprint of 1913 edition. 275 pp. Ten biographies of modern women who made vital contributions to religious thought: Anne Hutchinson, Lucretia Mott, Fanny Crosby, Susannah Wesley, and Maude Booth. Good bibliography of works consulted.

2227. Gibson, Elsie. WHEN THE MINISTER IS A WOMAN. New York: Holt, Rinehart and Winston, 1970. 174 pp. How ministerial status has affected the lives of women, based on 280 questionnaires. Information includes age, marital status, special problems or obstacles to women ordained in the ministry, and how women can make a distinctive contribution to their ministries.

2228. Graebner, Alan. AFTER EVE: THE NEW FEMINISM. Minneapolis, Minn.: Augsburg Publishing House, 1972.

2229. Hahn, Elizabeth. PARTNERSHIP. Geneva: World Council of Churches, Commission on the Life and Work of Women in the Church, 1954. Ratifies man's purpose and blesses woman for her fruitfulness and motherhood in man's conquest of the world.

2230. Hannon, Vincent Emmanuel. THE QUESTION OF WOMEN AND THE PRIESTHOOD. London: Geoffrey Chapman, 1967.

2231. Harkness, Georgia E. WOMEN IN CHURCH AND SOCIETY. Nashville, Tenn.: Abingdon Press, 1972. An ordained Methodist minister, she concludes that an equal position for women in the church and in society is in harmony with scriptural teachings and Christian doctrine.

2232. Heinrich, Sister Mary Pia. CANNONESSES AND EDUCATION IN THE EARLY MIDDLE AGES. Washington, D.C.: Catholic Univ. Press, 1924. 218 pp. A history of convent life and education for the feminine ministry.

2233. Henrichsen, Margaret. SEVEN STEEPLES: A MINISTER AND HER PEOPLE. New York: Harper, 1967. Autobiographical account of a woman minister.

2234. Hodgson, Leonard. THEOLOGICAL OBJECTIONS TO THE ADMISSION OF WOMEN TO HOLY ORDERS. Cambridge, England: R. I. Severs, 1967. Declares that women have a legitimate right to two important liturgical duties, prayer and prophecy, but not to the ministry.

2235. Hoppin, Ruth. PRISCILLA: AUTHOR OF THE EPISTLE TO THE HEBREWS, AND OTHER ESSAYS. Jericho, N.Y.: Exposition Press, 1969. Certain themes, such as the integration of women into Jewish assemblies, and the equality between men and women, are found in the Bible.

2236. Horner, Isaline Blew. WOMEN UNDER PRIMITIVE BUDDHISM: LAY-WOMEN AND ALMSWOMEN. New York: Dutton, 1930. 391 pp. Concludes that women's status greatly improved during the rise of Buddhism.

2237. Howard, Robert Wilmot. SHOULD WOMEN BE PRIESTS: THREE SERMONS PREACHED BEFORE THE UNIVERSITY OF OXFORD. Oxford: Blackwell's, 1949. 49 pp. First lecture advocates seminaries for women; the second offers various opinions as to what role women should play in the church; and the third presents an historical overview of why women have been denied access to the priesthood.

2238. Hughes, Elizabeth. HERTHA. Los Angeles, Calif.: Author, 1889. 81 pp. A spiritual interpretation of the woman question.

2239. Irvine, Mary D., and Alice L. Eastwood. PIONEER WOMEN OF THE PRESBYTERIAN CHURCH, UNITED STATES. Richmond, Va.: Presbyterian Committee of Publication, 1923. 399 pp. Short biographies of the achievements and contributions of women in the church.

2240. Kähler, Else. DIE FRAU IN DEN PAULINISCHEN BRIEFEN: UNTER BESONDERER BERUCKSICHTIGUNG DES BEGRIFFES DER UNTERORDNUNG. Zurich: Gotthelf Verlag, 1960. [Women in the Letters of Paul].

2241. K'ang Yu-wei. TA-T'UNG SHU: THE ONE WORLD UNITY OF K'ANG YU-WEI. Translated by Lawrence G. Thompson. London: Allen and Unwin, 1959. One of the last Confucians whose strict sexism is amply illustrated in this book.

2242. Key, Ellen. LOVE AND ETHICS. New York: G. P. Putnam's Sons, 1912. A Christian view of marriage and love.

2243. Kirby, Ellen. "Consciousness Raising for Women in the Church," RESPONSE: UNITED METHODIST WOMEN, vol. 4 (Feb. 1972), pp. 41-42. Short questionnaire and discussion questions for church groups.

2244. Lampe, G. W. H. THE CHURCH'S TRADITION AND THE QUESTION OF OF ORDINATION OF WOMEN TO THE HISTORIC MINISTRY. Cambridge, England: R. I. Severs, 1967.

2245. Levy, Gertrude R. GATE OF HORN: A STUDY OF THE RELIGIOUS CONCEPTIONS OF THE STONE AGE AND THEIR INFLUENCE UPON EUROPEAN THOUGHT. London: Faber and Faber, 1948. 349 pp. See especially her chapter entitled "The Mother Goddess."

2246. Loewe, Raphael. THE POSITION OF WOMEN IN JUDAISM. London: S.P.C.K., 1966.

2247. Lubac, Henri de. THE ETERNAL FEMININE. New York: Harper and Row, 1971; Paris: Aubier-Montaigne, 1968. Study of the poem by Teilhard de Chardin dealing with divine love, the Beatrix Theme, the Virgin Mary, and love—the great cosmic force—the Eternal Feminine.

2248. Lucka, Emil. THE EVOLUTION OF LOVE. Translated by Ellie Schleussner. London: Allen and Unwin, 1922. 303 pp. A philosophical and religious look at love and sex and the status of women.

2249. MacDonald, Elizabeth M. THE POSITION OF WOMEN AS REFLECTED IN THE SEMITIC CODES OF LAW. Toronto: Univ. of Toronto Press, 1931.

2250. McGrath, Albertus Magnus, O.P. WHAT A MODERN CATHOLIC BELIEVES ABOUT WOMEN. Chicago: Thomas More Press, 1972.

2251. McKenna, Mary L. WOMEN OF THE CHURCH: ROLE AND RENEWAL. New York: P. J. Kennedy, 1967.

2252. Maertens, Thierry. THE ADVANCING DIGNITY OF WOMAN IN THE BIBLE. Translated by Sandra Dibbs. De Pere, Wisconsin: St. Norbert Abbey Press, 1969. 241 pp. A reexamination of the Church's conception of woman: women in relation to husbands, church views on virginity, widowhood, motherhood, and the ordination of women into the ministry.

2253. Maimonides, Moses. THE CODE OF MAIMONIDES. BOOK FOUR: THE BOOK OF WOMEN. Translated by Isaac Klein. New Haven: Yale Univ. Press, 1972. Defines and supports the traditional Hebrew relationship of woman to man.

2254. Marans, Nelly. "Reflections on the Status of Women," WORLD ORDER, vol. 3, no. 1 (Fall 1968), pp. 23-26. Article in the magazine of the Baha'i faith, long an advocate of equality of men and women.

2255. Meyer, Donald. THE POSITIVE THINKERS. Garden City, N.Y.: Doubleday, 1965. 358 pp. For the most part, a theology of psychotherapy. A
study of the American quest for health, wealth, and personal power
from Mary Baker Eddy to Dr. Norman Vincent Peale. See the chapter
entitled "Troubled Souls of Females."

2256. Moll, Will. THE CHRISTIAN IMAGE OF WOMEN. Notre Dame, Ind.:
Fides, 1967. 168 pp.

2257. Monks of Solesmes, compilers. PAPAL TEACHINGS: THE WOMAN IN
THE MODERN WORLD. Boston: St. Paul Editions, 1959.

2258. Morris, Joan. "Female Rebellion and Spiritual Eruption in North America,"
WOMEN SPEAKING, vol. 2 (July-Sept. 1971), pp. 7-9. The author
finds a growing acceptance of women in the ministry, along with a
need for women to defend themselves in their struggle for equal participation in world affairs.

2259. Murray, Margaret Alice. PRIESTHOODS OF WOMEN IN EGYPT.
Oxford: International Congress of History and Religions, vol. 1, 1908.
220 pp.

2260. Nyberg, Kathleen Neill. THE NEW EVE: A FEMININE LOOK AT
CHRISTIAN STYLE. Nashville, Abingdon Press, 1967. 196 pp.

2261. Oden, Marilyn Brown. BEYOND FEMINISM: THE WOMAN OF FAITH
IN ACTION. Nashville, Tenn.: Abingdon Press, 1971. 112 pp.

2262. Phipps, William E. WAS JESUS MARRIED? New York: Harper, 1971.
239 pp. Examines the mind-body dualism and its influence on early
Christian traditions, and the distortion of sexuality in the doctrines of
the church.

2263. Pinkham, Mildreth Worth. WOMEN IN THE SACRED SCRIPTURES OF
HINDUISM. New York: Columbia Univ. Press, 1941. 239 pp. A study of
Hindu literature and history for the treatment of women.

2264. Prohl, Russell C. WOMAN AND THE CHURCH. Grand Rapids, Mich.:
William B. Eerdmans Publishing Co., 1957. 86 pp. Concludes it is time
for churches to put to use the mission potential they have in women
after discussing how women receive equal grace and equal responsibility
in the Kingdom of God.

2265. Raven, Charles E. WOMEN AND THE MINISTRY. New York: Doubleday,
1929.

2266. Reinhard, J. R. "Burning at the Stake in Medieval Law and Literature,"
SPECULUM, (April 1941), pp. 186 ff.

2267. Rice, John R. BOBBED HAIR, BOSSY WIVES AND WOMEN PREACH-
ERS: SIGNIFICANT QUESTIONS FOR HONEST CHRISTIAN
WOMEN SETTLED BY THE WORD OF GOD. Wheaton, Ill.: Sword of
the Lord Publishers, 1941. 91 pp. A fundamentalist point of view.

2268. Richardson, Aubrey. WOMEN OF THE CHURCH OF ENGLAND. London: Chapman and Hall, 1908. 352 pp. Traces the history of the influential women in the church from ancient times to the present.

2269. Richmond, Mabel. QUAKER WOMEN, 1650-1690. London: n.p., 1915.

2270. Royden, A. Maude. THE CHURCH AND WOMAN. London: James
Clarke, 1924. 255 pp.

2271. ———. SEX AND COMMON SENSE. New York: Putnam, 1922. 211 pp.
Discussions of the economic, ethical, and religious aspects of the
women's movement.

2272. Ryrie. Charles Caldwell. THE PLACE OF WOMEN IN THE CHURCH. Chicago: Moody Press, 1968. 155 pp.

2273. Scudder, Vida Dutton. THE PRIVILEGE OF AGE: ESSAYS SECULAR AND SPIRITUAL. New York: Dutton, 1939. 319 pp. The story of a Christian Socialist.

2274. Sheehan, Marion Turner, ed. THE SPIRITUAL WOMAN. New York: Harper, 1955. 167 pp. Anthology of 14 essays on such subjects as woman in the arts, woman and communism, and woman's spiritual role in society.

2275. Smith, Paul Jordon. THE SOUL OF WOMAN: AN INTERPRETATION OF THE PHILOSOPHY OF FEMINISM. San Francisco: Paul Elder, 1916. 66 pp. Review of the works of Ibsen, Browning, Strindberg, Maeterlinck, Olive Schreiner, Walt Whitman, and Ellen Key on feminism.

2276. Southard, Mabel M. THE ATTITUDE OF JESUS TOWARD WOMEN. New York: Doran, 1927.

2277. Stanton, Elizabeth Cady. THE WOMAN'S BIBLE. PART I AND PART II. 2 vols. New York: Arno Press, 1972. Reprints of the 1895 and 1898 editions. Comments on Genesis, Exodus, Leviticus, Numbers, and Deuteronomy, the Old and New Testaments from Joshua to Revelation. The publication of this book resulted in a split between orthodox and radical suffrage churchgoers, and marked a turning point from religion to practical politics in the women's movement.

2278. Steele, Robert. STORMING HEAVEN. New York: Morrow, 1970. 364 pp. Biographies of Aimee Semple McPherson and Minnie Kennedy, evangelists.

2279. Stendhal, Krister. THE BIBLE AND THE ROLE OF WOMEN. Philadelphia: Fortress Press, 1966. 48 pp. Translated from Swedish by Emilie T. Sander. Concerned with such questions as the ordination of women to the Christian ministry and the exegesis of the Pauline passages.

2280. Sudlow, Elizabeth W. CAREER WOMEN OF THE BIBLE. New York: Pageant Press, 1951.

2281. Suenens, Leon Joseph. NUN IN THE WORLD: NEW DIMENSIONS IN THE MODERN APOSTOLATE. Westminster, Md.: Newman Press, 1962. 175 pp. Monastic and religious life of women, with a good survey of the inner meaning of the religious vocation for women.

2282. Tatum, Noreen Dean. CROWN OF SERVICE. Nashville, Tenn.: Parthenon Press, 1960. 418 pp. The story of women's work in the Methodist Episcopal Church South, from 1878 to 1940.

2283. Thrall, Margaret E. ORDINATION OF WOMEN TO THE PRIESTHOOD: A STUDY OF THE BIBLICAL EVIDENCE. London: SCM Press, 1958. 115 pp. According to the Bible, she has found that women have every right to be ordained; because man and woman were created alike in the image of God, they both have an equal responsibility to serve Him.

2284. Tiemeyer, Raymond. THE ORDINATION OF WOMEN. Minneapolis: Augsburg Publishing House, 1970.

2285. Ulanov, Ann Belford. THE FEMININE: IN JUNGIAN PSYCHOLOGY AND IN CHRISTIAN THEOLOGY. Evanston, Ill.: Northwestern Univ. Press, 1971.

2286. United Presbyterian Church (U.S.A.). REPORTS OF THE TASK FORCE ON WOMEN, AND THE STANDING COMMITTEE ON WOMEN,

182nd GENERAL ASSEMBLY, AND THE 183rd GENERAL ASSEM-
BLY, 1970, 1971. New York: United Presbyterian Church, 1970, 1971.

2287. Ursulines of New York. IMMORTELLES OF CATHOLIC COLUMBIAN
LITERATURE COMPILED FROM THE WORKS OF AMERICAN
CATHOLIC WOMEN WRITERS. Akron, Ohio: D. H. McBride, 1897.
625 pp.

2288. Vreede de Stuers, Cora. PURDA: A STUDY OF MUSLIM WOMEN'S
LIFE IN NORTH INDIA. New York: Humanities Press, 1968. 128 pp.
Study of the religious and social reasons for screening women in the
Muslim faith.

2289. Wadia, A. R. THE ETHICS OF FEMINISM—A STUDY OF THE REVOLT
OF WOMAN. New York: Doran, 1923. Religious and ethical proposals for improving the condition of women.

2290. Walsh, James J. THESE SPLENDID SISTERS. Freeport, N.Y.: Books for
Libraries Press, 1970. 252 pp. Biographies of female religious leaders:
St. Bridget, St. Hilda, St. Scholastica, Mother Seton, the Irish Sisters of
Charity and Mercy, the nuns of the Battlefield, Mother Cabrini, etc.

2291. Webster, Thomas, Rev. WOMAN: MAN'S EQUAL. Introduction by Bishop
Simpson. Cincinnati: Hitchcock and Walden, 1873. 297 pp. The history
and condition of women from ancient times to the present, with evidence
from the Scriptures to support women's equal rights.

2292. Wedel, Cynthia. EMPLOYED WOMEN AND THE CHURCH. New York:
National Council of Churches of Christ in the United States of America,
1959. A Christian ethics for women in the home and in the world of work.

2293. White, Ebe Minerva. WOMAN IN WORLD HISTORY: HER PLACE IN
THE GREAT RELIGIONS. London: n.p., 1924. 416 pp.

2294. WOMEN AND THE WAY: CHRIST AND THE WORLD'S WOMAN-
HOOD, A SYMPOSIUM. New York: Friendship Press, 1938. 198 pp.

2295. Wyker, M. A. CHURCH WOMEN IN THE SCHEME OF THINGS. St.
Louis: Bethany Press Books, 1953. The role of women in the Church
and in society.

2296. Zerbst, Fritz. THE OFFICE OF WOMAN IN THE CHURCH. St. Louis:
Concordia Publishing House, 1955.

V. WOMEN IN MEDICINE AND HEALTH

The long-range goal of breaking through all the walls of male supremacy in medicine will be achieved at exactly the same pace social revolution occurs in all other areas.
—*Miriam Gilbert, R.N.*

2297. Abbott, Wallace C. "The Importance of Circumcision of the Female," THE MEDICAL COUNCIL, vol. 9 (Dec. 1904), pp. 437-439.
2298. Alpha Kappa Alpha Sorority. WOMEN IN MEDICINE. Heritage Series, no. 4. Chicago: Alpha Kappa Alpha Sorority, Inc., 1971. 32 pp. Black women in medicine; biographies of 26 women doctors.
2299. ———. WOMEN IN DENTISTRY. Heritage Series, no. 5. Chicago: Alpha Kappa Alpha Sorority, Inc., 1972. 27 pp. Negro women in dentistry.
2300. Anonymous. EMPLOYMENT OF FEMALES AS PRACTITIONERS IN MIDWIFERY. Boston: Cummings and Hillard, 1820. For evidence of male concern about women in the medical roles.
2301. Bardwick, Judith M. "Physiological Contributions to the Personality Development of Women." Paper presented at the American Psychological Association symposium "New Contributions toward a Psychology of Women," Aug. 1968.
2302. Bell, Enid H.C.M. STORMING THE CITADEL: THE RISE OF THE WOMAN DOCTOR. London: Constable, 1953. 200 pp. Women as physicians.
2303. Benedek, Therese F., and B. Rubenstein. THE SEXUAL CYCLE IN WOMEN: THE RELATION BETWEEN OVARIAN FUNCTION AND PSYCHODYNAMIC PROCESSES. Washington, D.C.: National Research Council, 1959.
2304. Beshiri, Patricia H. THE WOMAN DOCTOR: HER CAREER IN MODERN MEDICINE. New York: Cowles Book Co., 1969. 240 pp.
2305. Blackwell, Elizabeth. PIONEER WORK IN OPENING THE MEDICAL PROFESSION TO WOMEN. Hastings, England: K. Barry, 1895. 265 pp. Autobiography of the first woman doctor to receive a degree from an American university.
2306. Bloch, A. J. "Sexual Perversion in the Female," NEW ORLEANS MEDICAL AND SURGICAL JOURNAL, vol. 22, no. 1 (July 1894), p. 7. The usual Victorian notions that a woman was healthy only when she was sexless.
2307. Boston Women's Health Book Collective. OUR BODIES, OUR SELVES: A BOOK BY AND FOR WOMEN. New York: Simon and Schuster, 1973. 276 pp. Written by women for women to prove that women are the best experts on themselves and their feeling, and a polemic on the struggle for adequate health care. Includes chapters on female anatomy and physiology, and women and health care.
2308. Brey, Kathleen Healy. "The Missing Midwife: Why a Training Program Failed," SOUTH ASIA REVIEW, vol. 5 (Oct. 1971), pp. 41-52. States that a midwife program sponsored by the Indian government in 1956 failed because of inadequate research into the understanding by potential trainees of modern techniques of asepsis.
2309. Bullough, Bonnie, and Vern Bullough. "A Career Ladder in Nursing: Problems and Prospects," AMERICAN JOURNAL OF NURSING, vol. 71 (Oct. 1971), pp. 1938-1943. The history of nursing schools and the de-

velopment of three types of nurses: registered nurses, practical nurses, and nurse's aides.

2310. Campion, Rosamond. THE INVISIBLE WORM. New York: Macmillan, 1972. 96 pp. The story of one woman's revolt against 50 years of medical tradition: the radical operation that women fear most, mastectomy. Argues the right of each woman to choose.

2311. Carter, Charlene A. "Advantages of Being a Woman Therapist," PSYCHOTHERAPY: THEORY, RESEARCH AND PRACTICE, vol. 8, no. 4 (1971), pp. 297-300. Looks at the advantages of being a woman therapist by suggesting three types of patients for whom a woman therapist is better than a man, namely: women.

2312. Chambers, Carl. "Working Women and Drugs," LADIES HOME JOURNAL, vol. 89 (Mar. 1972), pp. 60+. The extent of drug use among working women.

2313. Church, Archibald. "Removal of Ovaries and Tubes in the Insane and Neurotic," AMERICAN JOURNAL OF OBSTETRICS AND THE DISEASES OF WOMEN AND CHILDREN, vol. 28 (1893), pp. 494-495. Pleads for the right to castrate nymphomaniacs.

2314. Cope, Zachary. FLORENCE NIGHTINGALE AND THE DOCTORS. London: Museum Press, 1958. 163 pp. A study of Nightingale, with a partial history of the development of nursing and medicine in the last half of the nineteenth century.

2315. Coppen, A., and N. Kessel. "Menstruation and Personality," BRITISH JOURNAL OF PSYCHIATRY, vol. 109 (1963), pp. 711-721.

2316. Cowan, John. THE SCIENCE OF A NEW LIFE. New York: Source Book Press, 1972. Reprint of the 1874 edition. 419 pp. An early "acceptable" book on marriage, contraception, pregnancy, sexual problems, and human anatomy.

2317. Crawley, Lawrence. "Sex Education for School Physicians: Report on an In-Service Training Course," JOURNAL OF SCHOOL HEALTH, vol. 42 (Jan. 1972), pp. 25-31.

2318. Dalton, Katharina. THE MENSTRUAL CYCLE. New York: Warner Paperback Library, 1972. 173 pp. Interesting theories on the influence of women's periods on men and children, as well as on women themselves in school, work, and other activities.

2319. Dawson, B. E. ORIFICIAL SURGERY, ITS PHILOSOPHY, APPLICATION AND TECHNIQUE. Edited by Minnie Elder Dawson. Kansas City, Mo.: Western Baptist Publishing Co., 1925. 1st ed., 1912. Chapter 2 and following chapters deal with the practice of circumcising girls to curb their "unappeasable" sexual drives.

2320. Edes, Robert T. "The Relations of Pelvic and Nervous Diseases," JOURNAL OF THE AMERICAN MEDICAL ASSOCIATION, vol. 31 (1898), pp. 1136 ff. Like most Victorian medicos, this one confuses causes and effects.

2321. Elliott, Grace Loucks. WOMEN AFTER FORTY. New York: Holt, 1936. 213 pp. A study of the psychological and physiological effects of menstruation and menopause.

2322. Engelmann, George T. "The Increasing Sterility of American Women," TRANSACTIONS OF THE SECTION ON THE DISEASES OF WOMEN OF THE AMERICAN MEDICAL ASSOCIATION (1901), pp. 271-295.

2323. ———. "Cliterodectomy," THE AMERICAN PRACTITIONER, vol. 25 (1882), pp. 3, 5. Paradoxically, he claims you can confine a woman's identity to the distinction of her sexual organs while, at the same time, maintaining she is sexless.

2324. Field, Mark G. DOCTOR AND PATIENT IN SOVIET RUSSIA. Cambridge: Harvard Univ. Press, 1957. 266 pp. Discusses the increasing role of women in the medical professions.

2325. Findley, Palmer. THE STORY OF CHILDBIRTH. New York: Doubleday, 1933. 376 pp. A history of childbirth practices.

2326. Frank, R. T. "The Hormonal Causes of Premenstrual Tension," ARCHIVES OF NEUROLOGY AND PSYCHIATRY, vol. 26 (1931), pp. 1053 ff.

2327. Frankfort, Ellen. VAGINAL POLITICS. New York: Quadrangle Books, 1972. How women are breaking the medical profession's grip on their bodies, their dignity, and their pocketbooks.

2328. Friedman, Alfred S., et al. THERAPY WITH FAMILIES OF SEXUALLY ACTING-OUT GIRLS. New York: Springer, 1971. 214 pp.

2329. Gardner, A. K. HISTORY OF THE ART OF MIDWIFERY. New York: Stringer and Townshend, 1852. A short pamphlet of a lecture delivered at the College of Physicians and Surgeons describing past inefficiences and present incapacities of women in the practice of obstetrics.

2330. ———. "The Physical Decline of American Women," THE KNICKERBOCKER, vol. 55, no. 1 (Jan. 1860), pp. 37-52. By a decidedly sexist doctor.

2331. Gendel, Evelyn S. "Fitness and Fatigue in the Female," JOURNAL OF HEALTH, PHYSICAL EDUCATION, AND RECREATION, Oct. 1971, pp. 53-54+. Discusses the need for physical education for American women, including various studies on the lack of physical education among women and how it leads to such common illnesses and complaints as backaches and cramps.

2332. Goldberg, Minnie. MEDICAL MANAGEMENT OF THE MENOPAUSE. Modern Medical Monographs. New York: Grune and Stratton, 1959.

2333. Gorney, Sondra, and Claire Fox. AFTER FORTY: HOW WOMEN CAN ACHIEVE FULFILLMENT. New York: Dial Press, 1973. Sound, sensible advice for women over forty about getting through the menopause, finding satisfactions in marriage after the children are grown, improving personal appearance, and much more.

2334. Green, R., and K. Dalton. "The Premenstrual Syndrome," BRITISH MEDICAL JOURNAL, vol. 1 (1953), pp. 1007-1013.

2335. Hansen, Lynn K., Barbara Garner, and Diana Hilton. HOW TO HAVE INTERCOURSE WITHOUT GETTING SCREWED. Seattle: Associated Students of the University of Washington, 1971.

2336. Hays, Elinor Rice. THOSE EXTRAORDINARY BLACKWELLS. New York: Harcourt, Brace and World, 1967. 349 pp. Emily Blackwell was a pioneer woman physician; Elizabeth, her sister, was the first woman in modern times to receive a medical degree.

2337. Hills-Young, E. "Female Circumcision in the Sudan," BIBLIOGRAPHIE ETHNOGRAPHIQUE DU CONGO BELGE, vol. 5, no. 1 (1949), pp. 13-15. Description of the operation performed on 4- to 10-year-old girls among the peoples of north and central Sudan.

2338. Hutton, Linda I. "Needed: Women Athletic Trainers," JOURNAL OF HEALTH, PHYSICAL EDUCATION, AND RECREATION, vol. 43 (Jan. 1972), pp. 77-78.

2339. Jaffe, R. B., G. Perez-Palacios, and G. Serra. "The Reproductive Cycle in Women." Pp. 1-22 in CONTRACEPTION: THE CHEMICAL CONTROL OF FERTILITY, edited by D. Lednicer. New York: Marcel Dekker, 1969.
2340. Janowsky, D. S., R. Gorney, and B. Kelly. "The Curse: I. Vicissitudes and Variations of the Female Fertility Cycle," PSYCHOSOMATICS, vol. 7 (1966), pp. 242-246.
2341. Janowsky, D. S., R. Gorney, and A. J. Mandell. "The Menstrual Cycle," ARCHIVES OF GENERAL PSYCHIATRY, vol. 17 (Oct. 1967), pp. 459-469.
2342. Jex-Blake, Sophia. MEDICAL WOMEN: A THESIS AND A HISTORY. New York: Source Book Press, 1970. 256 pp. Reprint of the 1886 edition. A comprehensive view of the question of women entering the medical profession, with a history of the victory in securing medical education for women.
2343. Kantor, H. I., Carmen M. Michael, S. H. Boulas, et al. "The Administration of Estrogens to Older Women, A Psychometric Evaluation," SEVENTH INTERNATIONAL CONGRESS OF GERONTOLOGY PROCEEDINGS, June 1966. The effects of hormonal treatment of older women.
2344. Kirk-Greene, A.H.M. "A Lala Initiation Ceremony," MAN, vol. 57 (1957), pp. 5-11. Ceremonies, such as puberty rites for girls, in an African setting.
2345. Kitzinger, Sheila. THE EXPERIENCE OF CHILDBIRTH. Baltimore: Penguin Books, 1964.
2346. Kupperman, H. S. "Sex Hormones." Pp. 494-502 in THE ENCYCLOPEDIA OF SEXUAL BEHAVIOR, edited by S. Ellis and A. Abarbanel. New York: Hawthorn Books, 1961. The effects of estrogens and other hormones in women.
2347. Kushner, Dan. "An Interloper in the Marital Bed (Troppi v. Scharf)," AMERICAN DRUGGIST, vol. 164 (Nov. 24, 1971), pp. 13-15. Discussion of the pill and its physiological and psychological effects on women.
2348. Laidler, P. W. "Native (Bantu) Beliefs Concerning Pregnancy and Child-Birth, Their Effects on Public Health Administration, and the Effects of Detribalisation or Urbanisation Upon these Ancient Customs and Upon Infant Mortality Rates," SOUTH AFRICAN JOURNAL OF SCIENCE, vol. 38 (1931), pp. 418-422. Notes on birth control and practices in S. Africa.
2349. Laigret, J. "De Quelques Coutumes Indigènes Concernant Les Accouchements," BULLETIN DE LA SOCIETE DE RECHERCHES CONGOLAISES (Brazzaville), vol. 6 (1925), pp. 11-14. Description of delivery of children "through the rear passage," when there has been a large tear in the tissue connecting the vagina and rectum. The child is delivered with the help of experienced midwives.
2350. Laslett, Peter. "Age at Menarche in Europe Since the Eighteenth Century," JOURNAL OF INTERDISCIPLINARY HISTORY, vol. 2 (Aug. 1971), pp. 221-236. A preliminary study implying that there has been a decline in the age at which women become mature from 17.5 years in Great Britain during the 1830s, to a figure below 15 years.

2351. Lear, John, and Will Jonathan. "The Unfinished Story of Thalidomide and the Feminine Conscience of FDA: Dr. Frances Oldham Kelsey," SATURDAY REVIEW, Sept. 1, 1962, pp. 35-43.

2352. Lee, P. "The Vulnerability to Trauma of Women in Relation to Periodic Stress." In MEDICAL COMMISSION OF ACCIDENT PREVENTION: SECOND ANNUAL REPORT. London: The Royal College of Surgeons of England, 1965-66. Women's menstrual cycles and their effects on trauma.

2353. Lefort, Pierre. "A Case of Excision of the Clitoris," MEDICAL REPOSITORY, vol. 4 (1818), pp. 84-87. A case of surgical treatment to cure a psychological disorder of a woman.

2354. Magnusson, Lucille. "The What and Why of AIAW (Association of Inter-Collegiate Athletics for Women)," JOURNAL OF HEALTH, PHYSICAL EDUCTAION, AND RECREATION, vol. 43 (Mar. 1972), pp. 71 ff.

2355. Mandell, A., and M. Mandell. "Suicide and the Menstrual Cycle," JOURNAL OF THE AMERICAN MEDICAL ASSOCIATION, vol. 200 (1967), p. 792. A study of the relationship between women's cycles and suicide.

2356. Mann, Constance. "The Lack of Girls' Athletics," THE PHYSICAL EDUCATOR, vol. 20 (Mar. 1972), pp. 9-10. Concludes that participation in competitive sports for girls is beneficial for their physical, social, and psychological development.

2357. Manton, W. P. "Mental Alienation in Women and Abdomino-Pelvic Disease," TRANSACTIONS OF THE SECTION ON OBSTETRICS AND DISEASES OF WOMEN OF THE AMERICAN MEDICAL ASSOCIATION (1909), no pages cited. An attempt to correlate the two.

2358. Masters, W. H., and M. H. Grody. "Estrogen-Androgen Substitution Therapy in the Aged Female: II. Clinical Response," OBSTETRICS AND GYNECOLOGY, vol. 2 (1953), pp. 139-147.

2359. Masters, W. H., and Virginia E. Johnson. "The Artificial Vagina: Anatomic, Physiologic, Psychosexual Function," WESTERN JOURNAL OF SURGERY, OBSTETRICS, AND GYNECOLOGY, vol. 69 (1961), pp. 192-212.

2360. Meigs, Charles D. WOMAN: HER DISEASES AND REMEDIES. Philadelphia: Blanchard and Lea, 1852. A gynecologically far-out study which states that women's generative organs exercise a "strange" influence over her heart, mind, and soul.

2361. Moos, R. "Psychological Aspects of Oral Contraceptives," ARCHIVES OF GENERAL PSYCHIATRY, vol. 19 (1968), pp. 87-94.

2362. Morris, Robert. "Circumcision in Girls," INTERNATIONAL JOURNAL OF SURGERY, vol. 25 (1912), pp. 135 ff.

2363. Nemilov, Anton Vitalievich. THE BIOLOGICAL TRAGEDY OF WOMEN. New York: Covici-Friede, 1932. 220 pp. Russian author develops the thesis that the biological nature of women has placed all the sexual burdens on women.

2364. Neugarten, Bernice L., and Ruth J. Kraines. "Menopausal Symptoms in Women of Various Ages," PSYCHOSOMATIC MEDICINE, vol. 27, no. 3 (1965), pp. 266-273.

2365. Nutting, Mary A., and Lavinia L. Dock. HISTORY OF NURSING. 2 vols. New York: G. P. Putnam's, 1907-1912.

2366. Packard, Francis R. HISTORY OF MEDICINE IN THE U.S. 2 vols. New York: P. B. Hoeber, 1931. Good general history.

2367. Palmer, Rachel L., and Sarah K. Greenberg. FACTS AND FRAUDS IN WOMEN'S HYGIENE: A MEDICAL GUIDE AGAINST MISLEADING CLAIMS AND DANGEROUS PRODUCTS. New York: Vanguard, 1936. 311 pp.

2368. Pierson, Elaine C. SEX IS NEVER AN EMERGENCY: A CANDID GUIDE FOR COLLEGE STUDENTS. Philadelphia: Lippincott, 1971.

2369. Pratt, E. H. "Circumcision of Girls," JOURNAL OF ORIFICIAL SURGERY, vol. 6, no. 9 (Mar. 1898), p. 390. Deals with female masturbation and how it raises women to a state of sexual craving, and thus, a threat to man.

2370. Sarrell, Phillip. "The University Hospital and the Teen-Age Unwed Mother," AMERICAN JOURNAL OF PUBLIC HEALTH, vol. 57 (1967), p. 1308.

2371. Shainess, Natalie. "A Re-Evaluation of Some Aspects of Feminity Through a Study of Menstruation: A Preliminary Report," COMPREHENSIVE PSYCHIATRY, vol. 2 (1961), pp. 20-26.

2372. Sherfey, Mary Jane. "The Evolution and Nature of Female Sexuality in Relation to Psychoanalytic Theory," JOURNAL OF THE AMERICAN PSYCHOANALYTIC ASSOCIATION, vol. 14, no. 1 (1966), pp. 28-128.

2373. Sherwood-Dunn, B. "Conservation of the Ovary: Discussion," TRANSACTIONS OF THE AMERICAN ASSOCIATION OF OBSTETRICIANS AND GYNECOLOGISTS, vol. 10 (1897), pp. 219-223. Defines the absence of sexual desire in women as normal; its presence, a disease.

2374. Southam, A. L., and F. P. Gonzaga. "Systemic Changes During the Menstrual Cycle," AMERICAN JOURNAL OF OBSTETRICS AND GYNECOLOGY, vol. 91 (1965), pp. 142-165.

2375. Staffieri, J. Robert. "Body Build and Behavioral Expectancies in Young Females," DEVELOPMENTAL PSYCHOLOGY, vol. 6 (Jan. 1972), pp. 125-27.

2376. Sutherland, H., and I. Stewart. "A Critical Analysis of the Premenstrual Syndrome," LANCET, vol. 1 (1965), pp. 1180-1183.

2377. Thomas, Adah B. PATHFINDERS: A HISTORY OF THE COLORED GRADUATE NURSES. New York: n.p., 1929.

2378. Tyler, Edward T. "How Soon Will We Have the 'Ideal' Contraceptive?" JOURNAL OF THE AMERICAN MEDICAL ASSOCIATION, vol. 219 (Mar. 6, 1972), p. 1333.

2379. Udry, J. Richard, and Naomi M. Morris. "Effect of Contraceptive Pills on the Distribution of Sexual Activity in the Menstrual Cycle," NATURE (London), vol. 227 (Aug. 1970), pp. 502-503. Progesterone as a depressant decreases sexual libido.

2380. Van der Warter, Ely. "The Fetish of the Ovary," AMERICAN JOURNAL OF OBSTETRICS AND THE DISEASES OF WOMEN AND CHILDREN, vol. 54 (July-Dec. 1906), p. 369.

2381. Wilson, Victoria. "An Analysis of Femininity in Nursing," AMERICAN BEHAVIORAL SCIENTIST, vol. 15, no. 2 (Nov.-Dec. 1971), pp. 213-

220. Advocates a sense of self-identity and independence, and challenges the culturally ascribed roles and expectations of nurturing and mothering.

2382. Zarechnak, Galina V. ACADEMY OF MEDICAL SCIENCES OF THE USSR: HISTORY AND ORGANIZATION, 1944-1959. Public Health Monograph, no. 63. Washington, D.C.: SUDOC, GPO, 1960, 48 pp. Indicates that the medical profession in the Soviet Union is dominated by women.

VI. WOMEN IN BIOGRAPHY, AUTOBIOGRAPHY AND MEMOIRS

It has been said that few biographies or autobiographies have been written by or about men and women whose lives are essentially placid, who are creatures of routine or the minions of institutions. The following biographical and autobiographical works were structured around a perception of change on both the social and personal or intellectual levels, and introduce thematically all sorts of social history and individual psychology. They are works that deal with women who lived and worked in America, immigrated from elsewhere, or lived abroad. The activities of these women include all occupations: scientists, writers, businesswomen, religious leaders, artists and entertainers, social reformers, sports figures, pioneers, journalists, musicians, politicians, society leaders, educators and scholars, and many others.

In selecting these works, we have not unwisely strived to limit our choices. We have tried to choose books representing all possible points of view, but have particularly singled out those works of and by women who helped shape or influence the cultural tendencies of all periods, who participated in great economic forces, in governmental forms and traditions, and in the social fabric of their communities, both local and national. In short, we have concentrated on those writings that relate their female subjects to history or define her position and significance in the broad stream of events.

The reader will notice that some biographies and autobiographies have been grouped in the history and political science sections, and others are scattered under other sections. To help the reader construct her own selected bibliography of sources in this category, we have constructed several indexes which list   xt authors, compilers, editors, persons mentioned, places, subjects, and topics.

There is properly no history, only biography.
                                        —*Emerson*

2383. Abbot, Willis J. NOTABLE WOMEN IN HISTORY: THE LIVES OF WOMEN WHO IN ALL AGES, ALL LANDS AND IN ALL WOMANLY OCCUPATIONS HAVE WON FAME AND PUT THEIR IMPRINT ON THE WORLD'S HISTORY. Philadelphia: Winston, 1913. 448 pp. Brief biographies, with a section on American feminists entitled, "Priestesses of the Woman's Cause."

2384. Adams, Elmer C., and Warren Dunham Foster. HEROINES OF MODERN PROGRESS. New York: Sturgis and Walton, 1918. 324 pp. Collection of biographical sketches of nineteenth-century American women such as Mary Lym, Harriet B. Stowe, Clara Barton, Jane Addams et. al., emphasizing their significance and their contributions to modern progress.

2385. Addams, Jane. TWENTY YEARS AT HULL HOUSE. New York: Macmillan, 1910. 462 pp. Autobiography of the founder of Hull House in Chicago, and recipient of the Nobel Peace Prize.

2386. Adelman, Joseph. FAMOUS WOMEN: AN OUTLINE OF FEMININE ACHIEVEMENT THROUGH THE AGES WITH LIFE STORIES OF FIVE HUNDRED NOTED WOMEN. New York: Woman's World, 1928. 328 pp. Short, well-written biographies of 500 women in education, science, literature, art, music, as well as famous queens, heroines, martyrs, explorers, social leaders, and historic personalities.

2387. Agate, James. RACHEL. New York: Benjamin Blom, 1969. 178 pp. Reprint of 1928 edition. The biography of one of the most celebrated French tragediennes (1821-1858), Elisa Rachel Felix.

2388. Alderson, Nannie T. A BRIDE GOES WEST. New York: Farrar, 1942. 273 pp. Autobiography of a Southern belle who moves to Montana in 1883. Details hardships and happy times of a woman who, though seemingly insignificant, nevertheless represented the life of our grandfathers and grandmothers.

2389. Alexander, Mithrapuram K. INDIRA GANDHI: AN ILLUSTRATED BIOGRAPHY. New Delhi: New Light, 1968. The biography of India's woman Prime Minister.

2390. Altemus, Jameson Torr. HELENA MODJESKA. New York: Benjamin Blom, 1971. 215 pp. Reprint of 1883 edition. The career of the famous Madame Modjeska, actress.

2391. American Association of University Women. NAMES REMEMBERED THROUGH AAUW FELLOWSHIPS. Compiled by Ruth Tryon. Washington, D.C.: AAUW Educational Foundation, vol. 1, 1958; vol. 2, 1970. Biographies of notable American women in education. Very handy reference work.

2392. Anderson, Margaret C. MY THIRTY YEARS' WAR: AN AUTOBIOGRAPHY. Westport, Conn.: Greenwood Press, 1970. Reprint of the 1930 edition. 274 pp. Describes her war against convention through her magazine THE LITTLE REVIEW, which did much to advance the cause of the arts and experimental journalism during its time.

2393. Anderson, Marian. MY LORD WHAT A MORNING. New York: Viking Press, 1956. 312 pp. Autobiography of the first black woman opera star to appear in Carnegie Hall.

2394. Anderson, Mary. WOMAN AT WORK: THE AUTOBIOGRAPHY OF MARY ANDERSON AS TOLD TO MARY N. WINSLOW. Minneapolis: Univ. of Minnesota Press, 1951. The life of the early reformer, a shoe worker and leader of her union, who became an early founding member of the National Women's Trade Union League, and Women's Bureau Director.

2395. Andrews, Mary R.S. A LOST COMMANDER: FLORENCE NIGHTINGALE. New York: Doubleday, 1933. 299 pp. Biography of the famous nurse of the Crimean War. The author takes issue with Lytton Strachey's character sketch of Nightingale in his EMINENT VICTORIANS.

2396. Angelou, Maya. I KNOW WHY THE CAGED BIRD SINGS. New York: Random House, 1969. 281 pp. Sensitive account of the joys and pains of growing up black and female in America.

2397. Anthony, Katherine. FIRST LADY OF THE REVOLUTION: A LIFE OF MERCY WARREN. New York: Doubleday, 1958. 258 pp. Carefully documented biography of an eminent literary figure of the Revolutionary War period; friend of Washington, Adams, and Hancock.

2398. ———. LOUISA MAY ALCOTT. New York: Knopf, 1938. 304 pp. Biography of the author of LITTLE WOMEN.

2399. ———. SUSAN B. ANTHONY: HER PERSONAL HISTORY AND HER ERA. Garden City: Doubleday, 1954. 521 pp. Delves into the fiber of Miss Anthony's beliefs and the core of her actions in the cause of woman suffrage.

2400. Antin, Mary. THE PROMISED LAND. Boston: Houghton Mifflin, 1912. 373 pp. Autobiography of the Russian-born immigrant to the United States, author, and interpreter of the immigrant. Speculates about the meaning of her immigrant experiences and her commitment to Americanism.

2401. Arendt, Hannah. RACHEL VARNHAGEN: THE LIFE OF A JEWESS. London: Published for the Leo Baeck Institute of Jews from Germany by the East West Library, 1957. 222 pp. Biography of Rachel Antonie Frederica Varnhagen von Ense, leader of a German salon in the last years of Frederick the Great and the first years of Wilhelmine Germany (1771-1833).

2402. Armes, Ethel, ed. NANCY SHIPPEN: HER JOURNAL. New York: Benjamin Blom, 1971. 394 pp. Reprint, 1935 edition. The diary of a fashionable Philadelphia belle, from 1777 to 1800, important for its information on colonial society during the early federal period of our history.

2403. Atherton, Gertrude. ADVENTURES OF A NOVELIST. New York: Liveright, 1932. 598 pp. Autobiography of the romantic novelist (1857-1948), often superficial and vain, but interesting in its revelations on literary matters.

2404. Austin, Mary. EARTH HORIZON: AUTOBIOGRAPHY. Boston: Houghton Mifflin, 1932. 381 pp. Reveals the spiritual and intimate side of the American novelist of the West (1868-1934), and how she "suffered from the contempt in which woman's talent was held."

2405. Bailey, Pearl. THE RAW PEARL. New York: Harcourt, Brace and World, 1968. 206 pp. Autobiography of the celebrated black singer, her struggle against racism, and to work.

2406. Balbabanoff, Angelica. MY LIFE AS A REBEL. New York: Harper, 1938. 324 pp. Autobiography of one of the leaders of the socialist movement in Italy.

2407. Barnes, Gilbert, and Dwight L. Dumond, eds. LETTERS OF T.D. WELD, ANGELINA AND SARAH GRIMKE. 2 vols. Gloucester, Mass.: Peter Smith, 1965. Important correspondence for any historian wishing to study the origins of the anti-slavery movement from primary sources.

2408. Bates, Daisy. THE LONG SHADOW OF LITTLE ROCK. New York: David McKay, 1962. 234 pp. Life story of the woman who was largely responsible for the integration of Little Rock High School in 1957.

2409. Bazin, Nancy Topping. "Virginia Woolf's Quest for Equilibrium," MODERN LANGUAGE QUARTERLY, vol. 32 (Sept. 1971), pp. 305-319. Good biographical and critical article on Virginia Woolf, the English novelist.

2410. Beach, Seth Curtis. DAUGHTERS OF THE PURITANS. Boston: American Unitarian Association, 1907. 286 pp. Collection of biographical sketches on Lydia Child, Dorothea Dix, Harriet B. Stowe, and others, emphasizing their personal, social, moral, and "transcendental" aspects.

2411. Beasley, Norman. MARY BAKER EDDY. London: Allen and Unwin, 1964. 371 pp. Life story of the founder of the Christian Science movement (1821-1910).

2412. Bell, Enid Moberly. JOSEPHINE BUTLER: FLAME OF FIRE. London: Constable, 1962. 268 pp. The life of the British social reformer and crusader against prostitution (1828-1906).

2413. Bell, Quentin. VIRGINIA WOOLF: A BIOGRAPHY. New York: Harcourt, Brace and Jovanovich, 1972. 314 pp. Recent biography of the English novelist by her nephew.

2414. Benson, E. F. CHARLOTTE BRONTE. New York: Benjamin Blom, 1932. 326 pp. Critical biography of one of England's great woman authors.

2415. Bernhardt, Sarah. THE ART OF THE THEATRE. New York: Benjamin Blom, 1933. 224 pp. Autobiography of the great international actress, with special comments on all her great roles.

2416. Betham-Edwards, Matilda. SIX LIFE STUDIES OF FAMOUS WOMEN. Freeport, N.Y.: Books for Libraries Press, 1972. 303 pp. Brief biographies of Fernan Caballero, Spanish novelist; Alexandrine Tinne, African explorer; Caroline Herschel, astronomer and mathematician; Matilda Betham, writer and biographer, friend of Charles and Mary Lamb; Elizabeth Carter, Greek scholar and linguist; and Marie Pape-Carpentier, educational reformer.

2417. Billington, Ray Allen, ed. THE JOURNAL OF CHARLOTTE L. FORTEN. New York: Crowell-Collier, 1961. Negro teacher and author (1837-1914) who pioneered in the education of blacks in the South.

2418. BIOGRAPHIUM FEMINEUM. THE FEMALE WORTHIES: OR MEMOIRS OF THE MOST ILLUSTRIOUS LADIES OF ALL AGES AND NATIONS. 2 vols. London: n.p., 1766. Interesting sketches on the Countess of Pembroke, the Duchess of Newcastle, and earlier and later women.

2419. Blackwell, Alice. LUCY STONE: PIONEER OF WOMEN'S RIGHTS. Detroit, Michigan: Gale Research Co., 1972. Reprint of 1930 edition.

2420. Blashfield, Evangeline Wilbour. PORTRAITS AND BACKGROUNDS. Freeport, N.Y.: Books for Libraries Press, 1971. Reprint of 1917 edition. 493 pp. Scholarly, but interesting accounts of the lives of four famous women, beginning with the tenth-century Benedictine nun and poetess in Germany, Hrotsvitha, and including Aphra Behn, English woman novelist; Aisse, the former Turkish slave girl raised in the French nobility in the period of Louis XIV; and Rosalba Carriera, the Venetian painter of miniatures and pastels.

2421. Bolton, Sarah Knowles. FAMOUS LEADERS AMONG WOMEN. Freeport, N.Y.: Books for Libraries Press, 1972. Reprint of 1895 edition. Biographical sketches of Madame de Maintenon, Catherine the Great, Dolly Madison, Lucy Stone, Julia Ward Howe, and Queen Victoria, among others; excellently written.

2422. ———. FAMOUS TYPES OF WOMANKIND. Freeport, N.Y.: Books for Libraries Press, 1971. Reprint of 1892 edition. 350 pp. Biographies of Queen Louise of Prussia, Susanna Wesley (mother of the Wesley brothers), Harriet Martineau, Jenny Lind, Dorothea Dix, and others.

2423. Bonham, Barbara. WILLA CATHER. Philadelphia: Chilton Press, 1970. 120 pp. Biography of the famous woman author of MY ANTONIA.

2424. Bosanquet, Theodora. HARRIET MARTINEAU. London: Etchells and McDonald, 1927. 255 pp. Biography of the English visitor to America (1802-1876), author of SOCIETY IN AMERICA.

2425. Boynick, David K. PIONEERS IN PETTICOATS. New York: Crowell, 1959. 245 pp. Sketches of American women who fought for equal rights and opportunities in such fields as law, and ministry, medicine, industrial engineering, aviation, and business.

2426. Bradford, Gamaliel. DAUGHTERS OF EVE. Boston: Houghton Mifflin, 1928. 304 pp. Seven biographies of some famous mistresses, including Catherine the Great, George Sand, and Sarah Bernhardt; bibliography lists more detailed sources.

2427. ———. PORTRAITS OF AMERICAN WOMEN. Freeport, N.Y.: Books for Libraries Press, 1969. Reprint of 1919 edition. 276 pp. Collection of short biographies of eight women, including Abigail Adams, H. B. Stowe, and Louisa M. Alcott.

2428. ———. PORTRAITS OF WOMEN. Freeport, N.Y.: Books for Libraries Press, 1969. Reprint of 1916 edition. 202 pp. Sketches of nine European women, including Lady Mary Montague (famous letter writer), Jane Austen, Mrs. Samuel Pepys, Madame de Sévigné (French letter writer), Madame de Choiseul (salonniere), and others.

2429. ———. WIVES. New York: Arno Press, 1972. Reprint of 1925 edition. 298 pp. Portraits of Theodosia Burr, Dolley Madison, Mary Todd Lincoln, Margaret Mansfield Arnold, Sarah Taylor Davis, Sarah Hildreth Butler, and Harriet Stanwood Blaine.

2430. Briant, Keith. MARIE STOPES: A BIOGRAPHY. London: Hogarth Press, 1962. 286 pp. Biography of the British pioneer of the birth control movement.

2431. Brown, Dee Alexander. THE GENTLE TAMERS: WOMEN OF THE OLD WILD WEST. New York: G. P. Putnam's Sons, 1958. 317 pp. Biographical accounts of the women who played a part in the building of the American West during the nineteenth century.

2432. Brown, Hallie Quinn, compiler. HOMESPUN HEROINES AND OTHER WOMEN OF DISTINCTION. Xenia, Ohio: Aldine, 1926. 248 pp. Biographies of black women by a black teacher and woman's leader who formed women's clubs for black women.

2433. Brown, Ivor. DARK LADIES. London: Collins, 1957. 319 pp. Biographies of Helen of Troy, Sappho of Lesbos, Cleopatra, and Shakespeare's "Dark Lady" in ROMEO AND JULIET and LOVE'S LABOUR'S LOST—who still remains a literary mystery.

2434. Buck, Pearl S. MY SEVERAL WORLDS: A PERSONAL RECORD. New York: John Day, 1954. 407 pp. The story of her childhood in China, in Europe, and at Randolph-Macon College in Virginia, and of her apprenticeship as an author.

2435. Burton, Margaret E. MABEL CRATTY: LEADER IN THE ART OF LEADERSHIP. New York: Woman's Press, 1929. 248 pp. About one of the leaders of the Young Women's Christian Association.

2436. Calisher, Hortense. HERSELF. New York: Arbor House, 1972. Autobiographical account of her progress as a woman and a writer, and the inseparability of the two; a woman's view of sex, politics, and other current topics.

2437. Carpenter, Adella P. ELLEN LOIS ROBERTS: LIFE AND WRITINGS, A SKETCH. Chicago: Woman's Missionary Society, Free Methodist Church, 1926. 191 pp. Biography of the wife of the founder of the Free Methodist Church in the United States, detailing her religious and missionary activities.

2438. Casey, Elizabeth. ILLUSTRIOUS IRISHWOMEN. 2 vols. London: Tinsley Brothers, 1877. Memoirs of some of the more celebrated Irish women from the earliest ages to the late nineteenth century, especially artists and women of letters, such as Lady Gregory.

2439. Cavanah, Frances. JENNY LIND'S AMERICA. Philadelphia: Chilton Press, 1969. 226 pp. Biography of the Swedish nightingale.

2440. Chao, Bu-wei Yang. AUTOBIOGRAPHY OF A CHINESE WOMAN. New York: John Day, 1947. The author was one of the early "emancipated," college-educated women of China in the 1920s.

2441. Chase, Ilka. PAST IMPERFECT. Garden City: Doubleday, 1942. 278 pp. Honest and witty autobiography of the writer, actress, and radio-television personality.

2442. Cheney, Ednah D., ed. LOUISA MAY ALCOTT: HER LIFE, LETTERS AND JOURNALS. Boston: Little, Brown, 1928.

2443. Chesnut, Mary B. A DIARY FROM DIXIE. New York: Appleton, 1905. 424 pp. A unique perspective from a well-born Southern lady on the life and times of the Civil War period and her struggle for the Southern cause.

2444. Chung, Hau-min, and Arthur C. Miller. MADAME MAO: A PROFILE OF CHIANG CH'ING. Hong Kong: Union Research Institute, 1968. Two accounts of a woman reputed to be the most influential politician in China since the Dowager Empress Tz'u Hsi and Madame Chiang Kai-shek.

2445. Clark, Septima Poinsette. ECHO IN MY SOUL. New York: Dutton, 1962. 243 pp. Autobiography of a black woman's struggle for her people.

2446. Clarke, Mary Cowden. WORLD-NOTED WOMEN: OR, TYPES OF WOMANLY ATTRIBUTES OF ALL LANDS AND AGES. New York: Appleton, 1857. 407 pp. Biographical portraits of 17 famous women throughout history, beginning with Sappho and ending with Florence Nightingale.

2447. Cochrane, Jeanie Douglas. PEERLESS WOMEN: A BOOK FOR GIRLS. London: Collins, 1904. Brief biographies of 12 women, including Mary Carpenter, Florence Nightingale, Elizabeth Fry, Frances Power Cobbe, Sarah Robinson, and Agnes Weston.

2448. Cole, Margaret. WOMEN OF TODAY. New York: Books for Libraries Press, 1968. Reprint of 1938 edition. 311 pp. Biographies of ten English women distinguished for their contributions to such fields as music, art, literature, and social reform, such as Edith Covell, Annie Besant, and Beatrice Webb.

2449. Colloque de Coppet. MADAME DE STAEL ET L'EUROPE. Paris: Editions Klincksieck, 1970. 398 pp. Biography of the famous intellect and salonniere in France during the regime of Napoleon.

2450. Cook, Edward. THE LIFE OF FLORENCE NIGHTINGALE. 2 vols. London: Macmillan, 1914.

2451. Cornell, Katharine. I WANTED TO BE AN ACTRESS: THE AUTOBIOGRAPHY OF KATHARINE CORNELL. New York: Random House, 1939. 361 pp. The life of the American actress, her early love for the theater, her training, and her career up to 1934.

2452. Costello, Louisa Stuart. MEMOIRS OF EMINENT ENGLISHWOMEN. 4 vols. London: R. Bentley, 1844. Biographies of notable English celebrities.

2453. Courtney, Janet E. THE ADVENTUROUS THIRTIES. London: Oxford Univ. Press, 1933. 279 pp. Biographical sketches of women involved in the women's movement in England during the 1830s: Caroline Norton, Harriet Martineau, Lady Ashburton, and others. Emphasis on women's role in politics and society and in the reforming spirit of the period.

2454. Cromwell, Otelia. LUCRETIA MOTT. Cambridge: Harvard Univ. Press, 1958. Biography of the pioneer woman's rights advocate.

2455. Curie, Eve. MADAME CURIE: A BIOGRAPHY. Translated by Vincent Sheehan. New York: Doubleday, Doran, 1937. 412 pp. Biography of the world-renowned woman scientist, winner of two Nobel Prizes.

2456. Dandre, Victor E. ANNA PAVLOVA IN ART AND LIFE. New York: Benjamin Blom, 1932. 410 pp. Biography of the great ballerina by her husband.

2457. Daniel, Sadie Iola. WOMAN BUILDERS. Washington, D.C.: Associated Publishers, 1931. 187 pp. Biographical sketches of seven Negro women eminent in their contributions in the development of educational programs for American Negro youth; includes Lucy Craft Laney, Maggie L. Walker, Janie Porter Barrett, Mary McLeod Bethune, Nannie Helen Burroughs, Charlotte Hawkins Brown, and Jane Edna Hunter.

2458. Daniels, Jonathan. WASHINGTON QUADRILLE: THE DANCE BESIDE THE DOCUMENTS. Garden City, N.Y.: Doubleday, 1968. 370 pp. Women who were leaders in Washington society, from the time of Lincoln to that of F.D.R.

2459. Dannett, Sylvia. PROFILES OF NEGRO WOMANHOOD. Westport, Conn.: Negro Universities Press, vol. 1, 1690-1900, 1964; vol. 2, 20th Century, 1966. Attractively compiled two-volume work covering numerous Afro-American women from 1690 to the present, with backgrounds of women in a wide range of fields and professions.

2460. Darton, John M. FAMOUS GIRLS WHO HAVE BECOME ILLUSTRIOUS WOMEN. Freeport, N.Y.: Books for Libraries Press, 1972. Reprint of 1864 edition. 312 pp. Brief biographies of 20 notable women, chiefly from the nineteenth century, such as Harriet Martineau, Queen Victoria, Madame de Staël, Jenny Lind, and the Princess of Wales.

2461. Davis, Almond H. THE FEMALE PREACHER, OR MEMOIRS OF SALOME LINCOLN, AFTERWARDS THE WIFE OF JUNIA S. MOWRY. New York: Arno Press, 1972. Reprint of the 1843 edition. The memoirs of an early American feminist and equal rights advocate.

2462. Dawson, Sarah. A CONFEDERATE GIRL'S DIARY. Boston: Houghton Mifflin, 1913. Author's journal of her experiences during the Civil War, with a good insight into the society of the South.

2463. Deachim, Jacob. "She Held a Mirror to the World: Margaret Bourke-White, 1904-1971," POPULAR PHOTOGRAPHY, vol. 70 (Jan. 1972), pp. 104-111. Biographical article on the famous LIFE photographer and Pulitzer Prize winner.

2464. de Beauvoir, Simone. MEMOIRS OF A DUTIFUL DAUGHTER. Paris: Editions Gallimard, 1956. Autobiography of the famous French author of THE SECOND SEX.

2465. ———. FORCE OF CIRCUMSTANCE. New York: G. P. Putnam's Sons, 1965. 658 pp. Continuation of her autobiography, MEMOIRS OF A DUTIFUL DAUGHTER.

2466. Der Ling, Princess. OLD BUDDHA: A BIOGRAPHY OF THE EMPRESS DOWAGER TZ'U HSI. New York: Dodd, Mead, 1928. 347 pp. Biography of the last Empress of China (1835-1908).

2467. Diamonstein, Barbaralee. OPEN SECRETS: NINETY-FOUR WOMEN IN TOUCH WITH OUR TIME. New York: Viking Press, 1972. 384 pp. The responses of 94 women to a questionnaire asking what women and men thought most gratifying about their careers, who influenced their careers, the causes they support, etc. Interviews with Joyce Carol Oates, Shirley Chisholm, Helen Gurley Brown, Bella Abzug, Betty Furness, Leontyne Price, Jessamyn West, Lucy Jarvis, and Coretta King, among others.

2468. Dorr, Rheta Childe. SUSAN B. ANTHONY: THE WOMAN WHO CHANGED THE MIND OF A NATION. New York: AMS Press, 1970. 359 pp. Reprint of the 1928 edition. Covers her early life through the period prior to passage of the 19th Amendment, and up to her death. Warm and flattering biography, but less cumbersome than those of Stanton, Gage and Harper, in their multivolume study.

2469. Douglas, Emily Taft. PIONEER OF THE FUTURE: MARGARET SANGER. New York: Holt, Rinehart and Winston, 1970. Biography and documentation of the life of the pioneer in birth control.

2470. Dreifus, Claudia. "St. Joan of the Bogside: An Interview with Bernadette Devlin," EVERGREEN REVIEW, vol. 15 (July 1971), pp. 25-50. The IRA, Sinn Fein, and the possibility of her martyrdom are discussed, along with information on her background and education.

2471. Duncan, Isadora. MY LIFE. London: Boni and Liveright, 1927. 359 pp. Posthumous autobiography of the American dancer, with a good account of her creativity and revolutionary concepts of dancing, as well as her ideas on beauty, love, and art.

2472. Dunham, Katherine. A TOUCH OF INNOCENCE. New York: Harcourt, Brace, 1959. 312 pp. Autobiography of Katherine Dunham, interpreter of Afro-American dance.

2473. Duniway, Abigail Scott. PATH BREAKING: AN AUTOBIOGRAPHICAL HISTORY OF THE EQUAL SUFFRAGE MOVEMENT IN PACIFIC COAST STATES. New York: Source Book Press, 1970. Reprint of the 1914 edition. 297 pp. Reminiscences of the Oregon suffrage leader, author of Oregon's Equal Suffrage Proclamation; brought Susan B. Anthony to the West Coast and organized women not only on the Pacific Coast, but all over America, for equal voting rights.

2474. Duster, Alfreda M., ed. CRUSADE FOR JUSTICE: THE AUTOBIOGRAPHY OF IDA B. WELLS. Chicago: Univ. of Chicago Press, 1970. Born of slave parents, she became an editor of the MEMPHIS FREE SPEECH newspaper, and launched a one-woman crusade against racism and injustice toward black people in America.

2475. Earhart, Amelia. LAST FLIGHT. Arranged by George P. Putnam. New York: Harcourt, Brace, 1968. Reprint, 1937 edition. 226 pp. Biography of the famous aviatrix, lost on her last around-the-world flight.

2476. Edge, Clara A. TAHIRIH. Grand Rapids, Mich.: Edgeway, 1964. Biography of the first feminist in Persia. She lived during the nineteenth century, was the only woman in the first small group of believers to cluster around the Bab, the Persian prophet of the Baha'i faith, and the first woman in Persia to unveil publicly.

2477. Ellis, Anne. THE LIFE OF AN ORDINARY WOMAN. Boston: Houghton Mifflin, 1929. 301 pp. Everyday accounts of miner's life in Colorado mining camps during her girlhood and her two marriages. Glimpses of all sorts of common mining-town people.

2478. ———. 'PLAIN ANNE ELLIS': MORE ABOUT THE LIFE OF AN ORDINARY WOMAN. Boston: Houghton Mifflin, 1931. 265 pp. Sequel to her earlier autobiography. "Her lean energy, her innate decency, her nervous eye for significant and commonplace detail give life to her books."

2479. Faber, Doris. THE MOTHERS OF AMERICAN PRESIDENTS. New York: New American Library, 1968. 271 pp. Rebecca Baines Johnson, Rose Kennedy, Ida Eisenhower, Eliza Ballou Garfield, Jessie Wilson, and the mothers of many other presidents are featured; excellent bibliography.

2480. Fauset, Arthur. SOJOURNER TRUTH. New York: Russell and Russell, 1971. 187 pp. A sentimental biography of Isabella Baumfree, known as "Sojourner Truth," a remarkable Negro woman.

2481. Fawcett, Millicent Garrett. WHAT I REMEMBER. New York: Putnam's 1925. 272 pp. Autobiography of an English leader in the struggle for woman suffrage.

2482. Fawcett, Millicent G., and E. M. Turner. JOSEPHINE BUTLER: HER WORK AND PRINCIPLES, AND THEIR MEANING FOR THE TWENTIETH CENTURY. London: Association for Moral and Social Hygiene, 1927. 164 pp. Biography of the English reformer and fighter against prostitution.

2483. Ferber, Edna. A PECULIAR TREASURE. New York: Doubleday, 1939. 398 pp. Autobiography of the Pulitzer Prize winning novelist (SO BIG, GIANT, THE ICE PALACE).

2484. Fernandez-Azabal, Countess Lilie de. THE COUNTESS FROM IOWA. New York: G. P. Putnam's Sons, 1936. Born in Iowa, she became an international actress, married into European royalty, saw and escaped the Russian Revolution, and married into a distinguished Spanish family. Interesting for its inside view of the highest society and its fall.

2485. Ferris, Helen, compiler. FIVE GIRLS WHO DARED: THE GIRLHOOD STORIES OF FIVE COURAGEOUS GIRLS AS TOLD BY THEM- SELVES. Freeport, N.Y.: Books for Libraries Press, 1971. Reprint of 1931 edition. 270 pp. Short autobiographical essays by Amelia Ear- hart, Louise DeKoven Bowen, Josephine DeMott Robinson, Elizabeth Marbury, and Marie, Grand Duchess of Russia.

2486. Fields, Annie, ed. HARRIET BEECHER STOWE: LIFE AND LETTERS. Boston: Houghton Mifflin, 1898.

2487. Flynn, Elizabeth Gurley. I SPEAK MY OWN PIECE: AUTOBIOGRAPHY OF THE "REBEL GIRL." New York: Masses and Mainstream, 1955. 326 pp. Account of the author's early youth, her socialist activities, agitation for the IWW, and her work in organizing the American Civil Liberties Union.

2488. Forten, Charlotte. THE JOURNAL OF CHARLOTTE FORTEN: A FREE NEGRO IN THE SLAVE ERA. New York: Dryden Press, 1953. 248 pp. The story of her fight against slavery.

2489. Frederick, Pauline. TEN FIRST LADIES OF THE WORLD. New York: Meredith Press, 1967. 174 pp. Biographies of Indira Gandhi, Mary Wilson,

Lady Bird Johnson, Yvonne de Gaulle, Carmen Franco, Jovanka Tito, Tahia Nasser, Fathia Nkruma, Madame Thant, and Imelda Marcos.

2490. French, Doris, and Margaret Stewart. ASK NO QUARTER. Toronto: Longmans Green, 1959. Well-documented life of Agnes McPhail, Canada's first woman Member of Parliament.

2491. Gaines, Ernest J. THE AUTOBIOGRAPHY OF MISS JANE PITTMAN. New York: Dial Press, 1971. 245 pp. The fictional life story of a 110-year old black woman.

2492. Geller, Gyula Gatson. SARAH BERNHARDT: DIVINE ECCENTRIC. New York: Benjamin Blom. Reprint of 1933 edition. 272 pp. An account of the actress's life, with a good description of the traits of her character that went to create the legend.

2493. Gibson, Althea. I ALWAYS WANTED TO BE SOMEBODY. New York: Harper and Row, 1958. 176 pp. Autobiography of the first black woman to become an international tennis champion.

2494. Gildersleeve, Virginia. MANY A GOOD CRUSADE. New York: Macmillan, 1954. 434 pp. Autobiography of a distinguished woman educator, retired Dean of Barnard College and founder of the WAVES, who helped draft of the United Nations Charter.

2495. Ginsburg, Mirra. DIARY OF NINA KOSTERINA. New York: Avon Books, 1972. The diary of a young Russian girl approaching womanhood during the days of Stalin; sensitive account of a young woman's response to a crucial time in history.

2496. Glasgow, Ellen. THE WOMAN WITHIN. New York: Harcourt, 1954. 307 pp. A completely honest portrayal of an interior world in the famous novelist (1873-1945). Excellent bibliography of her works and studies of her as a novelist.

2497. Goldman, Emma. LIVING MY LIFE. 2 vols. New York: Knopf, 1931. Unrestrained autobiography of the celebrated anarchist. It illustrates an era. [see 902]

2498. Goldmark, Josephine. IMPATIENT CRUSADER: FLORENCE KELLEY'S LIFE STORY. Urbana: Univ. of Illinois Press, 1953. 217 pp. The story of a woman who had probably the largest single share in shaping the social history of the United States during the first 30 years of this century.

2499. Gollack, G. A. DAUGHTERS OF AFRICA. New York: Negro Universities Press, 1969. Reprint of the 1932 edition. Biographies, ranging from ancient queens and traditional African women, to contemporary teachers, nurses, and mothers.

2500. Goodsell, Willystine, ed. PIONEERS OF WOMEN'S EDUCATION IN THE UNITED STATES: EMMA WILLARD, CATHERINE BEECHER, MARY LYON. New York: AMS Press, 1970. 311 pp. Biographies of three women eminent in the education of women.

2501. Gordon, Anna A. THE BEAUTIFUL LIFE OF FRANCES E. WILLARD. Chicago: Woman's Temperance Publishing Association, 1898. 416 pp. Educator and one of the first woman lobbyists to struggle for funding of America's first female seminary.

2502. Graham, Abbie. GRACE H. DODGE: MERCHANT OF DREAMS. New York: Woman's Press, 1926. Founder of numerous working girls' clubs, and one of the founders of Teachers College, Columbia University.

2503. Greenbie, Marjorie B. MY DEAR LADY: THE STORY OF ANNA ELLA CARROLL, THE "GREAT UNRECOGNIZED MEMBER OF LINCOLN'S CABINET." New York: Whittlesey House, 1940. Story of the woman who allegedly planned the strategy of Grant's Tennessee campaign and was a confidante of Lincoln's.

2504. Guedalla, Philip. BONNET AND SHAWL: AN ALBUM. New York: G. P. Putnam's Sons, 1928. 204 pp. Biographies of nine British women, including Jane Welsh Carlyle, Catherine Gladstone, Mary Arnold, Emily Tennyson, Mary Disraeli, and others.

2505. Hahn, Emily. THE SOONG SISTERS. New York: Doubleday, 1942. 349 pp. Popular biography of the three sisters who married Sun Yat-sen, Chiang Kai-shek, and H. H. Kung.

2506. Haig, Kenneth M. BRAVE HARVEST: THE LIFE STORY OF E. CORA HIND, LL.D. Toronto: Thomas Allen, 1945. 275 pp. Biography of a pioneer woman journalist, agricultural expert, and fighter for women's political rights in western Canada.

2507. Haight, Gordon. GEORGE ELIOT, A BIOGRAPHY. New York: Oxford Univ. Press, 1968. 616 pp. Excellent biography of the British novelist (SILAS MARNER, THE MILL ON THE FLOSS, etc.)

2508. Hall, Florence Howe. JULIA WARD HOWE AND THE WOMAN SUFFRAGE MOVEMENT. New York: Arno Press, 1969. 241 pp. Biography of the American poet (BATTLE HYMN OF THE REPUBLIC) and patriot.

2509. Hanaford, Phebe A. DAUGHTERS OF AMERICA: OR WOMEN OF THE CENTURY. Augusta, Maine: True, 1882. 730 pp. Very comprehensive and useful biographies of women in various fields of endeavor.

2510. HANNAH SENESH: HER LIFE AND DIARY. Introduction by Abba Eban. New York: Schocken Books, 1972. The story of Israel's national heroine who died in Hungary while organizing Jewish resistance to the Nazis.

2511. Hansberry, Lorraine. TO BE YOUNG, GIFTED AND BLACK. New York: Signet Books, 1969. 266 pp. Autobiography of a famous black writer (A RAISIN' IN THE SUN).

2512. Harper, Ida Husted. THE LIFE AND WORK OF SUSAN B. ANTHONY. 3 vols. Indianapolis: Hollenbech Press, 1898.

2513. Harveston, Mae Elizabeth. CATHERINE ESTHER BEECHER: A PIONEER EDUCATOR. Philadelphia: Science Press, 1932. 295 pp. Daughter of Lyman Beecher, sister of Harriet Beecher Stowe, and long an advocate of education for women in America.

2514. Hayek, F. A. JOHN STUART MILL AND HARRIET TAYLOR MILL. London: Routledge and Kegan Paul, 1951. 320 pp. Biography of the two most celebrated feminists in Britain. Harriet Taylor had a deep influence on Mill's thought.

2515. Hays, Mary. FEMALE BIOGRAPHY: OR MEMOIRS OF ILLUSTRIOUS AND CELEBRATED WOMEN OF ALL AGES AND COUNTRIES. 3 vols. London: R. Phillips, 1803; Philadelphia: Fry and Kammerar, 1807. Comprehensive biographies.

2516. Hellman, Lillian. AN UNFINISHED WOMAN: A MEMOIR. Boston: Little, Brown, 1969. Autobiography of the playwright (THE LITTLE FOXES).

2517. Higginson, Thomas Wentworth. MARGARET FULLER OSSOLI. Boston: Houghton Mifflin, 1884. 323 pp. A well-written observation of one of America's foremost personalities and women of letters.

2518. Hill, Octavia. LIFE OF OCTAVIA HILL AS TOLD IN HER LETTERS. Edited by C. Edmund Maurice. London: Macmillan, 1914. 591 pp. Story of a pioneer in housing reform and rehabilitation of slum tenements, and a life-long supporter of the woman's movement.

2519. Hobman, Daisy. OLIVE SCHREINER: HER FRIENDS AND TIMES. London: Watts, 1955. 182 pp. Biography of the British novelist and feminist.

2520. Holiday, Billie. LADY SINGS THE BLUES. New York: Lancer Books, 1969. Autobiography of one of black America's greatest blues singers.

2521. Holt, Rackham. MARY McLEOD BETHUNE. New York: Doubleday, 1964. 306 pp. Biography of the founder of Bethune-Cookman College and the National College Council of Negro Women.

2522. Horne, Lena. LENA. With Richard Schickel. New York: Doubleday, 1965. 300 pp. Autobiography of the famous black singer.

2523. Howe, Julia Ward. MARGARET FULLER (MARCHESA OSSOLI). Westport, Conn.: Greenwood Press, 1969. 298 pp. Reprint of 1883 edition. Considered Mrs. Howe's most important work.

2524. Hsieh, Ping-ying. AUTOBIOGRAPHY OF A CHINESE GIRL. London: Allen and Unwin, 1948. Biography of the famous Chinese novelist who fought in the KMT army during the 1920's.

2525. Hull, Helen. MAYLING SOONG CHIANG. New York: Coward-McCann, 1943. Biography of Madame Chiang Kai-shek.

2526. Humphreys, Mary G. CATHERINE SCHUYLER. New York: Scribner's 1897. Biography of the Revolutionary heroine and wife of Gen. Philip Schuyler, victor at the Battle of Saratoga.

2527. Hunt, Caroline L. THE LIFE OF ELLEN H. RICHARDS. Boston: Whitcomb and Barrows, 1912. 329 pp. Account of the American chemist and the founder of the home economics movement.

2528. Innis, Mary Quayle, ed. THE CLEAR SPIRIT: TWENTY CANADIAN WOMEN AND THEIR TIMES. Toronto: Univ. of Toronto Press, 1966. 304 pp. Collection of short biographies of 20 women of the past.

2529. Ireland, Norma Olin. INDEX TO WOMEN OF THE WORLD FROM ANCIENT TO MODERN TIMES: BIOGRAPHIES AND PORTRAITS. Westwood, Mass.: Faxon, 1970. 573 pp.

2530. Ishimoto, Shidzue. FACING TWO WAYS. New York: Farrar and Rinehart, 1935. 373 pp. Princess Ishimoto's enlightening autobiography of her role in the emancipation of Japanese women from traditional Japanese society.

2531. Jackson, Mahalia. MOVIN' ON UP: THE MAHALIA JACKSON STORY. New York: Hawthorne Books, 1966. 212 pp. Biography of the late gospel singer.

2532. Jacobs, H. H. FAMOUS AMERICAN WOMEN ATHLETES. New York: Dodd, Mead, 1964. 121 pp. Sketches of 13 American women who had careers in the world of sports.

2533. Jenkins, Hester Donaldson. AN EDUCATIONAL AMBASSADOR TO THE NEAR EAST: THE STORY OF MARY MILLS PATRICK AND AN AMERICAN COLLEGE IN THE ORIENT. New York: Fleming H. Revell, 1925. Biography of an outstanding woman educator.

2534. Johnson, Joseph. NOBLE WOMEN OF OUR TIME. London: Nelson, 1886. 406 pp. Brief accounts of some notable women reformers, including Agnes Jones, Mary Lyon, Fidelia Fiske, Catherine Tait, and others.

2535. Johnston, Johanna. MRS. SATAN: THE INCREDIBLE SAGA OF VICTORIA C. WOODHULL. New York: G. P. Putnam's Sons, 1967. 319 pp. Biography of a pioneer of women suffrage and equal rights (1838-1927).

2536. Johnstone, Grace. LEADING WOMEN OF THE RESTORATION. London: Digby, Long, 1892. 221 pp. Biographies of eminent British women, such as Lady Russell, Lady Warwick, Lady Maynard, Mrs. Godolphin, and others.

2537. Jones, Katherine M. HEROINES OF DIXIE: CONFEDERATE WOMEN TELL THEIR STORY OF THE WAR. Indianapolis: Bobbs-Merrill, 1955. 430 pp. A look at the Southern struggle from the autobiographical perspective of Southern women.

2538. Jones, Mary Harris. THE AUTOBIOGRAPHY OF MOTHER JONES. Chicago: Charles H. Kerr, 1925. 242 pp. Autobiography of an Irish-born agitator in the Colorado mining towns, Northern steel mills, and Southern textile centers, from the 1870's to the 1920's.

2539. Kamm, J. THE STORY OF MRS. PANKHURST. London: Methuen; New York: Meredith, 1968. 181 pp. The biography of the famous British feminist, Emmeline Pankhurst, founder of the Women's Social and Political Union, and ardent suffragette.

2540. Katasheva, L. NATASHA, A BOLSHEVIK WOMAN ORGANISER: A SHORT BIOGRAPHY. New York: Worker's Library, 1934. 63 pp. Communist pamphlet.

2541. Kearney, James R. ANNA ELEANOR ROOSEVELT: THE EVOLUTION OF A REFORMER. Boston: Houghton Mifflin, 1968. 332 pp. A scholarly investigation of Mrs. Roosevelt's prominent role in American society between 1933 and 1941.

2542. Keeler, Harriet L. THE LIFE OF ADELIA A. FIELD JOHNSTON. Oberlin, Ohio: Korner and Wood, 1912. 254 pp. The story of the Dean of Women at Oberlin College for 37 years and an outstanding educator.

2543. Keller, Helen. THE STORY OF MY LIFE. New York: Doubleday, 1947. 441 pp. Autobiography of Miss Keller's courageous struggle to overcome her handicaps. First published in 1903.

2544. Kemble, Frances Anne "Fannie". JOURNAL OF A RESIDENCE ON A GEORGIAN PLANTATION. New York: Harper and Row, 1863. 337 pp. Autobiographical account of the British visitor to America and her observations of life in the United States.

2545. Kennedy, David. BIRTH CONTROL IN AMERICA: THE CAREER OF MARGARET SANGER. New Haven: Yale Univ. Press, 1970. 320 pp. Biography of the American advocate of family planning and birth control, with bibliography of related materials and figures in the movement.

2546. Kenner, Zipora. "Women in the Knesset," ISRAEL MAGAZINE, vol. 3, (July-Aug. 1971), pp. 74-78. Short biographies of eight members of Israel's parliament.

2547. Koch, Harriet Berger. MILITANT ANGEL. New York: Macmillan, 1951. 167 pp. Biographical account of Annie Warburton Goodrich, pioneer of modern nursing training in the United States.

2548. Lader, Lawrence. THE MARGARET SANGER STORY AND THE FIGHT FOR BIRTH CONTROL. New York: Doubleday, 1955. 352 pp.

2549. La Marsh, Judy. MEMOIRS OF A BIRD IN A GILDED CAGE. Toronto: McClelland and Stewart, 1969. Autobiography of one of Canada's most interesting woman politicians, one-time mayor of Ottawa, and member of Parliament.

2550. Lane, Margaret. FRANCES WRIGHT AND THE "GREAT EXPERIMENT." Totowa, N.J.: Rowman and Littlefield, 1972. The story of her participation in the "Great Experiment" toward social reform and Utopian organization with Robert Dale Owen.

2551. ———. THE TALE OF BEATRIX POTTER. New York: Frederick Warne, 1946. 174 pp. Excellent biography of the author of children's books and the inventor of such characters as Peter Rabbit, Jemima Paddle-Duck, Cock Robin, and Mr. Tiggy-Winkle.

2552. Larcom, Lucy. A NEW ENGLAND GIRLHOOD. Boston: Houghton Mifflin, 1889. 274 pp. Valuable account of her years in Lowell, Massachusetts, chronicling the emotional and physical trials of the mill-girls in the Lowell area.

2553. Lash, Joseph P. ELEANOR: THE YEARS ALONE. New York: Norton, 1972. 368 pp. Conclusion to Lash's earlier work ELEANOR AND FRANKLIN, covering the last 17 years of her life. Interweaves history and personal biography in an excellent sketch of the first lady.

2554. Lerner, Gerda. THE GRIMKE SISTERS FROM SOUTH CAROLINA: REBELS AGAINST SLAVERY. Boston: Houghton Mifflin, 1967. 479 pp. Biography of Angelina and Sarah Grimké, famous abolitionists, detailing their struggle for political, religious, and equal rights.

2555. Lewis, Georgina King. ELIZABETH FRY. London: Headley, 1909. 176 pp. Biography of the British prison reformer.

2556. Lillard, Richard G. AMERICAN LIFE IN AUTOBIOGRAPHY: A DESCRIPTIVE GUIDE. Stanford: Stanford Univ. Press, 1956. 140 pp. A selected list of autobiographical works featuring many American and foreign women.

2557. Logan, Mary S. THE PART TAKEN BY WOMEN IN AMERICAN HISTORY. New York: Arno Press, 1972. Reprint of 1912 edition. Hundreds of entries, personal histories, causes and careers; especially valuable sections on outstanding Catholic and Jewish women.

2558. Longworth, Alice Roosevelt. CROWDED HOURS: REMINISCENCES. New York: Scribner's, 1934. 355 pp. Memoirs of the daughter of Theodore Roosevelt.

2559. Luhan, Mabel Dodge. INTIMATE MEMORIES, 1933-1937. New York: Harcourt, Brace, Kraus Reprint Co., 1971. She ran a literary salon in New York City; her memoirs span four volumes: Background, European Experiences, Movers and Shakers, and Edge of Taos Desert.

2560. Lurie, Nancy O., ed. MOUNTAIN WOLF WOMAN, SISTER OF CRASHING THUNDER. AUTOBIOGRAPHY OF A WINNEBAGO INDIAN. Ann Arbor: Univ. of Michigan Press, 1961. Excellent account of an Indian woman's life (1884-1960).

2561. Lyon, Mary. THE LIFE AND LABORS OF MARY LYON. New York: American Tract Society, 1885. 876 pp. Biography of the founder of Mount Holyoke College.

2562. MacClure, Victor. SHE STANDS ACCUSED: BEING A SERIES OF ACCOUNTS OF THE LIVES AND DEEDS OF NOTORIOUS WOMEN, MURDERESSES, CHEATS, COZENERS, ON WHOM JUSTICE WAS

EXECUTED. . . . Philadelphia: Lippincott, 1935. 240 pp. "a grisly book of murderesses."

2563. MacDonald, J. Ramsey. MARGARET ETHEL MACDONALD. New York: Thomas Seltzer, 1924. 239 pp. Biography of the British Socialist who struggled to improve the conditions of working women, make their position stronger in the Labour party, and who enthusiastically supported woman suffrage.

2564. Mackenzie-Grieve, Averil. THE GREAT ACCOMPLISHMENT. London: Geoffrey Bles, 1953. 290 pp. Five English women and their contributions to eighteenth century colonization movements.

2565. Marberry, M. M. VICKY: A BIOGRAPHY OF VICTORIA C. WOODHULL. New York: Funk and Wagnalls, 1967. 344 pp. Excellent biography of the woman suffragist, editor, nineteenth-century activist, and presidential candidate.

2566. Marreco, Ann. THE REBEL COUNTESS: THE LIFE AND TIMES OF CONSTANCE MARKIEVICZ. London: Weidenfeld and Nicolson, 1967. 330 pp. Biography of the Anglo-Irish aristocrat and her role in the Sinn Fein movement and the Easter Rising of 1916, her devotion to the Dublin poor, and her revolutionary activities.

2567. Marshall, Helen E. DOROTHEA DIX: FORGOTTEN SAMARITAN. Chapel Hill: Univ. of North Carolina Press, 1937. 298 pp. Biography of the advocate of humane legislation for improvement of American asylums.

2568. Martin, Ralph G. JENNIE: THE LIFE OF LADY RANDOLPH CHURCHILL. 2 vols. Englewood Cliffs, N.J.: Prentice-Hall, 1970-1971. The biography of Winston Churchill's mother, an astonishingly gifted woman.

2569. Maude, Aylmer. MARIE STOPES: HER WORK AND PLAY. New York: Putnam's, 1933. 299 pp. Biography of the foremost English advocate of birth control.

2570. Mavity, Nancy Barr. SISTER AIMEE. New York: Doubleday, 1931. 360 pp. Biography of Aimee Semple McPherson, the controversial California evangelist.

2571. McKee, Ruth K. MARY RICHARDSON WALKER: HER BOOK. Caldwell, Idaho: Caxton Printers, 1945. 357 pp. Story of one of the first women to cross the Rocky Mountains.

2572. McQuire, Judith W. DIARY OF A SOUTHERN REFUGEE DURING THE WAR. New York: Arno Press, 1972. Reprint of the 1867 edition. Southern lady tells the story of the dissolution of a homestead and of society during the Civil War.

2573. Mead, Margaret. BLACKBERRY WINTER: MY EARLIER YEARS. New York: Morrow, 1972. 305 pp. Autobiography of the famed American anthropologist, her childhood, education, marriages, and pioneering field experiences.

2574. Meltzer, Milton. TONGUE OF FLAME: THE LIFE OF LYDIA MARIA CHILD. New York: Crowell, 1965. Biography of the popular novelist (1802-1880), and pioneer children's magazine publisher. Her pamphlet on behalf of John Brown sold over 300,000 copies.

2575. Merriam, Eve. GROWING UP FEMALE IN AMERICA. New York: Doubleday, 1971. 308 pp. Biographies of Elizabeth Southgate, Elizabeth Cady Stanton, Maria Mitchell (astronomer), Dr. Anna Howard Shaw (minister and doctor), "Mother" Jones, and Mountain Wolf Woman (1884-1960).

2576. Messenger, R. THE DOORS OF OPPORTUNITY: A BIOGRAPHY OF DAME CAROLINE HASLETT. London: Macdonald, 1967. Electrical engineer, editor of the journal WOMAN ENGINEER, and advocate of careers for women in engineering in Britain.

2577. Meyer, Agnes E. OUT OF THESE ROOTS: THE AUTOBIOGRAPHY OF AN AMERICAN WOMAN. Boston: Little, Brown, 1953. 385 pp. Wife of the former owner of the WASHINGTON POST and an outspoken advocate of many social causes.

2578. Meyer, Bertha. SALON SKETCHES: BIOGRAPHICAL STUDIES OF BERLIN SALONS OF THE EMANCIPATION. New York: Bloch, 1938. 207 pp. Studies of famous Jewesses who influenced German literary and social life in the early nineteenth century.

2579. Middleton, Dorothy. VICTORIAN LADY TRAVELLERS. New York: Dutton, 1965. 182 pp. Such Victorian lady travellers as Isabella Bird, Marianne North, Fanny Bullock Workman, Mary Kingsley, and May French Sheldon are explored through their notebooks and travelogues.

2580. Migel, Parmenia. THE BALLERINAS: FROM THE COURT OF LOUIS XIV TO PAVLOVA. New York: Macmillan, 1972. 307 pp.

2581. Mishima, Sumie Seo. MY NARROW ISLE. New York: John Day, 1941. 280 pp. Autobiography of the life of a Japanese woman from the traditional Samurai class.

2582. Mitchell, David. THE FIGHTING PANKHURSTS: A STUDY IN TENACITY. London: Jonathan Cape, 1967. 352 pp. Biography of the British feminists and suffragists.

2583. Mitchell, Lucy Sprague. TWO LIVES: THE STORY OF WESLEY CLAIR MITCHELL AND MYSELF. New York: Simon and Schuster, 1953. 575 pp. Story of the remarkable marriage of two notable people: she, a writer and one of the most influential educators of our time; he, one of the leading economists.

2584. Mitford, Jessica. HONS AND REBELS. London: Gollancz, 1960. 222 pp. Autobiography of the British writer.

2585. Morny, Peter de. THE BEST YEARS OF THEIR LIVES. London: Centaur, 1955. 244 pp. A look at 29 women, most productive after the age of 40, among them Florence Nightingale, Elizabeth Fry, Emmeline Pankhurst, and Annie Besant.

2586. Moses, Anna Mary Robertson. GRANDMA MOSES: MY LIFE'S HISTORY. New York: Harper, 1952. 148 pp. Charming story of the famous American painter of primitives.

2587. Mozans, H. J. WOMEN IN SCIENCE. New York: Appleton, 1913. Biographical and historical review of the achievements of women in science.

2588. Nathan, Maud. ONCE UPON A TIME AND TODAY. New York: Putnam's 1933. 327 pp. Autobiography of a wealthy Jewish socialite, woman suffragist, and a founder of Barnard College.

2589. Nation, Carry A. THE USE AND NEED OF THE LIFE OF CARRY A. NATION. Topeka, Kans.: F. M. Steves, 1908. 396 pp. The story of the celebrated temperance advocate and feminist.

2590. Nestor, Agnes. WOMAN'S LABOR LEADER: THE AUTOBIOGRAPHY OF AGNES NESTOR. Rockford, Ill.: Bellevue, 1954. Trade union leader, president of the Chicago Women's Trade Union League from 1913-1948. Responsible for the 8-hour day in 1937; labored against child labor, minimum wages for women, and the establishment of the Women's Bureau in the Department of Labor.

2591. Nin, Anais. THE DIARY OF ANAIS NIN. 4 vols. New York: Harcourt, Brace and Jovanovich, 1968, 1969, 1970, 1971. The diaries of the Paris literary figure; covers the period 1931-34 (vol. 1); 1934-39 (vol. 2); 1939-44 (vol. 3); and 1944-47 (vol. 4).

2592. OUR FAMOUS WOMEN, COMPRISING THE LIVES AND DEEDS OF AMERICAN WOMEN WHO HAVE DISTINGUISHED THEMSELVES IN LITERATURE, SCIENCE, ART, MUSIC, AND THE DRAMA; OR ARE FAMOUS AS HEROINES, PATRIOTS, ORATORS, EDUCATORS, PHYSICIANS, PHILANTHROPISTS, ETC. Compiled by Harriet Beecher Stowe, Rose Terry Cooke, et al. Hartford, Conn.: Hartford Publishing Co., 1888. 715 pp. A well-written, comprehensive biographical study of such notables as Susan B. Anthony, Elizabeth C. Stanton, Catherine Beecher, Margaret Fuller, and others.

2593. Palencia, Isabel de. ALEXANDRA KOLLONTAI. New York: Longmans, 1947. 309 pp. Biography of the Soviet woman revolutionist, and first ambassador to a foreign country (1872-1952).

2594. Pankhurst, Dame Christabel. UNSHACKLED: THE STORY OF HOW WE WON THE VOTE. London: Hutchinson, 1959. 312 pp. The autobiography of the daughter of Emmeline Pankhurst, noted British feminist who worked with her mother for suffrage.

2595. Pankhurst, Emmeline. MY OWN STORY. New York: Source Book Press, 1970. Reprint of 1914 edition. 380 pp. The story of the making of a militant who founded the Women's Social and Political Union and of her fight for woman suffrage in England.

2596. Pankhurst, Estelle. THE LIFE OF EMMELINE PANKHURST: THE SUFFRAGETTE STRUGGLE FOR WOMEN'S CITIZENSHIP. London: T. W. Laurie, 1939. New York: Kraus Reprints, 1969. 179 pp.

2597. Parkman, Mary Rosetta. HEROINES OF SERVICE. Freeport, N.Y.: Books for Libraries Press, 1969. Reprint of 1917 edition. 322 pp. Biographies of Clara Barton, Mary Lyon, Alice Freeman Palmer, Jane Addams, Mary Antin, Marie Curie, and others.

2598. Patrick, Mary Mills. A BOSPHOROUS ADVENTURE: ISTANBUL (CONSTANTINOPLE) WOMAN'S COLLEGE, 1871-1924. London: H. Milford, 1934. 284 pp. The story of Mary Patrick's establishment of a woman's college in Turkey.

2599. Peck, Mary G. CARRIE CHAPMAN CATT: A BIOGRAPHY. New York: H. W. Wilson, 1944. 495 pp. An account of the one of the major personalities in the women's rights movement.

2600. Peel, Robert. MARY BAKER EDDY: THE YEARS OF DISCOVERY. New York: Holt, Rinehart and Winston, 1966. 372 pp. Discusses her life, her discovery of the relationship between science and religion, and her founding of the Christian Science Church.

2601. Perkins, A.J.G., and Theresa Wolfson. FRANCES WRIGHT: FREE ENQUIRER. New York: Harper, 1939. Scotswoman (1795-1852) who came to America in 1824, set up a Utopian colony in Tennessee, lectured throughout the East, and with Robert Dale Owen founded the magazine THE FREE ENQUIRER, in which she advocated birth control, atheism, and free public education for everyone.

2602. Phillips, Emma M. 33 WOMEN OF THE RESTORATION. Independence, Mo.: Herald House, 1960. 197 pp. Biographies of prominent British women.

2603. Phillips, M., and W. S. Tomkinson. ENGLISH WOMEN IN LIFE AND LETTERS. New York: Benjamin Blom. 430 pp. Reprint, 1926 edition. Fanny Burney, Dorothy Osborne, and others; a rich history of English-women in the seventeenth and eighteenth centuries.

2604. Pickett, La Salle C. ACROSS MY PATH: MEMORIES OF PEOPLE I HAVE KNOWN. Freeport, N.Y.: Books for Libraries Press, 1970. Reprint of 1916 edition. 148 pp. Collection of brief reflections on 25 American women of the nineteenth century.

2605. Pickford, Mary. SUNCHINE AND SHADOW: AN AUTOBIOGRAPHY. Garden City, N.Y.: Doubleady, 1955. 224 pp. The personal account of "America's Sweetheart" and her career in the movies.

2606. Pitman, Emma Raymond. ELIZABETH FRY. Wesport, Conn.: Greenwood Press, 1970. 269 pp. Reprint, 1884 edition. English prison reformer and philanthropist who worked to improve the conditions of women at Newgate prison; her methods were used throughout Europe.

2607. Popp, Adelheid. THE AUTOBIOGRAPHY OF A WORKING WOMAN. London: Fisher and Unwin, 1912. Memoirs of an Austrian socialist and writer who became a close associate of Frederick Engels'.

2608. Porter, Sarah H. THE LIFE AND TIMES OF ANNE ROYALL. New York: Arno Press, 1972. Reprint of 1909 edition. The life of a career woman in the middle of the nineteenth century who edited a publication which kept Washington and the Establishment on their toes.

2609. Reynolds, Myra. THE LEARNED LADY IN ENGLAND, 1650-1760. Gloucester, Mass.: Peter Smith, 1964. 489 pp. Scholarly studies of the achievements of such learned Englishwomen as Lady Jane Grey, the Duchess of Newcastle, Anne Killigrew, and Barthusa Makin. Informative bibliography of many miscellaneous books on women.

2610. Rheinhardt, Emil Alphons. THE LIFE OF ELEANORA DUSE. New York: Benjamin Blom, 1969. 293 pp. Reprint, 1930 edition. Biography of the great international actress, with long chapters on her relationships with Sarah Bernhardt and D'Annunzio.

2611. Richards, Laura E., and Maud Howe Elliott. JULIA WARD HOWE, 1819-1910. 2 vols. Boston: Houghton Mifflin, 1916.

2612. Rinehart, Mary Roberts. MY STORY: A NEW EDITION AND SEVEN-TEEN NEW YEARS. New York: Rinehart, 1948. 570 pp. The reflections of over 40 years of successful novel writing, with a lot of American history and culture interwoven in her memoirs.

2613. Rittenhouse, Mignon. THE AMAZING NELLIE BLY. Freeport, N.Y.: Books for Libraries Press, 1971. 254 pp. The story of the woman reporter who, in imitation of Jules Verne's hero Phineas Fogg, won worldwide fame by girdling the earth in 72 days.

2614. Robinson, Wilhelmena S. HISTORICAL NEGRO BIOGRAPHIES. New York: Publishers Co., 1969. 291 pp. Many short biographies of prominent black women in American history.

2615. Rollins, Charlemae Hill. FAMOUS AMERICAN NEGRO POETS. New York: Dodd, Mead, 1965. Biographies of 12 American black poets, including Jupiter Hammon, Phillis Wheatley, Frances Ellen Watkins Harper, Effie Lee Newsome, and Margaret Walker.

2616. Roosevelt, Eleanor. AUTOBIOGRAPHY. New York: Harper, 1961. 454 pp. An abbreviated edition of her multivolume autobiography, covering her entire life and providing a picture of the changing world seen through her eyes.

2617. Ross, Ishbel. CHARMERS AND CRANKS: TWELVE FAMOUS AMERI-
CAN WOMEN WHO DEFIED THE CONVENTIONS. New York: Harper
and Row, 1965. 306 pp. Biographies of Madame Jumel (wife of Aaron
Burr), Hetty Green (the Witch of Wall Street), Mrs. Frank Leslie
(LESLIE'S ILLUSTRATED NEWSPAPER), Margaret and Kate Fox
(spiritualists), Victoria Woodhull and Tennessee Claflin, Mrs. Jack
Gardner, Carry Nation, Nellie Bly, Isadora Duncan, and others.

2618. ———. CRUSADES AND CRINOLINES: THE LIFE AND TIMES OF
ELLEN CURTIS DEMOREST AND WILLIAM JENNINGS DEMOREST.
New York: Harper, 1963. 290 pp. The story of the inventors of the
paper pattern for sewing fashions, editors of DEMOREST'S MAGA-
ZINE, a fashion journal, and the role of Mrs. DeMorest as a business-
woman and fashion arbiter.

2619. ———. LADIES OF THE PRESS: THE STORY OF WOMEN IN
JOURNALISM BY AN INSIDER. New York: Harper, 1936. 622 pp.

2620. Roth, Lillian. I'LL CRY TOMORROW. New York: Fell, 1954. 347 pp.
The story of her unstable childhood, traumatic sex experiences, and
alcoholism; on to stardom on Broadway and in Hollywood, her decline
through alcoholism, and her comeback.

2621. Sachs Arling, Emanie. "THE TERRIBLE SIREN": VICTORIA
WOODHULL (1838-1927). New York: Arno Press, 1972. Reprint of
the 1928 edition. Member of the First International, candidate for
President of the United States, espouser of free love, socialism, birth
control, woman suffrage, and vegetarianism.

2622. St. Denis, Ruth. AN UNFINISHED LIFE: AN AUTOBIOGRAPHY.
New York: Harper, 1939. 391 pp. The story of the New Jersey farm
girl who triumphed in Paris and invented synchoric dancing.

2623. St. John, Christopher. ETHEL SMYTH: A BIOGRAPHY. London:
Longmans; 1959. 316 pp. Miss Smyth, composer and author, was also a
leading figure in the agitation for woman suffrage. She composed "The
March of the Women," which became the song of the movement in
Britain.

2624. Sanger, Margaret. AN AUTOBIOGRAPHY. New York: Norton, 1938.
Pioneer in the birth control movement in America.

2625. Sargeant, Winthrop. DIVAS. New York: Coward, McCann and Geoghegan, 1973. 192 pp. Glimpses into the lives of six major opera
sopranos: Joan Sutherland, Marilyn Horne, Beverly Sills, Birgit Nilsson,
Leontyne Price, and Eileen Farrell.

2626. Schmidt, Minna Moscherosch, compiler. 400 OUTSTANDING WOMEN
OF THE WORLD AND COSTUMOLOGY OF THEIR TIME. Chicago:
Author, 1933. 583 pp. Interesting selection of brief biographies of
women arranged by countries, including suffragists and reformers in
England, the United States, and Sweden; includes also a section of
American "colored" women.

2627. Scott, Denham. "Where Are They Now?" JOURNAL OF THE AMERI-
CAN AVIATION HISTORICAL SOCIETY, vol. 13, no. 3 (Fall 1968),
p. 212. Short biographical article of Miss "Tiny" Broadwick, the first
woman to parachute from a plane in 1913.

2628. Seyersted, Per. KATE CHOPIN: A CRITICAL BIOGRAPHY. Oslo: Norwegian Research Council for Science and the Humanities, 1969. 246 pp.
Biography of the short story writer of life in Louisiana (1851-1904).

2629. Shaw, Anna Howard. THE STORY OF A PIONEER. New York: Harper, 1915. 338 pp. The story of the influences that made her an abolitionist, a woman preacher, a physician, and an international leader of the suffrage movement.

2630. Sickels, Eleanor. IN CALICO AND CRINOLINE. Freeport, N.Y.: Books for Libraries Press, 1971. 274 pp. Reprint of 1935 edition. Collection of biographical episodes in the lives of American women from 1608 to 1865, including Anne Hutchinson, Billie Boyd (the Confederate Spy), and others. Successful in its attempt to exhibit the significant role of women in the great drama of America.

2631. ———. TWELVE DAUGHTERS OF DEMOCRACY. Freeport, N.Y.: Books for Libraries Press, 1968. 256 pp. Reprint of 1941 edition. Short biographies of women from 1865 to 1930.

2632. Smedley, Agnes. DAUGHTER OF EARTH. Old Westbury, N.Y.: Feminist Press, 1973. 432 pp. Semiautobiographical account of the first 33 years of her struggles as a radical and of her role in the Independence Movement in India. Her gravestone in Peking bears the inscription: "Friend of China."

2633. Smith, Florence. MARY ASTELL, 1666-1739. New York: Columbia Univ. Press, 1916. Full presentation of the life and works of Mary Astell, an early advocate of higher education for women.

2634. Smyth, Ethel. IMPRESSIONS THAT REMAINED: MEMOIRS. 2 vols. London: Longmans, 1919. Autobiography of the great English composer whose opera "DER WALD" was the only opera by a woman ever sung at the Metropolitan Opera House.

2635. Snyder, Agnes. DAUNTLESS WOMEN IN CHILDHOOD EDUCATION, 1856-1931. Washington, D.C.: Association for Childhood Education International, 1971. 405 pp. Historical and biographical studies of some women who devoted their lives to children's education: Elizabeth Palmer Peabody, Margarethe Schurz, Susan E. Blow, Kate Douglas Wiggin, Alice Temple, and others.

2636. Snyder, Charles McCool. DR. MARY WALKER, LITTLE LADY IN PANTS. New York: Vantage Press, 1962. 166 pp. America's first and only woman Medal of Honor winner, and champion of woman's rights.

2637. Sochen, June. THE NEW WOMAN IN GREENWICH VILLAGE, 1910-1920. New York: Quadrangle Books, 1972. 175 pp. Focuses on some early Village feminists: Crystal Eastman, Neith Boyce, Henrietta Rodman, and Ida Rauk, who struggled for a bloodless revolution to alter the status of women in American society.

2638. Sprague, Rosemary. GEORGE ELIOT: A BIOGRAPHY. Philadelphia: Chilton Press, 1968. 337 pp. Biography of the warm and feminine woman behind the masculine pseudonym.

2639. Stanton, Elizabeth Cady. EIGHTY YEARS AND MORE: 1815-1897. REMINISCENCES OF ELIZABETH CADY STANTON. London: Fisher and Unwin, 1970. 474 pp. Stanton's autobiography from childhood to her eightieth birthday; includes her views on the family, marriage and divorce, women and theology, and her role as founder of the Woman's Rights Convention in 1848.

2640. Stanton, Theodore, and Harriet Stanton Blatch. ELIZABETH CADY STANTON. 2 vols. New York: Arno Press, 1969. Reprint, 1922 edition. Letters, diaries, and reminiscences of the founder of the woman's rights movement.

2641. Stein, Gertrude. THE AUTOBIOGRAPHY OF ALICE B. TOKLAS. New York: Harcourt, Brace, 1933. 310 pp. Miss Stein and Miss Toklas were in the heart of the art movement in the early years of Picasso, Braque, Matisse, and others. Very revealing and well-written autobiography.

2642. Stern, Geraldine. DAUGHTERS FROM AFAR: PROFILES OF ISRAEL. New York: Bloch, 1958. 190 pp. Twelve profiles of the women who played a part in the birth of Israel.

2643. Stern, Madeleine B. THE LIFE OF MARGARET FULLER. New York: Dutton, 1942. 549 pp. Excellent sources and bibliography.

2644. ———. PURPLE PASSAGE: THE LIFE OF MRS. FRANK LESLIE. Norman, Oklahoma: Univ. of Oklahoma Press, 1953. 281 pp. The story of the fascinating widow who ran a publishing empire which became the official organ of the National Woman Suffrage Association.

2645. Stevens, Doris. JAILED FOR FREEDOM. Freeport, N.Y.: Books for Libraries Press, 1949. 388 pp. A look at the campaigns of the militant factions of the suffrage movement, 1913-1919. Included are Susan B. Anthony, Alice Paul (the "Militant General" of the suffrage movement), and others.

2646. Stowe, Lyman Beecher. SAINTS, SINNERS, AND BEECHERS. Freeport, N.Y.: Books for Libraries Press, 1970. 450 pp. Biographies of Catherine Beecher, Mary Foote Beecher (Grandmother of Charlotte Perkins Gilman), Harriet Beecher Stowe, Isabella Beecher, and several of the male Beechers.

2647. Strachey, Rachel Conn (Costelloe). STRUGGLE. New York: Duffield, 1930. 429 pp. Nancy Astor, Mary Wollstonecraft, Elizabeth Garrett Anderson, Florence Nightingale, and others are featured.

2648. ———. MILLICENT GARRETT FAWCETT. London: John Murray, 1931. 380 pp. Biography of a leader in the suffrage movement in Britain.

2649. ———. OUR FREEDOM AND ITS RESULTS, BY FIVE WOMEN: ELEANOR F. RATHBONE, ERNA REISS, RAY STRACHEY, ALISON NEILANS, MARY AGNES HAMILTON. London: Hogarth Press, 1936. 285 pp.

2650. Sugimoto, Etsu Inagaki. A DAUGHTER OF THE SAMURAI. Garden City, N.Y.: Doubleday, 1925. 314 pp. Contrasts her life in Japan with her life in America, and recounts her experiences as a Japanese language and history professor at Columbia University.

2651. Suhl, Yuri. ERNESTINE ROSE AND THE BATTLE FOR HUMAN RIGHTS. New York: Reynal, 1959. 310 pp. Biography of the Polish-born immigrant who pioneered in the Great Reform Movement of the nineteenth century, and agitated for abolition, equal rights, and Utopian socialist programs.

2652. Swann, Nancy Lee. PAN CHAO, FOREMOST WOMAN SCHOLAR OF CHINA, 1ST CENTURY A.D. New York: Century, 1932. 179 pp. Background and life of the most famous Chinese historian who invented the technique of dynastic histories of China with her father and brother.

2653. Swisshelm, Jane Grey. HALF A CENTURY. New York: Source Book Press, 1970. 363 pp. Reprint of the 1880 edition. Autobiography of her life and role in the abolitionist movement, and her role in the woman's rights movement.

2654. Sykes, Christopher. NANCY: THE LIFE OF LADY ASTOR. New York: Harper, 1972. 543 pp. Illustrated biography of the American-born Lady Astor, first woman member of the House of Commons and famed hostess to both the leading statesmen of her time and to the literary immortals of the "Clivedon Set."

2655. Tarbell, Ida M. MADAME ROLAND: A BIOGRAPHICAL STUDY. New York: Charles Scribner's Sons, 1896. Study of the famous French salonniere, literary figure, and writer.

2656. ———. ALL IN THE DAY'S WORK. New York: Macmillan, 1939. 412 pp. Author of the HISTORY OF THE STANDARD OIL COMPANY, and THE LIFE OF ABRAHAM LINCOLN, historian and editor (21 years on the staff of McCLURE'S, THE AMERICAN MAGAZINE, and fellow "muckraker" along with Lincoln Steffans, Ray Stannard Baker, and William Allen White.

2657. Terrell, Mary Church. A COLORED WOMAN IN A WHITE WORLD. Washington, D.C.: Ransdel, 1940. Autobiography of one of the first black woman graduates of Oberlin College, and first black woman member of the Washington, D.C. Board of Education; suffragist, president of the National Association of Colored Women, civil rights advocate, and the woman who won the right for blacks to eat in white restaurants in the District of Columbia.

2658. Thompson, Bertha. SISTER OF THE ROAD: THE AUTOBIOGRAPHY OF BOX-CAR BERTHA. New York: Sheridan, 1937. 314 pp. The memoirs of the daughter of "Mother Thompson," her thirty years as a hobo and prostitute in America.

2659. Todd, Margaret. THE LIFE OF SOPHIA JEX-BLAKE. London: Macmillan, 1918. 574 pp. Miss Jex-Blake was a pioneer in the advancement of women in the British medical profession, founder of the London School of Medicine for Women in 1874, and first woman to be admitted to medical practice through passage of the Russell Gurney Enabling Act of 1877.

2660. Tucker, Sophie. SOME OF THESE DAYS: THE AUTOBIOGRAPHY OF SOPHIE TUCKER. New York: Doubleday, 1945. 309 pp. Sentimental memoirs of the great vaudevillian and music-hall star.

2661. Van Hoosen, Bertha. PETTICOAT SURGEON. Chicago: Pellegrini, 1947. 324 pp. The autobiography of the woman physician who helped develop "twilight sleep," her training and practice in gynecology, her pioneering work in sex education, and her struggle against male dominance in Illinois hospitals.

2662. Vietor, Agnes C., ed. A WOMAN'S QUEST: THE LIFE OF MARIE E. ZAKRZEWSKA, M.D. New York: Arno Press, 1972. Reprint of the 1924 edition. How she became a doctor and the first woman physician of the N.Y. Infirmary for Women and Children, carrying her personal crusade into the big city where ignorance and poverty battered women and children into sickness and death.

2663. Visher, Stephen S. "Women Starred in 'American Men of Science,' 1903-1943." Pp. 148-149 in Stephen S. Visher, SCIENTISTS STARRED, 1903-1943. Baltimore: Johns Hopkins Press, 1947. The names and fields of 52 women are featured in this book of the most significant American scientists.

2664. Wagenknect, Edward C., ed. MARILYN MONROE: A COMPOSITE VIEW. Philadelphia: Chilton Press, 1969. 200 pp. Excellent biography of the actress, composed of essays by a number of authors.

2665. Wald, Lillian. HOUSE ON HENRY STREET. Boston: Little, Brown, 1915. 348 pp. A record of Miss Wald's twenty years of settlement house activity; offers many discussions of the social problems of the day.

2666. ———. WINDOWS ON HENRY STREET. Boston: Little, Brown, 1934. 348 pp. Continuation of the earlier book. Public Health Nursing and the United States Children's Bureau were originated on Henry Street.

2667. Wallace, Irving. THE NYMPHO AND OTHER MANIACS. New York: Simon and Schuster, 1971. 475 pp. Chronicles the true-life stories of more than 30 women who defied the social standards of their time—sexual, political, and intellectual—to go their own marvelously varied ways.

2668. Ward, Barbara E., ed. WOMEN IN THE NEW ASIA. Paris: UNESCO, 1963. Interesting collection of firsthand accounts of prominent Asian women.

2669. Wardle, Ralph M. MARY WOLLSTONECRAFT. New York: Coward, McCann and Geoghegan, 1972. 307 pp. A horrible childhood, a growing commitment to human rights, a flaming illicit love affair, and a brief, happy marriage are featured in this biography of one of the seminal spirits behind the feminist movement.

2670. Waters, Ethel. HIS EYE IS ON THE SPARROW: AN AUTOBIO-GRAPHY. Garden City, N.Y.: Doubleday, 1951. 278 pp. The success story of the black girl who became a star on the stage, screen, radio, and television.

2671. Watson, Paul Barron. SOME WOMEN OF FRANCE. Freeport, N.Y.: Books for Libraries Press, 1969. 269 pp. Seven essays featuring such famous French women as Madame de Deffand, Madame de Stael, Delphine Gay, Isabeau de Baviere, Marie d'Agoult, and Juliette Lamber.

2672. Webb, Beatrice. BEATRICE WEBB'S DIARIES, 1912-24. London: Longmans Green, 1952. 272 pp. The letters and diaries of the Fabian socialist, who along with her husband, Sidney, helped to found the London School of Economics.

2673. ———. OUR PARTNERSHIP. Edited by Barbara Drake and Margaret Cole. London: Longmans, 1948. 544 pp. Autobiography of a leading British socialist and her husband.

2674. Wells, Ida B. CRUSADE FOR JUSTICE: THE AUTOBIOGRAPHY OF IDA B. WELLS. Chicago: Univ. of Chicago Press, 1970. Autobiography of the great antilynching black crusader.

2675. Werlich, Robert. "The Strange Case of Doctor Mary Walker." Unpublished article, n.d. Available from Quaker Press, 3218 O Street, Washington, D.C. 20007. The story of the only woman to be awarded the Congressional Medal of Honor. Following the Civil War, she became a world-renowned champion of women's rights.

2676. West, Geoffrey. THE LIFE OF ANNIE BESANT. London: Howe, 1933. 295 pp. Mrs. Besant, in addition to being a leading theosophist and Indian leader, was also a free thinker, socialist, and early advocate of birth control.

2677. Wharton, Edith. A BACKWARD GLANCE. New York: Scribner's, 1964; Appleton, 1934. 385 pp. The memoirs of the novelist who died in 1937.

2678. Wheatley, Vera. THE LIFE AND WORK OF HARRIET MARTINEAU. London: Secker and Warburg, 1957. 421 pp. Biographical account of the the nineteenth-century English writer and agnostic.

2679. Whicher, George F. THIS WAS A POET: A CRITICAL BIOGRAPHY OF EMILY DICKINSON. New York: Scribner's, 1938. 337 pp. Background study of the eminent American female poet.

2680. Whitton, Mary O. THE FIRST FIRST LADIES, 1789-1865. New York: Hastings House, 1948. Short biographies of the wives and social backgrounds of America's first presidents.

2681. Willard, Frances E. GLIMPSES OF FIFTY YEARS: THE AUTOBIO-GRAPHY OF AN AMERICAN WOMAN. New York: Source Book Press, 1970. Reprint of the 1889 edition. By the outstanding American feminist and crusader for temperance and suffrage.

2682. Willard, Frances E., and Mary A. Livermore, eds. A WOMAN OF THE CENTURY: 1470 BIOGRAPHICAL SKETCHES ACCOMPANIED BY PORTRAITS OF LEADING AMERICAN WOMEN IN ALL WALKS OF LIFE. Buffalo, N.Y.: Moulton; Detroit: Gale Research, 1967. Reprint of the 1893 edition. 812 pp.

2683. Wilson, Edith Bolling Galt. MY MEMOIR. Indianapolis: Bobbs-Merrill, 1939. 386 pp. The memoirs of the wife of President Wilson.

2684. Wilson, Forrest. CRUSADER IN CRINOLINE: THE LIFE OF HARRIET BEECHER STOWE. Philadelphia: Lippincott, 1941. 706 pp. Probably the best biography of Mrs. Stowe.

2685. Wong, Jade Snow. FIFTH CHINESE DAUGHTER. New York: Harper, 1950. 246 pp. Autobiographical account of the San Francisco ceramic artist.

2686. Woodham-Smith, Cecil. FLORENCE NIGHTINGALE, 1820-1910. London: Constable, 1950. 600 pp.

2687. Woodward, Helen. BOLD WOMEN. Freeport, N.Y.: Books for Libraries Press, 1971. 373 pp. Witty profiles of Fanny Wright, Jane Grey Swisshelm, Sara Josepha Hale, Kate Field, Adah Mencken, Dr. Mary Walker, and Mrs. Tom Thumb.

2688. Wu Shu-chiung. YANG KUEI-FEI, THE MOST FAMOUS BEAUTY OF CHINA. London: Brentano, 1924. 103 pp. Biography of the eighth-century Chinese concubine traditionally credited with the demoralization of the T'ang Court, who paved the way for the rebellion which brought about the collapse of the dynasty.

2689. Wyndham, Horace. THE MAGNIFICANT MONTEZ (LOLA MONTEZ). New York: Benjamin Blom, 1935. 288 pp. The theatrical and personal life of Montez, as famous as a crusader for women's rights as for her life and her dancing.

2690. Yost, Edna. AMERICAN WOMEN OF SCIENCE. Philadelphia: Lippincott, 1955. 233 pp. Biographies of Ellen Richards, first woman in America to be granted a degree in science; Annie Jump Cannon, Harvard astronomer; Libbie Hyman, zoologist; Margaret Mead, anthropologist; and others.

2691. ———. WOMEN OF MODERN SCIENCE. New York: Dodd, Mead, 1959. 176 pp. Biographies of Gerty Cori, Nobel Prize winner, the only American winner; Lise Meitner, Austrian physicist; Chien Shiung Wu, Chinese nuclear physicist; Gladys Emerson, biochemist; Dorothea Rudnick, embryologist; and others.

VII. WOMEN IN LITERATURE AND THE ARTS

Most bibliographers are not equipped to make a representative selection of works dealing with women in literature and the arts, for the task requires the patient thoroughness to sift a mountain of publications and the tact to discriminate. We have attempted to furnish a compressed selection of works written about women—novels, plays, other literature and art forms. These works express women's deepest wishes and fears in terms of complexes, repressions, sublimations, compensations, and socially conditioned patterns of the subject's personality and character structure in terms of feminine interpretations. Also included are a number of critical studies of notable women writers and artists, especially as they deal with some of the ultimate psychological, philosophical, and ethical questions, beliefs, and values of women in general.

> *Men have had every advantage of us in telling thei. own story. Education has been theirs in so much higher a degree; the pen has been in their hands.*
> —*Jane Austen* (PERSUASION, 1818)

2692. Adams, Charles F., ed. CORRESPONDENCE BETWEEN JOHN ADAMS AND MERCY WARREN RELATING TO HER HISTORY OF THE AMERICAN REVOLUTION," JULY-AUGUST, 1807. New York: Arno Press, 1972. Reprinted from Collections of the Massachusetts Historical Society, vol. 4, 5th ser., Boston, 1878. The former president and this lady historian cross intellectual swords—to his disadvantage; reveals a remarkable lady and writer.

2693. American Music Conference. "The Women of Music," MUSIC JOURNAL, vol. 30 (Jan. 1972), pp. 9-24. A good general history of women in music.

2694. Aristophanes. LYSISTRATA. New York: Harcourt, Brace, 1954. 132 pp. Originally written four centuries before Christ, this ribald play centers around a sexual "strike" conducted by Greek women as a weapon to end war.

2695. Auchincloss, Louis. PIONEERS AND CARETAKERS. Minneapolis: University of Minnesota Press, 1965. 202 pp. The author feels that women possess a clearer sensitivity toward the American heritage in their writings. Examples of such women writers include Sarah Orne Jewett, Edith Wharton, Ellen Glasgow, Willa Cather, Katherine Anne Porter, Carson McCullers, and Mary McCarthy.

2696. Austen, Jane. PRIDE AND PREJUDICE. New York: Harcourt, Brace and Jovanovich, 1962. Classic novel of English society and woman's place in it.

2697. ———. SENSE AND SENSIBILITY. New York: Harper and Row, 1961. A famous novel of feminine sensibility.

2698. Bald, Marjory Amelia. WOMEN WRITERS OF THE NINETEENTH CENTURY. Cambridge: Cambridge Univ. Press, 1923. 288 pp. Discussions of Jane Austen, the Brontës, Mrs. Elizabeth Gaskell, George Eliot, Elizabeth Barrett Browning, and Christina Rosetti.

2699. Barnes, Daniel R. "Faulkner's Miss Emily and Hawthorne's Old Maid," STUDIES IN SHORT FICTION, vol. 9 (Fall 1972), pp. 373-377. Critique of Faulkner's and Hawthorne's treatment of women in their literature.

2700. Baym, Nina. "Hawthorne's Women: The Tyranny of Social Myths," CENTENNIAL REVIEW, vol. 15 (Summer 1971), pp. 250-272. Discusses Hawthorne's concept that women are slaves in society.

2701. ———. "The Women of Cooper's Leatherstocking Tales," AMERICAN QUARTERLY, vol. 23 (Dec. 1971), pp. 696-709. Discusses Cooper's treatment of women in his books.

2702. Bazin, Nancy Topping. "Virginia Woolf's Quest for Equilibrium," MODERN LANGUAGE QUARTERLY, vol. 32 (Sept. 1971), pp. 305-319. Excellent critical review of Virginia Woolf's novels, especially A ROOM OF ONE'S OWN and MRS. DALLOWAY.

2703. Behn, Aphra. WORKS. Edited by Montague Summers. 6 vols. London: Heinemann, 1915. Complete collection of the works of Aphra Behn, the first woman in England to earn her living by writing.

2704. Benn, J. W. THE WOMAN'S VIEW: AN ANTHOLOGY OF PROSE PASSAGES ABOUT WOMEN. London: Routledge and Kegan Paul, 1967.

2705. Bennett, Margaret. ALICE IN WOMANLAND: OR THE FEMININE MISTAKE. Englewood Cliffs, N.J.: Prentice-Hall, 1967. A satire.

2706. Berger, John. "Ways of Seeing: Women," THE LISTENER, vol. 87 (Jan. 20, 1972), pp. 75-76. The meaning of feminine viewpoints as revealed in writings by women about women.

2707. Brooks, Gwendolyn. SELECTED POEMS. New York: Harper Torchbooks, 1963. By the black poet on being a black woman and other themes.

2708. Bruere, Martha. LAUGHING THEIR WAY: WOMEN'S HUMOR IN AMERICA. New York: Macmillan, 1934. 295 pp. Humor, cartoons, and an overview of American female authors' satirical writings over the past hundred years.

2709. Bullard, Edgar J. MARY CASSATT: OILS AND PASTELS. New York: Watson-Guptill, 1972. 87 pp. Biographic text supplemented with 32 full-color plates of one of America's foremost woman painters.

2710. Calzini, Raffaele. LA BELLA ITALIANA DA BOTTICELLI A SPADINI [The Italian Women of Botticelli and Spadini]. Milano: Editoriale Domus, 1945. 180 pp. Discussions of women in literature and art.

2711. Camden, Carroll. "Iago on Women," JOURNAL OF ENGLISH AND GERMANIC PHILOLOGY, vol. 48 (1949), pp. 57-71. A critical study of Shakespeare's Iago and his conception of women.

2712. Cody, John. AFTER GREAT PAIN: THE INNER LIFE OF EMILY DICKINSON. Cambridge: Harvard Univ. Press, 1971. 538 pp. Critical study of the writings of Emily Dickinson.

2713. Colby, Vineta. THE SINGULAR ANOMALY: WOMEN NOVELISTS OF THE NINETEENTH CENTURY. New York: New York Univ. Press, 1970. 313 pp.

2714. Cole, William, and Florett Robinson, eds. WOMEN ARE WONDERFUL! A HISTORY IN CARTOONS OF A HUNDRED YEARS WITH AMERICA'S MOST CONTROVERSIAL FIGURE. Boston: Houghton Mifflin, 1956. 196 pp. Collection of caricatures extending from the 1820's to the 1920's.

2715. Cooper, Clarissa Burnham. WOMEN POETS OF THE TWENTIETH CENTURY IN FRANCE: A CRITICAL BIBLIOGRAPHY. New York: Morningside Heights Press, 1943. 317 pp.

2716. Cornillon, Susan Koppelman. IMAGES OF WOMEN IN FICTION:
FEMININE PERSPECTIVES. Bowling Green, Ohio: Bowling Green
Popular Press, 1972. 400 pp. Discusses the differences between fictional
women and our real lives; women in fiction as nonhuman artifacts for
the hero to test himself against, and the woman as person becoming her
own sort of woman.

2717. Crozier, Alice. THE NOVELS OF HARRIETT BEECHER STOWE. New
York: Oxford Univ. Press, 1969. 235 pp. Exegetical study of UNCLE
TOM'S CABIN and other writings.

2718. de Beauvoir, Simone. THE WOMAN DESTROYED. New York: G. P.
Putnam's Sons, 1969. 254 pp. The story of a middle-aged woman bent
on self-destruction because of her inability to cope with her life. An
excellent key to understanding her later book, THE COMING OF AGE.

2719. Dow, Blanche Hinman. THE VARYING ATTITUDE TOWARD WOMEN
IN FRENCH LITERATURE OF THE FIFTEENTH CENTURY: THE
OPENING YEARS. New York: Institute of French Studies, 1936. 289
pp. Women in French literature; history and criticism.

2720. Dreiser, Theodore. SISTER CARRIE. New York: Modern Library, 1927.
557 pp. Classic American novel of a small-town girl who goes to the big
city and becomes a prostitute.

2721. Drinker, Sophie Lewis. MUSIC AND WOMEN: THE STORY OF WOMEN
IN THEIR RELATION TO MUSIC. New York: Coward-McCann, 1948.
323 pp.

2722. Driver, Beverly. "Arthur Schnitzler's Frau Berta Garlan: A Study in Form,"
GERMANIA REVIEW, vol. 46 (Nov. 1971), pp. 285-298. Critical study
of the German playwright's handling of women.

2723. Dunnigan, Alice E. "Early History of Negro Women in Journalism,"
NEGRO HISTORY BULLETIN, 1965, pp. 178-179; 193, 197.

2724. Edwards, Lee R., Mary Heath, and Lisa Baskin, eds. WOMAN: AN
ISSUE. Boston: Little, Brown, 1972. 299 pp. Collection of stories,
poems, and essays which explore what it means to be a woman.

2725. Eliot, George. MIDDLEMARCH. New York: Harcourt, Brace and Jovanovich, 1962. Probably her best novel; portrays a whole community and
has been compared with Flaubert's MADAME BOVARY because of its
realism, especially in probing feminine character and social situations
of provincial life.

2726. Elson, Arthur, and Everett E. Truette. WOMAN'S WORK IN MUSIC:
BEING AN ACCOUNT OF HER INFLUENCE ON THE ART, IN
ANCIENT AS WELL AS MODERN TIMES. Boston: Page, 1931. 301 pp.
Summary of compositions by women with estimates of their rank in
comparison with male composers.

2727. Euripides. THE TROJAN WOMEN. London: Oxford Univ. Press, 1915.
93 pp. A powerful tragedy about the siege of Troy and the consequent
fate of its women at the hands of their male conquerors. Also, see his
MEDEA AND ELECTRA, which present conflicts and struggles within
women in terms of psychological motivations that are amazingly modern.

2728. FEMALE ARTISTS PAST AND PRESENT. Berkeley: Women's History
Library, 1972. Northwestern Univ. Special Collection Library, Evanston,
Ill.

2729. Fernando, Lloyd. "Special Pleading and Art in 'Middlemarch': The Relation Between the Sexes," THE MODERN LANGUAGE REVIEW, vol. 67 (Jan. 1972), pp. 44-49. Critique of George Eliot's novel.

2730. Fiedler, Leslie. LOVE AND DEATH IN THE AMERICAN NOVEL. New York: Criterion Books, 1960, 1966. 603 pp. Brilliant literary study of American literature; Fiedler asks where is our ANNA KARENINA, PRIDE AND PREJUDICE, MADAME BOVARY, or VANITY FAIR.

2731. Fisher, Dorothy Canfield. THE HOMEMAKER. New York: Harcourt, Brace, 1924. 320 pp. Father and mother change roles in this shocking and amazingly perceptive novel written over 50 years ago.

2732. Flaubert, Gustave. MADAME BOVARY. New York: Oxford Univ. Press, 1949. 403 pp. One of the most famous French novels of a woman driven by the tension between her real life and the romantic ideal—a tension that exists both in her own nature and in the social structure of her time.

2733. Foster, Jeannette H. SEX VARIANT WOMEN IN LITERATURE: A HISTORICAL AND QUANTITATIVE SURVEY. New York: Vantage Press, 1956. 412 pp.

2734. Gasiorowska, Xenia. WOMEN IN SOVIET FICTION, 1917-1964. Madison: Univ. of Wisconsin Press, 1968. 288 pp. History and criticism of Soviet literature.

2735. Glasgow, Ellen. THEY STOOPED TO FOLLY: A COMEDY OF MORALS. Garden City, N.Y.: Doubleday, 1929, 1938. 351 pp. Brilliant novel which serves as a study of the revolution in the moral codes governing feminine conduct in America.

2736. Glincher, Arnold B. LOUISE NEVELSON. New York: Praeger, 1972. Color and black-and-white illustrations of major works of one of America's greatest living woman sculptors. Selection of statements by the artist herself and about her art.

2737. Goldfarb, Russell M. SEXUAL REPRESSION AND VICTORIAN LITERATURE. Philadelphia: Bucknell Univ. Press, 1970. 222 pp. Critical study of Victorian attitudes in literature.

2738. Goulianos, Joan, ed. BY A WOMAN WRITT: LITERATURE FROM SIX CENTURIES BY AND ABOUT WOMEN. Indianapolis: Bobbs-Merrill, 1972. Anthology of basic readings. The works of earlier authors are more literary curiosities than literature, but some remarkable eighteenth-century women writers (Mary Shelley and Harriet Martineau) are included, as are writings by Kate Chopin and Dorothy Richardson from our own century.

2739. Gross, George C. "Mary Cowden Clarke, 'The Girlhood of Shakespeare's Heroines,' and the Sex Education of Victorian Women," VICTORIAN STUDIES, vol. 16 (Sept. 1972), pp. 37-58. Critique of Mary C. Clarke's portrayal of Victorian women and her attitude that Shakespeare was the male author who best understood women. Exaggerations and omissions from Shakespeare's views of women are also discussed.

2740. Gulliver, Lucile. LOUISA MAY ALCOTT: A BIBLIOGRAPHY. Boston: Little, Brown, 1932. Excellent source book of references and critical works dealing with this important American writer.

2741. Gwyn, Sandra. WOMEN IN THE ARTS IN CANADA. Ottowa Royal Commission on the Status of Women in Canada, 1971. The effects of women in Canadian arts, and why Canadian women, now and in the past, have been more successful in the arts than in any other competitive field.

2742. Hardy, Barbara. THE NOVELS OF GEORGE ELIOT: A STUDY IN FORM. London: Univ. of London, Athlone Press, 1959. 242 pp. Critical essays on ADAM BEDE, THE EGOISTS, SILAS MARNER, MIDDLE-MARCH, ROMOLA, THE MILL ON THE FLOSS, and other novels.

2743. Heilbrun, Carolyn G. TOWARD A RECOGNITION OF ANDROGYNY. New York: Knopf, 1972. Lays stress on sexual polarization in literature, i.e., the woman hero becoming the embodiment of the male writer's artistic vision. Discusses the writings of Shaw, Lawrence, Forster, Shakespeare, Malamud, Mailer, and Bellow, among others.

2744. Heller, Otto. "Women Writers of the 19th Century." Pp. 231-295 in O. Heller, STUDIES IN MODERN GERMAN LITERATURE. Freeport, N.Y.: Books for Libraries, 1967. Reprint, 1905 edition.

2745. Hess, Thomas B., and Linda Nochlin, eds. WOMAN AS SEX OBJECT. New York: Newsweek Books, 1972. 257 pp. Erotic elements of the female in the eighteenth, nineteenth, and twentieth centuries.

2746. Hirvonen, K. MATRIARCHAL SURVIVALS AND CERTAIN TRENDS IN HOMER'S FEMALE CHARACTERS. Helsinki: Soumailarnen Tiedecka-temia, 1968. 223 pp. The feminine characterizations in Homeric literature.

2747. Howard, Pamela. "MS. and the Journalism of Women's Lib," SATURDAY REVIEW, vol. 50 (Jan. 8, 1972), pp. 43-54. A study of the awareness which has been generated among the new women in America by an important shaper of media in American journalism.

2748. Howells, William Dean. HEROINES OF FICTION. 2 vols. New York: Harper, 1901. Women in literature and art.

2749. Hsia, C. T. "Residual Femininity: Women in Chinese Communist Fiction," CHINA QUARTERLY, vol. 13 (Jan.-Mar., 1963), pp. 158-179. Women characters from short stories show their adjustment of their feminine instincts and interests to the jealous demands of party and state; a year by year survey.

2750. Ibsen, Henrik. A DOLL'S HOUSE. Many editions available. This play, first published in 1879, is a very early pro-feminist drama of a woman who asserts her independence by finally leaving her husband. His other plays, such as GHOSTS, ROSMERSHOLM, and HEDDA GABLER, all turn to the theme of the individualism of women whose conflicts arise from the inconsistency of their natures with their desires.

2751. James, Henry. PORTRAIT OF A LADY. Numerous editions. First published in 1881, it is the story of Isabel Archer, an American girl of intelligence, who, given free choice to live her life as she will, makes an error and must in the end pay for it. The inner life of the heroine is portrayed with great psychological skill.

2752. Jameson, Anna Brownell. CHARACTERISTICS OF WOMEN: MORAL, POETICAL, AND HISTORICAL. New York: AMS Press, 1967. 391 pp. Essays on Shakespeare's female characters.

2753. Jessup, Josephine L. THE FAITH OF OUR FEMINISTS. New York: Biblo and Tannen, 1965. 128 pp. Biographical and critical studies of Edith Wharton, Ellen Glasgow, and Willa Cather, and of the roles of women as depicted in their novels.

2754. Kavanagh, Julia. ENGLISH WOMEN OF LETTERS. 2 vols. London: Hurst and Blackett, 1863. Biographical and critical essays on Mrs. Radcliffe and Jane Austen, among others.

2755. Kelly, Robert Gordon. "Mother was a Lady: Strategy and Order in Selected American Children's Periodicals, 1865-1890," ERIC, 1972. 321 pp. Examines children's books published during the Gilded Age, revealing the tensions and anxieties felt by social groups organized by a particular social ideal, namely, the traditional images of the gentleman and lady. Dissertation, Univ. of Iowa, 1970.

2756. Kramer, Marjorie. "Some Thoughts on Feminist Art," WOMEN AND ART (Winter 1971), p. 6.

2757. Kroeber, Karl. STYLES IN FICTIONAL STRUCTURE: THE ART OF JANE AUSTEN, CHARLOTTE BRONTE, GEORGE ELIOT. Princeton, N.J.: Princeton Univ. Press, 1971. 282 pp. Exegetical essays.

2758. Kushen, Betty. "Love's Martyrs: The SCARLETT LETTER as Secular Cross," LITERATURE AND PSYCHOLOGY, vol. 22, no. 3 (1972), pp. 109-120.

2759. Laffin, Garry S. "Muriel Spark's Portrait of the Artist as a Young Girl," RENASCENCE, vol. 24 (Summer 1972), pp. 213-223. Critical study of the writings of the noted British novelist.

2760. Lawrence, Margaret. THE SCHOOL OF FEMININITY: A BOOK FOR AND ABOUT WOMEN AS THEY ARE INTERPRETED THROUGH FEMININE WRITERS YESTERDAY AND TODAY. Port Washington, N.Y.: Kennikat Press, 1966. 382 pp.

2761. Lessing, Doris. THE GOLDEN NOTEBOOK. New York: Ballantine Books, 1962. Brilliant and disturbing novel about a woman writer in postwar London, with cleverly developed themes on politics, love, and independence interwoven.

2762. Lippard, Lucy R. "Sexual Politics, Art Style," ART IN AMERICA, vol. 59 (Sept.-Oct. 1971), pp. 19-20. Takes a look at discrimination against women in the art world.

2763. Livesay, Dorothy, ed. 40 WOMEN POETS OF CANADA. Montreal: Ingluvin Publications, 1971. 141 pp.

2764. Lowe, A. M. "Emma Bovary: A Modern Arachne," FRENCH STUDIES, vol. 26 (Jan. 1972), pp. 30-41. Critical study of Flaubert's famous woman character.

2765. MacCarthy, Bridget G. WOMEN WRITERS: THEIR CONTRIBUTION TO THE ENGLISH NOVEL, 1621-1744. Cork, Ireland: Cork Univ. Press, 1946. 288 pp. Considers those forces that affected women writers during the sixteenth, seventeenth, and eighteenth centuries, with excellent evaluations of the works of the Countess of Pembroke, the Duchess of Newcastle, Aphra Behn, Sarah Fielding, and others.

2766. ———. THE LATER WOMEN NOVELISTS, 1744-1818. Cork, Ireland: Cork Univ. Press, 1947. 296 pp. Discusses the Oriental novel, the novel of sentiment and sensibility, the domestic novels of Fanny Burney, the Gothic novels of Mrs. Shelley, and the novels of Jane Austen.

2767. McManmon, John J. "Phalli Non Erecti, Feminae Non Fecundatae, Et Entra Neutra," ANTIGIONE REVIEW, vol. 2 (Summer 1971), pp. 62-72. Short review of Pope's poem THE RAPE OF THE LOCK, criticizing the sexual identity in men and women.

2768. Malkin, Michael R. "The Dramatic Function of Matricide in the Greek Electra Plays," STUDIES IN THE HUMANITIES, vol. 3 (Oct. 1972), pp. 22-24.

2769. Manley, Seon, and Susan Belcher. O, THOSE EXTRAORDINARY WO-MEN! OR THE JOYS OF LITERARY LIB. Philadelphia: Chilton Press, 1972. 300 pp. Study of nineteenth- and early twentieth-century literary women, American, British, and European, who struggled to find fulfil-ment in their restricted areas.

2770. Mapes, Victor. DUSE AND THE FRENCH. New York: Benjamin Blom, 1969. 56 pp. Reprint, 1898 edition. Firsthand account of the furor that developed when Eleanora Duse invaded Sarah Bernhardt's Paris.

2771. Marder, Herbert. FEMINISM AND ART: A STUDY OF VIRGINIA WOOLF. Chicago: Univ. of Chicago Press, 1972. Excellent study of Virginia Woolf's feminist viewpoint in her novels.

2772. Mare, Margaret, and Alicia C. Percival. VICTORIAN BEST-SELLER: THE WORLD OF CHARLOTTE M. YONGE, 1823-1901. London: Harrap, 1947. 292 pp. Popular British writer of historical romances whose literary work and religious zeal formed her life.

2773. Masefield, Muriel Agnes. WOMEN NOVELISTS, FROM FANNY BURNEY TO GEORGE ELIOT. London: Nicolson and Watson, 1934. 224 pp. Literary criticism.

2774. Merriam, Eve. THE DOUBLE BED FROM THE FEMININE SIDE. New York: Marzani and Munsell, 1960. 160 pp. Feminist poems by one of the early leaders in the contemporary movement.

2775. ———. AFTER NORA SLAMMED THE DOOR. New York: World, 1964. 236 pp. Her chapter "Sex and Semantics" is worth reading.

2776. Mews, Hazel. FRAIL VESSELS: WOMAN'S ROLE IN WOMEN'S NOVELS FROM FANNY BURNEY TO GEORGE ELIOT. London: Athlone, Press, 1969. 209 pp.

2777. Moers, Ellen. "Women's Lit: Profession and Tradition," THE COLUMBIA FORUM, vol. 1 (Fall 1972), pp. 27-34.

2778. ———. "Women's Liberator," NEW YORK REVIEW OF BOOKS, vol. 18 (Feb. 10, 1972), pp. 27-31. Discusses Dorothy Richardson's novels as a vehicle for social reform in attacking sexual mores from an aggressive, feminist viewpoint.

2779. Moravia, Alberto. "Emma Unglued (Madame Bovary)," SATURDAY REVIEW, vol. 55 (Dec. 2, 1972), pp. 53-55.

2780. Morton, Frederick W., compiler. WOMAN IN EPIGRAM: FLASHES OF WIT, WISDOM, AND SATIRE FROM THE WORLD'S LITERATURE. Chicago: McClurg, 1898. 239 pp.

2781. Mull, Donald. "Freedom and Judgment: the Autonomy of Action in THE PORTRAIT OF A LADY," ARIZONA QUARTERLY, vol. 17 (Summer 1972), pp. 124-132. Critical study of James's heroine, Isabel Archer, and of her defense of the integrity of her spiritual self, a major theme of the novel.

2782. Murtaugh, Daniel M. "Women and Geoffrey Chaucer," ENGLISH LITER-ARY HISTORY (Johns Hopkins Univ.), vol. 38 (Dec. 1971), pp. 473-492. Study of the Canterbury Tales as transcending the division between the antifeminist and the courtly love traditions.

2783. Needham, Eleanor. ENGLISH FEMALE ARTISTS. 2 vols. London: Tinsley Brothers, 1876. Biographical and critical studies.

2784. Nemser, Cindy. "Critics and Women's Art," WOMEN AND ART, (Winter 1971), pp. 1+.

2785. ———. "Women Artists and the Whitney Museum," WOMEN AND ART, (Winter 1971), p. 6.

2786. Papashvily, Helen Waite. ALL THE HAPPY ENDINGS: A STUDY OF THE DOMESTIC NOVEL IN AMERICA, THE WOMEN WHO WROTE AND THE WOMEN WHO READ IT, IN THE NINETEENTH CENTURY. New York: Harper, 1956. 231 pp.

2787. Paradis, Suzanne. FEMME FICTIVE, FEMME REELLE. Montreal: Editions Garneau, 1966. Explores the consciousness of the Quebec woman by analyzing female characters in novels written by Quebec women writers.

2788. Peel, Maria. "Women's Lib in Lit," BOOKS AND BOOKMEN, vol. 17 (Nov. 1971), pp. 14-17.

2789. Phillips, James E. "The Background of Spenser's Attitude Toward Women Rulers," HUNTINGTON LIBRARY QUARTERLY, vol. 5 (1941), pp. 5-32. A critical study of Edmund Spenser's novels, especially THE FAERIE QUEENE.

2790. Pratt, Annis. "Women and Nature in Modern Fiction," CONTEMPORARY LITERATURE, vol. 13 (Aug. 1972), pp. 476-490.

2791. Reed, Evelyn. "Feminism and 'The Female Eunuch,' " INTERNATIONAL SOCIALIST REVIEW, vol. 32 (July-Aug. 1971), pp. 10-13+. Critical review of Germaine Greer's book.

2792. Revard, Stella. "Yeats, Mallarmé and the Archetypal Feminine," PAPERS ON LANGUAGE AND LITERATURE, vol. 8 (Fall 1972 Supplement), pp. 112-127.

2793. Richards, Marion K. ELLEN GLASGOW'S DEVELOPMENT AS A NOVELIST. New York: Humanities Press, 1971. 203 pp.

2794. Rogers, Katherine M. THE TROUBLESOME HELPMATE: A HISTORY OF MISOGYNY IN LITERATURE. Seattle: Univ. of Washington Press, 1968. 288 pp. Excellent literary study of women hatred in literature.

2795. Sachs, Hannelore. THE RENAISSANCE WOMAN. Translated from German by Marianne Herzfeld. New York: McGraw-Hill, 1971. 60 pp. Women in art during the Renaissance.

2796. Sato, Toshihiko. "Ibsen and Emancipation of Women in Japan," ORIENT/WEST MAGAZINE, vol. 9 (Sept.-Oct. 1964), pp. 73-77. Critical study of the influence of Ibsen on the feminist movement in Japan.

2797. Schneiderman, Beth K. BY AND ABOUT WOMEN: AN ANTHOLOGY OF SHORT FICTION. New York: Harcourt, Brace and Jovanovich, 1973. 352 pp. Twenty short stories sensitively examining what it means to to be a woman. Stories arranged around such topics as girlhood, marriage, fulfillment, and age. Includes a bibliography.

2798. Schopenhauer, Arthur. "Of Women." Pp. 198-215 in Arthur Schopenhauer, THE PESSIMIST'S HANDBOOK: A COLLECTION OF POPULAR ESSAYS. Lincoln: Univ. of Nebraska Press, 1964. Woman is by nature meant to obey because she needs a lord and master. An antifeminist essay, demonstrated by Schopenhauer's remark: " . . . the institution of the lady is a fundamental defect in our social scheme, and this defect, proceeding from the very heart of it, must spread its baneful influence in all directions."

2799. Schwieger-Lerchenfeld, Amand, Freiherr von. DIE FRAUEN DES ORIENTS IN DER GESCHICHTE, IN DER DICHTUNG UND IM

LEBEN [Women of the Orient in History, in Poetry, and in Life]. Vienna and Leipsig: A. Hartleben, 1904. 792 pp.

2800. Seidenberg, Robert. MARRIAGE IN LIFE AND LITERATURE. New York: Philosophical Library, 1970. 307 pp.

2801. Showalter, Elaine, ed. WOMEN'S LIBERATION AND LITERATURE. New York: Harcourt, Brace and Jovanovich, 1970.

2802. Sloman, Judith. "The Female Quixote as a Recurrent Character Type in 18th Century Novels and Plays," SAMUEL JOHNSON SOCIETY OF THE NORTHWEST (Calgary, Alberta, Canada), Oct. 1971, n.p.

2803. Smith, Henry Nash. VIRGIN LAND: THE AMERICAN WEST AS SYMBOL AND MYTH. New York: Random House (Vintage Books), 1950. 305 pp. Chapter 10, "The Dime Novel Heroine," pp. 126-135, has some interesting comments about phallic heroines in the popular culture of America. The works of many Victorian medical men have similar fantasies.

2804. Sparrow, Walter Shaw. WOMEN PAINTERS OF THE WORLD. London: Hodder and Stoughton, 1905. 332 pp.

2805. Sprague, Rosemary. IMAGINARY GARDENS: A STUDY OF FIVE AMERICAN POETS. Philadelphia: Chilton Press, 1969. 237 pp. The poetry of five women poets: Emily Dickinson, Amy Lowell, Sara Teasdale, Edna St. Vincent Millay, and Marianne Moore.

2806. Strindberg, August. GETTING MARRIED. Translated and edited by Mary Sandbach. New York: Viking Press, 1973. Thirty stories about the joys and sorrows of married life, the delights of sex, and the cruel effects of sexual repression, by a male liberationist who believed men's and women's equality were inextricably linked.

2807. Swan, Helena. GIRLS' CHRISTIAN NAMES: THEIR HISTORY, MEANING AND ASSOCIATION. London: Swan Sonnerschein, 1900. 515 pp. Unique volume tracing the origin, etymology, and historical and literary connotations of girls' names. Excellent for students of literature, mythology, religion, and history as a reference source.

2808. Thomson, Patricia. THE VICTORIAN HEROINE, A CHANGING IDEAL, 1837-1873. London and New York: Oxford Univ. Press, 1956. 178 pp. Critical study of women in British fiction in the nineteenth century.

2809. Todd, Robert E. "The Magna Mater Archetype in THE SCARLET LETTER," NEW ENGLAND QUARTERLY, vol. 45 (Sept. 1972), pp. 421-429.

2810. Tolstoy, Leo. ANNA KARENINA. New York: Random House (Modern Library Edition), 1947. A slice of nineteenth century Russian life, reflecting a conflict in the destructive power of love. Anna openly defies the established code of marriage, and her tragedy is still universal and modern.

2811. Trilling, Diana. "The Image of Women in Contemporary Literature." In THE WOMAN IN AMERICA, edited by Jay Lifton. Boston: Houghton Mifflin, 1965. pp. 52-71.

2812. Tyler, Parker. SEX, PSYCHE ETCETERA IN THE FILM. Baltimore: Penguin Books, 1971.

2813. Upton, George Putnam. WOMEN IN MUSIC. London: S. Paul, 1909. 221 pp. A list of prominent female composers during the past three centuries with critical evaluations of their works.

2814. Van Doren, Dorothy, ed. THE LOST ART: LETTERS OF SEVEN FAMOUS WOMEN. New York: Coward-McCann, 1929. 346 pp. Included are the letters of Lady Mary Wortley Montague, Abigail Adams, Mary Wollstonecraft, Jane Austen, Jane Welsh Carlyle, Margaret Fuller, and Charlotte Brontë.

2815. Violette, Augusta Genevieve. ECONOMIC FEMINISM IN AMERICAN LITERATURE PRIOR TO 1848. Orono, Maine: Univ. of Maine, 1925. 114 pp.

2816. Wade, Elizabeth. ANNE BRADSTREET: THE TENTH MUSE. London and New York: Oxford Univ. Press, 1972. 410 pp. Biographical and critical study of one of America's earliest poets.

2817. Wasserstrom, William. HEIRESS OF ALL THE AGES: SEX AND SENTIMENT IN THE GENTEEL TRADITION. Minneapolis: Univ. of Minnesota Press, 1959. 157 pp. Critical study of women in American literature.

2818. Waters, Clara Erskine Clement. WOMEN IN THE FINE ARTS FROM THE 7TH CENTURY B.C. TO THE 20TH CENTURY A.D. Boston: Houghton Mifflin, 1904. 395 pp. Art history with short biographies.

2819. Wharton, Edith. THE CUSTOM OF THE COUNTRY. New York: Charles Scribner's Sons, 1913. 594 pp. Study of an American woman counterpart to the masculine spirit of capitalist expansion, Undine Spragg.

2820. ———. THE HOUSE OF MIRTH. New York: Charles Scribner's Sons, 1933. 532 pp. Another study of a money-driven woman, Lily Bart. This book also discusses class limits, income limits, and race limits in which marriage becomes a way of finding a means of support and getting status within society.

2821. Wheatley, Phillis. POEMS OF PHILLIS WHEATLEY. Edited by Julian D. Mason. Chapel Hill: Univ. of North Carolina Press, 1966. 113 pp. Selections of one of America's early poets, with critical analyses.

2822. Willis, Eola. "The First Woman Painter in America," INTERNATIONAL STUDIO, (July 1927), pp. 13-20.

2823. Wood, Ann Douglas. "Mrs. Sigourney and the Sensibility of the Inner Space," NEW ENGLAND QUARTERLY, vol. 45 (June 1972), pp. 163-181. The writings of Mrs. Lydia H. Sigourney, popular pre-Civil War poet, offer important insights into the experience of nineteenth century women. She created a public image of the perfect wife and mother, and her writings consistently invoked the feminine virtues of domesticity, passivity, modesty, and dependence.

2824. Woolf, Virginia. A ROOM OF ONE'S OWN. New York: Harcourt, 1929. 199 pp. A brilliant novel conveying the longing, frustration, and rage of every woman and of the female creative writer.

2825. Wright, Celeste Turner. "The Amazons in Elizabethan Literature," STUDIES IN PHILOLOGY, vol. 37, no. 3 (1940), pp. 433-456. The Elizabethans regarded Amazons as picturesque ornaments to a pageant or a romance, but to their social system they were a dangerous example of unwomanly conduct and a violation of the traditional order.

2826. Wright, Frederick Adam. FEMINISM IN GREEK LITERATURE FROM HOMER TO ARISTOTLE. London: G. Routledge, 1923. 222 pp.

2827. Wylie, Philip. GENERATION OF VIPERS. New York: Rinehart, 1955. A study of "Mom-ism" in American society.

VIII. WOMEN IN PSYCHOLOGY

In this section we have tried to integrate very different experimental and theoretical articles dealing with the "psychology of women." What many people see in the personalities of women as dependence, passivity, and lack of self-esteem are, in many instances, the "psychological variables" that appear to differentiate women from men. We have examined much of the literature and have tried to select some of the traditional psychoanalytic studies. Some emphasize sex differences, but most of the following books and articles explore the psychological areas of women's lives, their egos, motives, goals, and personality qualities—in short, the psychological dynamics of today's woman. Most of the selections have been chosen for their contributions to the understanding of femaleness, and for the reason that they stress supposed traits of empathy, nurturance, and sensitivity.

"Das Ewig-Weibliche
Zieht uns hinan."

The Eternal-Feminine
Draws us upwards.
        —FAUST

2828. Adams, Grace. "Women Don't Like Themselves: Why Women Refuse to Be Led By Women," NORTH AMERICAN REVIEW, vol. 248 (Summer 1939), pp. 288-295. One of the early articles delving into the subject of women's self-esteem.

2829. Allport, Gordon. THE NATURE OF PREJUDICE. Garden City, N.Y.: Doubleday, 1958. 496 pp. A brief section on sex differences and concomitant stereotypes.

2830. Amir, Menachem. PATTERNS OF FORCIBLE RAPE. Chicago: Univ. of Chicago Press, 1971. 394 pp. A comprehensive work delving into all facets of rape, with considerations of various male and female personality characteristics of both victim and offender.

2831. Bachtold, Louise M., and Emmy E. Werner. "Personality Profiles of Women Psychologists: Three Generations," DEVELOPMENTAL PSYCHOLOGY, vol. 5 (Sept. 1971), pp. 273-278.

2832. Bardwick, Judith. PSYCHOLOGY OF WOMEN. New York: Harper and Row, 1971. 242 pp. Integrates psychological and medical data to explain the origin and development of sex differences and culturally defined roles in America. Excellent bibliography.

2833. Bardwick, Judith, Elizabeth Douvan, Matina S. Horner, and David L. Gutmann. FEMININE PERSONALITY AND CONFLICT. Belmont, Calif.: Brooks/Cole, 1973. 102 pp. Four experts trace aspects of feminine self-esteem, its origin, biological base, development, and vulnerability to threat and attack from a variety of sources, ranging from hormones to the social structure.

2834. Barnett, C. R., P. H. Leiderman, R. Grobstein, and M. Klaus. "Neonatal Separation: The Maternal Side of Interactional Deprivation," PEDIATRICS, vol. 45, no. 2 (1970), pp. 197-205.

2835. Benedek, Therese. STUDIES IN PSYCHOSOMATIC MEDICINE: PSYCHOSEXUAL FUNCTIONS IN WOMEN. New York: Ronald Press, 1952. Estimations of hormone production from psychoanalysis.

2836. Bennett, Edward M., and Larry R. Cohen. "Men and Women: Personality Patterns and Contrasts," GENETIC PSYCHOLOGICAL MONO-GRAPHS, vol. 59 (1959), pp. 101-155.
2837. Bosselman, Beulah Chamberlin. "Castration Anxiety and Phallus Envy: A Reformulation," PSYCHIATRIC QUARTERLY, vol. 34 (1960), pp. 252-259. Observations of anatomical difference in girls which induces feelings such as the female castration complex, which stimulates the Oedipus complex; a major motivating factor throughout feminine development.
2838. Brandon, Sydney. "Psychiatric Illness in Women," NURSING MIRROR, Jan. 21, 1972, pp. 17-18. Discusses the reasons more women need psychiatric help.
2839. Brody, Sylvia. PATTERNS OF MOTHERING: MATERNAL INFLU-ENCE DURING INFANCY. New York: International Universities Press, 1956. 446 pp.
2840. Brown, Daniel G. "Sex-Role Development in a Changing Culture," PSYCHOLOGICAL BULLETIN, vol. 55, no. 4 (1958), pp. 232-242.
2841. Carlson, Rae. "Understanding Women: Implications for Personality Theory and Research," JOURNAL OF SOCIAL ISSUES, vol. 28, no. 2 (1972), pp. 17-32. Urges a change in the present masculine psychological view of human nature, especially in research in feminine psychology.
2842. Chassequet-Smirgel, Janine. FEMALE SEXUALITY. Ann Arbor: Univ. of Michigan Press, 1970. Excellent study which may compare with Havelock Ellis's interpretations.
2843. Chesler, Phyllis. "Women as Psychiatric and Psychotherapeutic Patients," JOURNAL OF MARRIAGE AND THE FAMILY, vol. 33 (Nov. 1971), pp. 746-759.
2844. Coffin, Patricia. 1-2-3-4-5-6: HOW TO UNDERSTAND AND ENJOY THE YEARS THAT COUNT. New York: Macmillan, 1972. 160 pp. More in the area of child development, but an interesting record of the development of the author's daughter from ages 1 to 6 years, with notes by the daughter, now 18.
2845. Cohen, M. B. "Personal Identity and Sexual Identity," PSYCHIATRY, vol. 29 (1966), p. 1. Short article on male and female sexuality.
2846. Collins, Randall. "A Conflict Theory of Sexual Stratification," SOCIAL PROBLEMS, vol. 19 (Summer 1971), pp. 2-21. Basing his theory on Freudian and Weberian perspectives, the author maintains that there is a system of sexual stratification distinct from that based on economic, political, or status group position.
2847. Coppen, A., and N. Kessel. "Menstruation and Personality," BRITISH JOURNAL OF PSYCHIATRY, vol. 109 (1963), pp. 711-712.
2848. Deutsch, Helene. THE PSYCHOLOGY OF WOMEN: A PSYCHO-ANALYTIC INTERPRETATION. 2 vols. New York: Grune and Stratton, 1944. Psychological chronologue covering feminine psychosexual development from prepuberty to menstruation. Excellent discussions of female sexuality, homosexuality, and other sexually deviant patterns.
2849. Douvan, E., and J. Adelson. THE ADOLESCENT EXPERIENCE. New York: Wiley, 1966. 471 pp. Contains a chapter specifically devoted to adolescent feminine development.
2850. Earnest, Marion R. "Criminal Self-Conceptions of Female Offenders," THE WISCONSIN SOCIOLOGIST, Fall-Winter 1971, pp. 98-105. Ex-

plores and explains the presence or absence of a criminal self-conception among adult female offenders in a state institution.

2851. Ellis, Havelock. MAN AND WOMAN: A STUDY OF SECONDARY AND TERTIARY SEXUAL CHARACTERS. Boston: Houghton Mifflin, 1929. 495 pp. Contains the most extensive analysis of secondary and tertiary sex characteristics in men and women ever published.

2852. Entwisle, Doris, and Ellen Greenberger. "A Survey of Cognitive Styles in Maryland Ninth Graders: Four Views of Women's Roles," CENTER FOR THE STUDY OF SOCIAL ORGANIZATION OF SCHOOLS, Johns Hopkins University, report no. 89, 1970.

2853. Factor, Morris. "A Woman's Psychological Reaction to Attempted Rape," PSYCHOANALYTICAL QUARTERLY, vol. 53 (1954), pp. 243-244.

2854. Fleck, Stephen. "Some Psychiatric Aspects of Abortion," JOURNAL OF NERVOUS AND MENTAL DISEASES, vol. 151, no. 1 (July 1970), pp. 44-50.

2855. Frank, K., and E. Rosen. "A Projective Test of Masculinity and Femininity," JOURNAL OF CONSULTING PSYCHOLOGY, vol. 13 4 (Aug. 1949), pp. 247-256.

2856. French, E. G., and Gerald S. Lesser. "Some Characteristics of the Achievement Motive in Women," JOURNAL OF ABNORMAL AND SOCIAL PSYCHOLOGY, vol. 68 (1964), pp. 119-128.

2857. Freud, Sigmund. THREE ESSAYS ON THE THEORY OF SEXUALITY. New York: Basic Books, 1963. 130 pp. The differences between men and women, as seen within the psychoanalytic framework, are discussed, along with female erotogenic zones.

2858. –––. THE PSYCHOLOGY OF WOMEN: NEW INTRODUCTORY LECTURES ON PSYCHOANALYSIS. New York: Norton, 1933.

2859. –––. "Some Psychological Consequences of the Anatomical Distinction Between the Sexes," INTERNATIONAL JOURNAL OF PSYCHO-ANALYSIS, vol. 8 (1927), pp. 133-142. Deals with female penis envy, the Oedipal and Electra complexes.

2860. Glass, George S. "Psychiatric Emergency Related to the Menstrual Cycle," AMERICAN JOURNAL OF PSYCHIATRY, vol. 128 (Dec. 1971), pp. 705-711.

2861. Goldberg, Phillip. "Are Women Prejudiced Against Women?" TRANS-ACTION, (April 1968), pp. 28-30. His research indicates that women are prejudiced negatively against the intellectual attainments of other women, indicating that they accept the dominant social view of higher education as a masculine preserve.

2862. Grier, William H., and Price M. Cobbs. BLACK RAGE. New York: Basic Books, 1968. 179 pp. Good discussion of psychological effects of white racism on black women today.

2863. Hanford, J. M. "Pregnancy as a State of Conflict," PSYCHOLOGICAL REPORTS, vol. 22, no. 3, pt. 2 (June 1968), pp. 1313-1342.

2864. Harper, Juliet F., and John K. Collins. "The Effects of Early or Late Maturation on the Prestige of the Adolescent Girl," AUSTRALIAN AND NEW ZEALAND JOURNAL OF SOCIOLOGY, vol. 8, (June 1972), pp. 83-88. Study of how maturational rates interact with a broad complex of variables more important than prestige in determining social acceptance during adolescence.

2865. Heathers, G. "Emotional Dependence and Independence in a Physical Threat Situation," CHILD DEVELOPMENT, vol. 24 (1953), pp. 169-179. This study found evidence contrary to the stereotypical belief that girls are more fearful than boys in a physical threat situation.

2866. Herzberg, B., and A. Coppen. "Changes in Psychological Symptoms in Women Taking Oral Contraceptives," BRITISH JOURNAL OF PSYCHIATRY, vol. 116 (1970), pp. 161-164.

2867. Horner, Matina. "Woman's Will to Fail," PSYCHOLOGY TODAY, (Nov. 1969). pp. 36-38, 62. A take-off on Alfred Adler's "Will to Succeed." Women are threatened by success because outstanding achievement (academically or otherwise) is consciously or unconsciously equated with a loss of femininity and may lead to social rejection.

2868. Horney, Karen. FEMININE PSYCHOLOGY. New York: Norton, 1967. 269 pp. The author posits the theory that women are in fact envious of male attributes and the social and economic concomitants of male status.

2869. ———. "On the Genesis of the Castration Complex in Women," INTERNATIONAL JOURNAL OF PSYCHOANALYSIS, vol. 5 (1924), pp. 50-65. The phallocentric viewpoint of classical analysis.

2870. ———. "The Flight From Womanhood," JOURNAL OF PSYCHO-ANALYSIS, vol. 7 (1926), pp. 324-339. The female half of the race is not content with its sex because this is a man's world; therefore, their "motives for flight into male roles are later reinforced socially by the actual subordination of women."

2871. Jacobs, T. J., and E. Charles. "Correlation of Psychiatric Symptomatology and the Menstrual Cycle in an Outpatient Population," AMERICAN JOURNAL OF PSYCHIATRY, vol. 126 (1970), pp. 1504-1508.

2872. Jahoda, Marie, and Joan Havel. "Psychological Problems of Women in Different Social Roles," EDUCATIONAL RECORD, vol. 36 (Oct. 1955), pp. 325-335.

2873. Jarvis, Edward. "Of the Comparative Liability of Males and Females to Insanity, and Their Comparative Curability and Mortality When Insane," AMERICAN JOURNAL OF INSANITY, vol. 7 (1850), p. 158. The author feels that women are more prone to insanity.

2874. Joesting, Joan. "Comparison of Women's Liberation Members with Their Non-member Peers," PSYCHOLOGICAL REPORTS, vol. 29 no. 3, part 2 (Dec. 1971), pp. 1291-1294.

2875. Joesting, Joan, and Robert Joesting. "Future Problems of Gifted Girls," GIFTED CHILD QUARTERLY, vol. 14, no. 2 (1970), pp. 82-90.

2876. Johnson, Arthur. "Roundtable: The Significance of Extra-Marital Sex Relations," MEDICAL ASPECTS OF HUMAN SEXUALITY, vol. 3, no. 10 (1969), p. 33+.

2877. Johnson, Charles D., and John Gormly. "Academic Cheating: The Contribution of Sex, Personality, and Situational Variables," DEVELOPMENTAL PSYCHOLOGY, vol. 6 (March 1972), pp. 320-325.

2878. Jung, Carl G. ARCHETYPES AND THE COLLECTIVE UNCONSCIOUS. Princeton: Princeton Univ. Press, 1968. 461 pp. Articles by Jung and Kerenyi on the mother and kore-archetypes. See especially pp. 75-112 on mother archetypes and other interpretations of "dream" figures and representations. Excellent bibliography.

2879. Kagan, J., and H. A. Moss. BIRTH TO MATURITY: A STUDY IN PSYCHOLOGICAL DEVELOPMENT. New York: Wiley, 1962. 381 pp. Study of basic differences between men and women from a psycho-sexual-social development viewpoint, with predictions provided for eventual adult sexual behavior based upon male and female adolescent sexual patterns.

2880. Kirkpatrick, C. "Inconsistency in Attitudinal Behavior With Special Reference to Attitudes Toward Feminism," JOURNAL OF APPLIED PSYCHOLOGY, vol. 20 (1936 annual). pp. 535-552.

2881. Kitay, P. M. "A Comparison of the Sexes in Their Attitudes and Beliefs About Women," SOCIOMETRY, vol. 14 (1940 annual, pp. 399-407.

2882. Konopka, G. ADOLESCENT GIRLS IN CONFLICT. Englewood Cliffs, N.J.: Prentice-Hall, 1966. 177 pp. Study of the social and cultural factors in female delinquency. A chapter is devoted to the impact of cultural change on women's position.

2883. Kroth, J. A. "Relationship Between Anxiety and Menarcheal Onset," PSYCHOLOGICAL REPORTS, vol. 23 (1968), pp. 801-802.

2884. Kurtz, R. M. "Body Image—Male and Female," TRANS-ACTION, (Dec. 1968), pp. 25-27.

2885. Laing, Ronald D., and A. Esterson. SANITY, MADNESS AND THE FAMILY. New York: Basic Books, 1971. 288 pp. Research into the families of 11 schizophrenic women leads the authors to believe that this illness may be a means of dealing with what most women consider unlivable situations.

2886. Lester, D., and L. F. Orloff. "Personality Correlates of the Duration of Menses," PSYCHOLOGICAL REPORTS, vol. 26 (1970), p. 650.

2887. Lidz, Ruth. "Emotional Factors in the Success of Contraception," FERTILITY AND STERILITY, vol. 20 (1969), p. 761.

2888. Littig, Lawrence W. "A Study of Certain Personality Correlates of Occupational Aspirations of Black and White College Women," ERIC, 1971. 56 pp. Originally published by Howard University, Washington, D.C., 1971.

2889. Livingstone, Elizabeth. "Attitudes of Women Operatives to Promotion," OCCUPATIONAL PSYCHOLOGY, (Oct. 1953), pp. 191-199.

2890. Lynn, D. "A Note on Sex Differences in the Development of Masculine and Feminine Identification," PSYCHOLOGICAL REVIEW, vol. 66 no. 1 (Jan. 1959), pp. 126-135.

2891. McDavid, J. W. "Imitative Behavior in Preschool Children," PSYCHO-LOGICAL MONOGRAPHS, vol. 73, no. 486 (1959). This study indicates that preschool children are more likely to follow a female leader in the imitation of behavior.

2892. McKee, J. P., and A. C. Sheriffs. "The Differential Evaluation of Males and Females," JOURNAL OF PERSONALITY, vol. 25 (1957), pp. 356-371.

2893. Maddi, Salvatore R., and Luigi M. Rulla. "Personality and the Catholic Religious Vocation. 1: Self and Conflict in Female Entrants," JOURNAL OF PERSONALITY, vol. 40 (1972), pp. 104-122. To ascertain personality factors influencing choice of religious vocation, 283 women entering classes as nuns (religious group) and 136 Catholic females entering college (lay group) were given a series of personality inventories.

2894. Mai, F.M.M., R. N. Munday, and E. E. Rump, "Psychosomatic and Behavioral Mechanisms in Psychogenic Infertility," BRITISH JOURNAL OF PSYCHIATRY, vol. 120 (Feb. 1972), pp. 199-204.

2895. Malik, Har G. S. "Personality and Career Decision Making," ERIC, 1970, 9 pp. Study investigating the relationship between the level of anxiety and career decision-making ability for females and males. There was, in fact, no significant correlation between females or males, between the level of measured anxiety and decision-making ability.

2896. Mannes, Marya. "The Roots of Anxiety in Modern Woman," JOURNAL OF NEUROPSYCHIATRY, vol. 5 (1964), p. 412.

2897. Maslow, Abraham H. "Dominance, Personality and Social Behavior in Women," JOURNAL OF SOCIAL PSYCHOLOGY, vol. 10 (1939) pp. 3-39; vol. 16 (1942), pp. 259-294. The second article is entitled "Self-Esteem (Dominance-Feeling) and Sexuality in Women."

2898. Miller, Jean Baker, ed. PSYCHOANALYSIS AND WOMEN. Baltimore, Md.: Penguin Books, 1973, 415 pp.   pre-nata

2899. Milman, Donald S., and George D. Goldman, compilers and ed. MODERN WOMAN: HER PSYCHOLOGY AND SEXUALITY. Springfield, Ill.: C. C. Thomas, 1969. 275 pp. A thorough study of all aspects of female sexuality, including sections on women's attitudes toward child-bearing, expected sex roles, and the feminine personality.

2900. Money, John, and Anke A. Ehrhardt. MAN AND WOMAN, BOY AND GIRL. Baltimore, Md.: Johns Hopkins, 1973. Major thesis of the book is that the distinctions between the sexes are determined by the interaction of pre-natal and post-natal influences. Based upon clinical research and observation and the latest research in the social sciences.

2901. Moore, B. E. "Panel Report: Frigidity in Women," JOURNAL OF THE AMERICAN PSYCHOANALYTIC ASSOCIATION, vol. 9 (1961), pp. 571-584.

2902. Mullahy, Patrick. OEDIPUS, MYTH AND COMPLEX: A REVIEW OF PSYCHOANALYTIC THEORY. New York: Hermitage Press, 1948. 538 pp. Deals primarily with the psychosexual aspects of both males and females as theorized by such people as Freud, Jung, Rank, Horney, Fromm, and Sullivan.

2903. Neumann, Eric. AMOR AND PSYCHE: THE PSYCHIC DEVELOPMENT OF THE FEMININE. New York: Pantheon Books, 1956. Jungian interpretation of the transformation of feminine consciousness.

2904. Oakley, Ann. SEX, GENDER AND SOCIETY. New York: Harper and Row, 1972. 220 pp.

2905. Palubinskas, Alice. "Personality Changes in College Women During Four Years," PROCEEDINGS OF THE IOWA ACADEMY OF SCIENCE, vol. 59 (1952), pp. 389-391.

2906. Peck, Robert F. "A Cross-National Comparison of Sex and Socioeconomic Differences in Aptitude and Achievement." Paper from a symposium, entitled "Some Implications of Cross-national Research for a 'Universal' Theory of Coping Behavior," presented at the Annual Meeting of the American Educational Research Association, New York, N.Y., (Feb. 1971). Also available through ERIC. 13 pp.

2907. Perlstein, Gary R. "Certain Characteristics of Policewomen," POLICE, vol. 16 (Jan. 1972), pp. 45-46.

2908. Pohlman, Edward. PSYCHOLOGY OF BIRTH PLANNING. Cambridge, Mass.: Schenkman Publications, 1969. 496 pp.

2909. Poussaint, Alvin F. "The Stresses of the White Female Worker in the Civil Rights Movement in the South," AMERICAN JOURNAL OF PSYCH-IATRY, vol. 123 (Oct. 1966), pp. 401-407.

2910. Reik, Theodor. PSYCHOLOGY OF SEX RELATIONS. New York: Farrar and Rinehart, 1945. 243 pp. A former pupil of Freud, Reik intelligently discusses the relationship between love and sex, and criticizes his former mentor's libido theory. Deals with both sexes.

2911. ———. SEX IN MAN AND WOMAN. New York: Noonday Press, 1960. 186 pp.

2912. Rheingold, J. THE FEAR OF BEING A WOMAN. New York: Grune and Stratton, 1964.

2913. Roesgen, Joan. "How Much Relevance Can A Woman Take?" BULLETIN, AMERICAN SOCIETY OF NEWSPAPER EDITORS, no. 557 (Feb. 1972), pp. 4-5. Asks that newspapers interview women who are contemptuous or resentful of working wives. If women cannot cope with their own hangups or jealousy when another woman makes it to the top, how can they expect male bosses to understand them?

2914. Schein, Virginia E. "The Woman Industrial Psychologist: Illusion or Reality?" AMERICAN PSYCHOLOGIST, vol. 26 (Aug. 1971), pp. 708-712. Examines the scant representation of women as industrial psychologists in proportion to the large number of women in industry.

2915. Schwartz, Ellen Bay. "Psychological Barriers to Increased Employment of Women," ISSUES IN INDUSTRIAL SOCIETY, vol. 2, no. 1 (1971), pp. 69-73.

2916. Scienfeld, A., and J. E. Garai. "Sex Differences in Mental Behavioral Traits," GENETIC PSYCHOLOGY MONOGRAPHS, vol. 77 (May 1968), pp. 169-299

2917. Sears, R. R., J. Whiting, V. Nowlis, and P. Sears. "Some Child Rearing Antecedents of Aggression and Dependency in Young Children," GENETIC PSYCHOLOGY MONOGRAPHS, vol. 47 (1953), pp. 135-234. Maternal punitiveness was positively related to dependence in boys and negatively in girls.

2918. Seashore, Harold G. "Women are More Predictable Than Men," JOURNAL OF COUNSELING PSYCHOLOGY, vol. 9, no. 3 (1962), pp. 261-270.

2919. Sherfey, Mary Jane. "Evolution and Nature of Female Sexuality," JOUR-NAL OF AMERICAN PSYCHOANALYTIC ASSOCIATION, vol. 14, no. 1 (Jan. 1966), pp. 28-128.

2920. Sheriffs, A. C., and J. P. McKee. "Qualitative Aspects of Beliefs About Men and Women," JOURNAL OF PERSONALITY, vol. 25 (June 1957), pp. 451-464.

2921. Sherman, Julia Ann. ON THE PSYCHOLOGY OF WOMEN: A SURVEY OF EMPIRICAL STUDIES. Springfield, Ill.: C. C. Thomas, 1971. 246 pp. An anthology with excellent source materials.

2922. "Some Effects of the Derogatory Attitude Toward Female Sexuality," PSYCHIATRY, vol. 13 (1950), pp. 349-354.

2923. Stevens, Barbara. "The Psychotherapist and Women's Liberation," SOCIAL WORK, vol. 16 (July 1971), pp. 12-18. Analyzes the role of women in American society and the problems arising from oppressive sexual division. Suggests that therapists should support women patients trying to develop more positive roles for themselves.

2924. Storer, Horatio Robinson. THE CAUSATION, COURSE AND TREAT-
MENT OF REFLEX INSANITY IN WOMEN. Boston: Lee and Shep-
hard, 1871. Says that the significance men attach to the anatomy of
women increases in proportion to their devaluation of her mind.

2925. Symonds, Alexandra. "Phobias After Marriage: Women's Declaration of
Dependence," MENTAL HEALTH DIGEST, vol. 4 (Mar. 1972), pp.
31-34.

2926. Terman, Lewis M., and Catherine C. Miles. SEX AND PERSONALITY:
STUDIES IN MASCULINITY AND FEMININITY. New York: Russell,
1968. 600 pp. Reprint of the 1936 edition.

2927. Thompson, Clara. "Cultural Pressures in the Psychology of Women,"
PSYCHIATRY, vol. 5 (1942), pp. 331-339.

2928. –––. INTERPERSONAL PSYCHOANALYSIS. New York: Basic Books,
1964. Collection of papers edited by Maurice R. Green, which includes
a chapter on the psychology of women and the problems of womanhood.

2929. –––. ON WOMEN. New York: New American Library (Mentor Books),
1971. Selections by the author from her major work INTERPERSONAL
PSYCHOANALYSIS dealing with the psychological and sexual development of women from childhood and adolescence through maturity and
old age. Also includes sections on female homosexuals, single women,
married women, and the working woman.

2930. Thompson, Helen Bradford. THE MENTAL TRAITS OF SEX: AN EX-
PERIMENTAL INVESTIGATION OF THE NORMAL MIND IN MEN
AND WOMEN. Chicago: Univ. of Chicago Press, 1903. 188 pp. Concludes that social influences have determined the disparity in intellect
between men and women rather than inborn psychological characteristics of sex.

2931. Tuttle, Florence Guertin. THE AWAKENING OF WOMAN: SUGGES-
TIONS FROM THE PSYCHIC SIDE OF FEMINISM. New York: Abingdon, 1915. 164 pp.

2932. Weisstein, Naomi. "Kinder, Küche, Kirche as Scientific Law: Psychology
Constructs the Female," MOTIVE, vol. 29 (Mar.-April 1969), pp. 6-7.
Critique of classical psychological theory and interpretations.

2933. –––. "Woman as Nigger," PSYCHOLOGY TODAY, (Oct. 1969), pp. 20-
22, 58. The author asserts that, until social expectations for men and
women are equal, until we provide equal respect for both sexes, answers
to the question of what differences there are between men and women
will simply reflect our prejudices. She also attacks the theory that it is
woman's nature to be submissive and passive, posing instead the view
that sex differences do not necessarily imply differences in psychological
nature.

2934. Whalen, Richard E. HORMONES AND BEHAVIOR: AN ENDURING
QUESTION IN PSYCHOLOGY. Princeton, N.J.: Princeton Univ. Press,
1967.

2935. White, Martha S. "Psychological and Social Barriers to Women in Science,"
SCIENCE, vol. 170 (Oct. 23, 1970), pp. 413-416.

2936. Wright, Helena. SEX AND SOCIETY. Seattle: Univ. of Washington Press,
1968.

2938. Young, W. C., R. W. Goy, and C. H. Phoenix. "Hormones and Sexual Behavior," SCIENCE, vol. 173 (Jan. 17, 1964). pp. 212-219.

2938. Zilboorg, G. "Masculine and Feminine," PSYCHIATRY, vol. 7 (1944), pp.
257-296.

IX. WOMEN IN ANTHROPOLOGY

Anthropology allows us to meet other human beings across cultural boundaries. In the following selections we may learn about and understand women who are living out their lives in ways that are different from our own. Most of the studies in this section deal with women outside the American culture. Many deal with African women, and describe or explain their social behavior, environment, needs, and everyday problems. We have sought only works which have anthropological relevance, and though the references proceed in an order of selection sensible to us, we admit that our major emphasis has been directed toward those works which describe the position, role, functions and status of women in various contemporary and past cultures. It has been difficult to organize our selections across a broad geographic spectrum, for there is a paucity of materials relating to women in many areas. Many other alternative organizations were possible. It may be that our pigeonholes distort as well as enlighten, but we hope that the range of our selections has been judicious. Whether this *lacunae* reflects a decrease in the number of anthropological studies of women in general, or whether it is the result of the materials' inaccessibility to the authors, the users of this volume may also get some view of the critics who have offered to be their guides.

> *There was something formless yet complete,*
> *That existed before heaven and earth;*
> *Without sound, without substance,*
> *Dependent on nothing, unchanging.*
> *All pervading, unfailing.*
> *One may think of it as the mother of*
> *All things under heaven.*
>
> —Lao Tzu

> *... when Africans turn to their past they do not forget the part played by women in it, but on the contrary assign to them a place that in many respects is theirs no longer. Moreover, it should also show that there are no valid historical grounds for explaining the present lack of interest in political matters so often found among African women as being a heritage of the past.*
> —Annie M. D. Lebeuf

2939. Acquaye Elmina, J. R. "Fanti Native Customs About Conception and Birth," ANTHROPOS, vol. 23 (1928), pp. 1051-1053. Customs of the natives of the Gold Coast.

2940. Akeley, M.L.J. "The Swazi Queen at Home; Intimate Observations on Love, Life and Death in South Africa's Timeless Swaziland," NATURAL HISTORY, (June 1938), pp. 21-32. Interesting study with numerous illustrations, especially of the education of girls among the Swazi.

2941. Alberto, M. S. "Problemas do 'Bem Estar Rural' Moçambicano. A Mulher Indigena Mocambicana Perante a Estrutura Familiar da Tribo," BOLETIM DA SOCIEDAD DE ESTUDOS MOCAMBIQUE (Laurenco-Marques), vol. 24, no. 83 (1954), pp. 93-104. Concerning the position and social conditions of women within the tribal structure of the native family of Mozambique. The position of women is a subordinate one.

2942. Ames, D. "The Economic Base of Wolof Polygyny," SOUTH WESTERN JOURNAL OF ANTHROPOLOGY (Albuquerque), vol. 11, no. 4 (1955), pp. 391-403. Study of a Wolof woman of the Dakar region and the activities of some co-wives of her husband over a period of ten days.

2943. Appia-Dabit, B. "Quelques Artisans Noirs," BULLETIN DE l'IFAN, vol. 3, nos. 3-4 (1941), pp. 1-44. Descriptions of the prayers and incantations used by some women potters of French Guinea and Senegal.

2944. Aptekar, Herbert. ANJEA: INFANTICIDE, ABORTION AND CONTRACEPTION IN SAVAGE SOCIETY. New York: Godwin, 1931. 192 pp. A strong argument for birth control in modern society based upon the author's study of birth control and abortion in primitive society.

2945. Atangana, N. "La Femme Africaine dans la Société," PRESENCE AFRICAINE (Paris), n.s. 13 (1957), pp. 133-142. African woman in traditional society, with a study of marriage, polygyny, and other customs.

2946. Baege, B. DIE FRAU IM LEBEN DER NATURVOLKER. Jena: Thuringer Verlagsanstalt und Druckerie, 1931. 78 pp. The tribal life of women in the Transvaal region of South Africa.

2947. Bal, A. "La Claustration des Jeunes Filles Chez Les Ngbandi et Les Ngombe de Lisala" [The Confinement of Girls Among the Ngbandi and the Ngombe of Lisala], TRAIT D'UNION (Antwerp) vol. 3 (1934), pp. 3. Marriage customs of the Ngombe and Ngbandi in the Congo region.

2948. Balde, S. "La Femme Foulah et l'Evolution," L'EDUCATION AFRICAINE, vol. 98 (1937), pp. 214-219. Deals with the traditional education of Fulani girls, and with the women's emancipation movement to free themselves from the yoke of Fulani men.

2949. Barrow, T. Terence. WOMEN OF POLYNESIA. Wellington, New Zealand: Seven Seas, 1967. 240 pp.

2950. Baumann, H. "The Division of Work According to Sex in African Hoe Culture," AFRICA, vol. 1, no. 2 (1928), pp. 289-313. Article dealing with the role of women in the development of hoe culture in East and Central Africa.

2951. Bazelay, W. S. "Manyika Headwomen," NADA (Salisbury), vol. 17 (1949), pp. 3-5. Detailed study of the Manyika (Congo region) institution of headwomen, including biographical sketches of some important leaders.

2952. Beier, H. U. "The Position of Yoruba Women," PRESENCE AFRICAINE (Paris), n.s. 1-2 (1955), pp. 39-46. The traditional way of life of Yoruba women (Southern Nigeria), with descriptions of their political, economic, and religious status before and after the coming of the Westerners.

2953. Benedict, Ruth. AN ANTHROPOLOGIST AT WORK: WRITINGS OF RUTH BENEDICT. New York: Atherton Press, 1966. 583 pp. A biography of the noted anthropologist, edited by Margaret Mead.

2954. Beresford Stooke, G. "Ceremonies Designed to Influence the Fertility of Women," MAN, vol. 28 (1928), p. 177. Fertility ceremonies performed by the Akamba tribe of Kenya are said to be infallible.

2955. Binet, J. "Condition des Femmes dans la Région Cacaoyère du Cameroun," CAHIERS INTERNATIONAUX DE SOCIOLOGIE (Paris), vol. 20 (1956), pp. 109-123. A summary of the changes in the traditional activities of women in Cameroon, such as opportunities in trading, handicrafts, and field work.

2956. Blacking, J. "Fictitious Kinship Among Girls of the Venda of the Northern Transvaal," MAN, vol. 59 (1959), pp. 155-157. Study of a traditional initiation ceremony in which Venda girls are placed under the guidance of former initiates, the relationship lasting until marriage. Such rites are socially cohesive and politically influential for the girls.

2957. Bolamba, A. R. LES PROBLEMES DE L'EVOLUTION DE LA FEMME NOIRE. Elisabethville, Congo: L'Essor du Congo, 1949. 167 pp. The role of women in home and family and the education of young girls is discussed.

2958. Boyle, C. V. "The Marking of Girls at Ga-Anda," JOURNAL OF THE SOUTH AFRICAN SOCIETY, vol. 15 (1916), pp. 361-366. Description of tatooing practices of girls which have important social significance in that they show the stages of the social life of the girls from the time their marriages are arranged until they are married.

2959. Brausch, G. E. "Les Associations Prénuptiales dans la Haute Lukeyni," BULLETIN DES JURIDICTIONS INDIGENES ET DU DROIT COUTUMIER CONGOLAIS (Elisabethville), 15th year, vol. 4 (1947), pp. 109-129. Study of the sexual, social, and economic function of pre-nuptial association among the Nkutshu of the Congo.

2960. Briffault, Robert. "La Femmes dans L'Union Française," TROPIQUES (Paris) no. 379 (1955), pp. 2-91. Notes and essays on African women, their occupations, customs, dances, etc., with excellent illustrations.

2961. Burness, H. "The Position of Women in Gwandu and Yauri," OVERSEA EDUCATION, vol. 26, no. 4 (1955), pp. 143-152. The position of Hausa and Fulani women and their attitudes toward education today.

2962. Campbell, Joseph. THE MASKS OF GOD: PRIMITIVE MYTHOLOGY. New York: Viking Press, 1959. Classic study of mythology, with many illustrations of women's place and feminine themes within it.

2963. Ceston, J. M. "Le Gree-Gree Bush (Initiation de la Jeunesse) Chez Les Negres Golah, Liberia," ANTHROPOS (Freiburg), vol. 6 (1911), pp. 729-754. Initiation of girls into the life of the tribe.

2964. Cheron, G. "La Circoncision et l'Excision Chez Les Malinke," JOURNAL DE LA SOCIETE DES AFRICANISTES (Paris), vol. 3 (1933), pp. 297-303. Description of the ceremonies of cliterodectomy performed on girls between the ages of 13 and 15.

2965. Child, H. F. "Family and Tribal Structure: Status of Women," NADA (Salisbury), vol. 35 (1958), pp. 65-70. Formerly, every Matabele woman, of whatever tribe, remained a minor all her life.

2966. Cles-Reden, Sibylle von. THE REALM OF THE GREAT GODDESS. Englewood Cliffs, N.J.: Prentice-Hall, 1962. Brilliant anthropological study of primitive myth and societal organization.

2967. Collard, J. "La Femme dans la Sensibilité Bantoue," SYNTHESES (Brussels), 11th years no. 121 (1956), pp. 288-289. On relations between men and women. Wives are entirely dependent on their husbands, but mothers are not held in such strictly subservient positions.

2968. Comhaire, J. "La Vie Religieuse à Lagos," ZAIRE (Brussells), vol. 3, no. 5 (1949), pp. 549-556. Study of Yoruba market women who have formed a Woman's Party in which Muslim influences are considerable. Women of this party are very progressive and from an important class.

2969. Congres Colonial National, 12th Session. LA PROMOTION DE LA FEMME AU CONGO ET AU RUANDA-URUNDI. Brussells, 1956. Report of a questionnaire conducted in the Congo stressing the legal and customary status of women, social work as a means of education, education in the schools, and the training and role of European women for work in this region.

2970. Constance-Marie, Sister. "Het Jonge Meisje in Kongo" [The Young Girl in the Congo], NIEUW AFRIKA (Antwerp), 69th year (1953), pp. 163-169. Position of girls in tribal society, with a discussion of marriage and the role of the clan in the ceremony of marriage among the Bira of Ituri.

2971. Cornet, R. P. LA FEMME EN REGIME MATRIARCAL. Rapports et Comptes Rendus de la XXe Semaine de Missiologie de Louvain. Brussels: Edition Universelle, 1951. Women among the Bashila clan are regarded merely as an economic asset, and they are regarded as subordinate.

2972. Coulibaly, O. "Sur l'Education des Femmes Indigènes," L'EDUCATION AFRICAINE (Goree), no. 99-100 (1938), pp. 33-36. Study of the attitudes arising from the present education of girls which runs counter to the traditional system.

2973. Culwick, A. T., and G. M. Culwick. "Fostermother in Ulanga," TANGANYIKA NOTES AND RECORDS (Dar-es-Salam), vol. 1 (March 1936), pp. 19-24. Description of the foster mother system among the Wabena tribe.

2974. Cyfer-Diderich, G. "Le Statut Juridique de la Femme Indigène au Congo Belge," Conseil National des Femmes Belges, Brussells, 1950, 32 pp. The position of native women with emphasis on marriage customs, the rights and duties of wives, polygny and its effects, and how Congo women have been educated, emancipated, and assimilated culturally.

2975. Dartevelle, A. "La Femme: Etude de sa Condition et de sa Situation Sociale Chez les Ba-Vili (Congo Français)," BULLETIN DE LA SOCIETE ROYALE BELGE D'ANTHROPOLOGIE ET DE PRE-HISTORIE (Brussells), vol. 54 (1939), pp. 99-100. Summary of the position of women in society and in the family.

2976. Decapmaker. "Sanctions Coutumières contre l'Adultère Chez les Bakongo de la Région de Kasi," CONGO (Brussells), 1939, pp. 134-148. Description of the sanction applied to adulteresses before the arrival of the Europeans and since.

2977. De Man, M. "Het Social Statuut van de Vrouw in Belgisch-Kongo," ZAIRE (Brussells), vol. 4, no. 8 (1950), pp. 851-869. Good summary of the position of women of other races in comparison with that of the native women of the Belgian Congo.

2978. Devereaux, George. A STUDY OF ABORTION IN PRIMITIVE SOCIETIES: A TYPOLOGICAL, DISTRIBUTIONAL, AND DYNAMIC ANALYSIS OF THE PREVENTION OF BIRTH IN 400 PREINDUSTRIAL SOCIETIES. New York: Julien Press, 1955. 394 pp.

2979. Dietrich, Albrecht. MUTTER ERDE [Earth Mother]. Leipzig: Teubner, 1913. An explanation of the maternal origins of prophecy. Dreams are believed to exist, preformed in the earth, ready to emanate from the Earth Mother into the mind of the primitive dreamer.

2980. Dobson, B. "Woman's Place in East Africa," CORONA, vol. 6, no. 12 (1954), pp. 454-457.

2981. Donner, E. "Togba, a Women's Society in Liberia," AFRICA, vol. 11 (1938), pp. 109-111. Brief description of a women's society organized to protect the village against leopards and "human leopards" that exist among the Dan and Mano in Liberia.

2982. Doucy, A. "Reflexions sur le Role de la Femme Indigène au Congo Belge," BULLETIN DE L'UNION DES FEMMES COLONIALES (Brussells), 26th year, nos. 4-5 (1955), pp. 4-5. Some problems concerning the education of native Congolese women who continue to remain under the influence of their native clans despite nontraditional Western influences.

2983. Douglas, R. L. "Education for African Girls," WEST AFRICAN REVIEW (Liverpool), vol. 26, no. 335 (1955), pp. 743-748. The problem of women's education in the various British African territories.

2984. Driberg, J. H. "The Status of Women Among the Nilotics and Nilo-Hamitics," AFRICA, vol. 5 (1932), pp. 404-421. The position of women in this region is not an inferior one.

2985. Dupeyrat, A. SAVAGE PAPUA. New York: Dutton, 1954. Excellent anthropological study of Papuan tribes and the roles of women in them.

2986. Dutilleux, G. "La Femme Détribalisée du Centre Extra-Coutumier," BULLETIN DU CEPSI (Elisabethville), vol. 6, no. 14 (1950), pp. 100-114. Studies the problems posed by detribalized women in nontraditional surrounding, in particular, prostitution resulting from the shortage of women who have left the villages for the cities. The instability of marriage has resulted in conflicting ideas about the institution among men and women.

2987. ———. "L'opinion des Femmes du Centre Extra-Coutumier d'Elisabethville sur le Mariage la Famille, l'Education des Enfants," BULLETIN DU CESPSI (Elisabethville), vol. 17 (1951) pp. 219-223. Discusses some of the problems raised in the preceding article.

2988. Earthy, E. VALENGE WOMEN: THE SOCIAL AND ECONOMIC LIFE OF THE VALENGE WOMEN OF PORTUGUESE EAST AFRICA. London: Oxford Univ. Press, for the Internation African Institute, 1933. 251 pp. The social and economic life of Valenge women are discussed by a woman who lived among them as a missionary for 30 years.

2989. Eberhard, Wolfram. LOCAL CULTURES OF SOUTH AND EAST ASIA. Leiden: Brill, 1968. Translation of the prewar German edition, by the eminent sociologist at Berkeley. Researches the possible status of women in Neolithic China.

2990. Edme, P. "Kunda Kalumbi, Fille D'Afrique," JEUNE AFRIQUE, 7th year, vol. 19 (1953), pp. 41-46; vol. 20, pp. 32-35. The life of African girls.

2991. Ellison, R. E. "Marriage and Child-Birth Among the Kanuri," AFRICA, vol. 9, no. 4 (1936), pp. 524-535. Marriage and birth among a tribe of Northern Nigeria, illustrating how traditional Islamic practices have been modified and complemented by local custom and superstition.

2992. Elvin, Verrier. "The Vagina Dentata Legend," BRITISH JOURNAL OF MEDICAL PSYCHOLOGY, vol. 19 (1941), pp. 439 ff. The vagina is seen as a devouring organ in most primitive myths. It is even more capable of devouring if it has teeth.

2993. Ennis, E. L. "Women's Names Among the Ovimbundu of Angola," AFRICAN STUDIES (Johannesburg), vol. 4, no. 1 (1945), pp. 1-8. Study of women's names which reveal the customs, beliefs, and psychology of the Ovimbundu people.

2994. Evans-Pritchard, E. E. THE POSITION OF WOMEN IN PRIMITIVE
SOCIETIES AND OTHER ESSAYS IN SOCIAL ANTHROPOLOGY.
New York: Free Press, 1965. 260 pp. Anthology of 14 articles
written during the period from 1928 to 1963. Themes ranging from
cannibalism to anthropological methods.
2995. Farrand, Livingston. TRADITIONS OF THE QUINAULT INDIANS.
New York: Memoirs of the American Museum of Natural History, vol.
4, Jan. 1902.
2996. Fortes, M. THE DYNAMICS OF CLANSHIP AMONG THE TALLENSI.
London: Oxford Univ. Press, 1945. 270 pp. Chapter 9, pp. 147-153,
deals with the role of women in the clan organization and discusses the
concept of "clanswoman."
2997. Freud, Sigmund. TOTEM AND TABOO. New York: Norton, 1952.
Classic work, represented in anthropological studies as well as in psychoanalytical literature.
2998. Garnier, C. "Africaines 1955," TROPIQUES (Paris), 53rd year, no. 379
(1955), pp. 9-19. Popular article describing the women of French
Africa, their married lives, their occupations, and their character, based
on long observations by the author.
2999. Geigy, R., and G. Holtker. "Madchen-Initiationen im Ulanga Distrikt von
Tanganyika," ACTA TROPICA (Basel), vol. 8 (1951), pp. 289-344.
Description of the initiation of girls and fertility rites.
3000. Gerda, Sister. "La Femme Ruandaise Hier et Aujourd'hui," TRAIT D'
UNION (Antwerp), 7th year, vol. 44 (1957), pp. 11-14. Traces the former condition of women among the Tutsi tribe, and discusses the changes
in their lives with the advent of Christianity.
3001. Gessain, Robert. " 'Vagina Dentata' Dans la Clinique et la Mythologie,"
PSYCHOANALYSE (Paris), vol. 3 (1957), pp. 257-295.
3002. Gilles de Pelichy, Dom. "Condition de la Femme d'Aprés le Droit Coutumier de l'Ouest Africain," RAPPORTS ET COMPTES RENDUS DE LA
XXe SEMAINE DE MISSIOLOGIE DE LOUVAIN, Brussells, Edition
Universelle, 1951, pp. 155-177. Makes women look like miserable
creatures, but states that African customary laws pay great respect to
the dignity of women, especially mothers.
3003. Gluckman, M. "Zulu Women in Hoe Cultural Ritual," BANTU STUDIES
(Johannesburg), vol. 9 (1935), pp. 255-271. Study of the sexual division
of labor; the hoe culture is performed by women.
3004. Goodale, Jane C. TIWI WIVES: A STUDY OF THE WOMEN OF MEL-
VILLE ISLAND, NORTH AUSTRALIA. Seattle: Univ. of Washington
Press, 1971. 423 pp.
3005. Hamamsy, Laila Shukry. "The Role of Women in Changing Navaho Society," AMERICAN ANTHROPOLOGIST, vol. 59 (1957), pp. 101-111.
Concludes that the changing economic position and social organization
of the Navaho today is adversely affecting the women. They are losing
their economic independence, the satisfactions and rewards that
accompany their economic functions, and their security and power within the family structure.
3006. Hartley, C. Gasquoine. THE AGE OF MOTHER-POWER: THE POSITION
OF WOMEN IN PRIMITIVE SOCIETY. New York: Dodd, Mead, 1914.
356 pp.

3007. Hermann, Imre. "The Giant Mother, The Phallic Mother, Obscenity," PSYCHOANALYTICAL REVIEW, vol. 36 (1949), pp. 302-306. Female figurines of goddesses abstracted and reduced to stylized essentials are examined. Herman points out that this is how the mother appears to her child: huge breast, huge pelvis, huge genitalia.

3008. Kaberry, P. M. ABORIGINAL WOMAN SACRED AND PROFANE. Philadelphia: Blakiston, 1939.

3009. Kagame, A. "Les Organisations Socio-Familiales de l'Ancien Ruanda," MEMOIRES DE L'ACADEMIE ROYALE DES SCIENCES COLONIALES, Classe des Science Morales et Politiques, vol. 38, no. 3 (Brussells, 1954), p. 335. Chapter 2 deals with the family and kinship, in which it was found that Ruandan women do not belong permanently to their natal families, but rather, become completely under the influence of their husband's family when they marry.

3010. Kohen, Max. "The Venus of Willendorf," AMERICAN IMAGO, vol. 3 (1946), pp. 49-60. Sculptured female figure, highly stylized, about 30,000 B.C., found in Austria. The figure constitutes the earliest form of art in the archeological record. Male figures seem to be very rare.

3011. LAROUSSE ENCYCLOPEDIA OF MYTHOLOGY. New York: Prometheus Press, 1959. Many references to women in mythology and in anthropological studies.

3012. Layard, John. "The Incest Taboo and the Virgin Archetype," ERANOS JAHRBUCH, vol. 12 (1945), pp. 253-307.

3013. Leakey, Louis S. B. "The Kikuyu Problem of the Initiation of Girls," JOURNAL OF THE ROYAL ANTHROPOLOGICAL INSTITUTE, vol. 61 (1931), pp. 277-285. Discussion of the changes that have taken place in initiation rites since the arrival of Christianity. Hostile demonstrations resulted when the British tried suppressing such rites. Leakey suggests preserving the educational aspects of initiation ceremonies while casting off such practices as cliterodectomy.

3014. Leger, J. "La Femme en Pays Dogon," VIVANTE AFRIQUE (Namur), vol. 195, no. 22 (1958), pp. 10-12. Study of the privileged position of women among the Dogon.

3015. McLennan, John F. PRIMITIVE MARRIAGE: AN INQUIRY INTO THE FORM OF CAPTURE IN MARRIAGE CEREMONIES. Chicago: Univ. of Chicago Press, 1970. Reprint, 1865 edition. A destruction of the theory that the patriarchal family was the primordial unit in primitive society.

3016. MacPherson, K. MOTHERCRAFT IN THE TROPICS. London: Cassell, 1947. 205 pp.

3017. MacVicar, T. "The Position of Women Among the Wanguru," PRIMITIVE MAN (Washington), vol. 7, no. 2 (1934), pp. 17-22. Study of the family, economic, political, and religious life of a tribe of Tanganyikan women; they are inferior to the men, but are nevertheless able to participate in the public life of the tribe.

3018. Mair, L. "A Yao Girl's Initiation," MAN, vol. 51 (1951), pp. 60-63. Ceremony described by one who was present in the Tanganyika village.

3019. Malinowski, Bronislaw. THE SEXUAL LIFE OF SAVAGES IN N.W. MELANESIA. London: Routledge and Kegan Paul, 1968. 506 pp. Originally published in 1932. An ethnographic account of courtship, marriage, and family life among the natives of the Trobriand Islands, British New Guinea.

3020. ———. SEX AND REPRESSION IN SAVAGE SOCIETY. New York: Meridian Books, 1955. 251 pp. First published in 1927.
3021. ———. SEX, CULTURE, AND MYTH. New York: Harcourt, Brace and World, 1962. 346 pp.
3022. Marchal, R. P. "La Condition de la Femme Indigène. Etude sur le Problème de l'évolution des Coutumes Familiales dans quelques Tribus de l' A. O. F. Observations sur le Même Sujet Relatives a l'Algerie," CHRONIQUE SOCIALE DE FRANCE (Lyon, 1930). 24 pp. Two-part study of the position of girls and women among various tribes of the Sudan and the Upper Volta region.
3023. Marie-André du Sacré-Coeur. "La Condition de la Femme au Mossi," GRAND LACS (Namur), 54th year (1937-38), pp. 177-181. Brief notes on the position of women in Mossi society with a description of marriage customs.
3024. Messer, Mary Burt. THE FAMILY IN THE MAKING: AN HISTORIC SKETCH. New York: Putnam's, 1928. 359 pp. Traces the evolution of the family as a human institution from its earliest forms to the present, with chapters discussing the changing roles of women.
3025. Mulenzi, J. "La Femme dans la Société Ruandaise," ECHANGES (Paris), vol. 26 (1956), pp. 30-34. Analysis of the important role Ruanda women play in the education of their children.
3026. Nemo, J. "The Economic Role of Women." Pp. 67-74 in CONTRIBUTIONS A L'ETUDE DEMOGRAPHIQUE ET SOCIOLOGIQUE D'UNE VILLE DU TOGO, PALIME. Paris: Ministere de la France d'OutreMer, 1958. Discussion of the social significance of the economic activities of women in such areas as agriculture, dress-making, and small trade. Petty trading forms a key economic area occupied entirely by women.
3027. Neumann, Erich. THE GREAT MOTHER. New York: Pantheon Books, 1954. Brilliant study of the symbols of femininity through the ages: the Mater Genetrix, Mater Omnium (the All-Mother), and the Mother of Everything.
3028. Olivier, G., and L. Aujoulat. "L'Obstetrique en Pays Yaounde," BULLETIN DE LA SOCIETE D'ETUDES CAMEROUNAISES (Duala), vol. 12 (1945), pp. 7-71. Thorough study of marriage rites, initiation ceremonies, pregnancy, taboos, and confinement practices among Yao women of the Congo.
3029. Ominde, S. H. THE LUO GIRL FROM INFANCY TO MARRIAGE. New York: Macmillan, 1952. 69 pp. Study of the physical and mental development of East African girls from infancy to married life.
3030. Pailloux, R. "La Place de la Femme Chez les Babemba," GRAND LACS (Namur), vol. 10 (1953), pp. 9-16, 37-40. First part deals with the place of women in Babemba society; second part discusses the relation between husband and wife and between the mother and her children.
3031. Paulme, Denise, ed. WOMEN OF TROPICAL AFRICA. Translated by H. M. Wright. Berkeley and Los Angeles: Univ. of California Press, 1971. 308 pp. Reprint, 1963 edition. Collection of six essays by professional women ethnologists who conducted field work in French-speaking Africa. Deals with African women in everyday life, emphasizing the relative power and status of African women along with changes taking place in their traditional roles. Excellent bibliography.

3032. Peto, Andrew. "The Demonic Mother Image in the Jewish Religion," PSYCHOANALYSIS AND THE SOCIAL SCIENCES, vol. 5 (1958), pp. 280-287.

3033. Rank, Beata. "Zur Rolle der Frau in der Entwicklung der Menschlichen Gessellschaft," [The Role of Women in the Development of Human Society] , IMAGO, vol. 10 (1924), pp. 278-295. Historical examples of feminine transmission of power are cited, especially in Egypt, where queens probably have always been the true rulers.

3034. Rattray, R. S. ASHANTI LAW AND CONSTITUTION. Oxford: Clarendon Press, 1929. The importance of women in this matrilineal society are discussed.

3035. Reitzenstein, F. F. von. DAS WEIB BEI DEN NATURVOLKERN: EINE KULTURGESCHICHTE DER PRIMITIVEN FRAU [The Wife in the Tribe: A Cultural History of Primitive Women] . Berlin: Verlag Neufeld und Henius, n.d. 386 pp. A scholarly anthropological and sociological study of the family and cultural life of women among primitive peoples.

3036. Reyher, R. H. ZULU WOMAN. London: Oxford Univ. Press, 1948. The impressions of Christina Sibiya, the wife of a Zulu King.

3037. Reynolds, R. "Women in Africa: Notes on Religious and Social Trends," ANTIOCH REVIEW (Yellow Springs, Ohio), vol. 14 (1954), pp. 312-322. Compares the position of women and the changes brought about by Islam and Christianity in the former British territories of East and South Africa.

3038. Schmidt, W. "The Position of Women with Regard to Property in Primitive Society," AMERICAN ANTHROPOLOGIST, vol. 37, no. 2 (1935), pp. 244-256. Discusses the property rights of women among the South African pygmies, and among other hunters and pastoral tribes of the East African region.

3039. Shapera, I. MARRIED LIFE IN AN AFRICAN TRIBE. London: Faber and Faber, 1940. 364 pp. Descriptions of married life, husband-wife relations, relations between parents and children, and the legal status of married, divorced, and widowed women.

3040. Shaw, M. "Fertility Dolls in South Africa," NADA (Salisbury), vol. 25 (1948), pp. 63-68. Fertility dolls which women carry on their backs to prevent barrenness are illustrated from among such tribes as the Zulu, Swazi, Matabele, Basoto, Bechuana, Balenge, and Ovambo.

3041. Shropshire, D.W.T. THE BANTU WOMAN UNDER THE NATAL CODE OF NATIVE LAW. Lovedale, (South Africa): Lovedale Press, 1941. 47 pp. Description of customs relating to the position of women in Natal, along with a study of the family, widowhood, women's emancipation, and the care of children.

3042. Simons, H. J. "African Women and the Law in South Africa," THE LISTENER, vol. 55, no. 1416 (1956), pp. 626-627, 644. Native women in South Africa live under customary law, native law, and European law. The author contends that none of these systems accord them a legal position commensurate with the actual influence they wield in the village life.

3043. Smith, M. F. BABA OF KARO: A WOMAN OF THE MUSLIM HAUSA. London: Faber and Faber, 1954. 299 pp. Autobiography of a Hausa woman which is significant for the information she recalls about her childhood and the customs of her time.

3044. Strangway, A. K. "The Advance of African Women in Angola," AFRICAN WOMEN, vol. 1, no. 4 (1956), pp. 79-84. New responsibilities and a new division of labor between men and women are some of the advances being made by Ovimbundu women.

3045. Talbot, D. Amaury. WOMAN'S MYSTERIES OF A PRIMITIVE PEOPLE: THE IBIBIOS OF SOUTHERN NIGERIA. London: Cassell, 1915. 251 pp. Discusses the life of Ibibio women from birth to death, along with interesting tribal customs and religious ceremonies.

3046. Temple, O. "Women in Northern Nigeria," BLACKWOOD'S MAGAZINE (Edinburgh), vol. 117 (1914), pp. 257-267. The daily life of women of the Nupe tribe.

3047. Tyler, Edward B. PRIMITIVE CULTURE, 2 vols. New York: Holt, 1889.

3048. Weigert-Vowinkel, Edith. "The Cult and Mythology of the Magna Mater from the Standpoint of Psychoanalysis," PSYCHIATRY, vol. 1 (1939), pp. 347-378. Refers to woman's lack of state-building powers "because her libidinal interests do not extend beyond the home." National and ethical ideas are developed with reference to masculine gods. The Mother-deity remains "morally indifferent."

3049. Wittfogel, Karl A. "The Society of Prehistoric China," ZEITSCHRIFT FUR SOZIALWISSENSCHAFTEN, vol. 8 (1939), pp. 138-186. Somewhat dated, but scholarly theory of matriarchal society in neolithic China.

3050. Zimmer, Heinrich. MYTHS AND SYMBOLS IN INDIAN ART AND CIVILIZATION. Edited by Joseph Campbell. Washington, D.C.: Bollingen Foundation, 1946.

3051. ———. "Die Indische Weltmutter," ERANOS JAHRBUCH, vol. 6 (1938), n.p.

X. WOMEN IN ECONOMICS

Women comprise 42 percent of the labor force in the United States, and it has been estimated that a woman's work week averages slightly less than 100 hours. In prehistoric, ancient, medieval, and modern capitalist and socialist societies, the volume of work performed by women is enormous and incalculable if quantified in terms of productive labor. Despite these facts and figures, women in the United States and in most other countries find themselves either out of work, economically exploited, or excluded from full entry into the productive labor force on equal terms with their male counterparts and with equal pay.

The following books and articles deal specifically with those features of modern woman's situation as regards her economic oppression and discrimination, and with the historical factors that have determined her subordinate role in the family and in the labor force. Many of the references cited in the following subcategories propose and analyze solutions and changes in the socioeconomic system that promise an end to women's economic and legal oppression, and that foreshadow international campaigns for equal pay, equal work, and equal opportunities for women.

A. The Economic Position of Women—General

... it is pleasyng to God that all his Creatures be set in vertueux occupation and labour accordyng to their degrees.

> *(Petition of women silk weavers presented to Henry VI in 1455)*

The first premise for the emancipation of women is the reintroduction of the entire female sex into public industry.

> *—Friedrich Engels*

3052. Abbott, Edith. WOMEN IN INDUSTRY: A STUDY IN AMERICAN ECONOMIC HISTORY. New York: Source Book Press, 1971. 430 pp. Reprint of the 1910 edition. An important study of women's role in American industry from the colonial period to the early 1900's.
3053. Allingham, John D., and Byron G. Spencer. WOMEN WHO WORK. Ottawa, Canada: DBS Special Labour Force Studies, 1967, 1968. 280 pp. A two-part survey of patterns of employment of Canadian women.
3054. American Academy of Political Science. THE ECONOMIC POSITION OF WOMEN. New York: American Academy of Political Science, 1910. 193 pp. Anthology of essays, mostly by women, analyzing the position of women as producers in industry. Some contributors include: Helen L. Sumner, Mary Van Kleeck, Alice P. Barrows, M. Edith Campbell, and Josephine Goldmark.
3055. Anderson, Mary. WOMEN AT WORK. Minneapolis: Univ. of Minnesota Press, 1951. 266 pp. The story of the Women's Bureau, by its first director.
3056. Bell, Carolyn S. "Remarks on Women and Unemployment," CONGRESSIONAL RECORD, (March 30, 1972), pp. E3298-3300. Statement made for the RECORD on discrimination toward women in employment.
3057. Bentson, Margaret. "The Political Economy of Women's Liberation," MONTHLY REVIEW, vol. 24 (1969), pp. 13-27. On the economic role of women in American society.

3058. Bernard, Jessie. WOMEN AND THE PUBLIC INTEREST: Chicago: Aldine Press, 1971. 293 pp. Excellent study analyzing the public interest as regards women's rights, and women in the labor market.

3059. Beyer, Sylvia S. WOMEN'S JOBS, ADVANCE, AND GROWTH. Washington, D.C.: SUDOC, GPO, 1949. 88 pp. A survey of the extent of women's participation in the industrial and professional labor force.

3060. Branch, Mary S. WOMEN AND WEALTH: A STUDY OF THE ECONOMIC STATUS OF AMERICAN WOMEN. Chicago: Univ. of Chicago Press, 1934. 153 pp. Main topics covered are: women as taxpayers, women as owners of property, women as gainfully employed workers, women as buyers and managers of family income.

3061. Brittain, Vera. WOMEN'S WORK IN MODERN ENGLAND. London: Neil Douglas, 1928. 222 pp. A survey.

3062. Buckley, Louis F. THE EMPLOYED WOMAN. Washington, D.C.: Bureau of Employment Security, U.S. Department of Labor, 1965.

3063. Bullard, Washington I. WOMEN'S WORK IN WAR TIME. Boston: Merchant's National Bank, 1917. 85 pp. The record of American women's participation in the war effort.

3064. Bullock, Edna D., compiler. SELECTED ARTICLES ON THE EMPLOYMENT OF WOMEN. Minneapolis: H. W. Wilson, 1911. 147 pp.

3065. Burton, Margaret E. WOMEN WORKERS OF THE ORIENT. West Medford, Mass.: Central Committee on the United Study of Foreign Missions, 1918. 240 pp.

3066. Canada. Women's Bureau. "Women's Bureau '71." Introduction by Sylva M. Gelber. Ottowa: Department of Labour, 1972. 72 pp. Four papers covering statistics and other areas of interest in the employment of Canadian women.

3067. Clark, Alice. WORKING LIFE OF WOMEN IN THE 17TH CENTURY. London: Routledge, 1919. 335 pp. The author concludes that the advent of machinery and capitalism restricted the life of women economically and socially.

3068. Cohen, Wilbur J. WOMANPOWER POLICIES FOR THE 1970's. Washington, D.C.: U.S. Department of Labor, Manpower Administration, 1968. 40 pp. A seminar on womanpower policies and programs.

3069. Dardenne, E. "The Role of Women in African Social and Economic Development." In NEW EDUCATION FELLOWSHIP, 6th World Conference, Nice, France. London, 1932. n.p.

3070. De Graffenried, Clare. THE NEEDS OF SELF-SUPPORTING WOMEN. Washington, D.C., 1890. 10 pp. Studies the social and moral aspects of the employed female.

3071. Dellatol, Lesley. "Adam's Rib," SOUTH AFRICAN PANORAMA, vol. 16 (July 1971), pp. 10-13. Takes a look at the labor market and the potential of women's labor in the Third World.

3072. Dempsey, Mary V. THE OCCUPATIONAL PROGRESS OF WOMEN, 1910 to 1930. Washington, D.C.: SUDOC, 1933. 90 pp. An interpretation of census statistics of women in gainful occupations during a 20-year period.

3073. Devine, Edward T. THE ECONOMIC FUNCTION OF WOMAN. New York: Teachers College, Columbia Univ., 1910. 16 pp. More of a sociological than an economic study which stresses cooperation between the sexes.

3074. Dewar, Margaret. LABOR POLICY IN THE USSR, 1917-1928. London: Royal Institute of International Affairs, Chatham House, 1956. 286 pp. Detailed information concerning Soviet labor policies, conditions of work, wages and incentives, social and economic features, with much information on women.

3075. Dodge, Norton T. WOMEN IN THE SOVIET ECONOMY: THEIR ROLE IN ECONOMIC, SCIENTIFIC, AND TECHNICAL DEVELOPMENT. Baltimore, Md.: Johns Hopkins Press, 1966. 331 pp. Stresses the fact that Soviet women are an integral part of all sectors of the labor force as well as the professions, and that they can be expected to contribute significantly to Soviet economic growth and development in the future. Includes a bibliography of Russian-language sources.

3076. Donahue, Mary P. "Female Labor Force in the U.S.,"GEOGRAPHICAL REVIEW, vol. 61 (July 1971), pp. 440-442.

3077. THE ECONOMIC POSITION OF WOMEN, Proceedings of the Academy of Political Science, vol. 1, no. 1, 1910-11. 193 pp. New York: Columbia Univ. Helen Marot edited seventeen articles dealing with such topics as the historical development of women workers in the United States, vocational training for women, employment bureaus for women, with an excellent bibliography. though out of date.

3078. Edelman, Judy. WOMEN ON THE JOB: A MARXIST-LENINIST VIEW. New York: New Outlook, 1970. 21 pp.

3079. Elkan, W. "The Employment of Women in Uganda," BULLETIN DE L'INSTITUT INTERAFRICAIN DU TRAVAIL (Brazzaville), vol. 4, no. 4 (1957), pp. 8-23. Women in Uganda comprise a very small proportion of the total labor force and are excluded from industry. Discusses the prospects of employing more women in order to bolster the unstable labor force.

3080. Epstein, Cynthia F. WOMAN'S PLACE: OPTIONS AND LIMITS IN PROFESSIONAL CAREERS. Berkeley: Univ. of California Press, 1970. 221 pp.

3081. Eyde, Lorraine Dittrich. WORK VALUES AND BACKGROUND FACTORS AS PREDICATORS OF WOMEN'S DESIRE TO WORK. Columbus: Ohio State Univ., Bureau of Business Research, 1962. 88 pp.

3082. Fosbrooke, J. "Masai Women and Their Work," CROWN COLONIST, vol. 14 (1944), pp. 313-314. Short summary of the nature of women's work among this agriculturally important Kenyan tribal group.

3083. Fox, Genevieve M. WOMAN'S WORK FROM PRIMITIVE TIMES TO THE PRESENT: TOPICS AND REFERENCES FOR THE HELP OF DISCUSSIONAL GROUPS. Washington, D.C.: Industrial Committee War Work Council of the National Board, Y.W.C.A., 1919. 16 pp.

3084. Friedman, Bruno, ed. "Women in the Age of Science and Technology," IMPACT OF SCIENCE ON SOCIETY, vol. 20 (Jan.-Mar. 1970), 105 pp. Whole issue devoted to women in technological jobs. Articles on "Women in Space," "Feminine Intellect and the Demands of Science," "The Possible Biological Origins of Sexual Discrimination," "Women in Science," "Women and Work: The Effects of Technological Change," and "Women and Technology in Developing Countries."

3085. General Federation of Women's Clubs. WOMEN IN HIGH LEVEL POSITIONS (NATIONAL AND STATE.) Washington, D.C.: Author, 1954. n.p.

3086. Gilman, Charlotte Perkins. WOMEN AND ECONOMICS: A STUDY OF THE ECONOMIC RELATION BETWEEN MEN AND WOMEN AS A FACTOR IN SOCIAL EVOLUTION. Boston: Small, Maynard, 1898. 368 pp. Argues that marriage is essentially an economic relationship in which women are subordinated, and that the marriage institution has created a sexual over-specialization in women.

3087. Ginzburg, Eli. "The Changing Patterns of Women's Work," AMERICAN JOURNAL OF ORTHOPSYCHIATRY, vol. 28 (1958), pp. 313-321. A nonpsychological investigation exploring a series of theoretical questions bearing upon the development and utlization of women in an industrial society, concluding with an analysis of public policy and research into the changing patterns of women's work.

3088. Gross, Edward. "Plus Ca Change . . .? The Sexual Structure of Occupations Over Time," SOCIAL PROBLEMS, vol. 16, no. 2 (Fall 1968), pp. 198-207. Study of the differentiation of the sexes into male and female and the division of labor based on it.

3089. Guelfi, L. "La Femme Noire et Les Formes Modernes du Travail," CONSEIL NATIONAL DES FEMMES FRANCAISE (Paris), Oct. 1957, pp. 7-14. Brief study denoting the importance and the economic freedom of women in traditional African societies, with an assessment of the new forms of economic activities upon which African women are embarking: hospital work, research, office work, trade, domestic work, and industrial labor.

3090. Henderson, Julia J. "Impact of the World Social Situation on Women," THE ANNALS, vol. 375 (Jan. 1968), pp. 26-33. Reports that half the world's population lives below subsistence standards as far as food, housing, and employment are concerned, consequently, women are forced to supplement the family income. Discusses the role women are playing in developmental work and in the social revolution.

3091. Her Majesty's Stationery Office. SURVEY OF WOMEN'S EMPLOYMENT. 2 vols. London: H.M.S.O., 1965.

3092. Heywood, Anne. THERE IS A RIGHT JOB FOR EVERY WOMAN. Garden City, N.Y.: Doubleday, 1951. 192 pp.

3093. Hill, C. Russell. "Education, Health and Family Size as Determinants of Labor Market Activity for the Poor and the Non-Poor," DEMOGRAPHY, vol. 8 (Aug. 1971), pp. 379-388. Discusses labor supply decisions occurring in a family context.

3094. Hill, Joseph A. WOMEN IN GAINFUL OCCUPATIONS, 1870 to 1920. A STUDY OF THE TREND OF RECENT CHANGES IN THE NUMBERS, OCCUPATIONAL DISTRIBUTION, AND FAMILY RELATIONSHIP OF WOMEN REPORTED IN THE CENSUS AS FOLLOWING A GAINFUL OCCUPATION. Washington, D.C.: GPO, 1929. 416 pp. New York, Johnson Reprint, 1971.

3095. Hoffman, Anna Rosenberg. "A New Look at Women's Work." GREAT IDEAS TODAY, Part I. Chicago: Encyclopedia Britannica, 1961.

3096. Hopkins, Mary D. THE EMPLOYMENT OF WOMEN AT NIGHT. Washington, D.C.: U.S. GPO, 1928.

3097. Hutchins, B. L. WOMEN IN MODERN INDUSTRY. London: Bell, 1915. Study of British women in the industrial labor force.

3098. Hutchins, Grace. WOMEN WHO WORK. New York: International Publishers, 1934. 285 pp.

3099. Institute of Women's Professional Relations. PROCEEDINGS OF THE CONFERENCE ON WOMEN'S WORK AND THEIR STAKE IN PUBLIC AFFAIRS, March 28, 29, 30, 1935, Hotel Astor, New York City. New London, Conn.: Author, 1935. 327 pp.

3100. International Labour Office. "United States: Equality of Employment Opportunities for Women," INTERNATIONAL LABOUR REVIEW, vol. 105 (Feb. 1972), pp. 175 ff.

3101. ———. THE WAR AND WOMEN'S EMPLOYMENT: THE EXPERIENCE OF THE UNITED KINGDOM AND THE UNITED STATES. Montreal: International Labour Office, 1946. 287 pp.

3102. Johnstone, Elizabeth. "Women in Economic Life: Rights and Opportunities," THE ANNALS, vol. 375 (Jan. 1968).

3103. Kaberry, P. M. WOMEN OF THE GRASSFIELDS: A STUDY OF THE ECONOMIC POSITION OF WOMEN IN BAMENDA, BRITISH CAMEROON. Colonial Research Publications, no. 14. London: Her Majesty's Stationery Office, 1952. 220 pp. Discusses land tenure, women in agriculture, the division of labor, and standards of living.

3104. Klein, Viola. EMPLOI DES FEMMES, HORZIRES ET RESPONSIBILITIES. Washington, D.C.: Organization for Economic Cooperation and Development, OECD Publications Center, 1750 Pennsylvania Avenue, N.W., 1965.

3105. Levitin, Teresa. "Women in the Occupational World," ERIC, 1971. 11 pp. Paper arguing that women do not receive occupational rewards commensurate with their achievements, rewards that are allocated to equally qualified men.

3106. McMahon, Theresa S. WOMEN AND ECONOMIC EVOLUTION: OR THE EFFECTS OF INDUSTRIAL CHANGES UPON THE STATUS OF WOMEN. Bulletin of the University of Wisconsin, no. 496, vol. 7, Madison: Univ. of Wisconsin, 1912. 131 pp.

3107. Malcolm, Janet. "Women's Work," THE NEW REPUBLIC, Oct. 10, 1970, pp. 15-17.

3108. Mandel, William M. "Soviet Women in the Work Force and Professions," AMERICAN BEHAVIORAL SCIENTIST, vol. 15, no. 2 (Nov.-Dec. 1971), pp. 255-280. Data showing the rapid rate at which Soviet women have entered nearly all fields. Evidence that the government is sincere in seeking to eliminate barriers of male prejudice.

3109. Markus, Maria. "Women and Work (I) Feminine Emancipation at an Impasse," IMPACT OF SCIENCE ON SOCIETY, vol. 20, no. 1 (Jan.-Mar. 1970), pp. 61-72.

3110. Murdock, G. P. "Comparative Data on the Division of Labor By Sex," SOCIAL FORCES, vol. 15 (1937), pp. 551-553.

3111. Nader, Ralph. "How You Lose Money on Being a Woman," McCALL'S, Jan. 1972, pp. 65, 148.

3112. National Manpower Council. WOMANPOWER: A STATEMENT, WITH CHAPTERS BY THE COUNCIL STAFF. New York: Columbia Univ. Press, 1957. 371 pp.

3113. Neff, Wanda Fraiken. VICTORIAN WORKING WOMAN: AN HISTORICAL AND LITERARY STUDY OF WOMEN IN BRITISH INDUSTRIES AND PROFESSIONS, 1832-1850. New York: AMS Press, 1966. 288 pp. Reprint, 1929 edition. Study of the working woman and how she obtruded upon the sympathies of Victorian reformers. Women as workers did not harmonize with the philosophy of Victorian England, with its deification of the home and woman's place in it.

3114. Oppenheimer. Valerie K. "The Sex-Labeling of Jobs," INDUSTRIAL RE-LATIONS, vol. 7 (May 1968), pp. 219-234.

3115. Organization for Economic Cooperation and Development. EMPLOY-MENT OF WOMEN. Paris, Nov. 1968; Oct. 1970. 385 pp. Available from OECD Publications Center, 1750 Pennsylvania Avenue, N.W., Washington, D.C.

3116. Pan American Union. ALLIANCE FOR PROGRESS. OFFICIAL DOCU-MENTS EMANATING FROM THE SPECIAL MEETING OF THE INTER-AMERICAN ECONOMIC AND SOCIAL COUNCIL AT THE MINISTERIAL LEVEL. Punta del Este, Uruguay, 1961. Washington, D.C.: Pan American Union, 1961. American women found strong endorsement of their desire to participate in solving their countries' problems of preparing and executing plans for economic and social development whereby they would be placed on an equal footing with men.

3117. Penny, Virginia. THINK AND ACT. A SERIES OF ARTICLES PER-TAINING TO MEN AND WOMEN, WORK AND WAGES. Philadelphia: Claston, Remsen and Haffelfinger, 1869. 372 pp.

3118. Perella, Vera C. WOMEN AND THE LABOR FORCE. U.S. Department of Labor, Bureau of Labor Statistics. Washington, D.C.: SUDOC, GPO, 1968. 12 pp. Statistical summary.

3119. Perkins, Frances. PEOPLE AT WORK. New York: John Day, 1934. 287 pp. By the first woman Secretary of Labor, including discussions with a variety of American wage earners, with some references to women.

3120. Pidgeon, Mary E. CHANGES IN WOMEN'S EMPLOYMENT DURING THE WAR. U.S. Women's Bureau Bulletin, no. 253. Washington, D.C.: GPO, 1944. 29 pp.

3121. ———. CHANGES IN WOMEN'S OCCUPATIONS, 1940-50. U.S. Department of Labor, Women's Bureau, Washington, D.C., 1954. 104 pp.

3122. ———. WOMEN IN THE ECONOMY OF THE UNITED STATES OF AMERICA: A SUMMARY REPORT. Washington, D.C.: GPO, 1937. 137 pp.
TION, 1750-1850. London: Routledge, 1930. 342 pp. Part 1 discusses women in agriculture during the agrarian revolution; Part II discusses women in industry and trade, such as women textile workers, crafts women, businesswomen, and women workers in mines and the metal trades.

3124. Pogrebin, Letty Cottin. HOW TO MAKE IT IN A MAN'S WORLD. Garden City, N.Y.: Doubleday, 1970. 280 pp. Serious, yet partly tongue-in-cheek guide on how to get ahead in a predominantly male business world. world.

3125. Ramsey, Glenn V., et al. WOMEN VIEW THEIR WORKING WORLD: BASED ON A STUDY IN MENTAL HEALTH FOR THE TEXAS FED-ERATION OF BUSINESS AND PROFESSIONAL WOMEN. Austin, Texas: Hogg Foundation for Mental Health, Univ. of Texas, 1963. 47 pp.

3126. Rayburn, Letricia G. "Do Women Discriminate Against Each Other?" NATIONAL PUBLIC ACCOUNTANTS, vol. 16 (Oct. 1971), pp. 16-19. 663 replies to a questionnaire sent to members of the American Women's Society of Certified Public Accountants showing that the relations of women to supervisors of the female sex were not as good as those with men.

3127. Riesman, David. THE LONELY CROWD. New Haven, Conn.: Yale Univ. Press, 1962. 315 pp. Several chapters deal with women as leaders of opinion and discuss their role in contemporary literature, the work world, and women's stereotyped job functions, such as secretraries, clerks, etc.

3128. Rosenberg, Morris. OCCUPATIONS AND VALUES. Glencoe, Ill.: Free Press, 1957. In employment, masculine values and concerns take precedence over female concerns.

3129. Roundtree, M., and J. Roundtree. "More on the Political Economy of Women's Liberation," MONTHLY REVIEW, vol. 21 (1970), pp. 26-32. A reply to Margaret Benston's article arguing that women are no longer transient wage laborers; family standards of living depend on two permanent wage earners.

3130. Sandler, Bernice. "The Status of Women: Employment and Admissions," CONGRESSIONAL RECORD, Feb. 28, 1972, pp. S2750-S2752. Presents evidence to support the contention that the United States has relatively fewer professional women than other countries, such as Sweden, Denmark, Britain, France, Germany, and the Soviet Union.

3131. ———. "Women: The Last Minority," JOURNAL OF COLLEGE PLACEMENT, vol. 35 (Dec.-Jan. 1972), pp. 49-50+. Concludes that women are becoming more aware of the discrimination they face and have filed complaints so that more than $30 million of back pay has been awarded to them under the Equal Pay Act.

3132. Schreiner, Olive. WOMEN AND LABOUR. New York: Stokes, 1911. 299 pp. The author contends that the unrest among women is due to the fact that they are forced to live as parasites, a condition that must be remedied.

3133. Schultz, Theodore W. "Women's New Economic Commandments," BULLETIN OF THE ATOMIC SCIENTISTS, vol. 28 (Feb. 1972), pp. 29-32. Economic opportunities for women are delayed because of lags in social, legal, and economic adjustments.

3134. Shea, John R. "Years for Decision: A Longitudinal Study of the Educational and Labor Market Experience of Young Women," Vol. 1, Ohio State Univ. Center for Human Resource Research, 1971. 245 pp. Data collected in a 1968 interview survey of a national probability sample of young women 14-24 years of age were the basis for a 5-year study of employment and educational experience.

3135. Smuts, Robert W. WOMEN AND WORK IN AMERICA. New York: Columbia Univ. Press, 1959. 180 pp.

3136. Strachey, Rachel Conn (Costelloe). CAREERS AND OPENINGS FOR WOMEN. London: Faber and Faber, 1935. Guidebook of career openings for women seeking employment in Great Britain.

3137. Sullerot, Evelyne. HISTOIRE ET SOCIOLOGIE DU TRAVAIL FEMININ [The History and Sociology of Women's Work]. Paris: Gonthier, 1968.

3138. Sumner, Helen L. HISTORY OF WOMEN IN INDUSTRY IN THE UNITED STATES. U.S. Report on the Conditions of Women and Child Wage Earners, vol. 9. Washington, D.C.: GPO, 1911.

3139. Thompson, Edward. THE MAKING OF THE ENGLISH WORKING CLASS. New York: Vintage Books, 1966. 848 pp. History of the development of the English working class from 1792 to 1835.

3140. Thompson, Flora McDonald. "Letter from Flora McDonald Thompson, Petitioning the Secretary of Labor for the Establishment of a Bureau of Woman Labor in the Department of Labor." Washington, D.C.: GPO, 1913. 6 pp.

3141. Tickner, F. W. WOMEN IN ENGLISH ECONOMIC HISTORY. London: J. M. Dent, 1923. 236 pp. Scholarly and informative study.

3142. Tuckerman, Joseph. AN ESSAY ON THE WAGES PAID TO FEMALES FOR THEIR LABOR, IN THE FORM OF A LETTER, FROM A GENTLEMAN IN BOSTON TO HIS FRIEND IN PHILADELPHIA. Philadelphia: Carey and Hart; Boston: Carter and Hendee, 1830. 58 pp.

3143. Turner, Loretta E., ed. HOW WOMEN EARN A COMPETENCE. Oberlin, Ohio: News Printing Co., 1902. 320 pp.

3144. Turner, Marjorie B. S., and Irving Bernstein, eds. WOMEN AND WORK. Los Angeles: Univ. of California, Institute of Industrial Relations, 1964. 73 pp.

3145. United Nations. Economic and Social Council. Commission on the Status of Women. "Equal Pay for Work of Equal Value." New York: United Nations Publications, 1971. Progress report prepared by the International Labour Office on national and international action taken to achieve equal pay for equal work. Major developments in implementing the principle of equal pay are summarized for 81 countries.

3146. ———. PARTICIPATION OF WOMEN IN THE ECONOMIC AND SOCIAL DEVELOPMENT OF THEIR COUNTRIES. New York: United Nations Publications, 1971. 104 pp.

3147. U.S. Bureau of the Census. THE MAGNITUDE AND DISTRIBUTION OF CIVILIAN EMPLOYMENT IN THE USSR: 1928-1959. Prepared by Murray S. Weitzman and Andrew Elias. Washington, D.C.: GPO, 1961. 193 pp.

3148. ———. STATISTICS OF WOMEN AT WORK, BASED ON UNPUBLISH- ED INFORMATION DERIVED FROM THE SCHEDULES OF THE TWELFTH CENSUS: 1900. Washington, D.C.: GPO, 1907. 399 pp.

3149. U.S. Bureau of Labor. REPORT ON CONDITION OF WOMAN AND CHILD WAGE-EARNERS IN THE UNITED STATES. IN 19 VOL- UMES . . . PREPARED UNDER THE DIRECTION OF CHARLES P. NEILL, COMMISSIONER OF LABOR. 61st Cong., 2d sess. Senate document no. 645. Washington, D.C.: GPO, 1910-1913.

3150. ———. WORKING WOMEN IN LARGE CITIES. Washington, D.C.: GPO, 1889. 631 pp. Annual report of the Commissioner of Labor.

3151. U.S. Bureau of Labor Statistics. SUMMARY OF THE REPORT ON THE CONDITION OF WOMAN AND CHILD WAGE-EARNERS IN THE UNITED STATES. U.S. Bureau of Labor Statistics, Bulletin no. 175; Washington, D.C.: GPO, 1916. 445 pp. Women in Industry Series no. 5.

3152. U.S. Civil Service Commission. STUDY OF EMPLOYMENT OF WOMEN IN FEDERAL GOVERNMENT. Washington, D.C.: U.S. Civil Service Commission, Manpower Statistics Division, Dec. 1971. 236 pp.

3153. U.S. Congress. Joint Committee on Education and Labor. HEARINGS ON S.4002, A BILL TO ESTABLISH IN THE DEPARTMENT OF LABOR, A BUREAU TO BE KNOWN AS THE WOMEN'S BUREAU, 66th Cong., 2d sess. Washington, D.C.: GPO, 1920. 88 pp.

3154. U.S. Department of Health, Education and Welfare, Social Security Administration. A REPORT ON SOCIAL SECURITY PROGRAMS IN THE SOVIET UNION. Washington, D.C.: GPO, 1960. 157 pp. Much information on women.

3155. U.S. Department of Labor, Women's Bureau. "Background Facts on Women Workers in the United States." Washington, D.C.: SUDOC, GPO, 1970. 20 pp.

3156. U.S. Department of Labor, Women's Bureau, Work Standards Administration. "Changing Patterns of Women's Lives, 1970." Washington, D.C.: SUDOC, GPO, 1970.

3157. U.S. Department of Labor, Women's Bureau. COLLEGE WOMEN SEVEN YEARS AFTER GRADUATION: RESURVEY OF WOMEN GRADUATES, CLASS OF 1957. Washington, D.C.: Women's Bureau, 1966. 54 pp.

3158. ———. CONFERENCE ON MEETING MEDICAL MANPOWER NEEDS— THE FULLER UTILIZATION OF THE WOMAN PHYSICIAN. Washington, D.C.: SUDOC, GPO, 1968. 104 pp.

3159. ———. "Report on a Consultation on Working Women and Day Care Needs Held in Washington, D.C. June 1, 1967." Washington, D.C.: SUDOC, GPO, 1968. 86 pp.

3160. ———. "Dual Careers, A Longitudinal Study of Labor Market Experience of Women." Research Monograph no. 21. Washington, D.C.: SUDOC, GPO, 1970. Vol. 1, 284 pp.; vol. 2, 134 pp.

3161. ———. EXPLODING THE MYTHS. Report on the Conference on Expanding Employment Opportunities for Career Women. Washington, D.C.: SUDOC, GPO, Dec. 3, 1966. 67 pp.

3162. ———. "Facts About Women's Absenteeism and Labor Turnover," Wage and Labor Standards Administration. Washington, D.C.: SUDOC, GPO, August 1969.

3163. ———. "Fact Sheet on the Earnings Gap." Washington, D.C.: SUDOC, GPO, Feb. 1970. 5 pp.

3164. ———. "Guide to Conducting Consultation on Women's Employment with Employers and Union Representatives, 1971." Washington, D.C.: SUDOC, GPO, 1971. 15 pp.

3165. ———. HANDBOOK OF WOMEN WORKERS. Bulletin no. 290. Washington, D.C.: SUDOC, GPO, 1969. 321 pp.

3166. ———. JOB HORIZONS FOR COLLEGE WOMEN. Washington, D.C.: SUDOC, GPO, 1967. 83 pp.

3167. ———. LEGISLATIVE HISTORY OF THE EQUAL PAY ACT OF 1963 (AMENDING SECTION 6 OF THE FAIR LABOR STANDARDS ACT OF 1938, AS AMENDED), PUBLIC LAW 88-38, 88TH CONGRESS, H.R. 6060 and S. 1409. U.S. Congress. Committee on Education and Labor, 88th Cong., 1st sess. Washington, D.C.: SUDOC, GPO, 1963. 114 pp.

3168. ———. LABOR LAWS AFFECTING WOMEN, A CAPSULE SUMMARY BY VARIOUS STATES, 1944 TO PRESENT. Washington, D.C.: SUDOC, GPO, 1970.

3169. ———. NEGRO WOMEN . . . IN THE POPULATION AND IN THE LABOR FORCE. Washington, D.C.: SUDOC, GPO, 1968. 41 pp.

3170. ———. NEGRO WOMEN WORKERS IN 1960. Bulletin no. 287.
Prepared by Jean A. Wells. Washington, D.C,: SUDOC, GPO, 1964.
Compares 1960 data with those for 1940 and 1950 in order to determine the progress of Negro women workers during the past two decades.
3171. ———. THE SHARE OF WAGE-EARNING WOMEN IN FAMILY
SUPPORT. Bulletin no. 30. Washington, D.C.; SUDOC, GPO, 1923.
170 pp.
3172. ———. SUMMARY OF THE REPORT ON CONDITION OF WOMEN AND
CHILD WAGE-EARNERS IN THE U.S! Washington, D.C.; SUDOC,
GPO, 1916. 533 pp.
3173. ———. "Underutilization of Women Workers," Rev. ed. Washington, D.C.:
SUDOC, GPO, 1971. 25 pp. Brief description of statements and statis
tics documenting aspects of the underutilization of women workers.
3174. ———. UTILIZATION OF WOMEN WORKERS. Washington, D.C.:
Women's Bureau, Department of Labor, 1967.
3175. ———. WOMANPOWER COMMITTEES DURING WORLD WAR II,
UNITED STATES AND BRITISH EXPERIENCE' Bulletin no. 244.
Washington, D.C.: SUDOC, GPO, 1953. 73 pp.
3176. ———. WOMEN AT WORK: A CENTURY OF INDUSTRIAL CHANGE.
Bulletin no. 115. Washington, D.C.: SUDOC, GPO, 1933. 50 pp.
3177. ———. WOMEN'S OCCUPATION THROUGH SEVEN DECADES. Bulletin
no. 28. Washington, D.C.: SUDOC, GPO, 1947.
3178. ———. WOMEN—THEIR SOCIAL AND ECONOMIC STATUS: SELEC-
TED REFERENCES. Washington, D.C.: U.S. Department of Labor,
Dec. 1970. 41 pp. Selected list of publications dealing with foreign
women as well as U.S. women.
3179. ———. WORK LIFE EXPECTANCY AND TRAINING NEEDS OF
WOMEN. Manpower report no. 12. Washington, D.C.: SUDOC, GPO,
1967. 10 pp.
3180. U.S. Equal Employment Opportunity Commission. EQUAL EMPLOYMENT
OPPORTUNITY REPORT no. 3: JOB PATTERNS FOR MINORITIES
AND WOMEN IN PRIVATE INDUSTRY, 1969. 2 vols. Washington, D.C.:
SUDOC, GPO, 1971, 1972.
3181. ———. "Personnel Testing and Equal Employment Opportunity." Washington,
D.C.: SUDOC, GPO, 1971. 56 pp. Guidelines on employee selection
procedures.
3182. U.S. President's Commission on the Status of Women. REPORT OF THE
COMMITTEE ON FEDERAL EMPLOYMENT TO THE PRESIDENT'S
COMMISSION ON THE STATUS OF WOMEN. Washington, D.C.:
SUDOC, GPO, 1963. 195 pp.
3183. "Women in Sweden in the Light of Statistics." Stockholm: The Joint
Female Labour Council, Apr. 1971. 73 pp. Background facts on women
in the Swedish labor market, kinds of work, working hours, and labor-
market training. Very informative.
3184. Verway, David I. "Advance to the Rear for Women," BUSINESS TOPICS
(Michigan State Univ.), vol. 20 (Winter 1972), pp. 53-62. Article discussing the relative advances made by women with respect to the increase in their portion of the job market; from 28.6 percent in 1950,
they have increased to 37.7 percent in 1970.
3185. Vladeck, Judith. "The Equal Pay Act of 1963." Pp. 381-389 in PRO-
CEEDINGS: CONFERENCE ON LABOR, New York Univ., 1965.

3186. Weiss, E. B. "Female Earning Power May Equal Males as Early as 1985," ADVERTISING AGE, vol. 42 (Dec. 20, 1971), p. 26. Concludes that women will fill more white collar jobs, there will be more women in the professions, women will have fewer children, housewives will receive salaries, and above all, women's lib will achieve equal pay and there will be two heads of families.

3187. Weitzman, Murray S., Murray Feshbach, and Lydia Kulchycka. "Employment in the USSR: Comparative USSR-US Data." Pp. 591-667 in DIMENSIONS OF SOVIET ECONOMIC POWER. Washington, D.C.: GPO, 1962. Statistics on women are found throughout this article.

3188. Whiteside, Elena. "For Soviet Women: A 13-Hour Day," THE NEW YORK TIMES MAGAZINE, Nov. 17, 1963, pp. 28 ff.

3189. Wilensky, Harold L. "Women's Work: Economic Growth, Ideology, Structure," INDUSTRIAL RELATIONS, vol. 7 (May 1968), pp. 235-248. The author claims that more than a third of all people working or seeking work in the United States are women. At mid-century, the number of married women working exceeded the number of single women at work, a trend that is continuing.

3190. Williams, Gertrude. WOMEN AND WORK. New York: Essential, 1945. 128 pp. A plea for equal opportunity for women in industry, based upon experiences of women working during the war years.

3191. Yaffe, Barbara, and Byron Yaffe. "State Protective Legislation: An Anachronism under Title VII?" ISSUES IN INDUSTRIAL SOCIETY, vol. 2, no. 1 (1971), pp. 54-61. Discusses the conflicts between traditional state protective labor legislation and the recent congressional concern for eliminating discriminatory employment practices against women in this country.

3192. Youssef, Nadia H. "Social Structure and the Female Labor Force: The Case of Women Workers in Muslim Middle Eastern Countries," DEMOGRAPHY, vol. 8 (Nov. 1971), pp. 427-439. Analyzes the taboos and stereotypes concerning women entering the industrial labor market in Middle Eastern countries.

3193. Zellner, Harriet. "What Economic Equality for Women Requires: Discrimination Against Women, Occupational Segregation and the Relative Wage," AMERICAN ECONOMIC REVIEW, vol. 62 (May 1972), pp. 157-176.

B. Women and Job Discrimination

. . . far from woman's physical *weakness removing her from productive work, her* social
weakness has in these cases evidently made her the major slave of it.
—Juliet Mitchell

It's always been and always will be the same in the world: the horse does the work and
the coachman is tipped.
—Anonymous

3194. Association of American Colleges. "Federal Laws and Regulations Concerning Sex Discrimination in Educational Institutions." Prepared by
the Association of American Colleges, Project on the Status and Education of Women, Oct. 1972.
3195. ———. "Summary of Federal Policy Concerning Twenty-Five Affirmative
Action Issues in Employment." Prepared by the Association of American Colleges, Project on the Status and Education of Women, Nov. 1972.
3196. Barnier, Lucien. "A Woman in Charge of the Airplane," AFRIQUE
NOUVELLE, no. 1248 (July 14, 1971), p. 11. Takes a look at women
pilots and the difficulties they had to overcome.
3197. Brenner, Marshall H. "Management Development for Women," PER-
SONNEL JOURNAL, vol. 51 (Mar. 1972), pp. 165-169. Discusses ways
of increasing women's occupational opportunities in the light of discriminatory barriers such as stereotypes, role expectations, and
thoroughly internalized behavior patterns.
3198. Buckley, John E. "Pay Differences Between Men and Women in the Same
Job," MONTHLY LABOR REVIEW, vol. 94 (Nov. 1971), pp. 36-40.
Comparisons drawn between men's and women's wage levels in eight
office and two industrial occupations.
3199. Camargo, Dr. Alberto Lleras. "Twenty-Five Years of Work, 1928-1953,"
NEWS BULLETIN OF THE INTER-AMERICAN COMMISSION OF
WOMEN, no. 1 (July 1953). Most Latin-American countries have
passed laws that adequately protect the civil and political rights of
women regarding employment.
3200. Canada, Department of Labour, Women's Bureau. WOMEN IN THE
LABOUR FORCE, 1970: FACTS AND FIGURES. Ottawa: 1971. Includes comparisons of male-female wage rates over a wide range of
occupations.
3201. Clark, F. Le Gros. WOMAN, WORK AND AGE. London: n.p., 1962.
Study of the employment of working women throughout their middle
years.
3202. ———. THE ECONOMIC RIGHTS OF WOMEN. Liverpool: Univ. of
Liverpool Press, 1963. 18 pp.
3203. Clark, Patricia. "Sexism and the Secretary," DUNN'S REVIEW, vol. 99
(Jan. 1972), pp. 69-70. Discusses the repressive activities of sexist males
in prohibiting females, regardless of talents, to rise above the permanent
and unstimulating position of office secretary, and describes the condescending interactions between boss and secretary.
3204. Cohen, Audrey C. "A College for Human Services," IMPROVING COLLEGE
AND UNIVERSITY TEACHING, vol. 22 (Winter 1972), pp. 51-54. Discusses why women have been discriminated against at all levels of higher
education while denied access to careers for which they are suited by
talent and experience.

3205. Cohen, Malcolm S. "Sex Differences in Compensation," JOURNAL OF HUMAN RESOURCES, vol. 6 (Fall 1971), pp. 434-437. Paper examining some of the hypotheses frequently used to explain the large differences in earnings between men and women, relying on data from the "Working Conditions and Fringe Benefit Survey."

3206. De Vries, Margaret G. "Women, Jobs, and Development," FINANCE AND DEVELOPMENT, no. 4 (Dec. 1971), pp. 2-9. Identifies the nature of special problems of women in developing countries as economic development takes place, and stresses the importance of not neglecting the productive potentials of women.

3207. Eastwood, Mary. "Fighting Job Discrimination: Three Federal Approaches," FEMINIST STUDIES, vol. 1, no. 1 (Summer 1972), pp. 75-103. Discusses the problem of sex discrimination in employment.

3208. Ellman, Edgar S. MANAGING WOMEN IN BUSINESS. National Foremen's Institute, Bureau of Business Practice, National Sales Development Institute, Waterford, Conn., 1963. 155 pp. Study concerned with how women should be employed and managed.

3209. Emerson, John Philip. SEX, AGE AND LEVEL OF SKILL OF THE NON-AGRICULTURAL LABOR FORCE OF MAINLAND CHINA. Washington, D.C.: U.S. Department of Commerce, Bureau of the Census, 1965. Available from SUDOC, GPO. Contains statistical evidence that de facto discrimination against women still exists in Mainland China.

3210. "Employment Discrimination: The Burden is on Business, Griggs v. Duke Power Co.," MARYLAND LAW REVIEW, vol. 31, no. 3 (1971), pp. 255-272.

3211. Equal Employment Opportunity Commission. "Guidelines on Employee Selection Procedures." FEDERAL REGISTER vol. 35, no. 149 (Aug. 1, 1970), pp. 12333-12336.

3212. Fields, Cheryl M. "Few Academic Women Filing Complaints on Unequal Pay," THE CHRONICLE OF HIGHER EDUCATION, Jan. 8, 1973, p. 1.

3213. Friedman, Joel W. "Sex and the Law," INDUSTRIAL AND LABOR RELATIONS FORUM, vol. 7 (Oct. 1971), pp. 36-65. A discussion of law and the married woman, covering property and contractual rights, marriage and support laws, jury service, and how Title VII of the 1964 Civil Rights Act conflicts with state protective legislation. Good factual presentation of what constitutes Bona Fide Occupational Qualifications for women.

3214. Goldfarb, Anne, and Emma Bronson. "Pa Bell is a Rich White Man," WORKERS' POWER, April 30-May 13, 1971, p. 16. Single-page article denouncing Bell Telephone for discriminatory practices against blacks, Chicanos, and Puerto Ricans. WORKERS' POWER is a self-styled "revolutionary socialist bi-weekly published by the International Socialists" at Highland Park, Michigan.

3215. Gordon, Eugene, and Cyril Briggs. THE POSITION OF NEGRO WOMEN. New York: Workers Library, 1935. 15 pp. Short polemic which begins, "In a society based on production for profit to be both a woman worker and a Negro is to suffer a double handicap."

3216. Gould, Karolyn, and Kirsten Amundsen. "The Rise of Womanagement," INNOVATION, (Sept. 1971), pp. 14-22. Portrays the conflicts between men and women in management as a result of different cultural backgrounds.

3217. Harrison, Evelyn. "The Working Woman: Barriers in Employment," PUBLIC ADMINISTRATION REVIEW, vol. 24, no. 2 (June 1964), p. 78.

3218. HELP WANTED, FEMALE: A STUDY OF DEMAND AND SUPPLY IN A LOCAL JOB MARKET FOR WOMEN. New Brunswick, N.J.: Rutgers Univ., Institute of Management and Labor Relations, 1964. 94 pp.

3219. Jacobson, Carolyn J. "Some Special Problems the Older Woman Worker Encounters when Seeking Employment," INDUSTRIAL AND LABOR RELATIONS FORUM, vol. 7 (Oct. 1973), pp. 66-73.

3220. Kanowitz, Leo. "Some Legal Aspects of Affirmative Action Programs," UNIVERSITY OF CALIFORNIA, HASTINGS COLLEGE OF THE LAW, (Oct. 5, 1972), p. 3.

3221. Lobsenz, Johanna. THE OLDER WOMAN IN INDUSTRY. New York: Charles Scribner's Sons, 1929. 281 pp.

3222. Lopata, Helena Z. "Work Histories of American Urban Women," THE GERONTOLOGIST, vol. 2, no. 1 (Winter 1971), pp. 27-36. Concludes that the American social system has failed to prepare women adequately for its work structure and to utilize their labor potential in spite of the fact that most women hold jobs many years during their adult life.

3223. Mancke, Richard B. "Lower Pay for Women: A Case of Economic Discrimination?" INDUSTRIAL RELATIONS, vol. 10 (Oct. 1971), pp. 1316-1326. Discovers that it is not because of sex discrimination that women are paid less than men, but rather because firms employing women are faced with indirect labor costs higher than those employing equally productive men.

3224. Mead, Margaret. "The Life Cycle and Its Variations: The Division of Roles," DAEDALUS, vol. 96, no. 3 (Summer 1967), pp. 871-885. A prognosis that the rich societies will set international styles that will allow women to work and to function as independent individuals without the basis of sex discrimination.

3225. Pressman, Sonia. "Job Discrimination and the Black Women," THE CRISIS (Mar. 1970), pp. 103-108. Notes important statistical facts on black women in the American economy, and summarizes a number of rulings of the Equal Employment Opportunity Commission. Indicates federal and state statutes and municipal ordinances that may be utilized by black women who are the victims of sex discrimination in employment.

3226. Slevin, Dennis P. "What Companies are Doing About Women's Equality," PERSONNEL, vol. 48 (July-Aug., 1971), pp. 8-18. Reveals that some 40 corporations contacted were not eager to attack the problems of full utilization of women and were reluctant to comment on current programs.

3227. U.S. Civil Service Commission. "Equal Employment Opportunity in State and Local Governments—A Guide for Affirmative Action." Washington, D.C.: Bureau of Inter-Governmental Personnel Programs, SUDOC, GPO, 1970. 17 pp.

3228. ———. "Equal Opportunity in Employment." Personnel Bibliography Series, no. 38. Washington, D.C.: SUDOC, GPO, 1971. 135 pp.

3229. U.S. Congress. House Committee on Education and Labor. DISCRIMINATION AGAINST WOMEN: HEARINGS BEFORE THE SPECIAL SUBCOMMITTEE ON EDUCATION . . . ON SECTION 805 OF H.R. 160998, 91st Cong., 2nd sess., 1970, Washington, D.C.: SUDOC, GPO,

1970. Part I, 615 pp.; Part II, 1256 pp. Chairperson, Edith Green. OVERSIGHT HEARINGS ON DISCRIMINATION AGAINST WOMEN, HEARINGS BEFORE THE AD HOC SUBCOMMITTEE ON DIS-CRIMINATION AGAINST WOMEN, 92d Cong., 2nd sess., 1972. 409 pp. Washington, D.C.: SUDOC, GPO, 1972.

3230. ———. EQUAL PAY ACT OF 1963: HEARINGS ON H.R. 3861 AND RELATED BILLS TO PROHIBIT DISCRIMINATION, ON ACCOUNT OF SEX, IN THE PAYMENT OF WAGES. Washington, D.C.: SUDOC, GPO, 1963. 326 pp.

3231. U.S. Congress. House Committee on the Judiciary, Subcommittee no. 4. HEARINGS ON THE EQUAL RIGHTS AMENDMENT. Washington, D.C.: SUDOC, GPO, March 1971.

3232. U.S. Congress. Senate Committee on Labor and Public Welfare. EQUAL EMPLOYMENT OPPORTUNITY: HEARINGS BEFORE THE SUB-COMMITTEE ON EMPLOYMENT AND MANPOWER OF THE COMMITTEE ON LABOR AND PUBLIC WELFARE ON S. 773 AND S. 1937, 88th Cong., 1st sess. Washington, D.C.: SUDOC, GPO, 1963. 578 pp.

3233. U.S. Department of Labor, Women's Bureau. CONFERENCE ON EM-PLOYMENT PROBLEMS OF WORKING WOMEN, MICHIGAN STATE UNIVERSITY, 1961. Washington, D.C.: SUDOC, GPO, 1962. 23 pp.

3234. ———. "Policies of National Governments on Employing Women," WOMEN IN THE WORLD TODAY. International Report 3. Women's Bureau. Washington, D.C.: SUDOC, GPO, April 1964. 20 pp.

3235. ———. "Protective Labor Legislation for Women in 91 Countries," WOMEN IN THE WORLD TODAY. International Report 5. Women's Bureau. Washington, D.C.: SUDOC, GPO, Mar. 1963. 33 pp.

3236. ———. A REPORT: CHOICE OR CHANCE. CONFERENCE ON WOMAN'S DESTINY' UNIVERSITY OF WASHINGTON, 1963. Washington, D.C.: SUDOC, GPO, 1965. 86 pp.

3237. Wells, Jean A. "Automation and Women Workers," Women's Bureau. Department of Labor, 1970. 16 pp. Study of statistical data from 1958-1963 used to determine the repercussions of scientific and technological progress on the employment of women and their conditions of work.

C. Economic Effects of the Employment of Married Women

The fact is that the "woman's place is in the home" myth is a phony rationalization for paying lower wages and providing worse working conditions for women than men.
—Lyn Wells

3238. Andrews, Irene O., and Margaret Hobbs. ECONOMIC EFFECTS OF THE WAR UPON WOMEN AND CHILDREN IN GREAT BRITAIN. New York: Oxford Univ. Press, 1918.

3239. Blood, Robert O. "Long-Range Causes and Consequences of the Employ-ment of Married Women," JOURNAL OF MARRIAGE AND THE FAMILY, vol. 27 no. 1 (Feb. 1965), pp. 43-47. The author feels that employment of married women is producing more symmetrical family structures and more equality between husbands and wives and their families.

3240. Cain, Glen G. MARRIED WOMEN IN THE LABOR FORCE: AN ECO-
NOMIC ANALYSIS. Chicago: Univ. of Chicago Press, 1966. 159 pp.
Explains why the percentage of married women in the labor force has
risen since 1940, in order to interpret the economic growth and
cyclical behavior of national income, birthrates, personal distribution of income, and the effects of income taxes on the labor supply.

3241. Callahan, Sidney Cornelia. THE WORKING MOTHER. New York: Macmillan, 1971. 264 pp. Collection of essays on such questions as: is it
all right for a woman to work, reflections of a nonworking mother,
should mothers go back to school, careers and homes, and how women's
"second lives" can be creative.

3242. Columbia University. WORK IN THE LIVES OF MARRIED WOMEN:
PROCEEDINGS OF A CONFERENCE ON WOMANPOWER HELD
OCTOBER 20-25, 1957 AT ARDEN HOUSE, HARRIMAN CAMPUS
OF COLUMBIA UNIVERSITY. New York: Columbia Univ. Press, 1958.
220 pp.

3243. Cotton, Dorothy Whyte. THE CASE FOR THE WORKING MOTHER.
New York: Stein and Day, 1965. 185 pp.

3244. Coyle, Grace L. JOBS AND MARRIAGE: OUTLINES FOR THE DIS-
CUSSION OF THE MARRIED WOMAN IN BUSINESS. New York:
Woman's Press, 1928. 101 pp.

3245. Fogarty, Michael P. "Women at Work: The Small Child Gap and Other
Problems," PERSONNEL MANAGEMENT, vol. 4 (Feb. 1972), pp.
18-22. Discusses the PEP Report and their prediction that there is
likely to be a greater choice for working couples and an increase in
problems for personnel managers.

3246. Garza, Joseph M., and Rao Nandini. "Attitudes Toward Employment and
Employment Status of Mother in Hyderabad, India," JOURNAL OF
MARRIAGE AND THE FAMILY, vol. 34 (Feb. 1972), pp. 153-155.

3247. Her Majesty's Stationery Office. WOMAN, WIFE, AND WORKER.
London: H.M.S.O., 1965. Problems and consequences of married
women in the British labor force.

3248. Iglehart, John K. "Welfare Report: Congress Presses Major Child-Care
Program Despite White House Veto Threat," NATIONAL JOURNAL,
vol. 3 (Oct. 23, 1971), pp. 2125-2130. The administration is interested
in child care centers primarily for the role they could play in enabling
welfare mothers to work.

3249. Kieran, Sheila. THE NON-DEDUCTIBLE WOMAN: A HANDBOOK FOR
WORKING WIVES AND MOTHERS. Toronto: Macmillan, 1970. How
to manage money, housekeeping, and child care, and how to prevent a
husband's bruised ego when the wife goes to work.

3250. Lilienthal, Meta S. FROM FIRESIDE TO FACTORY. New York: The
Rand School of Social Science, 1916. 66 pp.

3251. Mott, Frank L. "Fertility, Life Cycle Stage and Female Labor Force
Participation in Rhode Island: A Retrospective Overview," DEMO-
GRAPHY, vol. 9 (Feb. 1972), pp. 173-185.

3252. Nye, Ivan F., and Lois W. Hoffman, eds. THE EMPLOYED MOTHER IN
AMERICA. Chicago: Rand McNally, 1964. 399 pp. Collection of
essays from several disciplines dealing with mothers at work, the effects
on the child, and attitudes of mothers and employers toward women in
the labor force.

3253. Organization for Economic Cooperation and Development. "Reentry of Women to the Labor Market After an Interruption of Employment." Washington, D.C.: OECD, 1971. 130 pp. Studies the problems involved in the reentry of women into the labor market and the extent to which there exists a demand for such reentry.

3254. Ostry, Sylvia. THE FEMALE WORKER IN CANADA. Ottawa: DBS, 1968. A Census Bureau monograph which discusses patterns of female employment, particularly the return of married women to the labor force.

3255. Pidgeon, Mary E. THE EMPLOYED WOMAN HOMEMAKER IN THE UNITED STATES: HER RESPONSIBILITY FOR FAMILY SUPPORT. Washington, D.C.: SUDOC, GPO, 1936. 22 pp.

3256. "The Place of Women in the Modern Business World as Affecting Home Life, the Marital Relation, Health, Mortality, and the Future of the Race," BULLETIN OF THE AMERICAN ACADEMY OF MEDICINE, vol. 9, no. 5 (1908), pp. 335-384.

3257. Rosenfeld, Carl, and Vera C. Perrella. "Why Women Start and Stop Working: A Study in Mobility," MONTHLY LABOR REVIEW, Sept. 1965, pp. 1077-1082.

3258. Schonberger, Richard J. "10 Million U.S. Housewives Want to Work." LABOR LAW JOURNAL, vol. 21 (June 1970), pp. 374-379.

3259. Schwartz, Jane. PART-TIME EMPLOYMENT: EMPLOYER ATTITUDES ON OPPORTUNITIES FOR THE COLLEGE-TRAINED WOMAN; REPORT OF A PILOT PROJECT. New York: Alumnae Advisory Center, 1964. 62 pp.

3260. Scofield, Nanette E., and Betty Klarman. SO YOU WANT TO GO BACK TO WORK. New York: Random House, 1968. 208 pp.

3261. Scott, Ann F. "Feminism vs. the Feds," ISSUES IN INDUSTRIAL SOCIETY, vol. 2, no. 1 (1971), pp. 32-46. Discusses women's struggle to realize equal rights. The work of the Office of Federal Contract Compliance, of the Equal Employment Office, and the Wages and Hours Division of the Department of Labor is outlined in the text.

3262. Shallcross, Ruth. SHOULD MARRIED WOMEN WORK? New York: Public Affairs Committee, 1940. 31 pp. Public Affairs Pamphlet No. 49.

3263. Silberberg, Marjorie M. "Career Part-Time Employment: Personnel Implications of the New Professional and Executive Corps," GOOD GOVERNMENT, vol. 88 (Fall 1971), pp. 11-19.

3264. Sweet, James A. FAMILY COMPOSITION AND THE LABOR FORCE ACTIVITY OF MARRIED WOMEN IN THE UNITED STATES. Ann Arbor: Univ. of Michigan, 1968.

3265. Tropman, John E. "The Married Professional Social Worker," JOURNAL OF MARRIAGE AND THE FAMILY, vol. 30 (Nov. 1968), pp. 661-665.

3266. U.S. Department of Labor. "Who Are the Working Mothers?" Wage and Price Standards Administration, Women's Bureau, Leaflet 37. Washington, D.C.: SUDOC, GPO, 1968.

3267. U.S. Department of Labor. Women's Bureau. WOMEN WORKERS IN THEIR FAMILY ENVIRONMENT. Washington, D.C.: SUDOC, GPO, 1941. 82 pp.

D. Women's Labor Unions and Organizations

Workers of the world—UNITE!
—Communist Manifesto

3268. Adams, Elizabeth K. WOMEN PROFESSIONAL WORKERS, A STUDY MADE FOR THE WOMEN'S EDUCATIONAL AND INDUSTRIAL UNION. New York: Macmillan, 1921. 467 pp. Addressed to undergraduates deciding on a profession, to college graduates not satisfied with their jobs, and to college teachers and employers.

3269. American Association of University Women. SUMMARIES OF STUDIES ON THE ECONOMIC STATUS OF WOMEN, COMPILED BY THE AMERICAN ASSOCIATION OF UNIVERSITY WOMEN. Washington, D.C.: GPO, 1935. 20 pp.

3270. ———. COUNSELING TECHNIQUES FOR MATURE WOMEN: A REPORT TO THE OFFICE OF MANPOWER, AUTOMATION AND TRAINING. Washington, D.C.: AAUW Educational Foundation, 1966. 447 pp. Collection of articles given at a professional meeting, dealing with counseling to help the mature women enjoy the fullest advantages of earning a living and living a satisfying personal life.

3271. ———. NEW CAREERS FOR WOMEN, 1970-80. Edited by Dora R. Evers. Washington, D.C.: AAUW Educational Foundation, 1966. 47 pp. Describes careers in engineering, astronomy, international affairs, higher education, social work, and other areas open to women.

3272. Andrews, John B., and W.P. D. Bliss. HISTORY OF WOMEN IN TRADE UNIONS IN THE UNITED STATES, vol. 10. Washington, D.C.: Department of Labor. Report on the Conditions of Women and Child Wage Earners, 1911.

3273. Boone, Gladys. THE WOMEN'S TRADE UNION LEAGUES IN GREAT BRITAIN AND THE UNITED STATES OF AMERICA. New York: Columbia Univ. Press, 1942; London: P. S. King, 1942. 283 pp. A history of these organizations from 1913 to 1929.

3274. Business and Professional Women's Association. PROFILES OF BUSINESS AND PROFESSIONAL WOMEN. Washington, D.C.: BPWA, 1970. 86 pp.

3275. Cleveland Chamber of Commerce, Committee on Industrial Welfare. A REPORT ON THE PROBLEM OF THE SUBSTITUTION OF WOMAN FOR MAN POWER IN INDUSTRY. Cleveland: Author, 1918. 49 pp.

3276. Cook, Alice H. WOMEN AND AMERICAN TRADE UNIONS. Ithaca, N.Y.: New York State School of Industrial and Labor Relations, 1968. Reprint Series, no. 237. Reprinted from THE ANNALS, vol. 375 (Jan. 1968), pp. 124-132.

3277. Dehareng, Marcelle. "Japanese Women at Work," FREE LABOR WORLD, Dec. 1971, pp. 8-10. Discusses the women's trade unions in Japan and how they help women workers.

3278. Drake, Barbara. WOMEN IN TRADE UNIONS. London: Allen and Unwin, 1920. 244 pp.

3279. Foner, Philip Sheldon. HISTORY OF THE LABOR MOVEMENT IN THE UNITED STATES. 4 vols. New York: International Publishers, 1947. 524 pp. Vol. 1: From Colonial times to the founding of the AFL—women and working conditions, trade unions; Vol. 2: Women in various unions and special problems of black women; Vol. 3: AFL from 1900-1909,

with emphasis on discrimination against women in the AFL, the number
of women in industry, status of unionism among women, and women's
strikes; Vol. 4: a study of the Industrial Workers of the World from 1905-
1917, woman suffrage, and the organization and work of the Women's
Trade Union League.

3280. Henry, Alice. THE TRADE UNION WOMAN. New York: Appleton, 1915.
314 pp.

3281. ———. WOMEN AND THE LABOR MOVEMENT. New York: Doran,
1923. 241 pp.

3282. Herron, Belva M. THE PROGRESS OF LABOR ORGANIZATION AMONG
WOMEN; TOGETHER WITH SOME CONSIDERATIONS CONCERNING
THEIR PLACE IN INDUSTRY. Urbana, Ill.: Univ. of Illinois Press, 1905.
79 pp.

3283. International Congress of Working Women. FIRST CONVENTION OF THE
INTERNATIONAL CONFERENCE OF WORKING WOMEN. 2 vols.
Washington, D.C.: International Congress of Working Women, 1919.

3284. Krout, Angeline. "Theme of Eighth Congress of Career Women Leaders:
Be Involved," THE SECRETARY, vol. 32 (Feb. 1972), pp. 6-7+.

3285. Lynd, Alice, and Staughton Lynd. RANK AND FILE. Boston: Beacon
Press, Sept. 1973. Personal histories of men and women who have been
involved in working-class organizing from the 1930's to the present

3286. Malkiel, Theresa. THE DIARY OF A SHIRTWAIST STRIKER. New York:
Cooperative Press, 1910. Concerns the reaction to the New York shirtwaist makers strike, in the words of one of the female strikers.

3287. O'Kelly, E. "Corn Mill Societies in Southern Cameroons," AFRICAN
WOMEN, vol. 1, no. 1 (1955), pp. 33-35. Women's societies originally
formed to play the role of cooperatives and to buy farm machinery.

3288. Pesotta, Rose. BREAD UPON THE WATERS. Edited by John N. Beffel.
New York: Dodd, Mead, 1945. 435 pp. A study of the American labor
movement. Special attention is given to the needle trades, by a young
woman who, from 1934 to 1944, was the only female vice-president of
of the International Ladies Garment Workers' Union.

3289. Rosenberg, Bernard, and Saul Weinman. "An Interview with Myra Wolfgang: Young Women Who Work," DISSENT, vol. 29 (Winter 1972), pp.
36. The international vice-president of the Hotel, Motel and Restaurant
Employees' Union speaks of the restaurant industry as provider of low
paying service jobs to women who need to work at odd hours.

3290. Schneiderman, Rose, and Lucy G. Schneiderman. ALL FOR ONE. New
York: P. S. Eriksson, 1967. 264 pp. Rose's accounts of her trade union
activities, including her part as president of the New York Women's
Trade Union League.

3291. U.S. Departmentof Labor. TOWARDS BETTER WORKING CONDI-
TIONS FOR WOMEN—METHODS AND POLICIES OF THE NATION-
AL WOMEN'S TRADE UNION LEAGUE. Women's Bureau Bulletin no.
252. Washington, D.C.: GPO, 1953.

3292. ———. A REPORT: UNIONS AND THE CHANGING STATUS OF
WOMEN WORKERS. Washington, D.C.: SUDOC, GPO, 1965. 29 pp.

3293. Van Etten, Ida M. THE CONDITION OF WOMEN WORKERS
UNDER THE PRESENT INDUSTRIAL SYSTEM. New York: Concord
Cooperative Print, 1891. 16 pp. An address delivered at the National
Convention of the American Federation of Labor.

3294. Williams, Maithy. "The Working Girls Strike," INDEPENDENT, vol. 67, no. 3186 (Dec. 23, 1909).

3295. "Women in Trade Unions," LABOUR GAZETTE, vol. 71 (Oct. 1971), pp. 682-685. Looks at the trend of female membership in unions in Canada and the United States.

3296. "Women's Work and Organizations," THE ANNALS, vol. 28, no. 2 (1906), 159 pp.

3297. "Women Workers," AMERICAN FEDERATIONIST, vol. 36 (Aug. 1929). Entire issue devoted to women workers and their trade unions.

3298. Wolfson, Theresa. THE WOMAN WORKER AND THE TRADE UNIONS. New York: International Publishers, 1926. 224 pp.

E. Women in Domestic Labor

> To make a happy fire-side clime
> To weans and wife,
> That's the true pathos and sublime
> Of human life.
> —Robert Burns

3299. Beecher, Catherine E. A TREATISE ON DOMESTIC ECONOMY. New York: Source Book Press, 1970. 465 pp. Reprint of the 1841 edition. Written for young ladies at home on a variety of subjects: domestic economy, household chores, and care of the family.

3300. Christensen, Ethlyn. "Household Employment: Restructuring the Occupation," ISSUES IN INDUSTRIAL SOCIETY, vol. 2, no. 1 (1971), pp. 47-53. Describes how the National Committee on Household Employment has been trying to stimulate and assist with the formation of community committees to help change public attitudes toward household employees and their working conditions.

3301. Johnson, Lucille L. "National Pilot Program of Household Employment: Final Report of the Experimental and Demonstration Projects," from GOVERNMENT REPORTS ANNOUNCEMENT, Dec. 25, 1971. 84 pp. The report describes the development of a national effort to solve the household services employment problem.

3302. Murray, K. C. "Women's Weaving Among the Yoruba at Omuaran in Ilorin Province," THE NIGERIAN FIELD, vol. 5, no. 4 (1936), pp. 182-191. Description of the work and economic activities of women weavers; illustrated.

3303. Nemo, J. "Contributions a L'Etude Demographique et Sociologique d'Une Ville du Togo: Palime," DOCUMENTS ET STATISTIQUES; no. 22, pp. 67-74. Paris: Ministère de la France d'Outre-Mer. Discusses the social significance of the economic activities of women in such domestic fields as agriculture, dressmaking, and petty trade.

3304. Schonberger, Richard J. "Inflexible Working Conditions Keep Women 'Unliberated'," PERSONNEL JOURNAL, vol. 50 (Nov. 1971), pp. 834-837. Talks about the ways in which the housewife can become liberated and have the same opportunities for advancement as the college woman has.

3305. Sloan, Edith B. "Keynote Address, First National Conference of Household Workers," NCHE NEWS, vol. 2, no. 7 (July 1971). Looks at the problems of the housewife and how she can liberate herself to demand the wages, benefits, and respect enjoyed by other workers.

3306. Sweet, James A. "The Employment of Rural Farm Wives." ERIC. Madison Institute for Research on Poverty, 1971. 54 pp. Analysis of data from the 1960 Census of Population and Housing, comparing the employment rates of married farm women with those of married nonfarm women.

F. Women in Business, Industry and Production

Women are the original moon-lighters.
          —*Len Bergstrom*

3307. Agassi, Judith B. "Women Who Work in Factories," DISSENT, Winter 1972, pp. 233-239.

3308. Ames, Azel. SEX IN INDUSTRY: A PLEA FOR THE WORKING-GIRL. Boston: J. R. Osgood, 1875. 158 pp.

3309. Anderson, Adelaide M. WOMEN IN THE FACTORIES (1839-1921). New York: Dutton, 1922. 316 pp.

3310. Anderson, Mary. "Women in Industry," AMERICAN FEDERATIONIST, vol. 32 (May 1925), pp. 333-335.

3311. Baker, Elizabeth Faulkner. TECHNOLOGY AND WOMAN'S WORK. New York: Columbia Univ. Press, 1964. 460 pp. The impact of industrial technology on women's labor. Limited to American women in the twentieth century.

3312. Baker, Helen. WOMEN IN WAR INDUSTRIES. Princeton, N.J.: Princeton Univ. Press, 1942. 82 pp. Discusses problems and adjustments made by companies employing women, selection procedures, training, hours of work, wages, health and safety, and care of children of working mothers in industry.

3313. Banning, Margaret C. WOMEN FOR DEFENSE. New York: Duell, 1942. 243 pp. Serious appraisal of womanpower and its usefulness during the beginning of World War II.

3314. Blood, Kathryn. NEGRO WOMEN WAR WORKERS. Women's Bureau Bulletin no. 205. Washington, D.C.: U.S. Department of Labor, 1945. 23 pp.

3315. Boserup, Esther. WOMEN'S ROLE IN ECONOMIC DEVELOPMENT. London: Allen and Unwin, 1970. 283 pp. The role of women in traditional agricultural society and in modern industrial societies is surveyed.

3316. Brooks, Tom. "The Terrible Triangle Fire," AMERICAN HERITAGE, vol. 8, no. 5 (Aug. 1957), pp. 54-57. New York failed to enact facotry safety legislation until it was shocked into action by the Triangle Shirtwaist Factory fire in 1911, in which 148 persons, mostly women, were helplessly trapped and killed within a few minutes.

3317. Brown, Jean Collier. THE NEGRO WOMAN WORKER. Women's Bureau Bulletin no. 165. Washington, D.C.: U.S. Department of Labor, 1938. 17 pp.

3318. Bruere, Martha. "The Triangle Fire," LIFE AND LABOR, vol. 1, no. 5 (May 1911), n.p.

3319. Butler, Elizabeth B. WOMEN AND THE TRADES. New York: Arno Press, 1969. 440 pp. Reprint of the 1909 edition. Diagnoses an American industrial district (Pittsburgh) and describes the economic effects of women employed there.

3320. Campbell, Helen Stuart. PRISONERS OF POVERTY, WOMEN WAGE WORKERS. THEIR TRADE AND THEIR LIVES. Westport, Conn.: Greenwood Press, 1970. 257 pp. Reprint of Boston, 1887 edition. The author was an important contributor to the literature on working women in the nineteenth century. Describes the social and labor conditions of women and was instrumental in bringing about reform legislation.

3321. ———. WOMEN WAGE-EARNERS: THEIR PAST, THEIR PRESENT, AND THEIR FUTURE. New York: Arno Press, 1972. 313 pp. Reprint of 1893 edition. Traces the way in which barriers to women's entry into the industrial labor force were removed, and the impact of women's entry into it.

3322. Crowley, Joan E., Teresa E. Levitin, and Robert P. Quinn. "Facts and Fictions about the American Working Woman." Research for the Employment Standards Administration, U.S. Department of Labor, Jan. 1973.

3323. Davis, Ethelyn. "Careers as Concerns of Blue-Collar Workers." Pp. 154-164 in BLUE COLLAR WORLD, edited by Arthur Shostak and William Gomberg. Englewood Cliffs, N.J.: Prentice Hall, 1964.

3324. Eaton, Charles H. THE INDUSTRIAL POSITION OF WOMAN. New York: W. R. Jenkins Press, 1890. A lecture delivered before the School of Social Economics, New York.

3325. Flynn, Elizabeth Gurley. WOMEN IN THE WAR. New York: Workers Library, 1942. 31 pp. Female contributions to the war effort.

3326. Gordon, Margaret S. "A Symposium: Women in the Labor Force," INDUSTRIAL RELATIONS, vol. 7 (May 1968), pp. 187-248.

3327. Greenbaum, Marcia L. "Adding 'Kenntnis' to Kirche, Küche and Kinder," ISSUES IN INDUSTRIAL SOCIETY, vol. 2 no. 1 (1971), pp. 61-68. Suggestions as to what employers can do to aid the woman worker in industry.

3328. Guilbert, Madeleine. LES FONCTIONS DES FEMMES DANS L'INDUS-TRIE. Paris: Mouton, 1966. 393 pp. Survey of French problems connected with women in industry.

3329. Hatcher, Orie L. RURAL GIRLS IN THE CITY FOR WORK: A STUDY MADE FOR THE SOUTHERN WOMAN'S EDUCATIONAL ALLIANCE. Richmond, Va.: Garrett and Massie, 1930. 154 pp.

3330. Hutchinson, Emilie J. WOMEN'S WAGES, A STUDY OF THE WAGES OF INDUSTRIAL WOMEN AND MEASURES SUGGESTED TO INCREASE THEM. London: Longmans Green, 1919; New York: Columbia Univ. Press, 1919. 179 pp.

3331. Josephson, Hanna Geffen. THE GOLDEN THREADS: NEW ENGLAND'S MILL GIRLS AND MAGNATES. New York: Duell, Sloan, and Pearce, 1949. 325 pp. Interesting history of the horrific conditions of female labor in nineteenth-century New England mills.

3332. Kelley, Florence. MODERN INDUSTRY IN RELATION TO THE FAMILY: A HEALTH EDUCATION ON MORALITY. New York: Longmans, 1914. Four lectures given at Columbia University on factory life by an early reformer.

3333. Klein, Viola. BRITAIN'S MARRIED WOMEN WORKERS. London: Routledge and Kegan Paul, 1965. Study of labor conditions in England's factories.

3334. Koontz, Elizabeth D. "The Progress of the Woman Worker: An Unfinished Story," ISSUES IN INDUSTRIAL SOCIETY, vol. 2, no. 1 (1971), pp. 29-31. Surveys the changes and trends in the role of working women since 1920.

3335. Larcom, Lucy. AN IDYLL OF WORK. Westport, Conn.: Greenwood Press, 1969. Reprint of 1875 edition. A narrative poem based on the authors's experiences in the Lowell mills which provides excellent accounts of working women in New England. An important source of information on factory conditions during the nineteenth century.

3336. Lattimore, Eleanor L., and Ray S. Trent. LEGAL RECOGNITION OF INDUSTRIAL WOMEN. New York: Young Women's Christian Association, Industrial Committee, War Work Council of the National Board, 1919. 91 pp.

3337. Laughlin, Clara E. THE WORK-A-DAY GIRL: A STUDY OF SOME PRESENT-DAY CONDITIONS. New York: Fleming H. Revell, 1913. 320 pp.

3338. Lee, Kendrick, "Women in War Work," EDITORIAL RESEARCH REPORTS (Washington, D.C.), vol. 1, no. 4, pp. 61-78.

3339. Levine, Louis. THE WOMEN GARMENT WORKERS. New York: Huebsch, 1924. A history of the women of the needle trades.

3340. LOWELL OFFERING: WRITTEN, EDITED AND PUBLISHED BY FEMALE OPERATIVES EMPLOYED IN THE MILLS. Series 1, nos. 1-4 (all published), 1840-41; series 2, vols. 1-5, 1841-45. Westport, Conn.: Greenwood Press, 1970. Reprint of 1840-1845 edition. Articles written exclusively by women employed in mills in Massachusetts. An important original source for research into working conditions of women in the 1830s and 1840s.

3341. McConnell, Dorothy. WOMEN, WAR AND FASCISM. New York: American League Against War and Fascism, 1935. 18 pp. Communist-front pamphlet protesting the use of women as cheap labor in factories and offices in the United States and in the fascist states.

3342. MacLean, Annie M. WAGE-EARNING WOMEN. New York: Macmillan, 1910. 202 pp. Introduction by Grace H. Dodge.

3343. ———. WOMEN WORKERS AND SOCIETY. Chicago: McClurg, 1916. 135 pp.

3344. McNally, Gertrude Bancroft. "Patterns of Female Labor Force Activity," INDUSTRIAL RELATIONS, vol. 7 (May 1968), pp. 204-218.

3345. Mahon, Lucy R. THE SHORTER DAY AND WOMEN WORKERS. Richmond, Va.: Virginia League of Women Voters, 1922. 26 pp.

3346. National Consumers' League. EARNING OF WOMEN IN FACTORIES AND A LEGAL LIVING WAGE. New York: Author, 1921. 27 pp.

3347. ———. EQUAL OPPORTUNITY FOR WOMEN WAGE EARNERS: FACTS VS. FICTION. New York: Author, 1920. 10 pp. An early polemic.

3348. National Federation of Settlements. YOUNG WORKING GIRLS: A SUMMARY OF EVIDENCE FROM TWO THOUSAND SOCIAL WORKERS. Boston: Houghton Mifflin, 1913. 185 pp. A survey of working conditions.

3349. National Industrial Conference Board. WOMEN WORKERS AND LABOR SUPPLY. New York: Author, 1936. 42 pp.

3350. Nearing, Scott. WOMEN IN AMERICAN INDUSTRY. Philadelphia and Boston: American Baptist Publication Society, 1915. 18 pp.

3351. Nelson, Nell [pseud.]. THE WHITE SLAVE GIRLS OF CHICAGO. NELL NELSON'S STARTLING DISCLOSURE OF THE CRUELTIES AND INIQUITIES PRACTICED IN THE WORKSHOPS AND FACTORIES OF A GREAT CITY. Chicago: Barkley, 1888. 139 pp.

3352. "Occupations of Women and Their Compensation: A Compilation of Essays by Prominent Authorities on All the Leading Trades and Professions in America in Which Women Have Asserted Their Ability, With Data as to the Compensation Afforded in Each One," THE NEW YORK TRIBUNE vol. 9, no. 12 (1898), 133 pp.

3353. Oppenheimer, Valerie K. THE FEMALE LABOR FORCE IN THE UNITED STATES: DEMOGRAPHIC AND ECONOMIC FACTORS GOVERNING ITS GROWTH AND CHANGING COMPOSITION. Berkeley: Univ. of California, Institute of International Studies, 1970. 197 pp.

3354. ———. "The Interaction of Demand and Supply and Its Effect on the Female Labor Force in the United States," POPULATION STUDIES, vol. 21, no. 3 (Nov. 1967), pp. 239-259. The demand for female labor is rising and this broadening demand for women workers has led to an increase in older married women entering the industrial labor market.

3355. Parker, Cornelia Stratton. WORKING WITH THE WORKING WOMAN. New York: Harper, 1922.

3356. Pidgeon, Mary E. EMPLOYMENT OF WOMEN IN THE EARLY POST-WAR PERIOD WITH BACKGROUND OF PRE-WAR AND WAR DATA. Washington, D.C.: U.S. Department of Labor, Women's Bureau, 1946. 14 pp. Statistical study.

3357. ———. NEGRO WOMEN IN INDUSTRY IN 15 STATES. Bulletin no. 70. Washington, D.C.: U.S. Department of Labor, 1929. 74 pp.

3358. Pruette, Lorine, ed. "Women in Industry," INDUSTRIAL PSYCHOLOGY, vol. 1 (April 1926), pp. 247-298.

3359. Russell, Thomas H. THE GIRLS' FIGHT FOR A LIVING: HOW TO PROTECT WORKING WOMEN FROM DANGERS DUE TO LOW WAGES. AN IMPARTIAL SURVEY OF PRESENT CONDITIONS, RESULTS OF RECENT INVESTIGATIONS, AND REMEDIES PRO-POSED. Chicago: M. A. Donahue, 1913. 200 pp.

3360. Spoor, Lillie M. WOMEN AND THE PROBLEM OF EARNING A LIV-ING. Denver, Colo.: Ward and Saunders, 1912. 62 pp.

3361. Sweden, National Labour Market Board. "Women and the Labour Market, Prejudice, Facts, Future." National Labour Market Board, 1969. 33 pp. Background data on women in the labor market.

3362. Trent, Ray S. WOMEN IN INDUSTRY. Bulletin of the Extension Division, vol. 3, no. 7. Bloomington: Indiana Univ. 1918. 59 pp.

3363. U.S. Department of Labor. "Background Facts on Women Workers in the United States." Washington, D.C.: SUDOC, GPO, 1970. 20 pp. Statistics on women in industry.

3364. Willett, Mabel Hurd. "Women in the Clothing Trade." In TRADE UNION-ISM AND LABOR PROBLEMS, edited by John Rogers. New York: Ginn, 1905. 628 pp.

3365. ———. THE EMPLOYMENT OF WOMEN IN THE CLOTHING TRADE. Studies in History, Economics, and Public Law, vol. 16, no. 2. New York: Columbia Univ., 1902.

G. Women in the Professions

The professions indeed supply the keystone to the arch of woman's liberty.
—*Julia Ward Howe*

3366. Coxhead, E. WOMEN IN THE PROFESSIONS. London: Longmans Green, 1961. 37 pp. A survey of women in the professions by job categories.

3367. Cussler, Margaret. THE WOMAN EXECUTIVE. New York: Harcourt, Brace, 1958. 165 pp. Case studies of women in a variety of white-collar positions in the eastern United States.

3368. Farley, Jennie. ACADEMIC WOMEN: FACTORS AFFECTING LEVEL OF LABOR FORCE PARTICIPATION. Ithaca, N.Y.: Cornell Univ., 1970. Pilot study sponsored by the Office of Research.

3369. Fidell, Linda S., and John De Lamater, eds. WOMEN IN THE PROFESSIONS: WHAT'S ALL THE FUSS ABOUT? Beverly Hills, Calif.: Sage, 1974. 144 pp. An anthology of essays devoted to women in the professions; includes such titles as "On the Status of Women," "Non-Academic Professional Political Scientists," "An Analysis of Femininity in Nursing," "Soviet Women in the Work Force and Professions," and "Women in the Professional Caucuses."

3370. Graham, Patricia A. "Women in Academe," SCIENCE, vol. 169 (Sept. 1970), pp. 1284-1290. Survey of current employment of women in colleges and universities, and why it is so low.

3371. Hughes, Helen MacGill. "Maid of All Work or Departmental Sister-in-Law? The Faculty Wife Employed on Campus," AMERICAN JOURNAL OF SOCIOLOGY, vol. 78, no. 4 (Jan. 1973), pp. 767-772. Personal account by the author of her position as assistant editor of the AMERICAN JOURNAL OF SOCIOLOGY. Seventeen years of editorial experience did not result in her being offered a job or position on the campus where the AJS was published, in spite of the permanent and professional nature of her work.

3372. Kahne, Hilda. "Women in the Professions: Career Considerations and Job Placement Techniques," JOURNAL OF ECONOMIC ISSUES, no. 3 (Summer 1971), pp. 28-45. Looks at the social structure and attitudes affecting career choice and job placement for women.

3373. Kass, Babette, and Rose C. Feld. THE ECONOMIC STRENGTH OF BUSINESS AND PROFESSIONAL WOMEN. New York: Columbia Univ. for the National Federation of Business and Professional Women's Clubs, 1954. 140 pp.

3374. Kay, M. Jane. "A Positive Approach to Women in Management," PERSONNEL JOURNAL, vol. 51 (Jan. 1972), pp. 38-41.

3375. Keniston, Ellen, and Kenneth Keniston. "An American Anachronism: The Image of Women and Work," AMERICAN SCHOLAR, vol. 33 (Summer 1964), pp. 355-378. Looks at the probelms professionally trained women have in obtaining jobs.

3376. Lewin, Arie Y., and Linda Duncan. "Women in Academia," SCIENCE, vol. 173 (Sept. 1971), pp. 892-895. A study of hiring decisions in departments of physical science.

3377. Lopate, Carol. WOMEN IN MEDICINE. Baltimore: Johns Hopkins Press, 1964. 208 pp.

3378. Loring, Rosalind, and Theodora Wells, eds. BREAKTHROUGH: WOMEN INTO MANAGEMENT. New York: Van Nostrand, Reinhold, 1973. How and why the admission of more women into the managerial ranks ensures greater productivity and profit for their organizations.

3379. Lowenthal, Helen. "A Healthy Anger," LIBRARY JOURNAL, vol. 96 (Sept. 1, 1971), pp. 2597-2599. Looks at the inequality of men's and women's roles in the field of library science.

3380. McLean, Beth B., and Jeanne Paris. THE YOUNG WOMAN IN BUSINESS. Ames: Iowa State Univ. Press, 1962. 304 pp.

3381. Mathews, John. "Female Rights and Faculty Rights," CHANGE, vol. 3 (Summer 1971), pp. 13-15. Summary of data presented to a House sub-committee on the case against the University of Michigan dealing with sex discrimination on college campuses.

3382. Mattfeld, Jacquelyn, and Carol G. Van Aken, eds. WOMEN AND THE SCIENTIFIC PROFESSION: THE MIT SYMPOSIUM ON AMERICAN WOMEN IN SCIENCE AND ENGINEERING. Cambridge: M.I.T. Press, 1965. 245 pp. Covers such topics as barriers to the career choice of women in engineering, how to enhance the roles of women in science, the present status of women scientists, and the pros and cons of employ-ing women scientists.

3383. Motz, Annabelle Bender. "The Roles of Married Women in Science," MARRIAGE AND FAMILY LIVING, vol. 23 (Nov. 1961), pp. 374-379.

3384. Nadelson, Carol, and Malkah T. Notman. "The Woman Physician," JOURNAL OF MEDICAL EDUCATION, vol. 47 (Mar. 1972), pp. 176-183.

3385. National Education Association. PROFESSIONAL WOMEN IN PUBLIC SCHOOLS, 1970-71. National Education Association Research Bulletin. Washington, D.C. vol. 49 no. 3 (Oct. 1971). pp. 67-68. 95.9 percent of full-time public school system women employees are teachers, nurses, and librarians.

3386. Parrish, John B. "Professional Womanpower as a Soviet Resource." QUAR-TERLY REVIEW OF ECONOMICS AND BUSINESS. vol. 4 no. 3 (Autumn 1964), pp. 55-61.

3387. Poloma, Margaret M., and Garland T. Neal. "Married Professional Women: A Study in the Tolerance of Domestication," JOURNAL OF MARRI-AGE AND THE FAMILY, vol. 33 (Aug. 1971), pp. 531-540. Special issue.

3388. Renshaw, J. E., and M. Y. Pennell. "Distribution of Women Physicians, 1969," WOMAN PHYSICIAN, vol. 26 (April 1971), pp. 187-195. Data on 24,000 women physicians compiled from AMA files.

3389. Sassower, Doris L. "The Legal Rights of Professional Women," CON-TEMPORARY EDUCATION, vol. 43 (Feb. 1972), pp. 205-208. Dis-cusses the protective forms laws take as they make arbitrary distinctions based on sex.

3390. Schiller, Anita. "Aware," AMERICAN LIBRARIES, vol. 2 (Dec. 1971), pp. 1215-1216. The number of key positions held by women profess-ionals is lower than at any point in recent history. This fact is explained and some views are aired on the subject.

3391. Schwartz, Bella. WOMEN IN SCIENTIFIC CAREERS. Washington, D.C.: National Science Foundation, 1961. 18 pp.

3392. Schwartz, Eleanor Brantley. "The Sex Barrier in Business," ATLANTA ECONOMIC REVIEW, vol. 21 (June 1971), pp. 4-9. A survey of 300

male executives from large corporations and 300 successful businesswomen to make recommendations for eliminating discrimination.

3393. Souter, L. S., and R. Winslade. WOMEN ENGINEERS IN THE USSR.
London: Caroline Haslett Memorial Trust, 1960. 28 pp.

3394. Tara, Bill. "The Art Director Ladies of Los Angeles," COMMUNICATION
ARTS, vol. 13, no. 2 (1970), pp. 84-90. Discussions by a group of
lady art directors on the problems of prejudice toward women in the
art director field.

3395. Theodore, Athena, ed. THE PROFESSIONAL WOMAN. Cambridge,
Mass.: Schenkman, 1971. 761 pp. Excellent collection of articles, with
an equally excellent bibliography of sources.

3396. Thomas, Dorothy. WOMEN LAWYERS IN THE U.S. New York: Scarecrow Press, 1957. 477 pp. General study of women in the legal profession.

3397. Tinker, Irene. "Non-Academic Professional Political Scientists," AMERI-
CAN BEHAVIORAL SCIENTIST, vol. 15 (Dec. 1971), pp. 206-212.
Sixty answers to a form sent to women in extra-academic positions in
government showing that discrimination exists for women in this field of
political science. Issue on Women in Professions.

3398. Tuttle, Helen W. "Women in Academic Libraries," LIBRARY JOURNAL,
vol. 96 (Sept. 1, 1971), pp. 2594-2596. A look at discrimination against
female academic librarians, from differences in income and position to
the make-up of the Association of Academic and Research Libraries and
the editorial staff of its publication.

3399. U.S. Department of Labor. CAREERS FOR WOMEN IN THE BIOLOGICAL
SCIENCES. Woman's Bureau, Washington, D.C.: SUDOC, GPO. 1961. 86 pp.

H. Women in the Semiprofessions

Women's values and goals make many of them tractable subordinates.
—Richard and Ida Simpson
("Women and Bureaucracy in the Semi-
Professions")

3400. Aguirre, Mme. Gertrude G. de. WOMEN IN THE BUSINESS WORLD; OR,
HINTS AND HELPS TO PROSPERITY, BY ONE OF THEM. Boston:
Arena, 1894. 322 pp.

3401. Alpha Kappa Alpha Sorority. WOMEN IN BUSINESS. Booklet no. 3.
Chicago: Alpha Kappa Alpha Sorority, Inc., 1970. 24 pp. Short sketches
of Negro women in executive and administrative positions.

3402. Basil, Douglas C. WOMEN IN MANAGEMENT. New York: Dunellen,
1972. 124 pp. Research study of attitudes toward women as
managers with profiles of the woman executive and a guide on
prejudice against women in management positions.

3403. Birdwell, Russell. WOMEN IN BATTLE DRESS. New York: Fine Editions Press, 1942. 198 pp. About the work of British women in various
branches of the military professions.

3404. Brandel, M. "The African Career Woman in South Africa," AFRICAN
WOMEN, vol. 2, no. 2 (1957), pp. 36-38. Study of the new, westernized
way of life of professional and semiprofessional women, particularly
nurses, teachers, and social workers.

3405. Buffington, H. Glenn. "Jean LaRene: Professional Pilot of the Golden Age,"
JOURNAL OF THE AMERICAN AVIATION HISTORICAL SOCIETY,

vol. 14, no. 1 (Spring 2969), pp. 47-49. Biographical article of a pioneer aviatrix.

3406. ———. "Louise Thaden," AMERICAN AVIATION HISTORICAL JOURNAL, vol. 12, no. 4 (Winter 1967), pp. 285-287. Woman aviatrix.

3407. ———. "Phoebe Fairgrove Omlie: USA's First Woman Transport Pilot," JOURNAL OF THE AMERICAN AVIATION HISTORICAL SOCIETY, vol. 13, no. 3 (Fall 1968), pp. 186-188.

3408. Etzioni, Amitai, ed. SEMI-PROFESSIONS AND THEIR ORGANIZATION. New York: Free Press, 1969. 328 pp. A scholarly and authoritative collection of six papers dealing with women's status in the semiprofessions and with the limits of professionalization.

3409. Herberg, D. M. THE CAREER PATTERNS OF FEMALE SOCIAL WORKERS. Ann Arbor: Univ. of Michigan. Department of Sociology, n.d. Information on the employment and the extent of underutilization of these women, and the determinants of their career decisions.

3410. Keyserling, M. D. EXPLODING THE MYTHS. Report of a Conference on Expanding Employment Opportunities for Career Women. Washington, D.C.: U.S. Department of Labor, Women's Bureau, 1967. 67 pp.

3411. Koontz, Elizabeth D. "The Extension Worker and the Changing Role of Women," JOURNAL OF HOME ECONOMICS, vol. 64 (Nov. 1971), pp. 588-590. Discusses the changes in the field of home economics as being more job-oriented training and not a preparation for homemaking.

3412. Kreps, Juanita. SEX IN THE MARKET PLACE: AMERICAN WOMEN AT WORK. Baltimore, Md.: Johns Hopkins Press, 1971. 117 pp. In addition to careers open to women, this book discusses the prejudices women confront in pursuing careers in the semiprofessions. Bibliography included.

3413. Lewis, Martha. "Nurse-Midwifery—A Growing Profession," THE CRISIS, vol. 78 (July 1971), pp. 155-157. Series of interviews with several professionals in the field of midwifery discussing their duties and the advantages in the field.

3414. Lockerby, Florence K. "Nurses' Roles Expanded," HOSPITALS, vol. 45 (Dec. 16, 1971), pp. 92+.

3415. Lubove, Roy. THE PROFESSIONAL ALTRUIST: THE EMERGENCE OF SOCIAL WORK AS A CAREER, 1880-1930. Cambridge: Harvard Univ. Press, 1965. 291 pp.

3416. MacKensie, R. Alex. "Are Executive Secretaries Obsolete?" PERSONNEL, vol. 48 (Sept.-Oct. 1971), pp. 60-64.

3417. Manette, Jan [pseud]. THE WORKING GIRL IN A MAN'S WORLD: A GUIDE TO OFFICE POLITICS. New York: Hawthorne Books, 1966. 223 pp.

3418. McCord, Bird. "Identifying and Developing Women for Management Positions," TRAINING AND DEVELOPMENT JOURNAL, vol. 25 (Nov. 1971), pp. 25+. Factors contributing to the shortage of management level women are studied, with examples from 150 companies.

3419. "Midwives in Canada," CANADIAN NURSE, vol. 67 no. 7 (July 1971), pp. 17-19. By P. Hays.

3420. Nekvasil, Charles A. "Sweet Young Things 'Invade' Industrial Selling (Omega Chemical Company)," INDUSTRY WEEK, vol. 172 (Jan. 17, 1972), pp. 45-46+.

3421. Nottingham, Ev. "Women's Lib and the Forest," AMERICAN FOREST, vol. 78 (Jan. 1972), pp. 8-11. Careers open for women in the conservation and forest fields.

3422. Pidgeon, Mary E. WOMEN IN THE FEDERAL SERVICE, 1923-1947. 2 vols. Washington, D.C.: GPO, 1949-50. Semiprofessional women in the federal service.

3423. Preston, Marilynn, Patricia Anstett, and Glenda Sampson. "Women in the Newsroom '71: Still Begging Crumbs," CHICAGO JOURNALISM REVIEW, vol. 4 no. 7 (July 1971), pp. 3-4. Describes the problems a newswoman has in working in the Chicago newsrooms.

3424. Pruette, Lorine, and Iva L. Peters, eds. WOMEN WORKERS THROUGH THE DEPRESSION, A STUDY OF WHITE COLLAR EMPLOYMENT MADE BY THE AMERICAN WOMAN'S ASSOCIATION. New York: Macmillan, 1934. 164 pp.

3425. Scotch, C. Bernard. "Sex Status in Social Work: Grist for Women's Liberation," SOCIAL WORK, vol. 16 (July 1971), pp. 5-11. Article describing the field of social work and why it remains a low paying field for women. The shortage of men in this predominantly female profession should advance many women field workers to administrative positions.

3426. Silver, Henry K., and Patricia A. McAtee. "Health Care Practice: An Expanded Profession of Nursing for Men and Women," AMERICAN JOURNAL OF NURSING, vol. 72 (Jan. 1972), pp. 78-80.

3427. Tierney, Patricia. THE LADIES OF THE AVENUE: THE ADVERTISING AGENCY JUNGLE DEFOLIATED BY AN INSIDER, A SUCCESSFUL WOMAN COPYWRITER. New York: Bartholomew House, 1971. The trials and tribulations of a woman advertising copywriter in this male-dominated area.

3428. Tolman, Mary H. POSITIONS OF RESPONSIBILITY IN DEPARTMENT STORES AND OTHER RETAIL SELLING ORGANIZATIONS: A STUDY OF OPPORTUNITIES FOR WOMEN. New York: Bureau of Vocational Information, 1921. 126 pp.

3429. U.S. Civil Service Commission. STUDY OF EMPLOYMENT OF WOMEN IN THE FEDERAL GOVERNMENT, 1968. Washington, D.C.: GPO, 1969. 237 pp.

3430. U.S. Department of Labor. CAREERS FOR WOMEN AS TECHNICIANS. Washington, D.C.: Women's Bureau, 1961.

3431. Van Schaick, Frances L. WOMEN IN HIGHER-LEVEL POSITIONS OF RESPONSIBILITY IN RELATED FIELDS OF BUSINESS AND INDUSTRY AND IN SPECIFIED AREAS. Washington, D.C.: 1950. 86 pp.

3432. Yanow, Jo. "But, Baby, Still a Long Way to Go," MADISON AVENUE, vol. 14 (July 1971), pp. 8-9+. Discusses the plight of women trying to compete with men in the advertising field.

XI. GENERAL REFERENCE WORKS ON WOMEN

The bibliographical and biographical references and lists of women's organizations, associations, collections, films, and periodicals in the next six sections attempt to incorporate as complete a cross-section of sources on women as is possible. The defects of any select bibliography are such that the reader who independently discovers a book that is relevant but unlisted does not know whether it has been rejected or simply overlooked. With the best will in the field of research endeavor, our selections will, nevertheless, contain omissions and errors. But that part of it which is comprehensive and representative should be a contribution, no matter how limited or unlimited its scope. Ignorance, rather than arrogance, has imposed further limitations upon our task of compilation. A sociologist, Robert Lynd, has cogently observed: "Research without an actively selective point of view becomes the ditty bag of an idiot, filled with bits of pebbles, straws, feathers, and other random hoardings." Our readers' concern over the hiatus of sources may stimulate future additions and corrections. To quote yet another compiler, Francis Bacon: "Truth will sooner come out from error than from confusion."

A. Bibliographies

There are books in which the footnotes, or the comments scrawled by some reader's hand in the margin, are more interesting than the text. The world is one of these books.
—*Santayana*

There is not so poor a book in the world that would not be a prodigious effort were it wrought out entirely by a single mind, without the aid of prior investigators.
—*Dr. Johnson*

3433. Ahlum, Carol, and Florence Howe, eds. THE NEW GUIDE TO CURRENT FEMALE STUDIES. Prepared by the Modern Language Association's Commission on the Status of Women, 1971. 30 pp. Available from KNOW, Inc., Box 10197. Pittsburg, Pa. 15232. Bibliography of over 600 courses on women offered in the United States and Canada.

3434. Astin, Helen. ANNOTATED BIBLIOGRAPHY OF RESEARCH ON WOMEN. Washington, D.C.: Univ. Research Corp., 1970.

3435. Astin, Helen, Nancy Suniewick, and Susan Dweck. WOMEN: A BIBLIOGRAPHY OF THEIR EDUCATION AND CAREERS. Washington, D.C.: Human Service Press, 1971. Bibliography of more than 350 works written after 1966.

3436. Bereaud, Susan. WOMEN IN EDUCATION: A BIBLIOGRAPHY. Ithaca, N.Y.: N.Y.: Cornell Univ. (Female Studies Program), 1971.

3437. Biggar, Jeanne C. BIBLIOGRAPHY ON THE SOCIOLOGY OF SEX ROLES. Charlottesville: Univ. of Virginia, Department of Sociology, 1970. Emphasis on women studies in college and university curricula.

3438. Bruemmer, Linda. "The Condition of Women in Society Today: An Annotated Bibliography—Part II," JOURNAL OF THE NATIONAL ASSOCIATION OF WOMEN DEANS AND COUNSELORS, vol. 33 (Winter 1970), pp. 89-95.

3439. Bureau International du Travail. BIBLIOGRAPHIE SUR LE TRAVAIL DES FEMMES, 1865-1965. Geneve: B.I.T., 1970. 252 pp.

3440. Business and Professional Women's Foundation. CAREER COUNSEL-ING: NEW PERSPECTIVES FOR WOMEN AND GIRLS; ANNOTA-TED BIBLIOGRAPHY. Washington, D.C.: Business and Professional Women's Foundation, 1972.

3441. ———. A SELECTED ANNOTATED BIBLIOGRAPHY: WOMEN EXECU-TIVES. Washington, D.C.: Business and Professional Women's Founda-tion, 1970. 26 pp.

3442. ———. A SELECTED ANNOTATED BIBLIOGRAPHY: WOMEN IN POSITIONS AT MANAGERIAL, ADMINISTRATIVE, AND EXECU-TIVE LEVELS. Washington, D.C.: Business and Professional Women's Foundation, 1966. 19 pp.

3443. ———. WORKING MOTHERS: ANNOTATED BIBLIOGRAPHY. Wash-ington, D.C.: Business and Professional Women's Foundation, 1968.

3444. Chatham Bookseller. WOMEN'S RIGHTS AND LIBERATION: OUT OF PRINT BOOKS AND PAMPHLETS. Chatham, N.J.: Chatham Book-seller, Catalog no. 22, n.d. Bibliography of out-of-print books and periodicals on women.

3445. Chmaj, Betty E. AMERICAN WOMEN AND AMERICAN STUDIES. Pittsburgh: KNOW, 1971. 258 pp. Includes essay and a major bibliography.

3446. Cisler, Lucinda. "Women: A Bibliography." Pp. 217-246 in VOICES OF THE NEW FEMINISM, edited by Mary Lou Thompson. Boston: Beacon Press, 1971.

3447. Cole, Johnneta B. "Black Women in America: An Annotated Bibliography," BLACK SCHOLAR, vol. 3 (Dec. 1971), pp. 42-53. Extensive annotated bibliography of articles, books, government publications, biographies, and autobiographies.

3448. Damon, Gene, and Lee Stuart. THE LESBIAN IN LIBERATION: A BIBLI-OGRAPHY. San Francisco: Daughters of Bilitis, 1967. 79 pp.

3449. Drake, Kirsten, Dorothy Marks, and Mary Wexford. WOMEN'S WORK AND WOMEN'S STUDIES. New York, N.Y.: Barnard College, Women's Center, 1971. 161 pp. Includes references on abortion, sex roles, marri-age and the family, women's vocations and careers, education, employ-ment, legal status, history, biography, literature, the arts, and the media; 1445 citations.

3450. Dubow, Rhona, compiler. THE STATUS OF WOMEN IN SOUTH AFRI-CA: A SELECT BIBLIOGRAPHY. Cape Town, S.A.: Univ. of Cape Town, School of Librarianship, 1965. 55 pp.

3451. Dupont, Julie A. WOMEN: THEIR SOCIAL AND ECONOMIC STATUS: SELECTED REFERENCES. U.S. Department of Labor, Women's Bureau. Washington, D.C.: SUDOC, GPO. Dec. 1970. 41 pp.

3452. ERIC Clearinghouse on Adult Education. "Continuing Education of Women," CURRENT INFORMATION SOURCES. Syracuse, N.Y.: Author, Dec. 1968. Documents dating from 1965-68 dealing with sex differences, social roles, employment interests and needs, programs, and women's education in foreign countries.

3453. Farians, Elizabeth. SELECTED BIBLIOGRAPHY ON WOMEN AND RELIGION. Washington, D.C.: National Organization for Women, Ecumenical Task Force on Women and Religion, 1971.

3454. Franklin, Margaret Ladd. THE CASE FOR WOMAN SUFFRAGE: A BIBLIOGRAPHY. New York: National College Equal Suffrage League, 1913.

3455. Frithoff, Patricia. A SELECTED ANNOTATED BIBLIOGRAPHY OF MATERIALS RELATED TO WOMEN IN SCIENCE. Lund, Sweden: Research Policy Program, 1967. 18 pp.
3456. Garai, Josef E. HUMAN RELATIONS BIBLIOGRAPHY. Brooklyn, N.Y.: Pratt Institute, 1970. Bibliography of studies on the psychology of women.
3457. George Washington University. DEVELOPING NEW HORIZONS FOR WOMEN: BIBLIOGRAPHY. Washington, D.C.: George Washington Univ., College of General Studies, 1970. 8 pp.
3458. Germany (Federal Republic), Bundestag Wissenschaftliche Abteilung. BIBLIOGRAPHIE ZUR SITUATION DER FRAU IN BERUF, FAMILIE, UND GESSELLSCHAFT. Bonn: Author, 1963. 33 pp.
3459. Goodland, R. A BIBLIOGRAPHY OF SEX RITES AND CUSTOMS. London, 1931.
3460. Göteborg University Library. THE WOMEN'S HISTORY COLLECTIONS. Göteborg, Sweden: Author, 1958-1971. Nine volumes have been published up to 1971. Bibliographic works as well as scholarly investigations in the field of women's history, particularly Swedish women.
3461. Harmon, Linda A., compiler. STATUS OF WOMEN IN HIGHER EDUCATION, 1963-1972: A SELECTIVE BIBLIOGRAPHY. Series in Bibliography, no. 2. Ames: Iowa State Univ. Library, 1972.
3462. Harper, Dee W., and Catherine L. Meeks. BIBLIOGRAPHY FOR THE SOCIOLOGY OF SEX ROLES. State College, Mississippi: Department of Sociology and Anthropology, Aug. 1972.
3463. Howe, Florence. FEMALE STUDIES II, III, IV. Available from KNOW, Inc., P.O. Box 10197, Pittsburgh, Pa. 15232.
3464. ———. A GUIDE TO CURRENT FEMALE STUDIES. Available from KNOW, Inc.
3465. Hughes, Marija Matich. THE SEXUAL BARRIER: LEGAL AND ECONOMIC ASPECTS OF EMPLOYMENT. Supplement no. 1 and supplement no. 2. San Francisco: Hastings College of Law, 1971, 1972. Very useful annotated bibliography of books, articles, pamphlets, and government documents dealing with sex discrimination, employment and education, and corrective legislation and judicial proceedings.
3466. Jackson, Clara O. A BIBLIOGRAPHY OF AFRO-AMERICAN AND OTHER AMERICAN MINORITIES REPRESENTED IN LIBRARY AND LIBRARY-RELATED LISTINGS. (Supplement no. 1 and supple-Series no. 7). Series no. 9. New York: American Institute for Marxist Studeis, 1972. Annotated entries with complete publication information on minority studies.
3467. Jacobs, Sue Ellen. WOMEN IN CROSS-CULTURAL PERSPECTIVE: A PRELIMINARY SOURCEBOOK. Urbana: Univ. of Illinois, Department of Urban and Regional Planning, 1971. Excellent handbook of sources.
3468. Johnsen, Julia E., compiler. SELECTED ARTICLES ON BIRTH CONTROL. New York: H. W. Wilson, 1925. 369 pp.
3469. Kanner, S. Barbara. "The Women of England in a Century of Social Change, 1815-1914: A Select Bibliography." In VICTORIAN WOMEN, edited by Martha Vicinus. Bloomington: Indiana Univ. Press, 1971. Contains 500 entries and other helpful sources for researchers.

3470. Kaplan, Edward H. WOMEN IN CHINESE HISTORY: AN ANNOTATED BIBLIOGRAPHY OF SOME ENGLISH-LANGUAGE WORKS. Program in East Asian Studies, publication no. 5. Bellingham, Wash.: Western Washington State College, Feb. 1971.
3471. Katz, Joseph. EDUCATIONAL AND OCCUPATIONAL ASPIRATIONS OF ADULT WOMEN. Stanford, Calif.: Stanford Univ., Institute for the Study of Human Problems, 1970. Annotated bibliography.
3472. Kieff, Miriam G., and Patricia A. Warren. POPULATION LIMITATION AND WOMEN'S STATUS: A BIBLIOGRAPHY, Princeton, N.J.: Princeton Univ., Educational Testing Service, Sept. 1970.
3473. Krichmar, Albert. THE WOMEN'S RIGHTS MOVEMENT IN THE UNITED STATES, 1848-1970: A BIBLIOGRAPHY AND SOURCE-BOOK. Metuchen, N.J.: Scarecrow Press, 1972. 445 pp.
3474. Laws, Judith Long. "A Feminist Review of Marital Adjustment Literature: The Rape of the Locke," JOURNAL OF MARRIAGE AND THE FAMILY, vol. 33, no. 3 (Aug. 1971), pp. 483-516.
3475. Leonard, Eugenie A., Sophie Hutchinson Drinker, and Miriam Young Holden. THE AMERICAN WOMAN IN COLONIAL AND REVOLUTIONARY TIMES, 1565-1860: A SYLLABUS WITH BIBLIOGRAPHY. Philadelphia: Univ. of Pennsylvania Press, 1962. 169 pp.
3476. Lynn, Naomi B., Anne B. Matasar, and Marie Barovic Rosenberg. RESEARCH GUIDE TO WOMEN'S STUDIES. Morristown, N.J.: General Learning Corp., 1974. 194 pp.
3477. Marshall, Judith M. STUDIES RELATING TO WOMEN'S NON-FAMILIAL ACTIVITY AND FERTILITY." Carolina Population Center Bibliography Series. Chapel Hill: Univ. of North Carolina, 1970.
3478. Matthews, William. AMERICAN DIARIES: AN ANNOTATED BIBLIOGRAPHY OF AMERICAN DIARIES WRITTEN PRIOR TO THE YEAR 1861. Berkeley: Univ. of California Press, 1945.
3479. Michigan State University Libraries. "Finding Women's Liberation Movement Materials in the Michigan State University Libraries," vol. 3. East Lansing: Michigan State Univ., 1972. Includes women's reference works and a list of concerned organizations and publishers.
3480. Miller, Elizabeth W., compiler. THE NEGRO IN AMERICA: A BIBLIOGRAPHY. Compiled for the American Academy of Arts and Sciences. Cambridge: Harvard Univ. Press, 1966. 190 pp. Excellent bibliography of references on race and social institutions and conditions. Includes sections dealing with Negro women in literature, folklore, and education, and with their economic status, political rights, and suffrage.
3481. National Council of Family Relations. ANNOTATED BIBLIOGRAPHY, FAMILY LIFE, LITERATURE AND FILMS. Minneapolis: Minnesota Council on Family Relations, 1971.
3482. Oetzel, Roberta. "Annotated Bibliography." Pp. 223-322 in THE DEVELOPMENT OF SEX DIFFERENCES, edited by Eleanor Maccoby. Stanford: Stanford Univ. Press, 1966.
3483. Radcliffe Institute. "Womanpower, Selected Bibliography on Educated Women and the Labor Force." Radcliffe Institute, 3 James Street, Cambridge, Mass. 1970.
3484. Rubin, Sarah. "List of Bibliographies Related to the Women's Movement." 1970. Available from KNOW, Inc. [see 3530]

3485. Schlesinger, Benjamin. THE JEWISH FAMILY: A SURVEY AND ANNOTATED BIBLIOGRAPHY. Toronto: Univ. of Toronto Press, 1971. 175 pp. Bibliographies of philosophy and religion, society and the family.

3486. Schuman, Pat, and Gay Detlefsen. "Sisterhood is Serious: An Annotated Bibliography," LIBRARY JOURNAL, vol. 96 (Sept. 1, 1971), pp. 2587-2590. Bibliography of 115 establishment and movement books and periodicals for women.

3487. Sells, Lucy W. SOCIOLOGISTS FOR WOMEN IN SOCIETY: CURRENT RESEARCH ON SEX ROLES. Berkeley: Sociologists for Women in Society, 1972. Wide-ranging bibliography, including papers presented at professional meetings, and lists of doctoral dissertations dealing with women in society.

3488. Sherman, Julia A. ON THE PSYCHOLOGY OF WOMEN: A SURVEY OF EMPIRICAL STUDIES. Springfield, Ill.: Charles C Thomas, 1971.

3489. Soltow, Martha Jane, compiler. WOMEN IN AMERICAN LABOR HISTORY 1825-1935: AN ANNOTATED BIBLIOGRAPHY. East Lansing, Mich.: Mich. State Univ. School of Indus. and Labor Relations, 150 pp. 1972.

3490. Spiegel, Jeanne. CONTINUING EDUCATION FOR WOMEN: A SELEC-TED ANNOTATED BIBLIOGRAPHY. Washington, D.C.: Business and Professional Women's Foundation, 1967. 17 pp.

3491. ———. A SELECTED ANNOTATED BIBLIOGRAPHY: WOMEN EXECU-TIVES. Washington, D.C.: Business and Professional Women's Founda-tion, 1970. 26 pp.

3492. ———. A SELECTED ANNOTATED BIBLIOGRAPHY: WORKING MOTHERS. Washington, D.C.: Business and Professional Women's Foundation, 1970. 24 pp.

3493. ———. SEX ROLE CONCEPTS: HOW WOMEN AND MEN SEE THEM-SELVES AND EACH OTHER. A SELECTED ANNOTATED BIBLIO-GRAPHY. Washington, D.C.: Business and Professional Women's Founda-tion, 1969. 31 pp. Includes books, pamphlets, reports, theses, articles, microfilm, etc.

3494. Steinmann, Ann. BIBLIOGRAPHY ON MALE-FEMALE ROLE RE-SEARCH. Maferr Foundation, Inc., 199 E. 58th Street, New York: New York, 1971. 13 pp.

3495. Strober, Myra. BIBLIOGRAPHY ON WOMEN IN THE LABOR FORCE (AND RELATED PROBLEMS). Berkeley: Univ. of California Press, 1970.

3496. Tobias, Sheila. FEMALE STUDIES I. 1970. Available from KNOW, Inc. Collection of college syllabi and reading lists collated and arranged by topic. [see 3530]

3497. ———. "The Study of Women," CHOICE, vol. 8 (Dec. 1971), pp. 1295-1301.

3498. Westervelt, Esther M., and Deborah A. Fixter. WOMEN'S HIGHER AND CONTINUING EDUCATION. New York: College Entrance Examina-tion Board, 1971. 78 pp. Annotated bibliography.

3499. Whaley, Sarah J. WOMEN STUDIES ABSTRACTS. P.O. Box 1, Rush, New York, 1972. A quarterly annotated bibliography.

3500. Wheeler, Helen R. "Some Sources of Information on Non-Sexist Media for School Libraries," LOUISIANA LIBRARY ASSOCIATION BULLE-TIN, (Winter 1972), pp. 113-119.
3501. THE WOMAN'S COLLECTION: A BIBLIOGRAPHY OF ALL MATTERS PERTAINING TO WOMEN'S INTERESTS. Greensboro: Univ. of North Carolina, 1937-40, 1944-49, 1950, 1952-53, 1955, and 1956. Compiled by Minnie Middleton Hussey. Bibliographies of all aspects of women in periodicals, pamphlets, biographies, histories (social and economic), and novels.
3502. WOMEN AND PSYCHOLOGY: ANNOTATED BIBLIOGRAPHY. Cambridge, Mass.: Goddard Graduate School, Feminist Studies Program, 1971.
3503. Women's Caucus for the Modern Languages. RESEARCH IN PROGRESS. Slippery Rock, Pa.: Slippery Rock State College, 1971. Periodical research in progress lists of works on women, women's studies, and women in literature.

B. Biographical Dictionaries

3504. AMERICAN MEN AND WOMEN OF SCIENCE. New York: R. R. Bowker, 1970.
3505. Chambers, W., and R. Chambers. CHAMBER'S BIOGRAPHICAL DIC-TIONARY. London: W. and R. Chambers, 1961. Revised periodically.
3506. Hale, Sarah Josepha. WOMAN'S RECORD, OR, SKETCHES OF ALL DISTINGUISHED WOMEN, FROM THE CREATION TO A.D. 1854. New York: Source Book Press, 1970. Reprint of 1855 edition. 912 pp. Exhaustive biographical dictionary.
3507. James, Edward T., and Janet Wilson James, eds. NOTABLE AMERICAN WOMEN, 1607-1950: A BIOGRAPHICAL DICTIONARY. 3 vols. Cambridge: Harvard Univ. Press, 1971. Contains biographies of 1,359 women; limited to women who died before 1950.
3508. Malone, Dumas, ed. DICTIONARY OF AMERICAN BIOGRAPHY. New York: Charles Scribner's, 1928-37.
3509. Murphy, Florence. THE NEGRO HANDBOOK. New York: Macmillan, 1949. 368 pp. Women are included.
3510. TWO THOUSAND WOMEN OF ACHIEVEMENT. Totowa, N.J.: Rowman and Littlefield, 1970.
3511. WHO'S WHO OF AMERICAN WOMEN: A BIOGRAPHICAL DICTION-ARY OF NOTABLE LIVING AMERICAN WOMEN. Chicago: A. N. Marquis, 1958-.
3512. WHO'S WHO OF AMERICAN WOMEN AND WOMEN OF CANADA. 1st ed. Chicago: A. N. Marquis, 1958-1959.
3513. Wilson, James G., and John Fiske. CYCLOPAEDIA OF AMERICAN BIO-GRAPHY. 12 vols. New York: Appleton, 1900. Contains many references to women in colonial times.

C. Directories of Women's Organizations and Institutes

3514. African Bibliographic Center. CONTEMPORARY AFRICAN WOMEN: AN INTRODUCTORY BIBLIOGRAPHICAL OVERVIEW AND A GUIDE TO WOMEN'S ORGANIZATIONS, 1960-1967. Compiled for the

Women's Africa Committee of the African-American Institute. Washington, D.C.: A.A.I., 1969. 59 pp.

3515. American Federation of Teachers, Women's Rights Committee
1012 14th Street, N.W.
Washington, D.C. 20005

3516. Association of American Colleges
1818 R. Street, N.W.
Washington, D.C. 20009

3517. Association of Women in Science
Department of Medicine
Stanford University
Stanford, Calif. 94305

3518. Bennett, S.R.I. WOMAN'S WORK AMONG THE LOWLY: MEMORIAL VOLUME OF THE FIRST FORTY YEARS OF THE AMERICAN FEMALE GUARDIAN SOCIETY AND HOME FOR FRIENDLESS. New York: American Female Guardian Society, 1877. 514 pp.

3519. Business and Professional Women's Association. INFO-DIGEST: WOMEN IN THE UNITED NATIONS. Washington, D.C.: Author, 1971.

3520. CATALYST. 6 E. 82nd Street, New York, N.Y. 10028. Nonprofit organization and a professional women's placement service and information center.

3521. Center for the American Woman and Politics, the Eagleton Institute of Politics. Rutgers Univ., Neilson Campus, New Brunswick, N.J. 08901.

3522. Chicago Women's Liberation Union
2875 W. Cermack, Room 9
Chicago, Ill. 60623

3523. Citizen's Advisory Council on the Status of Women, Washington, D.C. 20210. "One of the Council's primary purposes is to suggest, to arouse public awareness and understanding, and to stimulate action with private and public institutions, organizations and individuals working for improvement of conditions of special concern to women."

3524. Croly, Jane. THE HISTORY OF THE WOMEN'S CLUB MOVEMENT IN AMERICA. New York: H. G. Allen, 1898. 1185 pp.

3525. Crouch-Hazlett, Ida. "Women's Organizations," SOCIALIST WOMAN, vol. 2 (Sept. 1908), p. 11.

3526. Federally Employed Women (FEW)
Box 894, Ben Franklin Station
Washington, D.C. 20024

3527. International Council of Women. WOMEN IN A CHANGING WORLD. London: Routledge and Kegan Paul, 1966. 360 pp. The story of the International Council of Women since 1888.

3528. Interstate Association of Commissions on the Status of Women
District Building, 14th and E Streets
Washington, D.C. 20004

3529. Ireland, Norma Olin. INDEX TO WOMEN. Westwood, Mass.: Author, 1971. 1696 pp. An outstanding reference work.

3530. KNOW, Inc.
P.O. Box 10197
Pittsburgh, Pa. 15232

3531. Lord, Myra B. HISTORY OF THE NEW ENGLAND WOMAN'S PRESS ASSOCIATION, 1885-1931. Newton, Mass.: Graphic Press, 1932. 393 pp.

3532. The National Coalition for Research on Women's Education and Development, Inc.
State University of New York
Stony Brook, N.Y. 11790
Organization for research on women.

3533. National Organization for Women (NOW)
938 National Press Bldg.
Washington, D.C. 20004

3534. National Women's Political Caucus, 1302 18th Street, N.W. Suite 603, Washington, D.C. 20036. Represents women from every political party. Their purpose is to get women into significant decision-making positions at every level of government. Also publishes the NWPC NEWSLETTER.

3535. New York Radical Feminists
P.O. Box 621, Old Chelsea Station
New York, N.Y. 10011

3536. Radcliffe Institute
3 James Street
Cambridge, Mass. 12138

3537 Republican National Committee. THE HISTORY OF WOMEN IN REPUBLICAN NATIONAL CONVENTIONS AND WOMEN IN THE REPUBLICAN NATIONAL COMMITTEE. Washington, D.C.: Republican National Committee, 1968.

3538. Resource Center on Women, National Board, Y.W.C.A., 600 Lexington Avenue, New York, N.Y. 10002. Evaluates and updates new information on women and sets up affirmative action programs.

3539. Stone, Kathryn H. Meyers. WOMEN'S ORGANIZATIONS IN THE UNITED STATES. Washington, D.C.: U.S. Information Service, 1966. 36 pp.

3540. "Where to get help: Addresses of Selected National Women's Groups," MS. MAGAZINE, (Spring 2972), pp. 126-128.

3541. THE WHOLE WOMAN CATALOG, P.O. Box 1171, Portsmouth, N.H. 03801. Has listings of women's liberation groups around the country.

3542. Women's Action Alliance, 370 Lexington Avenue, New York, N.Y. 10017. A national information-referral service for women who want to contact other women working on mutual problems such as child care, abortion, women in unions, and the rights of women prisoners.

3543. Women's Bureau, Workplace Standards Administration, U.S. Department of Labor, Washington, D.C. 20210. Extensive offerings of publications on various subjects relating to women.

3544. The Women's Center
Barnard College
New York, N.Y. 10027

3545. Women's Equity Action League (WEAL), 1504 44th Street, N.W., Washington, D.C. 20007. WEAL prepared complaints against sex discrimination in employment, and gives information or helps other individuals and groups prepare complaints regarding the legal aspects of discrimination.

3546. WOMEN'S HALL OF FAME, Inc.
P.O. Box 335
Seneca Falls, N.Y. 13148

3547. Women's History Research Center, International Women's History Archives, 2325 Oak Street, Berkeley, Calif. 94708. Regularly publishes a catalog of books relating to women, a NEWSLETTER, WOMEN'S SONGBOOK, WOMEN IN WORLD HISTORY, and has a Tape Archive Index, Directory of Women's Films, and a Women's Periodicals Index. NOTE: The Women's History Library, Berkeley, Calif. has closed. The 2,000 subject file is now at Archive of Contemporary History, University of Wyoming, Laramie. The six-year feminist periodical collection is at Northwestern University's Special Collections Library, Evanston, Illinois.

3548. Women's National Abortion Action Coalition
150 Fifth Avenue, Suite 315
New York, N.Y. 10011

3549. WOMEN'S ORGANIZATIONS AND LEADERS—1973 DIRECTORY, available from TODAY PUBLICATIONS, National Press Building, Washington, D.C. 20004. Current listing of all organizations with special concern for women in all areas—government, industry, the professions, education, and politics.

3550. Wood, Mary I. THE HISTORY OF THE GENERAL FEDERATION OF WOMEN'S CLUBS FOR THE FIRST TWENTY-TWO YEARS OF ITS ORGANIZATION. New York: General Federation of Women's Clubs, 1912. 445 pp.

D. Women's Periodicals and Newspapers

3551. THE AFRO-AMERICAN WOMAN MAGAZINE
23 E. 42nd Street
New York, N.Y.

3552. APHRA
Box 273 Village Station
New York, N.Y. 10014
Literary magazine devoted to women and published by women.

3553. "BATTLE ACTS"
Women of Youth Against War and Fascism
58 W. 25th Street
New York, N.Y.

3554. CANADIAN NEWSLETTER OF RESEARCH ON WOMEN, Department of Sociology, University of Waterloo, Waterloo, Ontario. Excellent for on-going research, book reviews, bibliographies.

3555. Donnelly, Antoinette, and Alice Archibald, eds. THE WOMAN'S ALMA-NAC: THE THIRD ANNUAL BOOK OF FACTS FOR, BY AND ABOUT WOMEN, New York: Oquaga Press, 1939. 289 pp.

3556. EVERYWOMAN
1043B W. Washington Blvd.
Venice, Calif. 90291

3557. FEMALE LIBERATION
Box 300 Eshelman, University of California
Berkeley, Calif. 94720

3558. FORERUNNER. Volumes 1-7 published. New York, 1909-16. Reprinted by Greenwood Press, Inc. Westport, Conn. Liberal-radical pro-woman's rights monthly, edited by Charlotte Perkins Gilman. Advocated progress, social and intellectual equality for women, and nonviolent socialism.

3559. Greenwood Publishing Corporation. WOMEN'S RIGHTS STUDIES. West-port, Conn. This press has a microfilm collection of the most important periodicals on women's rights and feminism. First published in 1971.
3560. THE LILY, Seneca Falls, New York. Volumes begain in 1849. A ladies' journal edited by Amelia Bloomer, devoted to temperance and feminist causes.
3561. MOTHER EARTH BULLETIN. Series 1: volumes 1-12, 1905-1917; series 2: nos. 1-7, 1917-1918 (last published). Reprint by Greenwood Press, Westport, Conn., 1972. An anarchist literary and political monthly edited by Alexander Berkman and Emma Goldman, filled with articles on women's rights, birth control, marriage, and emancipation.
3562. MS. MAGAZINE, 370 Lexington Avenue, New York, N.Y. 10017. Gloria Steinem's glossy magazine devoted to women's struggle to be recognized as people by society.
3563. NEW ENGLAND FREE PRESS
Room 401, 791 Tremont Street
Boston, Mass. 02118
3564. NEW ENGLAND OFFERING: A MAGAZINE OF INDUSTRY. Vols. 1-3 all published. Lowell, Mass., 1848-1850. Reprinted by Greenwood Press, Westport, Conn. This journal superseded the LOWELL OFFERING thru which nineteenth-century women aired their comments on factory working conditions. Very important primary source for studying the working conditions of the female wage earner.
3565. New York Radical Women. NOTES FROM THE FIRST YEAR. New York Radical Women, 799 Broadway, Room 412, New York, N.Y. To date they have published NOTES FROM THE SECOND YEAR and NOTES FROM THE THIRD YEAR. Major writings of the radical feminists.
3566. Pankhurst, E. Sylvia, ed. THE WOMAN'S DREADNOUGHT, 1914-1924. Later known as WORKER'S DREADNOUGHT. Available from World Microfilms, 125 Tottenham Court Road, W. 1, London, England. For its first three years, this journal was concerned with the emancipation of women, ultra-socialist in its views. By 1917, it became the WORKER'S DREADNOUGHT, and strongly advocated universal suffrage and gener-al socialist principles. Provides important source materials, both for the study of Mrs. Pankhurst and her significant activities, and as a general background to the development of socialism and communism.
3567. Siefer, R., and J. Simmons, LOOK INTO THE UNDERGROUND . . . NEWSPAPERS: GUIDE TO UNDERGROUND NEWSPAPERS IN THE SPECIAL COLLECTIONS DEPARTMENT. Evanston, Ill.: Northwestern Univ. Library, June 1971. 60 pp. Lists over 500 English and North Ameri-can newspapers currently received.
3568. Stanton, Elizabeth Cady, Parker Pillsbury, Laura C. Bullard, and W. T. Clark. THE REVOLUTION (periodical), 8 vols. published, 1868-1872. Reprinted by Source Book Press, 185 Madison Avenue, New York, N.Y., 1972.
3569. THE SUFFRAGIST
Washington, D.C.
Published from 1914-1918.
3570. SYNDICALIST. Introduction by Melvyn Dubofsky, Univ. of Mass. Vols. 1-3, nos. 1-62 all published. Chicago, 1910-1931. Reprinted by Greenwood

Press, Westport, Conn., 1972. Very politically oriented paper. The issue of women's rights appears in many volumes, with contributions by such women as Emma Goldman.

3571. Wilde, Oscar, ed. THE WOMAN'S WORLD. 3 vols., published between 1888-1890. Reprinted by Source Book Press, 1972.

3572. WOMEN: A JOURNAL OF LIBERATION
3028 Greenmount Avenue
Baltimore, Md. 21218

3573. WOMEN AND ART: A NEWSPAPER QUARTERLY. Published by Woman Students and Artists for Black Art Liberation and Redstocking Artists. 89 E. Broadway, New York, N.Y. 10002.

3574. WOMEN LAWYERS JOURNAL, 1911-. Published by National Association of Women Lawyers. American Bar Center, 1155 E. 60th Street, Chicago, Ill. 60637.

3575. WOMEN'S JOURNAL OF THE ARTS
School of Art, California Institute of the Arts
2400 McBean Parkway
Valencia, Calif. 91355

3576. WOMEN'S RIGHTS LAW REVIEW, 1971-. Published by Women's Rights Law Reporter, Inc. 180 University Avenue, Newark, N.J. 07102.

3577. WOMEN'S STUDIES (periodical). Edited by Wendy Martin. Department of English, Queens College, New York, N.Y. Subscriptions to Gordon and Breach, 440 Park Avenue South, New York, N.Y. 10016.

3578. THE VOICE OF LABOR, 1919. National Women's Trade Union League. Chicago, Ill. The organ of the Women's Trade Union League.

E. Women's Collection and Libraries

3579. The Afro-American Woman's Collection. Bennett College Library, Bennett College, Greensboro, N.C. Includes materials by and about Negro women, chiefly American, during the eighteenth, nineteenth, and twentiety centuries. About 200 authors are represented, 325 books, 400 mounted clippings, and continually added to.

3580. American Association of University Women Library, 2401 Virginia Avenue, N.W., Washington, D.C. Collection of works on subjects ranging from women's education and community and family life to world problems.

3581. Ash, Lee, et al., compilers. SUBJECT COLLECTIONS: A GUIDE TO SPECIAL BOOK COLLECTIONS AND SUBJECT EMPHASES AS REPORTED BY UNIVERSITY, COLLEGE, PUBLIC AND SPECIAL LIBRARIES IN THE UNITED STATES AND CANADA. 3d rev. ed. New York: Bowker, 1967. 1221 pp.

3582. Berman, Sanford. WOMEN, SEXISM, THE FEMINIST MOVEMENT: A ROSTER OF MATERIALS AT THE MAKERERE INSTITUTE OF SOCIAL RESEARCH. Available from the MISR Library, P.O. Box 16022, Kampala, Uganda.

3583. Biblioteca Femina, Northwestern University Library, Evanston, Ill. Four collections showing the progress of women in all countries and in all fields of endeavor. Thirty-eight counties are represented. Chiefly historical, but includes special collections on women's liberation, feminism, and gay liberation.

3584. Boston Public Library. THE GALATEA COLLECTION OF BOOKS RE-
LATING TO THE HISTORY OF WOMAN IN THE PUBLIC LIBRARY
OF BOSTON. Published by the Trustees, Boston Public Library, 1898.
Catalog of about 5,000 items given to the Library by Thomas Wentworth
Higginson on the history of women.

3585. Business and Professional Women's Foundation Library, 2012 Massachusetts Avenue, N.W., Washington, D.C. Research materials in the area of
women's contributions to the cultural, economic, political, and social
development of the United States. 1200 volumes, a collection of unpublished doctoral dissertations on microfilm, and extensive vertical file
materials.

3586. College of Saint Catherine Library, 2004 Randolph Avenue, St. Paul,
Minn. Includes 564 catalogued volumes, some manuscripts, pictures, and
slides, with special emphasis on the psychological liberation of women
in the twentieth century.

3587. Colorado Woman's College, Permelia Curtis Porter Library, 7055 E. 18th
Avenue, Denver, Colo. Collection of over 1,000 catalogued volumes.

3588. Gerritson Collection, LA FEMME ET LA FEMINISME, University of
Kansas Library, Lawrence, Kan. Contains over 4,000 volumes of books,
pamphlets, and materials of the late nineteenth and early twentieth
centuries.

3589. Library of Congress, Washington, D.C. Special collections with materials
relating to women include the Susan B. Anthony Collection, the
National American Woman Suffrage Association Collection, and those
of Carrie Chapman Catt.

3590. National Woman's Christian Temperance Union, Frances E. Willard
Memorial Library for Alcohol Research, 1730 Chicago Avenue, Evanston,
Ill. 500 volumes from the archives of the Woman's Christian Temperance
Union.

3591. National Woman's Party, Florence Bayard Hilles Library, 144 Constitution
Avenue, N.E., Washington, D.C. 2,000 volumes of works by and about
women, with special reference to the suffrage and equal rights movement.

3592. New York Public Library, Schwemmer-Lloyd Collection. 3,000 items relating to women's work and activities, the changes in her position, her
efforts to achieve economic security, and the feminist movement in
foreign countries.

3593. Radcliffe College, Arthur and Elizabeth Schlesinger Library, 10 Garden
Street, Cambridge, Mass. Formerly known as the Women's Archives,
this is one of the largest collections in existence of materials on the history of American women from 1800 to the present. Includes over
12,000 volumes, 200 major collections, and 31 archives of important
women's organizations.

3594. Scripps College, Ella Strong Denison Library, Claremont, Calif. Library
has over 1,530 catalogued volumes and some manuscripts. Materials relating to the status, interests, and humanistic accomplishments of women.

3595. Sophia Smith Collection, Northampton, Mass. (Smith College Library),
1971. 4 vols., 65,000 cards. A printed list of the entire holdings of the
Sophia Smith Collection, probably the largest international collection
of materials devoted to the intellectual and social history of women.

3596. Source Book Press. THE SOURCE LIBRARY OF THE WOMEN'S MOVE-MENT. 450 West 33rd Street, New York, N.Y. 10001. Publishes reprints of important books by early feminists and women's suffrage leaders.

3597. Swarthmore College, Peace Collection, Friends Historical Library, Swarthmore, Pa. Contains the publications of some famous American women suffragettes, such as Jane Addams, Emily Green Balch, Rosika Schwimmer, Hanna Clothier Hull, Mildred Scott Olmsted, Anna Lee Stewart, and others.

3598. University of North Carolina, Woman's College Library, The Women's Collection, Greensboro, N.C. This library has been gathering materials in all areas pertaining to women since 1937. The library catalogue and annotated bibliographies have been issued since 1938.

3599. Woman's History Library. HERSTORY: MICROFILM COLLECTION. Berkeley, Calif. Published by Micro Photo Division, Bell and Howell Co. Wooster, Ohio. An exhaustive collection of publications including newspapers, journals, and newsletters, on women. [see 3547]

3600. Young Women's Christian Association, National Board Library, 600 Lexington Avenue, New York, N.Y. The library includes about 6,000 catalogued volumes. It is not a historical collection, but covers women in the contemporary world, her social, psychological, and political development.

WOMEN AND SOCIETY was delayed for several months by complications in the production schedule. In order to keep the volume as current as possible, we have added works which have come to our attention since our numbering of citations was completed in February 1974. We have dispensed with classifications and have simply listed the entries in this Addendum in straight alphabetical order by author, editor, or title as appropriate.

XII. ADDENDUM

"No girl was ever ruined by a book."

—James J. Walker
Mayor, New York City, 1926-1932

Adams, Hazard. LADY GREGORY. Lewisburg, Pa.: Bucknell Univ. Press, 1973. 106 pp. Brief but perceptive analysis of the noted Irish author with a good overview of her activities in several spheres and genres.

Alexander, Rodney and Elizabeth Sapery. SHORTCHANGED: MINORITIES AND WOMEN IN BANKING. Port Washington, N.Y.: Kennikat Press, 1973. 186 pp. Revealing study of discrimination in the banking business.

Alliluyeva, Svetlana (Stalina). ONLY ONE YEAR. New York: Harper and Row, 1970.

American Economic Association Committee on the Status of Women, "Combatting Role Prejudice and Sex Discrimination," (Parts I and II prepared by Kenneth Boulding and Barbara B. Reagan), THE AMERICAN ECONOMIC REVIEW, Vol. 63, No. 5 (Dec. 1973), pp. 1049-1061. Informative discussion of possible solutions to the problem of sex discrimination.

Anderson, Ellen, ed. GRADUATE AND PROFESSIONAL EDUCATION OF WOMEN. Washington, D.C.: American Association of University Women, 1974. 94 pp. Proceedings of AAUW Conference, May 9-10, 1974.

Banning, Evelyn I. HELEN HUNT JACKSON. New York: Vanguard, 1973. 248 pp. Biography placing Jackson's writings in the annals of American literature of the 19th century and describing her dedication to the rights of the native American Indian.

Baritz, Loren, ed. THE AMERICAN LEFT: RADICAL POLITICAL THOUGHT IN THE TWENTIETH CENTURY. New York: Basic Books, 1971. 522 pp. Contributors on women include Emma Goldman, Naomi Jaffe and Bernardine Dohrn, Robin Morgan, Kathy McAffe and Myrna Wood, Pat Mainardi, and Anne P. Koedt.

Bedford, Herbert. THE HEROINES OF GEORGE MEREDITH. Port Washington, N. Y.: Kennikat Press, 1974. 166 pp. Reprint of 1914 edition. Meredith's whole-hearted allegiance to the cause of feminism and his imaginative protraits of women are the subjects of this study.

Berendsohn, Walter A. SELMA LAGERLOF: HER LIFE AND WORK. Port Washington, N.Y.: Kennikat Press, 1974. Reprint of 1931 edition. Biography of the Swedish Nobel Laureate.

Berkin, Carol. WITHIN THE CONJURORS' CIRCLE: WOMEN IN COLONIAL AMERICA. Morristown, N.J.: General Learning Press, 1974.

Bernard, Jessie. THE FUTURE OF MOTHERHOOD. New York: Dial Press, 1974. 352 pp. Dissects the many social trends affecting motherhood, noting the coercive social forces which have pressured women to become mothers.

Berson, Barbara and Ben Bova. SURVIVAL GUIDE FOR THE SUDDENLY SINGLE. New York: St. Martin's Press, 1974. 224 pp. A liberated guide to divorce with chapters on sex, children, money, divorce, and lawyers.

Bickner, Mei Liang. WOMEN AT WORK: AN ANNOTATED BIBLIOGRAPHY. Irvine, Cal.: Univ. of Calif. Press, 1974. More than 600 entries with author, title, category, and key word index.

Billings, Victoria. THE WOMANSBOOK. Los Angeles: Wollstonecraft, 1974. 266 pp.

Borun, Minda. WOMEN'S LIBERATION: AN ANTHROPOLOGICAL VIEW. Pittsburgh: KNOW, Inc., 1972.

Boslooper, Thomas and Marcia Hayes. THE FEMININITY GAME. New York: Stein and Day, 1974. 256 pp. Sexism in sports, and how early conditioning of girls causes them to abjure competitive sports in the fear that competition is not ladylike.

Brée, Germaine. WOMEN WRITERS IN FRANCE: VARIATIONS ON A THEME. New Brunswick, N.J.: Rutgers Univ. Press, 1973. 90 pp. Survey of French women writers from medieval to modern times, with a witty and acute commentary on Colette and de Beauvoir.

Brockett, Linus Pierpont and Mrs. Mary C. Vaughan. WOMEN'S WORK IN THE CIVIL WAR: A RECORD OF HEROISM, PATRIOTISM, AND PA-TIENCE. Philadelphia: Zeigler, McCurdy, and Co., 1867. 799 pp.

Brooks, Gwendolyn. REPORT FROM PART ONE: AN AUTOBIOGRAPHY. Detroit: Broadside Press, 1972. 215 pp. Autobiography of her life, her view of her childhood, the black struggle, and black womanhood.

Buek, Alexandra and Jeffrey H. Orleans. "Sex Discrimination — A Bar to a Democratic Education: Overview of Title IX of the Education Amendments of 1972." CONNECTICUT LAW REVIEW, Vol. 6, No. 1 (Fall 1973), pp. 1-27.

Bunkle, P., N. Chick, A.D.M. Glass, M. Glass, M. E. Gordon, E. D. Penny, P. E. Penny, D. R. Perley, J. E. Perley, and J. E. Wells. WOMEN IN HIGHER EDUCATION. Report to Women's Rights Committee, New Zealand House of Representatives, on behalf of SEE. Palmerston North, New Zealand: Inter-University Committee for Sex Equality in Education, Jan. 1974. 60 pp.

Caine, Lynn. WIDOW. New York: William Morrow, 1974. 222 pp. Especially for women who must live their grief in a society that taboos death and shuns strong emotion.

Carden, Maren Lockwood. THE NEW FEMINIST MOVEMENT. Scranton, Penn.: Basic Books, 1973. 226 pp. A detailed study of the movement —structure, membership, and history of organizations that form a major part of present day feminism.

Carlson, Dale. GIRLS ARE EQUAL TOO: THE WOMEN'S MOVEMENT FOR TEENAGERS. New York: Atheneum, 1973. 146 pp.

Carnegie Commission on Higher Education. OPPORTUNITIES FOR WOMEN IN HIGHER EDUCATION: THEIR CURRENT PARTICIPATION. New York: Carnegie Foundation, 1973. 282 pp. Description of the continuing trends of increased participation of women in graduate studies and teaching.

Chaney, Elsa M. "Women and Population." In POPULATION AND POLITICS, edited by Richard L. Clinton. Lexington, Mass.: Lexington, 1973. 320 pp. Probes the normative and methodological dimensions of population research and policy, population problems in less-advantaged and industrialized countries.

Chun, Jinsie. I AM HEAVEN. Philadelphia: Macrae Smith Co., 1974. 276 pp. Portrait of the Empress Chao of the T'ang Dynasty in China.

Clarke, Isabel Constance. ELIZABETH BARRETT BROWNING: A PORTRAIT. Port Washington, N.Y.: Kennikat Press, 1973. 304 pp. Reprint of 1929 edition.

Colby, Vineta. YESTERDAY'S WOMAN: DOMESTIC REALISM IN THE ENGLISH NOVEL. Princeton, N.J.: Princeton Univ. Press, 1974. 269 pp. Discussion of novels by women and the roots of the Victorian novel's homeyness, attention to manners, education for women and domestic virtues.

Cole, Doris. FROM TIPI TO SKYSCRAPER: A HISTORY OF WOMEN IN ARCHITECTURE. New York: Braziller, 1973. 136 pp.

Confino, Michael, ed. DAUGHTER OF A REVOLUTIONARY: NATALIE HERZEN AND THE BAKUNIN-NECHAYEV CIRCLE. LaSalle, Ill.: Library Press, 1974. 416 pp. Correspondence, diaries, and documents of the eldest daughter of Alexander Herzen, 19th century Russian radical thinker.

Cook, Barbara and Beverly Stone. COUNSELING WOMEN. Boston: Houghton Mifflin, 1973. 114 pp.

Crafton, Allen and Robert E. Gard. A WOMAN OF NO IMPORTANCE. Madison, Wis.: Wisconsin House, 1974. 204 pp. The life story of May McDonald, a small town Wisconsin woman (1878-1950) and her confrontations with women's unequal treatment.

Crossland, Margaret. COLETTE: THE DIFFICULTY OF LOVING, A BIOGRAPHY. Indianapolis: Bobbs-Merrill, 1973.

Cunliffe, John William. LEADERS OF THE VICTORIAN REVOLUTION. Port Washington, N.Y.: Kennikat Press, 1973. 343 pp. Reprint of 1934 edition. Includes sections on woman suffrage, women's education, and some notable women of the age.

"Current Index to Journals in Education," Riverside, N.J.: Macmillan Information. Cumulative index (Printouts also available from computer service). Through Aug. 1974, 1,434 entries on women retrievable from key words: i.e., Women professors, Women teachers, Working women, Women's education, Women's athletics, Women's studies, Feminism, and Females.

da Costa, Maria Velho, Maria Isabel Bareno and Maria Teresa Horta. THE THREE MARIAS: NEW PORTUGUESE LETTERS. New York: Doubleday, 1975. The book is a collection of letters, verse, and essays by and about women. First published in Portugal in 1972, it was banned by the government as an outrage to public morals.

Dannett, Sylvia G. L., ed. NOBLE WOMEN OF THE NORTH. New York: T. Yoseloff, 1959. 419 pp. Women notable in the Civil War, their personal narratives of activities in hospitals, charities, etc.

David, Lester. JOAN: THE RELUCTANT KENNEDY. New York: Funk & Wagnalls, 1974. 264 pp. Wife of Senator Ted Kennedy.

Davis, Allen F. AMERICAN HEROINE: THE LIFE AND LEGEND OF JANE ADDAMS. New York: Oxford Univ. Press, 1973. 339 pp.

Davis, Angela. ANGELA DAVIS: AN AUTOBIOGRAPHY. New York: Random House, 1974. 400 pp. Her own account of her remarkable life as political theorist and activist, teacher and fugitive.

de Beauvior, Simone. ALL SAID AND DONE. New York: Putman's, 1974. 463 pp. Memoirs for the years 1962-1972. Translated from the French by Patrick O'Brian. Her fifth volume of autobiography.

de Castillejo, Irene Claremont. KNOWING WOMAN: A FEMININE PSYCHOLOGY. New York: G. P. Putnam's Sons, 1973. 188 pp. An inquiry into the psychology of women by a noted Jungian psychologist.

DeCrow, Karen. SEXIST JUSTICE: HOW LEGAL SEXISM AFFECTS YOU. New York: Random House, 1974. 329 pp. Interesting and valuable materials for U.S. women on their legal status in such areas as crime, education, marriage, credit, and employment.

de Mille, Agnes. SPEAK TO ME, DANCE WITH ME. Boston: Atlantic Little Brown, 1974. 404 pp. An account of Agnes de Mille, choreographer, from early dance steps to recent musicals such as CAROUSEL, including techniques and history.

Denmark, Florence, ed. WHO DISCRIMINATES AGAINST WOMEN? Beverly Hills, Calif.: Sage, 1974. 144 pp.

deRiencort, Amaury. SEX AND POWER IN HISTORY: HOW THE DIFFERENCES BETWEEN THE SEXES HAS SHAPED OUR DESTINIES. New York: McKay, 1974. Puts forth the theses that the survival of Western civilization depends on the recognition of and allowance for male and female differences.

Deutsch, Dr. Helene. CONFRONTATIONS WITH MYSELF. New York: W. W. Norton, 1973. 217 pp. Short autobiographical memoir of one of the first women analysts of the Freudian era.

Doumic, René. GEORGE SAND: SOME ASPECTS OF HER LIFE AND WRITINGS. Port Washington, N.Y.: Kennikat Press, 1973. 362 pp. Reprint of 1910 edition.

Dreifus, Claudia. WOMAN'S FATE. New York: Bantam Books, 1973. 288 pp. The record of her own consciousness raising group in which eight women explore their feelings on childhood, adolescence, sexuality, marriage, work and old age.

Dreitzel, Hans Peter, ed. SEXUAL REVOLUTION AND FAMILY CRISIS. New York: Macmillan, 1972. 350 pp. Number four in a series.

EDITORIAL RESEARCH REPORTS ON THE WOMEN'S MOVEMENT. Washington, D.C.: Congressional Quarterly, 1973. 180 pp. Reports on the status of women, marriage, child care, child adoptions, rape, prostitution, co-education, women voters, and women's consciousness raising.

Elliot, Linda Anne. "Black Women in the Media." In OTHER VOICES: BLACK, CHICANO, AND AMERICAN INDIAN, edited by Sharon Murphy. Dayton, Ohio: Pflaum/Standard, 1974. Pp. 47-52.

Epstein, Joseph. DIVORCED IN AMERICA: MARRIAGE IN AN AGE OF POSSIBILITY. New York: E. P. Dutton, 1974. 318 pp.

Feldman, Saul D. ESCAPE FROM THE DOLL'S HOUSE: WOMEN IN GRADUATE AND PROFESSIONAL SCHOOL EDUCATION. New York: McGraw-Hill, 1974. 208 pp. Excellent study of the professional education of women.

Ferguson, Mary Anne. IMAGES OF WOMEN IN LITERATURE. Boston: Houghton Mifflin, 1973. 437 pp. Collection of critical essays on the woman theme in literature.

Ferriss, Abbott L. INDICATORS OF TRENDS IN THE STATUS OF AMERICAN WOMEN. Scranton, Pennsylvania: Basic Books, 1971. 451 pp.

Flynn, John T. "Hetty Green: The Miser," in MEN OF WEALTH: THE STORY OF 12 SIGNIFICANT FORTUNES FROM THE RENAISSANCE TO THE PRESENT DAY. New York: Simon & Schuster, 1941. Pp. 215-249.

Freeman, Jo, ed. WOMEN: A FEMINIST PERSPECTIVE. Palo Alto, Calif.: Mayfield Publishing, 1974. Collection of papers on the effects of sexism, the status of women and the institutions and values that keep women in their place.

Friedman, Jean E. and William G. Shade. OUR AMERICAN SISTERS: WOMEN IN AMERICAN LIFE AND THOUGHT. Boston, Allyn and Bacon, 1973. 354 pp. Collection of readings on the problem of the representation of women in political, social, psychological, and economic history, as well as on attitudes toward women and their roles.

Furstenberg, George M. von. DISCRIMINATION IN EMPLOYMENT: A SELECTED BIBLIOGRAPHY. Listed in Council of Planning Librarians, EXCHANGE BIBLIOGRAPHIES. Monticello, Ill.: The Council, 1972. 24 pp.

Gager, Nancy, ed. WOMEN'S RIGHTS ALMANAC, 1974. Bethesda, Md.: Elizabeth Cady Stanton Pub. Co., 1974. 620 pp. State-by-state listing of information concerning demographic statistics, women officials, voting records of congressional members on women's issues, current legislation, and a chronology of women's events in 1973 and during two centuries of American and international feminism. With a bibliography of bibliographies.

Galenson, Marjorie. WOMEN AND WORK: AN INTERNATIONAL COMPARISON. Ithaca, N.Y.: N.Y. State School of Industrial and Labor Relations, Cornell Univ., 1973. 120 pp.

Gathorne-Hardy, Jonathon. THE UNNATURAL HISTORY OF THE NANNY. New York: Dial Press, 1973. 350 pp. Examines the institution of the British nursemaid.

Gelles, Richard J. THE VIOLENT HOME: A STUDY OF PHYSICAL AGGRESSION BETWEEN HUSBANDS AND WIVES. Beverly Hills, Calif.: Sage, 1974. 232 pp.

Giallombardo, Rose. THE SOCIAL WORLD OF IMPRISONED GIRLS: A COMPARATIVE STUDY OF INSTITUTIONS FOR JUVENILE DELINQUENTS. New York: John Wiley, 1974. 416 pp. Well-documented study of girls' prisons; a continuation of her earlier study.

_____. SOCIETY OF WOMEN: A STUDY OF A WOMEN'S PRISON. New York: John Wiley, 1966. 244 pp. Study of an adult female prison stressing why kinship, marriage, and family groups are the solution to the deprivations of prison life.

Gilder, George F. SEXUAL SUICIDE. New York: Quadrangle/The New York Times Book Co., 1973. 308 pp. Gilder has decided that women are morally and sexually superior to men by virtue of their "true" biological function through which they find profound fulfillment.

Ginsburg, Ruth Bader. CONSTITUTIONAL ASPECTS OF SEX-BASED DISCRIMINATION. St. Paul, Minn.: West Pub., 1974. 129 pp. An up-to-date legal study of women's rights.

Giroud, Francoise. I GIVE YOU MY WORD. Trans. by Robert Seaver. Boston: Houghton Mifflin Co., 1974. 280 pp. The autobiography of France's first State Secretary on the Condition of Women.

Gray, Virginia. "Women: Victims or Beneficiaries of U.S. Population Policy,"
POLITICAL ISSUES IN U.S. POPULATION POLICY, edited by Elihu
Bergman. Lexington, Mass.: Lexington, 1974.

Gridley, Marion Eleanor. AMERICAN INDIAN WOMEN. New York: Hawthorn, 1974. 178 pp.

Grimstad, Kirsten and Susan Rennie, eds. THE NEW WOMAN'S SURVIVAL
CATALOGUE. New York: Coward, McCann and Geohegan/Berkely
Pub., 1974. 223 pp. Catalogues and documents activities aimed at the
development of an alternative woman's culture.

"Guidelines for Equal Treatment of the Sexes in McGraw-Hill Book Co. Publications," NEW YORK TIMES MAGAZINE (October 20, 1974), pp. 38,
104-108.

Hahn, Emily. ONCE UPON A PEDESTAL: AN INFORMAL HISTORY OF
WOMEN'S LIB. New York: Thomas Y. Crowell Co., 1974. 279 pp.
Begins with colonial times and moves into the 19th century with portraits of Mrs. Trolloppe, Harriet Martineau, and Fanny Kemble, but
weak on 20th century women and the rebirth of feminism.

Hamilton, Alice. EXPLORING THE DANGEROUS TRADES: THE AUTO-
BIOGRAPHY OF ALICE HAMILTON, M.D. Boston: Little, Brown
and Co., 1943. 433 pp. Dr. Hamilton wrote on public health hazards
in trades and business.

Hare, Christopher. THE MOST ILLUSTRIOUS LADIES OF THE ITALIAN
RENAISSANCE. Williamstown, Mass.: Corner House, 1972. Reprint
of 1907 edition. 367 pp. A sweeping picture of the daily cares,
pleasures, and cultural contributions of women in 14th-16th century
Italy.

Harris, Seymour E. A STATISTICAL PORTRAIT OF HIGHER EDUCATION.
Report from Carnegie Commission of Higher Education. New York:
McGraw-Hill, 1972. 978 pp.

Haskell, Molly. FROM REVERENCE TO RAPE: THE TREATMENT OF
WOMEN IN THE MOVIES. New York: Holt, Rinehart & Winston,
1974. 388 pp.

Heffernan, Esther. MAKING IT IN PRISON: THE SQUARE, THE COOL, AND
THE LIFE. New York: Wiley-Interscience, 1972. 231 pp. Intensive
study of a women's prison, using data obtained by interviewing all the
inmates and from all the institutional records.

Hess, Thomas B. and Elizabeth C. Baker, eds. ART AND SEXUAL POLITICS:
WOMEN'S LIBERATION, WOMEN AS ARTISTS, AND ART HISTORY.
New York: Macmillan, 1973. 150 pp. Revised essays originally ap-
pearing in ART NEWS, Vol. 69, No. 9 (Jan. 1971). Includes bibliography.

Hogeland, Ronald W., ed. WOMEN AND WOMANHOOD IN AMERICA.
Lexington, Mass.: D. C. Heath, 1973. 183 pp. An anthology of readings on how to study women in American history, along with historical
discussions of the nature of their roles in the American experience.

Hochschild, Arlie, ed. "The American Woman," TRANS-ACTION, Vol. 8, No.
1/2 (Nov./Dec. 1970). 112 pp. Special combined issue. Contributors
include Arlie Hochschild, Joan Jordan, Unna Stannard, Jo Freeman,
Ruth B. Dixon, Marijean Suelzle, Linda J. M. La Rue, Nathan and Julia
Hare, Pauline Bart, Inge Powell Bell, and Anita Lynn Micossi.

Hoskins, Dalmer and Lenore E. Bixby. WOMEN AND SOCIAL SECURITY:
LAW AND POLICY IN FIVE COUNTRIES. Washington, D.C.: Social
Security Administration, SUDOC, GPO, 1973. 95 pp.

Howard, Jane. A DIFFERENT WOMAN. New York: Dutton, 1973. 416 pp.

Attempt to find out what American women are thinking as they become conscious of themselves as part of a new age.

Hunter, Alexander. THE WOMEN OF THE DEBATABLE LAND. Port Washington, N.Y.: Kennikat Press, 1972. 261 pp. Reprint of 1912 edition. Women in the Confederate States of America.

Iglitzen, Lynne and Ruth Ross, eds. WOMEN IN CROSS-POLITICAL PERSPECTIVE: FROM PATRIARCHY TO LIBERATION. Santa Barbara, Cal.: American Bibliographical Center, Clio Press, (forthcoming) 1975.

Infield, Glenn B. EVA AND ADOLF. New York: Grosset & Dunlap, 1974. 330 pp. Eva Braun, mistress of Adolf Hitler.

Israel, Stan, comp. and ed. A BIBLIOGRAPHY ON DIVORCE. New York: Bloch Pub. Co., 1974. 300 pp. 152 categories with annotations and complete tables of contents. Plus bibliography of 64 citations without detailed entries, 115 earlier U.S. publications and 76 worldwide publications on divorce.

Jacobson, Richard S., ed. "Women and the Law" TRIAL, Vol. 9, No. 6 (Nov./ Dec. 1973). pp. 10-28. Association of Trial Lawyers of America. Entire issue devoted to women. Contributors include U.S. Rep. Martha W. Griffith, Silvia Roberts, Dorothy Haener, Phyllis Schafley, U.S. Sen. Marlow W. Cook, Carol Burris, Allen R. Derr, Prof. Shirley R. Bysiewicz, Dan O'Leary, Lawrence J. Smith, Prof. Joe A. Moore, Prof. G. Lawrence Roberts, D. Grant Mickel, and Mary Velasco Mercer.

Janeway, Elizabeth. BETWEEN MYTH AND MORNING: WOMAN AWAKENING. New York: William Morrow, 1974. 279 pp. Includes such essays as "Realizing Human Potential," "Women's Place in a Changing World," and "Breaking the Age Barrier."

Jeter, Jeremiah Bell. A MEMOIR OF MRS. HENRIETTA SHUCK. Boston: Gould, Kendall and Lincoln, 1846. 251 pp. The first American female missionary to China.

Johnson, Paul. ELIZABETH I: A BIOGRAPHY. New York: Holt, Rinehart and Winston, 1974. 511 pp. The latest biography of a controversial queen, by the former editor of the NEW STATESMAN.

Jorns, Auguste. THE QUAKERS AS PIONEERS IN SOCIAL WORK. Port Washington, N.Y.: Kennikat Press, 1969. 268 pp. Reprint of 1931 edition. Shows a Quaker view of the position of women.

Josephson, Hannah Geffen. JEANNETTE RANKIN. Indianapolis: Bobbs-Merrill Co., 1974. 224 pp. Biography of the first woman elected to Congress in 1917 and later in 1941, who marched with NOW in New York and endorsed the presidential campaign of Shirley Chisholm.

Kallir, Otto. GRANDMA MOSES. New York: Harry Abrams, 1973. 360 pp. 253 illustrations, with text, of the American artist and her paintings.

Kane, Paula and Christopher Chandler. SEX OBJECTS IN THE SKY. Chicago: Follett, 1974. 160 pp. Another well-deserved dart to industries that package and market women as commodities, namely, the airlines.

Katz, Naomi and Nancy Milton, eds. FRAGMENT FROM A LOST DIARY AND OTHER STORIES. New York: Pantheon Books, 1973. 317 pp. Unique collection of writings from Asia, Africa, and Latin America which adds a vital literary dimension to our understanding of the liberation of women.

Kay, Herma H. SEX BASED DISCRIMINATION IN FAMILY LAW. St. Paul, Minn.: West Pub. Co., 1974. 306 pp.

Kemp-Welch, Alice. OF SIX MEDIEVAL WOMEN. Williamstown, Mass.: Corner House, 1972. 189 pp. Reprint of 1903 edition. Portraits of six women who played an important role in the period between the 10th and 15th century: Roswitha, a German nun; Marie de France, at the court of Henry II of England; Mechtild of Magdeburg, a mystic; Mahaut, Countess of Artois; Christine de Pisan, an Italian at the court of Charles V of France; and Agnes Sorel, confidante of Charles VII.

Kievit, Mary Bach. REVIEW AND SYNTHESIS OF RESEARCH FOR WOMEN IN THE WORLD OF WORK. ERIC. Clearinghouse on Vocational and Technical Education. Washington, D.C.: SUDOC, GPO, 1972. 96 pp.

Killian, Ray. WORKING WOMEN: A MALE MANAGER'S VIEW. New York: American Management Assn., 1971. 214 pp.

Klagsburn, Francine, ed. THE FIRST MS. READER. New York: MS. Magazine, 1973. A collection of articles from the first twelve issues of MS. 282 pp.

Kutner, Luis. THE INTELLIGENT WOMEN'S GUIDE TO FUTURE SECURITY. New York: Dodd, Mead, 1970. 202 pp. Common sense advice about wills, probate, estate and tax planning, insurance, finances, social security, etc.

Larrick, Nancy and Eve Merriam, comp. MALE AND FEMALE UNDER 18: FRANK COMMENTS FROM YOUNG PEOPLE ABOUT THEIR SEX ROLES TODAY. New York: Avon, 1974. 218 pp. Young people from all over America discuss themselves, each other, their parents, sex, and the changing male/female roles.

Le Masters, Ersel E. "The Battle Between the Sexes," THE WISCONSIN SOCIOLOGIST, Vol. 10, Nos. 2 & 3 (Spring/Summer 1973), pp. 43-55. Originally a chapter from BLUE COLLAR ARISTOCRATS: LIFE.

Lesser, Allen. ENCHANTING REBEL: THE SECRET OF ADAH ISAACS MENKEN. Port Washington, N.Y.: Kennikat Press, 1973. 224 pp. Reprint of 1947 edition. During Lincoln's day, she was a sex symbol, "actress," and dancer.

Lester, Richard A. ANTIBIAS REGULATION OF UNIVERSITIES: FACULTY PROBLEMS AND THEIR SOLUTIONS. A report prepared for the Carnegie Commission on Higher Education. New York: McGraw-Hill Book Co., 1974. 168 pp. A limited survey of effects of anti sex-discriminatory legislation on American universities.

Lieberman, Myron, ed. "Education and the Feminist Movement," PHI DELTA KAPPAN. Vol. LV, No. 2 (October 1973). Pp. 98-159. A special issue. Authors include Florence Howe, Betty Levy and Judith Stacey, Janice Law Trecker, Celeste Ulrich, Carol Kehr Tittle, Catherine Dillon Lyon and Terry N. Saario, Suzanne S. Taylor, Charlotte B. Hallman, Sheila M. Rothman, Guin Hall, Joseph M. Cronin, Florence C. Lewis, Sharlene Pearlman Hirsch, W. Michael Morrissey, June Marr, Gene A. Budig and Richard Decker, and Betty Wetzel.

Limmer, Ruth, ed. WHAT THE WOMAN LIVED. New York: Harcourt Brace Jovanovich, 1974. Selected letters of Louise Bogan, whose poetry suggested the lack of options that are a part of being a woman, but whose life exemplified the courage it took to write her poems.

Lindbergh, Anne Morrow. LOCKED ROOMS AND OPEN DOORS: DIARIES AND LETTERS OF ANNE MORROW LINDBERGH, 1933-1935. New York: Harcourt Brace Jovanovich, 1974. 352 pp.

Loeser, Herta. WOMEN, WORK, AND VOLUNTEERING. Boston: Beacon Press, 1974.

Lynch, Edith M. THE EXECUTIVE SUITE—FEMININE STYLE. New York: American Management Assn., 1973. 258 pp.

McBride, Angela Barron. THE GROWTH AND DEVELOPMENT OF MOTHERS. New York: Harper and Row, 1973. 153 pp.

McGovern, Eleanor with Mary Finch Hoyt. UPHILL: A PERSONAL STORY. Boston: Houghton Mifflin, 1974. 234 pp. Recollections of the wife of Sen. George McGovern, who was a presidential candidate in 1968.

McGuigan, Dorothy G., ed. NEW RESEARCH ON WOMEN: AT THE UNIVERSITY OF MICHIGAN. University of Michigan, Ann Arbor: Center for Continuing Education of Women, 1974. 289 pp. Proceedings from the conference – New Research on Women. Publication cooperation by the National Coalition for Research on Women's Education and Development.

McHugh, Mary. LAW AND THE NEW WOMAN. New York: Praeger, 1974. 160 pp. A report on the burgeoning opportunities for women in the legal profession.

McHugh, Mary. THE WOMAN THING. New York: Praeger, 1973. 127 pp. Praeger Choosing Lifestyles Series. Condenses and highlights advancing opportunities for women today.

Macleod, Jennifer S. and Sandra T. Silverman. YOU WON'T DO: WHAT TEXTBOOKS ON U.S. GOVERNMENT TEACH HIGH SCHOOL GIRLS, WITH "–SEXISM IN TEXTBOOKS: AN ANNOTATED SOURCE LIST OF 150+ STUDIES AND REMEDIES." Pittsburgh, Penn.: KNOW, Inc., 1973. 118 pp.

Madison, Dolly. MEMOIRS AND LETTERS OF DOLLY MADISON: WIFE OF JAMES MADISON, PRESIDENT OF THE UNITED STATES. Port Washington, N.Y.: Kennikat Press, 1971. 210 pp. Reprint of 1886 edition.

Mann, Peggy and Ruth Klüger. THE LAST ESCAPE: THE LAUNCHING OF THE LARGEST SECRET RESCUE MOVEMENT OF ALL TIME. Garden City, N.Y.: Doubleday, 1973. 518 pp. Records the activities of Ruth Klüger in the Mossad to smuggle Jews out of Europe and into Palestine just prior to the outbreak of World War II.

Marks, Arno F. "Man, Vrovw en Huishoud groep, de Afro-Amerikaanse Familie in de Samenlevina van Curacao" [Man, Woman and Household Group, the Afro-American Family in Curacao Society], RUKUNNERSITEIT LEIDEN, 1973. An English translation is in preparation, to be published in the VERHANDLINGEN series of the Royal Institute for Anthropology and Linguistics, Leiden, Netherlands.

Massell, Gregory J. THE SURROGATE PROLETARIAT: MOSLEM WOMEN AND REVOLUTIONARY STRATEGIES IN SOVIET CENTRAL ASIA, 1919-1929. Princeton, N.J.: Princeton Univ. Press, 1974. 486 pp.

Masson, Flora, THE BRONTES. Port Washington, N.Y.: Kennikat Press, 1970. 92 pp. Reprint of 1912 edition.

Maule, Frances. SHE STRIVES TO CONQUER. New York: Funk & Wagnalls, 1937. 301 pp. An analysis of the opportunities and pitfalls of employment in the business world from a "do's and don'ts" approach.

Mayer, Michael F. DIVORCE AND ANNULMENT IN THE 50 STATES. New York: Arno Press, 1967. 89 pp. Description of the various states' laws relating to divorce.

Mead, Margaret. RUTH BENEDICT. New York: Columbia Univ. Press, 1974.

180 pp. Biography of the noted anthropologist who broke out of the restrictions of the woman's role, but was continually at the mercy of male professionals.

Mellen, Joan. WOMEN AND THEIR SEXUALITY IN THE NEW FILM. New York: Horizon Press, 1974. 255 pp.

Mencken, Henry Louis. IN DEFENSE OF WOMEN. New York: Knopf, 1922. 210 pp. By the celebrated American cynic on the "Feminine Mind," "The War Between the Sexes," "Marriage," "Woman Suffrage," and "The New Age."

Millett, Kate. FLYING. New York: Knopf, 1974. 545 pp. An autobiography that explores her feelings, attitudes, way of life, and her sexual attitudes.

Mitchell, Juliet. PSYCHOANALYSIS AND FEMINISM. New York: Pantheon Books, 1974. 456 pp. Tries to rehabilitate Freud for feminists by developing a new "interface" between fathers and mothers in the family.

Moffat, Mary J. and Charlotte Painter. REVELATIONS: DIARIES OF WOMEN. New York: Random House, 1974. 448 pp. Diary selections organized under themes of love, power and work by such writers as Louisa M. Alcott, George Sand, Anais Nin, Virginia Woolf, and others. A book which rises above the usual narrow feminist definitions.

Money, Keith. THE ART OF MARGOT FONTEYN. New York: William Morrow, 1966. 261 pp. The biography, with beautiful photographs of the great British dancer. Commentary contributed by Ninette de Valois, Frederick Ashton, Keith Money, and Margot Fonteyn. Photographed by Keith Money.

Morrah, Dermot, et al. QUEEN'S VISIT: ELIZABETH 2ND IN INDIA AND PAKISTAN. New York: Asia Publishing House, 1974.

Mothersill, Mary, ed. "Women's Liberation: Ethical, Social, and Political Issues," THE MONIST, Vol. 57, No. 1 (Jan. 1973), pp. 1-114. Contributors are Christine Pierce, Virginia Held, Abigail L. Rosenthal, Mary Anne Warren, Jan Narveson, Thomas E. Hill, Jr., and Mary Mothersill.

National School Boards Association. WOMEN ON SCHOOL BOARDS. Evanston, Ill.: Author, 1974. A report.

Nettl, J. Peter. ROSA LUXEMBURG. Fairlawn, N.J.: Oxford Univ. Press, 1969. 557 pp. One of the pioneer women economists and German revolutionary communist.

Norman, Eve. RAPE. Los Angeles, Cal.: Wollstonecraft, 1973. Seeks answers to questions regarding a crime that deeply concerns all women.

North Carolina Museum of Art. WOMEN: A HISTORICAL SURVEY OF WORKS BY WOMEN ARTISTS. Raleigh, N.C.: North Carolina Museum of Art, 1972. 58 pp.

Oliphant, Mrs. Margaret. JEANNE D'ARC: HER LIFE AND DEATH. New York: AMS Press, 1974. Reprint of 1896 edition.

O'Neil, George and Nena O'Neil. OPEN MARRIAGE: A NEW LIFE STYLE FOR COUPLES. New York: M. Evans, 1972. 287 pp.

Peck, Ellen and Judith Senderowitz, eds. PRONATALISM: THE MYTH OF MOM AND APPLE PIE. New York: Apollo Editions, 1974. 333 pp. Advocates weighing alternatives to having children to arrive at a guilt-free decision.

Peters, Heinz Frederick. MY SISTER, MY SPOUSE. New York: Norton Library, 1974. 320 pp. Biography of Lou Andreas-Salome (1861-1937), who was loved by Nietzche, a confidante of Wagner, Rilke, Tolstoy, Rodin,

Strindberg, Buber, Hauptmann, and Freud.

Phillips, Leon. THE FIRST LADY OF AMERICA: A ROMANTICIZED BI-
OGRAPHY OF POCAHONTAS. Richmond, Va.: Westover Pub. Co.,
1973. 240 pp. Discloses the fascinating aspects of a personality that
rivals the modern woman in will and independence.

Plunket, Irene Arthur Lifford. ISABEL OF CASTILE AND THE MAKING OF
THE SPANISH NATION. New York: AMS Press, 1974. Reprint of
1919 edition.

Prywes, Ruth W. A STUDY ON THE DEVELOPMENT OF A NON-STANDARD
WORK DAY OR WORK WEEK FOR WOMEN. Report No. DLMA-91-
42-73-16-1. Graduate School of Social Work and Social Research, Bryn
Mawr College, Pa. Sponsored by the Dept. of Labor, Manpower Admin.,
Office of Research and Development. Washington, D.C.: SUDOC, GPO,
1974. 395 pp.

QUEST: A FEMINIST QUARTERLY. Washington, D.C., P.O. Box 8843.
Magazine published quarterly beginning in 1974, each issue having a
different theme. Vol. I, No. 1, "Processes of Change;" No. 2, "$$, Fame
and Power;" No. 3, "The Selfhood of Women;" No. 4, "Women and
Spirituality." Vol. II, No. 1, "Future Visions and Fantasies."

Radl, Shirley. MOTHER'S DAY IS OVER. New York: Charterhouse, 1973.
234 pp. A review of the myths of the "Mother" image.

Radloff, Barbara. "Political Woman: Public Role and Personal Challenges,"
CARNEGIE QUARTERLY, Vol. XXII, No. 3 (Summer 1974), pp. 1-5.

Ray, Gordon N. H. G. WELLS AND REBECCA WEST. New Haven: Yale Univ.
Press, 1974. 215 pp. Frank protrayal of the lives of the great science
fiction writer and Dame Rebecca West (Cicely Isabel Fairchild).

Richards, Caroline Cowles. VILLAGE LIFE IN AMERICA: 1852-1872. THE
DIARY OF A SCHOOL GIRL. Williamstown, Mass.: Corner House,
1972. Reprint of 1913 edition. 225 pp. Introduction by Margaret
Sanger. Caroline Cowles began her diary at the age of ten in Canandaigua,
N.Y. It provides a rich source of information on the style of life young
people experienced at that time.

Rivers, Caryl. APHRODITE AT MID-CENTURY: GROWING UP FEMALE
AND CATHOLIC IN POST WAR AMERICA. Garden City, N.Y.:
Doubleday, 1973. 283 pp.

Robinson, Mrs. Harriet (Hanson). LOOM AND SPINDLE, OR LIFE AMONG
THE EARLY MILL GIRLS. Boston: Crowell, 1898. 216 pp. Intro-
duction by Carroll D. Wright, with a sketch of "The Lowell Offering"
and some of its contributors.

The Roper Organization, Inc. THE VIRGINIA SLIMS AMERICAN WOMEN'S
OPINION POLL: A SURVEY OF THE ATTITUDES OF WOMEN ON
MARRIAGE, DIVORCE, THE FAMILY AND AMERICA'S CHANGING
MORALITY. Volume III. New York: Phillip Morris, Inc. (100 Park
Ave.), 1974. 123 pp.

Rosen, Marjorie. POPCORN VENUS: WOMEN, MOVIES & THE AMERICAN
DREAM. New York: Coward, McCann & Geoghegan, 1974. 416 pp.

Rosenberg-Dishman, Marie B., "Affirmative Action—Contexts and Compliance
for Local Governments," The MUNICIPALITY (Wisconsin), Vol. 69,
No. 12. (December, 1974). pp. 237, 246.

Rosner, Menahem. "Women in the Kibbutz, Changing Status and Concepts."
ASIAN AND AFRICAN STUDIES, Vol. 3 (Annual 1967). pp. 35-68.

Ross, Ishbel. THE PRESIDENT'S WIFE: MARY TODD LINCOLN. New York:
Putnam, 1973. 378 pp.

Rossi, Alice S., ed. THE FEMINIST PAPERS: FROM ADAMS TO DE BEAU-
      VOIR. New York: Columbia Univ. Press, 1973. 716 pp.
Russ, Joanna, "The Image of Women in Science Fiction," In RED CLAY READER
      7. Serial. Edited by Charleen Whisnant. Charlotte, N.C.: Southern
      Review, 1970. Pp. 34-47.
Russell, Letty M. HUMAN LIBERATION IN A FEMINIST PERSPECTIVE: A
      THEOLOGY. Philadelphia: Westminster Press, 1974. 224 pp. Places
      the women's movement into the context of other liberation movements
      in the Church, and outlines the common themes, perspectives, and
      methodologies for women to construct a viable past and future for
      themselves.
Scanzoni, John H. SEXUAL BARGAINING: POWER POLITICS IN THE
      AMERICAN MARRIAGE. Englewood Cliffs, N.J.: Prentice-Hall,
      1972. 181 pp.
Secrest, Meryle. BETWEEN ME AND LIFE: A BIOGRAPHY OF ROMAINE
      BROOKS. New York: Doubleday, 1974. 432 pp. Portrait of the
      female artist, obscure while in America, who became part of the world
      of Joyce, Pound, Gide, Colette, Valery, D'Annunzio, and Stein.
Seed, Suzanne. SATURDAY'S CHILD: 36 WOMEN TALK ABOUT THEIR
      JOBS. New York: Bantam Books, 1974.
Seidenberg, Robert. CORPORATE WIVES—CORPORATE CASUALTIES. New
      York: American Management Assn., Inc., AMA-COM, 1973. 177 pp.
Sewall, Richard Benson. THE LIFE OF EMILY DICKINSON. New York:
      Farrar, Straus, Girous, 1974. 2 vols. A monumental biography of the
      19th century American poet, following his 1963 collection of Dickin-
      son essays.
Sherwin, Robert Veit. COMPATIBLE DIVORCE. New York: Crown Publishers,
      1969. 308 pp.
Sidel, Ruth. WOMEN AND CHILD CARE IN CHINA. New York: Penguin,
      1973. 207 pp. Deals with liberation of women, marriage, pregnancy
      and childbirth, and the "Bitter Past."
Sklar, Kathryn K. CATHARINE BEECHER: A STUDY IN AMERICAN
      DOMESTICITY. New Haven: Yale Univ. Press, 1973. 356 pp. The
      latest biography of the early American feminist.
Sochen, June. MOVERS AND SHAKERS: AMERICAN WOMEN THINKERS
      AND ACTIVISTS, 1900-1970. New York: Quadrangle Books, 1973.
      320 pp. Survey of feminism with emphasis on women intellectuals
      who thought, wrote, and acted to elevate the status of women, with a
      discussion of some 30 selected feminists and their organizations.
Springer, John and Jack D. Hamilton. THEY HAD FACES THEN. Secaucus,
      N.J.: Citadel Press, 1974. All the lovely wistful moments in the movie
      houses of our youth in over 900 photographs of memorable ladies of
      the movies.
State Bar of Wisconsin. HANDBOOK OF DIVORCE PROCEDURE. 1973
      revised ed. Madison: Author, 1973. 112 pp.
Steegmuller, Francis. "YOUR ISADORA": THE LOVE STORY OF ISADORA
      DUNCAN AND GORDON CRAIG. New York: Random House, 1974.
      399 pp. Readable book about the phenomenal dancer and her relation-
      ship with the radical/humanitarian Craig.
Stein, Martha L. LOVERS, FRIENDS, SLAVES: NINE MALE SEXUAL TYPES.
      New York: G. P. Putnam's Sons, 1974. 225 pp. Despire its title, a
      study of call girls.

Strainchamps, Ethel, ed. ROOMS WITH NO VIEW: A WOMAN'S GUIDE TO
THE MAN'S WORLD OF THE MEDIA. Compiled by the Media
Women's Association. New York: Harper and Row, 1974. 320 pp.
Collection of 71 essays telling what it's really like for women to work
in television, newspapers, magazines, and book publishing; a picture of
what has been, and in some cases, still is.
Strauss, Robert P. and Francis W. Horrath. "Analyzing Economic Descrimina-
tion Against Blacks and Women with the Public Use Sample," REVIEW
OF PUBLIC DATA, Vol. 1, No. 4 (Oct. 1973), pp. 10-18.
Sullivan, Victoria and James Hatch. PLAYS BY AND ABOUT WOMEN: AN
ANTHOLOGY. New York: Random House, 1973. 425 pp.
Tak, Jean vander. ABORTION, FERTILITY, AND CHANGING LEGISLATION:
AN INTERNATIONAL REVIEW. Lexington, Mass.: Lexington, 1974.
175 pp. Includes bibliography.
Talmon, Yonina. FAMILY AND COMMUNITY IN THE KIBBUTZ. Cambridge;
Harvard University Press, 1972. 262 pp.
Thompson, Dorothy Lampen. ADAM SMITH'S DAUGHTERS: SIX DISTIN-
GUISHED WOMEN ECONOMISTS FROM THE 18TH CENTURY TO
THE PRESENT. Jericho, New York: Exposition Press, 1973. The six
"daughters" are Jane Haldimand Marcet, Harriet Martineau, Millicent
Carrett Fawcett, Rosa Luxemburg, Beatrice Potter Webb, and Joan
Robinson.
Thwaite, Ann. WAITING FOR THE PARTY: THE LIFE OF FRANCES
HODGSON BURNETT, 1849-1924. New York: Scribner's, 1974.
274 pp. A brisk and intimate portrait of the author of LITTLE LORD
FAUNTLEROY.
Tolchin, Susan and Martin Tolchin. CLOUT: WOMANPOWER AND POLITICS.
New York: Coward, McCann and Geoghegan, 1974. 320 pp. "A land-
mark analysis of where women stand in politics today and where they
are headed."
Tomalin, Claire, THE LIFE AND DEATH OF MARY WOOLSTONECRAFT.
New York: Harcourt Brace Jovanovich, 1974. 316 pp. Critical yet
sympathetic, well-documented and illustrated, the best since the more
idealized study of Eleanor Flexner.
Tripp, Maggie. WOMAN IN THE YEAR 2000. New York: Arbor House, 1974.
288 pp. 26 perceptive writers predict what may happen to women by
the beginning of the 21st century.
Tsuchigave, Robert and Norton Dodge. ECONOMIC DISCRIMINATION
AGAINST WOMEN IN THE U.S. Lexington, Mass.: Lexington Books,
1974. 152 pp.
Tufts, Eleanor. OUR HIDDEN HERITAGE: FIVE CENTURIES OF WOMEN
ARTISTS. New York: Paddington Press, 1973. 256 pp. Series of
biographical portraits of famous women artists, including Levina Teer-
ling (painter to Henry VIII); Elizabeth Vigee-Lebrun (portraitist to
Marie Antoinette); Angelica Kauffmann (one of the founders of the
Royal Academy in London); and Sofonisba Anguissola, who was ad-
mired by Michelangelo.
U.S. Citizen's Advisory Council on the Status of Women. WOMEN IN 1971.
Washington, D.C.: SUDOC, GPO, 1972. 61 pp.
U.S. Congress. Joint Economic Committee. HEARINGS ON THE ECONOMIC
PROBLEMS OF WOMEN. Ninety-third Congress, First Session. Part 1

(July 10-12, 1973). 220 pp.; Part 2 (July 24-26, 1973). pp. 221-241.; Part 3 "Statements for the Record," pp. 443-579. Washington, D.C.: SUDOC, GPO, 1973. Congresswoman Martha W. Griffiths presiding.

U.S. Congress. Senate Committee on Labor and Public Welfare, Subcommittee on Education. WOMEN'S EDUCATIONAL EQUITY ACT OF 1973. Ninety-third Congress, First Session. Hearings on S.2518 (Oct. 17 and Nov. 9, 1973). 426 pp. Washington, D.C.: SUDOC, GPO, 1973. Senator Walter Mondale presiding.

U.S. Department of Health, Education and Welfare. REPORT OF THE WOMEN'S ACTION PROGRAM. Washington, D.C.: U.S. Dept. of H.E.W. (Jan. 1972). Created in 1971, WAP was based on the premise that change was needed in the status of women both in HEW and in the outside world. Prognosis, poor; probable progress, slow.

U.S. Department of Health, Education and Welfare. RESEARCH IN EDUCATION: CUMULATIVE INDEX. Educational Resources Information Center (ERIC), National Institute of Education, Washington, D.C. Computer printouts available. Through July 1974, 1,210 entries on women retrievable from key words: women professors, women teachers, working women, women's education, women's athletics, women's studies, feminism, females.

U.S. Department of Labor. "American Woman at the Crossroads: Directions for the Future." Report of the 50th anniversary Conference of the Women's Bureau held at the Washington Hilton Hotel, Washington, D.C., June 11-13, 1970. Washington, D.C.: Women's Bureau, Employment Standards Administration (SUDOC, GPO), 1970. 126 pp. Extensive bibliography and listing of special collections on women, pp. 88-126.

Van Vuuren, Nancy. THE SUBVERSION OF WOMEN AS PRACTICED BY CHURCHES, WITCH HUNTERS, AND OTHER SEXISTS. Philadelphia: Westminster Press, 1973. 190 pp. Shows in detail how all our Western institutions have worked together through history to keep women subordinated. By the President of Pennsylvanians for Women's Rights.

Veroff, Joseph and Sheila Feld. MARRIAGE AND WORK IN AMERICA: A STUDY OF MOTIVES AND ROLES. New York: Van Nostrand Reinhold, 1970. 404 pp. Motives of affiliation, achievement, and power examined for interaction with role characteristics to affect experience of fulfillment and frustration in these roles. Large national sample.

Walters, Ronald G., ed. PRIMERS FOR PRUDERY: SEXUAL ADVICE TO VICTORIAN AMERICA. Englewood Cliffs, N.J.: Prentice-Hall, 1974. 175 pp. Selections included in this volume mark an important beginning in the study of the historical and cultural aspects of sexuality in American society.

Washington, Joseph R., Jr. MARRIAGE IN BLACK AND WHITE. Boston: Beacon Press, 1971. 358 pp. Author suggests racial conflict cannot be eliminated until we are willing to confront prejudice on its most personal level—by acceptance of intermarriage.

Whittaker, Peter. THE AMERICAN WAY OF SEX. New York: Berkley/G.P. Putnam's Sons, 1974. 256 pp. Interviews with women in the massage-parlor trade.

"Women Around the World," THE CENTER MAGAZINE, Vol. VII, No. 3 (May/ June 1974), pp. 43-80. Report of conference sponsored by the Center

for the Study of Democratic Institutions and the Univ. of California at
Santa Barbara on "Social and Political Change: The Role of Women."
Articles by participants Judith Van Allen, Rae Lesser Blumberg, Kay
Boals and Judith Stiehm, Lynn B. Iglitzin, Nora Scott Kinzer, Peter Merkl,
Sondra Herman and Alva Myrdal. Complete proceedings forthcoming.
WOMEN ON CAMPUS: THE UNFINISHED LIBERATION. New Rochelle,
N.Y.: Change, 1974. A number of distinguished—and successful—
women in American education today discuss the role of women in both
the present and future of American higher education.
Women on Words and Images. DICK AND JANE AS VICTIMS: SEX STEREO-
TYPING IN CHILDREN'S READERS: AN ANALYSIS. Princeton,
N.J.: Author, 1972. 57 pp.
THE WOMEN'S GUIDE TO BOOKS. New York: MSS. Information Corp.,
1974. A catalog, published quarterly, discussing novels, biographies,
books on film, law, ecology, poetry, sexuality, politics, education,
marriage, and divorce.
Women's History Research Center. FILMS BY AND/OR ABOUT WOMEN, 1972:
DIRECTORY OF FILM-MAKERS AND DISTRIBUTORS, INTER-
NATIONALLY, PAST AND PRESENT. Berkeley, California: Women's
History Research Center, 1972. 72 pp.
Wormser, Ellen, ed. "Women in Government: Public Policy Forum," THE
BUREAUCRAT. Vol. 1, No. 3 (Fall 1972). Entire issue devoted to
public policy formulation regarding women. Authors include: Ellen
Wormser, Glen G. Cain, Helene S. Markoff, Daisy B. Fields, Linda
Moore, Millicent Allewelt, Marjorie M. Silverberg, George S. Maharay,
Harry Flickinger, Gladys Rogers, Barbara Franklin, and Art Buchwald.
Yorburg, Betty. SEXUAL IDENTITY: SEX ROLES AND SOCIAL CHANGE.
New York: John Wiley, 1974. 227 pp. How and why sexual identity
and sex-typed role conceptions have varied throughout history. It
covers such topics as the biological bases of sexual identity, variations
in sexual identity in nonliterate, agricultural, and industrial societies,
and contemporary variations around the world and in America.

AUTHOR-ORGANIZATION INDEX

A

Abarbanel, A., 2346
Abbott, Edith, 1149, 1372, 3052
Abbott, John S. C., 133
Abbott, Wallace C., 2297
Abbott, Willis J., 2383
Abrahams, Sir Adolphe, 1288
Abram, A., 1680
Abrams, Ray H., 134
Abramowicz, Marc, 769
Abramson, Marcia, 1490
Abzug, Bella, 1088, 1466, 1490-1491, 2467
Achtemeier, Elizabeth, 2175
Ackworth, E., 135
Acquaye Elmina, J. R., 2939
Acrelius, Israel, 1988
Acton, William, 272
Adams, Abigail, 961, 1566, 2427, 2814
Adams, Charles F., 2692
Adams, Elizabeth K., 3268
Adams, Elmer C., 2384
Adams, Elsie, 1, 1261
Adams, Grace, 2828
Adams, Hazard, Adden.
Adams, James T., 1989
Adams, Mildred, 1332
Addams, Jane, 568, 880, 891, 907-908, 911, 925, 934-935, 954, 1372, 1431, 1825-1827, 1856, 1898, 1903, 2176, 2384-2385, 2597, 3054, Adden. (Davis)
Ade, Ginny, 1507
Adelman, Joseph, 2130, 2386
Adelson, J., 2849
African Bibliographic Center, 3514
Afro-American Woman's Collection, 3579
Agassi, Judith B., 3307
Agate, James, 2387
Agrippa, Marcus Vipsanius, 1543
Aguirre, Mme. Gertrude G. de, 3400
Ahlum, Carol, 3433
Akeley, M. L. J., 2940
Alberione, James, 2177
Alberto, M. S., 2941
Alcott, Louisa M., 1555, 2398, 2427, 2422, 2470, Adden. (Moffat)
Alcott, William A., 216-217
Alderson, Nannie T., 2388
Aldous, Joan, 2
Alexander, Mithrapuram K., 2389
Alexander, Ralph A., 612
Alexander, Rodney, Adden.
Alexander, Ruth, 389
Alexander, William, 1544
Algeo, Sara M., 1371
Ali, Ameer, 2178
Allen, Virginia, 1210
Allen, William H., 1289
Allewelt, Millicent, Adden. (Wormser)

Alliluyeva, Svetlana (Stalina), Adden.
Allingham, John D., 3053
Allport, Gordon, 2829
Almedingen, E. M., 2131
Almond, Gabriel, 1290 [Intro.]
Almquist, Elizabeth M., 3
Alpha Kappa Alpha Sorority, 1467, 1508, 2298-2299, 3401
Altbach, Edith Yoshino, 962
Altekar, A. S., 1619
Altemus, Jameson Torr, 2390
American Academy of Political and Social Science, ANNALS 59, 110, 130, 134, 279, 337, 369, 392, 1074, 1349, 1893, 3054, 3090, 3296 [Intro.]
American Anthropological Association, 705
American Association of University Professors, 706
American Association of University Women, 569, 661-662, 687, 707-709, 2391, 3269-3271
AMERICAN ASSOCIATION OF UNIVERSITY WOMEN JOURNAL, 17, 389, 700, 995
American Association of University Women Library, 3580
American Civil Liberties Union, 1035
American Economic Association Committee on the Status of Women, Adden.
American Federation of Teachers, Women's Rights Committee, 3515
AMERICAN FEDERATIONIST, 3297
American Female Moral Reform Society, 913
American Friends Service Committee, 770
American Historical Association, 710-711
American Music Conference, 2693
American Political Science Association, 712
American Sociological Society, 136
American University Law Review, 790
Ames, Azel, 3308
Ames, D., 2942
Amir, Menachem, 2830
Amundsen, Kirsten Steinmo, 1211, 3216
Anderson, Adelaide M., 3309
Anderson, Ellen, Adden.
Anderson, J. N. D., 1131
Anderson, Margaret C., 2392
Anderson, Marian, 2393
Anderson, Mary, 1509, 2394, 3055, 3310
Andreas, Carol, 473
Andrews, Irene O., 3238
Andrews, John B., 3272
Andrews, Mary R. S., 2395
Andrews, Matthew P., 2045
Angelino, H., 1775
Angelou, Maya, 2396
Angrist, Shirley S., 3
ANNALS, See American Academy of Political and Social Science

Anstett, Patricia, 3423
Anthony, Katherine Susan, 475, 2132, 2397-2399
Anthony, Susan Brownell, 963, 1043, 1366 [Intro.] , 1378, 1380, 1388, 1392, 1829, 1926, 2399, 2468, 2473, 2512, 2592, 2645
Antin, Mary, 2400, 2597
Appia-Dabit, B., 2943
Aptekar, Herbert H., 771, 2944
Aptheker, Herbert, 1621, 2082
Archer, Stevenson, 1403
Archibald, Alice, 3555
Archibald, Kathleen, 1212
Arendt, Hannah, 2401
Aretz, Gertrude, 1715
Arias, Jorge, 789
Aristophanes, 2694
Arkoff, A., 67
Arling, Emanie Nahm Sachs. See Sachs, Emanie.
Armes, Ethel, 2402
Armstrong, Ann, 1432
Army Air Force Historical Office, 2044
Arnott, Catherine, 4
Asbury, Herbert, 940
Ash, Lee, 3581
Ashton, Frederick, Adden. (Money)
Association of American Colleges, 3194-3195, 3516
Association for Women Psychologists, 713
Association of Women in Science, 3517
Astell, Mary, 218, 570, 2633
Astin, Helen S., 275, 714, 3434-3435
Atangana, N., 2945
Atherton, Gertrude, 5, 2133, 2403
Athey, Louis, 892
Atkins, Martha, 964
Auchincloss, Louis, 2695
Augur, Helen, 1990
Aujoulat, L., 3028
Austen, Jane, 1555, 2696-2698, 2754, 2757, 2814
Austin, Mary, 1381, 2404
Austin, William, 1622
Aviel, JoAnn F., 1448
Awobajo, Theophilus D., 965

B

Bach, Patricia Gorence, 1433
Bachofen, J. J., 1546 [Intro.]
Bachtold, Louise M., 1448, 2831
Backman, Margaret E., 6
Bacon, Francis D., 2179
Bacon, Margaret K., 7
Bader, Clarisse, 1681
Baege, B., 2946
Baig, Iara Ali, 1623 [Intro.]
Bailey, D. S., 2180
Bailey, Pearl, 2405

Bailyn, Lotte, 297
Bainton, Roland, 1682
Baird, Charles W., 1991
Baker, Elizabeth C., Adden. (Hess)
Baker, Elizabeth Faulkner, 3311
Baker, Helen, 3312
Bakke, E. Wight, 571
Bal, A., 2947
Balbabanoff, Angelica, 2406
Balch, Emily G., 934
Bald, Marjory Amelia, 2698
Balde, S., 2948
Baldwin, Alice, 1372
Bales, Robert F., 190
Ballin, A. S., 1777
Balsdon, John P. V. D., 1683
Banerji, J., 966
Banks, Joseph A., 773, 1830
Banks, Olive, 773, 1830
Banning, Evelyn I., Adden.
Banning, Margaret C., 3313
Baraka, Imamu Amiri, 1950
Barber, B., 1778
Barber, Kathleen Lucas, Intro. p. 26.
Barbour, Floyd, 295
Bardolph, Richard, 2083
Bareno, Maria Isabel, Adden. (da Costa)
Bardwick, Judith M., 2301, 2832-2833
Baritz, Loren, Adden.
Barker-Benfield, Ben, 393-394, 610
Barnard, Ella Kent, 1992
Barnes, Daniel R., 2699
Barnes, Earl, 1831, 3054
Barnes, Gilbert, 2407
Barnes, Hazel E., 2798
Barnes, L. A., 1775
Barnett, C. R., 2834
Barnier, Lucien, 3196
Baroja, Julio Caro, 1738
Barot, Madelaine, 2181
Barringer, Herbert R., 210, 270
Barrow, T. Terence, 2949
Barrows, Alice P., 3054
Barry, Herbert, 7
Bart, Pauline B., 111, 476, Adden. (Hochschild)
Bartell, Gilbert D., 395
Barth, Ilene, 572
Bartley, L., 1779
Basil, Douglas C., 3402
Baskin, Lisa, 2724
Bass, Bernard, 612
Batchelor, J., 1739
Bates, Daisy, 2408
Bateson, Mary, 1716
Batho, Edith C., 715
Battis, Emery, 2182
Baumann, H., 2950
Baumrind, Diana, 8
Bayer, Henry G., 1993
Bayles, George James, 1150
Baym, Nina, 2700-2701

Bazeley, W. S., 2951
Bazell, Robert J., 716
Bazin, Nancy Topping, 2409, 2702
Beach, Frank A., 396, 421
Beach, Seth Curtis, 2410
Beard, Charles A., 1519
Beard, Mary Ritter, 1372, 1534, 1547
    [Intro.], 1624, 1951, 3054
Beasley, Ina M., 337
Beasley, Norma, 2411
Beatty, Jerome, 276
Beauchamp, W. M., 2084
Beaver, Robert Pierce, 2183
Bebel, Auguste, 1548, 1952
Bedford, Herbert, Adden.
Beebe, Gilbert Wheeler, 774
Beecher, Catherine Esther, 573-576, 928,
    1404, 1679, 1717, 2500, 2513, 2592,
    2646, 3299, Adden. (Sklar)
Beedy, Helen C., 1994
Beeman, Alice L., 389
Behn, Aphra, 2420, 2703, 2765
Beier, H. U., 2952
Belcher, Susan, 2769
Belden, Jack, 1520, 1953
Bell, Carolyn Shaw, 3056
Bell, Enid H. C. M., 2302, 2412
Bell, Ernest A., 277
Bell, Inge Powell, Adden. (Hochschild)
Bell, Norman W., 137
Bell, Quentin, 1780, 2413
Bell, Ralcy Husted, 1832
Bell, Robert R., 397
Bem, Daryl J., 577
Bem, Sandra L., 577
Benedek, Therese F., 2303, 2835
Benedict, Ruth, 2953, Adden. (Mead)
Bengis, Ingrid, 398
Benjamin, Theodosia, 389
Benn, J. W., 2704
Bennett, Edward M., 2836
Bennett, John W., 9, 578
Bennett, Lerone, 2085-2086
Bennett, Margaret, 2705
Bennett, S. R. I., 3518
Bensman, Joseph, 369
Benson, E. F., 2414
Benson, Mary Sumner, 477, 1625
Benston, Margaret, 1251, 3057, 3129
Bercher, William, 1549
Bereaud, Susan, 3436
Berelson, Bernard R., 1291
Berendsohn, Walter A., Adden.
Beresford Stooke, G., 2954
Berger, Carruthers Gholson, 1204
Berger, John, 2706
Bergler, E., 1781
Bergman, Elihu, Adden. (Gray)
Berkeley: Women's History Library, 2728
Berkin, Carol, Adden.
Berman, Joan, 1985
Berman, Sanford, 3582

Bernard, Jacqueline, 929
Bernard, Jessie, 10, 219-220, 278, 337, 339,
    717, 3058 [Intro.], Adden.
Bernbaum, Ernest, 1405
Bernhardt, Sarah, 2415, 2426, 2492, 2610
Bernheim, Nicole, 1406
Berson, Barbara, Adden.
Bernstein, Irving, 3144 [Intro.]
Bernstein, Rose, 138
Berry, Jane, 579, 718
Besant, Annie, 815, 2448, 2585, 2676
Beshiri, Patricia H., 2304
Best, E., 1740
Betham-Edwards, Matilda, 2416
Bettelheim, Bruno, 329, 719
Betts, Annabel (Paxton), 1468
Beyer, Sylvia S., 3059
Bezucha, Robert J., 991
Bibbins, Ruth M., 1995
BIBLIOTECA FEMINA, Northwestern Univ.
    Library, Evanston, Ill., 3583
Bickner, Mei Liang, Adden.
Bieliauskas, Vytautas J., 11
Biggar, Jeanne C., 3437
Biller, Henry, 12
Billingsley, Andrew, 139
Billings, Victoria, Adden.
Billington, George, 1833
Billington, Ray Allen, 2417
Billington, Theresa, 1833
Bilshai, Vera, 1076
Binder, P., 1782
Binet, J., 2955
BIOGRAPHIUM FEMINEUM, 2418
Bird, Caroline, 221, 389, 1834 [Intro.]
Birdwell, Russell, 3403
Birney, Catherine H., 893
Bixby, Lenore E., Adden. (Hoskins)
Bjerregaard, C. H. A., 2184
Blackburn, Helen, 1333
Blacking, J., 2956
Blackwell, Alice, 967, 2419
Blackwell, Elizabeth, 2305, 2336
Blair, Emily Newell, 1292
Blake, Nelson M., 222
Blanc, C., 1783
Blanc, Madame Marie Therese de Solms, 478
Blandin, I. M. E., 580
Blashfield, Evangeline Wilbour, 2420
Blatch, Harriet Stanton, 1373, 1399, 1835,
    2640
Blavatsky, Helena P., 2185
Blease, Walter Lyon, 968
Bliss, Kathleen, 2186
Bliss, W. P. D., 3272
Bloch, A. J., 2306
Blood, Kathryn, 3314
Blood, Robert O., 3239
Bloor, Ella Reeve, 969, 1269, 1836
Blumberg, Dorothy R., 1837
Blumberg, Rae Lesser, Adden. ("Women . . .")
Blumenthal, Walter H., 1996

Blumer, Dietrich, 448
Boals, Kay, 1434, 1448, Adden.
  ("Women . . .")
Boatwright, Eleanor, 1077
Bode, Edward Lynn, 2187
Bode, Mabel, 2188
Boehn, M. von, 1784
Bogardus, Emory S., 2087
Bogue, Mary F., 140
Bohannan, Paul, 223
Bolamba, A. R., 2957
Bolton, Herbert E., 1997
Bolton, Sarah Knowles, 2421-2422
Bond, R. Warwick, 1549
Bonham, Barbara, 2423
Boone, Gladys, 3273
Booth, Meyrich, 1550
Booth, Viva B., 279
Borchers, G. L., 720
Borgese, Elizabeth Mann, 479
Boring, E. G., 723
Borun, Minda, Adden.
Bosanquet, Theodora, 2424
Boserup, Esther, 3315
Boslooper, Thomas, Adden.
Bosmajian, Hamida, 970
Bosselman, Beulah Chamberlin, 2837
Boston College Industrial and Commercial
  Law Review, 156
Boston Public Library, 3584
Boston Women's Health Book Collective,
  2307
Botkin, Benjamin A., 2088-2089
Bott, Alan, 1626
Boulas, S. H., 2343
Boulding, Kenneth, Adden. (Amer. Econ.
  Assoc.)
Boulting, William, 1838
Bourque, Susan, Intro. p. 23
Bouvier, Jeanne, 1954
Bova, Ben, Adden.
Bowen, Eliza S., 280
Bowen, Lucy de Koven, 2485
Boyd, Mary Sumner, 1314
Boyd, Rosamonde R., 337
Boyers, Robert, 369
Boyle, C. V., 2958
Boynick, David K., 2425
Brackett, Anna Callender, 581, 721
Bradbrook, Muriel C., 1839
Bradbury, Harriet B., 1551 [Intro.]
Braddon, Russell, 2046
Bradford, Gamaliel, 1684, 2426-2429
Bradford, Sarah H., 930
Bradlaugh, Charles, 815
Bragdon, Claude, 2189
Bragdon, Elizabeth, 281
Brailsford, Mabel R., 1998
Braithwaite, Richard, 1552
Branagan, Thomas, 971
Branch, E. Doughlas, 1627
Branch, Mary S., 3060

Brandel, M., 3404
Brandon, Sydney, 2838
Braun, Lily, 1436
Brausch, G. E., 2959
Breasted, Mary, 582
Breckinridge, Sophonisba P., 141, 480, 1149,
  1151-1152, 1374, 1535, 1553, 3054
Brée, Germaine, Adden.
Brenner, Marshall H., 3197
Breslin, John B., 775
Brew, M., 1785
Brey, Kathleen Healy, 2308
Briant, Keith, 2430
Brice, Raoul, 2047
Bridenbaugh, Carl, 1999
Briffault, Robert., 142, 224, 2960
Briggs, Cyril, 3215
Brinkley, Mrs. Hugh L., 894
Briscoe, Mary Louise, 1, 1261
Brittain, Alfred, 1554
Brittain, Vera, 583, 1840, 3061
Brockett, Linus Pierpont, 1407, Adden.
Brody, Sylvia, 2839
Bromley, Dorothy Dunbar, 776
Bronson, Emma, 3214
Brookes, Pamela, 1469
Brooks, Angie E., 337
Brooks, Geraldine, 2000
Brooks, Gwendolyn, 2707, Adden.
Brooks, Tom, 3316
Brophy, Brigid, 1555
Brown, Alberta, 282
Brown, Barbara A., 1153
Brown, Carol, 610
Brown, Charles Brockden, 1841
Brown, Daniel G., 2840
Brown, David G., 722
Brown, Dee Alexander, 2431
Brown, Donald R., 481
Brown, Hallie Quinn, 2432
Brown, Ivor, 2433
Brown, Jean, 3317
Brown, Judith, 506, 1886
Brown, Leando, 1375
Brown, Nona B., 1293
Brown, Norman K., 777
Brown, Norman O., 2190
Brown, Olympia, 1376
Brown, Mrs. Raymond, 1315
Browning, Hilda, 1955
Brownlee, Jean, 584
Bruce, H. Addington, 2001
Bruce, Margaret King, 337
Bruemmer, Linda, 3438
Bruere, Martha, 2708, 3318
Brumbaugh, Sara Barbara, 1294
Bruno, Anne, 1545
Bryan, A. I., 723
Bryant, Louise, 1262
Bryant, Willa C., 887, 972
Buchwald, Art, Adden. (Wormser)
Buck, Pearl S., 2434

Buck, Ross W., 13
Buckley, John E., 3198
Buckley, J. M., 1842
Buckley, Louis F., 3062
Buckmaster, Henrietta, 2090
Budig, Gene A., Adden. (Lieberman)
Buek, Alexandra, Adden.
Buffington, H. Glenn, 3405-3407
Buhle, Mari Jo, 1571, 1956
Bullard, Edgar J., 2709
Bullard, Laura C., 3568
Bullard, Washington I., 3063
BULLETIN OF THE AMERICAN ACAD-
    EMY OF MEDICINE, 3256
Bullock, Charles S., 1470
Bullock, Edna D., 3064
Bullough, Bonnie, 2309
Bullough, Vern L., 283, 1843, 2309
Bunce, Oliver B., 2048
Bunch-Weeks, Charlotte, 1844, 1849, 1985
Bunkle, P., Adden.
Bureau International du Travail, 3439
Burkhardt, James, 1490
Burkill, T. A., 2191
Burlingame-Cheney, Emeline, 1377
Burness, H., 2961
Burnett, Constance B., 1378
Burnham, Margaret, 1960
Burr, Andrew, 225
Burr, George Lincoln, 1741
Burress, Carol, Adden. (Jacobson)
Burton, Gabrielle, 284
Burton, Hester, 1241
Burton, John, 585
Burton, Margaret E., 2435, 3065
Bushnell, Horace, 1408
Business and Professional Women's Associa-
    tion, 285, 586, 724, 3274, 3519
Business and Professional Women's Founda-
    tion, 3440-3443
Business and Professional Women's Founda-
    tion Library, 3585
Butler, A. S. G., 955
Butler, Elizabeth B., 3319
Butler, Josephine E. G., 286, 955-956, 2412,
    2482
Butler, Pierce, 1685 [Intro.]
Buttles, Janet R., 2134
Buytendijk, F. J. J., 1845, 2192
Bysiewicz, Shirley R., Adden. (Jacobson)

C

Cade, Toni, 2091
Cain, Glen G., 3240, Adden. (Wormser)
Cain, Lynn, Adden.
CALCUTTA REVIEW, 273
Calderón, Mirta Rodríquez, 1284
Calderone, Mary S., 14, 369, 778
Calderwood, Ann, 753
Calhoun, Arthur, 143

Calisher, Hortense, 2436
Calkins, Grace Gilkey, 2193
Callahan, Sidney Cornelia, 287, 2194, 3241
Callwood, June, 1209
Calverton, Victor F., 226, 399, 886
Calzini, Raffaele, 2710
Camargo, Dr. Alberto Lleras, 3199
Camden, Carroll, 1686, 2711
Campbell, Amelia D., 2049
Campbell, Angus, 1295 [Intro.]
Campbell, Arthur A., 779
Campbell, Helen Stuart, 3320-3321
Campbell, J. G., 1742
Campbell, Joseph, 2962, 3050
Campbell, M. Edith, 3054
Campion, Rosamond, 2310
Campo de Alange, Maria de los Reyes
    Lafitte de Salamanca, Condesa del, 1556
Canada, Royal Commission on Status of
    Women in Canada, 1078
Canada, Department of Labour, 144-145,
    3200
Canada, Women's Bureau, 3066
Canadian Federation of University Women,
    726
Cannon, James, 1464
Cannon, Mary Agnes, 587, 1687
Caplow, T., 725
Caraway, Hattie, 1518
Carden, Maren Lockwood, Adden.
Carleton, R. O., 780
Carlier, Auguste, 1119
Carlson, Dale, Adden.
Carlson, Rae, 2841
Carlyle, Thomas, 1786
Carnegie Commission on Higher Education,
    Adden. (Lester)
Carpenter, Adella P., 2437
Carpenter, Edward, 400
Carr, Lucien, 2092
Carroll, Charles, 781
Carroll, Mitchell, 1554, 1688 [Intro.]
Carson, Josephine, 288
Carter, Charlene A., 2311
Cartwright, Julia, 2135
Casey, Elizabeth, 2438
Caspari, E. W., 401
Cassara, Beverly B., 15, 482, 1296
Cassell, Kay Ann, 1154
Castellani, Maria, 1957 [Intro.]
Castelnuovo-Tedesco, Pietro, 799
Castelot, Andre, 2136-2137
Castro, Fidel, 1252
CATALYST, 3520
Catlin, George, 1718
Catt, Carrie Chapman, 935, 1316, 1334-
    1335, 1378, 1401, 1425, 2599
Cavan, S., 483
Cavanah, Frances, 2439
Cavert, Inez, 2195
Ceballa Lopez, Fermin, 2196
Center for a Woman's Own Name, 1120

Center for Continuing Education of Women, 588
Center for the American Woman and Politics, Eagleton Inst. of Politics, 3521
Central Advisory Council for the Ministry of the Church Assembly, 2197
Central Statistical Board of the USSR, Council of Ministers, 146
Ceston, J. M., 2963
Chabaud, Jacqueline, 589
Chafe, William J., 878 [Intro.]
Chafetz, Janet S., 16
Chamberlin, Hope, 1471 [Intro.]
Chambers, Carl, 2312
Chambers, R., 3505
Chambers, W., 3505
Chandler, Christopher, Adden. (Kane)
Chandrasekhar, Sripati, 484, 782, 809
Chaney, Elsa, 1259, 1448, Adden.
Chao, Bu-wei Yang, 2440
Chapman, Charles E., 2002
Char, Walter F., 783
Charles, E., 2871
Charters, Jean, 1518
Chase, Ilka, 2441
Chase, Judy, 1213
Chassequet-Smirgel, Janine, 2842
Chasteen, Edgar R., 784
Chatham Bookseller, 3444
Chaton, Jeanne H., 337
Cheney, Ednah D., 2442
Cheron, G., 2964
Chesler, Phyllis, 18, 2843
Chesney, Kellow, 19
Chesnut, Mary B., 2443
Chesser, Eustace, 227, 402-405
Chester, Eliza, [Paine, Harriet E.], 590
Chester, Giraud, 895
Chew, Peter T., 289
Chicago Women's Liberation Union, 3522
Chick, N., Adden. (Bunkle)
Chideckel, Maurice, 406
Child, Frank S., 1743
Child, H. F., 2965
Child, Irvin L., 7
Child, Lydia Maria, 591, 1628 [Intro.], 2410, 2574
Chisholm, Shirley, 1088, 1155, 1472-1473, 1490, 1958, 2093, 2467
Chmaj, Betty E., 3445
Chombart de Lauwe, Paul-Henry, 147-148, 1557
Chomel, Marie Cecile, 1297
Chopin, Kate, 1846, 2628, 2738
Chou, Eric, 407
Christensen, Ethlyn, 3300
Christenson, C., 804
Chumacero, Rosalia d', 1629
Chun, Jinsie, Adden.
Chun, Victor K., 2050
Chung, Hau-min, 2444
Chung, Wen-hui, 2094

Church, Archibald, 2313
Church, Sen. Frank, 389
Church of England, Commission Appointed by the Archbishop of Canterbury and York, 2198
Chylinska, Kamila, 337
Cisler, Lucinda, 3446
Citizen's Advisory Council on the Status of Women, 485, 554-555, 1079, 1103, 1190, 3523, Adden.
Claflin, Tennessee C., 927, 973, 2617
Claflin, Victoria. See Victoria Woodhull
Clapp, Thomas, 2003
Clark, Alice, 1689, 3067
Clark, F. I., 1847
Clark, F. Le Gros, 3201-3202
Clark, Ida Clyde, 1263
Clark, Isabel Constance, Adden.
Clark, Patricia, 3203
Clark, Septima Poinsette, 2445
Clark, Shirley, 678, 756
Clark, W. T., 3568
Clarke, Amy K., 592
Clarke, Charles Walter, 956
Clarke, Mary Cowden, 2446, 2739
Clarkson, Adrienne, 1438
Claviere, R. de Maulde la, 1690
Clawson, Augusta, 290
Cleaver, Eldridge, 20, 2095
Clement, Jesse, 2004
Clephane, E., 408
Cles-Reden, Sibylle von, 2966
Cleveland Chamber of Commerce, 3275
Cleverdon, Catherine L., 1336
Clignet, Remi, 486
Clinton, Richard L., Adden. (Chaney)
Clough, Blanche Athena, 1242
Cobbe, Frances P., 593
Cobbledick, M. Robert, 1630
Cobbs, Price M., 2862
Cochrane, Jeanie Douglas, 2447
Cockburn, P., 726
Cody, John, 2712
Coffin, Patricia, 2844
Cohen, Audrey C., 3204
Cohen, Larry R., 2836
Cohen, Lucy M., 1259
Cohen, M. B., 2845
Cohen, Malcolm S., 3205
Cohen, Wilbur J., 3068
Colby, Vineta, 2713, Adden.
Cole, Arthur C., 594
Cole, Doris, Adden.
Cole, Hubert, 2138
Cole, Johnneta B., 3447
Cole, Margaret, 1328, 1474, 2448, 2673
Cole, William, 2714
Coleman, Emily R., 228
Collard, J., 2967
College of St. Catherine Library, 3586
Collins, John K., 2864
Collins, M., 727

Collins, Randall, 2846
Collis, Maurice, 2139
Colloque de Coppet, 2449
Collyer, A. O., 785
Colorado Woman's College, 3587
Colton, Olive A., 1298
Cometti, Elizabeth, 2051
Comhaire, J., 2968
Commander, Lydia Kingsmill, 786
Commissions on the Status of Women. See
    Place, Subject, Topic index.
Committee of Safety of 1908, 1370
Committee on Psychiatry and Law, Group
    for the Advancement of Psychiatry, 787
Committee to Organize the Advancement of
    Women, 1880-1881
Communist Party of Canada, 879
Communist Party, U.S.A., 1317
Conant, Margaret M., 21
Confino, Michael, Adden.
Conley, Frances, 389
Conrad, Earl, 1243
Conrader, Constance, 974
Constanco-Marie, Sister, 2970
Constantini, Edmond, 1475 [Intro.]
Converse, Florence, 595
Conway, Jill, 297, 1848
Cook, Alice H., 337, 3276 [Intro.]
Cook, Barbara, Adden.
Cook, D. E., 1810
Cook, Edward, 2450
Cook, Marlow W., Adden. (Jacobson)
Cooke, Joanne, 1849
Cooke, Rose Terry, 2592
Coolidge, Mary Roberts, 22, 1558
Coolidge, Olivia E., 1337, 1850
Cooper, Anna J. H., 487
Cooper, Clarissa Burnham, 2715
Cooper, Elizabeth, 291, 488
Cooper, James, 1851
Cooper, Jean, 23
Cooper, Sheila McIsaac, 1851
Cooperman, Irene G., 292
Cope, Zachary, 2314
Coppen, A., 2315, 2847, 2866
Corbin, John, 975
Corcos, Fernand, 2052
Cornell, Katharine, 2451
Cornell Law Review, 1193 [Intro.]
Cornet, R. P., 2971
Cornillon, Susan Koppelman, 2716
Costello, Louisa Stuart, 2452
Cott, Nancy F., 1852
Cotton, Dorothy Whyte, 3243
Couch, Elsbeth H., 229
Coughlin, Richard J., 489, 1959
Coulibaly, O., 2972
Coulter, Ellis M., 2053
Council for Exceptional Children, 596
Courtney, Janet E., 2453
Cowan, John, 2316
Cox, Harvey, 2200

Coxhead, E., 3366
Coyle, Grace L., 3244
Crafton, Allen, Adden.
Craik, Kenneth H., 1475 [Intro.]
Crankshaw, Edward, 2140
Crannell, Mrs. W. Winslow, 1409
Crawford, Marion, 2141
Crawford, Mary Caroline, 597
Crawley, Lawrence, 2317
Crockford, Richard E., 598
Croly, Jane, 3524
Cromwell, Otelia, 1379, 2454
Cronin, Joseph M., Adden. (Lieberman)
Crook, Margaret, 2201
Crooke, W., 1744
Crossland, Margaret, Adden.
Crouch-Hazlett, Ida, 3525
Crow, Duncan, 293
Crowe, Linda D., 121
Crowley, Joan E., 3322
Crozier, Alice, 2717
Crummell, Alexander, 2096
Cuber, John, 409
Cudden, J. A., 294
Cudderford, G., 1559
Cudlipp, Edythe, 976
Culver, Elsie Thomas, 2202
Culwick, A. T., 2973
Culwick, G. M., 2973
Cummings, Gwenna, 295
Cunliffe, John William, Adden.
Cunneen, Sally, 2203
Cunnington, C. W., 296, 1788-1789
Curie, Eve, 2455
Current Index to Journals in Education,
    Adden.
Curry, Douglas L., 1121
Cusack, Dymphna, 1853
Cussler, Margaret, 3367
Cutler, Amelia MacDonald, 1318
Cutler, John Henry, 490, 1631
Cyfer-Diderich, G., 2974

D

da Costa, Maria Velho, Adden.
DAEDALUS, 297
Daglish, R., 184
Dahlstrom, Edmund, 24
Dale, Marian K., 1691
Dall, Caroline W., 599, 1214
Dalla Costa, Mariarosa, 298
Dalton, Katharina, 2318, 2334
Daly, Mary, 2204-2206
Damon, Gene, 3448
Dancer-Fitzgerald-Sample, Inc., 564
Dandre, Victor E., 2456
Dangerfield, George, 1338
Daniel, E., 2207
Daniel, Sadie Iola, 2457
Danielou, Jean, 2208

Daniels, Arlene K., 345
Daniels, Jonathan, 2458
Dank, Barry M., 410
Dannett, Sylvia G. L., 2459, Adden.
Darcie, Abraham, 1560
Dardenne, E., 3069
Darmstadter, Ruth, 1490
Darrach, H., 2054
Dartevelle, A., 2975
Darton, John M., 2460
D'Arusmont, Frances Wright. See Wright, Frances.
Das, Sonya Ruth, 230
Datta, Kali Kinkar, 491
Davey, R. P. B., 299-300
David, Henry P., 788
David, Lester, Adden.
David, O., 492
David, Pauline G., 1156
Davids, Leo, 231
Davidson, Kenneth M., 1157
Davies, Emily, 600
Davies, H. O., 1339
Davis, Allen F., Adden.
Davis, Almond H., 2461
Davis, Angela Yvonne, 25, 977, 1960, Adden.
Davis, Ann E., 728
Davis, Elizabeth Gould, 1561 [Intro.]
Davis, Ethelyn, 3323
Davis, Hazel, 548
Davis, Katherine Bement, 411
Davis, Kenneth, 1439
Davis, Kingsley, 301
Davis, Paulina Wright, 978, 1854
Dawson, B. E., 2319
Dawson, Minnie Elder, 2319
Dawson, Sarah, 2462
Day, Dorothy, 1264
Deachim, Jacob, 2463
Deardorff, Meva R., 3054
de Beaumont, E., 2055
de Beauvoir, Simone, 26 [Intro.], 1555, 2464-2465, 2718, Adden.
de Castillejo, Irene Claremont, Adden.
Decapmaker, 2976
De Carturla Bru, Victoria, 979
Decker, Richard, Adden. (Lieberman)
DeCrow, Karen, 1265, Adden.
Decter, Midge, 27, 302, 329, 980
Deech, Ruth L., 1122
Deen, Edith, 2209
DeForest, John W., 1745
Degen, Marie Louise, 935
Degler, Carl N., 297 [Intro.], 1855
De Graffenried, Clare, 3070
Dehareng, Marcelle, 3277
de Koven, Anna, 1562 [Intro.]
DeLamater, John, 612, 3369
Delayen, Baston, 2142
Delgado Garcia, Ramiro, 789
Dell, Floyd, 880, 1856

Dellatol, Lesley, 3071
DeLora, Jack, 232
DeLora, Joann, 232
DeMan, M., 2977
de Mille, Agnes, Adden.
Dempsey, John J., 617
Dempsey, Mary V., 3072
de Negri, E., 1790
Denmark, Florence, Adden.
Denver Law Review, 1187 [Intro.]
Depatie, Francine, 1440
Derand, Marcelle S., 337
deRham, Edith, 303, 493
deRiencourt, Amaury, Adden.
Der Ling, Princess, 2466
Derr, Allen R., Adden. (Jacobson)
de Serviez, T. R. Nicholas, 2143
Detlefsen, Gay, 3486
deTocqueville, Alexis, 1441
Deutsch, Helene, 2848, Adden.
Deutsch, Ronald M., 412
de Valois, Ninette, Adden. (Money)
Devaux, Andre A., 2210
Devereaux, George, 2978
Devine, Edward T., 3073
De Vries, Margaret G., 3206
Dewar, Margaret, 3074
Dewey, Lucretia M., Intro. p. 15
Dexter, Elizabeth A., 1563, 2005
D'Héricourt, Madame, 2211
Diamonstein, Barbaralee, 2467
Diaz, Elena, 2119
Dibatista, Beverly, 234
Dickinson, Louisa, 601
Diener, Bertha (Eckstein-Diener, B. and Diner, Helen), 1564 [Intro.], 2144
Dienes, C. Thomas, 790
Dietrich, Albrecht, 2979
Dillon, Mary Earhart, 941
Dilts, Thomas H., 1158
Diner, Helen. See Diener, Bertha.
Dingwall, Eric John, 1565
Dirks, Sabine, 149
Ditzion, Sidney, 413
Dixon, Marlene, 981, 1266, 1857, 1900
Dixon, Ruth B., 233, 791, Adden. (Hochschild)
Djamour, J., 1123
D.-Johnson, Micheline, 1080
Dobson, B., 2980
Dock, Lavina L., 2365
Dodge, Mrs. Arthur M., 3054
Dodge, Bayer, 391
Dodge, Mary Abigail. See Hamilton, Gail.
Dodge, Norton T., 3075 [Intro.], Adden. (Tsuchigave)
Dodziuk-Kitynska, Ann, 150
Doely, Sara Bentley, 2212
Dohrn, Bernardine, Adden. (Baritz)
Dolan, Eleanor F., 602
Dollard, John, 494
Donahue, Mary P., 3076

Donaldson, James, 1692
Donnelly, Antoinette, 3555
Donner, E., 2981
Donovan, Frank R., 1566
Doo-hun Kim, 151
Dooley, W. H., 1791
Dorr, Rheta Louisechilde, 1380, 1858-1859, 2468
Dornberg, John, 982
Dorsen, Norman, 1862
Dorys, Georges, 304
Doucy, A., 2982
Douglas, Emily Taft, 2469
Douglas, R. L., 2983
Douglas, William, 2213
Doukhan-Landau, Leah, 1145
Doumic, René, Adden.
Dourlen-Rollier, Anne-Marie, 792
Douvan, Elizabeth, 2833, 2849
Dow, Blanche Hinman, 2719
Dowty, Nancy, 305
Doyle, Helen MacKnight, 1381
Drake, Barbara, 2673, 3278
Drake, Kirsten, 3449
Drake, Samuel G., 1746
Drake, St. Clair, 28
Dreier, Mary, 1860
Dreifus, Claudia, 1476, 2470, Adden.
Dreiser, Theodore, 2720
Dreitzel, Hans Peter, Adden.
Drezner, N., 419
Driberg, J. H., 2984
Drinker, Sophie Lewis (Hutchinson), 2006-2007, 2019, 2721, 3475
Drinnon, Richard, 1267
Driver, Beverly, 2722
Drumm, Stella M., 2020
Dubois, J. A., 1719
DuBois, W. E. B., 1632
Dubow, Rhona, 3450
Dubrovina, L., 603
Duchan, Linda, 3376
Duffus, R. L., 898
Dumas, Francine, 2214
Dumond, Dwight L., 2407
Dunbar, J., 306
Duncan, Isadora, 2471, 2617, Adden. (Steegmuller)
Dunham, Katherine, 2472
Duniway, Abigail Scott, 1382, 2030, 2473
Dunn, Erica, 1442, 1985
Dunnigan, Alice E., 2723
Duparcq, de la Barre, 2056
Dupeyrat, A., 2985
Dupont, Julie A., 3451
Duster, Alfreda M., 2474
Dutilleux, G., 2986-2987
Duverger, Maurice, 1443 [Intro.]
Dweck, Susan, 3435
Dyer, T. F. Thistleton, 1720

E

Earhart, Amelia, 2475, 2485
Earle, Alice, 2008
Earnest, Marion R., 2850
Earthy, E., 2988
Eastwood, Alice L., 2239
Eastwood, Mary O., 610, 1185, 1204, 3207
Eaton, Charles H., 3324
Eban, Abba, 2510
Eberhard, Wolfram, 2215, 2989
Ebbott, John F., 1146
Eckenstein, Lina, 307, 2216-2217
Eckert, Ruth E., 729
Eckstein-Diener, Bertha. See Diener, Bertha.
Eddy, Mary Baker, 2218, 2255, 2411, 2600
Edelman, Judy, 3078
Edes, Robert T., 2320
Edge, Clara A., 2476
Edme, P., 2990
Edmiston, Susan, 1124
Edmonds, Vernon H., 234
Edwards, Lee R., 2724
Effiger, John R., 1721 [Intro.]
Egle, William H., 2057
Ehrhardt, Anke A., 2900
Eicher, Joanne Bubolz, 1817
Eidlitz, Elizabeth M., 440
El-Badry, M. A., 793
Elder, Glen H., 29
Eley, G., 308
Eliot, George (Mary Ann Evan), 2507, 2638, 2698, 2725, 2729, 2742, 2757, 2773, 2776
Elkan, W., 3079
Ellet, Elizabeth F. Lummis, 1961, 2009, 2058
Ellington, George, 309, 1633
Elliot, Linda Anne, Adden.
Elliott, Grace Loucks, 1634, 2321
Elliott, Maud Howe, 2611
Ellis, Albert, 369, 414-415, 1792
Ellis, Anne, 2477-2478
Ellis, Evelyn, 310
Ellis, Havelock, 416, 849, 2851
Ellis, S., 2346
Ellison, R. E., 2991
Ellman, Edgar S., 3208
Ellmann, Mary, 30
Elson, Arthur, 2726
Elvin, Verrier, 2992
Emerson, John Philip, 3209
Emerson, Thomas I., 1153, 1862
Empey, Lamar T., 31
Engelmann, George T., 2322-2323
Engels, Friedrich, 152, 1926, 1976
Engle, Bernice Schultz, 2059
Ennis, E. L., 2993
Entwisle, Doris, 2852
Epstein, Cynthia F., 32-33 [Intro.], 1861, 3080

Epstein, Joseph, Adden.
Epstein, Sandra, 579
ERIC, Educational Resources Information
  Center, 684, 749, 757, 762-764, 3452
Erikson, Erik H., 297
Erikson, Joan M., 297
Ermath, Margaret S., 2219
Erskine, Hazel G., 34, 1521
Esselstyn, T. C., 369
Esterson, A., 2885
Etzioni, Amitai, 794, 3408
Evan, Mary Ann. See Eliot, George.
Evans, Frederick, 2220
Evans, J. D., 606
Evans, Wainwright, 250, 1329
Evans-Pritchard, E. E., 2994
Euripides, 2727
Ewart, Andrew, 2145
Ewen, Cecil Henry L'Estrange, 1747
Eyde, Lorraine Dittrich, 3081

F

Faber, Doris, 1340, 2479
Factor, Morris, 2853
Fairchild, J. E., 311
Fairchild, Mildred F., 175
Falk, Gail, 1153
Falk, Ruth, 1215
Fanon, Frantz, 495, 2097
Farber, Seymour M., 35, 36
Farello, Elene Wilson, 607
Farence, Patricia S., 608
Farians, Elizabeth, 3453
Farley, Jennie, 609, 3368
Farley, Luke A., 2221
Farmer, Leslie, 1545
Farmer, Lydia, 1863
Farnam, Anne, 1864
Farnham, Eliza Woodson, 1070, 2010, 2687
Farnham, Marynia, 439 [Intro.]
Farrand, Livingston, 2995
Farrell, Warren, 1448
Faulhaber, Michael Cardinal, 2222
Fauset, Arthur, 2480
Fava, S., 730
Fawcett, Millicent Garrett, 1341-1342,
  1400, 2481-2482, 2648
Federally Employed Women (FEW), 3526
Feeler, Felix (Rev. L. E. Keith), 1419
Feeley, Diane, 1985
Feld, Rose C., 3373
Feld, Sheila, Adden. (Veroff)
Feldman, Saul D., Adden.
Fell, Margaret, 2223
Felton, Gerald, 795
FEMINIST STUDIES, 610
Feminists on Children's Media, 37, 611
Fenberg, M., 496
Ferber, Edna, 2483
Ferber, Marianne, 741

Ferdinand, Theodore N., 369, 417
Ferguson, Mary Ann, Adden.
Ferm, Deane William, 418
Fernandez-Azabal, Lilie de (Countess), 2484
Fernando, Lloyd, 2729
Ferrara, Guglielmo, 2146
Ferriss, Abbott L., Adden.
Ferrers, Richard, 1635
Ferris, Helen, 2485
Ferris, P., 796
Feshbach, Murray, 3187
Festini, Nelly, 337, 1444
Fetscher, Iring, 177
Ficarra, Bernard J., 797
Fidell, Linda S., 612, 3369
Fiedler, Leslie, 2730
Field, Mark G., 2324
Fields, Annie, 2486
Fields, Cheryl M., 3212
Fields, Daisy B., Adden. (Wormser)
Fifield, Emily, 2224
Figes, Eva, 1567 [Intro.]
Figner, Vera, 1962
Filler, W., 419
Finck, Henry T., 1722
Findley, Palmer, 2325
Firestone, Shulamith, 38, 1002 [Intro.],
  1268, 1865
Fischer, Ann, 731
Fisher, Dorothy Canfield, 2731
Fisher, Marguerite J., 1299
Fisher, S., 420
Fishman, Nathaniel, 1159
Fiske, John, 2011, 3513
Fitzgerald, C. P., 2147
Fitzsimmons, John, 2225
Fixter, Deborah A., 3498
Flaubert, Gustave, 2725, 2732, 2764, 2779
Fleck, Stephen, 2854
Fletcher, Peter, 124, 466
Fletcher, R., 153
Flexner, Eleanor, 983, 1445 [Intro.], 1866
Flickinger, Harry, Adden. (Wormser)
Flora, Cornelia B., 1448
Florence, Lella Secor, 798
Flower, B. O., 1793
Flugel, J. C., 1794
Flynn, Elizabeth Gurley, 1269, 1522, 1617,
  2487, 3325
Flynn, John T., Adden.
Fogarty, Michael P., 154, 3245
Folsom, Joseph F., 1748
Folsom, Joseph K., 39, 155
Foner, Philip Sheldon, 3279
Fonteyn, Margot, Adden. (Money)
Foote, Cone and Belding Marketing Informa-
  tion Service, 545
Foote, Frieda L. See Gehlen, Frieda L.
Ford, Charles V., 799
Ford, Clellan S., 421
Forten, Charlotte, 2417, 2488
Fortes, M., 2996

Fosbrooke, J., 3082
Foster, Jeannette H., 2733
Foster, Warren Dunham, 2226, 2384
Fox, Ann, 156
Fox, Claire, 2333
Fox, Genevieve M., 3083
Fowler, William W., 2012
Francis, Ann, 1095
Francis, Philip, 1160
Francoeur, Robert, 422
Frank, K., 2855
Frank, R. T., 2326
Franken, Van Driel P., 312
Frankfort, Ellen, 2327
Franklin, Barbara, Adden. (Wormser)
Franklin, Margaret Ladd, 3454
Fraser, Lady Antonia, 2148
Fraser, Leila, 732
Frazer, Sir James G., 1749-1750
Frazier, E. Franklin, 157
Frazier, Thomas R., 981, 1278, 1867
Frederick, Pauline, 2489
Fredriksson, Ingrid, 40
Freedman, Ann E., 1153
Freeman, Jo, 339, 613, 1204, 1448, 1868,
    Adden. (Hochschild)
Freeman, M. D. A., 1125
French, Doris, 2490
French, E. G., 2856
Freud, Sigmund, 41, 423-424, 444, 1268,
    1567, 2190, 2857-2859, 2902, 2910,
    2997, Adden. (Mitchell)
Freud, Paul, 1862
Friderich, Nicole M., 337
Friedan, Betty, 41 [Intro.], 614, 1088
Friedman, Alfred S., 2328
Friedman, Bruno, 3084
Friedman, Jean E., Adden.
Friedman, Joel W., 3213
Frithoff, Patricia, 3455
Fritscher, John, 1751
Frölich, Paul, 1270
Froman, Lewis A., 881
Frost, David, 497
Frumkin, S., 1523
Fryer, Peter, 272, 800
Fuchs, Cynthia. See Epstein, Cynthia Fuchs.
Fuchs, Lawrence H., 2098
Fuentes, Sonia. See Pressman, Sonia.
Fujie, Yamaoto, 1613
Fujita, Taki, 337
Fukichi, Shigetaka, 1869
Fulford, Robert, 990, 1343
Fuller, Ann L., 733
Fuller, Margaret (Ossoli, Margaret Fuller),
    885, 1568, 1851, 2517, 2523, 2592,
    2643, 2814
Furness, Clifton J., 1723
Furth, Peter, 527
Furstenberg, Frank F., 801
Furstenberg, George M. von, Adden.
Furuya, Tsunetake, 1569

Fussell, G. E., 498
Fussell, K. R., 498
Fyfe, Henry H., 802

G

Gage, Jean, 1693
Gage, Matilda Joslyn, 1366 [Intro.], 1570
Gager, Nancy, Adden.
Gagnon, John H., 369, 425
Gaines, Ernest J., 2491
Galbraith, John Kenneth, Intro. p. 14
Gale, Zona, 900
Galenson, Marjorie, Adden.
Galkin, K., 615
Gallaher, Ruth A., 1081
Gallup, George, 313
Galway, Katherine, 678, 756
Gamble, Eliza Burt, 1870
Gamio, Manuel, 2099
Gannon, Martin J., 342
Garai, Josef E., 2916, 3456
Gard, Robert E., Adden. (Crafton)
Gardner, A. K., 2329-2330
Gardiner, Lady, 984
Gardner, Jo-Ann Evans, 734
Garma, A., 1795
Garner, Barbara, 2335
Garnett, Lucy, 1752
Garnier, C., 2998
Garza, Joseph M., 3246
Gasiorowska, Xenia, 2734
Gates, Nancy, 1490
Gathorne-Hardy, Johnathon, Adden.
Gattey, Charles Neilson, 899
Gaudio, Attilio, 985
Gavron, Hannah, 314
Gawthorpe, A., 315
Geairain, Jeanine, 803
Gebhard, P. H., 804
Geertz, Hildred, 158
Gehlen, Frieda L. (Foote), 1477-1478
Geiger, H. Kent, 159
Geigy, R., 2999
Gelber, Sylva M., 3066
Geller, Gyula Gatson, 2492
Gelles, Richard J., Adden.
Gendel, Evelyn S., 2331
Gendell, Murray, 805
General Federation of Women's Clubs, 3085
Georgeakis, G., 1753
George Washington Law Review, 1185
    [Intro.]
George Washington University, 3457
Gerber, Ellen W., 42
Gerda, Sister, 3000
Germany (Federal Republic), 3458
Gerould, Katherine Fullerton, 1300
Gerritson Collection, 3588
Gersch, Harry, 2013
Gerson, Menachem, 316

Gerstein, Hannelore, 616
Gessain, Robert, 3001
Giallombardo, Rose, Adden.
Gibson, Althea, 2493
Gibson, Colin, 160
Gibson, Elsie, 2227
Giele, Janet, 1871
Gigliotti, Cairoli, 1426
Gilchrist, B. B., 1872
Gilder, George F., Adden.
Gildersleeve, Virginia, 2494
Gilevskaya, S., 1025
Gilfond, Duff, 1479
Gilles de Pelichy, Dom, 3002
Gillespie, Dair L., 1900
Gilman, Charlotte Perkins, 43, 161, 900,
    1851, 1855-1856, 3086
Ginsburg, Mirra, 2495
Ginzberg, Eli, 317-318, 3087
Ginzburg, Ruth Bader, 1157, 1204, Adden.
Gittelson, Natalie, 426
Glasgow, Ellen, 2496, 2695, 2735, 2753,
    2793
Glass, A. D. M., Adden. (Bunkle)
Glass, D. V., 806
Glass, George S., 2860
Glass, M., Adden. (Bunkle)
Glasse, R. M., 235
Glen, Norval D., 236
Glincher, Arnold B., 2736
Gluckman, M., 3003
Godfrey, David, 990
Goldberg, Dorothy, 319
Goldberg, Marilyn Powers, Intro. p. 14
Goldberg, Minnie, 2332
Goldberg, Philip, 499, 2861
Golde, Peggy, 731
Goldfarb, Anne, 3214
Goldfarb, Russell M., 2737
Goldfield, Evelyn, 1908
Golding, Elizabeth B., 1536
Goldman, Emma, 901-902, 916, 1041, 1267,
    1271, 1617, 1856, 2497, Adden. (Baritz)
Goldman, George D., 2899
Goldman, Nancy, 320
Goldmark, Josephine, 903, 2498, 3054
Goldschmidt, Walter, 90
Goldstein, Mark L., 1217
Gollack, G. A., 2499
Gollancz, Victor, 1039
Goncourt, Edmond de, 500, 1636
Goncourt, Jules de, 500, 1636
Gonzaga, F. P., 2374
Good, Josephine L., 1301
Goodale, Jane C., 3004
Goode, William J., 33 [Intro.], 162-163,
    237, 1861
Goodhart, C. B., 1796
Goodland, R., 3459
Goodsell, Willystine, 2500
Goodwin, Grace Duffield, 1410
Gordon, Ann D., 1571

Gordon, Anna A., 2501
Gordon, David C., 321, 986, 1963 [Intro.]
Gordon, Eugene, 3215
Gordon, Linda, 1985
Gordon, Margaret S., 3326
Gordon, M. E., Adden. (Bunkle)
Gordon, Michael, 427
Gorecki, Jan, 1126
Gormly, John, 2877
Gorney, R., 2340-2341
Gorney, Sondra, 2333
Gornick, Vivian, 501 [Intro.]
Gosnell, Harold F., 1310
Gossmann, Elisabeth, 164
Göteborg University Library, 3460
Gotta, J. M., 821
Gough, Kathleen, 165
Gould, Karolyn, 3216
Goulianos, Joan, 2738
Gove, Walter, 44
Goy, R. W., 2937
Grady, Elaine, 617
Graebner, Alan, 2228
Graham, Abbie, 1383, 2502
Graham, Frank, 1480
Graham, Patricia A., 3370
Gray, Virginia, Adden.
Green, Edith, 1161, 1182, 1476, 1490,
    1493, 3235 [Intro.]
Green, Harry Clinton, 2014
Green, Mary Wolcott, 2014
Green, R., 2334
Greenbaum, Marcia L., 3327
Greenberg, Sarah K., 2367
Greenberger, Ellen, 2852
Greenbie, Marjorie B., 2503
Greene, Felix, 1127
Greene, Gael, 987
Greenfield, Lois B., 618
Greenstein, Fred, 882 [Intro.]
Greenwald, Harold, 322
Greenwood Press (Westport, Conn.), 3559
Greer, Germaine, 45, 2791
Greeting, Corinne, 988
Gregorovius, Ferdinand, 2149
Gregory, P. M., 1797
Grey, Mrs. William, 619
Gribble, Francis G., 2060
Gridley, Marion Eleanor, Adden.
Grier, William II, 2862
Griffiths, Martha, 1228, 1484, 1490, Adden.
    (Jacobson)
Grimes, Alan Pendleton, 889, 1427
Grimké, Angelina, 893, 931, 1617, 1851,
    2407, 2554
Grimké, Sarah M., 893, 931, 989, 1617,
    1851, 2407, 2554
Grimstad, Kirsten, Adden.
Grinnell, George N., 1724
Grobstein, R., 2834
Grody, M. H., 2358
Gross, Edward, 3088

Gross, George C., 2739
Gross, Irma H., 323
Grossholtz, Jean, Intro. p. 23
Grossman, Joel B., 1162
Groves, Ernest R., 46
Gruberg, Martin, 1481 [Intro.]
Gruchow, Nancy, 735
Grunfeld, Judith, 1218
Guazon-Mendoza, Maria Paz, 1344
Guedalla, Philip, 2150, 2504
Guelaud-Leridon, Francoise, 324
Guelfi, L., 3089
Guilbert, Madeleine, 3328
Gulik, Robert van, 428
Gulliver, Lucile, 2740
Gutmann, David L., 2833
Guttnacher, Alan, 194
Gwyn, Sandra, 990, 2741

H

Haavis, Mannila E., 325
Hacker, Helen M., 502
Hackett, Amy, 991
Haener, Dorothy, Adden. (Jacobson)
Hagood, Margaret J., 326
Hahn, Elizabeth, 2229, Adden.
Hahn, Emily, 2505
Haig, Kenneth M., 2506
Haight, Elizabeth H., 683
Haight, Gordon, 2507
Haldane, Charlotte, 166
Hale, Beatrice Forbes-Robertson, 620, 1874
Hale, Sarah Josepha, 1070, 1572 [Intro.],
  1725, 1875, 2687, 3506
Halifax, Lord, 1726
Hall, C., 1798
Hall, Florence Howe, 2508
Hall, Fred S., 1031
Hall, Granville S., 327
Hall, Guin, Adden. (Lieberman)
Hallam, Charlotte B., Adden. (Lieberman)
Halle, Fannina W., 503
Hamamsy, Laila Shukry, 3005
Hamid, M. A., 328
Hamilton, Alice, 934, Adden.
Hamilton, Cicely M., 1727
Hamilton, Gail (Mary Abigail Dodge), 888,
  1411
Hamilton, Jack D., Adden. (Springer)
Hammond, George P., 2015
Hanaford, Phoebe A. C., 2016, 2509
Haney, Jack, 621
Hanford, J. M., 2863
Hani, Setsuko, 167
Hannon, Vincent Emmanuel, 2230
Hanoi: Vietnam Women's Union, 1986
Hansberry, Lorraine, 1876, 2511
Hansbrough, Henry Clay, 2061
Hansen, Henny Harald, 1637-1638
Hansen, Lynn K., 2335
Harbeson, Gladys E., 47

Hardesty, Frances, 52
Hardie, Keir, 1163
Hardin, Garrett, 807-808
Harding, M. Esther, 48, 1754
Hardy, Barbara, 2742
Hare, Christopher, Adden.
Hare, Julia, 1639
Hare, Lloyd C. M., 1384
Hare, Nathan, 1639
Hareven, Tamara, 1446
Harkness, Georgia E., 2231
Harmon, Linda A., 3461
Harnick, E. J., 1799
Haroff, Peggy, 409
Harper, Dee W., 3462
Harper, Ida Husted, 1345, 1366 [Intro.], 2512
Harper, Juliet F., 2864
HARPER'S MAGAZINE, 329
Harriman, Florence, 1510
Harris, Ann Sutherland, 736-737
Harris, J. S., 49
Harris, Louis and Associates, 522-523
Harris, Sara, 330
Harris, Seymour, Adden.
Harrison, Evelyn, 3217
Harrison, G. B., 1785
Harry, M., 331
Harth, Erica, 610
Hartley, C. Gasquoine, 50, 3006
Hartley, Ralph Waldo, 942
Hartley, Ruth, 51-52
Hartmann, Heinz, Intro. p. 17
Harvard Civil Rights and Liberties Law Review,
  1862 [Intro.]
Harveston, Mae Elizabeth, 2513
Haskell, Molly, Adden.
Haskell, Oreola Williams, 1385
Hastings, Philip K., 1302
Hatch, James, Adden. (Sullivan)
Hatcher, Orie L., 3329
Hatcher, Robert A., 869
Hathway, Marion, 168
Hauferlin, C., 332
Haug, Marie R., 333
Hauge, John A., 1656
Havel, Joan, 63, 2872
Havens, Elizabeth M., 238
Hawes, E., 1800
Hawkins, Everett, 809
Hayek, Friedrich August, 2514
Hayes, Marcia, Adden. (Boslooper)
Hays, Elinor Rice, 1219, 1386, 2336
Hays, H. R., 53
Hays, Mary, 2515
Heath, Mary, 2724
Heathers, G., 2865
Hecker, Eugene Arthur, 1640 [Intro.]
Hect, J., 1641
Heer, David M., 810
Heffernan, Esther, Adden.
Heide, Wilma Scott, 1164
Heilbrun, Carolyn G., 2743

Heinrich, Sister Mary Pia, 2232
Heiss, Jerold, 169
Held, Virginia, Adden. (Mothersill)
Heller, Otto, 2744
Hellman, Lillian, 2516
Henderson, Julia J., 337, 3090
Henderson, Thomas F., 2151
Hennessey, Caroline, 429
Henrichsen, Margaret, 2233
Henriques, Fernando, 334-335, 430
Henry, Alice, 3280 [Intro.]-3281
Henshel, Anne-Marie, 239
Herberg, D. M., 3409
Her Majecty's Stationery Office (H.M.S.O.), 992, 1128, 1245, 3091, 3247
Herman, Sondra, Adden. ("Women . . .")
Hermann, Imre, 3007
Hernton, Calvin, 1877
Herron, Belva M., 3282
Herschberger, Ruth, 54
Herskovits, M. J., 240
Herzberg, B., 2866
Hess, Thomas B., 2745, Adden.
Hessel, Vitia, 170
Hewitt, John N., 2100
Hewitt, M., 171
Heys, Patricia Lee Findley, 1470
Heywood, Anne, 3092
Heywood, Thomas, 1573
Higginson, Thomas Wentworth, 622, 1420, 2517
Higham, John, 2101
Hiler, H., 1801
Hiler, M., 1801
Hill, C. Russell, 3093
Hill, Evan, 313
Hill, Georgiana, 1574, 1694
Hill, Joseph Adna, 3094
Hill, Octavia, 2518
Hill, Thomas E. Jr., Adden. (Mothersill)
Hills-Young, E., 2337
Hilton, Diana, 2335
Himmelheber, U., 336
Hinton, William, 1964
Hirning, L. C., 1802
Hirsch, Sharlene Pearlman, Adden. (Lieberman)
Hirvonen, K., 2746
Hjorth, Roland L., 172
Hoadly, Charles J., 1756
Hobbs, Margaret, 3238
Hobman, Daisy, 1346, 2519
Hochschild, Arlie, 55, Adden.
Hodgson, Leonard, 2234
Hoernle, A. W., 623
Hoffman, Anna Rosenberg, 3095
Hoffman, Lois W., 56, 3252
Hogeland, Ronald W., Adden.
Hoggan, Frances, 2102
Holden, James A., 2062
Holden, Miriam Y., 2019
Holding, E. M., 624

Hole, Christina, 1757
Hole, Judith, 1272
Holiday, Billie, 2520
Holliday, Carl, 1728, 2017
Hollis, Florence, 241
Holt, Rackham, 2521
Holtby, Winifred, 1642
Holter, H., 57
Holtker, G., 2999
Hoogenboom, Ari, 1597, 1848, 2126
Hoogenboom, Olive, 1597, 1848, 2126
Hoper, L. H., 1803
Hopkins, Mary D., 3096
Hopper, Janice H., 993
Hoppin, Ruth, 2235
Hopwood, Katherine, 625
Horne, Lena, 2522
Horner, Isaline Blew, 2236
Horner, Matina S., 58, 2833, 2867
Horney, Karen, 2868-2870, 2902
Hornig, Lilli S., 738
Horrath, Francis W., Adden. (Strauss)
Horrell, Muriel, 994
Horta, Maria Teresa, Adden. (da Costa)
Hosford, Frances Juliette, 626
Hoskins, Dalmer, Adden.
Hoshino, Ai, 627
Hosie, Dorothea, 1729
Hottel, Althea, 59, 337
Hotten, John C., 2018
Houghton, Ross C., 504
Houghton, Walter, 1878
Howard, G. E., 242, 3054
Howard, Jane, Adden.
Howard, Pamela, 2747
Howard, Robert Wilmot, 2237
Howe, Florence, 60, 628, 996, 3433, 3463-3464, Adden. (Lieberman)
Howe, Julia Ward, 629, 1372, 1387, 2421, 2508, 2523, 2611
Howe, M. A. DeWolfe, 1388
Howells, William Dean, 2748
Hoyt, Mary Finch, Adden. (McGovern)
Hsia, C. T., 2749
Hsieh, Ping-ying, 2524
Hubback, J., 338
Huber, Joan, 339
Hudson, K., 997
Hufstedler, Shirley M., 1166
Huggins, Ericka, 1960
Hughes, Elizabeth, 2238
Hughes, Helen MacGill, 3371
Hughes, Marija Matich, 3465
Hull, Helen, 2525
Hulton, Ann, 1965
Hume, Martin A. S., 2152
Humphrey, Grace, 1575, 1879
Humphreys, Mary G., 2526
Hunt, Caroline L., 2527
Hunt, Morton M., 61, 431-432
Hunter, Alexander, Adden.
Hurlock, Elisabeth, 1804

Husbands, Sandra A., 630
Hussey, Minnie Middleton, 3501
Hutchins, B. L., 3097
Hutchins, Grace, 3098
Hutchinson, Emilie J., 631, 3054, 3330
Hutton, J. Bernard, 2063
Hutton, Linda I., 2338
Hynes, Maureen, 998

I

Ibsen, Henrik, 2275, 2750, 2796
Ichihashi, Yamoto, 2103
Iga, Mamoru, 2104
Iglehart, John K., 3248
Iglitzen, Lynne B., 1448 [Intro.], Adden.
  (also "Women . . .")
Ilejiani, O., 340
Infield, Glenn B., Adden.
Inman, Mary, 1880-1881
Innis, Mary Quayle, 2528
Institute of Women's Professional Relations,
  3099
International Council of Women, 3527
International Federation of University
  Women, 632, 715
International Institute of Differing Civiliza-
  tions (INCIDI), 999, 1447
International Labour Office, 3100-3101
Interstate Association of Commissions on
  the Status of Women, 3528
Ireland, Norma Olin, 2529, 3529
Irvine, Mary D., 2239
Irwin, Inez Hayes, 1246, 1524, 1882-1883
Ishimoto, Shidzue, 2530
Israel, Stan, Adden.
Issaev, B., 1643
Itasca Conference on the Continuing Educa-
  tion of Women, 633

J

Jackson, Clara O., 3466
Jackson, Jacquelyne J., 173
Jackson, M., 1805
Jackson, Mahalia, 2531
Jacobs, H. H., 2532
Jacobs, Milton, 2105
Jacobs, Sue Ellen, 3467
Jacobs, T. J., 2871
Jacobson, Alver H., 62
Jacobson, Carolyn J., 3219
Jacobson, Richard S., Adden.
Jaffe, Naomi, Adden. (Baritz)
Jaffe, R. B., 2339
Jafri, S. N. S., 341
Jahoda, Marie, 63, 2872
Jaiswal, R. H., 811
Jakobovits, Immanuel, 812

James, Bartlett Burleigh, 1576
James, Bessie Rowland, 904
James, E. O., 1758
James, Edward T., 3507
James, Henry, 2751, 2781
James, Janet Wilson, 3507
Jameson, Anna Brownell, 2752
Jancar, Barbara, 1448
Janeway, Elizabeth, 64, Adden.
Janowsky, D. S., 2340-2341
Jaquette, Jane S., 1259, 1448
Jarin, Ken, 1490
Jarvis, Edward, 2873
Jaulin, R., 505
Javits, Jacob K., 1167
Jay, Anthony, 497
Jeffreys, Margot, 1511
Jenkin, Noel, 65
Jenkins, Elizabeth, 2153
Jenkins, Hester Donaldson, 2533
Jenness, Linda, 814, 1252, 1273
Jennings, Pauline, 1490
Jennings, M. Kent, 66, 883 [Intro.], 1525
Jenson, Oliver, 1885
Jessup, Henry Wynans, 1168
Jessup, Josephine L., 2753
Jeter, Jeremiah Bell, Adden.
Jex-Blake, Sophia, 2342, 2659
Joesting, Joan, 2874-2875
Joesting, Robert, 2875
Johnsen, Julia E., 3468
Johnson, Arthur, 433, 2876
Johnson, Charles D., 2877
Johnson, Dallas, 1536
Johnson, Helen, 1421
Johnson, Joseph 2534
Johnson, Julia T., 1169
Johnson, Lucille L., 3301
Johnson, Olive M., 1967
Johnson, Paul, Adden.
Johnson, Virginia E., 446-447, 2359
Johnston, Johann, 905
Johnston, Johanna, 2535
Johnston, John D., 1170
Johnstone, Elizabeth, 337, 3102
Johnstone, Grace, 2536
Jolson, Marvin A., 342
Jonathan, Will, 2351
Jones, Beverly, 506, 1886, Adden. (Cook)
Jones, Claudia, 343
Jones, Katherine, 2064, 2537
Jones, L. Bevan, 344
Jones, Mary Harris, (Mother Jones), 906,
  1537, 2538, 2575
Jones, Violet R. S., 344
Jordan, Joan, Adden. (Hochschild)
Jorns, Auguste, Adden.
Joseph, G., 507
Josephson, Hanna Geffen, 3331, Adden.
Joslyn, Kersten, 345
Judek, Stanislauw, 1512
Jung, Carl, 2878, 2902

Jutting, Van Bethem, 346

K

Kaberry, Phyllis M., 1695, 3008, 3103
Kagame, A., 3009
Kagan, J., 2879
Kähler, Else, 2240
Kahne, Hilda, 3372
Kalish, Richard A., 67, 347
Kallir, Otto, Adden.
Kally, Maureen M., 68
Kamm, J., 2539
Kamm, Josephine, 1887
Kandel, Denise B., 243
Kane, Paula, Adden.
Kaneko, Josephine C., 1968
K'ang, Yu-wei, 2241
Kanner, S. Barbara, 3469
Kanowitz, Leo, 1171-1174 [Intro.], 3220
Kantor, H. I., 2343
Kaplan, Edward H., 3470
Kaplan, Frances B., 1085 [Intro.], 1105
Kaplan, Justin, 1644
Kaplan, Temma, 1448
Kapur, Promilla, 244
Karim, Abdul K. N., 508
Karlen, Arno, 434
Karole, K., 836
Kass, Babette, 3373
Katasheva, L., 2540
Katayama, Tetsu, 1000
Katz, Daniel, 1502
Katz, Elihu, 1806
Katz, Joseph, 3471
Katz, Maude W., 1888
Katz, Naomi, Adden.
Kaur, Manmohan, 1889
Kavanagh, Julia, 2754
Kay, Herma H., 1157, Adden.
Kay, M. Jane, 3374
Kearney, James R., 2541
Keeler, Harriet L., 2542
Keir, Margaret S., 236
Keith, Rev. L. E. See Feeler, Felix.
Kellen, Konrad, 1645
Keller, Helen, 2543
Kellersberger, J. S., 509
Kelley, Florence, 892, 903, 1837, 2498, 3332
Kelly, B., 2340
Kelly, Robert Gordon, 2755
Kemble, Frances Anne (Fannie), 2544, Adden. (Hahn)
Kempton, Sally, 1088
Kemp-Welsh, Alice, Adden.
Keniston, Ellen, 3375
Keniston, Kenneth, 3375
Kenneally, J., 1412
Kennedy, David, 2545
Kennedy, John F., 1220

Kenner, Zipora, 2546
Kenney, Annie, 1389
Kenyatta, Mary, 1890
Kerstin, Aner, 1891
Kessel, N., 2315, 2847
Key, Ellen, 69, 174, 245, 348, 1667, 1892, 2242, 2275
Key, Mary R., 70
Keyserling, Mary Dublin, 3410
Kiba, Simon, 1001
Kieffer, Miriam G., 3472
Kieran, Sheila, 3249
Kievit, Mary Bach, Adden.
Killian, Ray, Adden.
King, Clyde L., 1893
King, William C., 1646 [Intro.]
Kingsbury, Susan H., 175
Kinsey, Alfred C., 435
Kinzer, Nora Scott, 1259, Adden. ("Women . . .")
Kirby, Ellen, 2243
Kirchwey, Freda, 349
Kirk, Russell, 1330
Kirkendall, Lester A., 436
Kirk-Greene, A. H. M., 2344
Kirkpatrick, Clifford, 176, 1577, 2880
Kirkpatrick, Jeane, 1482
Kirschner, Betty Frankle, 71
Kitay, P. M., 2881
Kitzinger, Sheila, 2345
Klagsburn, Francine, Adden.
Klarman, Betty, 3260
Klaus, M., 2834
Klein, Judy, 1442, 1985
Klein, Natasha, 2119
Klein, Vida, 548
Klein, Viola, 72, 95 [Intro.], 3104, 3333
Klimpel Alvarado, Felicitas, 1969
Klüger, Ruth, Adden.
Knapp, Charles L., 1170
Knorr, Norman J., 448
KNOW, Inc., 3530
Knowlton, Charles, 815
Knudsen, Dean D., 510
Koch, Harriet Berger, 2547
Koedt, Anne P., 1002 [Intro.], 1865, Adden. (Baritz)
Koeume, E., 511
Kohen, Max, 3010
Kohler, M., 246
Kok, G. H. S., 1082
Kolle, Oswalt, 73
Kollontai, Alexandra, 177, 350-351, 1262, 1513, 2593
Komarovsky, Mirra, 74-75, 125, 247, 339, 634
Komisar, Lucy, 1003
Konopka, Gisela, 2882
Koontz, Elizabeth D., 635, 3334, 3411
Kopp, Marie E., 816
Korshunova, Y., 1004
Koupernik, Cyrille, 437

Koya, Yoshio, 817
Koyama, Takashi, 512, 1894
Kraditor, Aileen S., 943 [Intro.], 1347, 1895
Krafft-Ebing, Richard von, 465
Kraines, Ruth J., 2364
Kramer, Marjorie, 2756
Krasnopolskii, A., 1005
Krause, Harry D., 1175
Krauss, Wilma, Intro. p. 23
Kreps, Juanita, 3412
Kresell, Judith, 612
Kresge, Pat, 389
Krichmar, Albert, 3473
Krige, E. J., 1759
Krige, J. D., 1759
Kroeber, Alfred L., 1807, 1814
Kroeber, Karl, 2757
Kronhausen, Eberhard, 438
Kronhausen, Phyllis, 438
Kroth, J. A., 2883
Krout, Angeline, 3284
Krueger, Lillian, 352
Kruschke, Earl R., 1303
Kulchycka, Lydia, 3187
Kuper, H., 248
Kupperman, H. S., 2346
Kuriansky, Joan, 1490
Kurland, Phillip B., 1862
Kurtz, R. M., 76, 2884
Kushen, Betty, 2758
Kushner, Dan, 2347
Kutner, Luis, Adden.

L

Labarge, Margaret W., 513
Labouret, H., 514
LABOUR GAZETTE, 3295
Lacey, W. K., 178
Ladd, William, 936
Lader, Lawrence, 818, 2548
Ladner, Joyce A., 77, 1970, 2106
Laffin, Garry S., 2759
Laffin, John, 2065
LaFollette, Suzanne, 1578 [Intro.], 1851
Lagno, Isadoro Del, 1696
Laidler, P. W., 2348
Laigret, J., 2349
Laing, Ronald D., 179, 2885
La Marsh, Judy, 2549
Lamb, Anthony B., 1176
Lamb, Harold, 2154
Lambton, Ann K. S., 515
Lampe, G. W. H., 2244
Lampson, Peggy, 1484
Landes, Ruth, 2107
Landes, R., 516
Landy, Laurie, 1274
Lane, Margaret, 2550-2551
Lang, Olga, 180
Langdon-Davies, John, 1579, 1808
Langmyhr, George, 819

Lanier, Alison R., 337
Lansing, Marjorie, 1448, 1896
Lantz, Joanne B., 517
Lapidus, Gail Warshofsky, Adden. ("Women . . .")
Lapin, Eva, 1221
Larcom, Lucy, 2552, 3335
LAROUSSE ENCYCLOPEDIA OF MYTHOLOGY, 3011
Larrabee, Eric, 518
Larrick, Nancy, Adden.
Larson, C. A., Intro. p. 19
Larson, T. A., 1422
La Rue, Linda J. M., Adden. (Hochschild)
Larus, John Rouse, 1580
Las Cases, Comte Emile, 2066
Lasch, Christopher, 1897-1898
Lash, Joseph P., 2553
Laslett, Peter, 2350
Laswell, Thomas E., 119
Latour, Therese Louis, 1697
Lattimore, Eleanor L., 3336
Laughlin, Clara E., 3337
Lauter, Paul, 996
La Violette, Forest E., 2108
Lawrence, Margaret, 2760
Lawrenson, Helen, 1899
Laws, Judith Long, 3474
Layard, John, 3012
Lazarsfeld, Paul F., 1291, 1806
Lazarsfield, Sofie, 78
League of Academic Women, 739
League of Women Voters, 1304-1306, 1539
Leakey, Louis S. B., 3013
Lear, John, 2351
Lebeson, Anita Libman, 2109
Lebeuf, Jean-Paul, 1809
Lederer, Wolfgang, 1581
Lednicer, D., 2339
Le Duan, 1971
Lee, George, 1275
Lee, Kendrick, 3338
Lee, N. H., 820
Lee, P., 2352
Lee, Sir Sidney, 2155
Lefcowitz, Myron J., 249
Leffler, Ann, 1900
Lefort, Pierre, 2353
Leger, J., 3014
Lehfeldt, H., 867
Leiderman, P. H., 2834
Leijon, Anna-Greta, 79
Leith-Ross, L., 1972
Leith-Ross, Sylvia, 1973
Lemaire, C., 353
LeMoyne, Jean, 80
Lenin, Vladimir I., 1260, 1976
Lenroot, Katherine F., 1518
Leonard, Eugenie A., 637, 1348, 2019, 3475
Lepper, Mary M., 1448
Lerner, Gerda, 1647, 2554 [Intro.]

Lerner, Max, 1648
Leslie, Eliza, 638, 1730
Lesser, Allen, Adden.
Lesser, Gerald S., 243, 2856
Lessing, Doris, 2761
Lester, D., 2886
Lester, Julia, 1649
Lester, Richard A., Adden.
Letourneau, C., 519
Lever, Janet, 639
Levine, Daniel, 907
Levine, Ellen, 1272
Levine, Isaac Don, 2067
Levine, Joseph M., 2156
Levine, Lena, 81
Levine, Louis, 3339
Levitin, Teresa, 612, 3105, 3322
Levy, Betty, 610, Adden. (Lieberman)
Levy, Gertrude R., 2245
Levy, Howard S., 1731-1732
Levy, Marion J. Jr., 181
Levy, Richard G., 1006
Lewin, Arie Y., 3376
Lewis, Edwin C., 354, 520, 737, 740, 748
Lewis, Florence C., Adden. (Lieberman)
Lewis, Georgina King, 2555
Lewis, Helen M., 1007
Lewis, John Wilson, 1178
Lewis, Martha, 3413
Library of Congress, 3589
Lichtenberger, James P., 1129, 1349
Lidz, Ruth, 2887
Lieberman, Myron, Adden.
Lifton, Robert Jay, 2811
Lilienthal, Meta (Stern), 1253, 1325, 3250
Lillard, Richard G., 2556
Limmer, Ruth, Adden. (Lieberman)
Lin, Yüeh-hua, 182
Lindbergh, Anne Morrow, Adden.
Linderman, Frank Bird, 2110
Lindsay, Jack, 2157
Lindsay, Malvina, 1307
Lindsey, Ben B., 250
LINK, 260, 377
Linn, James Weber, 908
Linton, E. Lynn, 1760
Lipman-Blumen, Jean, 82
Lippard, Lucy R., 2762
Littig, Lawrence W., 2888
Little, K. L., 521
Liu, William T., 860
Livermore, Henrietta W., 1320-1322
Livermore, Mary A., 1390, 1901, 2682
Livesay, Dorothy, 2763
Livingstone, Elizabeth, 2889
Lloyd, Trevor, 1350
Lobel, L. S., 1778
Lobsenz, Johanna, 3221
Lochner, Jim W., 821
Lockerby, Florence K., 3414
Loeb, Jane, 741
Loeser, Herta, Adden.

Loewe, Raphael, 2246
Logan, Mary S., 1582, 2557
Lombroso, Gina, 1413
Long, Kahlila D., 799
Long, Priscilla, 1008, 1908
Longford, Elizabeth, 2158
Longworth, Alice Roosevelt, 2558
Loosley, Elizabeth W., 373
Lopata, Helena Z., 251, 339, 355-356, 3222
Lopate, Carol, 3377
Lord, Myra B., 3531
Loring, Rosalind, 3378
Loth, David, 81, 1485
Louis Harris. See Harris, Louis.
Low, A. Maurice, 1308
Lowe, A. M., 2764
Lowenthal, Helen, 3379
Lubac, Henri de, 2247
Lubove, Roy, 3415
Lucas, Christopher, 1974
Lucas, Roy, 822
Lucka, Emil, 2248
Ludovici, Anthony M., 1414-1415
Ludwig, Emil, 2159
Luetkens, Charlotte, 1583
Luhan, Mabel Dodge, 2559
Lund, Caroline, 814, 1179
Lundberg, Ferdinand, 439 [Intro.]
Lurie, Nancy Oestrich, 2111, 2560
Lutz, Alma, 931, 1247, 1373, 1391-1392, 1835
Lyman, Susan E., 2068
Lynch, Edith M., Adden.
Lynd, Alice, 3285
Lynd, Staughton, 3285
Lyness, Jack, 1490
Lynn, D., 2890
Lynn, David B., 83
Lynn, Naomi B., 1448, 3476
Lyon, Catherine Dillon, Adden. (Lieberman)
Lyon, Mary, 1872, 2500, 2534, 2561, 2597
Lyon, Phyllis, 357
Lytton, Constance, 1393

Mc Mac

McAffe, Kathy, Adden. (Baritz)
McAleavy, Henry, 1131
McArthur, J. L., 2070
McAtee, Patricia A., 3426
McBreaty, James C., 643
McBride, Angela Barron, Adden.
McCandless, Boyd R., 461
MacCarthy, Bridget C., 2765-2766
MacClellan, Margaret E., 1083
McClung, Nellie L., 1395
McClure, Robert F., 644
MacClure, Victor, 2562
McConnell, Dorothy, 3341
McCord, Bird, 3418

McCracken, Elizabeth, 1586
McCrimmon, Abraham L., 1904
McCulloch, Albert, 1452
McCune, Shirley, 389
McDavid, J. W., 2891
McDermott, John F., Jr., 783
McDonald, Donald, 86
MacDonald, Elizabeth M., 2249
MacDonald, John Marshall, 1180
MacDonald, J. Ramsey, 2563
McFadden, Judith Nies. See Nies, Judith.
McFarland, C. K., 1537
McGee, Reece, 725
McGinnis, Robert, 210, 270
McGovern, Eleanor, Adden.
McGrath, Albertus Magnus, O. P., 2250
MacGregor, O., 252
McGuigan, Dorothy G., Adden.
McHugh, Mary, Adden. (also Baritz)
McKain, Walter C., 255
McKee, J. P., 87, 2892, 2920
McKee, Ruth K., 2571
McKeithan, Elsa, 734
McKenna, Mary L., 2251
Mackenzie, Norman I., 1584
McKenzie, Marjorie, 2113
Mackenzie-Grieve, Averil, 2564
MacKensie, R. Alex, 3416
McKnight, Robert K., 9
MacLean, Annie M., 3342-3343
McLean, Beth Bailey, 3380
MacLennan, John F., 253, 3015
Macleod, Jennifer S., Adden.
McMahon, Theresa S., 3106
McManmon, John J., 2767
McNally, Gertrude Bancroft, 3344
MacNamara, Donald E. J., 369
McPhee, William N., 1291
McPherson, K., 3016
McQuire, Judith W., 2572
McRobbie, Kenneth, 1700
McVeety, Jean, 1181
MacVicar, T., 3017
McWilliams, Nancy, 1448

M

Ma, Hsin-teh, 1975
Mace, David, 183
Mace, Vera, 183
Maccoby, Eleanor, 84, 3482
Macurdy, Grace H., 2160-2161
Maddi, Salvatore R., 2893
Madison, Dolly, 1566, 2429, Adden.
Madsen, William, 2112
Maertens, Thierry, 2252
Magnusson, Lucille, 2354
Magoffin, Susan Shelby, 2020
Maharay, George S., Adden. (Wormser)
Mahon, Lucy R., 3345
Mai, F. M. M., 2894

Maimonides, Moses, 2253
Mainardi, Pat, Adden. (Baritz)
Mair, L., 3018
Maison, Margaret, 1394
Maizels, Joan, 405
Majors, Monroe A., 2021
Makarenko, A. S., 184
Makonga, B., 524
Malcolm, Janet, 3107
Malfetti, James L., 440
Malik, Har G. S., 2895
Malinowski, Bronislaw, 224, 441-442, 3019-3021
Malkiel, Theresa, 3286
Malkin, Michael R., 2768
Malone, Dumas, 3508
Maloney M., 67
Mancke, Richard B., 3223
Mandel, William M., 612, 1009, 3108
Mandell, A. J., 2341, 2355
Mandell, M., 2355
Mandle, Joan D., 525, 1010
Manette, Jan (Pseud.), 3417
Manis, Laura G., 640
Manley, Seon, 2769
Mann, Constance, 2356
Mann, Herman, 2069
Mann, Jean, 1486
Mann, Peggy, 1487, Adden.
Mannes, Marya, 263, 2896
Mannin, Ethel E., 526
Manton, W. P., 2357
Mapes, Victor, 2770
Marans, Nelly, 2254
Maraventano, Frances, 1215
Marberry, M. M., 2565
Marble, Ann R., 2022
Marbury, Elizabeth, 2485
Marchal, R. P., 3022
Marchand, Henry L., 443
Marcus, Jacob R., 2023
Marcuse, Herbert, 444, 527
Marder, Herbert, 2771
Mare, Margaret, 2772
Marie-Andre Du Sacre-Coeur, Sister. See Sister Marie-Andre.
Marie, Grand Duchess of Russia, 2485
Marine, Gene, 1902
Markoff, Helene S., Adden. (Wormser)
Markowska, Danuta, 150
Marks, Arno F., Adden.
Marks, Dorothy, 3449
Markus, Maria, 3109
Marmor, Judd, 445
Marot, Helen, 3077
Marr, June, Adden. (Lieberman)
Marreco, Ann, 2566
Marshall, D., 1650
Marshall, Helen E., 2567
Marshall, Judith M., 3477
Martin, Anne, 1309
Martin, C., 804

Martin, Del, 357
Martin, Edward S., 1903
Martin, Gertrude S., 3054
Martin, Marion E., 1518
Martin, Ralph G., 2568
Martin, Wendy, 3577
Martineau, Harriet, 1585, 2422, 2424, 2453, 2460, 2678, 2738, Adden. (Hahn, Thompson)
Martines, Lauro, 1588
Marton, Elizabeth Homer, 1084
Marvick, Dwaine, 1451
Marx, Karl, 1976
Mary Ethel, Sister, 375
Marygrove College, 1698
Maryland Law Review, 3210
Masefield, Muriel Agnes, 2773
Maslow, Abraham H., 2897
Mason, Otis T., 1699 [Intro.]
Massell, Gregory J., Adden.
Masson, Flora, Adden.
Masson, Frederic, 2162
Masters, William H., 446-447, 2358-2359
Matasar, Anne B., 1448, 3476
Mather, Cotton, 641
Mathews, John, 3381
Mathur, Mary E. F., 85
Mattfeld, Jacquelyn, 3382
Matthews, William, 3478
Mattingly, Garrett, 2163
Maude, Aylmer, 2569
Maule, Frances, 1351, Adden.
Mauny, R., 530
Maurice, C. Edmund, 2518
Mavity, Nancy Barr, 2570
Maxeke, C. M., 531
May, Charles Paul, 1223
Mayer, August, 1651
Mayer, Michael F., Adden.
Mayer, P., 642
Mayhew, Henry, 358
Mayreader, Rosa, 1011
Mead, Margaret, 88, 256, 548, 823, 1085 [Intro.], 1088, 1105, 1515, 1668, 2573, 2690, 3224, Adden.
Means, Ingunn Norderval, 1323, 1453-1454
Meeks, Catherine L., 3462
Meggitt, M. J., 235
Mehta, Nandini, 89
Meigs, Charles D., 2360
Meigs, Cornelia, 645
Meijer, M. J., 1132
Meikle, Wilma, 1223
Mellen, Joan, Adden.
Meltzer, Milton, 2574
Mencken, Henry Louis, Adden.
Menon, Lakshmi N., 337
Menzies, Sutherland, 1905
Mercer, Mary Velasco, Adden. (Jacobson)
Mercier, P., 532
Merkl, Peter, Adden. ("Women . . .")
Merkle, Judith, 1257

Merriam, Charles E., 1310
Merriam, Eve, 2575, 2774-2775, Adden. (Larrick)
Merton, Robert, 301
Messenger, R., 2576
Messer, Mary Burt, 3024
Mestre, Carmen, 1012
Mews, Hazel, 2776
Meyer, Adolf, 824
Meyer, Agnes E., 2577
Meyer, Bertha, 2578
Meyer, Donald, 2255
Meyer, Jon K., 448
Meyersohn, Rolf, 518
Michael, Carmen M., 2343
Michael, Franz, 1977
Michaelson, Evelyn J., 90
Michelet, Jules, 1013
Michelson, Truman, 2114
Michigan Law Review, 1206 [Intro.]
Michigan Liquor Control Commission, 1217
Michigan State University, 742
Michigan State University Libraries, 3479
Mickel, D. Grant, Adden. (Jacobson)
Micossi, Anita Lynn, Adden. (Hochschild)
Middleton, Dorothy, 2579
Migel, Parmenia, 2580
Miles, Catherine C., 2926
Mill, Harriet Taylor, 1015, 1923, 2514
Mill, John Stuart 1014-1015, 1352, 1851, 1923, 2514
Millard, Betty, 1016
Miller, Alice D., 1353
Miller, Arthur C., 2444
Miller, Casey, 1017
Miller, Elizabeth W., 3480
Miller, Jean Baker, 909, 2898
Miller, Judy Ann, 1488
Miller, Nora, 646
Miller, Robert Stevens, 1182
Millett, Kate, 647, 1088, Adden.
Millman, Marcia, 91
Mills, Emma L., 2071
Mills, Herbert E., 648
Milman, Donald S., 2899
Milner, Esther, 92
Milton, Nancy, 533, Adden. (Katz)
Mink, Patsy, 1204, 1484, 1490
Minuchin, Patricia, 649
Miqueli, Violeta, 1761
Miron, E. L., 2164
Mishima, Sumie Seo, 359, 2581
Mitchell, A., 1489
Mitchell, David J., 1906, 2582
Mitchell, Hannah, 1355
Mitchell, Joyce M., 612
Mitchell, Juliet, 1018, 1254, Adden.
Mitchell, Lucy Sprague, 2583
Mitchell, Mildred B., 743
Mitchell, Robert E., 825
Mitford, Jessica, 2584
Mitscherlich, Alexander, 185

Miyake, Yujiro, 1019
Mochizuki, June, 640
Moers, Ellen, 2777, 2778
Moffat, Mary J., Adden.
Mohr, R., 449
Moll, Will, 2256
Molle, Jessie, 1526
Moller, Herbert, 2024
Money, John, 450, 2900
Money, Keith, Adden.
Monks of Solesmes, 2257
Monro, I. S., 1810
Monroe, Ernest R., 186
Montagu, Ashley, 93
Montefiore, Dora, 1907
Moody, Howard, 826
Moore, B. E., 2901
Moore, Frank, 2072
Moore, Joe A., Adden. (Jacobson)
Moore, Linda, Adden. (Wormser)
Moore, Malcolm A., 1147
Moos, R., 2361
Moran, Barbara K., 501 [Intro.]
Moravia, Alberto, 2779
More, Adelyne, 827
More, Hannah, 650
Moret, A., 1762
Morgan, Edmund S., 2025
Morgan, Elaine, 94
Morgan, Robin, 1020, 1276, 1849, 2125,
    Adden. (Baritz)
Morny, Peter de, 2585
Morrah, Dermot, Adden.
Morris, Clyde P., 187
Morris, Henry F., 1134
Morris, Joan, 2258
Morris, Margaret, 1978
Morris, Naomi M., 2379
Morris, Richard B., 1183
Morris, Robert, 2362
Morris, Roger R., 651
Morrissey, W. Michael, Adden. (Lieberman)
Morton, Frederick W., 2780
Morton, Ward M., 1356
Mosbacher, E., 185
Moses, Anna Mary Robertson, 2586, Adden.
    (Kallir)
Moss, H. A., 2879
Mothersill, Mary, Adden.
MOTHER EARTH BULLETIN, 3561
Mott, Frank L., 3251
Mott, James, 1396
Mott, Lucretia 931, 1378-1379, 1384,
    1396, 2226, 2454
Mottahedeh, Mildred R., 1248
Motz, Annabelle Bender, 3383
Moyer-Wing, Alice C., 1311
Moynihan, Daniel P., 188, 1659
Mozans, H. J., 2587
Mpongo, Laurent, 257
M'Rabet, Fadéla, 1587
MS. MAGAZINE, 3562, Adden. (Klagsburn)

Mueller, Kate, 652
Muggeridge, Kitty, 1455
Mulenzi, J., 3025
Mull, Donald, 2781
Mullahy, Patrick, 2902
Mullins, Carolyn, 653
Munaker, Sue, 1908
Munday, R. N., 2894
Mundt, Klara Muller, 2165
Murdock, G. P., 3110
Murphy, Florence, 3509
Murphy, Irene Lyons, 1184 [Intro.]
Murphy, Sharon, Adden. (Elliot)
Murray, K. C., 3302
Murray, Margaret Alice, 1763-1764, 2259
Murray, Pauli, 1185, 1204, 1862
Murtaugh, Daniel M., 2782
Myers, Albert Cook, 2073
Myrdal, Alva, 95 [Intro.], 828, Adden.
    ("Women . . .")
Myrdal, Gunnar, 534
Myrdal, Jan, 360

N

Nadarajah, Devapoopathy, 535
Nadelson, Carol, 3384
Nader, Ralph, 1490, 3111
Nagel, Stuart, 1186
Nandini, Rao, 3246
Napier, J., 1765
Narveson, Jan, Adden. (Mothersill)
NASSP, see National Association of
    Secondary School Principals
Nathan, Maud, 910, 1909, 2588
Nation, Carry A., 940, 2589, 2617
National American Woman Suffrage
    Association, 1357, 1910
National Association of Deans of Women,
    718
National Association of Secondary School
    Principals, (NASSP), 617, 664
National Coalition for Research on Women's
    Education and Development, Inc., 3532
National Consumers' League, 3346-3347
National Council of Family Relations, 3481
National Council of Women of the United
    States, 1811
National Education Association, 3385
National Federation of Settlements, 3348
National Industrial Conference Board, 3349
National Manpower Council, 3112 [Intro.]
National Merit Scholarship Corporation, 654
National Organization for Women (NOW),
    647, 655-656, 3533
National School Boards Association, Adden.
National Science Foundation, 744
National Woman's Christian Temperance
    Union, 3590
National Woman's Party, 3591
National Women's Political Caucus, 3534

Neal, Garland T., 3387
Nearing, Scott, 536, 3350
Needham, Eleanor, 2783
Neff, Wanda Fraiken, 3113
Neisser, Edith, 96
Neumann, Eric, 2903, 3027
Neuss, Margret, 361
Nevins, Winfield S., 1766
Newcomer, Mabel, 657
Newman, Pamela, 1062
New York City Commission on Human
    Rights, 1088
New York, Governor's Committee on the
    Education and Employment of Women,
    1249
New York: Prometheus Press, 3011
New York Public Library, 3592
New York Radical Feminists, 3535
New York Radical Women, 3565
NEW YORK TRIBUNE, 3352
New York University Law Review, 1170
    [Intro.]
Nicod, A., 538
Niemi, Richard G., 883 [Intro.]
Nies, Judith, (McFadden, Judith Nies), 1277,
    1491, 1514
Nin, Anais, 2591, Adden. (Moffat)
Nisbet, Robert A., 301
Nishimoto, Richard S., 2124
Noble, Jeanne L., 658, 2115
Nochlin, Linda, 2745
Norman, Eve, Adden.
Norris, Ada, 337
Norris, Kathleen, 937
Norris, Marianna, 1492
North Carolina Law Review, 822
North Carolina Museum of Art, Adden.
Norton, Caroline, 1652
Notman, Malkah T., 3384
Nottingham, Ev., 3421
Noun, Louise R., 1358
Novack, George, 1911
NOW. See National Organization for Women.
Nowlis, V., 2917
Noyes, Ethel J. R. C., 2026
Nuita, Yoko, 659
Nutting, Mary A., 2365
Nyberg, Kathleen Neill, 2260
Nye, Ivan F., 3252

O

Oakley, Ann, 97, 2904
Oakley, Violet, 911
O'Brien, John E., 258
Oden, Marilyn Brown, 2261
Oetzel, Roberta, 3482
O'Faolain, Julia, 1588
Ogg, Elizabeth, 1021
O'Hara, Albert R., 539, 1653
O'Kelly, E., 3287

Oldham, James C., 1187
O'Leary, Dan, Adden. (Jacobson)
Olin, Helen R., 660
Oliphant, Mrs. Margaret, Adden.
Oliva, Lawrence J., 2166
Olivier, B., 2207
Olivier, G., 3028
Oltman, Ruth M., 389, 612, 661-662
O'Malley, Austin, 829
O'Malley, I. B., 1912
Ominde, S. H., 3029
O'Neil, George, Adden.
O'Neil, Nena, Adden. (O'Neil)
O'Neill, Barbara P., 362
O'Neill, William L., 259, 884 [Intro.], 1278,
    1359, 1913
Oppenheimer, Valerie Kincade, 3114, 3353
    [Intro.] -3354
Orga, Irfan, 189
Organization of American States, Inter-
    American Commission of Women, 1089
Organization for Economic Cooperation
    and Development, 3115, 3253
Oriège, Guy d', 1589
Orleans, Jeffrey H., Adden. (Buek)
Orleans, Leo A., 830-831
Ormsbee, T. H., 1701
Orloff, L. F., 2886
Orth, Penelope, 363
Osofsky, Howard J., 420, 832
Osofsky, Joy D., 832
Ossoli, Mrs. Sarah Margaret Fuller. See
    Fuller, Margaret.
Ostrogorskii, Moseii Akovievich, 1188, 1914
Ostry, Sylvia, 3254
O'Sullivan-Beare, Nancy, 2027

P

Packard, Francis R., 2366
Packard, Vanco, 1812
Packer, Barbara, 663
Paine, Harriet E. See Chester, Eliza.
Painter, Charlotte, Adden. (Moffat)
Pailloux, R., 3030
Palencia, Isabel de, 2593
Palmer, Rachel L., 2367
Palubinskas, Alice, 2905
Pan American Union, 1022-1024, 1090-
    1094, 1189, 3116
Pankhurst, Dame Christabel, 1338, 1360,
    2582, 2594
Pankhurst, Emmeline, 1338, 1430, 2539,
    2582, 2585, 2595 [Intro.] -2596
Pankhurst, Estelle, 1338, 2582, 2596
Pankhurst, E. Sylvia, 1338, 1361, 1856,
    1915 [Intro.] , 2582, 3566
Pannell, Anne Gary, 912
Panofsky, Dora, 1767
Panofsky, Erwin, 1767
Panther Women, 1916

Papashvily, Helen Waite, 2786
Paradis, Suzanne, 2787
Paris, Jeanne, 3380
Park, Dabney, 746
Parker, Amelia C., 2074
Parker, Cornelia Stratton, 3355
Parker, Franklin, 664-665
Parker, Gail, 1917
Parkhurst, Jessie W., 98
Parkman, Mary Rosetta, 2597
Parmelee, Maurice, 3054
Parrinder, Edward Geoffrey, 1768
Parrish, John B., 389, 747, 3386
Parsons, Alice B., 1590, 1654
Parsons, Elsie Clews, 99, 1591, 3054
Parsons, Talcott, 100, 190, 540
Parton, Mary Field, 906
Passin, Herbert, 9
Patai, Raphael, 544
Patrick, Mary Mills, 1362, 2533, 2598
Patten, Simon N., 3054
Patterson, Samuel White, 666
Patton, James W., 1601
Paul, John E., 2167
Pauli, Hertha, 932
Paulme, Denise, 1979, 3031
Paulson, Ross E., 944
Pearsall, Ronald, 451
Peck, Ellen, 833, Adden.
Peck, Mary G., 2599
Peck, Robert F., 101, 2906
Pederson, Inger Margrete, 337, 1133
Peel, Maria, 2788
Peel, Robert, 2600
Pekin, L. B., 667
Peking: All-China Democratic Women's
    Federation, 1066
Pelrine, Eleanor Wright, 834
Pennell, M. Y., 3388
Penny, E. D., Adden. (Bunkle)
Penny, P. E., Adden. (Bunkle)
Penny, Virginia, 3117
Penzer, Norman M., 1733
Percival, Alicia C., 2772
Perella, Vera C., 3118, 3257
Perez-Palacios, G., 2339
Perkins, A. J. G., 1397 [Intro.], 2601
Perkins, Frances, 1517-1518, 3119
Perkins, Lisa H., 748
Perley, D. R., Adden. (Bunkle)
Perley, J. E., Adden. (Bunkle)
Perlstein, Gary R., 2907
Pescatello, Ann, 542, 1256
Pesotta, Rose, 3288
Peters, Heinz Frederick, Adden.
Peters, Iva L., 3424
Peterson, Esther, 297 [Intro.]
Peto, Andrew, 3032
Petrova, L., 1025
Phan Thi Mai, 1985
Phillips, Arthur, 1134
Phillips, Emma M., 2602

Phillips, James E., 2168, 2789
Phillips, Leon, Adden.
Phillips, M., 2603
Phillips, Marion, 1527
Phillips, Ruth, 1539
Phipps, William E., 2262
Phoenix, C. H., 2937
Pickett, La Salle C., 2604
Pickford, Mary, 2605
Pickles, Dorothy, 1456
Pidgeon, Mary E., 3120-3122, 3255, 3356-
    3357, 3422
Pierce, Christine, Adden. (Mothersill)
Pierson, Elaine C., 2368
Pietrofesa, John J., 668
Pillsbury, Parker, 3568
Pilpel, Harriet, 1135
Pinchbeck, Ivy, 3123
Pineau, Léon, 1753
Pinkham, Mildreth Worth, 2263
Pitman, Emma Raymond, 2606
Planned Parenthood-World Population, 835
Plant, Marjorie, 1655
Plato, 1592
Plunket, Irene Arthur Lifford, Adden.
Pogrebin, Letty Cottin, 3124
Pohlman, Edward, 2908
Pollack, Otto, 364
Pollard, Edward B., 1593 [Intro.]
Pollard, Penelope, 1026
Pollera, Alberto, 543
Poloma, Margaret M., 3387
Pomeroy, W. B., 804
Poole, Howard E., 102
Popova, Nina, 544
Popp, Adelheid, 2607
Porritt, Mrs. Annie G., 1351, 1428
Porter, Kirk Harold, 1363, 1918
Porter, Mary Cornelia, 1448
Porter, Sarah H., 2608
Potter, David M., 1656
Potvin, Raymond H., 873
Pouissant, Alvin F., 2909
Power, Eileen, 1702-1703
Power, James R., 2075
Prather, Jane, 612
Pratt, Annis, 2790
Pratt, E. H., 2369
Pratt, Lois, 103
Pressman, Sonia, 1204, 1224, 3225 (Fuentes,
    Sonia P.)
Preston, Marilynn, 3423
Prior, Margaret, 913
Pritchard, Ada, 1528
Prohl, Russell C., 2264
Proxmire, Ellen, 1529
Pruette, Lorine, 365, 3358, 3424
Pryor, Sara C., 2028
Prywes, Ruth W., Adden.
Pullai, Arpad, 1657
Pullen, Dale, 1490
Purcell, Susan Kaufman, 1255, 1448

Putnam, Emily James, 1594

Q

Quinn, Robert P., 612, 3322
Quisumbing, Lourdes R., 1734

R

Rabinowitz, Clara, 131
Rac, Frank, 1136
Racz, Elizabeth, 1027, 1919, 1985
Radcliffe College, 3593
Radcliffe Institute, 3483, 3536
Radl, Shirley, Adden.
Radloff, Barbara, Adden.
Rafiq, Bashir Ahmed, 1658
Rainwater, Karole K., 836
Rainwater, Lee, 191, 366, 836, 1659
Rakasataya, Amari, 337
Ralph, Diane, 1215
Ramelson, Marian, 1028
Ramos, Maria, 1660
Ramsey, Glenn V., 3125
Ramu, G. N., 192
Rank, Beata, 3033
Ransel, D. L., 1191
Rapoport, Rhona, 154
Rapoport, Robert N., 154
Rappaport, Philip, 1279
Rathbone, Eleanor R., 914, 1496, 2649
Rattray, R. S., 3034
Raushenbush, Esther, 329
Raven, Charles E., 2265
Ravenel, Florence Leftwich, 1029
Ray, Gordon N., Adden.
Rayburn, Letricia G., 3126
Reagan, Barbara B., Adden. (Amer. Econ.
  Assoc.)
Reed, Evelyn, 1280, 1980, 2791
Reed, Ruth, 193
Reeve, Tapping, 1192
Reeves, Nancy, 104 [Intro.]
Reich, Emil, 1595
Reich, Wilhelm, 452-453
Reid, Inez Smith, 2116
Reik, Theodore, 1769, 1813, 2910-2911
Reimar, Roberto Fernandez, 1981
Reinach, Adolphe, 2076
Reinhard, J. R., 2266
Reische, Diana L., 1596
Reitzenstein, F. F. von, 3035
Renard, Marie Thérèse, 1920
Rendon, Armando B., 2117
Rennie, Susan, Adden. (Grimstad)
Renshaw, J. E., 3388
Republican Party, National Committee,
  1530, 3537
Resnik, Byron J., 837
Resnik, H. L., 837

Resource Center on Women, 3538
Revard, Stella, 2792
Reyher, R. H., 3036
Reynolds, Myra, 1704, 2609
Reynolds, R., 3037
Rheingold, J., 2912
Rheinhardt, Emil Alphons, 2610
Rhondda, Viscountess, 1030
Rice, Clara C., 1735
Rice, John R., 2267
Richard, Jane, 1814
Richards, Britten D., 1148
Richards, Caroline Cowles, Adden.
Richards, Laura E., 2611
Richards, Marion K., 2793
Richardson, Aubrey, 2268
Richardson, Jane, 1814
Richardson, Stephen, 194
Richmond, Al, 1531
Richmond, Mabel, 2269
Richmond, Mary E., 1031
Rickert, E., 1815
Ridley, Jeanne Claire, 337
Riegel, Robert E., 105, 1423 [Intro.], 1816
Riesman, David, 297, 3127
Rinehart, Mary Roberts, 2612
Rischbieth, Bessie Mabel, 1921
Rittenhouse, Mignon, 2613
Rivers, Caryl, Adden.
Roach, Mary Ellen, 1817
Roberts, G. Lawrence, Adden. (Jacobson)
Roberts, Robert W., 195
Roberts, Silvia, Adden. (Jacobson)
Roberts, Thomas D., 838
Robertson, Constance Noyes, 915
Robertson, James A., 2029
Robin, Florence B., 329
Robins, Elizabeth, 1032
Robinson, Caroline Hadley, 839
Robinson, Florett, 2714
Robinson, Harriet H., 1364, Adden.
Robinson, Helen J., 2080
Robinson, Josephine DeMott, 2485
Robinson, Lora H., 749
Robinson, Marie N., 106
Robinson, Victor, 840
Robinson, Wilhelmena S., 2614
Roby, Pamela A., 669, 957-958
Rodocanachi, E., 1705
Roe, Dorothy, 1226
Roesch, Roberta F., 1922
Roesgen, Joan, 2913
Roessing, Jennie Bradley, 3054
Rogers, Gladys, Adden. (Wormser)
Rogers, Katherine M., 2794
Rogers, Walter C., 819
Rojas, Marta, 1284
Rokkan, Stein, 1324
Rollins, Charlemae Hill, 2615
Romain, Col. Charles Armand, 2077
Romer, Karen T., 750
Rongy, A. J., 841

Roosevelt, (Anna) Eleanor, 1439, 1446,
1457-1459, 2541, 2553, 2616
Root, Grace C., 945
Roper, Elmo, 1033
The Roper Organization, Inc., Adden.
Rose, Arnold, 107
Rosen, E., 2855
Rosen, Harold, 842
Rosen, Marjorie, Adden.
Rosenberg, Bernard, 369, 3289
Rosenberg, Carroll Smith, 108, 1597
Rosenberg-Dishman, Marie Barovic, 1034,
1460, 1493, 3476, Adden.
Rosenberg, Morris, 3128
Rosenfeld, Carl, 3257
Rosenthal, Abigail L., Adden. (Mothersill)
Rosner, Marjorie, Adden.
Ross, Ishbel, 2617-2619, Adden.
Ross, J. F. S., 1494
Ross, Nancy Wilson, 2030
Ross, Rugh, Adden. (Iglitzen)
Ross, Susan Deller, 1035, 1862
Rossi, Alice, 297, 546, 751-753, 844-845,
1015, 1923
Rostow, Edna G., 297
Roszak, Betty, 109
Roszak, Theodore, 109
Roth, Lillian, 2620
Rothfeld, O., 1818
Rothman, Betsy, 1095
Rothman, David J., 1141
Rothman, Shiela N., 1141, Adden. (Leiber-
man)
Rothschild, Joan A., 1540-1541
Rotstein, Abraham, 990
Rotzoll, Christa, 1036
Roundtree, J., 3129
Roundtree, M., 3129
Rover, C., 367, 1037, 1461
Rowbotham, Sheila, 1038, 1462
Royal Commission on Marriage and Divorce,
1128
Royce, Marion, 670
Royden, Agnes Maude, 671, 1039, 1331,
2270-2271
Rubenstein, B., 2303
Rubin, Isadore, 369
Rubin, Sarah, 3484
Rue, Vincent M., 1256
Rugg, Winnifred King, 1040
Ruhmer, W., 1706
Ruiz, Alonso C., 261
Rulla, Luigi M., 2893
Rump, E. E., 2894
Rumyantseva, M., 1004
Runge, Emily Foote, 3054
Russ, Joanna, Adden.
Russ, Lavinia, 368
Russell, Bertrand, 262
Russell, Dora, 1041
Russell, F., 1819
Russell, Letty M., Adden.

Russell, Thomas H., 3359
Rutko, Victor, 846
Ryan, M. S., 1820
Ryrie, Charles Caldwell, 2272

S

Saario, Terry N., Adden. (Lieberman)
Sachs, Emanie (Arling, Emanie Nahm Sachs),
2621
Sachs, Hannelore, 2795
Sagarin, Edward, 110, 369
Saghaphi, M. M. K., 370
St. Denis, Ruth, 2622
St. John, Christopher, 2623
Salaff, Janet Wietzer, 1257
Salazar, Fernando, 371
Sale, Edith T., 2031
Salmon, Lucy Maynard, 1661
Salper, Roberta, 672, 1924 [Intro.]
Samora, Julian, 2118
Sampson, Glenda, 3423
Samuelson, Agnes, 548
Sand, George (Amadine Aurore Lucie Dupin,
Baroness Dudevant), 1046, 1926, 2426,
Adden. (Doumic, Moffat)
Sander, Emilie, 2279
Sanders, Marion K., 329, 1312
Sandler, Bernice, 3130-3131
Sandlund, Maj-Britt, 673, 1096 [Intro.]
Sanger, Margaret, 196, 786, 816, 824, 847-
849, 1043, 1617, 1851, 1926, 2469,
2545, 2548, 2624, Adden. (Richards)
Sanger, William W., 1925
Sapery, Elizabeth, Adden.
Sarasvati, Pundita Ramabai, 547
Sargeant, Winthrop, 2625
Sarker, Subhash C., 850
Sarrell, Phillip, 2370
Sartin, Pierrette, 1042, 1227
Sassower, Doris L., 3389
Sato, Toshihiko, 2796
Scanzoni, John H., 197, Adden.
Schafley, Phyllis, Adden. (Jacobson)
Schein, Virginia E., 2914
Scheinfeld, Amram, 1598
Schickel, Richard, 2523
Schiller, Anita, 3390
Schlesinger, Benjamin, 1097, 3485
Schlossberg, Nancy K., 668
Schmalhausen, Samuel D., 399, 886
Schmidt, Dolores B., 674
Schmidt, Earl R., 674
Schmidt, Minna Moscherosch, 2626
Schmidt, W., 3038
Schneiderman, Beth K., 2797
Schneiderman, Lucy G., 3290
Schneiderman, Rose, 3290
Schneir, Miriam, 1043 [Intro.], 1926
Schoenfeld, Jermann, 1599 [Intro.]
Schonberger, Richard J., 3258, 3304

Schopenhauer, Arthur, 2798
Schreiber, Sarah Etta, 1707
Schreiner, Olive, 2275, 2519, 3132
Schrom, Nancy E., 1571
Schuck, Victoria, 754
Schuller, Mary Craig, 1662
Schulman, Alix Kates, 916
Schultz, Theodore W., 3133
Schuman, Pat, 3486
Schur, Edwin M., 198, 369, 851
Schurman, Ann Maria à, 1927
Schuster, Alice, 1258
Schwartz, Bella, 3391
Schwartz, Eleanor Brantley, 3392
Schwartz, Ellen Bay, 2915
Schwartz, Jane, 3259
Schwartz, Pepper, 639
Schwendinger, Herman, 454
Schwendinger, Julia, 454
Schwieger-Lerchenfeld, Amand, Freiherr
    von, 2799
Scienfeld, A., 2916
Scobie, Alistair, 1600
Scofield, Nanette E., 3260
Scotch, C. Bernard, 3425
Scott, A. C., 372
Scott, Anne Firor, 675, 890, 1044, 1928-
    1929, 3261
Scott, Clifford H., 455
Scott, Denham, 2627
Scott, Foresman, and Company, 1244
Scripps College, 3594
Scudder, Vida Dutton, 2273
Scully, Diane, 111
Seagoe, May V., 548
Seaman, Barbara R., 456, 1228
Sears, P., 2917
Sears, R. R., 2917
Seashore, Harold G., 2918
Secor, Cynthia, 750
Secrest, Meryle, Adden.
Seed, Suzanne, Adden.
Seeley, John R., 373
Seelye, L. Clark, 676
Seidelson, David E., 1137
Seiden, Rita, 369
Seidenberg, Faith A., 1193, 1204
Seidenberg, Robert, 2800, Adden.
Seip, Ellen Bonnevie, 1663 [Intro.]
Seler, Cecilia, 1664
Sells, Lucy W., 3487
Seltman, Charles, 1708
Senderowitz, Judith, Adden. (Peck)
Serra, G., 2339
Serebrennikov, G. N., 1045
Sessions, Ruth H., 917
Sewall, May Wright, 938
Sewall, Richard Benson, Adden.
Sewall, Samuel E., 1665
Seward, Georgene A., 112
Sexton, Patricia Cayo, 329
Seyersted, Per, 2628

Shade, William G., Adden. (Friedman)
Shaffer, Harry G., 755
Shaffer, Juliet P., 755
Shah, Diane K., 1195
Shainess, Natalie, 2371
Shallcross, Ruth, 3262
Shankweiler, Penelope J., 427
Shapera, I., 3039
Shapley, Deborah, 1229
Sharwin, Robert, 1196
Shaw, Anna Howard, 2575, 2629, 3054
Shaw, M., 3040
Shea, John R., 3134
Shedd, C. L., 1775
Sheehan, Marion Turner, 2274
Sheehy, Gail, 1281
Shelley, Mary Wollstonecraft (Godwin),
    2738, 2766
Sheresky, Norman, 263
Sherfey, Mary Jane, 457, 2372, 2919
Sherriffs, A. C., 87, 2892, 2920
Sherman, Julia Ann, 2921, 3488
Sherwin, Robert Viet, Adden.
Sherwood-Dunn, B., 2373
Shorter, Edward, 199
Showalter, Elaine, 2801
Shridevi, S., 677
Shropshire, D. W. T., 3041
Shuler, Nettie R., 1335, 1425
Sibler, Iriven, 2119
Sickels, Eleanor, 2630-2631
Sidel, Ruth, Adden.
Siefer, R., 3567
Sigworth, Heather, 1230
Sikora, Mitchell, 852
Silberberg, Marjorie M., 3263, Adden.
    (Wormser)
Sillen, Samuel, 1930
Silver, Henry K., 3426
Silverman, Phyllis R., 374
Silverman, Sandra T., Adden. (Macleod)
Sim, R. Alexander, 373
Simkins, Francis, 1601
Simmons, H. J., 1197
Simmons, J., 3567
Simmons, Jean, 389
Simms, Madeleine, 853
Simon, Rita, 678, 756
Simon, William, 369, 425
Simons, H. J., 1197, 3042
Simpson, Bishop, 2291
Sinclair, Andrew, 1046, 1424
Sioussat, Anna M., 2032
Sister Marie-Andre Du Sacre-Coeur, 528-
    529, 1450, 3023
Sister Mary Ethel, 375
Sklar, Kathryn K., Adden.
Skolnick, Arlene S., 200
Skolnick, Jerome H., 200
Slaughter, Diana T., 376
Slevin, Dennis P., 3226
Sloan, Edith B., 3305

Sloman, Judith, 2802
Slosson, Preston W., 1365
Smeal, Eleanor C., 1448
Smedley, Agnes, 2632
Smigel, Erwin D., 369
Smith, Anna Greene, 549
Smith, Catherine, 1490
Smith, D. L., 854
Smith, Ethel M., 1198
Smith, Florence, 2633
Smith, Henry Nash, 2803
Smith, Jessica, 550
Smith, Julia E., 1199
Smith, Lillian, 1666
Smith, Lawrence J., Adden. (Jacobson)
Smith, Margaret Chase, 1480, 1484, 1490, 1495
Smith, M. F., 3043
Smith, Munroe, 1416
Smith, Page, 1931
Smith, Paul Jordon, 2275
Smith, Raymond, 1138
Smith, Roy, 795
Smith, T. R., 1667
Smuts, Robert W., 3135 [Intro.]
Smyth, Ethel, 2623, 2634
Snow, Helen (Wales, Nym), 551
Snyder, Agnes, 2635
Snyder, Charles McCool, 2636
Snyder, Eloise C., 1200
Sochen, June, 1932, 2637, Adden.
Solton, Martha Jane, 3489
Somerville, Rose M., 679
Sone, Monica, 2120
Sontag, Susan, 552
Soong, Ching-ling, (Madame Sun Yat-Sen), 1047, 2505
Sophia Smith Collection, 3595
Sorensen, Robert C., 458
Sorokin, Pitirim A., 459
Source Book Press, 3596
Souter, L. S., 3393
Southam, A. L., 2374
Southard, Mabel M., 2276
Spacks, Patricia M., 113
Spargo, John, 1139, 1532
Sparrow, Walter Shaw, 2804
Spatt, Beverly Moss, 389
Spaull, Hebe, 939
Speer, David C., 264
Spencer, Anna Garlin, 918, 1602 [Intro.], 1709
Spencer, Byron G., 3053
Spiegel, Jeanne, 3490-3493
Spinner, Stephanie, 114
Spiro, Melford E., 201
Spoor, Lillie M., 3360
Sprague, Henry H., 1201
Sprague, Rosemary, 2638, 2805
Sprague, William Forrest, 2033
Springer, John, Adden.
Spruill, Julia C., 2034-2035

Stacey, Judith, Adden. (Lieberman)
Staffieri, J. Robert, 2375
Staines, Graham L., 612
Staley, Edgcumbe, 2169
Stalin, Joseph, 1976
Stambler, Sookie, 1282
Stammler, Wolfgang, 1603
Stampp, Kenneth, 2121
Stannard, Una, Adden. (Hochschild)
Stanton, Elizabeth Cady, 1043, 1366 [Intro.], 1378, 1391, 1398-1399, 1819, 2277, 2575, 2592, 2639-2640, 3568
Stanton, Theodore, 1048, 1399, 2640
Staples, Robert, 202
Starke, Barbara, 378
Starr, Rachel, 612
State Bar of Wisconsin, Adden.
State Government, 1518
Stavsova, Helen, 680
Stearns, Bertha Monica, 1933
Steegmuller, Francis, Adden.
Steele, Robert, 2278
Stein, Gertrude, 2641
Stein, Martha, Adden.
Steinem, Gloria, 1088
Steiner, Stan, 2122
Steinmann, Ann, 3494
Stembridge, Jane, 1985
Stendhal, Krister, 2279
Stenton, Doris Mary, 1604-1605
Stephens, Kate, 115
Stephens, Winifred, 1982
Stern, Bernhard J., 1668
Stern, Elizabeth G., 2123
Stern, Geraldine, 2642
Stern, Madeline B., 1934, 2643-2644
Stern, Meta Lilienthal. See Lilienthal, Meta.
Stevens, Barbara, 2923
Stevens, Doris, 2645
Stevens, Evelyn P., 1259
Stewart, Elinore, 2036
Stewart, Ella Seass, 3054
Stewart, Mrs. Eliza Daniel, (Mother Stewart), 946
Stewart, I., 2376
Stewart, Margaret, 2490
Stewart, William Rhinelander, 919
Stiehm, Judith, Adden. ("Women . . .")
Stockham, Alice B., 856
Stockholm: The Joint Female Labour Council, 3183
Stocks, Mary D., 1496
Stoller, R. J., 116
Stone, Betsey, 1179
Stone, Kathryn H. Meyers, 3539
Stone, Lucy, 967, 1219, 1283, 1378, 1386, 2419, 2421
Stopes, Marie Carmichael, 857-858, 2430, 2569
Storer, Horatio Robinson, 2924
Storrer, Anne-Marie, 859

Stowe, Harriet Beecher, 933, 1717, 2384, 2410, 2427, 2486, 2592, 2646, 2684, 2717
Stowe, Lyman Beecher, 2646
Strachey, Lytton, 2170
Strachey, Rachel Conn (Costelloe), 920, 947, 1049 [Intro.]-1050, 1400, 2467, 2647-2649, 3136
Strainchamps, Ethel, Adden.
Strangway, A. K., 3044
Strauss, Robert P., Adden.
Strickland, Bonnie R., 461
Strindberg, August, 2275, 2806
Strober, Myra, 3495
Stuart, Dorothy M., 117
Stuart, Janet Erskine, 681
Stuart, Lee, 3448
Stuart, Martha, 860
Stycos, J. Mayone, 789
Sudlow, Elizabeth W., 2280
Suelzle, Maryean, Adden. (Hochschild)
Suenens, Leon Joseph, 2281
Sugimoto, Etsu Inagaki, 2650
Suhl, Yuri, 921, 2651
Sullerot, Evelyne, 118, 3137
Sullivan, Victoria, Adden.
Summers, Montague, 2703
Summerskill, Edith, 1497
Sumner, Helen L., 3054, 3138
Sumner, William G., 682
Suniewick, Nancy, 3435
Sun Yat-Sen, Madame. See Soong, Ching-Ling.
Sussman, Marvin R., 333
Sussman, Robert, 1490
Sutherland, H., 2376
Sverdlov, G. M., 1005, 1140
Swaminathan, V. S., 1051
Swan, Helena, 1770, 2807
Swann, Nancy Lee, 2652
Swarthmore College, 3597
Sweden, National Labour Market Board of, 3361 [Intro.]
Swedish Institute for Cultural Relations with Foreign Countries, 861
Sweet, James A., 380, 3264, 3306
Sweetman, Maude, 1498
Swift, Kate, 1017
Swisshelm, Jane Grey, 922-923, 1070, 2653, 2687
Swords, Betty, 1935
Sykes, Christopher, 2654
Symonds, Alexandra, 2925
Symons, H. J., 1936-1937
Syrkin, Marie, 1499

T

Tait, Marjorie, 1313
Tak, Jean vander, Adden.
Talbot, D. Amaury, 3045
Tallman, I., 381

Talmon, Yonina, 119, Adden.
Tania, 1284
Tanner, Leslie B., 1938
Tara, Bill, 3394
Tarbell, Ida M., 382-383, 1435, 2655-2656
Tart, Marjorie, 1313, 1463
Tatarinova, Nadezhda, 1983 [Intro.]
Tatum, Noreen Dean, 2282
Taylor, G. Rattray Stirling, 460, 1285
Taylor, Ida Ashworth, 2171
Taylor, James M., 683, 1939
Taylor, Jean Anne M., 684
Taylor, Susie King, 2078
Taylor, Suzanne S., Adden. (Lieberman)
Tchernavin, Tatiana, 384
Tegg, William, 265
Temple, O., 3046
Terman, Lewis M., 2926
Terrell, May Church, 1367, 2651
Terry, Ellen, 924
Theobald, Robert, 1606
Theodore, Athena, 3395
Thieme, Hugo, 1607
Thomas, Adah B., 2377
Thomas, Anna L. B., 2037
Thomas, Antoine Leonard, 1736
Thomas, Dorothy, 3396
Thomas, Dorothy S., 2124
Thomas, Edith, 1286
Thomas, Katsy, 1545
Thomas, Norman, 66, 1525
Thomas, Paul, 1669
Thomson, Patricia, 2808
Thomson, Judith J., 862
Thompson, Bertha (Boxcar), 2658
Thompson, Clara, 2927-2929
Thompson, Dorothy Lampen, Adden.
Thompson, Edward, 3139
Thompson, Flora McDonald, 3140
Thompson, Helen Bradford, 2930
Thompson, Lawrence G., 2241
Thompson, Mary Lou, 120, 1052
Thompson, Norman L., 461
Thompson, William, 1670
Thrall, Margaret E., 2283
Thwaite, Ann, Adden.
Tickner, Frederick Windham, 1608, 3141
Tiemeyer, Raymond, 2284
Tien, H. Yuan, 863
Tierney, Patricia, 3427
Tietze, C., 864-867
Tims, Margaret, 925
Timms, Duncan W. B., 553
Timms, Elizabeth A., 553
Tingsten, Herbert, 1326 [Intro.]
Tinker, Irene, 612, 3397
Tittle, Carol Kehr, Adden. (Lieberman)
Tjan, Tjoe-som, 266
Tobias, Sheila, 3496-3497
Tobin, Kay, 462
Todd, John Rev., 463-464, 1053
Todd, Margaret, 2659

Todd, Robert E., 2809
Tolchin, Leon, Adden.
Tolchin, Martin, Adden.
Tolchin, Susan J., Adden.
Tolman, Mary H., 3428
Tolstoy, Leo, 2810
Tomalin, Claire, Adden.
Tomkinson, W. S., 2603
Torbert, Alice C., 2038
Torrey, Jane W., 734
Totaro, V., 720
Toussiant, Philippe, 868
Trahey, Jane, 1821
Trecker, Janice Law, 685, Adden. (Lieberman)
Trent, Ray, 3336, 3362
Trevelyan, George M., 1671
Trevelyan, Janet Penrose, 1417
Tripp, Maggie, Adden.
Trilling, Diana, 2811
Tropman, John E., 3265
Trotsky, Leon, 203
Trow, JoAnne J., 686
Trowbridge, Lydia Jones, 948
Truax, Ann, 758
Truette, Everett E., 2726
Trumball, Benjamin, 1141
Trumpeter, Margo, 121
Trussell, James, 869
Tryon, Ruth W., 687, 2391
Tsuchigrave, Robert, Adden.
Tuan Chi-hsien, 870
Tucker, Sophie, 2660
Tuckerman, Joseph, 3142
Tudor, Jeannette, 44
Tufts, Eleanor, Adden.
Turkey, Minstry of the Interior, 1609
Turner, E. M., 2482
Turner, Loretta E., 3143
Turner, Marjorie B. S., 3144 [Intro.]
Tuttle, Florence Guertin, 2931
Tuttle, Helen W., 3398
Tweedie, Ethel B., 2079
Tyler, Edward B., 3047
Tyler, Edward T., 2378
Tyler, Parker, 2812

U

Udry, J. Richard, 369, 2379
Ulanov, Ann Belford, 2285
Ulrich, Celeste, Adden. (Lieberman)
Ungor, Beraet Z., 337
United Nations, 379, 688-689, 959-960, 1054-1057, 1142-1143, 1202, 3145-3146
United Nations, Dept. of Economic and Social Affairs, Secretariat, 379
UNESCO, United Nations Economic and Social Commission, 122, 688-689

United Presbyterian Church (U.S.A.), 2286
U.S. Bureau of the Census, 871, 3147-3148
U.S. Bureau of Labor, 1239, 3149-3150
U.S. Bureau of Labor Statistics, 3151
U.S. Citizen's Advisory Council on the Status of Women, see also Citizen's Advisory Council on the Status of Women
U.S. Civil Service Commission, 1233-1234, 3152, 3227-3228, 3429
U.S. Communist Party, 1317
U.S. Congress, House Committee on Education and Labor, 3229-3230, 3235-3236
U.S. Congress, House Committee on the Judiciary, 3231
U.S. Congress, House Committee on Rules, 1203, 1940
U.S. Congress, Joint Committee on Education and Labor, 3153
U.S. Congress, Joint Economic Committee, Adden.
U.S. Congress, Senate Committee on Finance, 204
U.S. Congress, Senate Committee on Labor and Public Welfare, 3232, Adden.
U.S. Congress, Senate Judiciary Committee, 1235
U.S. Department of Commerce, Bureau of the Census, 1672
U.S. Department of Defense, 2080
U.S. Department of Health, Education and Welfare, 690, 872, Adden.
U.S. Department of Health, Education and Welfare, Social Security Administration, 3154
U.S. Department of Labor, 205, 691-692, 1058, 1236-1239, 1500, 1673-1674 [Intro.], 3155-3179, [Intro., no. 3165], 3266-3267, 3291-3292, 3363, 3399, 3430, Adden.
U.S. Department of Labor, Women's Bureau, 691, 1236, 1239, 1500, 2080, 3233-3236, 3453
U.S. Equal Employment Opportunity Commission, 1240, 3180-3181, 3211
U.S. Interdepartmental Committee on the Status of Women, 1104
THE UNITED STATES LAW WEEK, 813, 843, 855, 877
U.S., Office of the President, 206
U.S. President's Commission on the Status of Women, 693, 1105-1113 [Intro.], 1250, 3182
U.S. Supreme Court, 813, 1165, 1216, 1354
U.S. Women's Bureau, 2080
Unwin, Harriet, 1041
Upham, Charles W., 1771
Upton, George Putnam, 2813
Urlin, Ethel L., 267
Ursulines of New York, 2287
Useem, Ruth Hill, 694

V

Vaerting, Mathias, 123
Vaerting, Mathilde, 123
Valen, Henry, 1324, 1501-1502
Valparaiso University Law Review, 1204
Van Aken, Carol G., 3382
Van Allen, Judith, 1448, Adden.
  ("Women . . .")
Van Buren, E. Douglas, 1772
van der Valk, M. H., 207
Van Der Vries, Bernice T., 1518
Van der Warter, Ely, 2380
Van Doren, Dorothy, 2814
Van Ettin, Ida M., 3293
Van Fleet, David D., 762
Van Hoosen, Bertha, 2661
Van Kleeck, Mary, 3054
Van Laer, Arnold J. E., 2039
Van Rensselaer, Mrs. John King, 385
Van Schaick, Frances L., 3431
Van Vuuren, Nancy, Adden.
Varigny, Charles V., 1610
Vasquez, Enriqueta Lonquae, 2125
Vassar College, 695-696
Vaughn, Mary C., Adden. (Brockett)
Vavich, Dee Ann, 1059
Veblen, Thorstein, 556, 1675, 1780, 1822
Velazquez, Loreta Janeta, 2081
Velimesis, Margery L., 1205
Verba, Sidney, 1290 [Intro.]
Veroff, Joseph, Adden.
Verway, David I., 3184
Vicinus, Martha, 1676, 1941
Vickland, Ellen Elizabeth, 557
Vidal, Mirta, 386
Vietor, Agnes C., 2662
Vigman, Fred K., 1611
Vincent, Clark E., 208
Violette, Augusta Genevieve, 2815
Virginia Slims Polls, 522-523, Adden. (Roper)
Visher, Stephen S., 2663
Vladeck, Judith, 3185
Vogel, Ezra F., 137
von Krafft-Ebing, Richard, 465
Vreede de Stuers, Cora, 1368, 1942, 2288
Vroegh, Karen, 65

W

Waagenaar, Sam, 1612
Wade, Elizabeth, 2816
Wadia, A. R., 1943, 2289
Wadsworth, Benjamin, 209
Waggoner, Karen, 663
Wagenknect, Edward C., 2664
Wägner, Elin, 558
Wakamori, Taro, 1613
Wald, Lillian, 898, 2665-2666
Wales, Nym. See Snow, Helen.
Walker, Arda Susan, 1710

Walker, Kenneth, 124, 466
Walker, Lola C., 1401
Walkowitz, Judith R., 610
Wallace, Anthony F. C., 2126
Wallace, Irving, 2667
Wallach, Aleta, 1204
Wallin, Paul, 125
Walsh, James J., 2290
Walsh, William, 126
Walsh, William Thomas, 2172
Walters, Ronald G., Adden.
Ward, Arabella, 1601
Ward, Barbara E., 1944 [Intro.], 2668
Warden, J., 1779
Wardle, Ralph M., 2669
Ware, Caroline Farrar, 559
Warren, Constance, 697
Warren, Mary Anne, Adden. (Mothersill)
Warren, Patricia A., 3472
Warton, Jane, 1393
Washington, Joseph R., Adden.
Wasserstrom, William, 2817
Waterman, William Randall, 926
Waters, Clara Erskine Clement, 2818
Waters, Ethel, 2670
Watson, Paul Barron, 2671
Watts, Alan, 467
Webb, Beatrice, 880, 1455, 1856, 2448,
  2672-2673
Webster, Rev. Thomas, 2291
Wedel, Cynthia, 2292
Weibull, Curt Hugo J., 2173
Weigert-Vowinkel, Edith, 3048
Weinberg, Nancy, 1490
Weingarten, Violet, 387
Weininger, O., 468
Weinman, Saul, 3289
Weinstein, James, 1984
Weiss, E. B., 3186
Weiss, Jessica M., 1464
Weiss-Rosmarin, Trude, 560
Weisstein, Naomi, 1908, 2932-2933
Weitzman, Lenore J., 763, 1186
Weitzman, Murray S., 3187
Wells, Audrey Seiss, 1448
Wells, Ida B., 2474, 2674
Wells, J. E., Adden. (Bunkle)
Wells, Jean A., 698, 3237
Wells, Richard S., 1162
Wells, Theodora, 3378
Welter, Barbara, 127
Werlich, Robert, 2675
Werner, Emmy, 1448, 1503-1504 [Intro.],
  2831
Werner, Peter, 128
West, Anne Grant, 129, 614
West, Geoffrey, 2676
Westermarck, Edward, 268 [Intro.]-269
Westervelt, Esther M., 389, 3498
Westoff, Charles F., 873

Wetch, Galbraith, 1677
Wetzel, Betty, Adden. (Lieberman)
Wexford, Mary, 3449
Whalen, Richard E., 2934
Whaley, Sarah J., 3499
Wharton, Ann H., 2040-2041
Wharton, Edith, 388, 1372, 2677, 2695, 2753, 2819-2820
Wheatley, Phillis, 2615, 2821
Wheatley, Vera, 2678
Wheeler, Elizabeth H., 1662
Wheeler, Helen R., 3500
Whicher, George F., 2679
Whisnant, Charleen, Adden. (Russ)
White, Ebe Minerva, 2293
White, Elizabeth N., 2042
White, James J., 1206
White, Jean Bickmore, 1945
White, Lynn J., 699
White, Martha S., 2935
Whitehurst, Robert N., 436
Whiteside, Elena, 3188
Whiting, J., 2917
Whitman, Karen, 1985
Whittaker, Peter, Adden.
Whitton, Mary O., 1678, 2680
Whyte, William H., 561
Wicker, Rany, 462
Wides, Louise, 1490
Wieth-Knudson, K. A., 1614
Wilde, Oscar, 3571
Wilensky, Harold L., 3189
Willard, Emma, 1247, 1679, 2500
Willard, Frances E., 941, 947-953, 1388, 1819, 2501, 2681-2682
Willcoxen, Harriet, 1505
Willett, Mabel Hurd, 3364-3365
Williams, Fannie Barrier, 1061
Williams, Gertrude, 3190
Williams, Jesse Lynch, 1369
Williams, Josephine J., 548
Williams, Maithy, 3294
Williams, Mary W., 1711
Williams, Maxine, 1062, 2127
Williams, Penny, 1545
Williamson, G. C., 1712
Williamson, Robert C., 112
Willis, Eola, 2822
Wilner, Charles, 1144
Wilson, Alice, 617
Wilson, B. M., 1063
Wilson, Edith Bolling Galt, 2683
Wilson, Forrest, 2684
Wilson, James G., 3513
Wilson, Jennie L., 1207
Wilson, Justina Leavitt, 1327
Wilson, Roger H. L., 35-36
Wilson, Victoria, 612, 2381
Winch, Robert F., 210, 270
Winick, Charles, 130, 369
Winks, Robin W., 2128
Winslade, R., 3393

Winslow, Mary N., 1509, 2394
Winsor, Mary, 3054
Winter, Alice Ames, 1615
Wipper, Audrey, 1064
Wiseman, Jacqueline P., 211
Withers, Glenn, 234
Witke, Roxanne, 562
Wittenmyer, Annie, 953
Wittfogel, Karl A., 3049
Wolf, Margery, 212
Wolfson, Theresa, 1397 [Intro.], 2061, 3298 [Intro.]
Wollstonecraft, Mary, 983, 1043, 1065 [Intro.], 1285, 1851, 1926, 2647, 2669, 2814, Adden. (Tomalin)
Woman's History Library, 3599
Woman's Peace Party, 935
Women's Action Alliance, 3542
Women's Caucus for the Modern Languages, 3503
Women's Center, 3544
Women's Equity Action League (WEAL), 1208, 3545
Women's History Research Center, 3547, Adden.
Women's International Democratic Federation, 1069
Women's International League for Peace and Freedom, 911, 1826
Women's National Abortion Action Coalition, 3548
Women on Words and Images, Adden.
Wong, Jade Snow, 2129, 2685
Wood, Ann Douglas, 2823
Wood, Mary I., 3054, 3550
Wood, Myrna, Adden. (Baritz)
Woodbury, Helen L. S., 1429
Woodham-Smith, Cecil, 2174, 2686
Woodhull, Victoria (Claflin), 874, 905, 927, 2535, 2565, 2617, 2621
Woodroofe, Debby, 1946
Woodsmall, Ruth Frances, 390-391, 566
Woodward, Helen Beale, 1070, 1947, 2687
Woody, Thomas, 703, 1948
Woolf, Virginia, 1043, 1926, 2409, 2413, 2702, 2771, 2824, Adden. (Moffat)
World Council of Churches, 2199
Wormser, Ellen, Adden.
Wormer-Migot, Olga, 1618
Worthen, Samuel C., 1773
Worthington, C. J., 2081
Wortis, Helen, 131
Wright, Sir Almroth E., 1418
Wright, Carroll D., Adden. (Robinson)
Wright, Celeste Turner, 2825
Wright, Eleanor, 875
Wright (D'Arusmont), Frances, 897, 926, 1070, 1397, 1737, 2550, 2601, 2687
Wright, Frederick Adam, 2826
Wright, Helena, 469, 2936
Wright, H. M., 3031
Wright, Richardson, 2043

Wright, Thomas, 1713
Wu, Shu-chiung, 2688
Wughtman, John, 470
Wulffen, E., 471
Wyatt, Dorothea E., 912
Wyker, M. A., 2295
Wykes-Joyce, M., 1823
Wylie, Philip, 2827
Wyndham, Horace, 2689

XYZ

Yaffe, Barbara, 3191
Yaffe, Byron, 3191
Yale Law Journal, 1153
Yale University, Committee on the Status of
    Professional Women, 766
Yamada, Waka, 567
Yamakawa, Kikue, 1071
Yancey, William L., 1659
Yang, C. K., 213
Yanow, Jo, 3432
Yaukey, David, 876
Yetman, Norman, 1987
Ying-chao Teng, 1072
Yohalem, Alice, 318
Yorburg, Betty, Adden.
Yost, Edna, 2690-2691 [Intro.]
Young, Ann Eliza, 271
Young, Donald, 214
Young, K., 1824
Young, Leontine, 215
Young, Louise M., 392, 1073 [Intro.]-1074
Young, Miriam, 3475
Young, W. C., 2937
Young, Wayland, 472
Young Women's Christian Association,
    National Board Library, 3600
Youssef, Nadia H., 3192
Yu-lan Lu, 1075
Zacharis, John C., 1430
Zahm, John Augustine, 1714
Zapoleon, Marguerite Wykoff, 548, 704
Zarechnak, Galina V., 2382
Zavin, Theodora, 1135
Zellner, Harriet, 3193
Zerbst, Fritz, 2296
Zetkin, Clara, 1260, 1287
Ziebarth, Marilyn, 1949
Ziegler, Mel, 1466
Zilboorg, G., 2938
Zimmer, Heinrich, 1774, 3050-3051
Ziv, Avner, 132
Zuker, Marvin A., 1209

INDEX OF JOURNAL ISSUES ENTIRELY DEVOTED TO WOMEN

American Behavioral Scientist, 612, 3397
American Federationist, 3297
AAUW Journal, 389, 569, 700
American Journal of Sociology, 339
Annals, 59, 110, 130, 134, 214, 279, 337,
    369, 392, 1074, 1349, 1893, 3054,
    3090, 3296 [Intro.]
Aramco, 1545
Black Scholar, 3447
The Bureaucrat, Adden. (Wormser)
Casa De Las Americas, 1981
Chicago Journalism Review, 3423
Daedalus, 297
Ebony, 2085
Feminist Studies, 610
Impact of Science on Society, 3084
Journal of Marriage and the Family, 3374,
    3387. Special Issue: Sexism in Family
    Studies. (Because of nature of subject,
    virtually all issues deal with women.)
Journal of Social Issues, 548
The Monist, Adden. (Mothersill)
New Generation, 1828
Quest: A Feminist Quarterly, Adden.
Trans-Action, 1639
Valparaiso University Law Review, 1204
    [Intro.]
Woman: A Journal of Liberation, 1985

INDEX OF PERSONS NOT CITED AS AUTHORS

Aïsse, 2420
Anderson, Elizabeth Garrett, 2647
Anderson, Eugenie (Ambassador), 1484
Andreas-Salome, Lou, Adden. (Peters)
Andrew, Fanny Fern, 935
Anguissola, Sofonisba, Adden. (Tufts)
Anza, Juan Bautista de, 1997
Arnold, Margaret Mansfield, 2429
Arnold, Mary, 2504
Ashburton, Lady, 2453
Astor, Lady (Nancy), 2647, 2654
Austen, Jane, 2428, 2766, 2814

Baba of Karo, 3043
Bacon, Delia, 1070, 2687
Barrett, Janie Porter, 2457
Bart, Lily, 2820
Barton, Clara, 2384, 2597
Baviere, Isabeau de, 2671
Beatrice, 1714
Beecher, Isabella, 2646
Beecher, Mary Foote, 2646
Bellow, Saul, 2743
Betham, Matilda, 2416
Bethune, Mary McLeod, 2457, 2521
Bird, Isabella, 2579
Blackstone, Sir William, 496
Blackwell, Elizabeth, 2305, 2336
Blackwell, Emily, 2336
Blaine, Harriet Stanwood, 2429
Bloomer, Amelia Jenks, 899, 1819
Blow, Susan E., 2635
Bly, Nellie, 2613, 2617
Boadicea, 2060
Bodichon, Barbara, 1241
Bogan, Louise, Adden. (Limmer)
Bolton, Frances, 1484-1485
Booth, Maude, 2226
Borgia, Lucretia, 2149
Botchkareva, Maria, 2067
Bourke-White, Margaret, 2463
Boyce, Neith, 2637
Boyd, Billie, 2630
Bradstreet, Ann, 2816
Braun, Eva, Adden. (Infield)
Breckinridge, Madeline McDowell, 1374
Bridget, Saint, 2290
Broadwick, Miss "Tiny," 2627
Brontë, Charlotte, 2414, 2698, 2757, 2814,
    Adden. (Masson)
Brontë, Emily, 2698, Adden. (Masson)
Brooks, Romaine, Adden. (Secrest)
Brown, Charlotte Hawkins, 2457
Brown, Helen Gurley, 2467
Browne, Mary, 2042
Browning, Elizabeth Barrett, 2698, Adden.
    (Clarke)
Buford, Harry T. See Velasquez, Loreta
    Janeta, Author Index.

Burney, Fanny, 2603, 2766, 2773, 2776
Burnett, Francis Hodgson, Adden. (Thwaite)
Burr, Elisa Bowen Jumel (Mrs. Aaron Burr),
    2617
Burroughs, Nannie Helen, 2457
Butler, Sarah Hildreth, 2429

Caballero, Fernan, 2416
Cabrini, Mother, 2290
Calvert, Eleanor, 2038
Cannon, Annie Jump, 2690
Cannon, Dr. Martha Hughes, 1945
Carlyle, Jane Welsh (Mrs. Thomas), 2504,
    2814
Carpenter, Mary, 2447
Carriera, Rosalba, 2420
Carroll, Anna Ella, 2503
Carter, Mrs., 1841
Carter, Elizabeth, 2416
Carteret, Elizabeth, 2007
Cassatt, Mary, 2709
Cather, Willa, 2423, 2695, 2753
Catherine of Aragon, 2163-2164, 2167
Catherine II (the Great), 1191, 2131-2132,
    2166, 2421, 2426
Chao, Empress of T'ang Dynasty, Adden.
    (Chun)
Chapman, Maria Weston, 931
Chiang, Ch'ing (Madame Mao), 2444
Chiang, Mayling Soong (Madame Chiang
    K'ai-shek), 2444, 2505, 2525
Chaucer, Geoffrey, 2782
Choiseul, Madame de, 2428
Christina, Queen (Denmark), 2135
Christina, Queen (Sweden), 2171, 2173
Churchill, Lady (Jennie) Randolph, 2568
Clarke, Dr. E. H., 629
Cleopatra, 1543, 2130, 2134, 2142, 2157,
    2159, 2433
Clifford, Lady Ann, 1712
Clough, Anne Jemina, 1242
Cobbe, Frances Power, 2447
Coke, Sir Edward, 496
Colby, Clara B., 1376
Colette, Adden. (Crossland, Brée)
Comte, Auguste, 2211
Cooke, Cardinal Terence J.,
Cooper, Fenimore, 2701
Corbin, Margaret C., 2058
Cori, Gerty, 2691
Covell, Edith, 2448
Cratty, Mabel, 2435
Crosby, Fanny, 2226
Curie, Madame Marie, 2455, 2597

d'Agoult, Marie, 2671
D'Annunzio, Gabriele, 2610
Dante, 1714

Darragh, Lydia, 2054, 2058
Davis, Sarah Taylor, 2429
de Baviere, Isabeau, 2671
de Choiseul, Madame, 2428
Deffand, Madame du, 2671
de France, Marie, Adden. (Kemp-Welsh)
De Gaulle, Yvonne (Mrs. Charles), 2489
de Huech, Catherine, 924
de Maintenon, Madame, 2421
Demorest, Ellen Curtis, 2618
Demorest, William Jennings, 2618
de Pisan, Adden. (Kemp-Welsh)
de Sévigné, Madame, 2428
de Staël, Madame, 2449, 2460, 2671
Devlin, Bernadette, 2470
de Zaldivar y Mendoza, Doña Ana, 2015
Dickinson, Anna, 895, 1667
Dickinson, Emily, 2679, 2712, 2805, Adden.
   (Sewall)
Dido, 2133
Disraeli, Mary (Mrs. Benjamin), 2504
Dix, Dorothea, 2410, 2422, 2567
Dodge, Grace, 2502
Doña Felisa. See Rincon de Gautier, Doña
   Felisa.
Draga, Queen (Serbia), 2145
Duse, Eleanora, 2610, 2770

Eastman, Crystal, 2637
Eisenhower, Ida, 2479
Elizabeth I (of England), 2153, 2156,
   Adden. (Johnson)
Elizabeth II (of England), 1840, 2141,
   Adden. (Morrah)
Elizabeth (of Austria), 2130
Emerson, Gladys, 2691
Empress Wu (China), 2147
Estaugh, Elizabeth Haddon, 2005
Esther, Queen (Israel), 2130
Eurydice, Queen (Macedonia), 2161
Eustochium, 1714
Eve, 1769

Farrell, Eileen, 2625
Faulkner, William, 2699
Fawcett, Millicent Carrett, Adden.
   (Thompson)
Field, Kate, 1070, 2687
Fielding, Sarah, 2765
Fiske, Fidelia, 2534
Forster, Edward Morgan, 2743
Fox, Kate, 2617
Fox, Margaret, 2617
Franco, Carmen (Sra. Francisco), 2489
Franklin, Deborah (Mrs. Benjamin), 1566
Fromm, Erich, 2902
Fry, Elizabeth, 2447, 2555, 2585, 2606
Furness, Betty, 2467

Gandhi, Indira, 1505, 2389, 2489
Gannett, Deborah Sampson, 2058, 2069.
   See also: Sampson, Deborah.
Gardner, Mrs. Jack, 2617
Garfield, Eliza Ballou, 2479
Gaskell, Elizabeth, 2698
Gay, Delphine, 2671
Girardin, 2211
Gladstone, Catherine, 2504
Godiva, Lady, 1808
Godolphin, Mrs., 2536
Goesart v. *Cleary,* 1216 [Intro.]
Goodrich, Annie Warburton, 2547
Goodrich v. *Goodrich,* 1125
Grasso, Ella, 1490
Gray, Lady Jane, 2609
Green, Hetty, 2617, Adden. (Flynn)
Gregory, Lady, 2438, Adden. (Adams)
Griggs v. *Duke Power Co.,* 3210
Guevara, Che, 1284
Gulama, Mme. Ella Koblo, 1483

Hamilton, Mary Agnes, 2649
Hamilton, Elizabeth (Mrs. Alexander), 1566
Hammon, Jupiter, 2615
Hansen, Julia Butler (Congresswoman),
   1490, 1493
Harper, Frances Ellen Watkins, 2615
Hart, Nancy, 2053, 2058
Haslett, Dame Caroline, 2576
Hawthorne, Nathaniel, 2699, 2700, 2809
Heckler, Margaret M. (Congresswoman),
   1490
Helen of Troy, 2433
Herschel, Caroline, 2416
Hertha, 2238
Herzen, Natalie, Adden. (Confino)
Hicks, Louise Day (Congresswoman), 1490
Hilda, Saint, 2290
Hind, E. Cora, 2506
Hinestrosa, Francisca, 2029
Hitler, Adolf, Adden. (Infield)
Ho Chi Minh, 1986
Homer, 2746
Hooker, Isabel Beecher, 1864
Horne, Marilyn, 2625
Howe, Elias, 1803
Hoyt v. *Florida,* 1165
Hrotsvitha, 2420
Huech, Catherine de, 924
Hunter, Jane Edna, 2457
Hutchinson, Anne, 1040, 1990, 2182,
   2226, 2630
Hyman, Libbie, 2690

Irish Sisters of Charity and Mercy, 2290
Isabella, Queen (Spain), 2172, Adden.
   (Plunket)

Jackson, Helen Hunt, Adden. (Banning)
Jarvis, Lucy, 2467
Jefferson, Martha (Mrs. Thomas), 1566
Jerome, Saint, 1714
Jewett, Sarah Orne, 2695
Joan of Arc, 2065, Adden. (Oliphant)
Johnson, Ladybird (Mrs. Lyndon), 2489
Johnson, Rebecca Baines, 2479
Johnston, Adelia A. Field, 2542
Jones, Agnes, 2534
Josephine, Empress (France), 2136, 2138, 2162
Jumel, Madame (Mrs. Aaron Burr), 2617

Kauffmann, Angelica, Adden. (Tufts)
Kelsey, Dr. Frances Oldham, 2351
Kennedy, Joan, Adden. (David)
Kennedy, Minnie, 2278
Kennedy, Rose, 2479
Killigrew, Anne, 2609
King, Coretta, 2467
Kingsley, Mary, 2579
Korematsu v. U.S., Intro. p. 19
Kosterina, Nina, 2495
Kung, Madame H. H. See Soong, Ai-ling.

Lagerloff, Selma, Adden. (Berendsohn)
Lamber, Juliette, 2671
Laney, Lucy Craft, 2457
LaRene, Jean, 3405
Lawrence, D. H., 2743
Lee, Ann, 2220
Legouve, 2211
Leslie, Mrs. Frank, 2617, 2644
Lincoln, Mary Todd, 2429
Lincoln, Salome, 2461
Lind, Jenny, 2422, 2439, 2460
Lloyd, Nancy, 2037
Louisa, Queen (Prussia), 2165, 2422
Lowell, Amy, 2805
Lowell, Josephine Shaw, 919
Luxembourg, Rosa, 1270, 1275, Adden. (Nettl, Thompson)
Lym, Mary, 2384
Lysistrata, 2694

McCarthy, Mary, 2695
McCrea, Jane, 2062
McCullers, Carson, 2695
MacDonald, Margaret Ethel, 2563
McDonald, May, Adden. (Crafton)
McPhail, Agnes, 2490
McPherson, Aimee Semple, 2278, 2570

Madison, Dolly, 1566, 2421
Maeterlinck, Maurice, 2275
Magoffin, Susan Shelby, 2020
Mahaut, Adden. (Kemp-Welsh)

Mailer, Norman, 2743
Maintenon, Madame de, 2421
Makin, Barthusa, 2609
Malamud, Bernard, 2743
Marcos, Imelda (Sra. Ferdinand), 2489
Marcet, Jane Haldimand, Adden. (Thompson)
Maria Theresa (Austria), 2140
Marie Antoinette, 2137
Markievicz, Constance, 2566
Mary, Queen of Scots, 2148, 2151
Maynard, Lady, 2536
Mechtild of Magdeburg, Adden. (Kemp-Welsh)
Meredith, George, Adden. (Bedford)
Meir, Golda, 1487, 1499
Meitner, Lise, 2691
Mencken, Adah Issacs, 1070, 2687, Adden. (Lesser)
Millay, Edna St. Vincent, 2805
Minor v. Happersett, 1354
Mitchell, Maria, 2575
Mitchell, Wesley Clair, 2583
Modjeska, Helena, 2390
Monroe, Marilyn, 2664
Montague, Lady Mary Wortley, 2428, 2814
Montez, Lola, 2689
Moody, Lady Deborah Dunche, 2005
Moore, Marianne, 2805
Moses, Anna May (Grandma Moses), Adden. (Kallir)
Motte, Rebecca, 2058
Mowry, Junia S., 2461

Nammack, Elizabeth, 156
Nammack, Michael, 156
Nasser, Tahia (Mrs. Gamel Abdul), 2489
Natasha, 2540
Nechayev, Adden. (Confino)
Nefertiti, 2134
Nevelson, Louise, 2736
Newcastle, Duchess of, 2418, 2609, 2765
Newsome, Effie Lee, 2615
Nielans, Alison, 2649
Nightingale, Florence, 2060, 2314, 2395, 2446-2447, 2450, 2585, 2647, 2686
Nilsson, Birgit, 2625
Nkruma, Fathia (Mrs. Kwame), 2489
North, Marianne, 2579
Norton, Caroline, 2453
Noyes, John Humphrey, 915

Oates, Joyce Carol, 2467
Omlie, Phoebe Fairgrove, 3407
Oñate, Don Juan de, 2015
Osborne, Dorothy, 2603
Owen, Robert Dale, 2550, 2601
Owens, Bethenia, 2030

Palmer, Alice Freeman, 2597
Pan Chao, 2652
Pandora, 1767
Pape-Carpentier, Marie, 2416
Paul, Alice, 2645
Paula, 1714
Pavlova, Anna, 2456, 2580
Payne, Dorothy, 1992
Peabody, Elizabeth Palmer, 2635
Peale, Dr. Norman Vincent, 2255
Pembroke, Countess of, 2418, 2765
Penn, Hannah Callowhill, 2006
Pepys, Mrs. Samuel, 2428
Phillip v. *Martin Marietta,* Intro. p. 19
Pisan, Christine de, Adden. (Kemp-Welsh)
Pitcher, Molly, 2065, 2071
Pittman, Jane, 2491
Pius, Pope, 1787
Pocahontas, Adden. (Phillips)
Poole, Elizabeth, 2005
Pope, Alexander, 2767
Porter, Katherine Ann, 2695-2696
Potter, Beatrix, 2551
Price, Leontyne, 2467, 2625
Proudhon, Pierre J., 2211

Radcliffe, Mrs., 2754
Radice v. *New York,* Intro. p. 19
Raford, Mrs., 1375
Rankin, Jeanette, Adden. (Josephson)
Rauk, Ida, 2637
Reed v. *Reed,* Intro. p. 19
Reiss, Erna, 2649
Richards, Ellen H., 2527, 2690
Richardson, Dorothy, 2738, 2778
Riedesel, Baroness, 2074
Rincon de Gautier, Doña Felisa, 1492
Roberts, Ellen Lois, 2437
Robins, Margaret Dreier, 1860
Robinson, Joan, Adden. (Thompson)
Robinson, Sarah, 2447
Rodman, Henrietta, 2637
Roe v. *Wade,* 813
Roland, Madame, 2655
Rose, Ernestine Louise, 921, 2651
Rosen v. *Louisiana Board of Medical Examiners,* 843
Rosetti, Christina, 2698
Roswitha, Adden. (Kemp-Welsh)
Rousseau, Jean-Jacques, 1567
Royall, Anne, 904, 2608
Rudnick, Dorothea, 2691
Russell, Lady, 2536

Sacajawea, 2030
St. Bridget, 2290
St. Eustochium, 1714
St. Hilda, 2290
St. Jerome, 1714
St. Scholastica, 2290

St. Vincent Millay, Edna, 2805
Sampson, Deborah, 2058, 2069. See also:
Gannett, Deborah S.
Sappho of Lesbos, 2433, 2446
Schurz, Margarethe, 2635
Schuyler, Catherine, 2058, 2526
Scholastica, Saint, 2290
Semiramis (Assyria), 2130
Senesh, Hannah, 2510
Seton, Mother, 2290
Sévigné, Marquise de, 2428
Shakespeare, William, 2739, 2743, 2752
Shaw, George Bernard, 2743
Sheldon, May French, 2579
Shepherd, Father, 626
Shield, Pretty, 2110
Shippen, Nancy, 2402
Shuck, Mrs. Henriette, Adden. (Jeter)
Sibiya, Christina, 3036
Sills, Beverly, 2625
Simpson, Alan, 695
Smith, Abbey, 1199
Smith, Mrs. Pearsall, 920
Snell, Hannah, 2065
Soong, Ai-ling (Mrs. H. H. Kung), 2505
Soong, Ching-ling. See Author Index.
Soong, Mayling. See Chiang, Madame.
Sorel, Agnes, Adden. (Kemp-Welch)
Southgate, Elizabeth, 2575
Spalding, Eliza, 2030
Spark, Muriel, 2759
Spenser, Edmund, 2789
Staël, Madame de, 2449, 2460, 2671
State v. *Barquet* (Florida), 855
Stucky v. *Stucky,* 1121
Sullivan, Leonor K. (Congresswoman), 1490
Sutherland, Joan, 2625

Táhirih, 2476
Tait, Catherine, 2534
Teasdale, Sara, 2805
Teerling, Levina, Adden. (Tufts)
Teilhard de Chardin, Pierre, 2210, 2247
Temple, Alice, 2635
Tennyson, Emily, 2504
Thaden, Louise, 3406
Thant, Madame (Mrs. U), 2489
Theodora, Queen, 2145, 2154
Thomas, W. I., 454
Thumb, Mrs. Tom, 1070, 2687
Tinne, Alexandrine, 2416
Tito, Jovanko (Mrs. Joseph), 2489
Toklas, Alice B., 2641
Trollope, Adden. (Hahn)
Troppi v. *Scharf,* 2347
Truth, Sojourner (Isabella Baumfree), 929, 932, 2480
Tubman, Hariet, 930, 1243, 1617
Tutwiler, Julia S., 912
Tz'u Hsi (Dowager Empress of China), 2139, 2444, 2466

Van Rensselaer, Maria, 2039
Varnhagen, Rachel, 2401
Victoria, Queen, 1840, 2150, 2155, 2158,
    2170, 2174, 2421, 2460
Vigee-Lebrun, Elisabeth, Adden. (Tufts)

Wake, Nancy, 2046, 2065
Wales, Princess of, 2460
Walker, Margaret, 2615
Walker, Maggie L., 2457
Walker, Dr. Mary, 1070, 2636, 2675, 2687
Walker, Mary Richardson, 2030, 2571
Ward, Mrs. Humphrey, 1417
Ward, Lester Frank, 454-455
Warren, Mercy, 2397, 2692
Washington, Martha, 1566
Webb, Beatrice Potter, Adden. (Thompson)
Weld, T. D., 2407
Wells, H. G., Adden. (Ray)
Welsh, Kit, 2065
Wesley, Susannah, 2226, 2422
West Coast Hotel Co. v. *Parrish,* Intro.
    p. 16
West, Jessamyn, 2467
West, Rebecca, Adden. (Ray)
Weston, Agnes, 2447
Wharton, Edith, 2753
Whitman, Narcissa, 2030
Whitney, Anita, 1269, 1531
Wiggin, Kate Douglas, 2635
Wilhelmina, Queen (Holland), 2130
Wilson, Jessie, 2479
Wilson, Mary (Mrs. Harold), 2489
Wister, Sally, 2073
Wolfwoman, Mountain, 2111, 2560, 2575
Workman, Fanny Bullock, 2579
Worwick, Lady, 2536
Wu, Chien-Shiung, 2691
Wu, Empress, 2147

Yang, Kwei-Fei, 2688
Yonge, Charlotte M., 2772
Young, Brigham, 271
YWCA v. *Kugler,* 877
Zakrzewska, Marie E., 2662
Zaldivar y Mendoza, Doña Ana de, 2015

PLACES, SUBJECTS, TOPICS

Aboriginal, 1695
Abyssinia. See Ethiopia.
Abolitionists, 622, 1930, 1987, 2407, 2486,
2554, 2629, 2684. See Contents II.C.2.
Social Reformers, Abolitionists.
Abortion, 1209, 2854, 2944, 2978. See
Contents I.I. Birth Control, Abortion,
and Demographic Studies.
Actresses, 2387, 2390, 2415, 2441, 2451,
2484, 2492, 2592, 2605, 2610, 2664,
2670, 2770, Adden. (Agate, Lesser, Tak)
Adolescents, 77, 346, 604, 617, Adden.
(Carlson, Dreifus, Larrick, Merriam).
See Contents I.B. Family; I.G. Education
and Socialization.
Adultery, 413, 431, 1125, 2976
Advertising, 545, 833
Advertising Agencies, 3427, 3432
Affirmative Action, 738, 1208, 3195, 3220,
3227, Adden. (Lester, Rosenberg-
Dishman)
Afghanistan, 391, 566
Africa, 102, 225, 240, 246, 248, 336, 353,
449, 495, 505, 507, 509, 511, 514, 516,
519, 521, 524, 528-532, 538, 605-606,
623-624, 642, 846, 896, 965, 994, 1001,
1063-1064, 1131, 1134, 1177, 1197,
1319, 1339, 1437, 1450, 1600, 1662,
1677, 1762, 1768, 1790, 1809, 1936-
1937, 1966, 1970, 1972-1973, 1979,
2344, 2348-2349, 2489, 2499, 2939-
2943, 2945-2948, 2950-2952, 2954-
2961, 2964-2965, 2967-2977, 2980-
2984, 2986-2988, 2990-2991, 2993,
2998-3000, 3002-3003, 3009, 3013,
3017-3019, 3022-3023, 3025, 3027-
3031, 3034, 3036-3046, 3069, 3071,
3089, 3103, 3404, 3514. See individual
countries.
Aging, 255, 289, 323, 327, 333, 368, 552,
1002, 1634, 1779, 2321, 2333, 2343,
2358, 2929, 3201, 3219, 3221-3222,
Adden. (Dreifus, Janeway)
Ainu, 1739
Akamba, 2954
Alabama, 912
Algeria, 321, 495, 986, 1406, 1587, 1963,
2097
Alimony, 1144. See Contents I.C. Marriage
and Divorce; and II.D.3 Feminism:
Equal Rights—Marriage and Divorce.
Amazons, 1564, 2059, 2076, 2825
American Indians, 187, 1718, 1724, 2084,
2092, 2100, 2107, 2110-2111, 2114,
2126, 2560, 2575, 2995, 3005, Adden.
(Banning, Gridley, Phillips)
Anarchists, 901-902, 916, 1267, 1271,
2497, 3561, 3569
Anatomy, 13, 419-420, 2301, 2307, 2313,
2316, 2359-2360, 2362, 2373, 2375,

Anatomy, *continued*
2380. See Contents V. Women in Medi-
cine and Health.
Androgyny, 2743
Angola, 2993, 3044
Annulment, see Divorce.
Anomie, 553, 2097
Anthropologists, 705, 731, 771, 1807, 1814,
1870, 1979, 2573, 2690, Adden. (Mead).
See Contents IX. Women in Anthropology.
Anti-Feminism, 2093
Antinepotism, 756, 1230
Apache, 187
Appalachia, 774
Arabia, 267, 793, 985, 1545. See Saudi
Arabia.
Aragon, 2163-2164, 2167
Arapash, 88
Archeology, 1758
Architects, Adden. (Cole)
Argentina, 995, 1643
Art Directors, 3394
Arts, 1776, 2119, 2685, 2728, 2783-2785,
2818, 3573. Adden. (Hess, Secrest,
Sewall, Steegmuller, Sullivan, Thwaite,
Tufts, The Woman's Guide to Books).
See Contents VII. Women in Literature
and the Arts.
Ashanti, 3034
Asia, 235, 274, 291, 335, 370, 504, 1001,
1131, 1944, 1971, 1974-1975, 1985,
2668, 2799, 2989, 3065. See individual
countries.
Assam, 557
Assyria, 2130
Astronomers, 2416, 2575, 2690
Athletics, 42, 128, 2331, 2338, 2354, 2356,
2493, 2532, Adden. (Boslooper). See
Contents I.H. Women in Education; and
V. Women in Medicine and Health.
Australia, 1067, 1584, 1740, 1921, 2864,
3004
Austria, 1326, 1599, 2130, 2140, 2607,
2691, 3010
Aviators, 1222, 2044, 2050, 2425, 2475,
2485, 3196, 3405

Babembas, 3030
Babylonia, 117, 1664
Baha'i, 974, 1248, 2154
Balenge, 3040
Bali, 88
Ballerinas, 2456, 2580
Bankers, Adden. (Alexander)
Bantu, 531, 2348, 2967, 3003, 3041
Bashila, 2971
Basutoland, 1437, 3040
Beauty, 1675, 2688
Bechuanaland, 3040

Belgium, 147-148, 1557, 1993. See Congo
(Kinshasa).
Bengal, 491
Bible, 1749, 1769, 2191, 2207-2209, 2214,
2219, 2222-2223, 2231, 2235, 2240,
2252, 2277, 2279-2280, 2283. See
Contents IV. Women in Philosophy and
Religion.
Bibliographies, 268, 451, 658, 703, 806, 835,
864-865, 1758, 1801, 1810, 1817, 1843,
1849, 1904, 1948, 1979, 2019, 2077,
2101, 2106, 2226, 2291, 2609, 3178,
3228, 3395, 3567, Adden. (Bickner,
Gager, Israel). See Contents XI.A.
Bibliographies.
Biographies and Autobiographies, 607,
1835-1837, 1846, 1859-1860, 1879,
1882, 1934, 1961-1962, 2013, 2020,
2028, 2067, 2081, 2083, 2110, 2120,
2129, 2209, 2222, 2226, 2233, 2239,
2278, 2289, Adden. (Adams, Banning,
Berendsohn, Brooks, Chun, Clarke,
Confino, Crafton, David, A. F. Davis,
A. Davis, de Beauvoir, de Mille, Deutsch,
Doumic, Flynn, Giroud, Hamilton,
Infield, Jeter, Johnson, Josephson, Kallir,
Kemp-Welch, Lesser, Limmer, Lindbergh,
McGovern, Madison, Masson, Mead,
Millet, Money, Nettl, Oliphant, Peters,
Phillips, Plunket, Ray, Richards, Ross,
Secrest, Sewall, Sklar, Steegmuller,
Thompson, Thwaite, Tomalin, Tufts).
See Contents VI. Women in Biography,
Autobiography, and Memoirs; and III.L.
Women as Rulers.
Biologists, 3399
Bira, 2970
Birth Control, 197, 2194, 2430, 2469,
2545, 2548, 2944, 2569, 2585, 2601,
2676, 2908. See Contents I.I. Birth
Control, Abortion, and Demographic
Studies; and V. Women in Medicine and
Health.
Birthright Centers, 775
Black Americans, 20, 23, 25, 28, 77, 98,
139, 157, 169, 173, 188, 197, 220, 249,
282, 288, 295, 343, 355, 376, 487, 494,
534, 549, 658, 779, 801, 887, 892, 924,
928-933, 972, 977, 1002, 1007, 1061-
1062, 1155, 1243, 1367, 1451-1452,
1467, 1488, 1508, 1621, 1632, 1639,
1649, 1659, 1666, 1876, 1888, 1890,
1916, 1930, 1950, 1958, 1960, 1987,
2021, 2070, 2082-2083, 2085-2086,
2088, 2090-2091, 2093, 2095-2097,
2102, 2106, 2113, 2115-2116, 2119,
2121, 2127, 2298-2299, 2377, 2393,
2397, 2417, 2432, 2445, 2457, 2459,
2467, 2472, 2480, 2488, 2491, 2493,
2511, 2521-2522, 2531, 2614-2615,
2657, 2674, 2707, 2723, 2862, 2888,
3169-3170, 3214-3215, 3225, 3314,

Black Americans, *continued*
3317, 3357, 3401, 3447, 3466, 3480,
3509, 3551, 3579, Adden. (Davis,
Elliott)
Bloomers, 899, 1819
Books, 611, 1002, 1244. See Contents VII.
Women in Literature and the Arts.
Borneo, 267
Brazil, 1660, 1981
Buddhism, 2188, 2236
Bundu (Nigeria), 530
Burma, 1944, 2489
Burundi. See Ruanda Urundi.
Businesswomen. See Contents X.F. Women
in Business, Industry, and Production.
Byzantium, 1588, 2144-2145

California, 1382, 1531, 1997, 2002, 2094,
2129, 2570
Cameroun, 538, 1809, 2955, 3028, 3103,
3287
Canada, 80, 144-145, 239, 373, 513, 726,
834, 875, 879, 990, 998, 1078, 1080,
1083-1084, 1095, 1097, 1122, 1209,
1212, 1336, 1395, 1438-1439, 1512,
1528, 2128, 2490, 2506, 2528, 2549,
2741, 2763, 2787, 2802, 3053, 3066,
3200, 3254, 3419, 3433, 3512, 3554.
See Quebec.
Cannibalism, 2994
Capitalism, 1976, 3067
Caricatures, 2714
Castration, 419, 2837, 2869. See Circum-
cision; Cliterodectomy; and Contents V.
Women in Medicine and Health.
Catholic (Roman), 681, 775, 797, 829, 838,
1068, 1277, 1412, 1582, 2203, 2250,
2287, 2557, Adden. (Rivers). See
Churches; Convents, Nunneries and
Holy Orders; and Contents IV. Women
in Philosophy and Religion.
Cebu. See Philippines.
Celibacy, 2194, 2220. See Convents,
Nunneries and Holy Orders.
Ceylon (Sri Lanka), 1944
Chaldea, 267
Chemists, 2527
Chicanas, 386, 2125, 2087, 2089, 2112,
2117-2118, 2122, 2125, 3214
Childbirth, 194, 641, 2325, 2345, 2348-
2349, 2351, Adden. (Sidel). See
Maternity; and Contents V. Women in
Medicine and Health.
Child Care Centers. See Day Care.
Child Labor, 2590
Children's Books, 2551, 2755
Child Rearing, 1938, 2181, 2194
Chile, 1969
China (People's Republic), 180-182, 207,
213, 266, 360-361, 407, 428, 484, 533,
539, 551, 562-563, 830-831, 850, 863,

China, *continued*
870, 1047, 1066, 1072, 1075, 1127,
1131-1132, 1178, 1257, 1274, 1520,
1533, 1593, 1653, 1729, 1731-1732,
1853, 1953, 1964, 1974-1975, 1977,
2139, 2147, 2215, 2241, 2440, 2444,
2466, 2505, 2524-2525, 2632, 2652,
2685, 2688, 2691, 2749, 2989, 3049,
3209, 3470, Adden. (Chun, Jeter, Sidel)
China (Republic of). See Taiwan.
Chinese Americans, 2094, 2129
Christianity. See Churches; and Contents IV.
Women in Philosophy and Religion.
Christian Science, 2218, 2255, 2411, 2600
Churches, 463, 477, 624, 826, 918, 1554,
1570, 1630, 1787, 2181, 2186, 2195-
2196, 2201-2202, 2204, 2206, 2212,
2219, 2237, 2239, 2243-2244, 2251-
2252, 2262, 2264, 2268, 2270, 2272,
2292, 2295-2296. See individual de-
nominations; and Contents IV. Women
in Philosophy and Religion.
Circumcision, 2297, 2319, 2337, 2362,
2369, 2964. See Castration; Clitero-
dectomy; and Contents V. Women in
Medicine and Health.
Civil Rights Act of 1964, 1158, 1161, 1173,
1182, 1185, 1203, 1238, 3191, 3213
Civil Servants, 1212-1213, 1215, 1220,
1233-1234, 1509, 1511-1512, 3152,
3422, 3429
Civil War (U.S.). See War.
Cliterodectomy, 2323, 2353, 2964, 3013.
See Castration, Circumcision; and
Contents V. Women in Medicine and
Health.
Coitus, 2191, 2335, 2368, 2910-2911
Colleges, Barnard, 2588, 3544; Bennet,
3579; Bethune-Cookman, 2521; Bryn
Mawr, 645, Adde.. (Prywes); Cheltenham
Ladies, 592; Colorado Woman's, 3587;
Girton, 1839; Hunter, 666; Istanbul
Women's, 2598; Marygrove, 1698; Mount
Holyoke, 594, 1872; Oberlin, 626, 733,
2542, 2657; Radcliffe, 3483, 3536,
3593; Sarah Lawrence, 697; Saint
Catherine, 3586; Scripps, 3594; Smith,
601, 676, 3595; Swarthmore, 3597;
Vassar, 683, 695-696; Wellesley, 595.
See Contents I.I. Women in Education.
Colonizers, 2564
Colorado, 1429, 2477-2478, 2538
Commission, Japanese Women's, 1884
Commission on Marriage and Divorce, Royal
(Great Britain), 1128
Commission on the Status of Women,
American Economic Association, Adden.
(Amer. Econ. Assoc.)
Commission on the Status of Women, New
Hampshire, 1087 [Intro.]
Commission on the Status of Women, Mod-
ern Language Association, 3433

Commission on the Status of Women, Royal
(Canada), 1078, 1080, 2741
Commission on the Status of Women, U.N.
(United Nations), 1098-1102
Commission on the Status of Women, U.S.
(President's), 693, 1105-1113, 1250,
3182
Commissions on the Status of Women,
Interstate Association of, 3528
Commissions on the Status of Women,
State (Governors'), 1086-1087, 1114-
1116 [Intro.]
Committee on the Status of Women, Inter-
departmental (U.S.), 1104
Committee on Women, Standing: United
Presbyterian Church, U.S.A., 2286
Commission on Women, InterAmerican,
3199
Communists, 879, 1016, 1067, 1269-1270,
1317, 1522, 1531, 1836, 1953, 1955,
1975-1977, 2220, 2487, Adden. (Nettl)
Companionate Marriage, 250
Composers, 2634, 2726, 2813
Concubines, 486. See Harems.
Confederacy (U.S.), 1601, 2443, 2462,
2537, 2572, Adden. (Hunter)
Conference on Women's Work and their
Status in Public Affairs, 3099
Confucianism, 2241
Congo (Brazzaville), 509, 2951, 2969, 2975
Congo (Kinshasa), 257, 509, 524, 2947,
2951, 2957, 2959, 2969-2971, 2974-
2977, 2982, 2986-2987, 3002, 3023
Congres Colonial National, 2969
Congress Constitutif de L'Union des
Femmes de L'Ouest Africain, 896
Connecticut, 1743, 1756
Conservatives, Conservatism, 1330
Consumers, 910, 1675, 1909
Contraceptives, 2316, 2335, 2347, 2361,
2368, 2378-2379, 2866, 2944. See
Contents I.I. Birth Control, Abortion
and Demographic Studies; and Birth
Control.
Conventions. See Treaties.
Convents, Nunneries and Holy Orders, 307,
375, 624, 1702, 2217, 2232, 2234,
2236-2237, 2240, 2281, 2290, 2420,
2893
Counsellors (psychological), Adden. (Cook)
Courtship, 225, 1119
Crafts, 1701
Criminals (criminality), 303, 309, 315, 364,
471, 604, 919, 1193, 1205, 1633, 1996,
2562, 2850
Cuba, 1026, 1252, 1255, 1284, 1981, 1985,
2119
Cultural Congress of Havana, 2119
Curacao, Adden. (Marks)

Dahomey, 240, 332

Dan, 2981
Dancers, 2456, 2471-2472, 2689, Adden.
  (de Mille, Lesser, Money, Steegmuller)
Day Care, 145, 156, 172, 204-206, 707,
  Adden. (Sidel). See Contents I.B.
  Family.
Debutantes, 1591
Delaware, 1998
Delinquency, 2882, Adden. (Giallombardo)
Democrats, Adden. (McGovern)
Demographic Studies, 228, Adden. (Chaney,
  Gray). See Aging, Racism; and Contents
  I.I. Birth Control, Abortion and Demo-
  graphic Studies.
Denmark, 243, 254, 1614, 2135, 3130
Diplomats, 1484, 1513, 2593
Discrimination, 721, 732, 735, 739, 751,
  755, 765, 887, Adden. (Strauss). See
  Contents II.D. Feminism: Equal Rights;
  X.B. Women and Job Discrimination.
Divorce, 1156, 1895, Adden. (Berson,
  Epstein, Israel, Mayer, Roper, Sherwin,
  State Bar of Wisconsin). See Contents
  I.C. Marriage and Divorce; and II.D.3
  Feminism: Equal Rights—Marriage and
  Divorce.
Dogon, 3014
Domestic Servants, 1641, 1650, 1661
Dowry, 260
Drama, Adden. (Sullivan). See Contents VII.
  Women in Literature and the Arts.
Drugs, 2312, 2347, 2351, 2358, 2361, 2379
Duelists, 2055

Economic Role, 1778, 1937-1938, 1958-
  1959, 1967, 1983, 2115, 2271, Adden.
  (Strauss, Tsuchigave, U.S. Cong. Joint
  Econ. Comm.)
Economists, Adden. (American Economic
  Association, Thompson)
Education, 8, 102, 115, 1704, 1706, 1872,
  1875, 1927, 1931, 1939, 1942, 1948,
  2012, 2391, 2533, 2583, 2633, 2635,
  Adden. (Carnegie Commission, Feldman,
  Harris, Lester, National School Boards
  Assoc., U.S. Cong. Senate Comm. on
  Labor, U.S. Dept. H.E.W., Women on
  Campus, Women on Words and Images).
  See Contents I.G. Education and Social-
  ization; I.H. Women in Education; and
  II.D.7. Feminism: Equal Rights—Educa-
  tion.
Egypt, 449, 488, 504, 1762, 2130, 2134,
  2142, 2157, 2159-2160, 2259, 2433,
  2489, 3033
Emancipation, 1986, 2207
Engagement. See Courtship.
Engineers, 618, 719, 2576, 3382
Enlightenment, 1707
Episcopal, 1707, 2282

Equal Employment Opportunity Commis-
  sion, 3211, 3225
Equal Pay Act of 1963, 1173, 1236,
  3131, 3145, 3186, 3198, 3205, 3223,
  3230
Equal Rights Amendment (proposed), 1153,
  1164, 1167, 1179, 1190, 1194, 1862
Equality, Intro. p. 16, 1873, 1892, 1895,
  1903, 1923, 2225, 2231, 2235, 2254,
  2258, 2264, 2291
Erotica, 472, 2745
Eskimos, 233
Ethiopia, 267, 543
Ethnic Minorities, 1427, 1452, 2098. See
  Contents III.K. Women in Ethnic
  Minorities.
Europe, 199, 312, 806, 867, 939, 991,
  1082, 1713, 1721, 1764, 1768. See
  individual countries.
Euthanasia, 777
Evangelists, 2278, 2570
Explorers, 2386, 2416

Fascism, 1955, 1957
Faculty Wives, 755, 3371, 3381
Family, 2, 21, 39, 56, 98, 103, 224, 1256,
  1913, 2115, 2181, 3024, Adden.
  (Dreitzel, Kay, Roper, Talmon). See
  Contents I.B. Family.
Family Planning. See Birth Control.
Fanti, 2939
Farm Women, 326, 498, 646, 1318, 1586,
  3306
Fashion, 1591, 1675, 1715. See Contents
  III.C.3. Women in Fashion.
Feminists. See Liberation, and Contents
  II.D.1-9. Feminism.
Fertility, 779-780, 827, 873, 876, 2999,
  Adden. (Tak)
Fertility Rites, 2999
Films, 470, Adden. (The Women's Guide to
  Books, Women's History Research
  Center). See Motion Pictures, and
  Contents VII. Women in Literature and
  the Arts.
Florida, 2029
Folklore. See Contents, III.C.2. Women in
  Folklore and Witchcraft.
France, 324, 437, 443, 589, 769, 772, 803,
  859, 868, 995, 1013, 1027, 1029, 1042,
  1082, 1227, 1286, 1407, 1456, 1589,
  1607, 1685, 1690, 1697, 1710, 1721,
  1847, 1919-1920, 1954, 1982, 1985,
  1991, 2047, 2052, 2056, 2066, 2077,
  2136-2138, 2162, 2211, 2428, 2460,
  2489, 2591, 2597, 2610, 2655, 2671,
  2689, 2715, 2719, 2732, 2764, 2770,
  2779, 3130, 3328, Adden. (Brée, Crossland, Giroud, Oliphant)
Free Love, 350-351

Frigidity, 2901
Fulani, 2948, 2961
Future, 620, Adden. (Quest, Russell, Tolchin, Tripp, U.S. Dept. of Labor, Women on Campus)

Geishas, 330, 372, 642
Georgia (U.S.), 1077, 2053, 2544
Germany, 164, 176, 475, 616, 991, 1011, 1036, 1270, 1275, 1287, 1290, 1326, 1432, 1436, 1546, 1577, 1599, 1651, 1682, 1707, 1726, 2165, 2578, 2722, 2744, 2798, 3130, 3458, Adden. (Infield, Mann, Nettl)
Ghana (Gold Coast), 2489, 2939, 3034
Government, 1895. See individual states and countries.
Great Britain, 78, 117, 126, 153, 160, 171, 252, 272, 286, 296, 300, 311, 314-315, 338, 496-498, 583, 592-593, 600, 619, 667, 670, 727, 773, 796, 798, 812, 840, 853, 857-858, 914, 968, 983-984, 992, 997, 1014-1015, 1022, 1028, 1030, 1032, 1037-1039, 1049-1050, 1122, 1128, 1163, 1181, 1223, 1241-1242, 1245, 1285, 1288, 1290, 1328, 1331, 1333, 1338, 1341-1343, 1346, 1350, 1352, 1355, 1359-1361, 1389, 1393-1394, 1397, 1400, 1407, 1430,1461-1462, 1469, 1474, 1486, 1494, 1496-1497, 1511, 1523, 1527, 1552, 1559-1560, 1574, 1576, 1604-1605, 1608, 1620, 1626, 1635, 1641-1642, 1650, 1652, 1655, 1671, 1680, 1684, 1686, 1691, 1694, 1701, 1704, 1716, 1720, 1726, 1742, 1747, 1755, 1757, 1760, 1765, 1830, 1833, 1839-1840, 1851, 1887, 1905-1906, 1915, 1995-1996, 2018, 2079, 2141, 2148, 2150-2151, 2153, 2155-2156, 2158, 2170, 2174, 2197-2198, 2268, 2412-2414, 2424, 2428, 2430, 2450, 2452-2453, 2460, 2481-2482, 2489, 2504, 2507, 2514, 2518-2519, 2536, 2539, 2555, 2563-2564, 2568-2569, 2578, 2582, 2584-2585, 2594-2596, 2602-2603, 2606, 2609, 2623, 2626, 2634, 2638, 2648, 2654, 2659, 2672-2673, 2676, 2678, 2696, 2698, 2703, 2711, 2725, 2729, 2733, 2739, 2742, 2754, 2757, 2759, 2765-2767, 2771-2773, 2782-2783, 2789, 2808, 2814, 2824-2825, 3061, 3091, 3101, 3113, 3123, 3130, 3132, 3136, 3139, 3141, 3175, 3238, 3247, 3273, 3333, 3366, 3403, 3469, 3566, Adden. (Gathorne-Hardy, Masson)
Greece (Ancient), 1588, 1592, 1594, 2694, 2746, 2826
Greece, 178, 1664, 1688, 1692, 1753, 2059, 2160-2161, 2189, 2433, 2694, 2727, 2746, 2768, 2826

Group Sex, 395
Guilds, 1701
Guinea, 2943
Gynecology, 111, 419, 2661. See Contents V. Women in Medicine and Health.

Harems, 291, 294, 300, 331, 340, 370, 388, 1591, 1732-1733, 2752. See Concubinage.
Hausa, 2961, 3043
Hawaii, 2103
Hindu, 547, 1619, 1719, 2263. See Contents IV. Women in Philosophy and Religion.
History, Intro. pp. 6-13; 72, 117, 143, 178, 209, 228, 242, 259, 296, 311, 385, 443, 454, 460, 474, 477, 498, 500, 580, 587, 607, 641, 674, 703, 710-711, 806, 815-816, 842, 884, 1046, 1183, 1246, 1337, 1359, 1363, 1445, 1866, 1869-1871, 1874, 1879, 1887, 1889, 1907, 1910, 1912, 1919-1921, 1926, 1928-1929, 1932, 1946, 1949, 1951, 1963, 1969, 2128, 2175, 2182-2183, 2193, 2204, 2217, 2224, 2232, 2237, 2244-2245, 2262-2263, 2266, 2268-2269, 2282, 2291, 2293, 2314, 2325, 2329, 2365-2366, 2377, 2692-2693, 2714, 2723, 2728, 2752, 2818, 3035, 3137-3138, 3272-3273, 3279, 3475, 3537, 3547, 3584, Adden. (Berkin, de Riencourt, Friedman, Hogeland, Robinson, Thompson, Van Vuuren, Walters, Women's . . .) See Contents III.A-L. History.
Hoboes, 378, 2658
Holland. See Netherlands.
Home Economics, 2527
Honeymoon, 1591
Hong Kong, 825
Hormones, 2343, 2346, 2358, 2379, 2833, 2835, 2934, 2937
Household Workers, First National Conference of, 3305
Housewives, 314, 356, 365, 373, 381, 511, 564
Huguenots, 1991
Hull House, 1827

Ibibios, 3045
Ibo, 49, 1972
Illinois, 1149, 2661, 3351
Immigrants. See Ethnic Minorities.
Incest, 3012
Income tax (federal), 156, 172
India, 85, 89, 192, 244, 260, 273, 341, 344, 377, 391, 491, 508, 535, 547, 557, 566, 677, 782, 809, 811, 966, 995, 1051, 1505, 1619, 1623, 1669, 1681, 1719, 1744, 1818, 1889, 1944, 2263, 2288,

India, *continued*
  2308, 2389, 2489, 3050-3051, 3246,
  Adden. (Morrah)
Indonesia, 88, 158, 391, 566, 809, 1368,
  1942
Infanticide, 771, 2944
Insanity. See Mental Illness.
International Conference of Women Workers
  to Promote Permanent Peace, 938
International Congress of Women, 934
International Congress of Working Women,
  3283
International Court of Justice, 1054
Iowa, 1081, 1488, 2484
Iran (Persia), 391, 515, 566, 1735, 2476
Ireland, 1281, 2438, 2470, 2566, 2792,
  Adden. (Adams)
Islam. See Muslim.
Israel, 201, 305, 316, 1001, 1145, 1487,
  1499, 1612, 2130, 2510, 2546, 2642
Italy, 1290, 1413, 1682, 1690, 1696, 1705,
  1721, 1838, 1957, 2149, 2169, 2406
Ivory Coast, 507

Japan, 9, 167, 330, 359, 361, 372, 504, 512,
  567, 627, 659, 817, 995, 1000, 1019,
  1059, 1071, 1569, 1593, 1613, 1616-
  1617, 1739, 1869, 1884, 1894, 1951,
  2530, 2581, 2650, 2796, 3277
Japanese-Americans, 2103-2104, 2108,
  2120, 2124
Java, 158
Jews, 550, 560, 812, 1582, 2023, 2105,
  2109, 2123, 2235, 2246, 2249, 2253,
  2401, 2557, 2578, 3032, 3485, Adden.
  (Mann). See Contents IV. Women in
  Philosophy and Religion.
Journalists, 2392
Judges (judiciary), 1508
Jurors, 1165, 1200, 3213

Kanuri, 2991
Karezza, 856
Kentucky, 1374
Kenya, 511, 642, 1064, 2954, 3013, 3029,
  3082
Kibbutz, 201, 316, Adden. (Rosner, Talmon)
Kikuyu, 3013
Korea, 151
Kurdistan, 1637-1638

Labor (Trade) Unions, 1217, 1277, 1437-
  1438, 1517, 1836, 1860, 1960, 2394,
  2487, 2538, 2545, 2590, 3272, 3278-
  3283, 3285-3286, 3288-3298, 3316,
  3318, 3578
Lala, 2344

Laos, 1944
Latin America, 542, 780, 785, 789, 979,
  993, 1022-1024, 1026, 1089-1094,
  1189, 1256, 1259, 1284, 1660, 1674,
  1981, 2027, 3116, 3199
Law, 156, 790, 822, 1153 [Intro.], 1170
  [Intro.], 1185 [Intro.], 1187 [Intro.],
  1193 [Intro.], 1204 [Intro.], 1206
  [Intro.], 1620, 1652, 1888, 1936, 1959-
  1960, 2034, 2266, 3210, Adden. (Berson,
  De Crow, Giallombardo, Ginzburg,
  Israel, Kay, Lester, McHugh, Tak,
  Women's Guide to Books, Wormser).
  See Contents II.D.5. Feminism: Equal
  Rights-Legal Status.
Lawyers, 2425, 3396
League of Women Voters, 1294, 1539
Lebanon, 876, 995
Legislators. See U.S. Congresswomen, and
  U.S. Legislators, State.
Lesbianism, 357, 393, 406, 410, 424, 434,
  437, 445, 461-462, 1002, 1753, 1938,
  2306-2307, 3448, 3583. See Contents
  I.A. Sex Roles; I. E. Sexuality.
Liberation, Women's, 1, 23, 27, 86, 89, 108-
  109, 129, 284, 298, 302, 339, 359, 361,
  367, 456, 459, 506, 525-526, 564, 613,
  662, 750, 962, 966, 976-977, 980-981,
  988, 1002, 1010, 1020, 1062, 1215,
  1251, 1266, 1282, 1604, 1844-1846,
  1849, 1851-1852, 1855, 1857, 1865,
  1867-1868, 1876, 1886, 1890, 1896,
  1899-1900, 1902, 1904, 1916-1919,
  1922, 1924, 1932, 1935, 1938, 1950,
  1980, 2091, 2119, 2125, 2200, 2205,
  2228, 2238, 2271, 2275, 2289, 2747,
  2778, 2788, 2801, 2874, 2923, 3057,
  Adden. (Borun, Carden, Grimstad, Hahn,
  Iglitzin, Katz and Milton, Lieberman,
  Millet, Mothersill)
Liberia, 336, 2963, 2981
Librarians, 3379, 3398, 3500
Life Styles, 1875, 2010, 2035, 2094, 2112,
  2259, Adden. (Richards, Rosner, Russ).
  See Prostitution; and Contents I.A. Sex
  Roles, Characteristics and Differences;
  I.D. Life Styles; I.F. Class and Status.
Literature, Intro. p. 23; 1815, Adden.
  (Ferguson, Russ). See Contents VIII.
  Women in Literature and the Arts.
Love, 1700, 1722, 2242, 2247-2249, 2910
Lowell Mills, 2552, 3331, 3335, 3340,
  3564
Luo, 3029

Macedonia, 2160-2161
Maine, 1994
Malaysia, 1123, 1944
Mali, 896, 2964
Managers, 3367, 3373-3374, 3378, 3392,
  3402, 3431, Adden. (Lynch)

Manitoba, 1395
Manners. See Life Style.
Mano, 2981
Manus, 88
Manyika, 2951
Maoris, 1740
Marriage, 4, 29, 31, 62, 1031, 1151, 1727, 1772, 1895, 1913, 1942, 2115, 2242, 2925, 3086, Adden. (Dreifus, Editorial Research Reports, Roper, Scanzoni, Seidenberg, Sedel, Veroff, Washington, The Women's Guide to Books)
Married Women, 1159, 1168, 1171, 1511, 1727, 2252, 2925, 3039, 3333. See also Contents I.C. Marriage and Divorce.
Martyrs, 2386
Maryland, 1995, 2032, 2038, 2852
Marxists, 1279-1280, 1548, 1657, 1911, 1967, 1980
Massachusetts, 1040, 1201, 1364, 1405, 1412, 1540-1541, 1665, 1745, 1766, 1771, 1990, 2005, 2007, 2182, 2552, 3340, 3564, Adden. (David)
Mastectomy, 2310
Masturbation, 463, 2369
Matabele, 2965, 3040
Maternity, 50, 142-146, 166, 170, 174, 196, 352, 380, 591, 1140, 1651. See Family; and Contents I.B. Family; V. Women in Medicine and Health.
Mayors, 1492, 2549
Matriarchy, 80, 135, 142, 152, 173, 202, 1546, 1570, 1758, 2184, 2746, 2827, 2878, 2971, 3005, 3016, 3027, 3048-3049
Matricide, 2768
Media, 846, 1568, 1908, Adden. (Elliott, Strainchamps)
Melanesia, 88, 3019
Melville Island (Australia), 3004
Mende (Sierra Leone), 1483
Menstruation and Menopause, 2315, 2318, 2321, 2326, 2332-2334, 2339-2341, 2343-2344, 2346, 2350, 2352, 2355, 2358, 2364, 2371, 2374, 2376, 2379, 2847-2848, 2860, 2864, 2871, 2883, 2886
Mental Illness, 18, 44, 63, 837, 919, 2313, 2320, 2326, 2352, 2355, 2357, 2372, 2567, 2838, 2843, 2873, 2885, 2924
Mesopotamia, 1772
Methodist, 2243, 2282, 2437
Mexican-Americans, 386, 2087, 2089, 2099, 2112, 2117-2118, 2122, 2125, 3214
Mexico, 1290, 1356, 1629, 1664, 2020, 2027, 2099
Michigan, 2009
Middle East, 793, 1708, 1772, 3192. See individual countries.
Midwives, midwifery, 2300, 2308, 2329, 3413, 3419

Military, 1281, 1284, 1286-1287, 3403
See Contents III.D.3. Women as Soldiers and Spies.
Ministers (Cabinet and Parliamentary), 1516, 2490, 2546, 2549, 2654, 2575, 2629
Ministry, 2177, 2179, 2188-2189, 2197-2199, 2202, 2208, 2212, 2219, 2227, 2230-2234, 2237, 2244, 2252, 2258-2259, 2265, 2267, 2279, 2283-2284
See Contents IV. Women in Philosophy and Religion.
Minnesota, 729, 1949
Misogyny, 2794, Adden. (Mencken)
Missionaries, 1377, 2012, 2030, 2183, 2264, 2437, Adden. (Jeter)
Missouri, 1354
Mistresses, 363, 431, 433, 2421, 2426
Mohammedan. See Muslim.
Montana, 2388
Morality, 1119, 2215, 2221, 2242, 2271, 2289, 2292, 2410. See Prostitution; and Contents IV. Women in Philosophy and Religion.
Mormons, 271
Morocco, 2105
Mossi, 3023
Motion Pictures, 2812, Adden. (Haskell, Mellen, Rosen, Springer). See Films, and Contents VII. Women in Literature and the Arts.
Motherhood, 1727, 1994, 2014, 2181, 2229, 2252, 3006, Adden. (McBride, Radl). See also Maternity.
Movies. See Motion Pictures.
Mozambique, 2941, 2988
Mundugumor, 88
Musicians, 2448, 2592, 2693, 2721, 2726
Muslim, 149, 291, 299, 328, 344, 390, 515, 985, 1362, 1637-1638, 1658, 2105, 2178, 2288, 3192, Adden. (Massell). See Contents IV. Women in Philosophy and Religion.
Mythology, 2245, 2962, 2966, 2979, 2992, 3001, 3007, 3027, 3048, 3050. See Contents III.E. Women in Folklore and Witchcraft.

Nanny. See Nursemaid.
Natal, 246, 3041
National Women's Trade Union League, 1860
Navahos, 3005
Nazis, 1577
Nebraska, 1121
Netherlands, 2011, 2130
New England, 1746, 1989, 2025, 2552, 3331, 3564
New Guinea, 235, 3019
New Hampshire, 1087
New Jersey, 1748, 1773, 2005, 2007
New Mexico, 2015, 2020

Newspaperwomen, 1568, 2474, 2506, 2577, 2608, 2613, 2723, 3423, Adden. (Strainchamps)

New York, 193, 309, 385, 738, 755, 856, 910, 915, 957-958, 1088, 1249, 1315, 1542, 2005, 2039, 2042, 2049, 2062, 2068, 2074, 3316, 3318, 3535, Adden. (Richards)

New Zealand, 1740, 2864, Adden. (Bunkle)

Nigeria, 49, 240, 340, 528, 636, 995, 1790, 1972-1973, 2948, 2952, 2961, 2968, 2991, 3043, 3045-3046, 3302

Nghandi, 2947

Ngombe, 2947

Nilo-Hamitics, 2984

Nilotics, 2984

Nkutshu, 2959

Nineteenth Amendment, 1929

Norway, 1323-1324, 1453-1454, 1456, 1501-1502, 1663, 2750

Novelists, 2403, 2408, 2413-2414, 2416, 2420, 2423, 2428, 2483, 2496, 2507, 2519, 2524, 2574, 2612, 2638, 2677, Adden. (Brée, Colby, Crossland)

Nudity, 1796, 1798, 1802, 1808

Nursemaid, Adden. (Gathorne-Hardy)

Nurses (Nursing), 612, 767, 777, 783, 795, 898, 1390, 2309, 2314, 2365, 2377-2381, 2395, 2446-2447, 2450, 2547, 2585, 2597, 2686, 3369, 3414, 3426

Nymphomania, 2313, 2328

Occult, 2184-2185, Adden. (Van Vuuren). See Contents III.E. Women in Folklore and Witchcraft.

Ohio, 946, 1231, 1489, 2542

Oneida Colony, 856, 915

Ontario, 1528

Open Marriage, Adden. (O'Neil)

Opera, 2393

Oregon, 1382, 2473

Orgasm, 453

Ovambo, 3040

Ovimbundu, 2993, 3044

Pacifists, 1906, 2061, 3597. See Contents II.C.3. Social Reformers—Peace.

Painters, 2420, 2709, 2586, 2804, 2822-2823, Adden. (Kallir, Tufts)

Papal, 1787, 2204, 2257

Pakistan, 391, 508, 565-566, 1944, Adden. (Morrah)

Palestine. See Israel.

Panther Women, 1916

Papua, 88, 2985

Parliament (British), 1469, 1487, 1494, 1496-1497

Parturition. See Childbirth.

Party (political) Leaders, 1475, 1525. See Contents II.G.4. Politicians.

Party Activists, 3537

Party Conventions, 1292, 1301, 3537

Patriarchy, 1567, 3015

Pennsylvania, 1205, 1992, 2006, 2037, 2041, 2057

Penis (phallus) Envy, 2837, 2859

Personality development, 45, 51-52, 84, 92, 114, 640, 2301, 2356, 2375, 2839, 2844, 2848, 2879, 2891, 2900, 2917, 2929. See Contents I.A. Sex Roles; I.G. Women in Education; VIII. Women in Psychology.

Peru, 1444, 2027

Philippines, 1344, 1734, 1944, 2489

Philosophy, 1845. See Contents IV. Women in Philosophy and Religion.

Photographers, 2463

Physical Education. See Athletics.

Physicians, 1467, 1627, 2021, 2030, 2425, 2571, 2575, 2629, 2636, 2659, 2661-2662, 2675, 2687, 3377, 3384, 3388. See Contents V. Women in Medicine and Health; X.G. Women in the Professions.

Physicists, 2691

Pilots. See Aviators.

Pioneers, 1422, 1586. See Contents III.D. Women as Colonists and Pioneers.

Playwrights, 2516, 2694

Poets, 2420, 2615, 2679, 2707, 2712, 2715, 2763, 2774, 2805, 2816, 2821, Adden. (Clarke, Limmer, Lindbergh)

Poland, 150, 1126

Policewomen, 2907

Political Scientists, Intro. p. 23; 3369, 3397

Politicians, 1896, 1945. See Contents II.G. Politicians.

Politics, Intro. pp. 19-26; 1465, 1905, 1920, 1936, 1938, 1952, 1958, 2091-2093, 2098, 2258, 2277, Adden. (Radloff, Tolchin, "Women . . .", The Women's Guide to Books, Wormser)

Polls, 34, 522-523, Adden. (Roper)

Polygamy, 271, 486, 1936

Polygyny, 2942, 2945, 2974

Polynesia, 88, 1740, 2950

Portugal, Adden. (da Costa)

Portuguese East Africa. See Mozambique.

Pornography, 472. See Erotica.

Pregnancy, 2863, Adden. (Sidel)

Presbyterian, 2239

Priesthood. See Ministry.

Primitive, 1699, 1708-1709, 3006, 3008, 3019-3021, 3035, 3047

Prisons (prisoners), 1522, 2555, 2606, Adden. (Giallombardo, Heffernan)

Professionals, 32-33, 68, 275, 285, 310, 318, 339, 483, 548-549, 584, 586, 612, 615,

Professionals, *continued*
631, 653, 725, 734, 835, 1225, 1563,
3130, 3268-3269, 3369, 3274, Adden.
(Anderson). See Contents X.G. Women
in the Professions.
Prohibition, 1901, 2501, 2589, 2681-2682,
3560
Prohibitionists, 1901. See Contents II.C.4.
Social Reformers.
Property. See Contents II.D.4. Feminism:
Equal Rights—Property.
Prostitution, 272, 277, 283, 286, 301, 308-
309, 311, 322, 330, 334-335, 346, 358,
364, 379, 918, 1002, 1196, 1633, 1843,
1925, 2412, 2482, 2986, Adden. (Edi-
torial Research Reports, Stein, Whit-
taker). See Contents II.C.5. Social
Reformers—Prostitution.
Psychology, 1769, 1789, 1791, 1794-1796,
1799, 1804, 1813, 1820, 1845, 2059,
2104, 2124, 2190, 2255, 2285, Adden.
(Mitchell). See Contents VIII. Women
in Psychology.
Puberty, 2344, 2376, 3013. See Menstruation.
Publications, Adden. (Robinson). See Contents XI.D. Periodicals and Newspapers.
Puerto Rico, 1492
Purdah, 291, 328, 341, 2288
Puritan, 2025

Quakers, 920, 931, 1378-1379, 1384, 1396,
1992, 1998, 2011, 2037, 2073, 2269,
2454, 3597, Adden. (Jorns)
Quebec, 998, 1080, 1440, 2787
Queens, Adden. (Johnson). See Contents
III.F. Women as Rulers.
Quinault Indians, 2995

Racism, 1938, 1970, 2087, 2091, 2093,
2097, 2106, 2109, Adden. (Washington)
Radicals, 1897, 2101, Adden. (Baritz)
Radio, 846. See also Media, Newspaper-
women, and Television.
Rape, 308, 1180, 1195, 2830, 2853, Adden.
(Norman)
Reformers, 1928-1929, 1933, 2518, 2534,
2550, 2555, 2567. See Contents II.C.
Social Reformers.
Reformatories, 919. See Prisons.
Religion, 1726, 1769, 1787, 1791, 1818,
1895, 1943, 1953, 1998, 2025, 2037,
2101, Adden. (Quest, Russell, Van
Vuuren). See Churches; and Contents
IV. Women in Philosophy and Religion.
Renaissance, 587, 1594, 1611, 2795, Adden.
(Hare). See Contents III.C. Women
from Ancient Times Through Victorian.
Republicans, 1530, 3537
Revolutionary War. See Wars.

Revolutionists, 1027, 1270, 1275, 1284,
1286-1287, 1310, 1859, 1916, 1919,
2047-2048, 2051, 2540, 2593. See
Contents III.H. Women in Revolutionary
and Changing Societies.
Rhode Island, 918, 1371, 1602, 1990, 3251
Rhodesia, 2965
Rome, 1543, 1640, 1683, 1692-1693, 2143,
2146, 2149, 2154
Ruanda Urundi, 2969, 3000, 3009, 3025
Russia. See U.S.S.R. (Soviet Union)
Rwanda. See Ruanda Urundi.

Samoa, 88
San Francisco, 617
Saudi Arabia, 267, 985
Scandinavia, 475, 807, 1326, 1711, 1988
Scientists, 615, 719, 735, 744, 2455, 2587,
2592, 2597, 2663, 2690-2691, 2935,
3382-3383, 3391, 3504
Scotland, 1655, 1742, 1760, 1765, 2148,
2151
Sculptors, 2736
Seneca Falls. See Women's Rights Con-
ventions.
Senegal, 505, 2942-2943
Seraglio. See Harems.
Serbia, 2145
Serfdom, 228
Sex Education, 582, 2317, 2262
Sex Roles, 1778, 1877, 1913, 1953, 1957,
1959, 2024, 2126, 2180, 2201, 2203,
2207, 2210-2211, 2214, 2229, 2237,
2248-2249, 2251-2253, 2256-2258,
2295, 2832, 2840, Adden. (Quest,
Russ, Scanzoni, Seidenberg, Veroff,
Walters, Whittaker, "Women . . .",
Women on Words and Images, Yorburg).
See Prostitution, Contents I.A. Sex
Roles.
Sexism, 37, 121, 611, 674-675, 724, 765,
1017, 1157, 1244, 1265, 1938, 2091,
2241, 3203, 3582, 3500, Adden. (De
Crow, Freeman, "Guidelines . . .," Kane,
Macleod, Van Vuuren). See Contents
II.D. Feminism; III.B. The Position of
Women; X.B. Women and Job Discrim-
ination.
Sexual Intercourse. See Coitus.
Shakers, 2220
Sierra Leone, 521, 530, 1483
Sin, 2215
Singapore, 1123, 1944
Singers, 2393, 2405, 2520, 2531, 2660
Single Women, 371, 1021, 1171, 1181,
2929. See Spinsters.
Slavery, 25, 98, 516, 1649, 1832, 1930,
1987, 2088, 2090, 2121. See Contents
II.C.2. Social Reformers—Abolitionists
Socialists, 1018, 1139, 1253-1254, 1273,
1325, 1532, 1946, 1952, 1956, 1967-

Socialists, *continued*
   1968, 1971, 1976, 1984, 2200, 2274,
   2406, 2607, 2673-2674, 3525
Socialization, 7, 24, 138, 179, 190, 346.
   See Contents I.G. Education and
   Socialization; II.A. Women as Socializers.
Social Security, Adden. (Hoskins, Kutner)
Social Workers, 3425
Soldiers, 320, 1243, 2630. See Contents
   III.D.3. Women as Soldiers and Spies.
South (U.S.), 890, 972, 1586, 1666, 2462,
   2544, 3329, Adden. (Hunter)
South Africa, 240, 246, 248, 531, 1063,
   1197, 1437, 2940, 2946, 2956, 2958,
   3003, 3036-3038, 3040-3042, 3071,
   3404, 3450
South Carolina, 2078, 2554
Soviet Union. See U.S.S.R.
Spain, 73, 261, 371, 1012, 1556, 1721,
   2027, 2152, 2163-2164, 2167, 2172,
   2196, 2489, Adden. (Plunket)
Spies, 2063, 2081, 2630. See Contents
   III.J. Women as Soldiers and Spies.
Spinsters, 377, 918, 1021, 1080, 1171,
   1181, 1199, 1591. See Single Women.
Sports. See Athletics.
Sri Lanka. See Ceylon.
Status, 1605, 2092, 2095, 2105, 2107,
   2113, 2248, 2254, 2272, 2291, 2296,
   Adden. (Ferris, Sochen, U.S. Citizen's
   Council on the Status of Women, U.S.
   Dept. of Health, Education, and Wel-
   fare. See Committees on the Status of
   Women.
Sterility, 2322, 2894
Sterilization, 797, 869. See Birth Control
   and Castration.
Stewardesses, 1228
Stockbroker, 2081
Sudan, 240, 449, 606, 2337, 3022
Suffrage and Suffragettes, 1833, 1842, 1850,
   1858-1859, 1863-1864, 1883, 1892,
   1901, 1915, 1940, 2277, 2399, 2419,
   2454, 2468, 2481, 2512, 2535, 2539,
   2563, 2565, 2582, 2585, 2594-2596,
   2599, 2611, 2629, 2639-2640, 3568-
   3569, 3589. See Contents II.F. Woman
   Suffrage.
Suicide, 837, 2355, Adden. (Gilder). See
   Mental Illness.
Swaziland, 248, 2940
Sweden, 40, 69, 79, 223, 245, 254, 418,
   558, 673, 828, 861, 1096, 1891, 1988,
   2171, 2173, 2626, 2806, 3183, 3361,
   3460. Adden. (Berendsohn)
Swinging, 239
Syria, 504, 2160

Taiwan (Republic of China), 212, 870
Tallensi, 2996
Tamil (India), 535

Tanzania, 1970, 2973, 2999, 3017-3018
Tatmul, 88
Tchambuli, 88
Teenagers. See Adolescents.
Television, 1265, Adden. (Strainchamps)
Temperance. See Prohibitionists.
Tennessee, 2009
Texas, 2112, 3125
Thailand, 1944
Theater, 636
Theosophy, 2185, 2676
Therapists, 2311
Tiwi, 3004
Togo, 1449, 3026, 3303
Trade Unions. See Labor Unions.
Transsexuals, 448
Transvaal, 240, 2946, 2956
Treaties, 960, 992, 1056, 1101, 1143, 1189
Triangle Fire, 3316, 3318
Tropics, 999, 1447, 1979, 3016
Turkey, 149, 189, 299-300, 304, 391, 504,
   566, 1609, 1752, 2598
Tutsi, 3000
Tyre, 2133

Uganda, 3079, 3582
Unitarian, 2224, 2410
Universities: Akron, 762; California (Ber-
   keley), 759; Chicago, 745; Columbia,
   2502, 3242, 3332; Indiana, 757; Kansas,
   3588; Michigan (Ann Arbor), 537, 588,
   702, 765, Adden. (McGuigan); Michigan
   State, 694, 742; Minnesota, 758; North
   Carolina, 3501, 3598; Northwestern,
   3583; Ohio State, 1231; Oxford, 583;
   Pennsylvania, 764; Princeton, 656; San
   Diego State, 672; Valparaiso, 1204;
   Washington (Seattle), 760; Wisconsin
   (Madison), 660, 701, 761; Yale, 571,
   639, 663, 763, 766
Unwed Mothers, 138, 193, 195, 199, 208,
   215, 245, 617, 801, 821, 1099-1100,
   1175-1176, 2370, 1936
Upper Volta, 3022
U.S. Congresswomen, 1088, 1155, 1161,
   1182, 1204, 1228, 1466, 1468, 1470-
   1473, 1476-1480, 1484-1485, 1490-
   1491, 1493, 1495, 1500, 1503-1504,
   1514, 1518, 1940, 1958, 2093, 2467,
   Adden. (Josephson). See Contents II.G.
   Politicians.
U.S. Legislators, State, 914, 1482, 1488,
   1498, 1503, 1518, 1945, 2490, 2546,
   2549
U.S. Mayors, 1489, 1492.
U.S.S.R. (Soviet Union), 146, 159, 175,
   177, 183-184, 203, 350-351, 384, 481,
   503, 544, 550, 603, 615, 680, 810, 867,
   871, 969, 982, 995, 1004-1005, 1009,
   1025, 1045, 1076, 1130, 1140, 1191,

U.S.S.R., *continued*
1218, 1258, 1260, 1262, 1271, 1442,
1513, 1516, 1533, 1859, 1962, 1983,
2067, 2131-2132, 2166, 2324, 2382,
2485, 2495, 2540, 2593, 2734, 2810,
3074-3075, 3181, 3130, 3147, 3154,
3187-3188, 3369, 3386, 3393, Adden.
(Confino, Massell)
Utah, 1945

Valenge, 2988
Venda, 2956
Venereal Disease, 956, 2335, 2368
Venice, 2169
Victorian Attitudes, 2808. See
Contents II.B. Victorian Attitudes.
Vietnam, 489, 1060, 1944, 1959, 1971,
1981, 1985-1986
Viking, 1711
Violence, 258
Virginia, 2028, 2045
Virginity, 2252, 3012
Voluntarism, 345, 588
Voters. See Contents II.E. Women as
Voters; II.F. Woman Suffrage.

Wabena, 2973
Wales, 1747
Wanguru, 3017
War, 134, 1901, 1906, 2050, 2290, 2443,
2503, 2508, 2526, 2572, 2636, 2692,
Adden. (Dannett, Hunter, Mann). See
Contents III.J. Women as Soldiers and
Spies.
War Correspondent, 1859
War Wives, 292, 1221, 1601. See Contents
III.D.I. Women in Revolutionary and
Changing Societies.
Washington (state), 168, 1382, 1498
Welfare (aid to dependent children), 140,
1149
West (U.S.), 2431, 2571, 2803
West Virginia, 774
White Slave Traffic. See Prostitution.
Widows, 292, 355, 374, 380, 1152, 2252,
Adden. (Caine, Kutner)
Wifehood, 1727, 1903, 2008, 2012, 2213,
2267, Adden. (Seidenberg)
Winnebago (Indians), 2111, 2560, 2575
Wisconsin, 352, 1433, Adden. (Crafton)
Wolof, 2942
Women's Christian Temperance Union, 941,
947-953
Women's Peace Party, 935, 1826
Women's Party, 1519, 1524
Women's Rights Conventions:Seneca Falls
and Rochester, 1542
Women's Studies, 672, 679, 685
Workers, Intro. pp. 13-19; 290, 836, 938,
967, 969, 1217-1218, 1221, 1317, 1834,

Workers, *continued*
1860, 1938, 1975, 2034, 2081, 2115,
2292, 2889, 2929, 3340, 3564, Adden.
(Bickner, Galenson, Kievit, Killian,
Prywes, Robinson, Seed, Strainchamps,
Veroff). See Contents X.F. Women in
Business, Industry, and Production.
Working Mothers, 387. See also Day Care.
World Council of Churches, 2199, 2214,
2229
World War I. See War.
World War II. See War.
Writers, 2397-2398, 2400, 2403, 2409,
2416, 2428, 2434, 2436, 2442, 2448,
2464-2465, 2511, 2517, 2584, 2591,
2655, 2678, Adden. (Brée, Crossland,
Sochen, Sullivan, Thwaite, Tomalin)
Wyoming, 1409

Yao, 3018, 3028
Yemen, 331
Yoruba, 2952, 2968
Yugoslavia, 1456, 2485

Zaire. See Congo (Kinshasa).
Zulus, 3003, 3036, 3040